FOLIAGE PLANTS
for
DECORATING INDOORS

FOLIAGE PLANTS
for
DECORATING INDOORS

*Plants, Design, Maintenance
for Homes, Offices and Interior Gardens*

by
Virginie F. & George A. Elbert

TIMBER PRESS
Portland, Oregon

ISBN 0-88192-125-4
Printed in Hong Kong

TIMBER PRESS
9999 SW Wilshire
Portland, Oregon 97225

Library of Congress Cataloging-in-Publication Data

Fowler, Virginie, 1916-
    Foliage plants for decorating indoors : plants, design,
maintenance for homes, offices, and interior gardens / by Virginie
F. & George A. Elbert.
        p.   cm.
    Bibliography: p.
    Includes index.
    ISBN 0-88192-125-4
    1. House plants in interior decoration. 2. Foliage plants.
I. Elbert, George, 1911-   . II. Title.
SB419.25.F68 1989
635.9'65--dc19
                                              88-36580
                                                CIP

CONTENTS

ACKNOWLEDGMENTS

Indoor gardening amateurs, professional interiorscapers and botanical gardens owe much to the dedication of a few enthusiastic nurserymen who have, for years, acquired and maintained a supply of exotic plants. Most of our own foliage plants have been supplied by Ken Frieling and Tom Wynn of Glasshouse Works in Stewart, Ohio, and Joyce Logee Martin of Logee's greenhouses in Danielson, Connecticut. Our book was made possible by the availability of these rare plants.

We wish to express our appreciation to Richard Abel, publisher of Timber Press, who has displayed a miraculous combination of flexibility and cooperation.

Illustrations are by the authors unless otherwise credited. Line drawings by Mark Rabinow. Schematic drawings for the bulk of the color illustrations by Virginie Elbert.

Part I

INTRODUCTION

In less than 50 years plants have invaded American homes to such a degree that the popularity of indoor gardening now almost matches that of traditional outdoor gardening. At first it was assumed that the introduction of artificial light for plant culture would, in itself, spark an increasing interest in houseplants. That has not proved to be the primary influence. In fact, horticulture by artificial light has caught on very slowly. Two other changes in our mode of living were responsible for the boom.

One reason was the sterile environment imposed by modern living styles and design. In essence it involved the removal of decorative and cultural features from the indoor environment. The piano disappeared from the corner of the living room along with the curio cabinet and the paintings on the walls. The lines of furniture, even of so-called period reproductions, were simplified. Works of the hand, handicrafts, largely disappeared in the furnishings of most homes and have entered the realm of antiquarians and collectors. Something was required to fill the gap.

Fortunately, when the need arose, technology greatly improved the control of temperature indoors, summer and winter. As houseplants were, of necessity, tropical or subtropical in origin, very few had been able to survive for long in the irregular temperatures of homes before the 1940s. But from then on the environment became much more favorable and plants that formerly could be maintained only in heated greenhouses in winter proved adaptable to conditions in the modern home.

People instinctively turned to plants as a surrogate for what had been lost in decorative detail and adopted them as a sort of living furniture. As such they have suited the taste of the intervening years better than any other solution. The outdoors was, to some extent, brought indoors, and the tropical appearance of the plants exactly suited the romantic attitude toward the home that has persisted despite the imposition of efficiency and geometry in the environment.

Architecture of large buildings became even more severely rationalized than domestic design. In their bare offices secretaries began spontaneously to introduce greenery on desk and windowsill. Management finally discovered that plants were a necessity in the work place, satisfying the need for some suggestion of life and decoration in desolate surroundings. By stages that initiative has led now to the interior gardens that we call atria. In both offices and atria artificial light provides for maintenance, and the technology is now available to complement natural light in large spaces.

These developments have led to new professions—lighting designers expert in plant requirements, interior landscapers, maintenance specialists and a great number of what are, essentially, interior plant decorators.

We have been active in horticulture since our early years, took to indoor gardening as a hobby when we moved to a city home and, eventually, applied our knowledge and experience to the promotion of indoor gardening through organizational activities and our writings, consisting of both articles and books on the subject.

The present work is limited to foliage plants which are the mainstay of the houseplant industry. It should be understood, of course, that all the plants we discuss, except the fern alliance and other primitive plants, do produce normal flowers. The criterion for inclusion in our lists is that the plant be grown primarily for its decorative foliage. Actually, for most indoor gardeners, plants that have very decorative flowers are introduced into the home only as temporary decoration. We call some of these "gift plants" rather than houseplants because they are discarded after they have bloomed. Poinsettias, Exacum, Gloxinias, Chrysanthemums, Amaryllis, Azaleas and the like are treated in this way even when they can be bloomed more than once. Foliage plants, on the other hand, are acquired in the hope that they will last as at least semipermanent installations. And, though many succumb to accident or neglect, some are so adaptable and resistant to mistreatment that they can be enjoyed for many years.

We have attempted here to create a readable reference for all those who grow plants indoors. Information is drawn from our personal experience. The subjects and their treatment should be useful to interior landscapers, interior designers, plant-service personnel, commercial buyers and, above all, amateur indoor gardeners. We have done our best to help with selection, purchase, placement and maintenance in a variety of typical indoor environments. Additionally we have introduced some innovations that are intended to aid the tracking down of information that is needed and facilitate the acquisition of a realistic rather than theoretical understanding of indoor horticulture.

Vocabulary. We cannot avoid using Latin names for plants. The nomenclatural system introduced by Linnaeus has international validity while all other names change from region to region and language to language. Objections to and difficulties in learning the names are more psychological than real. They are names like any others. In the United States we are all used to personal names derived from dozens of foreign languages and, nevertheless, learn them without fussing about their strangeness.

It is another matter entirely when writers on horticulture use the jargon of botany in their descriptions. There are perfectly good English words for the appropriate nouns and adjectives. We consider it intellectual snobbery to expect an average reader or a professional plantsman without specific training in botany, to learn the vocabulary of the science when knowledge of the science is not necessary for carrying on the practical activities of the profession. Having to refer to specialized dictionaries for interpretations of words is an imposition and a discouragement. Our choice of vocabulary may not be as scientifically accurate, but it consists of common words that will be understandable at first sight to a far greater number of readers. Most florists, for example, who would find an academic botanical text hopelessly difficult, will have no trouble following ours. We must also state that botanists do not agree in practice on the precise use of the descriptive vocabulary, as can be illustrated by innumerable examples. We just make it easier to understand.

Plant names. We have throughout followed the names and spellings in *Hortus Third* and Jacobsen's *Lexicon of Succulent Plants* (see bibliography). Spellings of some species names in *Hortus Third* are controversial. We refer to the use of *sanderana* rather than the usual *sanderiana*. We have followed the book in eliminating the i after personal names, for better or worse. We have, on the other hand, made an exception in regard to these same latinized personal names by printing them in lower case rather than upper case. We believe that this avoids confusion and is easier to remember. *The International Rules of Nomenclature* permits either usage.

When the names of species have been changed and the older usage persists to any extent, we add alternatives, placing them between parentheses. Many names remain in limbo for years. Names that may be arbitrary or whose status as separate species is doubtful we have followed with a question mark between parentheses. This is done not so much out of academic rectitude as for an avoidance of confusion. Readers using different works of reference will often find the same plant under a different species name than that used in *Hortus Third*.

We use both the above-mentioned books as our authorities simply because they are the ones that are most accessible at present in libraries or by purchase.

Varieties and forms. Many plants that have been listed in botanies or catalogs as varieties or forms of species, as well as those species to which a Latin modifying adjective has been added to the species name, we have placed among the cultivars. Some have no botanical justification as natural variations of the botanical species. But even the ones that have some claim to validity can be segregated from the normal species more conveniently as cultivars. Some of our cultivars will, therefore, be found by readers in botanies and lexicons in lower case Latin following the species name.

Reliability of commercial labeling. We cannot guarantee that all our descriptions refer to the species or cultivar listed. Though more experienced than some, we have to take a proportion of the labeling on faith. The complexities involved in plant identification are so great that botanists, themselves, are uncertain as to the exact naming of some plants. We can hardly be expected to do better since we depend on their identifications.

Professional nurserymen face the same difficulty. Exotic nurseries and others frequently receive plants from foreign collectors and nurseries. These arrive unlabeled or with labels that, as often as not, are obviously mistaken. When no label is attached, the nurseryman, who rarely has access to a herbarium or the time to consult one, refers to one of the above-mentioned books or others, such as *Exotica* which is illustrated, and attempts to make an identification. If that fails, the name of the most similar plant is chosen and used in identifying it for the public. When different commercial growers receive plants from the same source, they are as likely as not to come to different conclusions. Thus identical plants may bear different species labels. Some just give up and use the generic name and add a cultivar name. However when a plant becomes popular it may be referred to the botanical department of a university where it is identified. The other growers then fall into line.

For the amateur indoor gardener or professional interior landscaper, labels can be equally misleading. To be sure of what one has, one must see the plants themselves, because then the matter of authenticity of name becomes secondary to the plant's appearance and prospective use in decoration. Of course, the more expensive the plant the greater assurance one will require that it is what it is claimed to be. In practice there is no guarantee that a correctly labeled plant will be more effective and reliable than a similar one that has been obviously named by a process of guesswork.

Selection of plants. Our choices of plants to include in our lists are, or course, arbitrary. The number of species in the tropics and subtropics is much greater than in the temperate zone. In warmer climates with greater rainfall mutation takes place much more rapidly. The number of untried plants is enormously greater than those in cultivation. Over a period of years many that are temporarily in collections disappear, replaced by others from the same or different genera. That happens because nurseries drop them, having found that they have no future in the market, and amateurs either lose the plants or prefer to replace them with later purchases. No listing, for these reasons, can be anything else than selective.

We can include only plants that are in cultivation at the time of writing, and even then, we either do not know of or overlook a goodly number. Nobody, in fact, knows them all. Cultural directions can nevertheless be valid for a majority of the plants in a genus and will apply as well to new introductions, due to similarity of type or habitat.

It will become obvious as one peruses our listings that some families and genera contain a richer trove of foliage houseplants than others. Their characteristics make them more adaptable to our growing environments. That is why we often refer to the possibility of other, related, plants as meriting trial indoors. For instance, the potential for growing tropical trees as juveniles indoors has hardly been touched as yet.

We think it may be worthwhile to set forth what, in our experience, are the true essentials for success with plants, without which all the books on indoor horticulture are in vain.

1. Learn to look. Fixing the image of a plant in the mind requires intense observation

which seems to be beyond the capacity of some but can be acquired. Not only does this exercise sharpen the awareness of differences between plants, it is also essential if one is to take note immediately of any changes in a plant's appearance; without which it is impossible to take the measures necessary for proper culture.

2. A number of decorative foliage plants can blush unseen and unattended for long periods of time. Those who look upon them merely as decorative stopgaps will pass them by day after day, and they will be none the worse until the most obvious signs of rigor mortis finally attract attention.

But plants are never inanimate. They are living creatures. Even a so-called Living Stone (Lithops) is internally active and, most implausibly, goes through a metamorphosis and a flowering. One cannot truly appreciate or fully enjoy plants without acquiring the habit of looking in on them every day, if but for a moment. You can never do justice to their vital needs without regular attention. Remember that plants in the outdoor garden benefit from the natural forces of nature. Indoors you are their only source of food, drink, frequently of light, of warmth and of protection against diseases and pests. Their dependence is complete.

Changes take place with startling suddenness. The good things are growth and the onset of bloom; the bad ones are signs of illness or the attacks of pests. A plant that has sulked for as long as a year inexplicably begins to grow with astonishing rapidity. A superbly grown specimen, treasured for its beauty and a source of personal pride, may wilt in a single day and present the challenge of diagnosing the problem in order to accomplish its recovery. To enjoy the pleasures plants can provide one must preserve their well-being. For this nearly daily attention is essential.

3. The closeness to plants that leads to understanding them is a natural consequence of conscientious care. We can state, without risk of hyperbole, that those who do care sooner or later come to view their houseplants as domestic pets in a way that outdoor gardeners, on account of the repetition of plants and their far greater numbers, never experience. Indoors the individual plant becomes the subject of interest and concern. Not everybody has the capacity for such intensity of involvement and a lot less will do for the maintenance of most of the standard indoor plants. But it is probably needed to understand the more difficult ones and for success in growing them.

Though our book has as its primary objective usefulness as reference on the identity and culture of foliage plants, we hope that some of our love for plants will also be communicated to the reader and contribute to a greater appreciation of their potential as an enrichment of our already far too artificial environment.

BUYING PLANTS

Selection of species or cultivars. The stereotype plants, only a handful from the total repertory that we list mostly as Cast Iron or nearly so, are the stock in trade of office and lobby plant decor. They are also the ones most frequently seen as medium to large specimens placed in corners or near windows to inject some life into dull social rooms in homes. They need no further recommendation.

As to the many other plants listed by us, we can at best offer a hint as to their possible uses. Every environment being different in decorative plan and in respect to factors more or less favorable to the health of particular plants, specific recommendations are manifestly impossible. Each situation must be studied in detail and plant selection be guided by the evidence of a combination of observations.

Pests. When one buys a plant at a nursery or a shop it is assumed that both soil and plant are free of infestations. In practice this cannot be taken for granted nor can it be justifiably expected. To be sure, the nurseryman should have drenched the soil with a pesticide and fumigated the plant. Most of them do. The treatments are most successful where large crops of single species are being grown. These more common plants usually reach us free of pests.

To buy the less common plants one must have recourse to nurseries that maintain a stock of many different species and cultivars. In that case there is no way to avoid entirely a risk of pests. If one selects plants personally at a nursery it is advisable to examine leaves and stems thoroughly for signs of animal life. That should be done properly with a loupe (small magnifying glass). A watering of the surface of the soil may bring little slugs and other creatures up from below. When the medium is ordinary garden soil one should be especially suspicious of the presence of cutworms and other pests that commonly occur in a garden. But even the most careful check will not eliminate the possibility that some insect or worm of the damaging sort is well hidden from discovery. A multitude can begin with a pair.

Pests often seem to remain dormant, or at least unnoticeable, for a long time after the purchase of plants and only make their appearance after months indoors. And it is impossible, when infestations do turn up of a sudden, to know whether they have come with that plant or arrived through the air or from some other plant. In short, some pest exposure is unavoidable. One must be prepared to take measures to eliminate them as recommended under Pests or by other means as they become available. Eradication is usually much more easily accomplished indoors than in a greenhouse where the sheer numbers of plants make complete discovery and elimination so difficult.

Light acclimatization. We discuss this elsewhere. It is generally expected that a nursery-grown plant will have been subjected to lower light intensities than those that are normal in greenhouses for a period of at least several weeks before being offered for sale. Contract purchases of large quantities of foliage plants usually require a period of light acclimatization. However the levels recognized as adequate in the trade are, in our opinion, far too high for the plants to adjust to many low light situations. A substantial part of all plant loss shortly after purchase can be traced not so much to inadequate light in the new home as to a severe shock from a sudden reduction in light intensity.

Cultural acclimatization. Unfortunately much nursery growing of plants is a race against time. The shorter the period between starting seeds or cuttings and marketing, the lower the cost of production. Forcing plants in the nursery cannot be offset by a short period of slowing up. The damage is permanent.

Forcing is accomplished by exposing plants to high light intensities and extreme humidity combined with heavy doses of nutrition and, not infrequently, additives to the soil that speed growth at the expense of vigor. Such plants betray their faulty culture through long spaces between joints, thin leaves, lighter than normal leaf color, softness of stems and branches. All the latter are obviously of very recent growth.

The treatment also produces weak root systems. Heavy top growth is unaccompanied by comparable root development because heavy feeding eliminates the need for them to spread out in search of nutriment. When the plants are suddenly moved to environments that offer lower light and humidity along with reduced fertilizer, roots are unable to support top growth. A common result is prompt loss of leaves. Often the only means of saving a plant is to prune it drastically to as much as half its original size. Cease fertilizing and maintain for some time in low light levels appropriate for that plant so that it has a respite and time to recover. The convalescence may be protracted as the whole plant must gradually adjust to the new situation. Excessive watering or sudden changes in temperature are usually lethal.

Reliability of supply. A contract for named species or cultivars should be a guarantee that the customer will be protected against substitution of similar but inferior plants. Nevertheless it has been widely publicized that interior landscapers, under stress of severe competition for business, agree to supply labeled plants of a specified quality but deliver different ones that they have picked up at substantial savings. It happens because of the almost total ignorance of many commercial buyers who know all about various kinds of equipment but nothing at all about plants. Many interior landscapers are almost equally incapable of judging plants as this is one of those businesses that amateurs can engage in with a minimum of training. In these instances nurserymen knowingly deliver an inferior product. One would be hard put to it to find a field where substitution of merchandise goes unnoticed more easily. The numerous first-rate nurseries and highly professional interior landscapers who maintain standards are, of course, the principal sufferers. Buyers often could not care less, being solely concerned with price.

Not only commercial buyers are the victims of these shenanigans, but also homeowners who employ a so-called expert to supply plants. The only way to protect oneself against exploitation in this manner is by checking references and being willing to pay a decent price for a superior product. Well-grown plants cannot be produced at rock-bottom prices. One must be prepared to pay more for reliability. But, of course, nothing takes the place of a careful check of the plants themselves by consulting outside experts.

LIGHT AND LANDSCAPING INDOORS

Much has been written about interior landscaping without taking into account that every aspect is related to the availability of sufficient light. The exercise of treating interior landscaping as merely a branch of outdoor landscaping, concerned with a more limited environment, solves nothing. The esthetic principles are but a matter of good intentions and "good taste," the latter of which is as nebulous as the former and a transitory affair in the bargain.

Contrary to outdoor light, natural light between four walls is always limited by window sizes, shapes, directions and degree of exterior obstruction. Plants must be clustered in relation to windows, and design has little scope except in the choice of plants capable of surviving in the available light.

Artificial light greatly expands the possibilities, but then the limitations are imposed by the light source itself. Those photographs in magazines showing decorator-designed rooms with plants prominently displayed without any visible source of special lighting can be misleading unless it is explained that they are placed only for the purposes of display.

Atria in tall buildings, which are nothing more than shafts with a transparent roof, a window, are no places for landscaping without the provision of complementary artificial lighting. They have come into being because of that alone. But atria and malls are only peripheral in the scope of this book. They are virtually the only places where the art of landscaping has any real application. The spatial conditions, however, are created by architects, and the making of these gardens requires the services not only of landscape gardeners and architects but also lighting and hydraulic engineers.

The above observations have convinced us that interior design with plants cannot be treated separately from lighting in a book that deals with most of the components of indoor gardening.

Natural Light

The relationship of natural light and plants indoors is both less and more complicated than that with artificial light. We are all aware that interior spaces depend on windows for daylight, whereas knowledge of the effect of artificial light sources on plant growth must be acquired. On the other hand artificial light is delivered by man-made tubes and bulbs that emit a definite quantum of illumination. Windows face different directions in relation to the sun, are small or large, are flush or recessed, clear or obstructed and exposed to more or less sunlight or overcast at different times of the year depending on local climate. There is, therefore, more data on artificial than natural light indoors that can be expressed quantitatively.

Exposure. A southern exposure receives the greatest amount of light for longer hours than the three others. The midday sun is the most intense. Morning light from the east is more at the blue end of the spectrum and the west, in the afternoon, at the red end. Midday is a mix of the two and, except under special atmospheric conditions, full spectrum.

The sun moves in an arc in the southern exposure; in east and west windows it covers only part of an arc, the one ascending and the other descending. In an east window in summer the light reaches plants first on the right side but for only a short time. The duration and intensity of the sunlight increases to the left. In a western exposure the right side also receives the first light which is also the most intense. It gradually decreases as the whole window is flooded. In winter the duration of sunlight in both east and west windows constantly decreases until 21 December and starts to increase thereafter. Plants that have become accustomed to bright light in east and west windows in summer may suffer from the shorter hours in winter and have to be moved to the south or supplied with supplementary artificial light. The north window receives no direct sunlight.

The intensity of light in an east, west or south window may be as great as out-of-doors for a short period during the day but for a shorter time. Plants receive it only on one side and must be turned frequently to preserve symmetry. Duration, compared with the outdoors, depends on the size and shape of the window. The longer and taller it is, the greater the duration and vice versa.

Windows that do not directly face a compass direction receive more or less light depending on orientation. A north window facing a bit east of the compass point receives a short period of direct sun in summer. If a west window is oriented slightly toward the north the hours of sun will be diminished. Observe the orientation of your windows. We often ask amateurs who have problems with their plants in what direction their windows face. Many have not the faintest notion. And yet the exposure must be known if they wish to choose the right plants for their exposures.

The sun at zenith is more vertical in summer than winter. This has the effect that the rays penetrate a shorter distance into a room in summer than in winter. When windows are recessed or there is any overhang, direct sunlight may enter only along a narrow band close to the window. In fact, since the sun is lower in winter and the angle is more near the horizontal, plants may receive longer hours of direct light at that time though it will be less intense. East and west are less affected by this change than south because the sun enters at a lower angle even in summer.

Obstructions of any kind from trees or buildings cut down on the duration of direct light and/or its intensity. Buildings may reflect more or less light depending on color and surface characteristics. Snow cover in winter greatly augments the intensity of sunlight in the country, especially in eastern, western and southern exposures.

Plants on a windowsill will always receive sunlight in the three exposures. But as we move them further into the room or to the sides of a window, it is the larger plants that benefit most from direct light. However, one must note the angle of the rays passing through the window. Only the upper half of a plant may be illuminated intensely in summer and the whole plant only in winter. Plants should be taller or be raised where back from but near to the window. Shorter plants can be further away. At some point the angle drops to the floor and offers no useful direct light at all. Placement of plants in respect to windows is subject to this rule; that is, unless one installs complementary artificial lighting.

A great deal more light is needed to induce plants to set buds and bloom than is required to maintain foliage plants. A southern exposure is recommended for those we rate as requiring 800–1,000 footcandles (fc). Most succulents require these levels. East and west will do for those needing from 500–800 fc and north for all the lower ratings. This is based on unobstructed, normal-sized windows. If they are larger, some of the high intensity plants may do well in east and west. Plants satisfied with a northern exposure may be adversely affected by a southern one. Leaves become bleached and growth inhibited. If one has only a north window it is wise to start with plants having the lowest light tolerance. If any of the other exposures is available one can experiment.

The following diagrams illustrate the scope and limitations of natural light from windows. They also suggest size limitations for plants in window-lighted rooms. Hours of light and number of sunny days varies according to latitude and climate. Variety of growing can be greatly increased by installing efficient artificial light sources.

This is a schematic representation of the range of window light inside a room. It tells us approximately the areas where we can place plants and the amount of light they will receive. Note that the top lines angle down and/or outward because the spaces directly on either side of the window are unlighted.

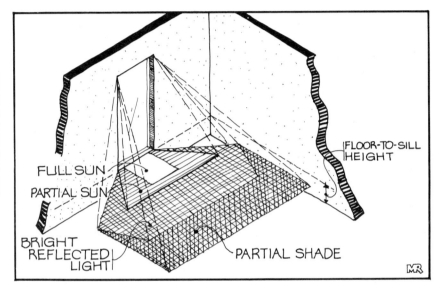

The general problem of light and plants is demonstrated by this simple diagram. A fixed light source, such as a lamp, is effective in an arc of approximately 90 degrees. The further the plant is away from the source the less light it receives until the limits of usable illumination are reached. In practice a window is not very different as a source of light for plants. The total amount of intensity and the duration are reduced as the plant is moved further and further away from the window.

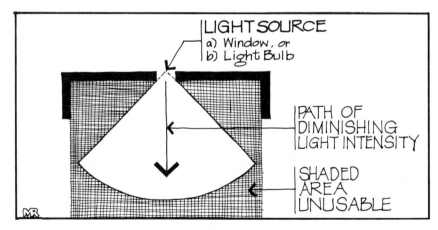

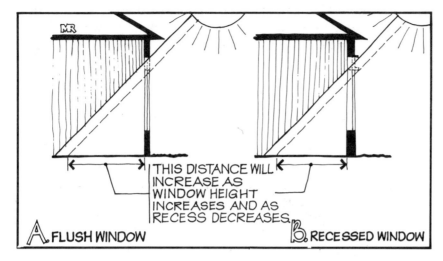

A. Flush window. B. Recessed window. The diagram shows how recessing of a window prevents daylight from reaching into a room. The higher the window relative to recessing, the further light will reach. Angled line A encloses the lighted area of the flush window. Angled line B encloses the lighted area of the recessed window. A reduction in window height will reduce both lighted areas.

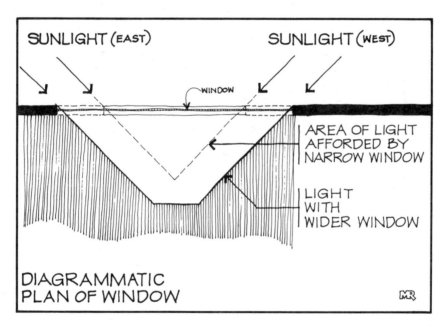

The diagram shows how a wider window provides a greater area of plant lighting during the day. Width of a window not only affects the angle of the lighting but also the duration of sunlight. The dark area is beyond range of light for plant maintenance.

Most of the time sunlight angles downward into a room. This means that the further it reaches into the room, the closer it is to floor level. Using plants with the same light requirement, the taller specimens must be close to the window. Inside the room a short plant may receive sufficient light where a tall one would not.

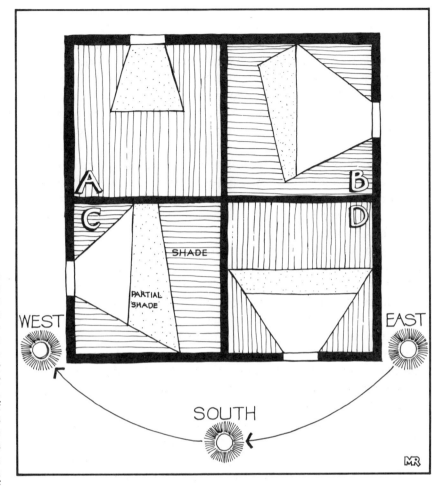

This diagram is meant as a guide to the placing of plants in a room according to the window exposure. The northern exposure, A, provides only Partial Shade, B and C, the eastern and western exposures, have a similar profile in reverse. However the east, in most regions, receives a shorter period of sunlight than the west. D is a southern exposure. The blank space directly in front is fully or partially sunlighted. Diagram E shows how a window to either side of center changes the shape of the usable space for plant maintenance. The bright light is cut off by the southern wall. The line to the north is longer because the sun comes around the window from the south. The situation is reversed with an eastern exposure. Plants can be grown in the shaded areas only if artificial lighting is provided.

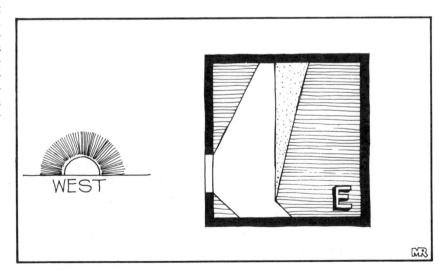

Artificial Light

Shortly after fluorescent tubes were first marketed around 1938, amateur growers of houseplants became aware that the artificial light produced freed them from the space restrictions of windowsills. African Violet enthusiasts were the first to take advantage of this new light source which caused their plants to flower throughout the year. With the fixtures suspended directly over them they also grew more symmetrically than on a windowsill. It now became possible to maintain plants indoors in rooms that were totally lacking in natural light.

Earlier, incandescent light had been tested for its effect on plant growth and found wanting. Why, then, was fluorescent light so much more effective? For a number of years, while amateurs experimented successfully with the new light source, no scientific explanation was forthcoming. Eventually researchers at the USDA in Beltsville, Maryland, discovered that the effectiveness of light on plant growth and bloom lay primarily in the blue and red wave lengths of the light spectrum.

Incandescent light, it turned out, was strong in the wave lengths from yellow to red but weak in blue. As the red end of the spectrum also produces heat, the bulbs could not be brought close to plants. There is no economical way to introduce blue into the emissions of incandescent bulbs. Fluorescent tubes, on the other hand, depend for color on the mixes of various fluorescent chemicals that coat the inner walls of the tubes. The proportions can be manipulated with greater ease to produce desired changes in the spectrum. The original fluorescent tubes just happened to possess a spectrum including sufficient intensity in the blue and red wave lengths to satisfy the light needs of shade-tolerant plants. The tubes were also much cooler than incandescent bulbs, making it possible to place them closer to the plants without causing damage.

Lighting manufacturers jumped to the conclusion that a fluorescent tube emitting mostly blue and red would be ideal for plant growth. It didn't work out that way. Deep red-purple lights became a fad for a while (they imparted a neon glow to flowers and to tropical fish, too) but were only a slight improvement over commercial fluorescent lighting. It gradually dawned on experts and amateurs alike that plants did, after all, benefit to some extent from other colors than red and blue in the spectrum. Ultraviolet light was lethal. But mixes containing a proportion of other colors in the spectrum than red and blue, such as near-violet, yellow to orange and far red, worked much better. The later Sylvania Gro-Lux tubes, for example, incorporated this improvement.

The popularity of blue-red fluorescent tubes faded when the light output of commercial lamps for use in workplaces (factories, shops, offices, etc.) was increased considerably, and the lights became much cheaper and were offered in a whole range of colors, some of which, alone or in combination, produced superior results with houseplants. Growers found that ordinary Cool White tubes worked well with foliage plants while those who wanted their plants to set buds and flowers had better results with a combination of Cool White and Warm White, installed alternately. Both these colors sold at the same price, were equally intense and the tubes lasted as long. Other colors were tried with moderate success, notably the bulbs designated Daylight. Some growers still use premium "growth tubes" but the majority has switched to the lower cost product. The only "growth tube" we have ever recommended is made by Verilux Inc., and we do so because of its natural color.

Though we are still in the early stages of the development of plant-lighting technology, the repertory of plants that flourish under currently available sources of artificial light is astonishing and increasing constantly. The introduction of high intensity discharge bulbs, which can be placed far above the plants, has made possible the maintenance of large plants under high ceilings and enabled landscapers to plant those huge indoor gardens that have become a feature of the latest public buildings.

Why artificial lighting works. The sun is obscured from time to time in summer and for long stretches in winter. Though artificial light with plant-growth capability is much less intense than sunlight, it shines every day throughout the year and can do so for a longer average period each day than natural light. The behavior of plants under artificial light indicates that longer periods of illumination compensate to some extent for the lower light intensity, making up most of the difference. With this in mind, a rough-and-ready calculation demonstrates why plants grow so well under relatively low artificial illumination indoors.

Multiply the footcandles of sunlight received by a plant in a greenhouse by the number of sunlit hours a day. 2500 fc and 8 hours is probably a fair estimate. Many nurseries expose their plants to higher intensities, but these are excessive in preparing the plants for adaptation to indoor conditions. Deduct from the total 30% for overcast days. Compare the total fc with artificial light calculated at only 800 fc but on a 16-hr. day. The result reveals that the amount of artificial light the plant receives is not much less than natural light.

Natural Light	Artificial Light
2500 fc	800 fc
× 8 hrs.	× 16 hrs.
20000 fc	
−30%	
14000 fc	12800 fc

The above calculation is based on the intensity of light emissions from fluorescent tubes. Multi-Vapor and Sodium bulbs are much brighter but the spectrums are somewhat less efficient so that results are much the same. However the bulbs can be effective at greater distances from the plants.

The spectrum. The wave lengths of the spectrum are measured in nanometers and are represented as a single strip from the invisible gamma rays and x-rays on the left, through the visible rays of near-violet, blue, green, yellow, orange, red and far red, continuing through invisible infra-red and radio waves to the right. It has been proved that plants alternate absorption of red and far red light according to need. Both aid in the formation of buds and flowers. They are less essential for foliage health than blue. Nowadays, because the tubes and bulbs being widely used to promote plant growth (fluorescent, multi-vapor bulbs with a reddish tint and, for special purposes, H.P. Sodium bulbs) have been sufficiently tested as effective for growth, growers pay less attention to spectrum charts than formerly.

Kelvins. The Kelvin scale is a measure of temperature that, among other uses, defines the temperature of a color or a combination of colors. Artificial light sources for general illumination and for photography are rated according to the Kelvins registered by their light emissions. The higher the Kelvin the more bluish the spectrum; the lower the Kelvin the more yellowish red the spectrum.

Sunlight, a combination of the total spectrum, is white, but the rays that reach us through the atmosphere change in color at different times of day and in different weather conditions. Six thousand to 6,500 Kelvins (K) is about equivalent to sunlight under an evenly overcast sky, and is almost white. Under artificial light with approximately the same reading, plants, soil, etc., appear much as we see them in natural light. Light approaching the 6,000 K reading proves to be excellent for plant growth. Slightly bluish light is effective with foliage plants while slightly reddish light promotes buds and flowers. The Kelvin range useful to plants lies between 5,500 and 6,500 K with maximum results close to 6,000. This acts as a rough guide in choosing artificial light sources.

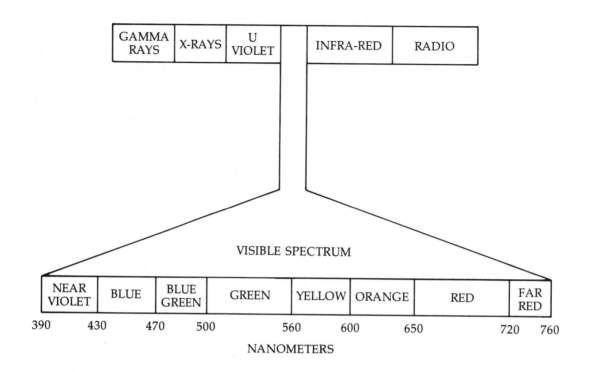

| GAMMA RAYS | X-RAYS | U VIOLET | | INFRA-RED | RADIO |

VISIBLE SPECTRUM

| NEAR VIOLET | BLUE | BLUE GREEN | GREEN | YELLOW | ORANGE | RED | FAR RED |

390 430 470 500 560 600 650 720 760

NANOMETERS

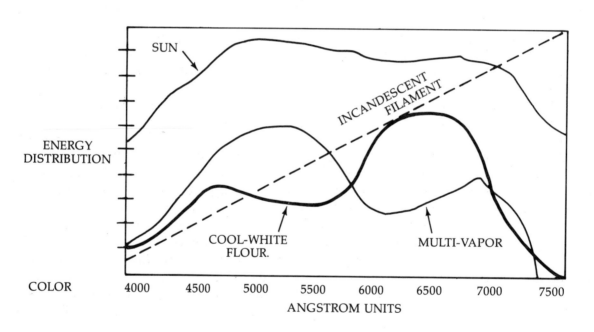

ENERGY DISTRIBUTION

SUN

INCANDESCENT FILAMENT

COOL-WHITE FLOUR.

MULTI-VAPOR

COLOR

4000 4500 5000 5500 6000 6500 7000 7500

ANGSTROM UNITS

Lumens and footcandles. These are the principal light measurements used by professionals and amateurs alike. One lumen is an amount of light equal to the emission of one international candle. It is an arbitrary measurement of the intensity of a lamp source. One footcandle (fc) is the amount of light striking an object one foot (30 cm) away from one standard international candle. It is an arbitrary measurement of the light received by an object from a source. The light output of tube and bulb is measured in lumens. The light requirements of plants and the amounts they receive from a source are measured in footcandles.

Measuring light for plants. The makers of moisture and pH meters produce inexpensive light meters that are only approximately accurate but adequate for home use. They measure only the footcandles, not the lumens, but that is what is really necessary.

The lumen rating is the total output of a lamp. But the lamp has a shape, tube or bulb, allowing light to be emitted in more than one direction. When a bulb has an internal reflector, it redirects part of the light emitted but only as it is reflected. There is bound to be some loss in doing so. Every shape diffuses to some extent so that the light is never directed at a single point, as does a laser. The total output of a Cool White fluorescent tube may be 2,800 lumens, but the emissions are spread over a total length of 48 in. (1.20 m). Therefore lumen output is, as far as the indoor gardener is concerned, only of interest as indicating relative intensity. It tells one that light source A is, say, twice as powerful as light source B.

The indoor gardener is interested in two factors; the amount of light actually reaching a plant and the growth-inducing quality of that light. The amount of light emitted by the section of a fluorescent lamp directly over a plant is considerably less than the total output of the tube. The light meter reading in footcandles provides the proper reading of that amount of light. The meter can be moved to different positions, directly under the lamps, between them or to the sides.

The output of many lamps suffers a reduction of about 10% within a relatively short period of use. Major manufacturers list in their catalogs not only the initial lumens but the average lumens over the life of the source. Subtraction of one from the other gives the percentage of the reduction. In practice the indoor gardener who chooses to make measurements at all should do so in footcandles after two months of daily use.

Most of the simpler meters register a maximum of 1,000 footcandles, which is sufficient for most measurements. If the indicator bumps up against the 1,000 footcandle mark, it will be evidence that the lamps are yielding more than most of our houseplants need for maintenance. Foliage plants usually can do with considerably less.

Light meters in general use measure only visible light. Part of the spectrum most effective in plant growth is beyond the visible range. A Verilux TruBloom or Sylvania Gro-Lus W-S lamp will register fewer footcandles than a Cool White tube but the efficiency of the two growth lamps will be equal or greater.

We wish to emphasize, then, that the measurement of light in relation to plants is no cut-and-dried matter, but one that involves judgement and experiment. Fortunately, as indicated below, the effectiveness of the major light sources is well known and most indoor gardeners find them very simple to work with. The following notes may be helpful.

1. The artificial light source has proved in practice to be effective in promoting plant growth.

2. The decline in light intensity with distance is measured with a light meter but in practice plants are placed in relation to known light sources according to well-tested information on their performances.

3. Environmental factors are taken into consideration by lighting engineers, for they have an effect on the footcandles of light that are delivered. For most indoor landscapers and for amateurs dealing with average situations, they do not have a significant influence on growth results with plants or at least not enough to warrant or create the necessity for complicated calculations.

4. The light requirements of some plants are known from testing and experience. If unknown it is often possible to reach an approximation by rating a plant's light needs in relation to one which it resembles or whose outdoor environment is similar. If that is too ambiguous, one falls back on experimentation based on observation.

Reduction of light with distance; rules and reality. The reduction of the intensity of light with distance from our two principal sources of artificial light obeys two different formulas.

Because of its length and shape a fluorescent tube is defined as a line source of illumination. The formula states that the footcandle illumination is in direct inverse proportion to the distance. Bulb sources are technically known as point sources. They obey the inverse square law that states that, with a point source of illumination the amount of light reaching an object is inversely proportional to the square of the distance.

We show two charts of fluorescent sources for which the calculations have been the same in the sense that they obey the rule, except that two line sources are used in both. Note the disparities between the two, even when only the distances in a direct line in the second chart are compared to the first. Simple as are these illustrations, they exemplify the difficulties in calculating footcandles delivered by a source and the confusion that can be created if all the conditions are not known. In the first chart we are told that the lamps have been used for 200 hours. That is really superfluous because we are given the footcandles at a distance of one inch.

Footcandle Illuminations of Cool, White Fluorescent Lamps at Different Distances

Distance from lamps (inches)	(1) Two lamps used for 200 hours	(2) Four lamps used for 200 hours	(3) Four lamps New
1	1100	1600	1800
2	860	1400	1600
3	680	1300	1400
4	570	1100	1260
5	500	940	1150
6	420	820	1000
7	360	720	900
8	330	660	830
9	300	600	780
10	280	560	720
11	260	510	660
12	240	480	600
18	130	320	420
24	100	190	260

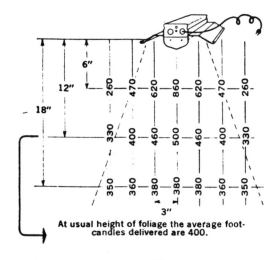

At usual height of foliage the average footcandles delivered are 400.

But we are not told whether a reflector is used, nor, if so, how far apart the tubes were set. In the second chart we can see that a reflector was used but again not how far they were apart. The calculations of footcandles for distances from the center of the tubes assume that measurements were taken directly under or to the sides of the center. They are no more than an extrapolation of the distance, the same as the calculation for the pure vertical relationship. In practice that does not take into consideration the fact that the ends of tubes not only give out less light but that a position under them receives light only from one side. The difference between the figures, say, at 6 in. (15 cm), may be due to older lamps having been used for the first chart and new ones for the second. Which is correct? Actually neither, though the first chart is more realistic. Our own measurements have shown an average of about 50 fc at 2 ft. (60 cm).

Note from the first chart that the addition of more tubes side by side does not cause a proportional increase in the number of footcandles delivered. There is a substantial increase, to be sure. The other advantage of using more than two tubes side by side is that houseplants that are in from the sides of the bank of tubes receive light of considerable intensity not only from above but at an angle. This results in the lower parts of taller plants receiving considerable illumination which results in their developing more uniformly and lower leaves and branches being longer lived.

Professionals calculate the amount of light reflected or absorbed by ceilings and walls. To learn how to make them one must go to an appropriate school. The vast majority of interior landscapers in practice have no more expertise in the subject than amateur indoor gardeners. The question for us is how one installs lighting for plants without the requirement for such knowledge.

The answer is given by the lighting equipment that is commonly used for plants in homes and commercial situations. These are fluorescent tubes and incandescent and metal halide bulbs.

The fluorescent tube is standard; Cool White and Warm White tubes and their equivalents emit a known output of light and indoor gardeners have been working with them for a long time. Hardly anyone measures the light or makes calculations yet the system works as well as if one had. Gro-Lux Wide Spectrum and Verilux TruBloom produce less light, but the growth effect on plants is about the same as for CW and WW.

Meters register about 1,000 fc very close to the tubes. At a distance of 24 in. (60 cm) it is reduced to 50–100 fc. Within this limited range of distance it is easy to set the lamps and plants at different relative distances according to their needs. When no accurate information is available on the light requirements of a species (estimates are always based on particular environments and may not apply to yours) one must experiment and judge by the behavior of the plants. One soon acquires a knowledge of how to arrange groups of plants of different sizes and species under different sets of tubes.

The situation is much the same for bulb sources. The 150 watt bulb is standard at the present time. How close plants can be placed to the source depends on the heat of the emissions and the degree to which the heat output is concentrated by the type of reflector or housing that is used. A crude estimate is a minimum distance of 1½ ft. (45 cm) and a maximum distance of 4 ft. (1.20 m). When bulbs are used as supplementary light, plants and bulbs can be set at a distance of 5–6 ft. (1.20 m–1.80 m) apart. The distance can be increased both for constant and supplementary use when more than one bulb is used. Because bulbs are so much more compact than fluorescent tubes and do not require bulky fixtures, they can be installed more easily. If light is inadequate, add more to track or as pin-ups. For most interior situations it is unnecessary to consult a lighting engineer. The real problems have to do with decoration. Thus the planning of light intensity for plant growth indoors is quite simple in practice.

The exceptions to the above occur when dealing with very big installations such as for atria and malls. The powerful bulbs that are often required do have bulky fixtures, and the services of lighting engineers and/or designers are required.

Virtually all indoor gardeners handle light sources in relation to their plants by rule of thumb. They soon become accustomed to manipulating both successfully. We have known no one who has installed lighting for plants for six months who has not become fully acquainted with the practical applications. Complete newcomers to indoor gardening are the ones, in our experience, who are convinced that they must have precise data in order to proceed. We have found that failures with plants are due not to ignorance regarding the technology of lighting, but to rudimentary understanding of other cultural requirements.

The infinite light source. If artificial light reduces so rapidly with distance from a line or point source, why is it that the intensity of sunlight does not decrease perceptibly between the top and bottom of a tree or building? The reason is that the sun is not a limited light source in relation to the earth but an infinite one. Light from it only decreases perceptibly over immense distances. We can create a partial equivalence by covering a surface, a ceiling for instance, with tubes or bulbs. Then, neither the line or point source formula applies. By actual measurement we can establish that there is a much smaller loss of intensity between source and object compared with lamps that are widely separated or occupy only part of the space above.

The principle can be put to work in illuminating plants. A single overhead source is less efficient that a cluster that covers a greater area. A plant then receives light from various angles as in nature and the total amount received by the total plant is greater. This is especially useful in the lighting of tall specimens.

Reduction of light through use. Manufacturers of lamps also state their rated life in use. It is usually on the conservative side. The fewer number of switchings on and off, the longer the lamp will last. A fluorescent lamp used for plants has a much longer life than an incandescent bulb. The latter are guaranteed for less than 1,000 hours, the former for 10,000–20,000 hours, a minimum of two years of normal daily use.

However they do suffer a loss of intensity during use. The biggest drop, up to 10%, occurs during the first 100 hours. After that the decline is gradual. When near maximum intensity is required for maintenance of plants, replace lamps after they have lasted 80% of their rated lives. Light output at that time will also be close to 20% below the original lumen rating. Most amateurs wait until a lamp blows out and commercial users generally do the same. Delay in replacement may be responsible for plants, failing to bud or bloom, but most foliage plants seem to suffer little harm. Still, for those who are concerned to keep their plants in top-notch condition, a timely change of lamps is advisable.

Lamps should be cleaned occasionally. Any dust or scum, sometimes hardly visible, causes a reduction in effective output of up to 30%.

Fluorescent tubes. The light output per watt of fluorescent tubes is about three times as great as that of incandescent lamps. The newer bulb sources of light include some that are even more efficient in terms of light output per watt consumed. However, the tubes are ideal for houseplants no more than about 24 in. (60 cm) in height. With taller plants in offices their output is just sufficient to maintain a very few species of shade-tolerant foliage plants.

The intensity of light from a fluorescent lamp is greatest at its center. The last few inches near the pins produce considerably less light. Therefore high light plants are grouped under the center and low light ones to the sides.

The straight tubes are manufactured in three principal wattages and lengths; 20 watt-24 in. (60 cm), 40 watt-48 in. (1.20 m) and 75 watt-96 in. (2.40 m). The two shorter sizes have two pins at each end; the 96-incher has a single pin at each end; hence different types of sockets. The three sizes are the most popular for commercial illumination and produce the highest intensities per watt at the lowest cost. The intermediate lengths and wattages are all less efficient and more expensive because of lower sales. As each of the major sizes can illuminate shelving of greater length, there are few situations where the odd sizes are needed.

U-shaped lamps are made in 20 watt-12 in. (30 cm) and 40 watt-24 in. (60 cm) lengths, measured from the base of the pins to the bend. They are considerably less efficient than the straight tubes. They require special fixtures and are used commercially in luminaires, or frames with diffusers, mainly for special problems in workplace illumination. They are rarely used with plants.

Circline lamps are in the form of a ring and screw into normal incandescent bulb sockets. There are two principal sizes; 22 watt-8 in. (20 cm) and 44 watt-10 in. (25 cm) diameters. Rated life is short and intensity low. There have been a number of attempts to manufacture light garden units incorporating these lamps, but results have been poor.

Sylvania Gro-Lux Wide Spectrum (W-S) tubes are also very effective in combination with Cool White, taking the place of Warm White. Excellent results have been reported.

Premium tubes, often advertised as "growth tubes", cost 2 to 3 times as much as standard commercial tubes. Of these more costly lamps we recommend unstintingly only the Verilux Tru-Bloom (See Verilux Inc. in Sources). It is the only one that we think yields results comparable to the combinations. The color of this tube closely approaches that of natural light. All other tubes emit colors that are noticeably unnatural in varying degrees; either too yellow or too blue, with the result that they distort the appearance of plants and clash with decor. With Tru-Bloom one sees the plants in the same hues as out-of-doors. Its visible intensity is less than Cool White or Warm White, hence less glaring. Footcandle readings may be as much as ⅓ lower than those for the commercial tubes, but the growth results, both for foliage and flowering, are the same. We prefer it for any installations in living areas. In use, Verilux tubes have proved much longer lasting than Cool White and Warm White.

The only other tube that has attracted attention is Vita-Lite. It is favored by cactus and bromeliad hobbyists, but we cannot recommend it for general plant maintenance. The more expensive high-output Vita-Lite tubes, on the other hand, provide good results with flowering houseplants.

Limitations of fluorescent tubes. Though the total light output of a fluorescent tube is high, it is spread along the whole length of the lamp. Hence the intensity at any point is quite low. They can be used in shelving set at approximately a maximum of 30 in. (60 cm) apart. This limits plants to a height of about 2 ft. (60 cm). In offices where there are a number of fluorescent fixtures spread across the ceiling, their effectiveness for growth extends to about 3 ft. (90 cm).

Recommended tubes. Two tubes, side by side, are a minimum for maintenance of foliage or flowering plants. The most reliable arrangement employs one Warm White for every Cool White tube. When multiples of two tubes are hung close together, Warm White and Cool White alternate. After years of testing premium "growth tubes", the USDA finally compared the combination Cool White/Warm White with the others and found them at least equivalent in growth effectiveness.

Some growers of foliage plants assert that they find Cool White tubes alone to be sufficiently satisfactory. In our opinion this depends on the specific species being grown. No doubt Cool White can maintain very low-light-tolerant plants, as is proven every day in office installations. But wherever the tubes are required to maintain a wide spectrum of foliage plants, we think it wise to use the combination which is also essential to produce flowering.

The convenient snap or stick-on single tubes or light sticks are of no use for plant maintenance in our opinion.

Higher intensity fluorescent lamps. Special tubes of two types have been installed for flowering plants in the past, but rarely at present, except for orchid culture. The additional light output costs relatively more initially and for electrical consumption over the long run. Their recessed double-contact design requires more expensive fixtures. Most growers have found that a greater number of standard tubes set side by side is just as effective. We do not recommend the special tubes for foliage.

The 48 in. (1.20 m) High Output tubes in Cool White or Warm White are rated 60 watts, 6300 lumens output and 12,000 hours life, compared with the standard 40 watt, 3200 lumens and up to 20,000 hours life.

Power Groove lamps are available in 48 in. (1.20 cm), 72 in. (1.82 cm) and 96 in. (2.34 cm) lengths. The 48 in. is rated 110 watts, 5100 lumens and 12,000 hours life. The extra lumen output results from the grooving of the tube which increases the fluorescent surface area.

Fluorescent fixtures. Fluorescent tubes are installed in sockets beneath long "stripfixtures" of metal, consisting of two parts, a cover and base, that fit together forming a box about 2 in. deep. Within the box is the ballast (a converter), the wires for the sockets at either end which are usually attached to them, and the two power lines. The box is held together by screws and wing nuts that are easy to unfasten.

To the two power lines, splice additional lengths of wire long enough to reach a wall plug. Attach male elements to the ends of the power lines and plug into a timer which fits into the nearest electric outlet.

Some fixtures are now made with the power lines already attached to the male plug. Attach to an extension cord long enough to reach a timer plugged into the wall outlet.

Installing the tubes. Sockets, called tombstones, project through openings in the bottom of the fixture at either end. Bi-pin tubes are lifted into the slots on the sockets and given a half twist. Single-pin and recessed tubes are installed by pressure.

Replacing sockets. Slotted tombstones have an annoying tendency to rust with age, making it difficult to twist the tubes and cause them to fit where ignition can take place. Sockets can be bought in hardware stores. Take along a tombstone to make sure that you are getting the same model. Remove the lower pan of the fixture, unscrew the old sockets; unscrew the wiring; wire the new sockets, slip into the slot provided for them and screw firmly into place.

Sometimes the screws holding the sockets work loose, causing the sockets to wobble so that the tubes no longer fit tightly between them. Remove the lower pan of the fixture and tighten the screws.

Rapid and Instant Start fixtures. Rapid Start fixtures have a hole in the bottom at one end into which an aluminum cylinder, the starter, fits by pressing and giving a right-hand twist. It assists in igniting the gas inside the tube. Especially at low temperatures newly installed tubes may take up to a minute to warm up. After that ignition is immediate. The cylinders must be replaced usually after two or three years in use. They are supplied in 15–20 watt and 30–40 watt models.

Instant Start fixtures do not have starters. Ignition is immediate. They are gradually replacing the Rapid Start fixtures.

Ballasts. The ballast is enclosed in a rectangular steel box, screwed inside the box of the fixture. If a ballast is of poor quality it may burn out after a long period of use and emit a tarry substance that smokes. The electrical connection is, simultaneously, burned out. The whole fixture must be replaced. It is difficult or impossible to know whether the fixture you are buying has been equipped with an inferior or superior ballast unless you are familiar with the different makes. Our own ballasts have never burned out after 15 years of service, but we do not know whether this is due to luck. Reports of burn-outs are rare. But they can happen. If the fixture is attached to a nonfireproof surface, there is a fire hazard. The best insurance against this occurrence is to check the quality of your ballast with an electrician. If inferior, it can be replaced by a more reliable model.

Remoting the ballast. The ballast contributes considerably to higher temperatures in the environment of the plants beneath the fixtures. Where this is recognized as a serious interference with maintenance, the ballast can be remoted. Remove from the box of the fixture by unscrewing it. Find or make a fireproof backing within 15 ft. of the fixture. Firmly attach the ballast to it. Unscrew the wires and splice on wire to reach the new location. The reduction of temperature in the vicinity of the plants will be 10 degrees or more. Remoting is most advisable where a large number of tubes are set side by side over the plants.

Number of tubes. Fixtures with and without reflectors are made in models that accept 1,

2 and 4 tubes. The 2s and 4s may have the tubes set side by side at different distances depending on the manufacturer, ranging from 3 to 6 in. between centers. The diameter of most tubes is 1½ in. (3.25 cm). For maximum intensity at close range, a short distance between the tubes is best. For longer distances a more open spacing is preferable. Though two tubes are usually sufficient for foliage plants, for plants over 18 in. (45 cm) in height or demanding greater intensities, four tubes or even two or more 4-tube fixtures side by side may be installed. You can also have multiple-tube lighting by placing single-tube strip fixtures, in any number side by side. Their wires can be accommodated by a fixture (available at hardware stores) that accepts a number of plugs.

Timers. A standard small-equipment timer, rated 1500 to 1875 watts, is capable of handling the input of several multiple fixtures. The total wattage of the tubes plus 10% should be less than the rating of the timer. Industrial-sized timers, with higher wattage capacity, are required for large installations. The small timers plug into the wall socket. Industrial timers must be attached to a wall with fireproof protection.

Both kinds of timers are equipped with one on and one off switch that can be set for any time of day and night. Special timers are available with multiple on-and-off settings. They are occasionally used for misters or humidifiers to turn them on and off a number of times every 24 hours. All automatic timers are also equipped with manual switches.

Attaching the fixture. The box cover is pierced at intervals with holes to which partly cut circles of the metal are still attached. Push them in with a screwdriver or pull out with pliers to provide ventilation to the box. The holes also serve as convenient means of attachment by S hooks and chains. Drill smaller holes in the cover to accommodate screws and attach the cover directly to a surface such as the underside of shelving. Lift the pan into place and attach tightly by means of the wing nuts.

Reflection. Because of its shape, a fluorescent tube emits as much light above as below. We employ it only to illuminate the area beneath, but half the light is wasted unless the up lighting is reflected downward. This can never be accomplished with complete success, but it is obvious that the more efficient the reflector used the greater the saving.

All strip fixtures are painted white, but the reflective surface is too narrow for maximum efficiency. Where strip fixtures are attached to a surface, the latter should be coated with matte titanium white paint. White enamel appears to be brighter and more reflective but is actually less so. Amateurs often suggest the use of mirrors, thinking them better. Not so, although mirrors can be attached to the back of the shelving space as a more attractive solution. A back wall of matte white, however, is more reflective.

Commercial fixtures are also available with white-painted reflectors already attached. These are in the shape of a hood and concentrate light more effectively than a flat surface. Paint the exterior of the reflector with a neutral color or one that matches decor.

Bulb sources of light. Although the decline in intensity with distance is greater for a point than a line source of light, bulbs are superior to tubes for the maintenance of plants above 2½ ft. (75 cm) in height and for those that are illuminated from a ceiling. Bulbs possess the advantage that very high light output can be packed into small units. They are much more adaptable to a variety of situations than fluorescent tubes when they can be angled to permit focussing for maximum effectiveness.

The other side of the coin is that it is difficult to change the spectrum to satisfy the needs of plants and that the colors they emit are frequently unflattering both to plants and humans.

High-wattage bulbs that require bulky fixtures containing converters are initially expensive and used mainly for very large garden projects.

Incandescent lamps. Those that are most frequently used for plant illumination in offices are designated R-Reflector Flood in catalogs. They are top-shaped, the front very wide and the neck and part of the swelling silvered as a built-in reflector. Spot PARs produce narrow beams and floods broad ones. They are recessed in ceilings or mounted in reflective cylinders or half globes, designed to project the light in a specific arc. On track, attached to ceilings, they can be moved and angled.

As already noted, incandescent has a poor spectrum for plant growth and is very hot. It also has the lowest light output per watt and the shortest life expectancy of any source used for plants. Yet PAR bulbs are widely used for area lighting and plant maintenance. However the plants are there only as an afterthought and are those with the lowest light requirement, restricting choice to a very few. A change to more efficient lighting for better results is not even considered.

150 watt R-Reflector Flood bulbs will just barely manage to maintain even Dracaenas and Syngoniums for a short time provided that the ceiling is not over 9 ft. (2.70 m) high and the plants with containers and on supports reach within 3–4 ft. (90 cm–1.20 m). Plants must be replaced at six-month intervals. They are returned to the nursery for recuperation. Three hundred and 500 watt PARs, set in clusters or rows, will maintain foliage plants for a while at a maximum distance of 10 ft. (3 m). They cannot be placed close to plants because of the heat.

When plants are placed directly beneath a single spot or flood, only the top branches and leaves receive sufficient light. Two lamps, one on either side, provide improved illumination for the whole plant. Replacement time can, thereby, be more than doubled.

In public places such as department stores, plants are often placed between rather than under light sources, and the latter are very widely spaced. The logical consequence is rapid deterioration. The best one can say for incandescent sources is that they are convenient means of illumination where plants are placed temporarily for function or decoration; but inefficient and costly in the long run.

Metal Halide lamps. These lamps are available in wattages from 175 to 1500 and produce about 20% more light per watt than fluorescent. For instance, the 400 watt lamp produces 40,000 lumens, equalling 100 lumens per watt, as against less than 80 lumens per watt for the most efficient fluorescent lamps. Rated life is 20,000 hours for lower wattages, decreasing to 3,000 hours for the 1500 watt bulbs. All use special ballasts and fixtures that increase initial cost considerably.

The light is strongest at the blue end of the spectrum but varies from lamp to lamp and is subject to changes in use. Nevertheless, the 1,000 watt High Output lamps are today the main source of supplementary illumination for large indoor gardens such as atriums. As a sole source the effect on plant growth is inadequate but, where there is considerable natural light, they supply a sufficient additive for long-term maintenance. Additional 400 watt bulbs are sometimes hung closer to the plants. Recognizing that the color is objectionable in its effect on the appearance of both plants and people, they are usually switched on only at night.

A more satisfactory solution is the use of Metal Halide in combination with High Pressure Sodium lamps (see in the following). The latter, are strong in yellow and emit some red parts of the spectrum. Together they meet the needs of trees and other large foliage plants. However, instead of bathing the whole area in metallic light, the combination makes everything look oddly yellowed and dessicated. Observe the Ficus trees (and people) in the Citicorp building atrium in New York City.

The lamps and the combination are of no value for use in the home.

Mercury Vapor lamps. Wonderlite. Standard mercury vapor lamps have various commercial uses, though they emit less light than fluorescent. For instance, 40 watt Cool and Warm White tubes have a rating of 3200 lumens, whereas 40-watt mercury lamps emit a maximum of 1500 lumens. They require special ballasts and fixtures. They have the advantage over other bulb sources that color can be controlled by the mix of gases within the bulb.

Manufacturers have also succeeded in producing bulbs that are self-ballasted and, therefore, requiring no special fixture, can be screwed into standard incandescent bulb sockets. They look like ordinary R-Reflector bulbs and the swelling is, likewise, coated as a reflector. With one exception, however, all multi-vapor lamps lack sufficient red light in their emissions to be efficient in plant maintenance.

The exception is the Wonderlite, available in 160 and 330 watt models (see Sources), whose manufacturers have succeeded in creating a bulb that emits a sufficient amount of red light to make it an excellent light source for plant growth and maintenance. So effective is the formula that it also sets buds and flowers. The color of the light is also pleasant and is acceptable in both public and living areas. As sales are not huge the lamp is expensive, but its 10,000-hour life expectancy reduces the long-term cost. The Wonderlite is constantly gaining wider acceptance by interior landscapers as its superiority becomes better known. It is the only bulb source of light we can recommend for home and office use.

Suspend the Wonderlite in a wide reflector shade over taller foliage plants; set two or more on a ceiling track to illuminate wall or corner gardens; give supplementary light to window gardens with a northern or obstructed exposure as well as on cloudy days.

First-time users of Multi-Vapor lamps should not be dismayed by one peculiarity. The bulbs take a few moments to warm up and reach maximum intensity. If switched off and then immediately on again, a few minutes will pass before the lamp ignites. This is not a practical handicap in use. Manufacture of the lamp is a very delicate operation and there are occasional failures. Steady improvement has been achieved in dependability. The manufacturer of the Wonderlite has been prompt in replacing faulty bulbs at no cost.

WONDERLITE SPECTRUM

— ·· — Photosynthesis
— — — Chlorophyll Synthesis
— · — ·· Phototropism
———— Photomorphogenesis-induction
— ···· Photomorphogenesis-reversal
·········· Photopic Vision
▬▬▬ Wonderlite's Relative Percent of Spectra

According to the Lighting Handbook (5th Edition) of the Illumination Engineering Society, "The action spectra of the five major photoresponses of plants show the utilization of energy in three major spectral regions (400 to 500 nm., 600 to 700 nm. 700 to 800 nm.)" As shown by the dark colored line on the top chart, the relative measurement of the **WONDERLITE** shows peaks of 80% or more in all three of the spectral regions of plant photoresponses.

High Pressure Sodium bulbs. Sodium lamps pack into a long bulb almost a third more light output than a fluorescent tube. The rated life is 24,000 hours. Special ballasts and fixtures are required. Wattage ranges from 35 to 1,000.

Alone they are impractical for plant maintenance indoors. Whatever their merits for out-door lighting, the color is unbearable in closed spaces. The red-yellow light is familiar as street and highway illumination. They have been used in shopping malls with trees. Combination with Metal Halide bulbs, as indicated above, is a practical, though hardly ideal, solution for large-scale indoor gardens.

PRACTICAL APPLICATION OF ARTIFICIAL LIGHT

Relativity of data on lighting vs. plants. Writers on gardening indoors are strongly tempted to lay down hard-and-fast rules based on precise technical data; for instance available footcandles and plant response, distance of the plants from a light source and the like. Such exactitude is a legitimate expectation in planning lighting for offices—or baseball fields. With plants that doesn't work. Experienced lighting experts understand that very complex factors are involved and that each situation requires, for precision of results, different calculations. It is one thing to estimate lighting for the mass production of a single plant species in an environment where all the elements can be measured and quite another to prescribe for all kinds of situations in homes and for a mixture of plant types.

All our own experience confirms this. Whatever figures we give on lights vs. plants are only approximations or based on a judgement of average situations. The actual ones vary to a greater or lesser degree. However, it can also be emphasized that these rough estimates work quite well and can be depended upon in most situations. If results fail to match expectations, adjustments can be made rather easily.

Lighting from below. A frequent question is whether artificial light from below contributes to the maintenance of plants. The answer is an unequivocal no. The chlorophyll layer of leaves is on the upper surface and benefits only from light shining upon it from above. Intense lighting from beneath a plant causes damage in the shorter or longer run. Soft lighting can be used safely, as long as it is not continuous, to create interesting silhouettes and shadows at night.

Amateurs have also occasionally installed fluorescent tubes in a vertical position with the idea of providing more uniform lighting on all parts of a tall plant. No damage occurs but the system is costly as the light must come from at least two sides. No improvement in growth or maintenance is perceptible.

Objections to use of fluorescent light in the home. Considering the huge number of American families that grow houseplants, it is an anomaly that only a small proportion install fluorescent lighting despite the evident advantages it offers over complete dependence on natural light. Cool houses and long stretches of cloudy weather in winter are conditions that a majority of tropical plants are unable to survive. Fluorescent tubes supply not only supplementary light but also higher and not excessive temperatures when they are most needed. Where windows face north or are seriously obstructed, growers must rely on a few species of plants whose only real merit is tolerance of unfavorable lighting conditions. The best decorative placing in rooms is frequently impractical because there is insufficient daylight.

The explanation for this avoidance of fluorescent lighting is twofold. The length of tubes and fixtures makes them ungainly and difficult to fit into standard interior decoration. And they are so little used for general lighting in the home that they are thought of as suited only to workplaces. The whole process of connecting them is alien. We have observed that even an ignorance of how to place a fluorescent tube in its sockets is widespread. That's considered a job for the electrician or superintendent. When houseplants are ailing from lack of sufficient light, the usual solution is to buy "growth bulbs" which, in our opinion, are of no avail, rather than try fluorescent tubes.

Willy-nilly, complementary fluorescent lighting must be provided for most kinds of foliage plants in windows with obstructed light. Performance is improved in northern exposures. In the interior of rooms where little daylight penetrates, fluorescent lighting is essential for growing the smaller houseplants.

Complementing window lighting. When window light is inadequate install fluorescent tubes. A 20-watt, 24 in. (60 cm), 2-tube fixture will be sufficient to provide complementary lighting for any width from 24–40 in. (60–100 cm). From 41 to 65 in. (102.5–162.5 cm) use a 48 in. (1.20 m) fixture. From 72 to about 90 in. (1.80–2.25 m) use a 3-24 in. or 1-24 in. and 1-48 in. (60 cm and 1.20 m) fixture. From 90 in. to a few inches beyond 100 in. (2.25–2.50 m) a 96 in. fixture is best. Intermediate tube lengths produce less light for the wattage used. These are only guidelines and are not to be taken as gospel.

Attach the fixture to a valance strong enough to bear the weight. It does not matter if the fixture must be wider than a window. Just make the valance a few inches longer. Attach the fixture by screws or hang it by chains so that it can be raised or lowered.

In a very poorly lighted window it may be necessary to provide 10 hours of artificial light throughout the year. Where some sunlight is available, 4 hours in summer and 9–11 hours in winter may be about right. Adjustments can be made depending on plant response. The longer hours that we suggest may seem excessive considering that in parts of rooms where plants are even more dependent on artificial light, the on period is much the same. However they are usually necessary because window fixtures are set at a greater distance from the plants.

Fluorescent shelf lighting. Among the few places where fluorescent fixtures can be related to furnishings in the home is in shelving, whether built from scratch or adapted. The shape of a fixture fits neatly into the space and the distances between shelves is just right for good growing of smaller houseplants—those that are less than 2 ft. (60 cm) high.

One can also buy fully equipped stands and 2-, 3-, or 4-shelved units with trays, manufactured for the sole purpose of growing houseplants. Unfortunately the designs have been utilitarian and difficult or impossible to match decoratively with existent furniture. Nevertheless, most avid indoor gardeners prefer these units. From time to time there have been attempts to market decorative units in wood or of metal with wood finishes, but the cost has been high and the appearance not attractive. We discuss shelving units below, but first, it is necessary to indicate the limitations imposed by shelf lighting on the sizes of plants.

Limits of plant size and shelf spacing. For shelves 1 ft. (30 cm) wide, use a pair of fluorescent tubes. For greater widths figure an additional tube for every extra 4–6 in. (10–15 cm). In planning a shelf garden the limitation on plant height is set by the light output of the tubes. Using Cool White/Warm White tubes that limit is roughly 30 in. (75 cm) from the bottom of the pot to the top of the plant. The distance between shelves is restricted roughly to 34 in. (85 Scm). Permissible width of a plant is a few inches more than that of the shelf. Figure a 16 in. (40 cm) wide plant, allowing some overhang, as maximum on 12 in. (30 cm) shelving.

A general rule is that low, wide plants benefit most from 2-tube fixtures. Narrow, tallish plants, over 15 in. (37.5 cm) excluding pot, usually lose lower leaves. For these it is better to use wider shelving and increase the number of tubes so that more light is supplied at an angle, effectively framing them with illumination.

Within these limitations shelves can be adjusted to the height of plants; shorter distances for short ones and wider spacing for tall ones. The practice is to gang up plants of similar size and light requirement. However, one short plant may need intense light and a close setting whereas another may well need much less and be a further distance away from the light source. Small differences are overcome by raising plants on temporary supports. As they increase in size the supports are removed and, eventually it is frequently necessary to move them to wider-spaced shelving.

Adapting storage shelving to fluorescent fixtures and plants. Storage shelving is mostly 10–12 in. (25–30 cm) wide and 30–36 in. (75–90 cm) long. It may be of fine, finished woods, of bolted or fitted metal or plastic. Distances between shelves may be permanent or adjustable. Both types can be used but adjustable shelving offers obvious advantages for indoor gardening.

Fixtures need not approximate closely the length of shelving. Twenty-four in. (60 cm) fixtures are ample for 36 in. (75 cm) shelving and 48 in. (1.20 m) fixtures fit 72 in. (1.80 m) shelving. As noted previously these size fixtures and their tubes are more efficient than in-between sizes. The space beyond the ends of the tubes is useful for the lower-light-tolerant foliage plants.

When the only available shelving is located in living or other social rooms, converting it to light-gardening purposes seems impossible without simultaneously damaging the fine-quality materials of which it is made or forcing the displacement of books, art objects or sound/video equipment. Some moving to other locations is inevitable, but there are compromises that work well in most instances. It is, for example, unnecessary or even inadvisable to convert the whole unit to plants. A part may be sufficient; materials can be protected and the result of a mix of plants and objects of art or books enhances rather than detracts from the appearance.

To protect the sensitive surface of a base shelf, cover it with thick vinyl plastic sheeting, a pane of acrylic or glass, cut to size. As further insurance use attractive shallow trays. Saucers are riskier as they often overflow in watering. Cover metal shelving with a polyurethane paint in a color that matches the decor. Undersides of shelves painted white act as reflectors. Give at least two coats to base shelves. Even the simplest shelving is absorbed into its surroundings if the color is right.

In any shelving complex the sections devoted to fixtures and plants should be chosen with some consideration of the sizes you wish to grow. That depends on the distances between shelves or their adjustability. We have discovered that the combination of plants with lights on one or more shelves and books as well as other objects on others makes enchanting decoration. There is also the advantage that the lights are frequently sufficient for reading and for a substantial part of room illumination at night. We wish that furniture manufacturers and furniture stores would get together to offer the public the option of growth-light installations in bookcases and storage wall combinations. Recently there has been considerable use of shelf lighting for decorative reasons but without consideration of the possibility of growing plants. Of course, the total use of shelving for plants is a satisfactory option at all times.

Building shelving with fluorescent fixtures. Construction of your own shelving is one of the simpler projects in carpentry. There are a number of systems that permit 1 in. (2.5 cm) adjustments in height. Formica surfaces on wooden shelves are impervious to drip. Making your own shelving gives you greater control over the size of the unit, permitting you to fit light gardens into awkward places. We have a space at the end of a pantry where shelving has provided us with extra room for plants which could only be gained in this way. Part of the unit is even overlapped by a storage cabinet. Yet it is accessible and fills a dead storage area with light and greenery.

Valances. We have mentioned these before. They are an amenity that we recommend wherever there are lighted shelving units above 4 ft. (1.20 m) high when the lights can be seen from a seated position. The valances for shelving are battens added to the outer edge of the shelf. On the roof of a unit the valance overhangs the fixture and tubes attached to it. Further down, in order to hide trays or saucers, it can also extend to 2 inches (5 cm) above. The correct amount of overhang is about 6 in. (15 cm) at 6 ft. (1.80 m). For shelving lower down you must experiment by checking from chairs in the room the width of valance that will hide the light.

Manufactured growth stands. Growth stands are not sold at present through either the furniture or lighting sections of department stores. Some specialty lighting stores market the simplest type, a 2-tube, 24-in. (60-cm) fixture in a rectangular reflector, raised on legs. It can be set on the floor or a table and is easily assembled and portable. You must supply a tray for the plants. All larger stands can be bought only through a handful of distributors, are shown in some seed catalogs, or bought directly from the manufacturers who advertise in specialty indoor-gardening plant magazines issued by various horticultural hobby societies.

The larger models are generally 24 or 48 in. (60 cm or 1.20 m) long and 12 or 20 in. (30 or 50 cm) wide. Metal or plastic trays are supported on the tubular metal shelf framework. Two- to 5-tier units are available. Additional shelf units can usually be added to the basic 2-level unit. Within the limitations of the framework, distances between shelves are adjustable. The finish is chrome or white enamel. All have 2-tube fixtures. If more tubes are desired for the 20 in. (50 cm) wide shelving, buy only the supporting structure and install 4-tube fixtures bought from commercial electric supply stores. The manufacturer or distributor will not supply the 4-tube fixtures.

The units are rather like hospital equipment but not bulky. They can be quite inconspicuous if painted to match walls or furniture. The plants themselves overcome any incongruity. Most foliage plants will do well in these units, but the distance allowed between shelving is limited.

Automatic light gardens. We have not seen them lately but from time to time manufacturers have attempted to introduce enclosed units that they promote as automatic light gardens. Various controls are supposed to provide a risk-free terrarium environment for plants using fluorescent lighting. In the past these have been expensive disasters. Before investing in any such equipment find some way to check results achieved by previous customers. The designs are those of competent engineers who, unfortunately, have had no experience with plants.

Other home installations. With ingenuity you can find various places for fluorescent fixtures and plants in a home.

Light a terrarium by means of a grow stand.

Install a fixture in the flue of an unused fireplace. Arrange plants in a tray beneath or enclose them in a terrarium.

A friend has converted shelves of a highboy very prettily into a little light garden.

Cover the ceiling of a windowed bay with fluorescent fixtures hidden by sheets of parawedge diffusers (*see* in the following). They supply extra light further back from the windows and improve performance near the windows on overcast days. The whole bay can be planted with large foliage plants.

Utilize excess closet space by installing shelving and fixtures.

Place plants on half-high room dividers—counters and such. Suspend fixtures from the ceiling. Bulb light can also be used for this purpose but the shape of the fluorescent fixture is more suitable.

Use attics and cellars for large numbers of shelved units. Cellars require heating; attics cooling and ventilation. Grow plants to put on display in other parts of the house. Rotate them as they deteriorate while on display. Start plants from seeds and cuttings. Experiment with new plants.

Plants in offices. Plants are an almost automatic requirement in offices, and ceiling fluorescent fixtures are the universal sources of light in the workplace. As ceilings are rarely more than 9 ft. (2.70 m) high and usually only reach 8 ft. (2.40 m), plants are placed on partial dividers or file cabinets in a range of 4½ to 6 ft. (1.35–1.80 m) tall. Diffusers under the fluorescent tubes reduce illumination, but at 2–3 ft. (60–90 cm) below there is a minimum of 40 fc available; just enough to maintain some very low-light-tolerant plants, such as some Dracaenas or Aglaonemas, for a while.

The tubes are usually Cool White or Vita-Lite. Even if the CW/WW combination were to be specified by the plantscaper or architect, it would not be installed because most office workers are accustomed to Cool White. This requires that the task of maintenance be taken over by a service organization that waters, grooms and rotates the plants. Workers are grateful for any greenery at all. No improvement is expected because additional cost for superior lighting cannot be justified as economically advantageous. And one has to face the fact that changes in the lighting system might very well cause more distress to workers than the ordinariness of the plants.

Plants under fluorescent in stores, restaurants, etc. The same systems are used in stores as in offices. On street floors a greater concentration of ceiling fixtures produces somewhat more light. Plants are placed on dividers separating sales strips on adjacent aisles. The choice of plants is broader because they are meant to fit seasonal or holiday decorative schemes and are maintained for only a few weeks. Hence, spreading palms and other more exotic greenery are used.

In restaurants basket plants are sometimes hung from the ceiling. Being closer to the tubes, Boston Ferns, Swedish Ivy and similar plants can thrive for as long as six months without notable deterioration. Spathiphyllums, Homalocladiums, darker green Aglaonemas and a few other shade plants last well in low dividers. Tall Dracaenas also can be maintained for a while in areas that receive little or no daylight.

Para-wedge diffusers. For decorative purposes the most interesting of the diffusers is called para-wedge, which also comes under a variety of trademarked names. It is plastic sheet ⅜–½ in. (9.35–12.5 mm) thick, cut in a square waffle or hexagon design. The side walls of the openings are mathematically curved and covered with a highly reflective metallic coating. The diffuser not only effectively hides the light source; it virtually obliterates awareness of it. Seen from below at an angle of 30 degrees or more, a ceiling covered with the material appears to be black. It is used extensively in prestige situations such as banks, where a patterned ceiling without glare is desired. This diffuser can be used instead of valances to hide tubes and fixtures in high-placed shelving units in the home.

Bulbs for houseplants. There has been relatively little exploitation of the potential of bulb sources of light for plants in the home. The broad and tall plants, to which bulbs offer greater freedom in placing and more efficient lighting, are located near windows, serving as surrogates for old-fashioned heavy curtains. The advantages of complementary illumination is usually overlooked. Floor gardens along walls or in corners are rare, as they involve more expense and ingenuity. Rock-built wall gardens are certainly a luxury. However, the interior plantscaper should always keep these possibilities in mind. So often period social rooms are as cluttered with furniture and bric-a-brac as those of the Victorian era, and more modern styles of decorations are frequently so ascetic as to be sterile. Indoor plantings are a spectacular solution to both the above extremes.

Inadequacy of incandescent bulbs. We have already expatiated on the shortcomings of the incandescent spectrum. If this source is delivered with considerable intensity some beneficial effect on maintenance can be noted. The reason is that, if a light source has, like incandescent or high pressure sodium, very little blue light compared to yellow through red, simply increasing the amount of light does the same for blue and is tolerable if the heat generated by the red rays is not too great.

The least wattage that is used is 150. Tall plants quickly lose leaves without two bulbs angled so as to reach down on both sides.

Reflector floods and spots need no housing. Nonreflecting lamps require small reflectors. They are attached to ceiling track where they can be moved and angled, or recessed into the ceiling where they can only be angled. The maintenance of the gardens mentioned above is impossible with this type of lighting.

Applications with Wonderlite bulbs. As previously noted, we consider the Wonderlite the only bulb source that does a good job of maintaining foliage (and flowering) plants in home and business environments. We do not doubt that technological advances will result in other lamps for the purpose, but we see no alternative to the Wonderlite for the present. With it indoor gardens are able to flourish for any length of time.

Substitute the lamp for fluorescent fixtures in complementing window light. Maintain gardens further back from windows, on tables or stands. Since tall plants suffer at windows in summer from the fact that the verticality of sunlight penetrates only a very short distance into rooms, bulbs will supply the direct illumination that is needed. In winter they are helpful on overcast days.

Attach 160- or 330-watt bulbs to ceiling track, spacing them 4 ft. apart. This is very approximate. More precise settings are possible by measuring light along the space devoted to plants, shifting the position of the lamps to balance the footcandle intensity at plant level. The length of time the lamps should be lit depends on window exposure, time of year and plant reactions; in other words pretty much trial and error.

Floor and corner gardens. To make a floor garden, enclose a space in a low wall of suitable material. Calculate that behind the wall pots will be either close to floor level or set on top of a fill material. That decision regulates the height of the wall. Line the interior with a metal pan, the sides nearly as high as the wall or use heavy, durable plastic sheeting. Fill the space with pebbles, sand, marble chips or other loose materials that either permit circulation of air or permit quick evaporation of water. Plunge the pots or set them on top. Saucers can also be used. Tall plantings are lighted from ceiling track with Wonderlites. If small plants are planned, build a frame deep enough and wide enough to hold track and bulbs. Attach to the wall or provide supports. Track is advisable so that the lamps can be moved for maximum effectiveness. This system works in the same way for corners, which are frequently the best available spaces in a room. Experiment with a 5-ft. (1.50 m) spread between bulbs. If that is inadequate extras can be added.

Table gardens. Large coffee tables of glass, marble or travertine support a number of medium-tall plants up to 4 ft. (1.20 m) in height including pots. Suspend a Wonderlite in a broad reflector shade over the group.

Wall gardens. It is difficult but not impossible to build wall gardens in a living room. The problems are of a kind best solved by a professional. Design involves a floor-level trough with waterproof lining, protection of the wall with plastic sheeting and side frames, arrangement of real or artificial rocks in a crude wall and the provision of a recirculating pump that moves water in the trough to the top of the garden whence it trickles down by a number of pre-arranged paths to the trough. The trick is in canting the rocks so that the water is distributed widely at the top and is then made to flow by a number of routes. The spaces between the rocks are filled with sphagnum moss and soil. The pockets are planted and must receive regular watering.

The lighting is on track attached to the ceiling and should consist of 160-watt bulbs for higher positions and 330 or higher wattages for lower positions. The idea is not merely theoretical for it has been carried out in various ways and worked successfully. A considerable amount of trial and error is involved in finding plants that survive in these conditions.

Bulbs in stores and offices. Large plants are tucked into corners of department store floors, placed on either side of escalators to direct attention to their presence or lined up to guide traffic. Their functions are much the same in other public buildings. Where they are set has little to do with the distribution of existing lighting and it is rare, indeed, that additional lighting is installed to aid in maintaining them for a longer period. Service companies rotate them as they deteriorate. One need only keep track of the relationship between ceiling lighting and plants in those places to be aware of the incongruity and the unlikelihood of any change in current practices.

In executive offices there is plenty of opportunity for handsome plantings along the lines described above for homes. Methods and means are the same. As part of the perks of status in businesses these offices usually enjoy window light. That can be exploited and bulbs on track installed as complementary lighting.

For office decoration with plants, the function of interior landscapers is usually confined to choosing plants for size, shape and tolerance of the existing lighting. Often they are in charge of the crews that service the plants with watering, feeding, grooming, removing and replacing. Their knowledge is essential to the proper performance of these tasks, but hardly creative. Little scope for creativity is generally accorded by managements. If superior bulbs or tubes are installed, more often than not the superintendent replaces them, as soon as the first batch has failed, with ordinary light sources. Inertia is a major handicap to any improvement in the system. Hence the sameness of most office plant decor.

INTERIOR LANDSCAPING WITH FOLIAGE PLANTS

An industry has grown up in recent years consisting of nurseries producing plants for cultivation indoors, distributing wholesalers and retailers, interior landscape designers, architects, engineers and plant lighting specialists and service organizations. For these and kindred operations the title of Interior Landscape Industry has been adopted and we speak of interior landscapers. To suggest that all professional plant installation in commercial and domestic situations is interior landscaping, in the same sense as we speak of outdoor garden landscaping, is misleading. The term applies with some justification to the plantings of large atriums and enclosed malls but is thoroughly inappropriate for the infinitely greater use of plants in other commercial and all domestic situations. Plant decorating and plant decorator are more correct as descriptions of the functions of experts in this field. The distinction highlights the essential difference between outdoor and indoor designing with plants. We use interior landscaping and landscaper only because of the convention, as a change would only create confusion.

Large-scale atrium gardens are intended as outdoor tropical or subtropical landscaping and planting adapted to architecturally enclosed spaces. Designs are derived from outdoor-garden prototypes. The elements are beds, massed shrubs and trees, walls, troughs, patterned walkways, terraces, waterfalls and streams. To accomplish such artistic and technical feats indoors has required the employment of architects, professional landscapers, engineers and other technical assistance recruited from many fields of expertise.

Ways of overcoming the problems encountered in producing and maintaining such works have been dealt with in specialized books and numerous articles. Throughout this book there is information regarding plant material, the environment and culture which should be useful to interior landscapers. In this section we discuss briefly large indoor gardens, especially some recurrent causes of the failures that have occurred. Office, shop, restaurant and most other commercial installations require little more than knowledge of a very limited plant repertory and a modicum of ingenuity and good taste. We have touched on this already. A more complex matter is the use of foliage for the decoration of homes.

Functional plant categories. It is natural to attempt the formulation for plant decoration of a body of rules and a set of categories that make planning virtually automatic. Systematization is helpful in many fields but it has never been applied successfully to interior decoration with or without plants. We give a few very elastic suggestions that are worth keeping in mind

1. *Architectural plants.* Plants that complement or mask architecture. Modern walls and angles are often blank spaces and geometric lines. Plants of sufficient height and width, with thick, densely leaved, branching systems and organic contours, perform a real service in interrupting verticality and hiding meaningless or unattractive angles. They can be used singly or in clusters. Leafy vines on supports serve the same purposes. Other functions include service as room dividers or directional indicators, for example, as lead-ins to stairs or escalators or double-rowed as pedestrian traffic lanes.

2. *Sculptural plants.* Plants of all sizes possessing a striking and distinctive shape. This may be natural or artificial. A *Ficus* grown naturally may be architectural; shaped by trimming, it becomes sculptural.

3. *Screening plants.* Plants that create an effect of softness, of loose form and transluscence. Their small leaves allow light to pass between, creating complex shadows. Vines are useful screens, trailing over the sides of balconies.

4. *Bedding plants.* All those, modest in size, that are most effective when massed in the foregrounds of garden designs in the same way that they are used outdoors. Most of these achieve an individual personality in rooms where they can be placed in positions to be appreciated as such. The majority of smaller plants of all shapes belong to this category.

5. *Specimen plants.* A poor designation for lack of a better. We apply it to those cultivars that have a very distinctive appearance not typical of the species, for example variegation. This trait is frequently regressive and makes the plants more demanding of special cultural conditions. Hence they are, if produced in quantities, less reliable or, if not, require the ministrations of knowledgable and conscientious growers. The most spectacular of these are, therefore, relatively scarce in the shops. But they are the favorite plants of those who like to experiment with novelty or are attracted by striking colors and shapes. At nurseries they come and go as their ability to survive varies. Some, however, have the potential to become standard indoor-gardening plants once superior clones are selected for propagation. In our lists of plants we include many that, at the present time, have only a potential; but among these may be found the plants of the future.

Commercial Indoor Gardens

Size and Proportion. Plain, mountain and sea views are so vast that we say that the human being is "lost" in them. We can only marvel at their appearance in different atmospheric conditions but we cannot relate the size of our own bodies to these huge features. Pyramids and skyscrapers are artificial works that have little meaning for us except as awe-inspiring in size. Usually we try to shape the spaces surrounding us in such a way that we can relate space and the objects in it to our own bodies and level of vision. A 200-foot tree is too big to be grasped because only its girth and a sense of the height of its bare trunk are visible as a whole. As a whole we can see very big objects only at a distance. The closer they are the smaller they must be and, along with closeness, comes the appreciation of detail. When we plan our surroundings we choose proportions intuitively.

In an outdoor garden we arrange plants so that those nearest to the path or edge of a lawn are the lowest, with their height increasing with distance. Large trees are viewed across lawn or pond. An exception is when we plant tall shrubs on either side of a path; but then they serve a different function by forming a living wall. Small plants must be massed in the garden because they are dwarfed by their surroundings. They must be very close before we can examine their shapes and colors.

Atrium gardens. Indoors the proportions of an outdoor garden are approximated only in atria. There, too, very large plants, such as trees, only function as "shading" or as irregular living walls. They can be seen in their entirety only if they are placed at the ends or sides of gardens. They should be carefully chosen for height and width to match the size of the space, and the positioning of entrances to the garden should present a vista in which they relate to other tall plants that act as transitions from still smaller ones. Big as an atrium's dimensions may be, they are not to compare with the outdoors. The tall-tree effect is achieved with smaller ones than we allow to grow outdoors. It is true that the shaft of the atrium may be very high but the rest of the enclosure is limited in size so that we are conscious of only part of the shaft's height. We cannot compete; we can only compromise.

The situation is changed when trees are the only feature of a garden. Their function is to form a canopy of greenery. The atrium of the IBM building in New York provides the ambience of a bamboo grove in which the plants have been geometrically spaced. The large *Ficus* in the Citicorp building is more formal still, the tall trunks leaving space for tables. Both solutions hide the shaft above. There is no attempt to create a naturalistic garden which demands herbs, shrubs and small tree, mostly no higher than eye level. Other elements of gardens may be a rock wall with waterfall, pools and streams. The paths and levels must be carefully directed close to these features so that the pleasure is not confined just to some instant view but can dwell on details.

Street-floor gardens. Two large street-floor gardens suggest the difficulty in executing such projects and some of the mistakes that are frequent in designing large commercial gardens. Street-floor gardens are transitional between atria and domestic and office plantings. The garden in the Chemcorp building in New York is in a huge lean-to greenhouse projecting from the tower at street level. Greenhouse efficiency is vitiated by a roof that is too high and a space that is too narrow. The exterior appearance is unattractive because of the large size and prominence of the supporting members.

If a firm invests in one of these costly affairs one presumes that it expects some benefit through institutional publicity. To accomplish this, the garden must be made attractive and inviting from the street side as well as within. Any such intention is defeated because the tall plants are placed close to the windows. They form a wall of undifferentiated greenery that turns the windows into mirrors. Within, the tall plants on the street side cut off the light while the inner side is terraced and intended to contain smaller but more colorful plants. For the latter insufficient artificial light has been provided. What there is causes a yellow half light that is positively gloomy to anyone coming in from the street.

The shape of the space prohibited the use of very tall plants. The lean-to is sufficiently high but the space too narrow. The plants used are seen only as a nearly black, undifferentiated wall of greenery. The 3-ft. plants on the terraces therefore look even smaller, being dwarfed by the proportions with which they compete.

To make any inside space sufficiently bright when seen from the street, very intense artificial lighting, as in storefront display windows, is required. Colorful, low plants should have been massed close to the windows and bathed in sufficient illumination to match the outdoor light. The relatively tall plants, not as high as those actually used, could be massed in the corners. Much more light on the terraces would improve the appearance and growth. Even at best this garden must depend very heavily on temporary plantings, replaced at regular intervals. The darkness of the area was brought into additional prominence because the adjacent banking space with large unobstructed windows on the street was so much lighter, and a row of Aglaonemas in pots along the broad sill looked more cheerful and brighter than anything in the garden.

Another instructive example is one of the early attempts installed at the Ford Foundation building. This one depends for light on extremely high south-facing windows partly blocked by buildings across the street. The garden is arranged in semicircular terraces opposite the windows and backed by story after story of balconies that are part of the communication between offices. The ceiling is so high that suspending additional lighting has been a problem. Furthermore, and more serious, those in charge wanted to create a temperate zone garden and apparently were not warned of the consequences. As the building is heated for comfort in winter, the original plantings could not survive. The most obvious rule, to use plants compatible with the environment, had been broken. The cost of upkeep must have been considerable. Despite many changes and its prominent position it has attracted little attention or favorable comment.

Both gardens may have been much improved at this writing, but the original mistakes indicate the pitfalls awaiting those who attempt such projects without knowledge or consideration of actual plant needs.

The most successful of the recent atrium gardens have been mostly in the South where there is more sunlight and less severe, long-lasting changes in exterior temperatures. Much progress has been achieved in overcoming problems of maintenance. Plants have been chosen with more care. Lighting technology has improved. Most of the atriums are daylighted by means of ample shafts and provided with architectural features permitting the use of adequate lighting fixtures that are placed so that they are not excessively obtrusive.

Decorating with plants in the home

While it is true that all gardens are artificial, outdoor ones and atriums can suggest a natural setting. In street-floor gardens this is already more difficult to achieve. Domestic situations allow no scope for truly natural effects. Compositions with plants are determined by the surroundings and are essentially abstract. Assuming that they are placed according to some plan, the sizes and shapes of plants depend on the furnishings which, in turn, are strictly dependent on our personal needs.

In rooms the walls are rarely more than double our own height; the ceiling is the indoor sky; chairs, tables, mantels, even windows, all are measured in human proportions. Within these dimensions plant size assumes an entirely different role than out-of-doors or in places large enough to give an illusion of great space. A small tree that reaches to the ceiling seems crushed by it and altogether out of proportion to everything else in the room. That is because we, ourselves, are not far form the ceiling and are very conscious of it as a barrier and protection. We are too close to walls to actually pay much attention to anything that is at ceiling level. We are comfortable only with objects that are standing at eye level or only a little above.

The space in even a large domestic room causes us instinctively to adjust our sense of proportions. Plants that appear insignificant in a garden assume much greater importance when placed on a side table or in a window. A 3–4 ft. shrub in its container is a big object; one that is 6 ft. tall may be incongruously out of proportion to an "interior landscape." Even the massing of like plants is out of place. In our rooms a single plant is sufficiently noticeable.

Therefore the decorative art consists in the arrangement of choice individual plants in relation to each other and to the surroundings. Certainly, one can achieve quite pleasant effects by grouping different kinds of plants any which way on a windowsill, shelf or table; but that is not decorative design. Planned decoration with plants obeys the same rules of formality as setting a dining table for a special occasion.

A professional plant decorator (or plantscaper) should be able to choose plants that adapt well to different cultural environments, find or make space for them, install additional lighting if necessary and, perhaps, service them regularly. These are technical matters. Artistic choices and arrangements require a different kind of knowledge and talent. Style and taste are personal but the problems of decorating with plants are also always subject to technical imperatives.

Rooms have windows mostly on one or two sides. These being the only sources of natural light, we automatically group plants close to them. In other areas they must be fitted into empty spaces between furniture and be lighted artificially. Or we can utilize wall shelving, also by installing artificial light.

Rarely can plants be the dominant feature of the rooms we live in. They are usually subsidiary to the furniture and merely complementary. Their role is, however, not different from other decorative features, which is to blend in with and enhance the ambience. That is why finding locations for plants, and arranging and lighting them in the home, calls for considerable ingenuity and a realization of the inherent limitations.

In those homes where plants are valued more highly than average and are given constant care, the potential for experimentation with tropical and subtropical material is greatly increased and the repertory becomes more varied than for any other use, but at some sacrifice of interest in esthetic arrangement. Numerous dedicated hobbyists have become familiar with the whole spectrum of foliage plants for indoor gardening. Location in relation to available natural light, the possibilities offered by artificial light sources, the means of changing the indoor environment to meet plant needs, the challenge to increase space for cultivation and display, are subjects under constant review. Professional assistance is required only where the demands exceed owners' means of execution.

Interior decorating literature frequently presents solutions that are more esthetic than practical. We refer especially to illustrations that show plants placed in situations that are chosen solely because they look well in a photograph. The most common fault is that they have no visible source of light for maintenance. The limitations imposed by domestic architecture are considerable and should not be represented as of no consequence. They can be overcome to some degree by various means some of which we describe below.

Plants in windows. We have already discussed the characteristics of window light in our section on Natural Light. Hours of daylight and the seasonal angle of the sun influences the placement of plants, small or large, for maximum benefit. Here are some of the options.

1. Tall plants (*Dracaena, Polyscias, Dieffenbachia,* cluster palms, etc.) placed on the floor directly in front of a window. Usually the plants reach close to the top of the window. It creates a rather messy curtain of greenery but is a way of blocking an unattractive view. Few people go to the trouble of rotating the plants at regular intervals of time. This is a very common device that is easy but ugly.

2. Tall plants placed on either side of the window and smaller plants on the sill. This makes design sense and can be varied in a number of ways.

a. Shelving attached at different levels to hold small herbs and trailing vines. A number of models are available on the market. Glass is the most decorative material

b. Projecting window greenhouses. They increase window space and plants receive longer hours of daylight. However, some provision must be made to protect plants from intense sun in summer. A wash of water solvent paint will filter the light.

c. Extending the sill into the room. This can be done with a shelf permanently screwed to supports. You can also use fixtures with collapsible elbow joints which permit folding down the shelf when not in use. Build a rectangular or semicircular table at windowsill height. Casters make it movable. Support larger tables on metal sawhorses set on wood blocks with casters. Hide the sawhorses with a skirt made of lengths of tatami or other material. A very considerable amount of space is gained in these ways.

Shelves or tables are especially useful if there is a radiator at the window. Make them a few inches higher than the radiator and place a small fan where it will drive heat out from under the table into the room. Another solution is to put insulating material into the space between the radiator and the table.

d. Hanging baskets at different levels close to the window.

e. Vines grown around the window frame on aluminum trellis.

f. A 3–6 in. high frame constructed on the floor and lined with heavy-weight plastic. Fill with a light mulch. Place taller plants on the sides and smaller ones, to above windowsill level, in the middle. Employ basket plants or vines against the panes. If a deeper frame is built, pots can be plunged into the mulch.

g. Broad troughs with metal or plastic lining installed to stand at windowsill level. This is a good solution for very wide windows.

For all arrangements maintenance will be simplified if Wonderlite bulbs are attached to the ceiling or side walls to shine towards the window so that the room side of the plants receives growth lighting on overcast days and for display at night.

Plants can be placed in windows anywhere in the house—in bedrooms, bathrooms, kitchens and, of course, family rooms. There is a special pleasure to waking up in winter with a view of a tropical plant. Herbs with decorative foliage are both useful and esthetic in a kitchen.

The fireplace syndrome. Normally the existing arrangement of furniture takes precedence over plants, which we place near windows, in corners and, ultimately, wherever there is sufficient unobstructed space. Obviously they cannot be allowed to interfere either with traffic or seating. However, they do offer the possibility of liberating furniture positioning in living rooms from the fireplace syndrome. This is the custom of being seated facing away from windows. It dates from the time when the only source of heat was a fireplace. At the same time, it formed a natural social grouping.

A fireplace is still a good spot to gather around. But it is no longer a necessity or a universal feature of living rooms. Windows are relatively leakproof. Yet we still group seating facing the wall opposite windows, replacing the fireplace with shelf units containing the TV and stereo sets, partly from habit. Most rooms no longer have a piano in a corner or display cabinets. The excess spaces are frequently left empty.

Must seating congregate around the stereo set? With the elimination of most traditional decorative furniture, can seating be changed and plants, artificially lighted, play a more important part in interior design? Can the major grouping of seating be placed off center allowing space for one or more minor groupings? In short, can plantings become a major focus of room design? These are questions raised by our ability to grow them under artificial light.

Position, size and eye level. The choice of indoor plants involves consideration not only of furniture style—its lines and shapes—but matching shape and size in relation to our level of vision. As all plants have limited ranges of growth but do increase within them, all dimensions are temporary. The best one can do is to approximate a harmony of the spatial and visual elements. Every plant has a different decorative potential and, for many, this changes according to the stage of growth. Numerous plants used indoors are, at maturity, very large ones. They are impractical except as juveniles. As the stock of nurseries changes constantly one can rely on them for the "right" sized plant only when mass-production plants are being chosen. For a desirable size of other plants, one must often shop extensively. A few examples of position and size in relation to eye level illustrates our point.

1. Place small, herbaceous, compact and creeping plants close to eye level on tables and window or wall shelving. Look upon them as the equivalent of bibelots that are displayed in cabinets; from a distance they are unidentifiable and, to be appreciated, must be examined closely. Provide neat, decorative potting, utilizing minimum-sized containers. Arrangement is instinctive, in such a way that forms and colors complement and enhance each other.

2. Place plants with horizontal, spreading growth below eye level. The foliage is ornamental only when seen from above. *Dracaena marginata* 'Tricolor' looks fine as a short-stemmed plant. Its attraction, the colorful stripings of the leaves, looks beautiful from above. When the leaves are raised above eye level by a pedestal or a long stem only their backs are seen. *Aglaonema* 'Silver Queen' is a splendid, medium-sized spreading plant but would be totally uninteresting if the leaves were perched on a long stem. Other examples are young fan palms and cycads. Note that it is the attitude of the leaves which makes a low position mandatory. When long leaves curve over and hang down, the plant can be raised to higher levels. Many variegated plants should be displayed only as juveniles.

3. Place tall plants with bare stems at a distance and on the floor, with part of the stem hidden by furniture. Out of doors a view of the whole plant is set against other greenery or the sky. Indoors where ceilings are low and walls the background, stems are unattractive. It is the clustering of foliage at the top and its position relative to ceilings and the height of furniture that are important. Examples: single-stemmed palms, *Dieffenbachia*, tall *Dracaena marginata* or *massangeana*.

4. Raise clustered or shrubby plants so that the tops are somewhat above eye level but not so high that the base of stems is directly in the line of vision. Examples: cluster palms,

Pittosporum, Dizygotheca.

5. Place plants with solid, geometrical masses of greenery so that they reach no higher than standing eye level.

6. Hang baskets with short, spreading plants half way up a window. Those with long trailers hanging down belong near the top of the window.

Effect of artificial light on interior decoration with plants. The scope for decorating with plants is greatly increased when we use artificial lighting which allows us to grow in any part of rooms, even without any natural light whatsoever. It increases the choices from one to three because, in addition to growing near windows, we can combine daylight with artificial lighting or plan exclusively on the latter. But if one wishes to embark seriously on plant decoration we are obliged, as already indicated, to attach a greater importance to plants than is required for decorating by natural light alone. We presuppose the plants, taking up considerably more space, which necessitates changing our habitual placement and use of furniture. Shelf, wall, corner and floor gardens are not practical possibilities without this change in values.

The fear of mess. Introducing greater numbers of plants also threatens to violate deep-seated conceptions of proper domestic management.

For most Americans the living room is an inviolable place. It represents family status as much or more than the family car. Once it has been furnished it is on display but rarely used. We have created the family room for socializing, leaving the living room to be used only on state occasions. To do indoor gardening in such a room threatens its immaculate appearance. A similar prejudice bars plants from a bedroom except for temporary display. Even the kitchen is not exempt from the fear of disorder that might follow the introduction of plants.

This attitude explains why plants used in most interior decoration are usually the same as those supplied to offices. The professional interior plantscaper has little more to do than choose large foliage plants and set them near windows. In big pots or tubs with saucers to match, they last a long time and need only be watered and occasionally, fertilized.

Despite these prejudices there are already many homes where plants are being grown as well as displayed in various rooms by people who consider them sufficiently decorative to ignore convention. The trend has been aided by modern design which is so lacking in what is considered superfluous decoration that plants become a necessity in order to humanize the environment. We also know of some who grow in rooms with wall-to-wall carpeting and period-style furniture yet manage to avoid visible consequences of handling media, the chief sources of grime. They keep them on shelving, broad windowsills, tables, have growth or complementary lighting and do their cultural chores, except for watering and fertilizing, in the kitchen.

For those who cannot bear to face the challenge, plants can be grown in a cellar or attic. Cellars, as long as they are heated, are ideal as they offer plenty of room for growing. Attics must be heated in winter but their chief disadvantage is the accumulation of heat in summer. That can be taken care of through air conditioners and fans. Plants grown in these areas can be displayed throughout the house even without special lighting. They can be returned to cellar or attic at regular intervals when they need revival.

Hiding the light source. Modern electrical lighting is an unavoidable anachronism in any rooms styled for a period before its invention. Decorators have dealt with the problem by equipping chandeliers with false candles or installed innocuous reflective bowls near the ceiling equipped with bulbs. As table lamps they have used ceramic or metal antique or reproduction bases equipped with shades "in the style of" and incandescent bulbs. For instance, a Rococo or Louis Seize effect is achieved by using a decorated chinoiserie porcelain vase for a base and a shade with an appropriate fabric covering. Early American decor may call for a metal stand with a glass shade adapted to a bulb. Much use is made of fluorescent tubes supported by valances. The light is reflected from the ceiling, providing an even glow. The table lamp light is well hidden by the shades which extend below eye level when seated. The tubes in the valance cast their light upward.

When we wish to maintain plants, the light must angle downward from a higher level except in low shelving and must be treated somewhat differently.

Make valances wider and higher to accommodate reflector bulbs attached beneath the support for the fluorescent tubes. Such valances are usually painted to match wall color, making them relatively unobtrusive. The placement of the lamps is related to the number and spacing of the plants below. For a 10-foot ceiling, allowing for the lower position of the bulbs, 160 watt Wonderlites are adequate and higher wattages are also practical to illuminate a floor or corner garden. In a corner the valance is extended into a triangle or an arc as the outer edge to illuminate the similar space below.

A wall garden requires a combination: fluorescent tubes directly over the upper reaches, as they are cooler and the light less concentrated; bulbs angled from the sides for plants on a lower level.

Period settings range from the very formal and cluttered to a more open style. The former leaves little scope for plants except in odd corners or some adventitious space. Formal plants must be chosen to match the environment. Niches are easy to handle with hidden bulbs over conical or columnar foliage plants, a solution far more attractive than pharmaceutical jars or vases with artificial flowers. When there are cabinets or shelving, the normal use of fluorescent tubes with valances where necessary presents no special problem.

Plants are also placed atop table structures serving the purpose of dividers between seating areas, for example couches set back to back. The surface should be no higher than the backs of couches or chairs. Plants can be lighted from bulbs recessed in ceiling fixtures.

Compared with period decor, modern rooms usually offer an embarrassment of space to fill. The simple geometrical lines and cool colors cry out for the contrasts of organic forms. There is much more daylight because the windows are either uncovered or have translucent curtains. Modern decorators are accustomed to placing plants at windows *faute de mieux*. Visible artificial light sources are acceptable. Ceiling track, pin-up fixtures and hanging metal shades are normally employed so that the addition of fixtures for plant lighting goes virtually unnoticed. Of course, all lights must be angled to avoid glare. Humidity, too, can be raised without causing damage to possessions while contributing to the health of humans as well as plants. Modern decor is so adaptable to plants and vice versa that with careful planning, a room can be turned into a furnished indoor greenhouse considerably more attractive than greenhouses usually are. Nevertheless this potential has rarely been exploited.

The following series of drawings (by Mark Rabinow from our *The House Plant Decorating Book*, published by Dutton in 1977) are suggestions for the use of plants in homes. They also provide simple ideas for the arrangement of furniture in typical rooms, mandated by a desire to use the decorative potential of plants to the full.

A surprising amount of space can be gained by means of a window greenhouse. It projects beyond the exterior wall of the building and is reached by the sun from three sides. At midsummer the intensity of the light may be sufficient to burn some plants and it may be necessary to provide some means of filtering the light—even whitewashing part of it. On the other hand, if the greenhouse is facing north supplemental fluorescent light will be needed in order to bloom plants. The drawing shows where these should be located.

A bedroom window. It faces south and has a storm window. The lower sash can, therefore, be raised extending the sill outward. A shelf supported by brackets adds to the usable space and can be surfaced with plastic tiling. Hanging plant cuts glare. Plants are kept low in front and higher on the sides so that the cityscape shows in the center. The plants on the shelf should be considered as foreground of the outside scene. They all have different forms of leaves and textures with African Violets, small and large palm trees, and Nolina to add interest. The hanging plant is a Browallia, with blue flowers.

susans they can be turned at intervals to maintain their shape. For evening illumination there is a hanging lamp over the table and two spotlights near the window.

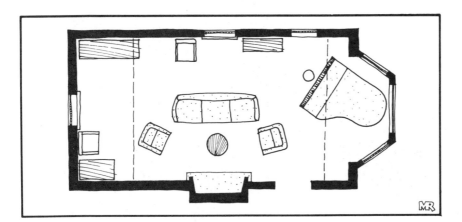

The conventional solution. Seating is clustered around the fireplace. The rest of the space is filled by a piano and pieces of furniture which usually have no use. Lines drawn across the plan suggest how the room would look without a bay or if it were shortened at one end.

A large room with bay. Conversation seating is provided in front of the fireplace. One end of the room is separated by a short divider and becomes an intimate alcove for reading, TV viewing, or hi-fi listening. At the other end of the room there is also a small room divider, this time of potted plants, and the bay, too, has greenery and flowering plants creating another socially useful grouping. Plants at the window opposite the fireplace take the place of heavy curtains. There is room for entertainment in various ways. The plants add decisive color and formal accents.

Bays in modern high-rise apartments are quite common. Here is a simple solution to bay window plantings. Build planter frames to windowsill level with inset troughs ten or twelve inches deep. Fill part-way with long-fiber sphagnum moss (natural dried sphagnum) and set in your pots. Then build up the moss around the pots until their tops are completely hidden. Keep the moss moist and you will not have to water the plants as often. Also the moisture will increase the humidity in the area. Grow foliage or flowering plants, placing the lower ones in the center and the taller ones along the sides of the windows.

A deep window embrasure in the corner of a living room or study offers the opportunity to create a place for comfortable seating, a place to enjoy the sun's warmth and a riot of colorful foliage and flowers. Especially in winter you will enjoy the tropical coloring while watching the snow swirling outdoors. Phalaenopsis and Paphiopedilum orchids look wonderful in such a setting. And in the early spring you can force tulips and hyacinths in low wide pots. The plants will be just high enough to cut the glare for reading. A coffee table between two high-backed chairs can bear a feathery fern or a cluster of pots containing pileas with contrasting colors and textures.

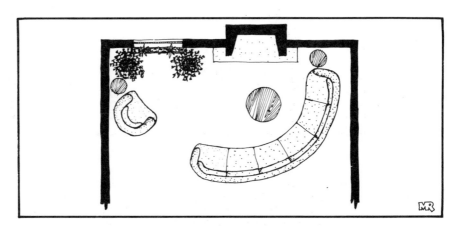

Palms would be good choices for the plants flanking the window. The arrangement of furniture is best for a rather small living room. If the floor plan is extended on the side of the room to the right of the fireplace there would be room for a separate social area such as we have shown in other illustrations.

The half-oval platform at the end of the room at windowsill height and the other arrangements are described in the text. The long coffee table is faced on entering the room from a wide doorless archway from the hall. The hall thereby becomes more useful for stand-up conversation at larger parties while the other end of the room gains in intimacy. The large plant to the right of the platform extends the greenery relieving the severity of the central grouping of plants.

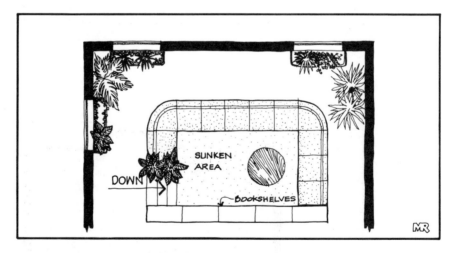

A conventional living room shape has been converted by means of plants and a sunken area surrounded by seating into a tropical ambience hitherto only possible and rarely achieved in a greenhouse. As plants have become the principal decorations of the room, eliminating occasional furniture, there is scope for plenty of imagination in their use. Palms, ficus, large succulents, ferns on stands, small leafy trees, tall aroids, dracaenas, vines on standards, polyscias, podocarpus—these and many others are suitable. What you select should depend on the actual spaces to be filled, the size of the windows, and the position in relation to other plants. Also the proportions of the plants must be related to the size of the room and the height of the ceiling.

46

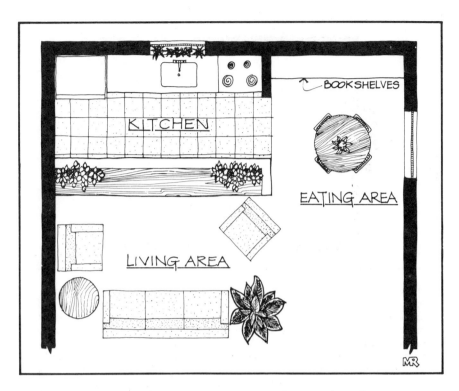

The living-dining-kitchen room is a common feature of small apartments. Plants introduce a valuable amenity and offer possibilities of lively decor (with the use of overhead spot lighting) which would be impossible otherwise in such close quarters. Line unoccupied sections of wall with attractive storage modules.

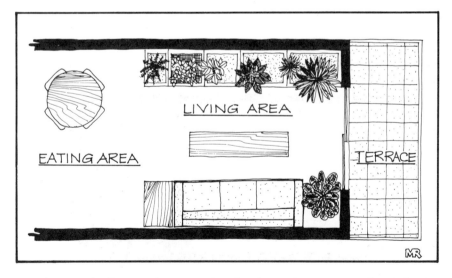

In planning the floor garden remember that the section nearest to the window receives less light than those which are partway into the room, but that the ones furthest along the wall from the window have progressively less light. This means that if you wish to have a tall plant in the corner it must reach out directly in front of part of the window. Otherwise supplementary illumination must be provided by spots or floods. The central section can be relatively low. If sufficient fluorescent illumination is attached to the wall above, low flowering plants can be grown. The higher parts of the garden, built up with feather rock, slag, or entirely of soil can bring plants requiring more light closer to the lamps.

47

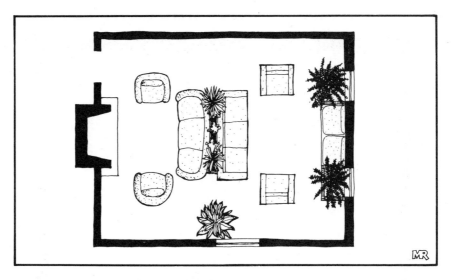

Depending in part on how much light you want in the room, the two windows opposite the fireplace can hold collections of small plants or large ones which form pillars of foliage that almost shut out the light. They frame a comfortable banquette against the wall between the windows. In the approximate center of the room is a planter lighted by overhead spotlights, or hanging, shaded lamps, flanked by couches, one facing the windows, the other the fireplace. They need not be of the same shape. There is another large plant in a tub next to the window on the side wall. Two back-to-back social areas are created in this way and the smnaller furniture is grouped in the two areas. Thus the space is more efficiently utilized while leaving ample wall space for storage or occasional furniture.

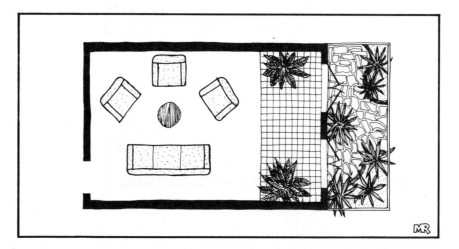

Frenchwindows looking out on a garden can be utilized for the development of the indoor/outdoor effect by providing a wide indoor apron of tiling or paving stones and by the use of large shrubs and vines. Vines can be planted between the windows so that they partly extend into them. The plants must be large ones because rooms with French windows are high ceilinged and usually large in area. Two big tubs will be sufficient then create the seating arrangement in the middle of the room. Concealed lighting over the tiled floor provides a dramatic effect at night.

Modular boxes at floor level hide the pots. Three-foot plants break the hard lines of the room and the empty expanse of the window. Plants hang from hooks under the valance, which also conceals supplementary floodlights.

The separate tropical garden corner away from it all. A shallow sunken area on top of a storage cabinet holds plants. Hanging plants screen the light and a large palm tree helps to create an intimate reading area.

A windowed alcove is set off by an archway. Plants permit seating without glare. Flood-lights at night make the view entrancing from an adjoining room while helping to maintain the plants.

Floor-to-ceiling windows separate the room from a terrace (or a patio). Without the plants along the side windows, indoors and outdoors would be separated so that each would have an existence of its own. It requires an effort to sit near the window and the bright light is disturbing. One looks out for only a moment to see a happening or to note the weather. The moment we have plants the situation is transformed. Now the outdoors expands indoors and vice versa. The planters and their greenery or flowers are part of our room and also lead the eye naturally to sky and scenery; in summer to a terrace or patio garden. Seating near to the window becomes not only acceptable but attractive. The floor gardens on either side of the door have tiled walls and are planted with low greenery or flowers. In summer outdoor planters in the terrace continue and reinforce the indoor/outdoor feeling. One or more large foliage plants in tubs carry the eye upward and screen the light. Indoors and outdoors the floor can be tiled or paved with flagstones.

A large, small-paned window supplies sufficient light for the development of a garden area to balance the bookcase on the other side of the fireplace. Low- and medium-light plants are contained at floor level behind an edging of bricks. The wall behind the floor garden can be faced with tiles or bricks. A lavabo is filled with trailing plants. Overhead floods are for nighttime or gray day lighting.

The pleasurable sensation of being surrounded by plants in winter while looking out on a cold sky and landscape or cityscape is a new experience brought about by the plant revolution. As in many modern apartments, glass doors and small terrace are located at one end of a long living room. Our drawing shows one way in which the space can be turned into a delightful sunny, separate social area with plants on two sides and the terrace a potential garden in summer. The wall on the left is built up with sections of cork tile holding orchids and bromeliads which are given supplemental lighting by means of floods. Plants hang in baskets at the end of the room and a large sculptural plant fills the angle between door and window. A large potted plant stands beside the couch. Tiling covers the floor in front of the cork wall and the window.

An atticstudio living room with dormer window extended by a skylight. The flooring is of flocked white vinyl squares, surrounding a central area of ceramic tile with raised sides. Plants are on the extended windowsill in the embrasure, on the floor in the enclosure, and hanging from the beams in baskets. Wicker garden furniture fits the mood of the room.

An attic or second-floor bedroom with 12-inch-wide frame around the slanted window. The shelf is supported by brackets. Plants are on the shelf, hung from the top area, and also from brackets at the sides of the window.

Dormer, showing how a "ceiling" of glass panes can be installed for a "greenhouse" area.

An attic bedroom has two small slanting windows in an embrasure. This has been turned into a storage wall with plants. On the floor there are storage modules. Hanging plants are in front of the windows. In the center, shelving is provided with fluorescent fixtures which grow and bloom still more plants.

In a bedroom the storage area between bed and window has plants on top.

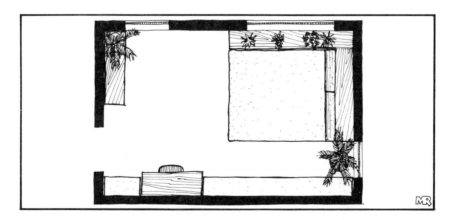

Floor plan of a bedroom. The storage space described in Figure 40 is on the long side of the bed and is lighted by a window. This is a satisfactory arrangement which permits you to free the opposite side of the room where the bed is normally placed. The cabinet, about a foot higher than the bed level has two shelves for books on either side of a two-door storage space. The chest is against the opposite short wall next to the other window. Plants make this a more livable, lively bedroom.

Double-decker window shelves, which can be used in other rooms, are particularly useful in the bathroom. In some modern homes there are ceiling skylights in the bathroom which give enough natural light for larger plants. Large bathrooms in older houses with good-size windows can accommodate large low-light plants. Ferns in baskets will thrive behind frosted windows.

ACCLIMATIZATION

Acclimatizing greenhouse and outdoor-grown plants in preparation for being moved indoors should be a primary task of nurseries. However, concern for the ultimate consumer conflicts with the economics of production. High light intensities increase the rapidity of growth in the early stages and reduce costs. In a competitive environment producers, with few exceptions, choose the cheaper way.

Full sunlight in the tropics can rise to above 10,000 fc intensity. The reaction of the plants is to develop thick, small, closely set leaves, a device that prevents damage to the cells active in metabolism. The phenomenon is most prevalent among desert plants, the leaf succulents, but also affects vines, trees and shrubs that are exposed to very bright sun. For this reason most nurserymen choose the middle way and protect their plants to some extent from extreme exposure. Nevertheless, the levels are way above those possible indoors. The combination of high humidity and intense lighting in greenhouses results in fast growth and wide spaces between joints.

Indoors at a window, light intensity may reach 5,000 or more fc, but the periods of exposure are much shorter than out-of-doors. Artificial light rarely provides more than 800–1,000 fc, and usually rather less but for longer periods. The effect of low light is to make leaves thinner, larger and greener, while stems are narrower and the whole plant taller. The worry for indoor growers is principally the trauma suffered by a plant that is suddenly moved from intense sunlight to low light conditions. It is responsible for the failure of many houseplants in all categories. The damage is not usually immediately apparent. It often occurs months later with a sudden collapse.

Researchers have developed lists of light levels for nurserymen growing tropical plants for market. Without exception these indicate 1500 fc or higher. For some plants the transition to the indoors after such exposures to light during their growing period is only moderately traumatic, but for others it is severe. A level of 4,000–5,000 fc for *Ficus* accounts for the frequent immediate loss of leaves when the plants are moved indoors. The same is true of many palms. A rate of 3,000–6,000 fc for *Dracaena marginata* is sufficient to cause cessation of active growth when the plants are exposed to the lower levels of intensity. Corn Stalk plants, with inadequate roots to begin with, fail to develop them properly but may linger on for as long as a year. When such Cast-Iron plants suffer one can imagine the problems with others that are less tolererant of such treatment.

The solution has been to shade the plants for a period of 6 weeks to 3 months before sending them to market. Some nurserymen are conscientious in doing so; others are not. It is very difficult to tell the difference between a high-light-grown plant and one that has been shaded properly because improper fertilizing and other factors can cause elongation of stems and thinning of leaves. For instance, sugar in one form or another has been fed to plants in order to speed growth with disastrous results for the consumer. Excessive fertilizer can produce similar bad results.

Commercial interior landscapers can specify proper acclimatization techniques and make sure that they have been carried out. Amateurs are more or less at the mercy of the nurseryman or florist.

Signs of poor acclimatization are: branching that is widely separated on the stem, thin and juicy stems, light-colored leaves and a greater spread between them. Spotting of leaves is a sign of the onset of infection, the presence of pests or virus infections.

We reproduce a list of recommended light levels for the acclimatization of foliage plants. Many nurseries grow under much higher intensities and make no attempt to reduce them for acclimatization. This confirms that so-called acclimatization is usually done at very much higher levels of light than can be achieved indoors.

Suggested light for production of some potted acclimatized plants.

Botanical name	Light intensity (foot-candles)
Aeschynanthus pulcher	1500–3000
Aglaonema spp.	1000–2500
Aphelandra squarrosa	1000–1500
Araucaria heterophylla	4000–8000
Asparagus spp.	2500–4500
Brassaia spp.	3000–5000
Calathea spp.	1000–2000
Chamaedorea elegans	1500–3000
Chamaedorea erumpens	3000–6000
Chlorophytum comosum	1000–2500
Chrysalidocarpus lutescens	4000–6000
Cissus rhombifolia	1500–2500
Codiaeum variegatum	4000–8000
Coffea arabica	1000–2500
Cordyline terminalis	1500–3500
Dizygotheca elegantissima	2000–4000
Dieffenbachia spp.	1500–2500
Dracaena deremensis (cultivars)	2000–3500
Dracaena fragrans (cultivars)	2000–3500
Dracaena marginata	3000–6000
Dracaena—other species	1500–3500
Epipremnum aureum	1500–3000
Ficus benjamina	4000–6000
Ficus elastica (cultivars)	5000–8000
Ficus lyrata	4000–6000
Fittonia verschaffeltii	1000–2500
Gynura aurantiaca	1500–3000
Hedera helix	1500–2500
Hoya carnosa	1500–3000
Maranta spp.	1000–3500
Monstera deliciosa	2000–4000
Nephrolepis exaltata (cultivars)	1500–3000
Peperomia spp.	1500–3000
Philodendron scandens oxycardium	1500–3000
Philodendron selloum	3000–6000
Philodendron spp.	1500–3500
Pilea spp.	1500–2500
Pittosporum tobira	3000–6000
Polyscias spp.	1500–4500
Sansevieria spp.	1500–6000
Schlumbergera truncata	1500–3000
Spathiphyllum spp.	1500–2500
Syngonium podophyllum	1500–3000
Yucca elephantipes	2500–4500

Copyright 1985. Horticultural Research Institute. Charles A. Conover and Richart T. Poole. Agricultural Research Center of the U1 of Florida

THE MEDIUM

It is commonly assumed that the species we grow indoors would do better if we could exactly duplicate the soil they are used to in nature. Beside the impracticability of matching the natural soil for every species, the cliche ignores the vast differences between a natural and an artificial, or indoor, environment. The suitability of any one spot in nature where a plant can survive successfully depends on many factors besides the composition of the soil. One that meets the general characteristics that we indicate below is quite adequate for most tropical plants.

Tropical plants are of two kinds; terrestrials that grow in soil, just like those in temperate climates, and epiphytes which live on the boughs and in the crotches of trees. Forest soil is very low in nutrition due to the frequent rains that leach out the chemicals. But the constant falling of vegetation from above, combined with rapid decompostion due to high temperature and humidity speeding up bacterial action, provides a thin layer rich in nutrition. Remove the forest and it is almost impossible to raise crops. The ancient Mayas burned the forest to gain potash and were able to grow crops for a few years, after which they had to move on.

Epiphytes are perched on spongy masses of decayed vegetation made up of the decomposed remains of previous generations. In addition there is a constant fall of decaying leaves and flowers from higher up or carried by the wind.

Another mistaken impression is that there are long-lasting, naturally nutritive soils. In temperate zone farming, even what are considered the richest soils have always required annual additions of nutrients for every crop accomplished by leaving fields fallow or enriching them with organic or inorganic fertilizers. It is, rather, the mechanical structure of soils and an absence of injurious chemical content that matters.

As far as indoor gardening is concerned, we must emphasize that for the culture of tropical and subtropical plants, temperate zone soils will not do any better than the basic forest soils of the tropics. They are heavy, poorly aerated yet dry out very rapidly. We attempt, rather, to approximate epiphytic conditions through the use of a very fibrous material such as peat, combined with inorganic materials such as perlite and vermiculite, about which more below. The resultant soil is light, airy and moisture retentive. It can be combined in various proportions to satisfy plants from the thin upper layer of the forest floor or the vegetable trash in the upper reaches of the trees.

In some country districts in the North, one can compound similar soils by mixing sand, humus or compost and topsoil. However, collecting these components is not practical for greenhouse production or for urban dwellers.

John Innes composts, made of normal loam, sand and additives, have been traditional in English horticulture. Now it has become evident that however excellent for outdoor gardening, the use of these mixtures has probably been responsible for consistently poor results with tropical plants. The first systematic compounding of artificial media for tropicals was done at Cornell University. They consist of the three basic materials of all modern greenhouse media with the addition of a number of other ingredients. Nowadays, simpler formulas are the rule and are generally designated as houseplant mixes.

Large commercial operations, growing great numbers of one or more closely related species, learn through experience and the aid of scientists the optimum formulas to maximize their production. Professional interior landscapers and amateurs alike depend more on prepared mixes or their own compounding, varying them as experience dictates.

Close observation of plants over a number of years endows one with a kind of sixth sense for the proper texture of a medium compatible with individual plants. That cannot at present be systematized. We only wish to emphasize that no formula is rigid, even for the packaged materials. Different environments and cultural methods affect the performance of any medium that is used. All our formulas, therefore, are only suggestions and, with the range of ingredients, should be varied according to the user's perceptions of the particular needs of plants.

Principal components

Peat moss. Peat moss is so vital to the formulation of artificial soils that we would be hard put to it to find a substitute should the supply ever be exhausted. Fortunately, that is still in the far distant future.

Sphagnum peat is a product of the decomposition of sphagnum moss, the fastest growing and largest of the mosses, which covers vast stretches of bog in the Northern Hemisphere. It is brown in color, fibrous and absorbs and holds large quantities of water. The nutritive value is very low, and the pH tends to become more acid with time in pot. Sphagnum peat moss, as sold in packages and bales, is cleaned, and when not compressed, fluffy material. The German moss is preferred, when not too costly, because of its finer texture, but American material is usually satisfactory.

Sedge, a grassy member of the *Cyperaceae,* also lays down peat. It has a more acid pH and is considered inferior except for acid-loving, woody plants, such as members of the Ericaceae, Azaleas, Rhododendrons, etc.

Vermiculite. Vermiculite is made from mica, a silica crystal in the form of closely packed, extremely thin, transparent sheets. When subjected to high temperatures, the "books" as they are called, exfoliate or separate. Industrial mica comes in large sheets, the horticultural grade in small ones. High-grade horticultural mica looks like small, silvery, accordion-pleated cubes, consisting of many small sheets. The mineral does not absorb water but the many surfaces hold moisture by surface tension. It is crisp and brittle, breaking up in a mix with time.

Cube mica has almost disappeared as the best mines have become exhausted. The current product is in the form of chips that are chemically neutral. Smaller amounts than formerly are being used in packaged houseplant mixes. Inexperienced growers, attracted by its low price, sometimes use insulation-grade vermiculite which is produced in enormous quantities. The material is dull gray, chalky, larger in size and mushy. It contains various amounts of chemical impurities that are harmful to plants. It should not be used at all. Whenever it is available, buy large-cube material.

Bark. Fir and presumably other bark chips have been included recently in commercial mixes. Being light in weight and not very water absorbent they have to some extent replaced perlite in formulas and even proved of value in the culture of succulents. But this has been in greenhouses where a low continuous moisture level is maintained in pots. For indoor use it is rather on the acid side and dries out too fast for most tropicals. In our opinion packaged media containing bark should be avoided.

Perlite. When obsidian, a volcanic stone, is subjected to intense heat it becomes pure white and takes the form of exceedingly light, firm, gritty granules. These are graded by size and sold in packs or bales. It takes the place of sand in mixes permitting better aeration of the soil, absorbing and holding more moisture and being sufficiently hard to fool a plant used to sand. The light weight is an added advantage.

Most perlite now contains a large amount of the fines or dust that should have been sieved out before packaging. When handled the perlite dust becomes airborne and is irritating to the nose and eyes. Included in a mix it can be damaging to some plants. Remove it, leaving only clean, large granules. Do not attempt to sieve the dry material by shaking. Place in a sieve and run water through until the dust has been removed. Use the wet perlite in mixes.

Perlite is also suspected by some growers of accumulating and storing deleterious chemical salts. Also, as pointed out under *Potting,* it floats and congregates when heavily watered, leaving air spaces in a mix through which the liquid drains without completely moistening the rest of the mix.

Despite these disadvantages, it is indispensable unless pumice is available and can be substituted. Other materials, such as polystyrene pearls, are a nuisance.

Pumice. This familiar lava stone, when crushed to horticultural-sized pieces, is very light and porous, but firm and gritty; much more so than perlite and preferable because it lacks the other's disadvantages. It is somewhat heavier but not excessively so. Inexpensive on the West Coast, the freight charges because of its bulk and weight prevent it from being carried by Eastern distributors.

Sand. The English have horticultural grades of sand; we do not. Builder's sand is about the best we can get. A good quality is clean (though not sterilized), sufficiently gritty and with a good particle size. There exist graded sieve sizes in construction sand, but they are not readily available in small enough quantities for home use. Commercial interior landscapers can usually buy the particle size they consider necessary.

Another option is bird gravel. It is really a coarse sand that is very clean and uniform. There are two types; one with and one without seed. Ask for the seedless kind as otherwise your pots will be full of grassy plants.

Sand is very heavy and evaporates moisture too quickly for most tropical plants. It is useful as a counterweight for tall plants in small pots. It is a substitute for perlite. For succulents it is a necessary ingredient of the mix.

Other components of mixes

Garden topsoil. Sometimes called "rich loam," garden topsoil is not usually rich and contains various organisms and dries out to a hardness injurious to most houseplants. It is normal procedure to repot plants from nurseries that are in ordinary soil. After the plants are acclimatized, wash the roots and replant in a houseplant mix.

Nevertheless, we recommend it for some plants that prefer a medium of this type. Mix in peat moss to enrich it with fibrous material. A good proportion is 1 part peat to 4 parts topsoil. The formula varies according to the degree of succulence of the plant, the less succulent requiring more peat.

Sterilize garden soil in a 180°F (82°C) oven for a half hour.

Live sphagnum moss. The material is available only in northern country districts in bogs. It can be kept alive for about 6 months in containers by adding water. It is excellent for rooting soft cuttings. Some tropical plants, mostly aroids, do very well in it. It is rarely used directly in mixes.

Long-fiber sphagnum moss. This is dried and partly cleaned sphagnum moss containing long strands of the plant. It is used for the same purposes as live moss. Plants liable to fungal diseases are protected by the material which possesses the characteristic of resisting invasion by fungi. The water absorption is very high, and aeration is good as long as it is not packed too hard in the pot. Excellent for some aroids.

Milled sphagnum moss. This is dried sphagnum moss ground to a fineness close to dust.

It has the same resistance to fungi as long-fiber moss. For that reason it is an excellent medium for seeding and for propagation with cuttings. The material clings firmly to roots yet the plant can be lifted out without damage. Because of its extreme dryness milled sphagnum moss should be placed in a container, watered, covered and left overnight to soak up the moisture. It can replace peat in mixes. Both long-fiber and milled sphagnum are available in small packages and bales.

Lime. Because of the use of sphagnum peat moss the pH of mixes turns acid with time. For those plants that prefer a more neutral, more alkaline soil, horticultural lime is added to the mix. Lime comes in several forms, among them as dolomitic lime in chips and powder. Crushed egg shells are an excellent source. The proportion is usually 1 or 2 tablespoons of lime to a quart of mix.

Packaged media

A majority of growers use already packaged mixes compounded by any number of firms serving the nursery and houseplant industry.

A distinction must be made between packaged material that consists of ordinary garden or other soil with additives and those that are composed of the basic components we have listed. The former should be rejected. True houseplant mixes are packaged with the components printed on the label.

Compounding mixes

It is much easier to adjust the formulas of media to the needs of plants by mixing your own. The ingredients, sphagnum peat moss, vermiculite, perlite or pumice or sand, can be bought in separate packages. Put the dry ingredients into a container, stir them together well and add water at the rate of about a drinking glass to a quart. When allowed to stand overnight, the moisture will permeate the mass.

Using only peat moss, vermiculite and one of the gritty materials, it is customary to designate the formula simply by numbers representing the proportions by volume. For instance, 1-1-1 is 1 part moss, 1 part vermiculite, 1 part perlite. 2-1-2 is 2 parts peat moss, 1 part vermiculite, 2 parts perlite. Pumice or sand can be substituted for the perlite. Formulas employing other ingredients must be spelled out.

For our foliage plant list we have proposed "standard" mixes that work well in our experience.

Houseplant Mix #1 (1-1-1). 1 part peat moss, 1 part vermiculite, 1 part perlite. A light mix popular with nurseries growing small or juvenile tropical plants. For indoor use with mature fleshy herbs it is rather too light and dries out rapidly in low humidity. It is excellent as a medium for first plantings of seedlings or cuttings. Frequently works well with epiphytic (tree growing) plants. A good medium for succulents that do not require extreme dryness.

Houseplant Mix #2 (2-1-1). 2 parts peat moss, 1 part vermiculite, 1 part perlite. Gritty sand or pumice may be used instead of either vermiculite or perlite for some plants. A good general purpose mix for nonwoody foliage plants.

Houseplant Mix #3 (3-2-1). 3 parts sphagnum moss, 2 parts vermiculite, 1 part perlite, gritty sand or pumice. Best for shrubby, woody plants, most vines and some trees.

Cactus & Succulent Mix #1 (1-1-2). 1 part peat moss, 1 part vermiculite, 2 parts gritty sand. The sand can be replaced by either perlite or pumice, preferably the latter. Add lime when soil tests pH6 or less.

Cactus & Succulent Mix #2. 2 parts sterilized garden soil, 1 part peat or milled sphagnum moss, 1 part gritty sand. Add lime when soil tests pH6 or less.

Sterilized Garden Soil Mix. Garden soil should not be used straight indoors but always mixed with peat moss and/or perlite. 1 part peat moss to 5 parts soil is a good proportion. If the soil is heavy the formula should be 1 part perlite and 1 part peat moss to 5 parts garden soil. Add lime if the reaction is acid. Packaged houseplant mixes, often called peat-lite mixes, have a history of changing formulas according to the price and availability of the ingredients. Percentages of the components are rarely, if ever, listed on the label. Whether one brand or another will prove best suited to a particular environment or collection of plants is, therefore, unpredictable. Nurserymen have their favorite brands, but their preferences are no guarantee of good results in an indoor environment. Occasionally these mixes have contained chemical impurities or additives injurious to certain plants. The main problem has been that they are often too heavily loaded with peat moss and/or bark. Recently the vermiculite has been very low grade and the perlite too small grained. If you have become familiar with the texture and appearance of Houseplant Mixes #1, 2 and 3, made with good grades of vermiculite and perlite, you should be able to match them by adding these components in different proportions to the packaged mixes. We find that such amendments work much better.

Following is a partial list of manufacturers of packaged mixes and their brand names.

Conrad Fafard, Inc., Growing Mix No. 2 and Agro-Mix; Fisons-Western Corp., Sunshine Mix; Lambert Peat Moss, Inc., Lambert Potting Mix; Premier Brands Inc., Pro-Mix.

Containing sphagnum peat moss and vermiculite: A. H. Hoffman, Inc., Fertilmix; Jiffy Products of America, Jiffy Mix.

Containing sphagnum peat moss, vermiculite, perlite, sand and bark: Grace Horticultural Products, Peters Professional and Terralite.

Containing slow-release fertilizers: Hyponex Corp., Professional Mix; Jiffy Products of America (peat moss and vermiculite), Jiffy Mix Plus; Michigan Peat Co., Baccto Professional Planting Mix. No nutrient should be added for at least 6 months.

POTTING

Potting is choosing of a container for size and shape suitable to the needs of a plant and filling it with medium so that the roots are in close contact. It is one of the most frequent chores in caring for any large collection of plants.

Reasons for Repotting

Whether you buy foliage plants at a nursery or a florist, closely examine the medium and the state of the roots. Accepting potting on faith accounts for the loss of many recently acquired plants. If only we could do our check up at the point of purchase. We have not yet found a nursery or florist willing to knock the plant out of its pot for us. So we have to do it at home. The faults in the original potting that we may uncover are the same that occur during our own care of plants. They usually call for repotting.

1. Improper soil. The buyer of nursery plants encounters two kinds of natural media that are equally unsuited to indoor growing. One is a typical northern type that is usually low in pH, that dries out rapidly indoors and becomes almost brick hard at the same time. It is much more liable to contain harmful pests than artificial soils.

It presents a real problem for it is difficult to separate roots from the material. When decanting is attempted roots are broken off by the solid lumps to which they are attached. Yet repotting is necessary except for a few very acid plants that manage to survive in the stuff. After the plant has become acclimated, a matter of about a month, water heavily and immediately remove the roots and soil from the pot with the help of a long knife worked along the inner wall. Let roots and soil fall into a bowl, add room temperature water and gently shake the roots free. Discard the old medium. Repot carefully, spreading the roots, with houseplant mix. Set the plant in indirect light and keep above 70°F (22°C) for 2–3 weeks. If leaves wilt cover with transparent plastic.

There is also a kind of southern bog soil that has been used for potting large plants. The unwary associate dark brown or nearly black soil with high nutrition. This material is not only lacking in natural fertilizers but is very quick to dry out and compact. It is usually lethal to any plant growing indoors. However, the plant can be knocked out of its container easily, most of its clinging soil removed and repotted in normal mix.

A third menace is an artificial soil consisting of very coarse peat moss, wood shavings and other ingredients. It is very light and will settle in a container to as little as two-thirds of its original volume in a matter of a few months. Working around the roots with a trowel, you can often lift out the plant.

2. Pot-binding. Seedling plants grown to minimum salable size are usually potted in extremely light peat moss mix that promotes fast growth. The roots are often pot-bound. Pot-binding is the condition when roots permeate the medium completely and circle the bottom of the container. The plant should be knocked out of its pot and the tangle of roots in the bottom

carefully unravelled and spread. Repot in the next-size-larger pot with additional mix with a higher proportion of peat moss. It is unnecessary to remove the old soil. Even for larger plants some nurseries use an excessively light mix. The procedure is the same.

Give particular attention to plants that have been maintained at the nursery for a long time. Moss or algae forms on the surface of the medium which will be found to contain a concentration of salts and to be very acid. A strong acrid odor is the indication. Such plants are often also pot-bound. Leach the soil thoroughly, allow to stand for an hour or two and then decant. Repot in a larger size container, spreading roots.

Seedlings started in peat pellets frequently are unable to work their roots free. Remove the plastic net and repot with normal mix.

Pot-binding requires repotting. Nurseries often plant two or three specimens in a single container to make a showier impression in a shorter period of growth. That leads quickly to severe pot-binding. Decant the plants and separate them carefully. Repot separately.

3. Root problems. When a plant stops growing for no apparent reason, sulks or wilts the problem may be due to dying-off of roots. Knock the plant out of its pot. If sections of soil separate and contain dead roots something is wrong. The causes, of course, are many—overfeeding, insects or root-boring worms, fungus infections, etc. Take some of the soil and examine it under a 10-power loupe for pests. If these are not apparent, discard all soil not attached to roots, break off any rootlets that are dead and repot in fresh medium. Mix in a soil fungicide labeled to control root-rotting diseases as directed. If pests are present wash the roots thoroughly.

We have already mentioned root- or pot-binding. When the roots of plants reach the bottom and sides of containers they continue to grow, intertwining and forming a mesh that squeezes the medium ever tighter toward the center of the pot. Aeration is cut off and the plant eventually strangles itself. In the later stages of pot-binding the pot holds less water which is exhausted more rapidly so that, unless the plant receives frequent attention, one may find that it has died of underwatering.

A pot-bound plant can exist for a while if constantly watered and fed to take care of any top growth. Many plants prefer snug potting, but they must be serviced more frequently than others. If roots are visible through the bottom holes of containers, the plants are ready for repotting.

Clay or plastic pots? Standard clay pots have been almost entirely superseded by plastic. The familiar reddish ceramic containers are thick walled, heavy, narrow bottomed and broad topped. The rim is also thick and broad to prevent breakage. The clay is sufficiently low fired to absorb and sweat moisture. This latter characteristic has made them useful in greenhouses where the high humidity keeps the pots cool and moist while excess water is quickly sweated out and evaporated. It can be argued that the color and texture of clay pots is more esthetic than the harsh brilliance of plastic. Despite these virtues they are now principally used indoors for succulents because the soil dries out faster in the low humidity.

Plastic pots are lighter in weight, enclose more space for volume and retain moisture in the medium for a much longer time. They do not discolor or become moldy. Pests do not multiply on their surfaces. Also they are less costly. The chief objections are to their appearance. Standard sizes are usually sold in just two colors, white and dark green, neither of which enhances the appearance of plants. Most of the other colors, when available, are ghastly. We still keep a stock of very decent dark brick red pots we bought a number of years ago.

Plastic screening. Formerly, in order to prevent roots or soil from protruding through the holes in pots, it was the custom to cover them with pebbles or a single stone when there was only one. This was necessary because roots growing out of the pots would anchor themselves in the dirt and moist planking of nursery benches. That is quite unnecessary nowadays. Our peat mixes do not drain out through the holes even when totally dry and roots have nothing to grow into in our trays. We do use a small piece of plastic screening to cover holes when the medium is very sandy, as for succulents.

Drainage material. Traditionally, clay pot shards or large gravel has been placed in the bottom of pots to assist in drainage and aeration. The practice was appropriate at a time when garden soils were used much more than at present. They either hardened excessively or became water soaked. Drainage reduced the depth of the medium in the pot thus reducing the risk of soil remaining soaked too long.

Today we do not use drainage material at all. Our houseplant media are sufficiently water absorbent and also porous. The elimination of drainage saves space and permits us to use smaller pots. Plastic and the absence of drainage cuts down on the weight of large pots for big plants. Finally, the fact that the medium is pressed against the bottom holes permits us to see when roots have filled the pot and are trying to escape, very useful to warn us of pot-binding.

Potting sticks. Potting sticks are necessary to aid proper packing of medium into containers and around the roots of plants. They are round lengths of wood, or dowels, that are bevelled at one end to a blunt, flat-sided point. We use diameters of ¼–1 in. (6.25 mm – 2.5 cm), the largest size usually being made of a length of broom handle. They should be 6–15 in. (15–37.5 cm) long. Make your own and keep an assortment for different size pots.

Container size. In most cases the choice of a pot is dictated by the size and shape of roots. Pots range from 1¼ in. (3.125 cm) to 15 in. (37.5 cm) in the low range and then on up to containers big enough to hold fair-sized trees.

In the smaller range shapes are square or round. Depth is equal to width in the standard pots. So-called azalea pots are ⅔ to ½ as deep. Deeper pots hold plants with long narrow root systems; azalea pots those with shallow, spreading roots.

The pot should be big enough for the roots and allow some space for growth. Fast growers need more room than slow growers. Correct potting requires that the container be neither so small as to bind the roots nor so large that the amount of extra soil accumulates unused moisture which the roots can't handle, a frequent cause of fungal diseases. For a plant with damaged roots a smaller pot is advisable. Where much of the root is lost, the reduction in size of pot may have to be considerable, usually accompanied by a trimming of some of the top growth so that the remaining roots are not required to supply as much nutrition and moisture as before.

Decanting plants. Removing plants from pots with peat medium is easy but doing so with minimum damage to roots requires care and practice.

With pots that can be lifted without difficulty we "knock" the soil out by holding the plant upside down and banging the edge of the pot on a hard surface. However, that is not all there is to it.

Water the soil thoroughly and let stand for at least an hour. Lift the pot with one hand, turn it over, holding the plant stem with fingers of the outspread palm which should cover the surface of the soil. Have a bowl ready to receive any loose soil and the plant. Gently knock the edge of the pot on the edge of a solid surface while turning it. The root ball should slip out in a solid mass. If it is resistant, run a long knife along the inner wall of the pot to loosen it. Then resume knocking.

The soil will remain a solid mass if roots extend to the bottom of the pot. Otherwise, the unattached part will split off. Set the plant as upright as possible in the bowl.

Set very large plants in big pots or tubs on their sides and beat the exterior of the container while rolling it over. A long narrow spatula may be needed to loosen the soil from the wall of the container. Decanting may be a job for two or more persons who simultaneously pull at the plant and the pot. Patience is repaid by minimum damage.

If the soil in a pot is dry it will break up under stress and destroy roots. If it is too wet, the heavy lumps breaking away will do even more damage. Loosening the soil around the inner wall of the pot might appear to be the best first step for all decanting, but it should be avoided if possible as that, too, severs roots.

Succulents planted in sandy soil are an exception. The medium should remain dry. Run a knife around the inner wall of the pot, lay it on its side with the bottom end raised at a low angle. Knock gently while turning. One hand should protect leaves from damage.

Potting seedlings and cuttings. Remove seedlings from the propagation box after they have at least two real leaves, cuttings when there is new top growth and tugging indicates the presence of roots. Lift out with a houseplant trowel, taking along as much attached medium as you can. In a pot big enough for the roots, pour medium part way so that with the roots spread out, the joint between stem and root will be a little below the rim. Hold the plant by a leaf or leaves, not by the stem. Add enough medium so that the plant can stand up by itself. With a small potting stick, push soil downward along the inner wall of the pot and lever it inward. Fill in with soil until the packing is firm. If peat pellets are used, cut the net away from the roots before potting.

Potting larger plants. The procedure is the same as for seedlings with two exceptions. The plant can be held by its stem and the packing of the soil is much more critical. In regard to the latter we have made comments in other sections about the risk of leaving vacant spaces in the packing of the medium.

For larger plants in particular, do not use soaking-wet medium for potting. It should be just moderately moist and still fluffy in texture. The wet soil would be liable to pack too hard. The moist medium is easier to handle but can leave air spaces. Use the appropriate size potting stick and fill in with soil very carefully. After packing, water the soil thoroughly and poke it all around the edge with the stick. Where soft spots are discovered add more soil.

Interior landscapers have developed various techniques for packing, transporting and planting very big specimens. Careful packing of the roots should preserve most of the root ball. During planting as little strain must be put on it as possible.

Planting baskets. What are currently called baskets are really no more than plastic pots, wider than deep, with inward-curved sides and a detachable saucer and a wire hanger. The procedure for planting is no different than for other pots.

More decorative are wicker, cedar wood and wire baskets. The narrow frames leave wide gaps through which peat mixes would fall if an inner covering were not provided. The best material for the purpose is sheet moss, a kind that grows in the North on rocks and is sold in bags. Moisten it well, allow to drain and then line the basket completely. Then partly fill the container with medium, making room for the roots of plants and adding more soil to top off. Long-fiber sphagnum, moistened and spread on the sides, will also do.

9

CONTAINERS

At horticultural industry shows the booths selling containers are the most numerous of all. An amateur attending one of these professional events is astonished to see such a wealth of different sizes, shapes and materials. The choices available to nonprofessional indoor gardeners in shops and the catalogs of suppliers seem very few indeed by comparison. They are mostly strictly utilitarian in the catalogs and garishly colored in variety stores. The trade, on the other hand, can count on finding containers to serve esthetic needs and designed to meet the decorative styles in vogue.

Nurseries deliver most of their plants in standard white or green plastic pots. Indoor gardening suppliers list the usual sizes we have mentioned in Potting. The shapes are all square or round and the colors invariably green and white. Nurseries also deliver some of their plants in ugly, dull black and green ribbed pots, made of a thin and flexible plastic with side openings in the base. They are much used in mass-production operations but present the buyer with the necessity of prompt transplanting to more presentable containers.

The thickness of the plastic for a reasonably solid 4 in. (10 cm) pot is about 1.5 mm. A rolled edge or a 0.5 in. (1.25 cm) projecting band at the top adds to rigidity. Lately pots have been offered with thinner walls which crack very easily. No doubt competition will cause a further deterioration in quality. The new types are already little better than plastic party cups. In fact we use the latter for most of our seedlings and juvenile plants when they need less than a 4 in. (10 cm) diameter pot because they are cheap and sold everywhere in supermarkets and variety stores. But they are of no use for display. The discarded standard pots at florist shops are also inexpensive. They should be washed in chlorinated water before use.

Selections of colored plastic pots are offered by variety stores. Our objection is to their colors. The shades are bright and clean but no better for display than standard pots because the colors clash with greenery. It is a recognized principle that containers be graceful but unobtrusive. Their purpose is to enhance the decorative qualities of plants, not to compete with them for attention.

Problems arise when we want to buy decorative pots that are compatible with plant forms and colors. They are sometimes to be found in shops selling decorating supplies and gifts. In the wholesale florist markets of cities are stores that specialize in containers. Many types of bowls would be suitable as temporary display pots if they had bottom holes. One can cut a hole in ceramics with an electric punch drill and a special bit but doing so requires practice. Ceramic containers usually suffer from the disadvantage for longer use of being glazed inside. Metal ones also lack porosity. So most of the containers are useful only as cover pots.

Japanese pots. Containers imported from Japan that are glazed matte brown are usually called bonsai pots. Many of the shapes are too shallow and of no use for normal growing indoors. But there are any number of others that are superb both for growing and display. The color is a neutral shade that enhances foliage. Sets of small pots for tiny trained plants are ideal for the display of trimmed foliage plants.

Less frequently seen are pots in Sung-type soft blues, grays and greens and decorated pots on which the designs are sufficiently detailed so as not to make a splash of color. The Japanese also make large, heavy glazed pots, up to 2 ft. (60 cm) in diameter, usually straightsided and in matte, simple colors. They are big enough for large shrubs or small trees.

Hand-thrown pots. Some domestic potteries turn out containers of good design, usually lightly glazed or not at all. Occasionally good glazed ware can be found.

Troughs. Molded troughs in classical designs are imported mainly from Italy. They can be used as window boxes and on balconies. They are also decorative on window sills.

Baskets. See Potting.

Cover Pots. Cover pots or cachepots are one means of overcoming a shortage of decorative containers. Any container becomes a cover pot when it can hide an ordinary pot. A bottom hole is not required. That gives much greater latitude of choice, shape, size and material. As it is only a temporary housing there need be less worry about using choice-quality art works.

All kinds of pots, urns, baskets, bowls and vases of glazed or unglazed ceramic ware, straw, cork, copper, brass, cast-iron and molded plastic are usable. The search for cachepots offer antique shop rummagers a field day. Gift shops have decorated and handcrafted ceramics. Manufacturers for the trade turn out slick modern designs for the up-to-date decorator. There is no end to the possibilities.

Beside esthetic considerations, which are strictly personal, the principal task is matching the cachepots to standard pot sizes. That is not easy by visual judgment alone. Measurements of width and depth are essential. The interior pot must be below the rim of the cachepot. And the latter greatly increases the volume of the container which may cause it to overwhelm a particular plant.

When the display is very temporary, one need only set the utilitarian pot inside the cachepot and be careful in watering that no considerable amount of liquid remains in the bottom. For longer periods the space between pot and cover pot should be filled with moist long-fiber sphagnum moss to keep the pot cool and reduce evaporation. It also prevents the inner pot from shifting within the cachepot. To mask the inner pot, put a layer of live sphagnum moss, sheet moss or moist sphagnum moss on top.

Architectural troughs. Architectural troughs are very large containers, square or oblong in shape and usually quite deep. They are used for indoor landscaping as units of the design and may be set at various levels. For some time such troughs were also installed in office-building lobbies, usually at about waist level, to enliven a sterile area.

The troughs may be constructed with drainage outlets, a layer of coarse drainage material and topped off with medium. Plants grow either directly in the soil or in pots that are plunged below the surface. There may be provision for automatic watering. Those in lobbies have frequently been no more than supports for pots buried in mulching material. The outer facings are of polished stone sheathing. Lighting in atria is provided by daylight and complementary artificial lighting. In lobbies, incandescent lamps have been used.

We have observed that most lobby installations soon became unusable because of inadequate lighting and neglect. The troughs are practical and decorative if growth lighting and regular servicing are provided.

Pedestals for containers. Pedestals must be provided for free-standing, low-stature, spreading plants situated in open spaces where they compete with other large-size objects or must be out of the way of traffic.

Amateurs are largely dependent on makeshift solutions—stools, upturned round metal baskets and chance purchases of old pedestals. The interior decorating and landscape design trade has access to many lines of usually cylindrical or square pedestals finished in chrome, straw, cork and other materials. Here, too, accessory shops in wholesale florist sections of cities may be your best bet for finding better-looking plant and pot supports. Furniture shops, it should be added, often show old-fashioned wicker stands.

10

TERRARIUMS

In the second quarter of the 19th century a London physician, Dr. Nathaniel Ward, noted a seedling sprouting and putting out leaves in a sealed glass bottle which was being used for an entomological experiment. Thus the terrarium was born, for Dr. Ward proceeded to test the growing of plants in larger and larger closed transparent containers. They were dubbed Wardian cases, were manufactured in quantity and became very popular in Victorian living rooms. The method contradicted deep-seated preconceptions about plant needs. The cases proved that they could live in an enclosed atmosphere for years without any attention as long as the interior moisture conditions were right, the ambient air temperature met their needs and there was enough light to sustain growth. The cases could not be exposed to sunlight because heat accumulated inside and boiled the plants. But, as long as the light was indirect, the plants were happy.

True Wardian cases, of wood with glass panes, are still occasionally used by orchid hobbyists, but terrarium has become the accepted word to describe any transparent, closed container in which plants are grown. In the 1970s they became very popular and were made in many shapes and sizes. The market was also swamped with glass bowls crowded with foliage plants. Although they were left open, they were sold as terrariums. The plants soon strangled each other, and consumer enthusiasm evaporated. Terrariums ought to be revived because they have a great potential as easy-to-maintain plant decor. The practical possibilities of making really large ones have never been tested.

A terrarium works when the soil within is just barely moist. This is the critical factor. If it is too wet fungus will develop and the plants will rot. When it is correctly adjusted the plants within the container simply recirculate oxygen and carbon dioxide in a highly humid atmosphere that is ideal for tropical plants and at the same time reduces the need for light. Without direct sun many plants will flower in a terrarium environment.

Containers for terrariums. Even the hardest plastic sheets or panes craze very quickly from the action of soil and chemically treated water. One can clean a dirty pot, but the damage to a plastic terrarium is permanent. Nevertheless, because plastic is cheaper, it is a good choice where the object is utilitarian.

Young plants from seeds and cutting get a good start, sick ones recover and very delicate plants can be maintained in prime condition until they are ready for use in a terrarium garden or brought into the open. There are many kinds of small plastic containers on the market that are essentially terrariums. They are usually molded of very thin, light plastic, the bases opaque and the tops clear, "miniature greenhouses" for instance. Plastic storage boxes from the variety store serve the same purposes. They are very useful and economical for propagation and maintenance of small plants. We emphasize the distinction that decorative terrariums do not use plastic and are planted as displays and miniature gardens in glass containers.

Clear glass is the only permanent material for terrariums. Round bowls and vases of any size are attractive for the purpose but, because of their curving sides, present a distorted image of the plants. The ideal shape is rectangular, usually oblong and the best proportions are those of tropical fish tanks which are made in many sizes. The frames are of metal or opaque plastic, and the bottom plate is usually a solid sheet of a black, rubbery plastic material. On special order they can be made as large as you wish. They are usually sealed with silicone resin which prevents leakage but is not very strong. Tanks must always be placed on a flat surface as large or larger than width and length, otherwise, the bottom plate, because of the weight, will separate sooner or later from the frame.

Terrariums are also made with leaded glass in shapes that are usually tall and polygonal. Our objection to these admittedly finely crafted containers is that the leading interferes with vision and the showiness detracts from the plants they contain.

Culture in plastic terrariums. From our description of plastic terrariums the reader who judges that they may be much the same as propagation boxes, as mentioned under *Propagation,* would be right. They are standard indoor gardening equipment. Clear plastic containers, as small as cocktail glasses and as big as clothing storage boxes, have the same purpose. The smaller ones are used for seeds and cuttings planted in milled sphagnum moss, peat moss or houseplant mixes. As long as the medium is not too wet and care is taken that the boxes do not overheat, they are the best containers for propagation. Of course, the smaller glass tropical fish tanks are equally adaptable.

We rarely put soil in the larger boxes. The transplanted seedlings and rooted cuttings in their pots are simply watered, placed in the box and covered. Keep away from sun and maintain at 68°F (20°C). If signs of mildew appear, spray with an appropriate fungicide. Otherwise, leave the plants in peace until they are big enough to be accustomed gradually to normal room conditions.

Shallow pans covered with plastic domes make safe havens for the more delicate tropicals, such as Episcias, Sonerilas, some Begonias and the like that need high humidity.

Terrarium gardens. Terrarium gardens are among the most satisfying of all horticultural displays indoors, are easy to set up and need only occasional care.

The simplest arrangement, a very satisfactory one, is rarely exploited. Cover the bottom of the terrarium with pebbles. Any natural ones will do, but the Japanese smooth white or black ones about an inch in length, sold in bonsai stores, are especially attractive. Candy colored plastic cubes are not.

Set on this base as many plants in pots as can be arranged without crowding. The size of the terrarium dictates the size and shape of the plants which should also be culturally compatible. Carefully chosen pots are very essential for a truly ornamental effect. Water the pots and cover. If the soil in the pots dries out after a week or two, water them and pour a small amount of liquid on the pebbles. Repeat if dryness recurs but be careful not to exceed minimum moisture needs. Set in bright reflected light or under a pair of fluorescent tubes.

The benefits of a controlled environment are more than matched by the startling beauty of the staging, for the plants are framed as in a shadow box and no extraneous objects impinge on our visual image. Thus all the individuality of the plants—texture, form and color—are enhanced.

This type of arrangement is a formal garden and best suited to miniature plants. In large terrariums one can imagine the same principle applied to larger compositions.

A more challenging type of garden is a miniature landscape planned to be as natural as possible. The rectangular shape of the container places limitations on any plan. Refinements of design depend on the choice and placing of materials and plants.

The first step is to lay down a thin bed of small pebbles or perlite as drainage insurance for any free moisture in the medium. The next is to build up contours with sphagnum peat moss or standard houseplant mix which has been sufficiently moistened to form slopes without crumbling. If plants are to be set directly into the medium the water used should contain fertilizer diluted at one quarter the recommended amount.

There is no point in an arrangement on the flat. To display plants from one side they must be shown one above the other. The slopes also increase the plantable areas. These hills therefore rise from a flat space in the middle of the composition or to either side. When covered with white pebbles they simulate a pond. The slope rises in the rear of the tank and around the sides. The taller plants you intend using will have to be placed in the lower areas.

Thin, flat, disklike stones are inserted horizontally into the medium to support it where the slope is most steep. Have a stock of different sizes handy. You may also want to have curious or grotesque or colorful larger stones to be set upright as peaks. Often a single well-chosen rock is effective especially to further the illusion of the miniaturization of plants masquerading as trees or shrubs. They can be collected on trips to the country.

Before planting, set plants in pots approximately where you want them to go and make the fine adjustments in position before attempting actual planting. When ready make holes in the medium, decant the plants and pop the root balls into place. A light watering is advisable.

Once the plants have become adjusted to their new home they will grow normally. When branches spread you can trim them. Roots, however, cannot be controlled; they will spread and overlap in the medium with those of neighbors. If any of them dies or if they must be replaced for some other reason, you must dig up roots, a chore which is difficult in those close quarters and involves considerable damage to other plants as well as to delicately balanced slopes and terraces. Yet terrarium enthusiasts have always planted in this way and been satisfied as long as the crimes were rare and reparable.

We have discovered that it is far more satisfactory to bury the pots directly in the soil. Doing so removes the serious problems we mention previously for pots can be hauled out, moved or replaced at will. Roots of one plant do not encroach on others. The pots provide a much firmer anchorage for a plant within the composition. A very favorable effect of their use is that the growth of the plants will be restrained and the risk that it will outgrow its usefulness greatly reduced.

It is essential that the medium in the pots be evenly and firmly packed, for the plants are dependent in a terrarium on the small amount of moisture that is available, and it is essential that this be retained. Water the medium thoroughly before planting and bury the pots just deep enough so that their rims are no longer visible. Rather snug potting makes for smaller containers that are easier to fit into the limited spaces.

It is better to start off with very little moisture in the medium surrounding the pots. If the pots start to dry out they can be watered and if this is kept up a few times as needed the terrarium will become properly balanced so that there will be neither shortage nor excess. When the temperature drops at night expect that the glass will cloud up. That is normal. However, large drops collecting on the cover are an indication of too much moisture. The cover may be opened when atmospheric temperature rises over 80°F (27°C), but after the hot spell passes it is usually necessary to rebalance the moisture in the container.

The completed terrarium garden should be a miniature landscape that is replete with textures, shapes and details that catch the eye. Tiny figures of people, animals and bridges can be added. We don't believe that these should be cute but miniatures that are appropriate for the setting. It should be possible to look into a terrarium and imagine oneself as a tiny visitor in a dramatic natural setting.

We list terrarium plants in the Introduction to the Plant List, below. These all require tropical conditions for we do not favor temperate zone plantings dependent on the use of small, wild plants that are collected in woods. They do not last for long unless given very cold conditions in winter.

The terrarium should be placed in bright indirect light or beneath a fluorescent fixture or a Wonderlite bulb. Do not place the light source so close that it heats up the interior of the container. The high humidity inside a terrarium causes the plants to react more efficiently to light so that the intensity need not be as high as when the plants are on shelves. One hundred to 150 fc is usually ample.

Very large terrariums could be sensational in public places. They can be recessed into walls or freestanding. The larger area for planting suggests the possibility of placing the high points of the composition in the center so that the landscape can be viewed from all sides. If the cover is attached to thermostatic lifting equipment (as for greenhouses and hotbeds) the units would need very little attention over long periods and function far better than the often miserable plantings that are exposed to drafts, pollution and neglect.

TRAINING

Training an indoor plant goes beyond grooming, whose sole purpose is neatness. It seeks to restrict size and/or shape a plant to a preconceived form. The highest art has been achieved with topiary and bonsai techniques, both of which are very specialized operations requiring great skill and experience. Some of the methods can also be applied to more limited objectives, such as dwarfing plants, preventing them from outgrowing their usefulness as decoration, enhancing their appearance by limited shaping that simultaneously increases branching and causes more compact growth.

Bonsai and topiary employ a small range of species proven by long experience to be especially adaptable to drastic pruning and shaping. Our knowledge of the huge repertory of foliage houseplants that we train, often more from necessity than esthetics, is less dependable. Single-stemmed plants such as many aroids, the palms and most ferns cannot be trained at all. For the majority of crawling and hanging plants, training is only a part of grooming because we trim merely in order to shorten. Real training encourages branching and is applied mainly to shrubs and trees.

For many years we harbored the illusion that any branching plant, especially woody ones, could be trained to shape and induced to produce more branches by judicious pruning. When the growing tip of a stem or branch is removed a signal is sent to the incipient buds at one or more joints below that causes them to grow into branches. Each leaf joint, whether opposite or alternate, is capable of producing a branch. On some plants adventitious buds between joints are stimulated to do the same.

All of this can and does happen, but, as we learned in due course, by no means always. Some species react automatically while others do not. If we have a branching plant with opposite leaves, we expect that two branches will appear at the joints after trimming. We may hope that the next lower joint will also be activated. Occasionally a joint will produce more than one branch. When the leaves are alternate, two joints must be productive if there is to be an increase in branching. The actual results vary between species. Failures and successes occur also within the same species with different plants. We don't know whether this is caused by some real difference between the plants or is fortuitous.

We have pruned a Begonia species for years until it has a thick trunk with short branches covered with leaves. Its ability to put out new growth at the joints after dozens of prunings has been astonishing. That is not at all typical of the genus. There are shrubs whose stems or branches we can trim over and over again that never fail to continue multiple branching as long as we cut back to a fresh joint.

On the other hand, there are many plants that become woody when still young and, if trimmed, stop producing branches altogether. With the tip of the stem removed they appear to become semidormant and cannot be revived. Such plants, in fact, soon die. What they require is to be allowed to grow normally. If there is any trimming it must be superficial.

Some tall trees branch well as juveniles and can be pruned quite drastically. But, if one cuts the tip of the stem of a young Mango after it has produced several leaves, it will usually put forth only one shoot at the next lower leaf joint which will grow straight up as a continuation of the stem. The symmetry is destroyed without halting upward growth or causing more branching. We are not even sure that this is behavior common to all Mangos. There are many strains and some may act quite differently.

A Jacaranda will do the same but also produce one or more rather weak branches below the top joint. When the tips of some plants are cut, the tip joint does not grow as a continuation of the stem. Instead, a fast-growing branch appears that takes off at an acute angle. The permanent damage to the shape of the plant is considerable. On some plants when the stem tip is removed branches grow from several joints and, instead of spreading like the others below, grow straight up.

The lessons learned from the negative effects of trimming are: that it does not always produce branching or a more compact form; that more harm than good may be done; that where we have no prior knowledge of the effects of pruning, we must treat it as an experiment and change our future handling of the plant in accordance with the result; that success in training depends as much on the choice of plant as in pruning. And all this adds up to the advisability of growing several plants of a kind from seed or cuttings so that one has sufficient material with which to experiment. In our cultural list we attempt to characterize plants as suitable or not for training.

Bonsai technique not only dwarfs plants, it obeys traditional sets of rules pertaining to dynamic symmetry and asymmetry. Houseplant training is more practically oriented, the object being to maintain a suitable size without distortion, enhance the symmetry and cause a thicker, more branching and leafy habit.

🙲🙲🙲 12 🙲🙲🙲

TEMPERATURE

Temperature in greenhouses is carefully regulated with no other object than the health of the plants. The indoor temperature of homes and public places is, with rare exceptions, controlled to suit our comfort. If we wish to grow plants we are obliged to choose those that manage to survive in the conditions that we impose. This fact is fundamental to an understanding of the problems we face matching plants to the temperatures of our artificial environments.

The warmth of American homes and public buildings in winter is notorious. The majority maintain a minimum of 60–65°F (16–18.5°C) at night. It is cooler, of course, close to open windows and in drafty situations, but the plants are usually placed where they have some protection against extremes. This range happens to coincide with minimum average temperatures at sea level in the tropics which are defined as approximately the latitudes between the equator at 0° and the tropics of Capricorn and Cancer 23.7° 36' north and south.

Tropical plants near the northern and southern limits of the range experience extremes of low temperatures occasionally that may damage foliage but do not destroy roots.

The coincidence of similar minimum average temperatures indoors and in tropical habitats accounts for our ability to grow tropical plants indoors that, in the past, were only feasible in warm greenhouses. Achieving the accompanying high humidity has proved more difficult. Europeans maintain lower average temperatures in winter and have been less successful.

A very crude estimate states that temperature averages decrease 1°F (.06°C) for every 330 ft. (110 m) increase in altitude. This means that if the mean temperature at sea level is 65°F (18.5°C) it will be 60°F (16°C) at 1650 ft. (550 m), 55°F (13°C) at 3300 ft. (1100 m), 50°F (10°C) at 4950 ft. (1650 m) and 45°F (7°C) at 6600 ft. (2200 m). Extremes can be 10°F (6°C) or more lower. The principal high mountains in the tropics are located in Central America, northern South America and on some Pacific islands. Temperature at sea level may be cooled by prevailing winds passing over cold ocean currents or through high mountains.

Summer temperatures are another matter. It is a peculiarity of temperature distribution that maximum averages in the tropics at sea level rarely go above 90°F (33°C) and are mitigated in most places by continuous breezes. The discomfort felt on the west coast of Africa is mainly due to high humidity. Moreover, where extremely oppressive atmospheric conditions prevail, the vegetation is less varied. Most of the plants we grow come from somewhat higher elevations with climates more comfortable both for humans and plants.

Most tropical plants are adversely affected by protracted periods of temperatures over 85°F (29.5°C). It is an anomaly that U.S. temperatures in summer frequently rise to and stay above this level for a week or more at a time in July and August. Even New York City and Boston experience such periods, and they are common in the plains states. Open windows and fans are usually enough to reduce the levels sufficiently in homes. In some cities, such as Houston or Dallas, air conditioning is absolutely necessary for humans as well as plants. Public buildings everywhere are usually air conditioned, which reduces humidity but does prevent overheating. Nevertheless, probably more tropical plants are killed by summer heat indoors than by winter cold. When plant activity ceases injurious fungi grow more speedily in the presence of moisture. Disease becomes rampant when measures are not taken to reduce temperatures and reactivate the plants (see Ventilation).

The subtropics stretch between latitudes 23°F' and 36° north and south of the equator. Average minimal temperatures are no lower than 40–45°F (4–7°C) for any month of the year. However, at the northern and southern limits, severe winter weather may drop the thermometer for a short time to freezing. At high altitudes the plants may be hardy, like those of the temperate zone.

As one moves north and south of the equator temperature differences between the seasons of the year and even the highs and lows of a single day increase. It thus becomes more difficult to predict the tolerances of individual species because they, too, are less uniform in their reactions. Those nearer the tropics are usually much more sensitive to cold than those nearer the temperate zone. Tropical plants grown indoors are of all types, but most of our subtropicals are shrubs and trees with very few herbs by comparison.

Most of the subtropical plants we grow indoors originate in the Mediterranean basin, South Africa, Madagascar, Central to South coastal China, Japan, Southern Australia, New Zealand, Southern Brazil and Mexico. They are not easy to maintain in warm homes where we grow tropicals because they suffer from central heating in winter and even more from temperatures much over 80°F (27°C) in summer.

However many homes and buildings throughout the United States experience low average temperatures in winter from choice or for reasons of economy. The minimum average is about 50°F (10°C) at night. Occasionally it may dip to near 40°F (4°C). The warmer minimum is not harmful to most subtropical plants; the cooler minimum is, and will damage all but subtropicals from high altitudes or a handful of plants that are on the borderline between the subtropics and the temperate zone at sea level.

Day/night temperatures. Tropical and subtropical plants experience a 10–15°F (6–8.5°C) drop in temperature at night which is virtually mandatory for their maintenance indoors. This occurs naturally in most homes and public buildings. However, there are periods in the temperate zone during midsummer when the drop is from a temperature, say, of 96°F (35°C) to 86°F (30°C). Both levels cause many plants to cease activity and can be damaging. During such times air conditioning or fans must be active day and night.

Temperature categories:

Warmhouse. Summer max. 90°F (33°C). Winter min. 60°F (16°C). These are typical of ideal conditions for tropical plants growing at sea level up to about 1200–1500 ft. (360–450 m).

Intermediate house. Summer max. 80°F (27°C). Winter min. 50°F (10°C). The range of the minimum might be better stated as 50–55°F (10–13°C) because there is considerable variability in this group of plants. The range stretches into the warmer subtropical plants and higher elevations in the tropics. 80°F (27°C) is a sort of cut off for these plants which succumb to long periods at higher levels. Many orchids require this range which is that of the lower rain forest conditions. Most plants that we call cool growing fit this category.

Cool house. Summer max. 80°F (27°C). Winter min. 40°F (4°C). These are temperatures that are associated with plants from such habitats as Japan, Southern Australia, New Zealand, South Africa. Most of these will be perfectly happy with a minimum of 55°F (13°C) but the upper level of 80°F (27°C) must be adhered to even more strictly than among the intermediate plants. The majority of plants that belong to this category do not do well in warm homes.

Heat from artificial light. All artificial sources emit heat. The closer they are to the plants and the more confined the space the greater the build-up of temperature. Fluorescent installations are especially liable to create excessive temperatures. They are commonly 10–20°F (6–12°C) higher under the fixtures than elsewhere in a room. Bulb sources can be even more damaging because of the greater concentration of heat rays over a smaller area. (See Ventilation.) Fans or other means of keeping the air moving on warm days in summer or high-temperature central heating in winter are essential to prevent drying or burning of foliage.

Placement vs. temperature. Hot air rises; cool air drops. The higher a plant stands in a room the warmer the temperature; the nearer the floor the cooler it is. The differences are significant. Placing the plants correctly is particularly important in summer. Plants more sensitive to high temperatures should be near the floor. Exceptions? Heated floors which are equivalent to radiators, the air is then somewhat cooler nearer the ceiling. The only real protection against overheating is constant air movement.

Radiators. These are usually set below windowsills. Pots, soil and roots are super-heated if set directly above them. Humidity in the air is sharply reduced.

Place hollow tiles over the radiator and trays half filled with water above them. Variety stores sell wire supports on legs. Place these in or over the trays with pots and saucers on top. A small fan directed at the area disperses the heat. Put a sheet of metal or plywood behind the radiator to direct heat into the room. A nearby humidifier can replace the water-filled trays.

Tips on temperature:

1. The effect of excessive heat is difficult or impossible to observe immediately. If a plant starts to droop it is usually evidence that root rot has already set in and the situation become incurable. This is because the plants cease activity and fungi, aided by heat, multiply and attack in greater numbers, hence the frequent losses during July/August in temperate latitudes.

The effect of a few degrees of excessive coolness may be more immediately noticeable in discoloration and loss of leaves. But fungal action is slower, and removal of a plant to a warmer place will usually save it, though often at the price of some trimming to relieve any damaged roots of part of the aboveground amount of plant they must support. A cool spell of short duration may, in fact, affect only the top of a plant. The rule is that the deeper the roots, hence the greater amount of soil, the less vulnerable the roots are to a drop in temperature. This is because it takes the soil longer to cool off. However the warm-growing tropicals are very susceptible to sudden drops in temperature.

2. When plants are discovered to be suffering from either too much heat or cold they should not be heavily watered in the hope of reviving them. The effect will be just the opposite. If the soil is damp at all, the plant should not be watered. If the medium is bone dry that may be the cause of the damage rather than the temperature.

3. The task of the indoor gardener would be simplified if the temperature environment where the plant was collected could be pinpointed. A warm-growing genus frequently includes species that grow in cooler regions and at higher altitudes than others; and vice versa. Where such plants have not been grown in sufficient quantities to establish their tolerances, the indoor gardener has no means of knowing them and must experiment. Hence the wisdom of prompt propagation and testing under varying conditions.

4. For many tropicals a combination of high humidity and high temperature is very beneficial. But when the temperature rises above the level to which the plant is normally tolerant, very high humidity becomes a liability. It further increases fungal activity especially in respect to stems and leaves. Above 85°F (29.5°C) a drop in humidity may save many a tropical from damage.

5. When the temperature is very high more light speeds up metabolism or helps to prevent it from ceasing. Plants in low light are more likely to suffer damage from high temperatures.

6. The chief virtue of air conditioning is the maintenance of moderate temperatures. There is much less loss during hot summers. However, for maximum results, the lower humidity it creates must be raised by means of humidifiers or other means.

7. Note our remarks under Ventilation. Air movement is one of the best means of combatting excessive heat. Even cool-growing houseplants may do well in warm homes if the ventilation is adequate.

13

WATERING

It is one of the cliches of plant care that more are killed by overwatering than any other cause. Our own experience has convinced us that neglect is the principal culprit. This is one chore that must be attended to without fail and at the right time. Light may not be sufficient for a while or fertilizer forgotten, and many plants will survive unfavorable temperature changes if not protracted; on the other hand, a plant's real need for water cannot wait.

The factors that play a role in watering needs are (1) the size of the plant, (2) the size of the pot and its content of medium, (3) the water-holding capacity of the medium, (4) the temperature, (5) the speed of growth and (6) whether the species is a light or heavy consumer of water. Keeping track of this complex of influences is easy when there are few plants to care for; one soon learns to recognize a shortage of moisture and the intervals of time before it recurs after watering. In many commercial situations the plants, pots and medium are uniform, so that servicing can be scheduled correctly. But when there is a large collection of different exotic plants, the problem of watering at the right time requires constant vigilance and observation in each individual case.

Careful packing of soil. As advised under Potting, make sure that there are no gaps in the soil that allow water to run through without moistening it. Water drips down from the holes in pots when packing is complete and firm. It pours through when it is too loose or when there are gaps. Use a potting stick to find the holes and add soil as needed. Potting should be checked 2 or 3 times at intervals of 3 weeks. Very frequently gaps develop after a while. Failure to notice the condition is a frequent cause for mysterious decline in plants. This does not happen with garden soil but is a characteristic problem of the artificial mixes. The reason is that when the soil is watered the perlite floats, some of it moving upward to the surface and some congregating. Both actions leave gaps that must be corrected.

Packing of the soil should be firm but not forced. Very loose packing of mixes should be avoided indoors. When the pots are on capillary mats, in shallow reservoir pots or are watered from below in saucers, once the supply is exhausted the drying out of lightly packed soil will be so rapid that a complete state of aridity may catch you unawares. Some nurseries pack soil very loosely around young plants. That speeds root formation and is permissible in greenhouse conditions. In the low humidity and with the less constant attention they receive indoors, plants suffer when moisture is exhausted in short order.

Artificial soils also contain a large proportion of peat moss. When it dries out completely, water absorption becomes difficult. When using mixes do not water from the top when the medium is completely dry. Set the pot in a saucer filled with water so that the moisture can be absorbed slowly. It is a sound rule never to allow mixes containing peat moss to become absolutely dry.

Temperature of the water. Always use room-temperature water or slightly warmer. Draw it from the warm water faucet. Having been previously heated, the liquid contains fewer chemical impurities. Letting water stand over night before use permits evaporation of chemical additives in the supply.

Salt accumulation. When a plant has lived in a container for six months or more, a crystalline crust builds up on the inner side of the rim. Moisture pulled up by surface tension evaporates and deposits the residue of rime. It is a good indicator of the amount of free salts that are released from soil and fertilizer by water. There is always an accumulation that is ultimately dangerous or even fatal to the roots of a plant. It breaks down tissue and may contain an excess amount of elements that are harmful. Palms, for example, are well known to react unfavorably to the presence of boron.

Watering techniques differ in the degree to which they assist salt accumulation. One of the prime causes of the deterioration of plants in large containers is the harm done by the salt content of the soil. The universal remedy is leaching, which is nothing more than periodic flooding of the soil with fresh water so as to flush out the excess salts.

Ideal moisture. Ideal moisture for a majority of foliage plants is even moisture. That is, soil in much the state of a sponge that has been squeezed. There is no free liquid; the medium is neither wet nor partly dry but simply damp. This condition permits air to circulate around the particles of light materials that we use as media. It encourages root growth and inhibits the spread of fungi and algae.

Soaking-wet soil is equivalent to standing the roots of plants in water. Outdoors rain drains off or sinks quickly deeper into the earth, leaving the root area just moist. As the surface dries out the nether moisture gradually rises until there is no more to draw on. Indoors there is no such action. The soil may remain soaking wet because we water too frequently or the pot is allowed to sit in a saucer with excess water. Reservoir pots and capillary matting can be lethal to some plants because the soil never has a chance to lose sufficient moisture. Wet conditions, if protracted, result in the loss of roots and the development of stem rot. As with most generalities there are exceptions, namely semiaquatic plants which benefit from constant moisture.

If watering takes place before the soil is partly dry at root level, absorption is delayed and a soaking-wet condition persists. Since water falls by gravity and evaporation rises into the air, it is the surface that becomes dry first. The dry soil attracts moisture from below with the result that the root level is gradually deprived of water. This is like the outdoors except the depth of the soil is so much less that the process is much more rapid. However, if the plant has stopped growing or grows very slow or the pot very big, the process will take place very much more gradually. Do not expect pots to dry out all at the same time. Those who imagine that it is proper to water all pots at regular intervals are heading for trouble. Ascertaining moisture conditions below the surface of the soil has always been critical to watering conditions, for each pot and plant reacts differently except in mass-production situations where plants and pots are all the same.

Testing soil moisture. Experienced growers claim to be able to tell the amount of moisture in a pot by its weight. Others poke a finger into the medium. But no other means is as reliable and easy as the use of a moisture meter, the only one of a number of inexpensive soil-testing gadgets that we have found to be consistently accurate. The type with two prongs and without batteries is as good as any. It immediately indicates the degree of soil moisture when plunged into the medium. A pointer on a dial registers the degree of moisture to the right and degrees of dryness to the left. Water when the indicator is close to the borderline of dryness. The test should be taken about two-thirds the depth of the pot.

Full and partial watering. Water thoroughly so that it flows out of the bottom of the container, even with succulents. Salts trapped in the soil are leached out, preventing accumulation. Do not try partial watering. You can't possibly estimate the right amount. Salts concentrate above any level of the soil where water penetration has stopped.

Top or bottom watering. Top watering is better for the plant. Bottom watering is frequently more convenient. If the soil draws its water from below, salt build-up is inevitable. It reaches dangerous proportions very quickly when fertilizer is applied regularly. Whatever the disadvantages, the method is preferred by many indoor gardeners because it is the only way to have a reservoir of water for the plants to draw on and, thus, reduce the frequency with which they must be served. If you do water from the bottom, flush the soil at least every three months to remove the residue of fertilizer.

Bottom-watering methods. It is assumed and claimed that moisture is supplied by bottom watering only when it is needed, and therefore the plant benefits from a continuous but not excessive supply. This is, of course, an illusion, since the media we use will attract water until it is soaking wet and the reservoir keeps it that way. A number of popular foliage plants do manage well enough with the system to give an appearance of general effectiveness. It is when we increase our repertory of houseplants to include less tolerant species that we become aware of its inadequacy. That having been said, we list below some of the means by which to extend the supply of water to plants.

1. *Capillary matting.* This is inexpensive, mildew- and rot-resistant cloth available from firms selling indoor gardening accessories. Cut it to fit the bottom of trays. It is a means of watering a large number of small plants simultaneously, retains moisture well and supplies additional humidity. Though the least risky system of bottom watering, the cloth does become algae ridden and acts as a thoroughfare for insects. Frequent washing of the cloth is recommended.

2. *Wick watering.* The wicks are lengths of thick, soft, mildew-resistant, moisture-absorbent material. They are sold by indoor gardening suppliers but can also be made from such materials as discarded pantyhose. One end of the wick is poked through a hole in the bottom of a pot until it is half way to the top. Fill the bottom with soil and fix the roots of the plant in place with additional medium. The other end of the wick should dangle far enough below the bottom of the pot to reach water in a deep saucer or tray. The method is satisfactory for plants that do not mind a continuous supply of water.

The methods of expert indoor gardeners are constantly being modified as they gain new insights into the needs of their plants. Recently those who have been accustomed to wicking only their gesneriads and other soft-stemmed tropicals have been applying the method to woody shrubs. This has been the result of the observation that, though not tolerant of heavy and continuous soakings, shrubs are most often killed by a short period of near or complete dryness, overnight for example. Wicking guarantees a regular supply of water. It is not an ideal solution because these plants prefer the natural rhythm of drenches and gradual drying out. But it does prevent that sudden loss which all indoor gardeners fear most of all.

3. *Pots with attached saucers.* They are plastic pots with deep snap-on saucers. The close fitting of the saucers to the body of the pot reduces evaporation. Variety stores and florists usually carry various sizes and styles. However the actual capacity of the saucers is small and the supply does not last long. It is a convenient system with only the disadvantages of bottom watering.

4. *Reservoir pots.* There are a number of systems of two basic types on the market. One is a pot with double bottom and/or walls. Water is poured through a tube into these spaces and is released to the plant by means of variously designed holes or plugs. The water level is indicated on a transparent tube or by a float. The units are bulky and, because of the complex construction, much more expensive than normal pots. For that reason they have appealed more to decorator/plantscapers than to the average indoor gardener. For the professional clientele they have been made in large sizes and a variety of colors and materials.

Separate reservoirs to be inserted into large pots are also available in a number of sizes. They are simple plastic tanks with holes in the cover and a tube in which a float is inserted to indicate the water level. They are placed in the bottoms of the pots with the tube projecting over soil level. They are not expensive and offer the advantage that they can be reused after the original pot has been discarded. A disadvantage is that if the soil becomes completely dry, the water in the refilled reservoir may not be able to moisten the soil either because the holes are clogged or the dry material resists impregnation.

Both methods completely enclose the water supply, thus preventing evaporation. But both also result in the use of pots much bigger than a plant of a given size normally requires.

Frequency of watering. We have already mentioned that a precise watering schedule is possible only where pots and plants are uniform and growing in the same environment. Indoor landscaping firms also know the length of time between waterings for their standard office installations. But not even the most experienced indoor growers can work out an unvarying schedule for a mixed collection of house plants, much less prescribe it for anyone else. Each environment is different, the temperature changes seasonally and all the factors of pot size, medium and consumption rate come into play. Scheduling must be based on the actual state of the soil in each pot. A daily check of moisture in pots is absolutely essential for good maintenance of mixed plantings.

Retention of water by the medium. (1) Garden soils dry out rapidly indoors in pots. (2) Mineral ingredients of mixes such as vermiculite, perlite, sand and pumice, dry out very fast; vermiculite a little slower than the others. Water retention of all of these is low though absorption is rapid. (3) Wood and bark chips absorb moisture slowly but do not retain it very long. (4) Peat moss and sphagnum mosses absorb more moisture and retain it longer.

Hence the greater the amount of peat/sphagnum products in a mix, the longer the water will last in a pot. It should also be noted that loose packing dries out much faster than firm packing of soils.

Pot size and watering. It stands to reason that a small plant in a large pot with extra soil around the roots will go without watering for a longer time than one that is closely fitted in its container. Firms that supply and service commercial plantings usually over-pot in order to reduce the frequency of waterings. It should be emphasized however that, with few exceptions, plants thrive better in pots that are not much bigger than their minimum requirement. There is always the danger with over-potting that the soil will stay too wet too long during a period when the plant is relatively inactive. Indoor gardeners prefer small pots as they take up less room and are lighter to handle.

Rates of plant absorption. Some plants drink more rapidly or copiously than others. Appearance is not a reliable guide. A dry-leaved plant such as *Lantana,* or a rubbery one like *Phyllanthus* may require twice as frequent waterings as juicy-leaved plants. *Dieffenbachias* are slow drinkers and object to excess. One species of a genus may drink much more than another, despite great similarities in other respects. *Calathea princeps* will drink less in a small pot than *Calathea warscewicziana* in a big one. With the aid of a moisture meter one can quickly identify the fast- and slow-drinking plants.

Manual and automatic watering. Commerical growers of small and medium-sized houseplants mass them and water automatically. Sometimes they bury soaker hoses that release water slowly into medium deep enough to plunge the pots. Hanging baskets and pots on benches are serviced by means of lengthy hoses that are pierced at intervals by capillary tubes, usually with weights attached. Each one of the tubes is dropped onto the surface of a pot. When water is turned on the whole lot receives moisture at the same time. If a schedule has been established, the flow is controlled by a timer. Indoor gardeners with a large number of plants would welcome a similar system, but despite many attempts, none have proved satisfactory.

Plastic, small-gauge hoses for attachment to home faucets are offered in many seed and indoor garden supply catalogs. Equipped with a rigid, tubular wand they eliminate the back and forth from kitchen or bathroom with a watering can. They come with faucet adapters which fit some and not others. They are useless if the right fitting has not been supplied. We consider the trigger mechanism on the wand to be flimsy and subject to malfunction. However, they are a convenience not to be overlooked.

One firm provides a gallon bottle as a reservoir, a long plastic tube and a well-made wand that releases water by trigger action. We have used one for years in watering small pots. The bottle must be positioned higher than the plants.

In both pieces of equipment the narrow tubes sooner or later become clogged with dark green algae. Separate the tube from the wand and drop it into a pot of boiling water for 3 minutes. Remove and, when the tube has cooled, roll it between thumb and forefinger while holding one open end under a hot water faucet so that the algae is flushed out.

Watering cans of various sizes with long nozzles but without roses (perforated water diffusers on the ends of the nozzles) are still the mainstay for both professional plant service personnel and amateurs.

Large public indoor gardens employ various designs for watering based on one system. Noncorrosive grating is put down over a catch basin with an outlet to the drainage system of the building. Gravel and other drainage material is layered above it and a deep layer of soil tops it off. Watering is manual with hoses or automatic by means of metal or plastic pipes pierced with small holes and buried in the soil. Drip action keeps the soil moist.

Effects of temperature. It is an old rule to water more in summer than winter. But central heating and low humidity in winter often combine to dry out soil more rapidly than warm, fresh, humid air. Therefore a better statement of the rule is simply: Water is exhausted more quickly at high temperatures than low. Pots exposed to the sun may require two waterings a day in summer.

Effect of light on the consumption of water. Plants consume more water on sunny days than overcast ones. This is one of the factors that demonstrates the folly of attempting to establish a strict watering schedule.

Humidity. High humidity reduces evaporation and slows plant absorption of moisture.

Plant activity. When plants are in active growth they consume more water than when inactive. Watch their growth rates as a guide to the giving or withholding of moisture. When leaf buds cease to develop it is an indication of the onset of a resting period, complete dormancy or disease. Roots are no longer called on to nourish new growth and metabolism is slowed. Watering before the soil has lost most of its moisture will help bring on or aggravate disease.

In the tropics more than one wet or dry season is a common occurrence during the year. The seasonal timing of this alternation differs geographically. Local plants are used to these cycles which are usually of shorter duration than the four seasons in the North and much more irregular in their timing. The most noticeable effect is that of the dry seasons. At that time many plants lose their leaves but replace them a few weeks to a couple of months later. Others just stop growing for the same period.

Indoors the effects of this phenomenon are less noticeable because we grow many different kinds of tropical plants and the loss of leaves or a slowdown in growth is usually confined to one species at a time. Furthermore, our very different conditions seem to shorten the resting periods. All the more reason to take notice if activity stops. The loss of leaves should be checked for cause as, in particular instances, it may result from other influences such as pests, disease, underwatering, excessively low temperatures, etc. However, if these factors have been eliminated, you must assume that the plant has automatically reacted, similarly to those in our own spring and fall, to the expectation of a change in season; in this case to a dry one. Watering should be reduced to the minimum short of absolute dryness. Resume normal watering when leaf buds start to grow again. Once the seasonal behavior of a plant has been established it is a good idea to note the dates of beginning and ending for future reference.

Impurities in water. Most water these days is contaminated in one way or another. Even rainwater cannot be trusted because it has proved lethal to forests in parts of the Northern Hemisphere. Which chemicals in acid rain are the more destructive is still a matter of debate. Urban water supplies vary, some being safer than others. Chlorine evaporates when water is allowed to stand for a while in air. Fluorine is now a universal additive. Its effect on different plants has not been fully researched. Filtration processes and water softeners may utilize chemicals that do more harm than good. In large sections of the country the water supply is called hard, that is to say loaded with alkalinity.

If your own experiences and that of other growers confirm damage done by the water supply, there is no other recourse than to consult experts who are familiar with local conditions. In first line are the county agents of the U.S. Dept. of Agriculture. They are in constant touch with nurseries and agriculturists who supply information when there is anything drastically wrong with the water they use. The county agent has the means to test water and to secure information as how best to deal with chemical imbalance. There are various ways of removing impurities or neutralizing them.

As a backup there are the agricultural horticultural departments of universities and colleges. A local botanical garden may also be able to offer useful information.

Excessive acidity or alkalinity of soils as well as water are such common phenomena that the proportions have been worked out for chemical soil additives that correct the imbalance. But it is a mistake to use them without knowledge of actual need based on the pH of the soil or water you are using. It is better to consult the authorities we have mentioned than to follow formulas that have been published and which have only a general and approximate application to individual needs.

Spraying and misting. Spray is in the form of large drops very similar to a drizzling rain that drips quickly off leaf surfaces but accumulates in the joints of leaves, especially rosettes of new leaves. Manual sprayers are sold in variety stores where they are sometimes called misters. In hot weather or when the humidity indoors is below 50%, a daily spraying is beneficial to foliage plants. Blasting the undersides of leaves helps keep mites and some other insects under control. Tiny amounts of fertilizer added to the water are absorbed by leaves. Watch out, however, for water collecting in joints where it can cause rot. A paper handkerchief quickly absorbs any excess.

True mist is a cloud of particles of moisture so light that they remain partly suspended in the air and contribute to ambient humidity. Manual sprayers equipped with a nozzle that can be tightened to reduce the size of moisture particles, are rarely effective for long, soon becoming clogged. There are electric sprayers of the type used for the application of disinfectants in hospitals (similar to paint sprayers) that produce a true mist cloud. Plugged into an automatic timer they can be set to emit bursts of 2 or 3 seconds' duration every half hour. However they emit so much moisture that use must be confined to specially prepared rooms. The water pressure from faucets in most homes is not sufficiently strong to produce mist from a hose with a special mist attachment.

The best way to mist is by means of a humidifier placed close to the plants. It does double duty, maintaining a higher level of general room humidity and emitting a continuous, limited mist cloud directly over the plant area. Furniture and books in a room will not be adversely affected.

The humidifier should have a minimum of one-gallon capacity and should turn off automatically if the water is exhausted. Attach to an automatic timer and operate during daylight hours. The "ultrasonic" machines are very efficient but usually have small reservoirs. Floor models with fans also do a good job. The improvement in texture and growth habit of tropical foliage plants when grown in high humidity (over 50%) and misted is very noticeable.

Hydroculture. Hydroculture has a great attraction for science-oriented amateurs and owes most of its modest commercial success to that fact. In our opinion, performance by no means matches the claims.

Hydroculture is not hydroponics. The latter is a continuous system of water plus nutrient treatment. Hydroculture is static, employing a container, an inner basket of plastic to hold the plant and a filling of baked clay pebbles or other inert materials. The water level is maintained at all times and nutrients are added in tiny amounts. Containers and pebbles must be flushed and cleaned from time to time.

The system offers no advantages in our opinion other than a reservoir of water so large that servicing is considerably reduced. The disadvantages are also considerable. The cost of each unit is much higher than a normal pot. Compared to the large size of the containers the amount of space left for roots is comparatively small. Unless the instructions regarding nutrients and water changes are followed to the letter, salts build up and the water becomes contaminated with organic matter that absorbs nutrients and may initiate plant diseases.

Observing their use by others we have noted that only the most common members of the Araceae and Liliaceae usually survive for long. And such means are hardly necessary to grow these carefree plants. We find that some disciplined and conscientious growers have been moderately successful using the method. By and large, however, the persistence of these gadgets on the market depends on attracting new purchasers who are without previous experience in growing houseplants. We do not recommend them.

Watering succulents. As we list only some of the leaf succulents and not the stem succulents the problems of watering these desert plants are somewhat reduced. Inured to extreme deprivation one might think that their watering needs would be satisfied by a very short season during which growth takes place. That this is not the case was proved to us by our leaving a number of healthy plants, used to complete droughts for long periods, waterless while on vacation for 5 weeks at a time when we expected them to be dormant. On our return every one was shrivelled and dead.

We can only guess that indoor conditions differ from the habitats in a number of ways and that the same behavior as in the desert cannot be expected in the house. It is also too easy to forget the nightly dews and, for those plants that are near a coast, the mists driven in from the sea that always provide a little moisture to the leaves. Thus, the fact that a year or more may go by without rain falling in the desert is not a reliable indicator. For they do not depend entirely on the thick, juicy reservoirs of their leaves. We have observed this time and again over the years. There is also considerable variation between species depending on the amount of rainfall in their habitats. For instance, broad-leaved Sansevierias grow where there usually is ample rainfall. The more cylindric the leaves, the drier the habitat.

We have found just two indicators for watering with these plants, and one is related to the other. The normal healthy leaf is turgid or bloated and is an indicator that more water is not required. One must not water even if the plant seems to be growing. On the other hand, when one or more of the lower leaves starts to shrivel ever so slightly, water is needed. In many leaf succulents the sign is simply a thinning or a modest creasing of the taut surface. Even if these changes are noted, water only on sunny days. Soak the soil thoroughly so that the liquid drips from the bottom of the pot. The shrivelled leaves will fill out completely in from a few hours to overnight. Keep pots in warm, sunny locations so that excess moisture evaporates more rapidly.

Dormancy is indicated by leaves remaining fat for a long time although the soil has become completely dry. During this period a light spraying in the morning of sunny days will do no harm.

There are a number of exceptions to these rules. Growing leaves, for instance, are a better signal to water for Sansevierias, whose shrivelling is difficult to observe. The same is true of Aloes and Agaves. Fall-winter dryness and spring-summer watering is relatively safe. There are leaf succulents that rarely go completely dormant indoors. Aeoniums require winter sun and watering followed by much reduced moisture in summer.

Going away. The problem of what to do with plants during vacations or an enforced absence has always bedeviled indoor growers. Plant sitters, whether friends or people employed for the purpose, are generally incapable of doing the job right, even though following watering instructions is all that is expected from them.

Many suggestions have been offered from time to time but we have found only one that is really dependable. That is to apply the principle of terrarium culture; enclose the plants in some way so that moisture does not evaporate. As we know (see Terrarium Culture), when plants are sealed into a container soil moisture is not consumed but is recirculated.

Recently a piece of equipment that does the job rather well has been sold through stores and mail order catalogs. It is called a plant tender or tent, and it comes in a narrow cardboard tube. When pulled out a sort of furled umbrella is revealed, with metal ribs covered by clear plastic and a zipper on one side that reaches from bottom to top. Contrary to an umbrella, however, the gadget that opens it is in the top instead of the bottom. When a rod is pulled up, the ribs spread and a stopper inside is lifted into the knob at the top to hold the shape. What one ends up with is a plastic tent with a sheet of plastic at floor level. Sizes are approx. 2 × 2 ft. (60 × 60 cm) and 3 × 3 ft. (90 × 90 cm). A large number of small and big plants fit into the ample space. After use, the tent is collapsed, furled and replaced in the tube. We have left our plants in the tents for 6 weeks with no losses. They could have survived even longer.

Before leaving water the pots thoroughly. Set them inside the tent and close the opening. Place anywhere in rooms that have some natural light but never where the tent is exposed to direct sunlight. Near a north window is a good place.

Perfection cannot be expected. Tent care can go awry if air temperatures rise over 80°F (27°C). Inside the tent it will be still warmer. In late spring and summer, therefore, 6 inches of the zipper should be opened. Small pots evaporate fast. If these are placed in a tent they should be enclosed in larger containers with moist long-fiber sphagnum moss. When the absence is over 3 weeks at that time of year, someone should look in every week and check two things, 1) whether the heat is becoming too great for the plants, in which case the zipper should be opened more and 2) whether any of the pots has dried out. If so they should be thoroughly watered. Even a plant sitter can hardly go wrong. After 3 weeks the visitor can also water succulents that are not placed in tents.

If tents are unavailable the same principle can be applied in various ways. Houseware and variety stores carry packs containing large sheets of transparent, light-weight plastic. Place plants on shelves of bookcases; hang plastic sheeting over the open sides and seal with adhesive tape. Use a bath tub covered with plastic sheeting. It is also not at all difficult to put together a rectangular frame of any size, made with lengths of light weight wood. Cover with plastic, top and sides. These enclosures are usually effective for 2 weeks without supervision. After that they should be checked once a week. Remember to leave some small opening during the warm months.

Large plants, 3–8 ft. (90 cm – 2.40 m) in big pots or tubs containing standard houseplant mix will remain moist for at least 3 weeks summer or winter. Extend the period to 6–8 weeks by covering the surface with plastic sheeting so that evaporation is reduced. Fix the sheeting to the rim of the container and around the stem of the plant with adhesive tape.

14

FERTILIZER

Plants in active growth soon exhaust whatever nutrients are available in most natural soils. That has been demonstrated throughout the history of agriculture. Lacking the ability to enrich them with organic or inorganic nutrients, whole communities have been forced to move from place to place in order to occupy unexhausted land. Deprivation of nutrients is very much more rapid indoors, where the quantity of medium assigned to each plant is limited.

Where there is a convenient supply of decomposed organic matter with which to enrich a normal soil no additional nutrients may be needed for a while. In the longer run, however, the supply must be replenished, and that is not possible with either humus or compost because of their bulk. If one insists on organic fertilizers it becomes necessary either to make nutritive brews from compost or depend entirely on manures, bone meal, dried blood and the like which are used in small-scale agriculture.

No doubt intensive agriculture benefits from the recycling of vegetable waste. However, for most indoor gardeners, compost is unavailable. Because most organic fertilizers are low in chemical content they can be used in large amounts, which suits them to outdoor gardening. But, again, they are both too bulky and too weak to satisfy the needs of tropical and subtropical plants. Even if they were, that the materials are hard to find in the shops and, when available at all, are packed in quantities too large for indoor use, makes them quite impractical. Artificial soils and chemical fertilizers can be bought everywhere in small amounts. Both professional nurserymen and amateur indoor gardeners have found them quite satisfactory for growing tropical and subtropical plants and ever so much more convenient.

The elements most essential for plant nutrition are nitrogen, phosphorus and potassium in forms that can be absorbed and converted into the various compounds providing the means to complete a plant's normal life cycle. In addition, certain other elements, called trace elements, such as iron, sulfur, copper, manganese and magnesium must be present in small quantities.

The big question is, how much of each element is best for a species or cultivar. When nurserymen grow quantities of one species, extensive research and testing usually yields a formula which is almost precisely suited to its needs. For the majority of plants, however, we have little to go on except the fortunate fact that they do rather well on simple formulas consisting of the three basic elements with an occasional dosage of trace elements.

Botanists have published illustrations of leaves damaged by a lack of one or another of the elements. In practice they are of little use, as leaves of plants show varying patterns of damage, making the specific cause usually quite unidentifiable. For certainty, complex analytical tests are required.

Some nutrient formulas are advertised as improving the vigor of all plants equally well. *Caveat emptor* is our best advice. The claims for one formula are the same as for another. They can't both be equally right. Of one thing we are sure; species in many or all instances prefer a particular mix of nutritive elements, and no one thus far has discovered the perfect formula for all.

What can happen if a formula is not quite right is illustrated by the experience of a very conscientious nurseryman who, after long testing, found one commercial fertilizer that yielded superior growth of a major crop. Several years later, using the same fertilizer, all the plants died. Tests proved that the cause was a slight increase in the amount of a trace element included in the formula. When growing many different plants, indoor gardeners rarely suffer such experiences because they usually use several formulas and change from one to another rather haphazardly during a season. Many use simple formulas without trace elements and incur no problems. Should one or another plant among many suddenly die, the cause would be impossible to trace. The system, if one can call it that, works fairly well and, for the present, is about all one can expect.

Uncertainty about the effects of fertilizers is one of the reasons why professionals and amateurs alike are wary of plants that have not proved capable of tolerating almost any combination of elements in the nutritional formula. But the packaged fertilizers that are marketed most widely do give good results in most instances. Results are average, and, on the whole, little damage is apparent from lack of proper nutrition. It is best to use fertilizers very moderately or not at all rather than to dose heavily. The very small dosages we suggest, which are much less than recommended on labels, are more than adequate.

Basic elements

Nitrogen. Essential for the development of stems, branches, leaves and the green color of the latter, the green form of chlorophyll. It facilitates metabolism of the other elements. Excessive use results in too rapid, weak growth and flaccid leaves, causing the plant to be less resistant to disease. Nitrogenous compounds acidify soil and must be used less with alkaline plants. Acid plants require larger amounts.

Phosphorus. Encourages root formation but is principally required for budding and flowering. More frequently used with alkaline plants.

Potassium. Appears to promote sturdy growth. Presence of the other elements is necessary for its metabolism. Only recently have high potash fertilizers become more easily available to horticulturists.

Calcium. Contributes to the formation of the walls of cells. Generally available in near neutral medium. Added as lime it reduces acidity.

Trace elements. Tiny amounts can be beneficial or even essential to some plants. Excess can prove toxic.

Iron. Only small amounts are required but it is very necessary for acid-loving, woody plants to maintain green leaves and sturdy growth. Deficiency of iron is the easiest to detect, as green leaves turn yellowish. But there are other causes for this discoloration that must be eliminated before iron can be pinpointed as the cause.

It is fed to plants in a micronized or chelated (to assist its metabolism) form. Both are available in small packaged amounts. A pinch for a 4 in. (10 cm) pot once a year is sufficient; other size pots in proportion.

Magnesium. Assists the assimilation of phosphorus and is needed for chlorophyll formation. Lack of this element results in bleaching of older leaves, known as chlorosis, while iron deficiency affects newer leaves.

Manganese. The action is similar to that of iron.

Sulfur. Aids formation of organic compounds. Usually available from chemical compounds of the principal elements.

Aluminum. May be necessary in very small amounts for some acid plants. Strongly acidifying and therefore toxic to high-pH, acid-neutral plants. Counteracted by adding lime to the soil.

Boron. Required by some plants but has been found harmful to palms. Lately it has been suspected of damaging other groups of genera.

The pH factor

pH is an arbitrary scale for measuring the degree of acidity or alkalinity of substances. It is widely used in agriculture and horticulture because the degree of acidity/alkalinity affects the availability to plants of the essential elements in plant nutrition.

Everyone who engages in horticulture sooner or later becomes aware that no single factor in culture stands alone. All the major processes react with each other. pH is no exception. It enters into the inter-reactions between a plant and the medium in which it grows, with the water it receives and the fertilizer with which it is fed. Even light or the lack of it, temperature and humidity play roles.

The pH scale is numbered from 1 to 14. 7.0 pH is neutral, neither acid or alkaline. Nevertheless, any plant that prefers a range between pH 6.5 and 7.0 is considered alkaline. Lower numbers are increasingly acid. The range for most acid plants is between pH 5.0 and 6.0.

pH is measured by testing equipment available as kits from seed catalogs and supply houses. Less expensive are pH meters, similar in appearance to moisture meters. The number is indicated on a dial. Litmus paper, sold in rolls at tropical fish stores, changes color when in contact with moisture. A short strip partly buried in moist soil yields an approximate reading. The pH number is ascertained by comparing the color of the paper with a chart printed on the label of the package.

A pH of 6.5 was long considered a good average level for most plants, based on the use of natural soils. Later it was demonstrated that in houseplant soil mixes containing greater amounts of organic material in the form of peat moss, bark or wood chips, plants react differently and absorb nutrient chemicals more readily at pH 5.5–6.0. We suspect that choices of plants and media used in past experiments have affected the results and that anything conclusive awaits further study.

Unfortunately, very little has been published regarding the ideal pH for most of our houseplants. We ourselves go by the assumption that shrubs and vines are usually acid demanding but that most of the rest of our tropical plants are nearer neutral. Because of the heavy rainfall in tropical forests the soil is leached of its chemicals rather quickly and is nearer neutral most of the time. Trees both inland and on coasts are also more frequently rather alkaline in their preferences.

The media we use indoors are compounded to be close to pH 6.5. But the peat moss content gradually acidifies when it is subjected to moisture for a long time. In addition, we must take into consideration that faucet water is very hard in some parts of the country, in other words alkaline, and that it is near neutral in others. Only natural rain affected by industrial pollutants is definitely acid. Alkaline water builds up the alkalinity of soil and raises the pH.

This leaves the matter up in the air and by no means as clear as was believed in the past. Here are our own suggestions based on the assumption that the medium being used tests approximately 6.5 pH when fresh.

1. For most vines and shrubs fertilize with 30-10-10 or equivalent. Dose with iron twice a year. The same for any other plants about which it is known that they prefer acid conditions.

2. For most tropical trees use 20-20-20 except palms which should have high potash formulas.

3. Plants that prefer a soil to be near neutral should be fed with 15-30-15 or equivalent, with one tablespoon of dolomite lime chips or crushed egg shell added to each quart of mix.

4. If the local water is very hard, that is to say high in calcium, consult the county agent or nearby college botany department for advice on the best acidifier and the right quantities to use in order to maintain the pH in your media at proper levels.

Chemical fertilizers

Indoor gardeners, professional and amateur, prefer to buy chemical fertilizers that have been compounded by horticultural scientists and in quantities suitable to their needs. Convenience and average good results are the main reason for their popularity. One can buy nitrates, phosphates, and potash separately in packages. Professionals have access to packaged sources of trace elements. Yet very few, if any, horticulturists mix their own compounds from these ingredients.

There are numerous packaged liquid, powdered, granular and crystalline chemical compounds on the market that are relatively safe in use and that are packaged for a variety of quantitative needs. The amounts required indoors for houseplants are tiny compared with agriculture. The fertilizers are measured out in drops or from fractions to whole teaspoons per gallon of water instead of pounds. The labels of packaged fertilizers usually list the principal ingredients and sometimes the trace elements, and they specify an amount to be diluted in water.

We do not advise buying any fertilizer whose label does not list the ingredients, nor any that is not completely soluble in water. Fertilizers listing trace elements are preferable to those that do not.

Contents of fertilizers. The available nitrogen, phosphorous and potassium in packaged fertilizers are listed on their labels in that order as percentages. Thus it has become standard practice to refer to the contents by the percentages themselves. For instance, 15-30-15 means that the fertilizer contains those percentages of the basic elements; in this instance, 15% nitrogen, 30% phosphorous pentoxide and 15% potassium oxide. The total is therefore 60%. The labeling procedure is invariable.

The percentages are useful in comparing prices of packaged fertilizers. If the weights and prices of two brands are the same, the one with the higher total percentage of ingredient is the less expensive. We would not stress price if we were able to discover any noticeable differences in quality among the leading brands. We have found them essentially alike as long as they meet the criteria noted above. Years of contacts with growers have not revealed any important differences. In fact we are especially wary of any product that goes by a cute name and makes exaggerated claims, often using purple prose as a substitute for proper labeling.

The endorsements of professionals and amateurs alike, prove equally dubious. They are generally based on short-term experience, tests with selected plants and special environments. Later it is found out that results in use are much the same as with other fertilizers. As long as the essential elements are present they do the job. The only harmful effects we have encountered involved an excess of one or another trace element on a species. Much more scientific evidence is needed before the superiority of one or another brand of fertilizer can be proved.

Standard formulas. The three most popular formulas of chemical fertilizers are 20-20-20, 15-30-15 and 30-10-10. The first is a general fertilizer. Equivalents are other even percentages for which we have used the designation "balanced." This is probably the safest formula to apply on foliage plants except those requiring especially high acid reactions (low pH). The second is more frequently used to induce budding and flowering as well as for plants preferring near neutral pH. The third, which is more acidifying, we use on most vines and shrubs and some trees that prefer acid conditions. There are many fertilizers that, using slightly different proportions, approximate the effects of the above.

High-potash fertilizers are scarcer and there is less experience in using them indoors. They should be helpful in promoting sturdy, compact growth. At present the principal ones on the market are Peters 7-6-19 and Phostrogen 10-10-27.

The leading liquid fertilizer is Schultz Instant, with a rating of 15-30-15. Sturdy, listed in horticultural supply catalogs, is an organic, high-phosphorous and -potassium formula, 0-15-

14. Fish emulsion is 5-1-1; weak but useful for promoting greenness. Liquid seaweed has little chemical content but is considered a conditioner or catalyst, perhaps for other chemical or organic fertilizers.

To make your own fertilizer compounds buy soluble nitrates, phosphates and potash in packages as small as 1 lb. (453.60grams). The concentration of each is 44%. Add trace elements. Sterns Miracle-Gro Therapy provides a combination of trace elements. It contains chelated iron, zinc, copper and manganese.

The slow-release fertilizer, Osmocote 14-14-14, in the form of soluble beads, is much used as an additive to commercial soil mixes. Each dosage lasts 3-4 months. Sprinkle on the surface of soil in pots. The sticks now being sold widely in variety stores are an expensive but convenient source of fertilizer. They work on the slow-release principle but are a very expensive source of nutrition. We avoid both these fertilizers because we have heard of cases of overdosage. This probably occurs because the chemicals are released too rapidly. Little or no information is offered as to ways to reduce the recommended amounts for plants with lower requirements.

Frequency and amounts to use The labels on packaged fertilizers state a dosage per gallon of water but nothing specific about frequency; that is to say, how often the fertilizer/water mix should be applied. Are we to fertilize with every watering or only after we have watered a certain number of times without fertilizer? Does time between fertilizings play a role? Are there situations that mandate no fertilizer at all.

For standard, slow-growing plants that we list as Cast Iron, a treatment with the dosage recommended on the labels of the packages once a month is ample and can usually be stretched to once every 2 months during the winter without starving or overfeeding them. With slow-release fertilizers which are especially convenient for commercial plantings, the advice of the technical personnel of the manufacturers can probably be followed. That may come to mean no more than 3 or 4 applications a year.

Where mixed collections of plants are involved, consider the Cast-Iron plants as a separate category and apply fertilizer as suggested above. Other plants, however, usually include more temperamental exotics that, if we knew their real quantitative needs, would oblige us to follow a different schedule for each plant. The larger the collection, the more difficult this would be. Actually, the necessary information is very scant at present.

We believe that there are only two convenient choices: either to apply the fertilizer once a month in the full amount recommended or to do so with every watering and leach the plants more often. If the latter method is chosen the amounts of fertilizer used with each watering must be greatly reduced; but there is a limit beyond which measurement becomes so fine as to be totally impractical. That being the case, we have found that one-eighth (⅛th) of the recommended dosage with every watering works on average quite well but should be followed by a thorough leaching, preferably every 3 months or a minimum of at least every 6 months.

Neither these or any other schedules are perfect. In practice growers learn to adjust the amounts and frequency of fertilization to the behavior of the plants. As any schedule based on plant reactions depends as much on the specific environment as the species of plant, its use by other growers may produce different results.

The above suggestions are anything but immutable and must be adjusted according to circumstances. Two points to remember are: 1) Fertilize when plants are growing actively. Cease fertilizing when growth stops, no matter how long that lasts; 2) Do not fertilize tropical plants when the temperature is above 85°F (29.5°C) or below 60°F (16°C).

Pre-fertilized plants. Plants bought from a florist or nursery frequently are dosed with slow-release fertilizer before having been brought to market. Additional feeding will aggravate the trauma suffered in transferring to a home or office. Nurserymen will know whether this has been done; florists generally do not. If the plants have been treated, feeding indoors should not start until after 6 months. We can only issue the warning to find out about prior fertilizing if you can. At purchase time you may also be able to find out what fertilizer has been used.

Plants bought at a nursery that have algae or moss on the surface of the soil or whose pots have encrusted rims have been held for a long time. Their soil usually does not contain slow-release fertilizers. It is more likely that they have been starved in order to inhibit fast growth while waiting for a buyer. Leach these plants well at home and put them on a regular fertilizer schedule promptly thereafter.

Stabilizing plants. We constantly speak of growing plants indoors, though realistically we know that there are times when we wish the growth to be minimal. The fact is that the whole interior landscape industry and most owners of decorative foliage plants make their selections on the basis of a certain size that fits a planned decorative scheme. They want them to remain that way as long as possible. A fast-growing plant defeats the intended use when it outgrows the size we consider ideal. In large landscapes and in living rooms alike, they must be replaced when they grow too big to handle or simply look out of proportion to their surroundings.

One way to retard growth or at least maintain plants virtually unchanged in size, is to prune them regularly. Unfortunately we can't do it to all plants, for instance single-stemmed ones such as palms or Dieffenbachias. Another way is to pot them tightly or even allow them to become partially pot-bound. Finally, one can reduce feeding until there is evidence that the need is desperate.

Cast-Iron plants can survive for a long time on nothing else but standard houseplant media and water. Less tolerant plants, of which there are many more, endure deprivation in varying degrees. The signs of starvation are seen in smaller new growth, by yellowing and by browning of tips and edges of leaves. In themselves small leaves can be an advantage, but the other signs signal greater danger. On the other hand some aroids will lose their large leaves more rapidly if undernourished and replace them with new foliage that is no longer of a size or texture to be decorative as originally intended. A danger at any time is that the plant may be weakened and liable to infection.

Because our own growing space is inadequate for the large numbers of plants we accumulate, we have often been obliged to attempt preventing some from growing ever larger. We reduce the amounts of fertilizer and the frequency of feeding until growth ceases or is very much reduced and keep the plants in small pots as long as possible. From then on we watch their general health and fertilize only when some sign of starvation first appears. With constant care we are usually successful in maintaining the plants very close to the size they attained before our undernourishing regimen started.

After being subjected to this treatment plants frequently remain seemingly incapable of rapid growth even after normal fertilizing resumes. It is a risk one must take to maintain some plants for a very long time.

15

HUMIDITY

In the tropics and subtropics from which we derive most of our indoor plants aerial humidity averages 60–65% and may run considerably higher for long periods of the year. Deprived of it many of the plants suffer severely, remain stunted or easily succumb to disease. Tropical plants are considerably more dependent on a humid atmosphere than those of the temperate zones. A major reason is the lack of nutrition in the soil due to the leaching action of heavy rainfalls. It is through their leaves that they absorb sufficient nutrition from the atmosphere to meet part of their needs.

During the day, fine particles of decomposed matter, produced in vast quantities in tropical forests, are held in suspension by the humid air. Humidity also keeps the surfaces of leaves fresh and active in receiving the nutritive dust. At night it is fixed on leaf surfaces by heavy dews.

Indoors the humidity level for much of the year is 30% or lower; there is no dew and the air contributes no nutrition.

We satisfy the need for nutrients by supplying more of them to the roots than is usually available in nature. The leaves initially develop normally. However, though no longer required to absorb nutrients, leaves still must perform the essential function of metabolizing by means of light the elements we now supply only to the root system. The health of leaves is, therefore, all-important. For many tropical plants a high level of humidity is required in order that they may carry out this function normally. When humidity is low the layer of cells containing chlorophyll is damaged or destroyed through desiccation, and the plant will eventually die as surely as if we were to deprive it of all nutrition.

The degree to which high humidity levels of 60 to 80% contribute to the efficiency of energy production becomes obvious when plants are grown in terrariums. The light requirement is greatly reduced. Compared with 30% humidity, a level of 70% reduces the light requirement by as much as 40% with the minimum at 50 fc. There are also risks in high humidity. They occur when the temperature is below or above plant tolerance. With most tropicals this can be stated as below 55°F (27°C). At these levels metabolism slows and high humidity causes root and/or stem rot.

Though moist air is as healthful for humans as it is for plants, it is often avoided because of the notion that it is harmful to furniture and books to say nothing of the added expense of providing it. Business rejects humidifying out of hand. In large public plantscapes it has only recently become possible to increase humidity through changes in design. The following are some of the means used in homes and public places for that purpose.

The most primitive method for supplying humidity to house plants is to fill the bottoms of trays with an inch or more of pebbles or gravel and add water to just below the surface. Evaporation raises the humidity of the air around pots set on the surface. The heavy weight of the material and the difficulty of keeping it free from algae and insects are definite disadvantages.

Capillary matting is inexpensive rot- and mildew-resistant cloth that is laid on the bottom of trays. When wetted it provides a continuous supply of moisture to the soil in pots and a considerable increase in ambient humidity. Some small tropical herbs flourish on the mats. For others the supply of moisture is too great. The mats also become algae ridden and must be periodically cleaned. Insects spread more easily from one plant to another.

The modern practice is to line trays with plastic crate. This is approximately ⅜ in. (9.35 m) thick plastic sheet with square holes used as a light diffuser under fluorescent fixtures in offices and elevators. It can be cut to size to fit the trays. The water level is kept below the surface of the sheet and provides humidity. The plastic must also be cleaned periodically but a bottle brush and very hot water does the job quickly. It is light in weight and permanent.

Humidifiers are still more effective and less bother. Room size usually has a capacity of 3 gallons. Under certain conditions such installations are practical for interior landscapes.

Lately watercourses and pools have become more popular. In place of troughs with stone facings in some sterile arrangement planted with selections from a small list of indestructibles, more imaginative and naturalistic gardens have proved feasible. The protection of four walls and winter heating combined with the higher humidity creates a tropical environment. We are beginning to see gardens modelled on the innovations of Roberto Burle Marx, the great Brazilian landscaper. With further improvements in techniques and more experience with the available plant material, there is no limit to the possible range of esthetic effects.

In many instances in our cultural list we have specified minimum humidity of 50–60% for plants. Some of these can do with less as long as there is continuous air movement. But the benefits of higher levels cannot be exaggerated and are proved by the more lively appearance of foliage and its longer life.

16

VENTILATION AND AIR MOVEMENT

All leaves of plants utilize light to convert aerial oxygen, moisture and minute quantities of organic and inorganic materials into energy. They respire by breathing in principally oxygen and expelling oxygen and carbon dioxide. Any interference with respiration causes it to slow or come to a halt. A constant flow of air over the leaves ensures the proper functioning of respiration.

When the air is still, leaves become enclosed in a thin layer from which oxygen has been exhausted and in which residue gases and carbon dioxide are concentrated, effectively stopping the normal process of interchange.

In natural habitats plants experience an atmosphere that is in constant motion, feeding the leaves with oxygen, etc., and carrying off the gases they expel. Moisture is evaporated. The Bromeliads are plants that live mostly from airborne products. Spanish Moss requires nothing else for survival. Indoors still air reduces the vigor of plants making them more vulnerable to disease. In large cities and industrial areas pollution compounds the problem, allowing noxious gases to replace oxygen and depositing fine particles of acid products on leaves. For these reasons it is essential for plant hygiene to keep the air moving and to bring in as much fresh air as possible without reducing temperatures to levels uncomfortable for ourselves and damaging to our plants. Even where pollution is rampant, it is better to ventilate well than to try to keep it out.

As usual with all rules regarding plants there are exceptions. Plants of the tropical forest floor, such as some Acanthaceae, Gesneriaceae, Selaginellas and Begonias, do not require much ventilation. They prefer still, humid, but clean air. Hence they are best suited to the environment of a terrarium when their size and growth habit permits. As terrariums are partly or completely enclosed, pollution is less of a problem. See Terrarium Culture.

It should be evident from the above that ventilation supplies fresh air which must enter buildings through openings such as windows or doors. In order for it to do so, it must push the air inside the building out in some other direction. Ergo, without a through draft an open window can supply neither much fresh air nor much air circulation/movement.

With fans we create air movement. For that reason they are helpful in preventing the kind of leaf asphyxiation we have described. But, as long as the air itself is not replaced, much of the benefit is dissipated. Accordingly, it is clear that to have fresh air *and* movement, there should be a through draft and that fans can assist by simultaneously pulling in outside air and assisting it in moving on and out.

1. In summer keep windows open as much as possible but reduce the risk from driving winds and rain by inserting adjustable screening. There should be open windows at different exposures to produce through drafts. If that is impossible, large fans in areas away from windows where the air becomes stagnant will increase ventilation and circulation.

2. Plants under artificial light are exposed to temperatures in any season that are higher than the rest of a room. In summer the level can be very dangerous to plants. Shelving, in particular, traps heat as well as still air. Excessive temperatures may occur in winter when heat-

ing is maintained in the 70s (above 28°C). Place small fans so that the moving air passes between the lights and the tops of the plants. They should be in operation by day and on hot, still nights. Whisper fans, used to cool heavy computer equipment are almost silent and the cost of operation is minimal.

3. In winter open a window at night at one end of a living floor and another in a room that is not in a direct line. Direct passage can cause severe drafts. Indirect ones reduce the risk. Maintaining tropical plant minimum temperatures is more essential than ventilation or air movement. How much ventilation is possible depends on exterior as well as interior temperatures.

4. In winter plants should not be exposed to frequent opening of doors to the outside.

Air conditioning. The air conditioned room is, in respect to ventilation, air movement and temperature, a controlled environment.

The equipment installed in apartments and homes is used in summer to suck in outside air and, in doing so, to cool it. In winter, the same process can counteract high temperatures produced by central or baseboard heating. A thermostat is the means by which the unit is adjusted to provide a desired temperature level at will. To be effective windows must remain closed.

The fan in the unit keeps air moving inside the room. The filter removes some pollution and some airborne pests. Temperature can be maintained at below 80°F (27°C) and above 60°F (16°C), all of which is to the good. The only adverse influence is the absorption of humidity in the air. To keep most tropical plants in good health a humidifier must be in operation, raising the level to at least 50%.

Air conditioning in large office buildings serves the double purpose of cooling in summer and warming in winter. In the interest of economy most of the units recirculate and re-use the air. The effect on humans and plants is uncertain but not very harmful. Cast-Iron plants do well on the whole. However, the humidity is very low and humidifiers are rarely installed even in executive offices. That eliminates all but the most tolerant foliage plants.

17

DISEASE

In other sections (see Water, Temperature, Soil, Fertilizer, etc.) we have mentioned causes of disease in plants. As to the organisms causing the sickness, in many instances only a plant pathologist can make definitive diagnoses. We are neither plant pathologists nor knowledgeable on the subject. Our encounters with it have been infrequent and have taught us little more than the mistakes we may have made in culture causing the debility that permitted the disease to take hold. There are certainly many fewer diseases affecting houseplants than garden flowers, vegetables or trees.

Virus

There is nothing you can do about plant viruses, but some information about them can be useful in selecting plants and in guessing the reason for inexplicably abnormal growth behavior.

Viruses are the smallest of micro-organisms that invade plants and are transmitted from generation to generation. They are innumerable and their effects range from beneficial through mild, specific damage to the complete destruction of plants. A virus may slow growth, distort flowers or leaves, cause growths atypical of a plant form, cause spotting and short life to leaves. It may do just enough general damage to make it easier for bacteria or fungi to invade a plant.

Plants in nature often are infested with a host of viruses that reduce their vigor without causing massive damage. Plenty of seemingly normal plants are infected. Viruses may also cause mutations, often regressive ones. If the effect is to make them more rather than less attractive to the grower, they are selected and propagated as cultivars. Many cultivars we list are undoubtedly the result of virus action.

Viruses can be transmitted from one plant to another in cultivation when the grower fails to sterilize cutting tools. When we use the same scissors or knife in trimming we may be transferring viruses.

There are at present no chemical means of destroying viruses without killing the plant. We have no antibodies to deal with them. Considerable, but not complete, success has been achieved through tissue culture. Micro-thin slices of the meristem, or leading growth cells of stems, are often temporarily free of virus and these can be grown successfully in laboratory conditions. The new plants usually prove to be more vigorous than their parents.

Subtle changes created by viruses account for some differences in vigor between clones of the same species. Plants from different nurseries may differ because they were originally collected from separate habitats, but also one plant may be relatively free from virus compared with the other. Amateurs are aware from experience that a plant of one nurseryman can be invariably more adaptable than the same species from other sources. As we have pointed out elsewhere, in buying plants one should always be on the lookout for superior clones.

Fungus

We know nothing about bacterial action which, if it exists in our plants, we lump with fungus. From the lists of diseases and causes that have been published we have the impression that bacteria play a relatively minor role where houseplants are concerned.

All fungi, of course, are relatives of mushrooms but exceedingly small. Their spores are everywhere in the air and in soil. They invade roots wherever they have been damaged. On leaves or stems their spores lodge in lesions and spread through the tissues. Standing water on the softer surfaces of plants is sufficient with some species to facilitate the entry of fungus mycelia or roots.

They cause discoloration and short life in leaves; they reduce stems to watery mush; they destroy all or parts of roots; they prevent germination of seeds or kill off the seedlings. Plants that are weakened by improper environments or the wrong treatment become easy victims. In fact, it would appear that when fungi gain a hold it is usually the grower's fault.

Time and again, after the fact, we have traced damage to our plants to some mistake: too much fertilizer; over watering at low temperatures; lack of ventilation at high temperatures frequently combined with very high humidity. We believe this is valid throughout horticulture. A plant that is healthy to begin with and is maintained properly rarely becomes a host to fungi.

As for the vulnerability of species, we have examined any number of lists relating particular ones to specific fungal diseases. One gains the impression that the only plants that have been fully tested are flowering gift plants and those grown for cut flowers. There is virtually no information available for about 95% of the foliage plants on our list. But we have come to the conclusion, from the diseases that are mentioned, that most of those that occur indoors are caused by a small number of fungi and their relatives. Furthermore, the symptoms, when lumped together, are relatively few in number.

The most popular foliage plants are adaptable to various environments and are rarely attacked by fungi. Although the more exotic species and cultivars are frequently vulnerable, amateurs who grow a great variety rarely use fungicides at all. The need doesn't arise that often if culture is reasonably good.

Some plants are sensitive to particular fungicides the way they are to insecticides. Fungicide spraying may be more damaging than the simple removal of an affected part of a plant. A change in cultural treatment can also inhibit and eventually eliminate milder attacks of fungi.

Damping off. Seeds and seedlings are affected, the damage taking place very rapidly. Seeds just don't come up. The effect of the fungus can be observed on large seeds that fail to germinate. They are mushy, usually ill smelling and covered with grayish mold. Seedlings that have germinated just collapse as the fungus attacks the remains of the seed and the new roots.

A number of fungi are responsible, including *Pythium,* and *Rhizoctoria* species and *Botrytis cinerea.* By the time the damage occurs identifying the organism is of no avail.

Prevention is the best cure. Use packaged houseplant seeding mix and sterilize it in a 180°F (105°C) oven for a half hour. Or plant in milled sphagnum. The medium should be just barely moist. Any excess is risky for the plant whether fungi are present or not. Seed may require soaking before planting.

Do not permit the temperature inside the propagation box to rise over 80°F (28°C) or drop below 60°F (16°C). Very high humidity must be avoided. Its presence indicates an excess of moisture in the soil. Do not remove the cover until seedlings have two real leaves.

Soaking seed before planting in a solution of Benomyl may act as a preventative.

Powdery and downy mildew and gray mold. The three are quite visible once they have infested a plant. Powdery mildew appears as a grayish layer completely covering green leaves. The other two are seen as masses of grayish-white filaments on leaves. Powdery mildew seems to be produced by several fungus species, downy mildew by *Peronospora* species and gray mold by *Botrytis cinerea.*

In all our growing indoors we have encountered powdery mildew only once. It attacked a Cast-Iron plant that was kept in deep shade and subjected to rather low temperatures while being watered regularly. We suspect that it is, indeed, rather uncommon among houseplants. We washed off the leaves of our plant in warm, soapy water. Some were lost but most recovered well, and we had no further trouble. The same fungi may act differently on other plants and in other environments.

Powdery and downy mildew indoors seems to attack plants in propagation boxes or terrariums that are kept too wet and warm. Leaves turn black and rot. If the damage is localized rotten leaves may be removed and the rest of the plant sprayed with rubbing alcohol. One can also spray with an appropriate fungicide. You will find these listed by greenhouse and houseplant supply firms which will also describe the specific uses of the chemicals.

But the most effective procedure is, after taking the measures described above, to ventilate the container and dry out the soil and provide against overheating when the cover is again replaced.

Root and stem rots. These are caused by, among others, *Pythium* and *Phytophora* species. Stem rot may appear suddenly at the joint of stem and root. The base of the stem turns black and/or mushy. The infection may have spread upward from below. To find out one must decant the plant and examine the roots. Most often they are infected. No fungicide is going to cure the condition where houseplants are concerned.

If there are several sections of connected roots, the apparently healthy parts can be separated, washed off, doused with a fungicide and replanted in fresh, sterile soil. One or more parts may eventually sprout if the infection has not already invaded the tissues. Cut off the apparently healthy upper parts of the plants, treat like the roots and attempt to propagate them in fresh, sterile soil. Results depend on the progress of the disease. Usually the plant is a total loss, but the effort may be worthwhile if a valuable plant is at stake.

When the infection occurs at one or more joints the procedure is the same. The diseased parts cannot be saved. The healthy ones are iffy but might come through if cut off and propagated promptly.

Fungicide sprays and drenches can prevent disease but rarely cure it. When very large plants such as shrubs or trees are attacked, treatment can prevent spreading. But nothing much can be done for the sizes of plants grown in a house. When a whole plant receiving normal care loses leaves or droops the cause is root rot. There is no way to save it.

Attacks of rotting fungus can be prevented by good cultural practices. The environmental causes of rot are the same as for other fungal diseases. Fungi multiply and gain access in low light, excessive moisture, high humidity, heat or cold outside the tolerance of the plant. Lesions produced by pests, fertilizer or salts offer entry of fungi to the tissues of plants.

Even the best treatment available does not work against the susceptibility of a few houseplants. Some winter-blooming Begonias are an example.

Fungicide sprays and drenches do protect plants against infection. They can be applied at regular intervals according to the manufacturers' recommendations. Some professional interior landscapers treat their plants with fungicide before installation. Very few amateurs bother at all. For the latter, propagating cuttings offer a practical alternative. If one plant becomes infected another is ready to take its place.

Fungicides. There are many other individual disease fungi by which plants are more or less affected. Wilt causes the whole plant to droop and die while leaves turn yellow. There are more localized fungus infections of leaves that spot them and sap their energy causing them to die. Occasionally they take the form of tiny mushrooms, visible through a loupe.

As the grower cannot usually anticipate what fungus to expect, the choice of a fungicide is in large measure dictated by the breadth of the fungal spectrum which it prevents or inhibits.

Manufacturers and compounders sell fungicides that are mixes of several compatible chemicals each of which inhibits the spread of one or more fungus species.

Two basics have long been Benomyl (Benlate) and Captan which can be used as sprays or drenches with long-lasting effect. Banrot is highly recommended as a preventive for infections of the roots of shrubs and trees. Read the lists of diseases on fungicide labels and choose brands that are formulated to treat the diseases we have mentioned and others. Follow instructions for use as too strong or too frequent dosages can be damaging.

18

PESTS

Where do pests come from? We buy plants from nurseries that either periodically fumigate their greenhouses or treat plants with powerful pesticides before sending them to market. Most indoor growers use artificial soil that everybody assumed has been sterilized before packaging. Why, then, do pests appear with such regularity not only in country homes but apartments and offices many stories high above street level, even with air conditioning and all windows hermetically sealed?

There are two main sources, the air and seeds, as well as the plants themselves. Most of the eggs and young of small insects are so light as to be easily airborne and some pass through a stage during which they are equipped with wings. Being minute they enter buildings through any crack and are circulated by air conditioning both summer and winter. Every time a door is opened or people come into a building from the outside, insects are wafted or carried in.

Insects and other pests survive in and on the surface of seeds that have not been properly sterilized. Even when plants have been fumigated or treated with powerful insecticide sprays some pests escape by taking refuge in the tiniest of crevices where moisture may form a barrier to the poisonous materials.

A secondary source is soil that has become infested with the eggs or larvae of insects or contains worms or slugs.

For these reasons every grower of plants must be watchful on a day-to-day basis that leaves are clean of any traces of insects. The sooner one can spot an infestation the easier the cure. Once it is severe the chances of other plants being implicated increases day by day. When a plant with normal treatment fails to grow and sulks the soil should be decanted and examined closely for small slugs and harmful worms.

Beware especially of well-intentioned gifts of plants whose leaves or soil may contain an accumulation of different pests.

None of our houseplant pests do anything but attack the plants. One need not fear that they will make themselves at home with you or become a general nuisance. All are small and are dependent on plants for their survival.

The absence of predators. Houseplants are mercifully free of those large animals such as weevils, slugs and caterpillars that plague vegetables and other plants outdoors. But though ours are small, they are no less a nuisance because there are no predators indoors, and without our intervention, they can invade any number of plants in a very short time. We are handicapped in combatting them with pesticides because we share a common home or work place and in eliminating them, must be careful not to poison ourselves. Nurserymen can spray and fumigate in a way that is out of the question for us.

Predator insects are now being used to an increasing extent to control pests in agriculture. But a home or office is no place for ladybugs and even less for praying mantises. Herbs have been used to keep down some pests in the garden; Marigolds, for instance. But, though one can grow and bloom Marigolds indoors, there is no practical way to utilize their powers if, indeed, they are as real as claimed.

Our first indoor garden under artificial light came about because a friend gave us a collection of orchids. Her professional work tabooed the use of any form of pesticide so spiders were brought in from the country to deal with insects. The spiders arrived along with the orchids. No doubt they consumed their share and they were no bother, but it was soon apparent that the insects were winning out and so completely that there was no alternative to getting rid of the orchids. It was a mistake that we were not tempted to repeat.

Pesticide safety. By now everyone is worried about using any pesticide indoors because of the uncertainty regarding the effects on our own health. Some are recognized as highly poisonous; others very much less so. However, with the standard chemical pesticides it must be taken into account that those involving no risk for one person may be really dangerous for another.

With elaborate precautions any pesticide can be handled safely. Complete body covering and gas masks are standard equipment for professionals handling very toxic materials. To amateurs that seems an absurd amount of trouble, and professional service people cannot apply these materials in the workplace. For a long time amateurs were rather careless in the use of sprays. Now the concensus is to avoid them entirely. That, in our opinion, is to go to the other extreme. In order to kill pests one must accept the fact that the killing material is poisonous to some extent. Many supposedly nontoxic substances that are part of our daily lives and are in constant use are injurious to those few who suffer an allergic reaction. The sensible approach is to avoid pesticides when any other method of eradication is effective and to use them only in a form or as a substance that reduces risk to a minimum.

We consider a minimum risk to be the use of products whose probable effects on humans are well known. We are reminded of a horticultural friend who believes a mix of rubbing alcohol with water and some detergent to be very effective in eradicating pests. He may be right and the idea could be valuable. But certainly the brew is not for drinking; it can be extremely painful if it comes into contact with eyes, and some people may be affected by the fumes or develop skin rashes or other symptoms. We do consider the formula, nevertheless, relatively nontoxic and less of a risk by far than dealing with very complex formulas whose long-term effects are not predictable.

Finding the pests. Except for mites and nematodes all our mature houseplant pests are visible to the naked eye. Their young are not. To see mites or baby pests of any kind, a magnifying glass is necessary. However, the ordinary large type of round or rectangular magnifying glass does not provide sufficient magnification. 10× or 10 time magnification is the minimum. For this purpose one uses 10× (power) jeweler's loupes or old-fashioned thread counters. The former cover a larger area and are easier to use. Photography supply shops now carry a 10× loupe with attached flashlight. Other loupes are sold by optical and educational scientific supply companies. When buying loupes, check the clarity of magnification over the whole surface. Poorly made ones are fuzzy around the edges. No amateur or professional horticulturist should be without one.

Patience with pests In the home patience is a virtue when dealing with pests. Too many growers give up after a few attempts at eradication and throw out a plant. Nurserymen are more concerned with controlling insects, not that they wouldn't prefer to get rid of them entirely. But they know that a complete job is too time consuming and costly in other ways. Hobbyists can take their time. On occasion we have fought a whole year for the survival of a favorite or rare plant. Sometimes a single spraying or soil drench is sufficient but, more often, it must be repeated even when using the most effective pesticides. It is easy to be deceived by a temporary disappearance of a pest. One may believe that it is gone for good. A few weeks later the little devils are back again. It can be disheartening but don't give up. Keep watching and treating until examination of leaves and the healthy appearance of the whole plant proves that the treatment has finally succeeded.

Mealybugs. Mature mealybugs are visible as oval, very slow-moving creatures covered with white powder, as gobs of white goo with which they cover themselves or, when stripped of both the goo and powder by a wet brush, as delicately pink. They are found on the undersides of leaves, especially along the midrib and joints of stalks. Look for them, too, in between clasped young leaves. They attack a great many houseplants but avoid others completely.

They are sucking insects that leave no marks as do mites but simply sap the strength of leaves by attacking the base of the stalk until the leaf drops off, or the midrib so that it turns yellow and dries. They do not destroy a plant as quickly as do mites. But if they become numerous they consume all new leaves and growth ceases, the plant is weakened and becomes less resistant to disease. Furthermore mealybugs spread rapidly from plant to plant so that eventually they become unmanageable.

Removing mature bugs from plants with smooth stems and broad leaves is possible with a ½ in. (1.25 cm) oil paintbrush dipped in rubbing alcohol, followed by a good scrubbing of stems and stalks. On all others it is difficult to get at the young which seek protection and shelter in tight joints and in the interstices of the rough bark of shrubs where they are especially difficult to eradicate.

We spray with Safer Insecticidal Soap or Ced-O-Flora and wash the plant with clear water the following day. Several applications at intervals of a week may be required. Occasionally we have a plant that needs treatment for months before we are sure that all danger of a recurrence is past.

Mites. Mites belong to the spider family and, some, like their relatives, spin threads. The two-spotted mite, the most common, is 8-legged, watery colored, has 2 dark spots on its back and moves about rapidly. Red and black mites are much smaller and occasionally other kinds turn up. All can be seen rather easily with a loupe because of their color and motion. The young are microscopic.

Signs of their presence are white threads on the undersurfaces of leaves, especially near the midribs, and dots of transluscence on thinner leaves that result from the killing of individual cells. When the leaves of small plants suddenly turn yellow look for mites. Palm leaves become dusty gray. Larger, thicker leaves show networks of transluscence. On Alocasias mites may also be active on the upper surfaces.

They thrive in hot, dry atmospheres. High humidity slows them down. Frequent washing of the undersides of leaves with strong jets of water is temporarily effective but rarely eradicates them. The specific pesticides are changing. Inquire about the latest ones.

Scale. Oval, flat or domed plates, ranging in color from transluscent to dark brown. They attack along the midribs of leaves and on juicy stems, adhering tightly to the surface. In small numbers they destroy only a few leaves but multiply rapidly until a surface may be completely coated with them. Favorite hosts are the finer-leaved ferns. The specific pesticide is Malathion, which is damaging to ferns. A stiff brush dipped in rubbing alcohol scrapes away most of these creatures and should be followed by washing in strong jets of water.

Whitefly. Pretty, little flying insects that lay masses of bubble eggs on the bottoms of leaves and reproduce at an astonishing rate. They prefer thin-leaved herbs, especially aromatics of the mint family. Take immediate action if they appear. Yellow-colored adhesive tapes attract the flyers and there are a number of specific sprays on the market. House and Garden Raid can be used if it does not damage the plant itself.

Nematodes. These tiny, wormlike animals are in a class by themselves for destructiveness and deserve star billing though they occur very rarely nowadays in nursery-shipped plants because of stringent regulations.

We have had only one experience with them and that was with an aboveground type. When we examined the leaves of a plant that looked sick through a loupe, we observed enormously agile, colorless worms writhing on the edges. Normally they are virtually invisible, and the evidence of their presence is small, swollen nodes on roots, usually noticed only after the plant wilts. An infestation is invariably lethal. Though there are nemacides to combat them, the danger of their spreading to other plants is so great that this is one instance when we must recommend getting rid of plant and pot immediately. They are most likely to appear in natural potting soils.

Aphids. Really an outdoor pest that turns up occasionally on plants from nurseries that employ natural soils. They are oval, greenish, and have a little pipe sticking out the rear. Indoors they are easily removed by flushing a plant a few times with a strong jet of water. Act quickly because they will spread to other plants.

Slugs and snails. These, too, usually arrive with natural soils. The snails live frequently in live sphagnum moss. Slugs are slimy creatures like snails without their shells. We have to deal only with small ones indoors. They rise to the top when water is poured into a pot filled with soil and can be picked off manually. They feed on soft plant tissues. The little snails can also be picked off and crushed in the house. They're a real nuisance in greenhouses, for instance midst a crop of orchids, but are not much bother indoors.

Fungus gnats. They turn up occasionally in potting soils and are mainly irritating because they multiply and fly around. A good pesticidal drenching of the soil gets rid of them. They look like other gnats and are black.

Springtails. When you water they hop into the air. A pesticidal soil drench finishes them off. Those little white buggies that run around the moist bottoms of pots and appear briefly on the surfaces of potting soils can be treated in the same way.

Pesticides

Unless the invaders are nematodes do not get rid of plants immediately just because they are hosts to one of the other pests we list. They can all be eliminated by various means and with a little patience.

Amateurs have tried out simple formulas of their own to take the place of packaged pesticides. Abe Cohen of Bronx, New York, suggests the following spray that has been tried successfully by other amateurs. It is claimed to be effective against major houseplant pests.

2 tablespoons (.242 deciliters) liquid Ivory Hand Soap

3 ounces (75.05 grams) rubbing alcohol.

Add water to make one quart (1,057 liters) liquid.

Sprays. The two most harmless to humans seem to be the following.

Safer Agro-Chem's Insecticidal Soap. A good general purpose spray. Drench plants thoroughly. Although the content is only fatty-acid salts it can be irritating to nasal membranes and to eyes. Some plants suffer leaf damage. When testing a different plant, spray a few leaves. If damage is visible within a couple of days it is advisable to wash off that plant in clear water 3 hours after each application of the spray. Several applications at intervals of a week are needed to rid shrubs and some other plants of infestations.

Ced-O-Flora. An oily, kerosene and borax spray that is relatively harmless to humans. With patience it is effective in eliminating the three worst pests mentioned above. Do not use on palms.

Systemics. Systemic pesticides are applied to the soil in pots. When the soil is watered they enter the plant via its roots and spread through stems, branches and leaves which become poisonous to pests that feed on them. A single application is claimed to last 3–6 months. The action is not immediate. Two to three weeks may be required before the plant becomes toxic. Needless to say pests can do a lot of damage in that interval. Nevertheless we prefer these forms of pesticides with high toxicity to the sprays since they are safer to handle.

The material comes in the form of granules or solid sticks. Follow directions as to quantities and handling. The granules are applied to the surface of soil and worked into it. It is then moistened. We have found that a malodorous gas is emitted. The narrow sticks are simply stuffed into the soil. We do not recommend any one systemic product and advise reading labels carefully to determine the specific pests they are meant to destroy. We have used Hyponex Bug Darts and found them convenient but expensive. It is difficult to judge the effectiveness of the systemics because of the delay in their action.

Soil drenches. Some liquid pesticide sprays can be diluted according to instructions and poured into wet soil to kill minor pests. We have found Ortho's Isotox sprays particularly good for this purpose, but advise checking with your local nursery.

Quarantining. It is good practice to quarantine new plants from whatever source against the risk of pests invading the clean plants in a stock or collection. At a warehouse that can be done in a separate room where they can be sprayed and/or fumigated. In the home it is usually difficult to find a place that can be kept separate and closed for the purpose. Plastic plant tenders or tents offer a ready-made, space-saving solution. Plants can be incarcerated within by simply closing the zipper. If pests appear try pesticide drenches or sprays inside the tent. Remove the plants only after a delay of several days with no reappearance of the infestation.

Professional use of pesticides. A primary rule of interior landscape gardening and service is not to use spray chemicals in a home, workplace or public planting if it can possibly be avoided. When absolutely necessary it should be done at night or over a weekend. We remember an attempt to deal directly with fungus gnats in the pots of office plants. It almost caused a riot and justifiably.

An interior landscaper who maintains a greenhouse to acclimate plants or a warehouse to store them may spray or fumigate as a precaution. Much more powerful pesticides are usual in such situations. Choice of the chemical and methods of use are based on experience or the advice of the staffs of manufacturers.

Plants received from nurseries should be scrutinized with the utmost care for any signs of pests. Even if these are not in evidence it is the custom to use a systemic pesticide in every pot that is moved to a permanent location. As part of servicing it should be applied on a regular schedule when effectiveness is due to wear off.

19

PROPAGATION

Why Propagate? Propagation is a process of litte interest to interior landscapers. If they are employed in designing and installing, they order their plants from nurseries. The same can be said for those that stock and acclimate plants for their projects. Only nurseries that also engage in interior landscaping become involved in propagation, and their activity is outside the scope of this book.

It is a different matter for amateurs, even those whose plants are supplied by a professional. Of course, there is always the option of replacing losses by buying new ones, and that is what most people do. However, the rarer plants, those not grown in commercial quantities, are often available for only a short time. Experienced horticulturists know that there is no other way to guarantee continuity except through propagation.

Plant loss is normal. Amateurs frequently forget that plants can die from simple old age. More often the loss occurs because of accidents, neglect, or poor cultural methods, insects and diseases as well as a host of other possibilities. As living organisms they are always at risk.

Indoor gardeners who have become interested in the hobby or have a sense of pride in maintaining healthy, interesting plants, are conscious that propagation is necessary chore and, at the same time, one that makes good economic sense and is a great deal of sheer fun. Furthermore, they find that starting plants from scratch frequently produces better-looking and more reliable specimens than those purchased from a nursery. The change of environment from greenhouse to home always involves some trauma. Plants that start their lives and grow on in a single environment prove more adaptable and long lived. Our rule is to propagate any newly acquired plant as soon as possible. For every worthwhile plant there should be a backup of one or more, ready to take its place if it should fail or outgrow the space assigned to it.

Methods of Reproduction

Other than growing from seed the following are the principal means of propagation:

1. Stem or branch tip cuttings. This is the most common method.

2. Leaf cuttings. Possible with leaf succulents and a limited number of other tropical plants.

3. Division. Common for plants that grow in tufts, with underground runners or with pups or offsets.

4. Soil layering. A frequent method for plants with surface runners.

5. Air layering. Useful when some thick-stemmed plants become too big.

Stem or branch tip cuttings. The best time to take cuttings is when a plant is in rapid growth, usually during the warm months of the year. Note, however, that some erratically alternate active and inactive periods, especially indoors.

With a sharp knife or scissors cut a stem or branch at an acute angle just below the tip group of joints. In some plants 3 or 4 joints are sufficient. In others, where the distance between the joints are short, the cut may be made 5–10 joints from the tip. The length of the cutting should not be less than 1½ in. (3.75 cm).

Do not cut single-stemmed plants that lack branches, palms for instance, as that will destroy them. Canes are also damaged by the process but if there is a sufficient number the disfigurement of one will make little difference. As for branching shrubs or herbs, there are usually branches longer than others that can be shortened without sacrificing the esthetic appearance. When you trim branches to improve the shape, use the cuttings for propagation.

The lower two joints of a cutting should be firm. Extreme tips with very new growth are usually too soft. Do not use cuttings with wider spaces between the joints than those of the rest of the plant. Soft growth is the consequence of inadequate light accompanied by excess moisture and/or fertilizer. Harden your plant by modifying its culture before attempting to take cuttings. On the other hand, it should be noted that stems and branches that have turned woody are more difficult to root.

Before planting the cutting remove the leaf buds at the tip.

When branches are very long it is often possible to divide them into several lengths to be planted as cuttings. In dividing the branch be careful, after removing each section, to square off the upper end and cut the lower end at an angle. Do this in order to avoid planting the cutting upside down.

Note that cuttings consisting of the top joints of the stem of a plant, grow straight upward after being rooted. Those taken from the tips of side branches not infrequently continue to grow at an angle and, therefore, less symmetrically.

Containers for propagating cuttings. Any container is suitable for propagation with soil as long as it is deep enough to hold medium for roots and enough space above for the exposed section of the cuttings(s), a little room for growth and a transparent cover. The bottom may be opaque, translucent or transparent.

Little cuttings from creeping plants do well in a 1½ in. (3.75 cm) diameter pot with a clear plastic party glass upended over it. Or use a small plastic glass with another, slightly larger one, on top.

Cover deep pots or other containers with a sheet of glass or plastic wrap. Plastic bread and various other types of storage boxes, available in the housewares department of stores, are adaptable to use as propagators.

Drainage holes in the bottom of the containers are not necessary.

Propagating Media See Media.

1. Milled Sphagnum Moss. A good medium for many types of cuttings especially those prone to fungus diseases. Fill the container to the required depth and add water at the rate of ¾ of a normal drinking glass to a quart of the material. Cover tightly overnight. The following day the sphagnum should be evenly saturated and just barely moist to the touch. This is the ideal state for any medium used for propagation. It there is any excess of moisture pour it off and expose the sphagnum to the air until it dries sufficiently.

2. Live sphagnum moss. In much of the north of the USA this is available in bogs. But you'll have to gather it yourself. It must be kept very moist in order to survive. Very good for most cuttings.

3. Long-fiber sphagnum moss. Also a good medium. Wet thoroughly, squeeze out excess moisture and pull apart until it is light and fluffy.

4. Peat pellets. Excellent for shrubby cuttings, one to a pellet. Place pellet in water for a few minutes until it has swollen and is soft. After planting the cutting place in a covered container. Note: Before transplanting the rooted cutting cut away the plastic net around the pellet. The net may be bio-degradable in the greenhouse, but indoors it becomes a straightjacket as roots increase in size.

5. Perlite. Pour the perlite into a fine sieve and run water through it to drain off the fine dust. Allow to dry until it is barely moist before using.

The Texas method. For small quantities of stem or nonsucculent leaf cuttings the method has been successful. Use styrofoam pots or drinking cups. Punch a few holes around the container close to the bottom. Punch another set halfway up the sides. Fill the bottom with sterile, dry medium such as perlite, fine gravel, bird gravel without seeds, chicken grit or sand. From the level of the upper set of holes fill with moist, milled sphagnum moss, peat moss, or houseplant mix. Plant cutting and set container in a saucer or tray with sufficient water to cover the bottom holes. The propagator is not covered and must be kept at a temperature of min. 70°F (22°C) for most cuttings.

Planting. Remove at least one set of leaves from the bottom of the cutting. At least one joint should be bare. Dip the bottom end in a hormone powder (Hormodin, Rootone). Poke into the medium if it is soft or make a fine hole for the cutting with a thin dowel. Cover container with transparent plastic or glass. Watering will not be necessary unless the cover is left open.

In each medium plant the cuttings so that the bottom joint is covered. Never expose the container to sunlight.

Place in indirect or reflected sunlight or under 400 fc of fluorescent light. Tropical plants require a minimum of 70°F (23°C). Cool-growing plants should be propagated at about 60°F (16°C) and not above 75°F (24.5°C).

Transplanting cuttings. Do not disturb the cutting until growth is visible. Then you may give a gentle tug to it. If there is resistance some root has formed. Tug a little more firmly. If the plant does not move it is ready for transplanting. Partly remove the cover for a period of a week, increasing the opening slightly each day. Then dig up the cutting and plant in a small pot. Always handle by a leaf; not the stem.

Handle cuttings in peat pellets by removing the net from the pellet and planting as is in a pot.

Water. Rooting cuttings in water has rarely been described or recommended. We have found it remarkably rapid and efficient for a great number of soft-stemmed herbs such as some Geraniums, gesneriads, many aroids that have adventitious roots or tendrils, Syngonoums, Grape Ivies, *Hedera* and many others. Even the soft tip growth of tropical trees, Jacaranda for instance, often quickly put out roots. It is the simplest of all procedures. However it does not work with hard wood cuttings.

Choose a glass sufficiently large to hold the cutting without tipping over. Take a good-sized cutting, not less than 4 in. (10 cm) long. Remove the lower leaves so that there is at least 1½ in. (3.75 cm) of bare stem. Pour enough room-temperature water into the glass to submerge the bare part of the stem. Add a very small pinch of Transplantone or rooting hormone powder to the water. Place the plant and container in bright indirect daylight or 300–400 fc of artificial light. The air temperature should be 72–75°F (23–24.5°C). Replenish water as it evaporates. Replace water after 4 weeks. The development of roots will be visible. When they are an inch (2.50 cm) or more long, the cutting can be planted.

Leaf Cuttings. Leaf succulent plants are most frequently reproduced by means of leaf cuttings. The thick leaves of the *Crassulaceae* and others break off the stems or branches very easily. Lay them on sand, vermiculite, perlite or sterilized seed mix. Place them where they will receive 400–800 fc of light in 72–85°F (23–29.5°C). Mist lightly every day until roots and leaf pairs appear.

The leaves of very few other foliage plants can be propagated. Begonia leaves with stalks are planted up to the base of the leaf in houseplant mix and subjected to terrarium conditions. The leave of *Zamioculcas* need only be poked into the moist mix. Leaves of Sansevierias are cut into sections and planted in the same way. Be very careful to differentiate the bottom from the top of the section in planting.

Division. Of all methods of reproduction, division is the simplest and safest procedure and should be employed whenever possible. Many plants multiply themselves by vegetative means (colonize). On some plants pups develop at the base of the stem. Others have underground runners that reach out from the mother plant and then rise to the surface where they develop normal stems, branches and leaves. The pups or offsets start to grow their own roots as soon as they have surfaced. Allow the new plant sufficient time to develop enough root to support itself. There is no need to be in a hurry. When the pup has a full complement of vegetative parts above ground, sever the runner close to the mother plant. Wait another two weeks or so before digging up the plant with as much root as possible and moving it to a separate pot.

Soil Layering. When plants have long, flexible branches, place a pot filled with moist medium within reach, where a section of the branch can come into contact with the soil. Score the joint(s) with vertical cuts by means of a sharp knife. Dust them with hormone powder. Bend the branch sufficiently to bury the joint(s) in the medium and pin down with hairpins or bent wire. When the joint(s) have rooted cut the branch on the side toward the mother plant and transplant it to a pot.

The procedure is the same with those plants that have long aboveground runners, whether with joints or with only a cluster of leaves at the tip. The sole difference is that the runner should not be damaged by scoring. Just fix the runner in the soil until rooted. Several runners can be rooted at the same time in different pots.

Air Layering. We use this method with tropical plants and shrubs that have soft, juicy wood, when the diameter of the stem or branch is at least 0.5 in. (1.25 cm). It comes in handy when a large plant has become too tall or spread too far. By its means one can make a fresh start, especially with single-stemmed plants having tall, bare stems and foliage concentrated at the top.

Remove all discolored or dried lower leaves. Bare the highest joint below those with young, well-developed leaves. (1) Scrape or cut away the bark below the chosen joint or (2) draw a sharp knife vertically across the joint, making several cuts around the stem or branch or (3) make a shallow upward cut on either side of the stem past the joint, long enough to be lifted by the tip.

Dust the wound thoroughly with hormone powder. Then wrap moist, long-fiber sphagnum moss around the wounded section. When using Method No. 3, force some of the moss under the cuts. Cover the joint tightly, top and bottom, with a sheet of clear plastic. Seal the loose end of the plastic sheet with adhesive tape. Within 3–8 weeks roots will become visible through the plastic. Remove the wrapping carefully and cut the stem just below the roots. Pot up in the usual way.

Growing from seed. Indoors the propagation box (plastic storage box or miniature plastic greenhouse) is ideal for sowing seed. Our favorite medium is milled sphagnum moss which is well known to inhibit powdery mildew, the greatest enemy of seedlings.

Tropical seeds vary widely in viability and germination time. The safe course is to plant immediately after receipt or after prompt special treatment. Seed with hard outer skins take an excessive length of time to germinate unless prepared for seeding. Seek the advice of seedsmen or nurserymen in special cases. There are two principal methods. In one cover the seed with water just short of boiling and allow to soak 2–3 days. In the other, using a triangular file, cut a nick in both broad sides of the seed until the flesh is just exposed. Do not damage the narrow side. Soak in room temperature water 2–3 days before planting.

Fill the propagation box to a depth of 2–3 in. (5–7.5 cm) with milled sphagnum moss and pour in ¾ of a measuring cup of water. Cover and allow to stand over night. Spread the seed on the surface and cover with a very thin layer of the dry moss. Cover the box and place in a temperature of 72–82°F (23–28°C) under minimum 400 fc. Do not expose to direct sun. In winter, bottom heat by means of electric cable (sold by seedsmen) may be necessary.

As soon as seedlings have 2–4 real leaves, loosen the soil with a narrow instrument and lift seedlings from the moss, holding them by their leaves, not stems. Transplant temporarily either further apart in another propagation box or to individual small pots filled with moist houseplant soil. Cover for a few days, then grandually expose.

Much the same method is used with standard seedling mixes available in the market.

Part II

20

INTRODUCTION TO THE PLANT LIST

The Cultural Guide

We explain in the following the cultural guide that precedes descriptions of the species in our alphabetical list of genera. This general way of specifying the cultural needs of plants has long been in common use. It achieves any considerable degree of precision only when the list of species and cultivars is short and consists of plants with very similar requirements. The more species and cultivars there are, the greater the likelihood of differences in culture and the less reliable this kind of guide becomes. It is used, nevertheless, because readers find that it is a quick way of checking the approximate conditions of culture and assists in the search for suitable plants to place in various indoor environments. We have tried in the species and cultivar descriptions to specify ways in which some diverge from the average behavior of the genus.

The reader should be aware that the geographical origins of species may make a pronounced difference in the cultural needs of particular clones. In practice we learn about them only by comparing the behavior of plants acquired from different nurseries. Some have been collected at high, others in low, altitudes, near the cool or warm latitudes of their range or on the windward or leeward sides of hills. The effect of such habitats is reflected in their tolerance of our variable indoor environments.

The guide works rather well, nevertheless, because the lower demands placed on foliage plants indoors have the effect of broadening the range of conditions under which they can be grown successfully. They are not expected to bloom and fruit, need not grow at maximum speed and, all in all, are satisfactory if they remain healthy.

1. Genus name. See Glossary. Genus is the most convenient categorization for botanical references. It consists of one or more species.

2. Family name. The family is the larger category, to which the genus belongs. See Glossary.

3. Country or region of origin. Some genera have very extensive or even worldwide distribution. We indicate the narrower ranges of species.

4. Common name. Every language uses different common, or colloquial, names for plants. In English some are more widespread than others. They have no scientific validity and frequently cause confusion. Not only are some common names strictly local, the same ones are often applied to totally different plants. For some they are convenient means of identification, especially when the Latin is considered more difficult to remember. As they are also listed in our index they are a help in finding plants in the cultural list. The Latin names have international validity and obey botanical rules.

5. Type of plant. Tree, shrub, herb, vine, etc.

6. Natural light requirement. The indoor natural light needs of the plants we list are arbitrarily rated on the assumption that they are at a window which has a glass area at least 30 in. (75 cm) wide and 65 in. (1.60 m) high.

Full sun. A summer exposure in a south, east or west window. If small, the plant is on the windowsill; if large, it stands directly in front of and close to the window. In winter the plants may have insufficient direct light in an east or west exposure so that it may be necessary to move some of them to a south window or install complementary light. For most of the year there should be a minimum average of 5 hours of direct sunlight on clear days. We assume that the plants can do with somewhat less in midwinter, but a protracted period of overcast may be harmful.

Partial sun. In east or west exposure summer and winter or a position somewhat further away or to the sides of windows where the period of direct sunlight is shorter than for full sun. Plants should received 3 hours of direct sun on clear days.

Filtered sun. A position in any exposure close to a window but receiving no more than 1 or 2 hours of direct sunlight on clear days. The rest of the time the plant should be protected against direct sunlight by intervening plants, a curtain or an exterior obstruction.

Shade. A northern exposure and also east and west in midwinter. A position that does not receive direct sunlight. A number of foliage plants can thrive in this condition.

In practice these four situations are modified in any number of ways; partial or complete obstruction from buildings, overhangs, trees and hills. These diminish natural light to an extent that is usually very difficult to estimate. The effect on plants must be discovered through experience. Environmental conditions, especially temperature and humidity, affect plant reactions to an available quantity of light. Our categories, therefore, are only a very crude guide to the relative light needs of the plants.

7. Artificial light intensity. Those footcandle measurements given apply only to the needs of plants that are grown entirely under artificial illumination. They are estimates based on experience with the genus under artificial light indoors using normal day lengths of 12–16 hours and are valid only for maintenance. Almost invariably the levels in nurseries are considerably higher. Outdoors these plants undergo entirely different lighting conditions. Intensity may be much greater, offset by overcast periods. Brightness is reduced in locations on the north sides of hills (reversed in the Southern Hemisphere), and obstructions shorten the effective day length. Some plants are unable to endure high light intensities. Others are accustomed to so much direct sunlight that the greatest practical intensity of artificial light indoors (in homes), about 1,000 fc, is only barely sufficient for maintenance with a long day length and unvarying daily illumination. Exceptions from typical light conditions for a genus are noted in species descriptions when known.

8. Daily hours of light. These are calculated for plants dependent exclusively on artificial lighting. We have used a span of 10–16 hours but very low-light-tolerant plants have to manage with 8–10 hours in offices. At best the numbers are guesses based on experience; actual results depend on the individual environment. On windowsills or in atria, where light intensities and/or day length is inadequate, complementary lighting must be added. The amount of total light for maintenance is calculated by combining the total of natural and artificial footcandles of illumination. The efficiency of the artificial light spectrum must also be taken into consideration. Day length is not given for every genus. It is given only when it has been established with some measure of reliability, primarily for plants that have been in cultivation in great numbers for a long time.

9. Temperature tolerance. Minimum and maximum temperatures are estimated for indoor conditions. Neither is absolute. However, the ranges may be relied on for safe maintenance. Temperatures below or above the ranges indicated can usually be tolerated for short periods of a few hours to a full day. But during that time plant activity ceases, and they become virtually defenseless to diseases.

Warm house. Minimum 60°F (16°C). Maximum 90°F (33°C). This is the typical tropical plant range of safe tolerance, based on habitat in the wild.

Intermediate house. Minimum 55°F (13°C). Maximum 80°F (27°C). Appropriate for plants at elevations in the tropics of 1500–2500 ft. (approx. 450–750 m) and borderline regions at sea level between the tropics and subtropics.

Cool house. Minimum 40°F (4°C). Maximum 80°F (27°C). For plants from the subtropics or with tolerance that permits them to grow in the South Temperate Zone. Some of these plants can tolerate short freezes but usually only if they have a well-developed and protected root system.

10. Humidity. Percentage of aerial humidity is noted only when the genus requires higher levels than those normally prevalent indoors, namely 35% in winter though frequently much higher in summer. Tropical humidity is 65% or higher most of the time. 50% is minimal.

11. Medium. Indoor gardeners know that the natural "fertility" of a medium is rapidly depleted in use and must be replenished with organic or inorganic nutrients. It is evident, therefore, that the mechanical characteristics of a medium determine its long-term suitability for growing different species under different conditions. The essential components are a compacting, water-storing material and a gritty, loose, aerating material. The properties of each in a medium determine its suitability for specific plant needs. We repeat this information because the availability and quality of media is in a constant state of flux.

Houseplant Mix 1. 1 peat moss, 1 vermiculite, 1 perlite or pumice or gritty sand. A medium suitable for seeding, rooting cuttings, the growing on of soft-stemmed tropical herbs and even for some moisture tolerant succulents.

Houseplant Mix 2. 2 parts peat moss, 1 vermiculite, 1 perlite or pumice or gritty sand. A good mixture for most of the larger, nonwoody tropical plants.

Cactus & Succulent Mix 1. 1 peat moss, 1 vermiculite, 2 gritty sand or perlite or pumice. A general purpose succulent mix. The peat moss proportion can be increased for succulents that have short dormancies.

Cactus & Succulent Mix 2. 2 sterilized garden soil, 1 peat moss or milled sphagnum moss, 1 gritty sand.

Sterilized Garden Soil. Good garden topsoil well sterilized. We recommend it for a few plants that prefer normal soil characteristics.

Packaged Houseplant Medium. There are a number of branded products on the market. The packages should state that the contents are made of peat moss, vermiculite and perlite. We consider wood and bark additives inferior. They are more commonly used than formerly. The advantage of a packaged mix as a labor saver is obvious but we consider the Houseplant Mix formulas much more reliable for indoor growing. Perlite and vermiculite of large particle size is becoming more and more difficult to find. Peat moss is not being listed in most supply catalogs. The houseplant mix blenders have therefore turned to bark and wood along with inferior vermiculite and perlite. By shopping around, however, most people can find the necessary ingredients. You will have better results if you mix your own.

Note: Although bark and wood in foliage plant media do not retain sufficient moisture for indoor environments and possess other disadvantages, cactus and succulent growers have been using them in combination with sand and perlite. They report good results.

Sphagnum moss. Milled sphagnum moss is a good medium for growing seed and rooting cuttings. Damp-off is rarely experienced. Long-fiber sphagnum moss is also a satisfactory rooting medium for tropical herb cuttings and a growing medium for some aroids and ferns.

12. Method of propagation. Seeds and/or cuttings. See Propagation.

13. Ease or difficulty of cultivation. Cast Iron is the easiest category. It refers to plants that have become stereotypes in commercial interior landscaping because of their tolerance of a wide variety of conditions and considerable neglect. Ratings from easy to difficult are our own estimates based on experience. However, where plants are exposed to different environments and culture a grower may well have results that contradict our own. Too many factors are

involved to treat such ratings as gospel.

14. Number of species in the genus and in cultivation. Especially in the larger genera no listing of cultivated plants can be entirely accurate. Growers constantly experiment with species and market those that they hope will prove popular. Almost as many species disappear from cultivation each year as are introduced and achieve some acceptance from the trade and the public.

Note: Height and spread of plants. It would be very useful if we were able to specify the indoor dimensions and the proper pot size for each species and cultivar. Experienced growers realize that this is impossible. Nurseries deliver plants with pots in an unpredictable range of sizes that is constantly changing in response to judgment of the sizes that are expected to attract consumers. The same plant may be produced in a small size for windowsill growers, medium for inner room or office decoration and large for major interior landscaping projects. Offerings by the trade are in constant flux.

Many of the plants we list are not grown in large numbers for market. They are available only from nurseries specializing in tropical plants and are sold as rooted cuttings. Some of these are large shrubs, vines or trees at maturity. Indoor gardeners grow them to the size they prefer, which may be from a few inches to several feet in height or spread. We have Polyscias that are 10 years old and beautiful at 12 inches. Florists sell the same plant to 8 feet in height and interior landscapers may seek specimens that are much larger still.

The reader must use a bit of imagination in judging the potential indoor sizes from descriptions. Height in nature gives a clue. An 80-foot tree is obviously grown indoors to less than the height of ceilings. An upright palm has a wider spread than most indoor-grown trees as juveniles and a fan palm will usually be still broader. Use tells something about size; for instance basket or terrarium plants. Wherever possible we have indicated dimensions that should be helpful in judging the range of sizes of a species or cultivar grown indoors.

21

ENVIRONMENTAL REQUIREMENTS

Selected plants listed by certain major environmental requirements.

Plants with Cast-Iron Culture

Aglaonema	Ehretia
Aloe	Ficus
Aspidistra	Homalocladium
Beaucarnea	Polyscias
Begonia aconitifolia	Sansevieria
Brassaia arboricola	Spathiphyllum
Cordyline	Zamioculcas
Dracaena	

Plants that Tolerate Low Light—Less than 400 fc

Aeschynanthus	Cyanastrum	Homalocladium	Philodendron
Aglaonema	Dieffenbachia	Homalomena	Pilea
Amorphophallus	Dracaena	Kaempferia	Plectranthus
Anthurium	Ehretia	Leea	Polyscias
Aspidistra	Equisetum	Macodes	Rhoicissus
Beaucarnea	× Fatshedera	Maranta	Schismattoglottis
Begonia	Ficus	Monstera	Scindapsus
Calathea	Fittonia	Myrtus	Siderasis
Chlorophytum	Haemaria	Pellionia	Spathiphyllum

Herbs Tolerant of Temperatures Below 55°F (13°C).

Acanthus	Haworthia
Acorus	Ligularia
Aechmea	Mimosa
Aeonium	Myrsine
Aloe	Myrtus
Ballota	Ophiopogon
Carex	Pelargonium
Dianella	Reineckia
Dioscorea	Rhoicissus
Dyckia	Sageretia
Equisetum	Senecio
× Fatshedera	Zamia
Geogenanthus	

Herbs to Maintain at 60°F« (16 °C)

Some of these plants will tolerate lower temperatures for a short period but all do better in warm conditions.

Acalypha	Dracaena	Monolena	Schismattoglottis
Acanthus	Ehretia	Monstera	Scindapsus
Aeschynanthus	Epipremnum	Muehlenbeckia	Spathiphyllum
Aglaonema	Episcia	Nautilocalyx	Stromanthe
Aloe	Hemigraphis	Neoregelia	Syngonium
Alternanthera	Hoffmannia	Pellionia	Tetrastigma
Anthurium	Homolomena	Peristrophe	Tradescantia
Bertolonia	Hoya	Philodendron	Trevesia
Caladium	Iresine	Pilea	Triolena
Calathea	Kaempferia	Piper	Vriesea
Callisia	Kalanchoe	Raphidophora	Zamioculcas
Carludovica	Lavandula	Reineckia	Zanthosoma
Dianella	Macodes	Rhoeo	Zenophia
Dieffenbachia	Maranta	Sansevieria	Zebrina

Shrubs Tolerant of Temperatures Below 50°F (10°C).

Acacia	Laurus
Ardisia	Mimosa
Aucuba	Myrsine
Begonia	Nandina
Buxus	Osmanthus
Chlonanthus	Pittosporum
Cleyera	Podocarpus
Coprosma	Rosmarinus
Elaeagnus	Ruscus
Euonymus	Sageretia
× Fatshedera	Serissa
Fatsia	Synadenium
Helichrysum	Tetrapanax

Shrubs Requiring Temperatures Over 60°F (16°C), or Higher Minimum Temperatures

Acalypha	Myrciaria
Blakea	Nicodemia
Brassaia	Pereskia
Carissa	Phyllanthus
Eugenia	Piper
Excoecaria	Polyscias
Leea	Pseuderanthemum
Murraya	Tupidanthus

Trees Accepting Temperatures Below 60°F (16°C)

Temperatures of 45°F (7°C) acceptable in winter but higher temperatures tolerated in summer.

Agathis	Grevillea
Albizia	Harpephyllum
Araucaria	Ilex
Arbutus	Melia
Citrus	Osmanthus
Coffea	Pandanus
Corynocarpus	Pittosporum
Cycas	Podocarpus
Encephalartos	Yucca
Eriobotrya	

Trees Requiring 60°F (16°C) or Higher Minimum Temperatures

Adenanthera	Jacaranda
Brassaia	Mangifera
Bucida	Manilkara
Carica	Meryta
Chorisia	Pandanus
Coccoloba	Persea
Cussonia	Pimenta
Dioon	Rademachera
Dizygotheca	Tamarindus
Ficus	

Plants Requiring More Than 50% Humidity

Alocasia	Colocasia	Homalomena	Rhodospatha
Alpinia	Ctenanthe	Macodes	Schismattoglottis
Amorphophallus	Cyrtosperma	Monolena	Soleirolia
Anoectochilus	Dizygotheca	Monstera	Strobilanthes
Anthurium	Episcia	Nautilocalyx	Trevesia
Bertolonia	Equisetum	Neoregelia	Xantheranthemum
Campelia	Geogenanthus	Philodenron	Xanthosoma
Carica	Guzmannia	Pilea	
Chirita	Haemaria	Pseuderanthemum	
Cissus	Hoffmannia	Rhektophyllum	

Plants for Terrariums

Anoectochilus	Euphorbia	Iresine	Reineckia
Begonia	Ficus	Macodes	Serissa
Caladium	Fittonia	Maranta	Soleirolia
Carissa	Geogenanthus	Monolena	Strobilanthes
Chamaeranthemum	Haemaria	Pellionia	Xantheranthemum
Chirita	Hemigraphis	Pilea	
Episcia	Homalomena	Polyscias	

Succulent Plants

Abromeitiella	Dorstenia
Adansonia	Ficus
Adenia	Gasteria
Aeonium	Gastrolea
Agave	Haworthia
Aloe	Hechtia
Beaucarnea	Hoya
Bowiea	Kalanchoe
Calibanus	Peperomia
Crassula	Pereskia
Cussonia	Senecio
Cyanotis	Yucca
Dioscorea	

Plants Resistant to Pests

Abromeitiella	Cyanotis	Lavandula	Pseuderanthemum
Adenia	Dianella	Leea	Rosmarinus
Agave	Elaeagnus	Mangifera	Sageretia
Aglaoneoma	Euonymus	Myrsine	Sansevieria
Aloe	Excoecharia	Pandanus	Scindapsus
Beaucarnea	Graptophyllum	Pelargonium	Setcreasia
Begonia	Guiacum	Peperomia	Yucca
Brassaia	Guzmannia	Pereskia	Zamioculcas
Calibanus	Hechtia	Pilea	
Cordyline	Homalocladium	Pittosporum	
Cryptanthus	Ilex	Podocarpus	

Plants with a Period of Semidormancy

Acalypha
Acanthus
Aeonium
Agave
Aloe
Calathea
Ctenanthe
Kalanchoe
Maranta
Melia
Stromanthe

Plants with a Period of Dormancy

Adansonia
Adenia
Bowiea
Caladium
Crassula
Dioscorea
Euphorbia

Abromeitiella chlorantha

Acalypha wilkesiana. Photo Gordon Courtright

Acanthus mollis

Acorus gramineus variegatus

PLATE 1

Adansonia digitata. Baobab. Photo Gregory A. Koob

Adenia 'Snowflake'

Adenia spinosa

Aechmea 'Burt'

PLATE 2

Aechmea 'Mend'

Aechmea chantini

Aechmea ornata. Porcupine Plant

Aeonium arboreum 'Schwarzkopf'

PLATE 3

Aeonium haworthii

Aeonium tabulaeforme

Aeschynanthus marmoratus

Agave americana marginata

PLATE 4

Agave angustifolia marginata

Agave colorata

Agave horrida

Agave parrasana

PLATE 5

Aglaonema commutatum

Aglaonema nitidum 'Curtisii'

Aglaonema 'Manila'

Aglaonema pseudobracteatum

PLATE 6

Aglaonema 'Silver Queen'

Aglaonema modestum variegatum

Aglaonema costatum

Alocasia micholitziana 'Green Velvet'

PLATE 7

Alocasia sanderana

Alocasia cuprea

Alocasia portei

Alocasia longiloba x sanderana

PLATE 8

Plants Easily Propagated from Cuttings

Acalypha
Aglaonema
Alocasia
Alternanthera
Begonia
Bignonia
Brassaia
Chamaeranthemum
Cissus
Coleus
Cordyline
Cryptanthus
Dichondra
Ehretia
Epipremnum

Episcia
Eugenia
Excoecharia
Evodia
× Fatshedera
Ficus
Fittonia
Gynura
Haemaria
Hemigraphis
Homalocladium
Hypoestes
Iresine
Jacaranda
Kalanchoe

Lavandula
Leea
Monstera
Nautilocalyx
Pellionia
Peperomia
Pereskia
Peristrophe
Philodendron
Pilea
Plectranthus
Polyscias
Pseuderanthemum
Raphidophora
Rhodospatha

Rhoicissus
Rosmarinus
Ruscus
Scindapsus
Senecio
Setcreasia
Siderasis
Strobilanthes
Tetrastigma
Tradescantia
Triolena
Tristania
Xantheranthemum
Zebrina

Plants Propagated by Division or Offsets

Abromeitiella
Acorus
Aechmea
Aglaonema
Alocasia
Aloe
Amomum
Amorphophallus
Aspidistra
Caladium
Calathea
Campelia
Carex
Carludovica
Chlorophytum
Chryptanthus
Ctenanthe
Cyanastrum
Cycas
Cyrtosperma
Dianella
Dichorisandra
Dioon
Dioscorea
Dracaena (some)
Dyckia

Encephalartos
Equisetum
Euonymus
Gasteria
Haworthia
Hechtia
Homalocladium
Maranta
Murdannia
Ophiopogon
Oplismenus
Psilotum
Reineckia
Rhektophyllum
Rhoeo
Sanchezia
Sansevieria
Schismattoglottis
Soleirolia
Spathiphyllum
Vriesea
Xantheranthemum
Xenophia
Yucca
Zamia
Zamioculcas

List of Indoor Foliage Plant Seed

This is only a partial list to suggest the variety of available foliage plant seed.

Anyone contemplating growing woody plants from seed should do some research as to germination techniques before purchasing. It should be noted that many tropical seeds are viable for only a short period. An example is *Trevesia,* which must be airmailed promptly in moist packing and planted immediately. Other seeds have extremely hard shells which must be nicked or soaked in water to encourage germination which is frequently very much delayed. Species and cultivars of a single genus may differ widely in type of seed and the treatment they require. Seed catalogs contain useful information and the seedsmen can be consulted.

Included here are some genera not included in our plant list.

Acacia	Cupressus	Musa
Achras	Cussonia	Myrsine
Adenanthera	Cycas	Myrtus
Agave	Dianella	Nandina
Aglaonema	Dioon	Pachypodium
Anthurium	Dodonaea	Pandanus
Aralia	Dracaena	Pelargonium
Araucaria	Elaeagunus	Persea
Ardisia	Eriobotrya	Philodendron
Beaucarnea	Erythrina	Pithecelobium
Begonia	Eucalyptus	Phoenix
Bombax	Eugenia	Phytolacca
Brassaia	Euphorbia	Piper
Bromeliads	Ficus	Pittosporum
Calathea	Grevillea	Plectranthus
Calothamnus	Griselina	Podocarpus
Calpurnia	Guaiacum	Pritchardia
Carica	Harpephyllum	Psidium
Carissa	Hedera	Raphiolepis
Carludovica	Hypoestes	Reinhartia
Cassia	Ilex	Schefflera
Ceiba	Juniperus	Spathiphyllum
Ceratonia	Kalanchoe	Strelitzia
Chamaecyparis	Kentia	Syngonium
Chamaedorea	Lavandula	Tamarindus
Chlorophytum	Leea	Thea
Chorisia	Livistona	Trevesia
Chrysalidocarpus	Macadamia	Tupidanthus
Citrus	Mangifera	Yucca
Coleus	Meryta	Zamia
Coprosma	Monstera	
Cordyline	Murraya	

22

LEAF CHARACTERISTICS

These lists group genera that include plants with special leaf characteristics.

Examples of Plants with Compound Leaves
(Ferns and Palms not included)

Acacia
Acanthopanax
Adansonia
Adenanthera
Albizia
Anthurium
Brassaia
Harpephyllum
Leea
Melia
Mikania

Philodendron (Most commercial cultivars have simple leaves.)
× Polyscias
Pseudopanax
Rademachera
Rhoicissus
Syngonium (Only if grown as a totem [most cultivars])
× Trevesia
Tupidanthus
Zamioculcas

Herbs with Colored Leaves

Acalypha
Aechmea
Alpinia
Alternanthera
Begonia
Bertolonia
Bignonia
Caladium
Calathea
Canistrum
Coleus
Cordyline
Cryptanthus
Ctenanthe
Dichorisandra

Episcia
× Fatshedera, variegated
Fittonia
Graptophyllum
Guzmania
Gynura
Haemaria
Hemigraphis
Hoffmannia
Homalomena
Hoya
Hypoestes
Iresine
Macodes
Nautilocalyx

Neoregelia
Pereskia
Pilea
Piper
Pseuderanthemum
Rhektophyllum
Rhoeo
Setcraesia
Siderasis
Sonerila
Strobilanthes
Viresea
Zebrina

Shrubs with Colored Leaves

Acalypha
Aucuba
Breynia
Cleyera
Coprosma

Excoecharia
Pereskia
Pseuderanthemum
Sanchezia

Plants with Leaves Variegated in White, Yellow or Silver

Acalypha
Acorus
Aechmea
Agave
Aglaonema
Alpinia
Ananas
Arundinaria
Begonia
Caladium
Calathea
Callisia

Campelia
Carex
Chirita
Chlorophytum
Coprosma
Dianella
Dieffenbachia
Dracaena
Epipremnum
Euonymus
Ficus
Geogenanthus

Graptophyllum
Hoya
Ligularia
Murdannia
Myrsine
Myrtus
Neoregelia
Ophiopogon
Oplismenus
Pandanus
Peperomia
Peristrophe

Piper
Pisonia
Polyscias
Reineckia
Rhodospatha
Sansevieria
Senecio
Stenotaphrum
Xanthosoma
Zebrina

Plants with Aromatic Leaves

Ballota
Citrus
Coleus
Helichrysum
Lavandula
Myrtus
Osmanthus
Pelargonium
Rosmarinus

Plants with Grasslike Leaves

Acorus
Amomum
Arundinaria
Beaucarnea
Carex
Chlorophytum
Cyperus
Dianella

Equisetum
Nolina
Ophiopogon
Oplismenus
Psilotum
Reineckia
Stenotaphrum

124

23

GROWTH CHARACTERISTICS AND DECORATIVE POTENTIAL

The following selective lists group foliage plants according to habit and potential use.

Architectural Plants

Ardisia	Elaeagnus	Ilex	Podocarpus
Beaucarnea	Eugenia	Laurus	Polyscias
Brassaia	Euonymus	Leea	Spathiphyllum
Cordyline	Ficus	Myrsine	Tristania
Dizygotheca	Fortunella	Nandina	
Dracaena	Guiacum	Pittosporum	

Sculptural Plants

Acanthus	Coccoloba	Nolina	Trevesia
Adenia	Colocasia	Pandanus	Tupidanthus
Aeonium	Cycas	Pittosporum	Xenophia
Agathis	Dieffenbachia	Podocarpus	Yucca
Agave	Euphorbia	Polyscias	Zamia
Araucaria	Ficus	Sanchezia	
Beaucarnea	Gasteria	Tetrapanax	

Screening Plants

Acacia	Grevillea
Adenanthera	Jacaranda
Albizia	Leea
Asparagus	Murraya
Boweia	Tamarindus
Dizygotheca	

Miniature Plants

Abromeitiella	Carex	Hedera	Senecio
Acorus	Carissa	Myrtus	Serissa
Alternanthera	Crassula	Pelargonium	Soleirolia
Begonia	Ficus	Pellionia	Sonerila
Bertolonia	Fittonia	Peperomia	
Buxus	Gasteria	Pilea	
Caladium	Haworthia	Reineckia	

Plants Amenable to Trimming

Acacia	Cleyera	Ilex	Polyscias
Adenanthera	Coprosma	Kalanchoe	Rosmarinus
Albizia	Ehretia	Lavandula	Sageretia
Brassaia	Elaeagnus	Murraya	Serissa
Bucida	Excoecharia	Myrtus	Synadenium
Buxus	Guaiacum	Nicodemia	
Carissa	Hypoestes	Pereskia	

Plants for Dish Gardens

Abromeitiella	Gasteria
Acorus	Haworthia
Agave parviflora, etc.	Iresine
Aloe	Kalanchoe
Begonia	Maranta
Bertolonia	Ophiopogon
Calathea	Pellionia
Carissa	Pilea
Cryptanthus	Polyscias
Cyanotis	Rosmarinus
Dyckia	Sansevieria
Ehretia	Soleirolia
Episcia	
Fittonia	

Plants for Pseudo-Bonsai

Buxus
Carissa
Chamaecyparis
Guiacum
Juniperus
Myrtus
Pithecellobium
Polyscias
Rosmarinus
Serissa

Basket Plants

Aeschynanthus	Cyanotis	Kalanthoe	Scindapsus
Asparagus	Epipremnum	Oplismenus	Setcreasia
Begonia	Episcia	Pellionia	Siderasis
Calathea	Excoecharia	Peperomia	Soleirolia
Callisia	Fittonia	Pilea	Stenotaphrum
Chlorophytum	Gynura	Plectranthus	Tetrastigma
Cissus	Hemigraphis	Rhoiscissus	
Coleus	Hoya	Sageretia	

Plants for Massing

Aglaonema (low to medium)
Aphelandra (low)
Bamboo (high)
Begonia (low)
Brassaia (medium to high)
Bromeliads (low)
Caladium (low)
Codiaeum (low to medium)
Cordyline (low to medium)
Dieffenbachia (medium to high)
Dizygotheca (high)
Dracaena (medium to high)
Excoecharia (low to medium)
x Fatshedera (medium to high)
Ficus (low to high)
Hemigraphis (low)
Ilex (medium to high)
Leea (medium)
Nothopanax (high)
Oreopanax (high)
Philodendron, Selfheading (low)
Pittosporum (low to medium)
Podocarpus (medium)
Polyscias (medium to high)
Sanchezia (low to medium)
Sansevieria (low)
Spathiphyllum (low to medium)
Tetrapanax (medium)

Plants for Groundcovers

Alternanthera
Bromeliads
Calathea
Callisia*
Chamaeranthemum
Chlorophytum

Codiaeum
Coleus
Epipremnum*
Ficus
Iresine
Hedera

Maranta
Pellionia
Peperomia
Pilea
Plectranthus*
Pseuderanthemum

Scindapsus*
Setcreasia*
Strobilanthes
Tradescantia*
Zebrina*

*These are better known as basket plants but can also trail over the surface of the soil, rooting at the joints.

Trailing Plants

Aeonium
Aeschynanthus
Bertolonia
Callisia
Ceropegia
Chamaeranthemum
Chlorophytum
Cissus
Coleus
Coprosma
Cyanotis
Dichondra
Dichorisandra
Epipremnum
Episcia
Ficus
Fittonia

Gynura
Haemaria
Hedera
Hemigraphis
Impatiens
Pellionia
Peperomia
Plectranthus
Rhipsalis
Scindapsus
Senecio
Setcreasia
Soleirolia
Strobilanthes
Syngonium
Tradescantia
Zebrina

Low, Broad Plants

Acanthus
Aechmea
Aeonium
Agave
Aglaonema
Ananas
Begonia
Caladium
Canistrum
Carludovica
Ceratozamia
Cycas
Dieffenbachia
Dioon
Dracaena
Dyckia
Hechtia
Hoffmannia
Maranta
Neoregelia
Rhoeo
Vriesea
Xanthosoma
Zamia

Vines

Amydrium
Anthurium
Asparagus
Bignonia
Boweia
Cissus
Dichondra
Dioscorea
Ficus
Hedera
Hoya
Mikania
Muehlenbeckia
Pereskia
Philodendron
Piper
Raphidophora
Rhodospatha
Rhoicissus
Scindapsus
Senecio
Syngonium
Tetrastigma

Aquatic & Semiaquatic Plants

Acorus
Carex
Carludovica
Cyperus
Dianella
Equisetum
Myriophyllum
Pistia

24

CULTURAL PLANT LIST

Abromeitiella. **Bromeliaceae.** Argentina. Small succulent pot plant. Partial to full sun. 700–1,000 fc. Temperature min. 40°F (4°C). Houseplant Mix #1. Propagation from offsets. Easy. 4 or more species in cultivation.

A. brevifolia, Dense fountain rosette of narrow, triangular 2" leaves with spiny edges, quite green.

A. chlorantha. Similar to above but leaves more grayish.

Colonizing by offsets. Keep rather dry and mist frequently during warm months. Flowers insignificant. Good plant for dish gardens.

Acacia. **Leguminosae.** Mimosa. Mostly Australia and Central America. Shrubs or small trees. Full sun. To minimum of 1,000 fc. Minimum 40°F (4°C). Houseplant Mix #2 with sand. Propagation by seed. Easy to difficult. 800 species of which some potentially useful as foliage indoors.

The Acacias are branching, spiny shrubs and treelets with long compound leaves composed of small narrow leaflets that fold together at night. Some are widely grown, especially in the Mediterranean basin, for the showy masses of perfumed white or yellow flowers. *A. dealbata* is commercially grown in France for perfume.

The best-known flowering plants come from southern, temperate Australia and require temperatures that approach freezing in winter.

A number of members of the family with similar foliage are grown as miniatures indoors without much trouble and are quite decorative. Species from northern Australia and the warmer parts of Central America and the Caribbean islands may prove useful indoors provided they are given a southern exposure in domestic situations or planted in equivalent sunlight in commercial locations.

The plants are rapid growing and relatively short-lived. They respond to pruning. They are also drought resistant, growing new leaves quickly when watering is resumed. To maintain foliage, however, even moisture is advisable. Fertilize with high nitrate formula 3 or 4 times a year. Plants are hosts to various spider mites and should be sprayed regularly with water and a pesticide. Immerse seed in boiling water to aid sprouting. Allow water to cool and soak for several days until the seed swells. Buying plants is easier.

We believe that these are excellent screening plants because of their airy foliage.

We list below only warm-growing species. These do have white or yellow blooms but are not grown for the purpose. Indoors flowering is unlikely except with greenhouse culture. Note that roots are deep growing.

A. baileyana. Tree to 15' (4.5 m) with grayish-green, double compound leaves, the leaflets ¼" (6.25 mm) long.

A. latifolia. Woody shrub to 15' (4.5 m) with leaflets to 6" (15 cm) long and 2" (5 cm) wide. Warm growing. Minimum 60°F.

Other tropical Acacias worth considering are *A. auriculiformis* (N. Australia), *A. caffra* (tropical Africa), *A. sutherlandii* (N. Australia), *A. tortuosa* (W. Indies), *A. torulosa* (N. Australia).

Acalypha. **Euphorbiaceae.** Jacob's Coat. South Seas. Shrub with branching canes. Partial to full Sun. 800+ fc 16 hours daily. Temperature min. 60°F (16°C) in winter, 70°F (22°C) in summer. Humidity min. 50%. Medium; 4 parts sandy sterilized garden soil, 1 part sphagnum peat moss. Propagation from heel cuttings. Difficult. More than 400 species of which only 2 are widely grown.

A. hispida. Large shrub with green leaves grown for its long pendant, narrow foxtail clusters of tiny red flowers. Strictly a greenhouse plant in the North though a recently introduced dwarf cultivar may prove to be a better houseplant.

A. wilkesiana. Offsetting shrub to 10' (3 m). Widely grown as a hedge or tall clump in the South for its brilliantly colored leaves. Leaves broadly oval, thin, finely toothed, 5–6' × 2½" (12–16 cm × 6 cm); stalks 1" (2.5 cm). Blade unevenly divided into areas of copper, red and green. There are several popular stabilized cultivars but also frequent sports with different coloring.

'Godseffiana', green with ivory edging, the edges scalloped.

'Heterophylla'; narrower, pendant, toothed leaves with cream or green edges.

'Hoffmannii'; leaves curled-contorted, bright

green, with prominent toothing; sometimes creamy edged. A very handsome type that blends well with other greenery.

'Macafeana'. Copper Leaf. Red leaves with bronze marbling.

'Obovata'. Leaves green, broadly spoonshaped with cream edge.

These cultivars are sold as 1' or 2' (30 or 60 cm) houseplants. Keep evenly moist, not soggy. Very heavy feeders requiring balanced fertilizer at one quarter the strength recommended with every watering. Lower leaves brown and drop when light is inadequate. Cut canes to soil level in late fall. After a rest of less than a month rootstocks will put up new canes. Heel cuttings root easily in water or moist medium. Plants are subject to mites and fungus diseases indoors.

Juvenile plants in 4–6" (10–15 cm) pots are showy indoors, grown in a sunny window or under lights. Periodic propagation by means of cuttings is advisable.

Too vulnerable for interior landscape use in the North except as temporary decoration. Better suited to conditions in southern states.

Acanthus. **Acanthaceae.** Mediterranean to tropical Africa. Large-leaved herb. Filtered sun. 200–500 fc 12 hours daily. Temperature and medium; see below. Propagation by seeds and division. Difficult. 20 species of which 2 are suitable for indoor culture.

Note the different environmental requirements of the species.

They make good, temporary sculptural plantings that can be massed in troughs. Both the species below are much-neglected, fast-growing foliage showpieces.

A. mollis. The Artist's Acanthus or Architect's Plant. The dark green leaves are broadly lanceshaped to 24" (60 cm) long with 5 or 6 deeply cut, jagged, dramatically symmetrical lobes on either side of the blade. Stalks to 1' (30 cm), curved outward. The plants grow in low rosettes to 4' (1.20 m) wide from thickened, spreading roots. The tall flowering spike consists of tubular, lipped white flowers.

A Mediterranean plant, it requires cool winters and good air movement at all times. Keep evenly moist. Will rarely flower indoors but it does (or is allowed to) the medium should dry out between waterings for about 6 weeks in the spring. Fertilize monthly except November to March with 20-20-20. Min. temperature 40°F (4°C). Plant in 4 parts Sterilized Garden Topsoil, 1 part sphagnum peat moss and 1 tbsp. lime to the quart.

'Frieling's Sensation'. Margins richly variegated with ivory and cream.

A. montanus. Mountain Thistle. Tropical Africa. Stem woodier; leaves narrower and covered with spines. Grows to 4' (1.20 m) in a year. Min. 55°F (13°C). Keep rather pot-bound and water sparingly. Fertilize with 20-20-20 every 2 months. Humidity min. 45%. If a more compact plant is desired fertilize only 2 or 3 times a year. Flowers are pink.

Because of their height and/or spread, these plants can be grown under fluorescent light only as juveniles.

Acorus. **Araceae.** Grassy Sweet Flag. E. Asia. Miniature grassy herbs. Partial to full sun. Min. 800 fc 14–16 hours daily. Temperature min. 40°F (4°C). Medium: 3 parts sandy garden top soil, 1 part sphagnum peat; or Houseplant Mix #2. Propagation by division. Moderately difficult. 2 species of which one grown indoors.

A. gramineus. The green-leaved species which grows to 18" (45 cm) is not cultivated indoors. The dwarfs are more suitable and attractive. We lead off with 'Variegatus' because it is the easiest to maintain.

'Variegatus'. In our opinion the most beautiful of the grassy plants. Leaves from a large, flat, brown, branching rhizome that clings to the surface of the soil like a limpet. Each short branch produces a tuft of straight leaves angling outward, each to 10" (25 cm) long and ¼" (6.25 mm) wide, shiny green with white edges. As the rhizome spreads so do the leaves in a widening arc. Thus the plant requires a broad, shallow, preferably decorative, pot.

The genus is semiaquatic. The cultivar should be kept moist at all times, even by immersing the base of the pot in a saucer filled with water. Keep in partial to full sun or close to the fluorescent tubes. Protect from summer heat with fans or good ventilation. Fertilize with a relatively high phosphate/potash formula such as Hyponex 7-6-19. Feed not more than once a month. Sections of rhizome can be cut free with roots and potted up. Do this during the warm season.

'Pusillus'. Leaves 3" (7.5 cm) long and less than ¼" (6.25 mm) wide. Shining green. The following cultivars derived from 'Pusillus' vary in size, but none are larger than the parent cultivar.

'Masamune'. Leaves edged with white.

'Oborozuki'. Light tan leaves with fine green stripes.

'Tanimanoyuki'. Leaves yellow striped.

'Yodonoyumi'. Light tan stripes.

These tiny, esoteric plants are for the collector and dish garden afficionado. They are even more sensitive to summer heat and should be kept under 75°F (24.5°C) if possible. They should also not be exposed to as much light as 'Variegatus'. Filtered to Partial sun is sufficient.

A. Morrowii. See Carex.

Adansonia. **Bombaceae.** Africa, Madagascar, Australia. Succulent trees. Full sun. Min 50°F (10°C). Sterilized Garden Soil. Succulent Mix #2. Propagation from seeds. Difficult. 9 species of which one is occasionally grown indoors.

A. digitata. Baobab Tree. Famous for its enormously swollen trunk. This is strictly a horticultural curiosity sometimes offered by nurseries. It can be maintained in a sunny window.

The tree grows to 60' (18 m) but no more than 10' (3 m) indoors, which is sufficient to form an enlarged trunk. Handshaped leaves with 5–7 leaflets, each 5" (12.5 cm) long, elliptic, on 6–12" (15–30 cm) stalks. Keep moist in summer and feed with high-middle-number formula once a month. Goes dormant in winter; water should be withheld once the stem has thickened.

Adenanthera. Leguminosae. Bead Tree Tropical Asia and Australia. Tree. Filtered to partial sun. 400–800 fc 14 hours daily. Temperature min. 60°F (16°C). Packaged Houseplant Medium. Houseplant Mix #2 with sand. Propagation from cuttings and seed. Easy. 4 species of which one grown indoors.

A. pavonina. Sandalwood. Tree to 50' (15 m). Leaves compound, Leaflets oval in alternate pairs, to 1½" (6.25 cm) long. Culture as for *Tamarindus*. Soak seeds in hot water before planting.

Leaves fold at night. Decorative use is similar to the other compound; small-leaflet **Leguminosae** which are mainly screening plants and grown as juveniles in pots.

Adenia. Passifloraceae. East Africa, Madagascar, Burma. Vines and shrubs with grossly thickened stems and thorns. Succulent. Partial to full sun. Warm to rather cool growing. Cactus & Succulent Mix #2 without lime. Propagation mostly by cuttings. Easy. 20 or more species of which a few are cultivated indoors.

A. spinosa. Transvaal. This species may serve as an example of the genus. Other species are listed below. The Adenias are extremely succulent, forming thickened stems that range from bottleshaped to those shaped like formless boulders up to 39" (1 m) high and 8' (2.4 m)! in diameter, sometimes with a smooth, other times with a bumpy surface. Branches often cover the whole surface and these may be either very long or quite short, often with thick thorns, sometimes with tendrils.

The plants available from nurseries are mostly juveniles which bear no resemblance to the mature plants, are grown in small pots and make attractive specimens. For instance, at maturity *A. spinosa* has a tuber 6' (1.80 m) across, with a smooth green rind, covered with branches and very spiny. The leaves are small, oval and short lived.

Specimens of juveniles supplied to us have had bottleshaped tubers 8" (20 cm) high, with a rubbery, brownish green skin which is very smooth. The single branch grows like a vine to a length of 2' (60 cm), has thin, soft spines and tendrils. Mature plants have hard thorns with thick bases. Leaves are 3-lobed, about 1½" (3.75 cm) long and quite soft textured. Leaves at top of branch are oval and the same size.

Other species that have been offered recently are *A. fruticosa, glauca, keramanthus, venenata* and *volkensii.* Consult Jacobsen for details.

During the growth period keep moist and fertilize once a month with a high phosphate-potash formula. As soon as leaves start to yellow cease watering. Trim back the longer stems. The chief attraction of these plants is the sculptural tuber (thickened stems).

Aechmea. Bromeliaceae. Living Vase. Tropical America. Aerial rosette plants. Full sun. 1,000 fc 14–16 hours daily. Temperature min. 50°F. (10°C.). Humidity 50%+. Osmunda Fiber or Houseplant Mix #3 with sand. Propagation by offsets or seeds. Long-term maintenance difficult.

Florists usually sell *Aechmeas* in flower or seed, both of which are often colorful and long lasting. We are concerned here with those that also have decorative leaves. They can be grown to nearly full size rather easily. It is more rewarding for the amateur to start with young plants directly from the nursery. The attractive markings––dark bands on gray or green––fade unless given bright greenhouse or window light.

Aechmeas are very ornamental for trough gardens and temporary displays. Plants are purchased in bloom which lasts 2–4 months, following which the leaves remain showy for 4–6 months. To maintain, simply fill the vase with water to overflowing. Fertilize at every watering with high nitrate fertilizer at ⅛ the concentration recommended on the label. Only *Aechmea fasciata* and its cultivars are at present available in sufficient numbers for commercial use.

A. 'Burgundy'. (*A. distichantha* × *A. weilbachii*). Loose upright rosette of narrow, long, spine-edged leaves, shiny-tawny red when grown in bright light. Plant 18" high, 24" wide (45 cm high, 60 cm wide.).

A. caudata 'Variegata'. Upstanding rosettes of 2' × 3' (60 × 7.5 cm) leaves, with alternate yellow and green vertical stripes.

A. chantini. Very symmetrical rosette of 12" × 2" (30 × 5cm) leaves, strapshaped and blunt tipped. Olive green, horizontally banded with pinkish gray to near black in some clones. Height 1', spread 2' (30 × 24 cm). The contrast in color between the broad, evenly spaced bands can be startling and highly ornamental.

A. fasciata. Leaves 2' × 3–4" (60 × 7.5 cm). Leathery, spreading, gray, with irregular silver banding. The flowering is like a torch crowned with an ice cream sundae, decorated with touches of pink, blue and silver. The massive sculpture of the leaves sets it apart. The most popular florist plant.

'Albo-marginata'; silvery banding and vertical white stripes. 'Variegata' is similar.

A. fosterana. Rosette erect, tubular. Leaves 2' × 4" (60 × 10 cm), striped horizontally in brownish purple. Large purple spot near tip.

A. 'Foster's Favorite' (*A. fosterana* x *A. orlandiana*).

Narrow-leaved, upright urns, entirely lacquered burgundy red. Produces many offsets. Height 2", spread 1' (60 × 30 cm). Especially handsome as a basket plant.

A. orlandiana. Open rosette with leaves 1' × 1¼" (30 × 3 cm), yellow-green, crossbanded in chocolate. Black spines along the margin.

Aeonium. Crassulaceae. Mostly Canary Islands. Shrubby leaf succulents. Part to full sun. Min. 800 fc for 14–16 hours daily in summer and min. 12 hours in winter. Temperature min. 45°F (7°C). Humidity

50%+. Cactus and Succulent Mix #2. Propagation from stem cuttings and leaves. Difficult. Sculptural pot plants. 38 species, 5 cultivated indoors.

The Aeoniums are thick-stemmed, erect or prostrate succulents carrying at the tips of the bare branches, with dramatic decorative effective, flat rosettes 4–10" (10–25 cm) in diameter. They require maximum sunlight indoors. Spectacular plants for temporary displays but unsuitable for permanent installations. Winter bloom.

The Canary Islands are subtropical, moist and warm in midsummer, relatively dry for most of the year. Water no more than once a month February to June and September through November, whenever soil is dry from the beginning of June through August, and not at all in December and January; but misting is beneficial.

They can endure high temperatures in summer with good air movement but must have cool nights, down to 45–50°F (7–10°C) in winter. Fertilize in summer twice a month using 15-30-15 at ¼ strength. Mealybugs are a problem, especially destructive if they get into the soil. Remove from leaves and stems with a brush soaked in alcohol and drench the soil with a general pesticide. Test any fungicide or pesticide spray on a leaf before applying to the whole plant. Avoid Malathion entirely.

Branching is encouraged by cutting out the growing tips of the rosettes—the young leaves in the center. To preserve the appearance of the foliage remove any flower stalks. Propagate in summer by rooting rosettes with a short length of branch, after the cut has callused, in slightly moistened sand. Or lay leaves on moist sand and maintain a temperature of 75°F+ (24°C+.) until rooted. Spray soil surface when dry.

A. arboreum. Morocco. Branched to 3' (90 cm). The rosettes consist of 2–4" (4/5-1-4/5 cm) wedgeshaped leaves, shiny brownish green to black-purple. Plants with a dark shade of purple are called 'Atropurpureum'. 'Schwarzkopf', nearly black, is the plant usually sold in the shops. Variegated and crested plants, much favored by collectors, occur. Difficult because of the need for careful watering. Roots easily rot with any excess moisture, especially during the cool months.

A. decorum. Canary Islands. Much branched shrub to 2' (60 cm) with many rosettes 4–5" (10–12.5 cm) in diameter, the leaves spoonshaped 1–2" (2.5–5 cm) long, bluish with red edges. Stems encircled by lines of hard, whitish scales.

A. haworthii. Canary Islands. Similar to the above, but leaves wedgeshaped, almost as broad as long, and the stems without scales.

A. tabuliforme. Canary Islands. Saucer Plant. Green throughout. Sprawling to 3' (90 cm) unless trimmed back. The 6–12" (15–30 cm) rosettes are very flat, consisting of closely packed roundish wedge-shaped, geometrically overlapping, fringed leaves 3–5" × 1½" (7.5–12.5 × 4 cm).

A. undulatum (pseudo-tabuliforme). Green Platters. Like *tabuliforme* but rosettes to 12" (60 cm). Leaves 4– 6" × 1½–2" (10–15 × 4–5 cm), glossy, yellowish green. Not branching; instead, it suckers from the base and spreads to 5' (1.5 m) unless drastically trimmed or grown as a juvenile.

Aeschynanthus. **Gesneriaceae.** Lipstick Plant. Mostly S.W. Pacific. Trailing aerial plant. Filtered sun. Minimum of 65°F (17.5°C). 40% humidity. Houseplant mix #3 with lime. Propagation from stem cuttings. Easy.

Most *Aeschynanthus* are grown for their long, tubular, orange or red flowers in clusters at the tips of branches. There are over 100 species of which only one at present is grown for foliage.

A. longicaulis (marmoratus). The many whiplike stems, to 24" (60 cm) and spreading 30" (75 cm) in clusters from underground runners, bear opposite, short-stalked elliptic leaves to 1½" (4 cm). Trim branches for more compact growth. The top surfaces of the leaves are green but the undersides are yellowish barred with dark maroon. Seen in day or night light the pattern shows up clearly. Keep evenly moist and fertilize six times a year with a balanced formula. The blooms are green. At temperatures over 85°F (29.5°C) leaves may shatter but recovery is usually rapid.

This shade-tolerant basket plant is a greater favorite with interior landscapers than home gardeners. Maintenance presents few problems. Fast growing but easily trimmed.

Agathis. **Araucariaceae.** Kauri. Phillipines, Australia and New Zealand. Tall tree. Partial to full sun. 600–1,000 fc. Temperature min. 50°F (10°C). 3 parts Packaged Houseplant Medium to 1 part gritty sand. Propagation from seed. Fairly easy. 30 species of which one is grown indoors.

A. robusta. Queensland Kauri. Grown as a juvenile pot or tub plant. Leaves opposite, elliptic, stiff, to 4" × ½" (10 × 1.25 cm), stalkless. The branches are spiraled and alternate; an undisciplined arrangement. Do not trim. Prefers temperature below 80°F (27°C). Sensitive to pollution which results in leaf browning.

Agave. **Agavaceae** (not *Amaryllidaceae* or *Liliaceae*). Tropical America. Mostly large rosette succulents. Full sun. 800–1,000 fc 14–16 hours daily. Temperature hardy to 32°F (0°C). Houseplant Mix #2 with sand or Succulent Mix #3. Propagation by offsets. Moderately easy. Sculptural display or decorative pot plants. 300 species of which at least 20 are widely cultivated but fewer indoors.

The rosettes of the larger plants achieve spread of up to 9' (2.5 m). Leaves usually curved outward on larger plants and inward on smaller ones. Mostly spiny edged. Juveniles in 4–8" pots (10–20 cm) will grow well with 800–1,000 fc, but half grown to mature plants, unless receiving full sunlight, usually remain in a state of suspended activity and do not survive for very long. Best plants for indoor culture are those from warm habitats. Water sparingly during the summer and not at all in winter. Apply a balanced fertilizer only during the growth period and not more than twice a season.

Full-grown large plants are suitable only for lobbies and atria in tubs. Juveniles can be kept dwarf for a long time by underpotting.

A. americana. Century Plant. Huge gray leaves, 5' × 10" (1.5 m × 25 cm) curve out and downward; margin toothed.

'Aureo-marginata' and 'Marginata'. Both have yellow marginal stripes.

'Medio-picta'. Yellow stripe down center of leaf.

'Picta'. Green with silvery-blue powdered surface; margins grayish to white; teeth brown.

'Striata'. Vertical yellow lines. Produces many offsets.

Specimens of *A. americana* and other variegates are exellent interior landscape plants, to be replaced at 6-month intervals and grown for a while in full sun before being reused. They are very durable with this treatment.

A. angustifolia. At maturity a ferocious, spherical cluster of whitish powdered, sharp pointed, gray-green leaves, 30" × 3" (75 × 7.5. cm); black toothed along the margins and with a thick black tip spine. Spread is about 3' (90cm).

'Marginata' has white edges and is the variety usually seen. Widely grown as an ornamental in the tropics where eggshells are laid over the points to warn the unwary. A fine sculptural subject for a succulent display.

A. attenuata. Long elliptic leaves to 30", lacking teeth; powdery gray or whitish. Spread 2½' (75 cm).

A. parrasana. This and *A. potatorum* are two of the most beautiful succulents for pots. Both belong to a group of species that spread broad, lanceshaped leaves from a tightly furled cone in the center and, as they open outward, retain the impression of the wavy edges and spines of the previously opened leaves. They are distinctly bluish, 12 × 6" (30 × 15 cm), height 10" (25 cm), spread 15" (37.5 cm), with light brown, curved teeth. The tip spine is 1" (2.5 cm) long. Leaves are held upright, forming a compact rosette.

A. potatorum. Similar to the above but somewhat greener and with reddish brown teeth, the tip spine 1½" (4 cm). It is more demanding of 40° to 50°F (4° to 10°C) in winter.

Among a number of similar species are *A. gracilipes, macrantha* and *parryi.*

A. stricta. Globular rosette of numerous leaves 15 × ⅜–⅝" (37.5 × 10–15 mm), gradually tapering and ending with a 1" (2.5 cm) spine.

'Nana', with 6" (15 cm) leaves is well suited to pot culture.

A. univittata (lophantha). The mature plant is a rosette a yard (90 cm) across, the leaves spiny, 12–18 × 1½" (30–45 × 4 cm), green with light colored vertical stripes. There are cultivars with more distinct variegation that are very showy. Warm growing. Min. 50°F (10°C).

A. victoriae-reginae. Most unusual of the Agaves.

The many 6" (15 cm) leaves form a tight globular rosette up to 14" (35 cm) across. The upper surface of the leaf is somewhat concave. The cross section is that of an inverted, truncated pyramid that, just short of the tip, becomes triangular. The upper surface is marked by 2 converging snow white lines, while others appear on all the lower edges and meet at the blunt tip. Extremely slow growing. There are a number of variations including the former *A. fernandi-regis,* which has recently lost its status as a species.

Some Agaves are distinguished by loose threads all along the edges of the leaves. They are fancied by collectors and are generally sold as juveniles. We list them separately below. They are usually sold as 3–4" (7.5–10 cm) high juveniles.

A. filifera. Rosette of 10–15 × 1½" (25–37.5 × 4 cm) leaves, green or purplish with a nearly 1" (2.5 cm) spine at the tip.

A. parviflora. Dwarf. Leaves 4 × ½" (10 × 1.25 cm); green, marked with vertical white lines.

A. toumeyana. Leaves to 12 × 1" (30 × 2.5 cm), spine ½" (1.25 cm). Keep cool in winter.

Aglaonema. **Araceae.** Chinese Evergreen. Tropical Asia, Philippine Islands. Mostly large-leaved, spreading herbs. Shade to filtered sun. Minimum 50 fc (12 hrs.) Temperature 50°F (10°C). Packaged Houseplant Medium or Houseplant Mix #2. Propagation by stem cuttings or division. Cast Iron. 50 or more species of which 9 or 10 are grown indoors.

Chinese Evergreens are currently the most popular decorative foliage plants in their size category; for 5–12" (12.5–30 cm) pots; height and spread rarely greater than 3 feet (90 cm). *A. commutatum,* dark leaved and straggling, was one of the early, reliable Victorian houseplants. Clusters of long-lasting, large red berries were the chief attraction.

Aglaonemas seemed fated to join Aspidistras as the last resort of those who required an indestructible plant, whatever its appearance. *A. commutatum* 'Silver Queen', a far cry from the species, appears to have been hybridized by Robert McColley at his Bamboo Nursery in Florida in the early 1960s. It was not produced on a commerical scale until the 1970s and achieved its great popularity no earlier than 1978. *Hortus Third,* published in 1976, does not mention it. In any event, this one important plant has led the way for modern interest in the whole genus which has focused attention on the immense potential that it possesses.

Aglaonemas form a thick, shallow root from which grow the stalked, mostly lanceshaped leaves in more or less tight spirals. Most species and cultivars need little attention and survive most forms of neglect. Even those with considerable variegation tolerate light levels as low as 50 fc and flourish in a north window. At 100–400 fc they develop larger, healthier leaves. They need only shallow potting with enough room to permit the roots to spread and produce offsets. Any standard houseplant mix seems to work equally well. The soil should be kept moist but not soggy. They will survive a week or more of dry soil without suffering much permanent damage. Though resistant to low temperatures, long exposure to 50°F (10°C) or less should be avoided.

For fast growth they can be fertilized frequently. To slow growth, feed only once a month with 20-20-20 at ¼ strength. Propagation is by means of heel or mallet cuttings in any moist medium or plain water. Plants with suckers are easily divided. Mites are occasional visitors, and mealybugs find refuge in the clasping bases of the leaves. But they are not favorite hosts for either, and a course of frequent sprayings with suitable pesticides will eradicate them quickly. They are rarely attacked by fungal diseases unless over-watered at low temperatures.

Nine or 10 species are in active cultivation. In addition explorations in S.E. Asia and the Philippines have brought back many variations. Hybridization and the occurrence of spontaneous variation contribute to the increasing number of leaf patterns. These consist of spottings, blotchings and streakings of light green, chartreuse or silver against dark green or the reverse. Partial or complete absence of chlorophyll and changes in pigmentation are common. In fact the instability of these plants is such that many of the horticultural names are arbitrary and the botanical ones blurred. Taxonomic methodology, as it has been used in the past, is no longer adequate to deal with these situations. The genus is a mine of beautiful foliage plants, many of which are still untested. New forms will undoubtedly gain commercial acceptance with time.

Aglaonemas are sold in pots as individual stems, as colonies and as collections of rooted cuttings:

A. brevispathum. Thailand. White-spotted leaf like *A. costatum (see below),* but identification is uncertain and the plant is rare in cultivation. Much the same as *A. hospitum* which is generally lumped with *A. costatum* in catalogs.

A. commutatum. In one way or another most of the plants active in commerce are of this species or hybridized with it. The distinction between plants deriving from natural variation or hybridization or from hybridization and variation in the greenhouse is unclear. Named plants issued one year look different a couple of years later. Orderly presentation has been attempted but failed, and we cannot expect to do any better. Buyers should see the plants rather than depend on names.

A. commutatum, the original Chinese Evergreen is from the Philippines. Upright or sprawling. Leaves dark green to 12 × 4" (30 × 10 cm), lanceshaped. Stalks to 6". Flowers insignificant. Large red berries are attached to an upright stalk. Long lasting. The true species is probably not in cultivation.

In listing the varieties and cultivars we follow Roy N. Jervis' *Aglaonema Grower's Notebook* of 1980 in part. We hold the opinion that the category "variety" no longer has validity. All forms in cultivation except original species must be considered cultivars. Dr. Jervis, on page 11, appears to hold to this view.

Variety *commutatum* is closest to the species. Leaves very dark green, lanceshaped with a shallow waist toward the tip, the veins discontinuously lighter colored. Dull plants but virtually indestructible.

Variety *elegans.* Leaves broader. Veins silvery and more continuous. 'Queen Juliana' has larger leaves but is very compact. Still frequently seen on the market.

'Malay Beauty' and 'Pewter'. Blades to over 12" (30 cm) and more attenuated. The variegation begins to approach that of the best current clones. Broad herringbone bands of light blotches with irregular dark spots, patterning very irregular. 'Malay Beauty' more silvery. 'Pewter' more gray. Very vigorous, relatively tall growing plants.

'Pseudobracteatum' is still very much in evidence along with 'Snow Queen' and 'White Rajah'. Leaves are lanceshaped on long stalks and marked with the broad, herringbone pattern except that the tint is yellowish, on both the blade and the stalk. When more yellow you are dealing with 'Pseudobracteatum' and, if more cream or near white, with one of the other two. The survival of these cultivars seems to us to be based more on their quick-growing quality than anything else. Plants are anything but compact and make an elongated-unsymmetrical impression.

The so-called 'Maculatum' type has more oval leaves with a short point, rather leathery blades and some light feathering along the veins. The background color is very dark green.

A. 'Picturatum' leaves are lanceshaped but narrower and more symmetrical than the others. Varieties of this cultivar have turned out all silver or all aluminum color. One clone was dubbed 'Mutton-fat Jade'. 'Alumina' and 'Moonglow' have been others. None have been commercially important.

Also belonging to the 'Picturatum' group is 'Treubii'. If you see a plant with markings somewhat like 'Fransher' (below) but with the blades much smaller, it is probably 'Treubii'. Nice for a small pot and quite carefree.

Hybrids involving *A. commutatum* cultivars are, in most instances, so closely related in appearance to natural variations that one must doubt that they are more than crosses between *A. commutatum* clones. The list is, nevertheless, important for it not only represents the results of breeding efforts but success in achieving plants with great popular appeal and excellent growth characteristics.

A. × 'Fransher'. Supposed to be a hybrid between *A. tricolor* (?) and *A. commutatum* 'Treubii'. It looks like a large, robust 'Treubii', the leaves to 12" (30 cm), with considerable greenish white variegation amid irregular stripes and blobs of green. It has proved a very sturdy plant, easy to grow and equally easy to maintain. It is the best of the older "hybrids."

A. × 'Manila'. ('Manila Bay'?): The leaves are very leathery, the shape oval-pointed up to 12" (30 cm) long, the green very dark but with large patches of silver that give it a very rich, even aristocratic, appearance. Growth is compact and culture virtually carefree. It may be that this plant does not grow fast enough for the nurseries. It should be more popular and would be a good alternative to 'Silver Queen'.

A. × 'Silver King' and 'Silver Queen'. Virtually identical plants, typically named differently by their presumed originators. The leaf type is long, narrow lanceshaped, the edges green and green irregular herringbone pattern with very bright silvery areas in between. The plants are symmetrical and compact. Slow growing indoors. They have proved immensely popular. No other foliage plant of this size, requiring so little light, is as colorful. Splendid in rows of 6" pots or in tubs with several plants. Even 5" potted plants are attractive. The name 'Silver King' has virtually disappeared from the market in favor of 'Silver Queen'.

A. costatum. An obviously different species with leaf blades to 6" (15 cm) and stalks to 8" (20 cm). Blades are narrow to broadly lanceshaped. The feature is white spotting and white along the midvein. There are several cultivarts based on the amount of spotting and the feathering of the midvein. 'Hospitum', at times considered a separate species, seems only to have smaller spots but on both surfaces.

These plants are suited to a 4–6" (10–15 cm) shallow pot as the main root crawls on the surface of the soil, putting up a leaf at every joint. Keep quite moist at all times. Tolerant of low light and high temperatures. Nice for a dish garden.

A. crispum. A large plant, to 5' (1.5 m), the blades 12 × 5½" (30 cm × 13.75 cm), broadly oval, of heavy texture. Stalks thick to 8" (20 cm) long. Typically the blade is edged with green and the midrib feathered with green while the spaces between are silvery gray with a greenish tinge. Handsome, rich but dark and more sensitive to watering and temperature than some of the other species. Cultivars are 'Chartreuse Halo', 'Emeralds on Ice', 'Fantasy' and Harlequin'. Produces large red berries. Better suited to greenhouse than domestic use or interior landscaping.

A. marantifolium. A large, all green plant that may have been used for hybridization but is rarely cultivated.

A. modestum. A smaller plant than most, the stem thin and growing to 2' (60 cm) in height. Leaves broadly lanceshaped, 10" (25 cm) long and half as wide. The green species is not commercially grown.

'Shingii'. The center of the blade and the tip are creamy white. Parts of the edge are soft green. Makes a pretty small pot plant when young, but later on must be supported. Its useful life is short.

A. nitidum. There are two cultivars of interest. 'Curtisii'. In our opinion the most beautiful of the Aglaonemas. Leaves borne nearly erect, growing in a dense, symmetrical spiral. Blades to 12 × 3½" (12 × 8.75 cm). Quite elliptical. The background green is grainy with almost a cloth texture and the neat, thin, herringbone veining is whitish. Thus the decorative quality is very different from other Chinese Evergreens and should prove especially useful in formal decoration. Maintenance is simple.

Other variations of the species are supposed to have gray to white spotting but are rarely seen.

'Ernesto's Favorite' is notable for the broad, dark green margin and the broad silvery stripe down the middle. Very sensitive to temperature and watering, it has remained quite rare.

A. pictum. Broad, lanceshaped leaves to 6½ × 2½" (16.25 × 6.25 cm), dark green, soewhat quilted, with blotches of gray. Cultivars offer different variegation patterns but the results are not impressive.

A.rotundum. Leaves nearly round, 5 × 4" (12½ × 10 cm), dark green with pink midrib and veins, purple below. Some clones have larger leaves. It makes a very attractive mound of ornamental foliage of smaller size than most of the species. Minimum temperature 65°F (18.5°C). Minimum humidity 50%. Requires very well aerated mix. A beauty but not easy to maintain.

Having achieved such success in the market there is a grave danger that Aglaonemas will suffer the fate of some formerly popular plants. There is the risk, for instance, that variegation will be carried too far, resulting in less attractive plants with less adaptability, as has happened with several of the other aroids. A. 'Silver Queen' is medium fast growing. To speed up commercial production for the market, several rooted cuttings that have been excessively forced are being stuffed together into pots to give an effect of ample foliage. These clusters are unsymmetrical and much less attractive than single well-grown plants. Plantscapers should resist such methods and be especially careful to buy plants that are properly grown and subjected to a sufficient period of low light.

The above advice applies as well to indoor gardening amateurs. Look at the stems of Aglaonemas before buying. They should be thick and the leaf spiral very tight otherwise the plants simply will not last.

Albizia. **Leguminosae.** Powder Puff Tree. India, Africa. Tree. To 8–10" (2.40–3.00 m) indoors. Filtered sun. 600 fc 12 hours daily. Min. 50°F (10°C) indoors. Houseplant Mix #2 with sand. Moderately easy. Propagation from stem cuttings. Over 100 species; one grown indoors.

A. julibrissin. This is one of the less tender species. The compact 'Rosea' is grown as far north as New Jersey, where it is deciduous, for its pink "powder puff" flowers. Indoors it remains evergreen at temperatures above 50°F (10°C). Leaves are up to 1' (30 cm) in length, the leaflets to ½" (1.25 cm) long and very narrow. Graceful and feathery. Quite fast growing unless trimmed.

Some of the other Albizias might make even better indoor foliage plants. A. stipulata could be a good prospect as it is naturally warmer growing. It has very velvety, hairy branches and small leaves. Use as a screen or for pseudo-bonsai.

Alocasia. **Araceae.** Tropical Asia. Large-leaved herb. Max. 4' (1.20 m) high indoors. Partial sun. Min. 500 fc 14 hrs daily. Temperature min. 60°F (16°C). Humidity min. 50%. Houseplant Mix #2 with lime. Sphagnum Moss. Rather difficult. Propagation from offsets, tubers, heel cuttings. 70 species of which about 20 are occasionally grown indoors.

Alocasias grow from thick, shallow roots, the short trunks fleshy, bearing prominent scars from dead leaf stalks. Leaves Large, heart to arrowshaped, facing outward on long, erect stalks that are attached below the cleft (peltate). Similar in shape to many other aroids, they are distinguished by their frequently thick texture and shiny or dull, leathery or metallic surfaces with prominent veining patterns.

We have always esteemed them the most aristocratic of the aroids. Formerly maintainable only in warm, humid greenhouses, awareness that they can perform rather well in a normal environment indoors is of quite recent date. Except in atria with controlled temperature and humidity, they are not yet viable as plantings. Further breeding, it is hoped, will produce clones having greater tolerance of a variety of environments. With ingenuity Alocasias can be used very effectively by plantscapers indoors. Amateurs will be attracted to the challenge represented by these extraordinarily handsome plants.

In our experience Alocasias are by no means as tolerant of low light as they are said to be. They will survive even in a north window, but they do not thrive. If they have insufficient light, leaf stalks grow very long and are weak. With Partial Sun and a minimum of 600 fc they remain more compact, are more vigorous and leaves are retained longer.

Watering is not easy because, like Dieffenbachias, Alocasias suffer from being waterlogged for even a relatively short time. A dependable sign is that the stalks of lower leaves flop over and gradually are followed by others. When the leaves die off the stem is denuded. The plant can be revived if the soil is kept barely moist, but recuperation takes months. In short, it is much safer to allow the soil to dry out completely for several days than to keep it soaked.

A means of counteracting a tendency to overwater is to use Houseplant Mix #1. Another is to pack the roots rather loosely with long-fiber sphagnum moss and allow it to dry out between waterings.

Fungus diseases attack the roots. Well-aerated soil is one preventative. Use coarse-grade perlite and some charcoal in the mix. Drench the soil with fungicides. The plants should be kept moist, but water in the morning and preferably not on cloudy days or when the humidity outside is unusually high. Underwatering is preferable during the dog days of late July and August. Keep windows open or get the fans going. The rot rarely affects the stem itself. When leaves are completely lost and roots have disappeared, plant the stump of stem in lightly packed sphagnum moss kept just moist and maintain a temperature of 70–75°F (22–24.5°C). Be patient; leaves and roots will appear eventually.

The most damaging pest is mite, usually the two-spotted variety. They appear on both surfaces of the leaves, preferring, contrary to general experience, the upper. Spray with a miticide or use a systemic pesticide.

Fertilize once a month with 20-20-20 at the rate of ¼ tsp. to a gallon. Add 1 tbsp. dolomite lime to a quart of medium. This is not necessary if your water is hard. Leach the soil thoroughly twice a year. Cut off flowering stalks as they only interfere with growth. Reduce the leaf size of the bigger plants by underpotting and reduced feeding.

Some species produce tubers that can be separated. Others colonize. Sections of stem can be sprouted with patience in long-fiber sphagnum moss. When the stem becomes too long, cut below the oldest leaf and immerse in water where it will put forth roots.

Like several other aroid genera, *Alocasia* is extremely variable even where asexually reproduced plants are concerned. The most recent study is "The Cultivated Alocasia" by David Burnett of Sydney, Australia, issued as Volume 7, No.3 and 4 of *Aroideana,* publication of The International Aroid Society. We have referred to this work elsewhere not only because of the plant subject but also Dr. Burnett's remarks about naming and labeling that are so much in the vein of our own, the whole matter of plant differentiation in some genera having become more and more confused as we become better informed about wild populations and artificial breeding proceeds apace. The following list, therefore, is only a selection of what we consider important at the moment and is a good example of the difficulties we, or any writer, now faces in venturing to describe and recommend plants for specific purposes. The list consists of those we consider outstanding for color, shape or texture. There are many other Alocasias worth a trial.

Note: Description is further complicated by the fact that some plants display quite differently shaped leaves as juveniles and adults. In general we have to follow what we believe to be a consensus of nursery labeling.

A. × 'amazonica'. (*A. lowii* × *A. sanderana*). Probably the most popular *Alocasia* in cultivation. The hybrid (?) has been around for a long time, but there is no record of how it came about. The leaf blades are narrowly to broadly heartshaped with well-developed, upright lobes. To 24 × 11" (60 × 27.5 cm). Shallowly but definitely lobed below. Principal veins thick and quite brilliantly white against lacquered, rich, dark green surface. The reverse is purple and displays a close pattern of transverse veins. Stalk to 15" (37.5 cm), brown spotted near base. Exceedingly variable, there are any number of cultivars but these are not very stable.

The plant is robust and probably the easiest to maintain of the whole genus. Young plants are very elegant, and larger ones have leaves that are almost overwhelming in their solidity and powerful design. Some of the cultivars have a more silvery blade surface.

A. × *chantrierana (chantrieri).* Heartshaped leaf, oval

Alocasia guttata 'Imperialis'

Alocasia korthalsii

Alocasia cucullata 'Crinkles'

Aloe harlanii

PLATE 9

Aloe aristata

Aloe rauhii

Aloe variegata. **Partridge Breast Aloe**

Alpinia zerumbet variegata

PLATE 10

Alpinia purpurea

Alternanthera ficoidea. Joseph's Coat

Ananas comosus 'Tricolor.' Pineapple

Anthurium crystallinum

PLATE 11

Anthurium veitchii

Anthurium warocqueanum

Anthurium clarinervium (leuconeurum)

Aphelandra 'Apollo'

PLATE 12

Araucaria heterophylla (excelsa). Norfolk Island Pine

Ardisia crenata. Coral Berry

Asparagus densiflorus 'Myers.' Foxtail Fern

Arundinaria (Sasa) pygmaea. Dwarf Bamboo

PLATE 13

Asparagus racemosus

Asparagus macowanii (myriocladus)

Aspidistra elatior 'Milky Way'

Aspidistra elatior variegata

PLATE 14

Aucuba japonica. Gold-dust Plant. Photo Gordon Courtright

Ballota nigra. Black Horehound

Bambusa oldhamii. Photo Gregory A. Koob

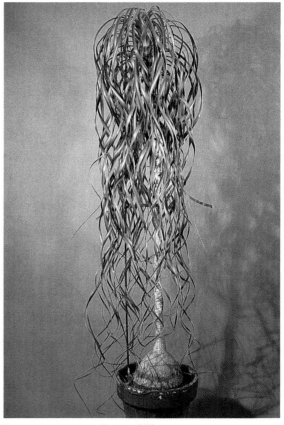

Beaucarnea recurvata. Ponytail Plant

PLATE 15

Begonia aconitifolia. Old plant trained as bonsai

Begonia 'Kew'

Begonia undulata

Begonia 'Tingley Mallet'

PLATE 16

in shaped with short basal lobes. 12" (30 cm) or more long. Major veins horizontally curved, the tips marking the undulating edge. Quilted between veins. Midrib and lobe ribs white, side veins grayish. The plant produces underground tubers.

A. × chelsonii. Has been listed as a hybrid, but this is questioned. The leaf is close to oval with almost no cleft at the base and with a short narrow point. 15 × 7" (37.5 × 17.5 cm), convex. Background color rich metallic green. Midrib raised, greenish white. Side veins silvery. Reverse purple. Stalk 15" (37.5 cm), purplish. Very slow growing, but considered easy.

A. cucullata. Chinese Taro. Quite a different plant than the others. Stalks are stiff and spreading, growing in a tight spiral and the broad leaves are carried quite horizontally. Blades heartshaped, max. 11 × 7" (27.5 × 17.5 cm), somewhat cupped, green. The stalks to 12" (30 cm) or more. Slow growing and bushy. Also very tolerant of cool conditions down to 40°F (4°C). Very attractive as a 6" pot plant. Leaves are long lasting.

A. cuprea. Borneo. Relatively compact plant. Leaf blades almost oval and only shallowly notched; convex. 12 × 6" (30 × 15 cm) or larger. Surface coppery to nearly black with sunken veins. A species that, for a change, is quite stable. It is easily grown and has been popular with horticulturists for a long time. Small pot plants of the species are very distinctive.

A. 'Fantasy'. A plant of unknown origin. There is a large and a dwarf type, the latter being the more popular. Heartleaved with broad, long, round-tipped lobes, somewhat cupped and with a short, abrupt point. 8 × 4" (20 × 10–12.5 cm). Side veins few. Midvein green with silver overlay and very broad. Side veins broad, silvery. Blade deep purple below. Stalks long and bright pink. Texture of leaves unusually thick.

A. guttata var. *imperialis.* Leaves reach max. 10" (25 cm) in length. The outline is broadly heartshaped, deeply cleft with broad lobes, convex. Midrib and principal side veins deeply imbedded. Texture thick and leathery. Transverse veins in curving patterns. Surface blue-gray, blue-black near the veins. Reverse light to dark purple. Stalks purple spotted. Still a relatively rare plant. The horizontal attitude of the leaf blades when young adds to its attractions as a pot plant. Resistant to pests.

A. 'Hilo Beauty'. Irregularly heartshaped leaves with blunt tips. The whole surface is marked with shapeless islands of ochre against emerald green. Showy but not elegant. Both species and cultivar are especially resistant to mites.

A. korthalsii. Sarawak (?). Plants very similar to *A. lowii* which comes from the same area. The matter is complicated by variability of a high order. It seems to be a plant with somewhat cupped leaf blades 1" (30 cm) by 7" (17.5 cm). Plants we have observed with this label had leathery, gray blades, purple beneath, with a rich pattern of transverse veins. It is said to resemble *A. × chelsonii.*

A. longiloba. A name applied to a whole host of differently leaved plants with a general tendency to have large, arrow-shaped-triangular leaf blades, with long, often spreading, basal lobes. Surfaces are grayish to lacquered dark green. There are many named cultivars but all relatively rare and purely for collectors. It is in such congregations that the shrewd nurseryman often finds clones with combinations of superior characteristics. But none of these have become popular as yet.

A. lowii. Another "congregation" accorded a species name. Here the situation is so confusing that even Dr. Burnett does not presume to describe a typical plant. However it can be stated that leaves are huge at maturity 2' (60 cm) or more and different from juvenile leaves. The outline of the leaf is generally curved, hence heartshaped, with a distinct cleft. Transverse veins frequently are prominent. Ease of maintenance differs. When you buy a plant listed as *A. lowii* you would be wise to see it rather than depend on a listed name which may be merely a catch-all. It is, however, a superb example of the dilemma faced by the "science" of taxonomy in the modern world of horticulture.

A. micholitziana. Green Velvet. It is a measure of the confusion as to names among horticulturists that magnificent specimens of this distinctive plant were exhibited at the Chelsea Show in London under the label of *A. amazonica,* with which it shares hardly any resemblance. *Hortus Third* describes it as similar to *A. sanderana* which is even worse. In the United States this species is often called *A. maxkowskii,* which is no improvement.

The species is certainly variable enough, from long arrowshaped to quite oval in outline. The best clones are of the latter shape, 12–16 × 6–7" (30–40 × 15–16.5 cm), somewhat convex, the cleft moderately deep and the lobes rounded; the edge gently undulating and turned downward; the surface an especially rich, green velvet; principal veins thick, few and nearly pure white-crystalline; blades carried vertically on 12–18" (30–45 cm) stalks. Fine specimens are glorious. We have found this a type not at all difficult to maintain. But see that you acquire a superior clone.

A. portei. The leaves are so distinctive that one must question its relationship to other Alocasias. Blades may grow to 3' (90 cm) on stalks that are as long or longer. Long-arrowshaped in outline but with horizontal, deeply cut lobes with undulating edges. The leaf is bright green and rather thin in texture. Makes a good pot plant but elongates rapidly and must be protected against fungus. Has been attributed to the genus *Schizocasia.*

A. sanderana. A favorite of horticulturists that strongly resembles *A. × amazonica* but with deeper lobes so that the appearance of the blade is much leaner. The pattern is stronger and more attractive than the hybrid, but maintenance is not as easy due to fungus.

Aloe. **Liliaceae.** Mostly Africa and Madagascar. Rosette succulents from very small to very large. Partial to full sun. Min. 500 fc. Min. 40°F (4°C). Cactus and Succulent Mix #2. Easy. Propagation by offsets and seeds. 250 or more species of which a large number in cultivation.

Aloes are popular throughout the tropics as garden ornamentals. They are mostly stiff-leathery leaved succulents, frequently spiny. The flowering stalk is stout and tall carrying numerous, nearly overlapping, pendant, tubular yellow to orange flowers. Indoors they are grown for their foliage which is sculptural and spectacular in large specimens and very neat for small pot plants.

Plantscapers have not used them much in the North because they do not blend easily with soft tropical foliage. With improved lighting of atriums and the development of more indoor gardens of scale in the South we may see more of them. Mixed with palms, other succulents and other woodier tropical foliage they should fit very well into arrangements.

Amateurs interested in succulents grow them in fair quantity and there is always demand for dwarfs and juveniles as small, carefree potted plants. But they are little used as large sculptural decoration.

Aloes can be maintained under 500 fc of fluorescent lighting. But better growth and color is achieved at higher levels. Underlighted, some species will elongate and leaves turn soft, making them vulnerable to attacks of fungus. They also lose the gray or powdery surfaces that are a major attraction.

Excessive watering will produce similar effects. Water lightly every 3 weeks from November to February; increase gradually during the spring months until you are watering thoroughly once a week from June to September, then back to light watering in the fall. Another system is to water frequently only during growth. Fertilize no more than 2 or 3 times a year with a balanced formula. Work dolomite lime into the soil once a year at the approximate rate of 1 tbsp. to the quart of medium.

In the following listing we have omitted climbing, sprawling plants as of little interest to indoor gardeners or plantscapers.

Large Plants
A. africana. S. Africa. Stem 6–12′ (1.80–3.6 m). Rosettes of 25–40 leaves, 26 × 5″ (65 × 12.5 cm). Bluish. Toothed.

A. bainesii. S. Africa. To 60′ (18 m), with thick trunk. Leaves in tight rosettes, 40″ (1 m) long. Fine display plant when partly grown.

A. comosa. S. Africa. To 6′ (1.80 m). Leaves 14–20″ (35–50 cm). Bluish. Edges toothed.

A. dichotoma. S. Africa. To 30′ (9 m). Trunk thick. Spiral rosettes. Leaves 14 × 2″ (35 × 5 cm). Small, hard teeth.

A. ferox. S. Africa. To 15′ (4.5 m) or more. Leaves 36 × 6″ (90 × 15 cm). Surface pimpled. The variegated form with vertical light stripes is attractive. Much grown as a 5 or 6 leaved juvenile in small pots.

A. marlothii. S. Africa. 6–12′ (1.80–3.6 m). Rosettes dense. Leaves 24 × 4″ (60 × 10 cm). Bluish. Sharply toothed. Usually grown as a juvenile.

A. plicatilis. S. Africa. To 15′ (4.5 m). Opposite strapshaped leaves, closely layered, 12 × 2″ (30 × 5 cm), bluish green. Handsome. Will bloom in a sunny window.

A. thraski. 6′ (1.80 m) or more. Leaves 4′ × 13″ (1.20 m × 32.5 cm). Very concave. Small toothed. Good display plant.

Medium-sized Plants
A. barbadensis. S. Africa. Commonly called Aloe Vera. Famous for its medicinal and cosmetic virtues but one of the less attractive Aloes. Sold as a juvenile when its leaves are narrow, concave, upright, light green with white spots. The whole leaf turns gray as it matures to 20–30″ (50–75 cm).

A. barbertoniae. S. Africa. Dense rosette of leaves max. 16 × 4″ (40 × 10 cm) with a long hair at tip. White spotted in horizontal bands.

A. capitata. Madagascar. Stemless rosette. Leaves to 28 × 2″ (70 × 5 cm). Thick, red tipped. There are several varieties.

A. dawei. Uganda. Short-stemmed, branching leaves to 20 × 3″ (50 × 7.5 cm), bluish, toothed.

A. harlana. S. Africa. Leaves to 20 × 6″ (50 × 15 cm). The juvenile plants in the trade have broad, short, triangular leaves stacked in a rosette to several inches high, the background light green and covered with numerous vertical hatchings in dark green. Toothed. The surface shiny. One of the most spectacularly marked of the pot-sized aloes.

A. peglerae. Stemless. Leaves 14 × 2″ (35 × 5 cm). Boatshaped beneath.

A. striata. S. Africa. Leaves 20 × 6″ (50 × 5 cm) with a bluish cast and streaked in a lighter shade.

All the above are most often sold as juveniles, the leaves much shorter and rarely more than 1′ (30 cm) across.

Small-sized Plants.
These are sculptural little pot plants suitable for dish gardens. A few are so brightly spotted that they merit individual display. Must be dried out between waterings. Effective when massed.

A. aristata. S. Africa. Stemless. Offsetting and colonizing. Leaves 2–4 × ½″ (5–10 × 1.25 cm), with long hairs from the tips. Incurving. An excellent house and bedding plant.

A. ausana variegata. S. Africa. Leaves 5 × 2″ (12.5 × 5 cm), broadly triangular. Distinctly white dotted in rows.

A. brevifolia. S. Africa. Colonizing. Leaves 7½ × 1″ (18.75 × 2.5 cm), thick; underside boatshaped.

A. haworthioides. Madagascar. Densely packed little rosettes. Leaves 1 × 2½ × ⅜″ (2.5 × 6.25 cm × 9.37 mm). The thin edges are lined with white hairs. Leaf surface white beaded. A gem but difficult to water properly. Has definite dormant period.

A. jucunda. Somalia. A popular dwarf. Leaves 2–5 × 1″ (5–12.5 × 2.5 cm), liberally spotted with white dots. Edges toothed. Easy and very attractive.

A. krapohliana. S. Africa. Stemless rosettes. Leaves 2–4″ × 1″ (5–10 × 2.5 cm). Covered with bluish powder. Edges reddish. Toothed.

A. laeta. Described as stemless but ours were definitely stemmed and leaf joints separated. Leaves 6–9″

(15–22.5 cm) long. Attenuated. Surface pimpled and edges toothed.

A. longistylis. S. Africa. Stemless. Leaves 4–6 × 1″ (10–15 × 2.5 cm). Striped vertically. Pimpled, mostly on the under side.

A. rauhii. Madagascar. Leaves separated and spiraled; held horizontally, 3–4 × 1″ (7.5–10 × 2.5 cm). Very blue and covered with white spots. Showiest of the lot.

A. saponaria. S. Africa. Dense rosette. Leaves 6–8 × 2–3″ (15–20 × 5–7.5 cm), thick, gray-green, covered with light oblong spots in rows.

A. squarrosa. Socotra and Zanzibar. Short stemmed. Leaves 4–8 × ¾″ (10–20 × 18.6 cm). Lightly spotted in parallel lines.

A. suprafoliata. Leaves opposite, horizontal, closely packed over each other, 13 × 3″ (32.5 × 7.5 cm). Concave, deep green, large toothed. A most curious and sculptural small aloe. Keep very dry in dormancy. We have encountered clones that are very narrow leaved and others with very thick ones. The latter are handsomer.

A. variegata. S. Africa. Partridge Breast Aloe. Leaves in a spiral of threes, closely packed and upright, 5 × 1½″ (12.5 × 3.75 cm), very concave, folded, clasping. Dark to bluish green with white oblong spots in horizontal bands beneath. A beautiful plant that also blooms well.

This entire group is colorful and shapely, well worth more attention. There are a number of other species and many varieties.

Alpinia. **Zingiberaceae.** Ginger Lily. Asia and Pacific Islands. Tall, leafy herbs. Partial to full sun. Temperature min. 60°F (16°C). Humidity min. 50%. Houseplant Mix #3. Propagation by division. Difficult. 250 species; a half dozen occasionally grown indoors.

Alpinias are valued in the tropics for their lush leaves and frequently richly colored flowers. They are ill-suited to northern environments being especially subject to fungus due to low temperatures and periods of overcast. In the South where atriums or malls may have good natural light and warmth, they may be used as tall bedding plants for background foliage. Flowers are not usually to be expected indoors.

The plants grow as tall canes bearing alternate, lanceshaped, clasping leaves. They require constant moisture, high humidity and heavy feeding with balanced formulas.

A. purpurata. South Seas. Red Ginger. Grows to 15′ (4.5 m) but usually less. Leaves 2½′ × 6″ (75 × 15 cm). Green, sometimes reddish.

A. sanderae. Variegated Ginger. Thin canes to 39″ (1 m). Leaves 9 × 3″ (22.5 × 7.5 cm), thin, mostly white with green stripes angled toward the midrib. Can be grown under fluorescent light as a juvenile and makes a colorful foliage pot plant. However, it is subject to fungus and not frequently seen.

A. tricolor. To 8′ (2.40 m). Leaves 10 × 1½″ (25 × 3.75 cm), variously striped with pale green, yellow or white.

A. zerumbet (nutans). Shell Ginger. Leaves 24 × 5″ (60 × 12.5 cm). Leaves white with green stripes.

Alternanthera. **Amaranthaceae.** (Achyranthes in hort.) Tropical America. Small, colorful ornamentals. Full sun. Min. 800 fc. Min. 60°F (16°C). Sterilized garden soil with peat. Propagate from seeds and cuttings. 100 species of which 2 are widely grown.

Alternantheras, treated as annuals, make good outdoor edging plants. Flowers small, clustered; without petals. Indoors they need full-window sunlight. As they are quick growing and weak stemmed, trim to make them bush out. They propagate easily from stem cuttings in houseplant mix or sterilized garden soil, kept moist and over 72°F (23°C). Fertilize with high potash formula.

A. dentata. West Indies and east coast of S. America. Called "Indoor Clover" for the small, cloverlike flower clusters, similar to but less showy than the related Globe Amaranth. Lance leaves to 2½ × 1″ (6.25 × 2.5 cm), normally green. Will tolerate temperatures down to 50°F (10°C).

'Rubiginosa' Purplish-red leaves.

'Ruby'. Leaves deep red.

A. ficoidea. A number of varieties are improperly listed as species, including *bettzickeana* and *amoena*.

Fleshy, weak-stemmed, branching plants with small, short stalked, more or less elliptic, leaves clustered at the joints. Popular as a summer-garden edging plant but even more so as a houseplant, despite a disorderly growth habit and the need for constant trimming. For good health it requires full sun. Chief attraction is the availability of cultivars with colorful leaves.

'Amoena'. Leaves rose.

'Aurea Nana'. Yellow leaves.

'Bettzickiana'. Bright red.

'Versicolor'. Zoned red and copper.

New shades occur frequently and spontaneously at nurseries.

Subject to browning leaves from underwatering and rotting of stems (fungus) when overwatered. Plants sold by nurseries and florists are usually small and potbound. They do not take kindly to repotting. Subject to mite and white fly infestation. Sensitive to urban pollution. But they can grow very well and quite showily in a bright country window.

Amomum. **Zingiberaceae.** False Cardamom. Java. Grassy herb. Partial sun. Min. 45°F (7°C). Houseplant Mix #3. Propagation by division. Rather easy. 100 species of which one is grown as a substitute for cardamom.

A. compactum (cardamomum) 3′ (90 cm), grassy plant, similar to *Zingiber officinale*. The thin, spiky, 4–5″ (10–12.5 cm) leaves alternate; pleasantly aromatic. Dormant part of the winter. Water regularly when in growth. Sparing high phosphate/potash feeding. Subject to mite infestation. Divide in winter. A very temporary plant indoors and grown mostly as a curiosity. For true cardamom see *Elettaria*.

139

Amorphophallus. **Araceae.** Devil's Tongue. Southern Asia and East Indies. Tuberous aroid. Max. 3–4' (90–1.20 cm) indoors. Filtered sun or 300 fc. Temperature min. 65°F (18.5°C). Humidity 50%. Houseplant Mix #3. Easy. Propagation by offsets and bulbils. 90 species of which 2 or more grown indoors.

In *A. titanum* the genus produces the largest of all flowers. In the spring, shops sell imported tubers of smaller, related species that, when exposed without soil to light and warmth, shoot up a short-lived, large brownish spathe (modified leaf) with purple spots, enclosing a still-longer spadix (flowering stalk). If the tuber is potted up after flowering, a single leaf appears promptly on a tall, erect stalk. It is held horizontally, is up to 4' (1.20 m) across, circular and divided into 3 branches bearing many leaflets. This decorative display lasts until October when water is withheld and the leaf dies down. Remove the tuber from the pot and store dry in a plastic bag at min. 55°F (13°C) until about March, when it sprouts again.

A. bulbifer. Tuber to 6" (15 cm) diameter. Stem to 3' (90 cm). Leaf blade 2' (60 cm) diameter bearing bulbils in joints which can be planted.

A. rivieri. (Sauromatum guttatum.) Voodoo Lily. Tuber to 10" (25 cm) diameter. Stem to 4' (1.20 m). Leaf blade to 4' (1.20 m) wide.

These are strictly novelty plants but easy and appealing.

Ananas. **Bromeliaceae.** Pineapple. Brazil. Rosette plant with long, succulent, spiny leaves. Full sun. Min. 800+ fc. Temperature min. 50°F (10°C). Humidity min. 50%. Houseplant Mix #2. Easy with adequate light. Propagation from offsets. 9 species; 2 grown as pot plants.

Cut off the leafy tip of the fruit with its cluster of hard, spiny leaves, allow the pulp to dry out for a few days and then plant in houseplant mix. This unusual cutting does root most of the time and will grow for a while as a novelty. Unfortunately the leaves are unattractive. Quite another matter are the handsome, variegated-leaved plants.

A. bracteatus. Red or Wild Pineapple. Brazil. It has showy red flowers lacking in *A. comosus.*

'Striatus'. Leaves with a bright white border. As juveniles leaves are 6–10" (15–25 cm) long, forming a rosette that is attractive in a small pot. At maturity the length of the spiny leaves is 3' (90 cm) and the width 1½" (3.75 cm) in a tightly spiralled, spreading rosette 4' (1.20 m) or more in diameter. The plant usually produces offsetts, and these can be separated and potted up.

A. comosus. The edible pineapple is about the same size as the above.

'Variegatus'. Leaves edged in ivory.

'Porteanus'. Central yellow stripe.

Recently plants have appeared in the market with small, very red fruit and silvery, frosted leaves. The fruit is often sold attached to stalks for vase display.

Keep moist in summer and quite dry in winter. The leaves benefit from regular mistings. Fertilize with high nitrate formula once a month in summer.

Splendid low, spreading display plants that should be replaced at 6-month intervals unless kept in bright sunlight as, otherwise, they lose color. Vacationed in sun they recover their beauty. On display they do not need high humidity and should be watered every 2 weeks at most, as roots will rot with wet soil in low light.

Anthurium. **Araceae.** Tropical America. Low herbs with small to very large leaves. Shade to filtered sun. 100–500 fc. Temperature min. 60°F (10°C). Humidity min. 40%. Houseplant Mix #2 or 3 with lime. Also terrestrial orchid mix and sphagnum moss. Propagation from offsets, heel cuttings and division. Easy to difficult. 600 species of which only a few widely grown.

This is a fascinating genus with great future potential, but at present, most species are grown indoors only by botanical gardens and hobbyists.

The most popular species is the flowering *A. andreanum,* the Flamingo Flower, from Columbia but now widely grown in the tropics for the colorful, long-lasting flowers that are shipped to market. *A. scherzeranum,* similar but much smaller, also with colorful flowers, is frequently seen in greenhouses and can be grown indoors with little difficulty. The flowers of the rest of the genus are insignificant, but the foliage is beautiful and varied. Of these there are 8 species with velvety, heartshaped leaves and a unique pattern of white or crystalline silvery veins that are spectacular ornamentals. Assumed to require the high humidity of a greenhouse, they have only recently attracted the attention of plantscapers and indoor gardeners. It has been shown that, maintained at normal tropical temperature and in soil free of excessive salts, they adapt very well. No doubt as selection proceeds even more tolerant plants will be developed.

The other foliage Anthuriums offer advantages that may earn them popularity in the long run. The vast majority have never been given a trial. Most leaves are thick and leathery, making them resistant to insects. The plants are also quite disease resistant. Growth is very slow and internodes usually short. The blades are very long lasting; a full year being not unusual. Those that may seem too large at maturity for pot culture are attractive as juveniles. Slow growth, it is true, is mated to slow propagation, but this handicap will prove insignificant when tissue culture is carried on in quantity.

Species that have similar-looking leaves are often difficult to tell apart. For the indoor gardener or plantscaper it is the decorative qualities and ease of culture that count. Thus the groupings of leaf shapes and growth habit in our descriptions makes practical sense.

Culture is very much the same as usual for aroids. Garden soil or Florida muck won't do. It must be porous, fibrous and well aerated. Sphagnum peat moss, vermiculite and perlite in even proportions works well. Bark can be mixed with the peat moss. Pumice replaces perlite. Osmunda fiber is always a satisfactory medium.

A temperature of 65 to 85°F (18.5–29.5°C) is the ideal; below 50° (10°C) most of the plants suffer Sunlight over 2,000 fc for an extended period may lead to spotting. The best level is 600 to 1,000 fc of indirect or artificial light. Keep constantly moist. Regular misting is helpful. During midwinter, the short semidormant period when growth stops, moisture should be given at longer intervals though soil should never be allowed to dry out completely.

Brown spots on the blades are caused by either sunburn or excess salts. The pots should be well leached every 3 months. The plants are rarely attacked by mites; more often by scale. Because the leaves are relatively few and possess large surfaces they can be swabbed. Safer Insecticidal Soap and Malathion can be used.

Propagation is slow but sure. The best procedure is to make heel or mallet cuttings, dust with hormone powder and plant in long-fiber sphagnum moss, or live moss if you can get it, at a minimum 72°F (23°C) and 400 fc of light. Upper parts of plants with stems that have grown too long can be cut off and treated the same.

Tight potting encourages growth of new leaves but limits their size. Roots are spreading, not deep; therefore relatively shallow pots are best. Pack the soil loosely, but be careful to leave no empty spaces in the pot.

Note that leaves in bud sometimes have difficulty unfolding and tear themselves in the process. This may be the result of insufficient light or humidity.

CRYSTALLINE-VEINED SPECIES

A. clarinervium. S. Mexico. Heartshaped. 5–7" (12½–17½ cm) long, 4–5½" (10–13½ cm) wide. Stalks sturdy to 8" (20 cm). Three thick veins on either side of the midvein, arising from the attachment of the stalk and curving toward the tip, are joined by shorter veins that form rough rectangles. Texture stiff, leathery. Color medium to olive green. Surface somewhat velvety. Veins whitish crystalline.

A. cordatum. S. Brazil. Arrowshaped leaf with spreading lobes. Veining thick, simple, crystalline. Color olive green. The size is between *clarinervium* and *crystallinum.*

A. crystallinum. Colombia. The species most frequently grown. Heartshaped to 20 × 12" (50 × 30 cm). Sturdy stalks to 20" (50 cm). Veining like *clarinervium.* Surface a richer emerald green and more velvety. Among the most beautiful of all foliage plants.

A. forgettii. Colombia. Short, lanceshaped because there are no basal lobes. Stalk is attached near the base of the leaf (peltate). About the same size as *A crystallinum,* but veining is less complicated; two pairs on either side of the midvein extending only to the edge, and there are fewer crossveins. Surface velvety, veins silvery.

A. grande. Bolivia. Heartshaped. Very similar to *crystallinum* but middle lobe longer pointed and lacks the crossveining.

A. leuconeurum. Mexico. Heartshaped with a wide notch and long basal lobes. 5–7" (12–18 cm). Stalks slender, to 15" (37½ cm). Surface velvety. Texture leathery. Veins emanating from base; simple, curved toward tip.

A. magnificum. Colombia. Very similar to *crystallinum* except blades somewhat larger and leaf stalks four angled.

A. warocqueanum. Colombia. Very long heartshaped. 36 × 12" (108 × 30 cm). Shimmering, emerald green. Side veins simple from midvein; pale white. 'Robustum' is a selected clone. Because of length the plant must be raised on a pedestal or suspended. A magnificent display plant.

THE OTHER SPECIES

We have arranged other cultivated species by leaf shape except for two types that are best separated by their growth habits. This will make it easier to differentiate between similar plants.

Arrowshaped

A. hygrophyllum. Ecuador. Semiaquatic. Variable shaped leaves with widespread lobes on thin stalks.

A. peruvianum. Peru. Very dark green, small leaves. Basal lobes narrowing but rounded; spread very wide. 7" (17½ cm) long. Middle lobe pointed. Stalks 5" 12½ cm).

A. pulchrum. Ecuador. Robust plant with leathery leaves. Lobes rounded, spread wide, short. Middle lobe pointed. The many fine veins depressed. Edge flattened.

A. sagittatum (rubrinervium). Guiana. 15–18 × 10" (37½–45 cm × 26 cm). Stalks to 18" (45 cm). Veins and stalks reddish. Vein along edge.

Elliptic-leaved

All are quite alike, with rather leathery, shiny, smooth blades.

A. harrisii. Brazil. Strap Flower. Blades 12–15 × 4" 30–37½ × 10 cm). Moderately long elliptic. Stalks 6" (15 cm).

A. microphyllum. S. Brazil. Blade 6 × 3" (15 × 7½ cm). Stalks 6–8" (15–20 cm). Thick.

A. loefgrenii. S. Brazil. Long elliptic like *harrisii* but stiffer, leathery, with pale midvein.

A. longilaminatum. Brazil. 28 × 5" (70 × 12½ cm). Stalks to 16" (40 cm). Almost strapshaped.

A. offersianum. Leathery, shiny leaves, 6–8" (15–20 cm) long and half as wide. On stout stalks to 8" (20 cm).

A. pittieri. Costa Rica. Leathery, shiny, leaves. 12 × 3½" (30 × 8¼ cm).

A. ptarianum. Venezuela. Creeper, climber. Short, lanceshaped to broad elliptic. 8–12 × 6" (20–30 cm × 15 cm). Stalks 24" (60 cm). Berries red. Requires very high humidity.

A. reticulatum. Colombia. Pendant, long elliptic. 18 × 3½" (45 × 8–¾ cm). Stalks short.

A. rigidulum. Costa Rica to Colombia. Clustering epiphyte with small, leathery, elliptic leaves on short stalks. Blades 4–6" (10–15 cm).

A. scolopendrium. Costa Rica to Brazil. Long elliptic. Short stalked. Dark green with a marginal vein.

A. spathulatum. S. Venezuela. Small leaves on thin

stalks. Shiny; the midvein depressed. Blades 6 × 3″ (15 × 7½ cm).

A. trinerve. Brazil and Guiana. Blade 4–7″ (10–17½ cm) long with broad midvein and the 2 others less so. Dark green; pale below. Stalks thick, 10″ (25 cm), further thickened at joining to blade.

Halberdshaped

A. bogotense. Colombia. 18″ (45 cm) or more long. Basal lobes long, rounded, incurving. Middle lobe, long pointed. Stalks as long or longer than blades.

A. bullatum. (or × *bullatum*). 18–24″ (45–69 cm) long. Basal lobes rounded; middle lobe broad. Veins depressed, corrugated.

A. denudatum. Colombia. Basal lobes spread horizontally; middle lobe narrow, pointed. Soft textured.

A. longilinguum. Brazil. Shape like *bogotense.* Leaves clustered, 15–18″ (37½–45 cm) long. Basal lobes long, round tipped. Middle lobe pointed. Glossy green; leathery.

A. signatum. Venezuela to Ecuador. Kidneyshaped lobes almost equal in size with lanceshaped middle lobes. Veins depressed. Stems covered with fibers.

A. subsignatum (*wrightii*). Costa Rica. 'Cowface'. So-called because the long basal lobes are turned upward toward the longer middle lobe. Diameter 12″ (30 cm). Stalks as long as leaves.

Handshaped

Varying from simple compound leaves to ones that are like snowflake designs in their complexity. The simpler designs are potential pot and display plants. The more complex ones are suitable as greenhouse ornamentals.

A. eminens. Bolivia. Spidery-looking plant with very long, very narrow, strapshaped leaflets.

A. fissum (*A. palmatum*). W. Indies. Possibly the same as *A. palmatum.* 12″ (30 cm) in diameter. Segments 7, spoonshaped, the bottom two widely spread and with 2 pointed lobes. Creeper, with stem up to 36″ (90 cm) long.

A. fortunatum (*A. pedatum*) (*elegans* in horticulture). Colombia. Segments 8–15″ (20–37½ cm) long, short, strapshaped. Stalks to 20″ (50 cm).

A. helleborifolium. E. Mexico. Similar to *pedatoradiatum* but smaller. 7–11 narrow segments. Stalks 20″ (50 cm).

A. holtonianum (*A. clavigerum*). Panama and Colombia. Glossy green. 5–9 segments, deeply lobed. Middle segment 25″ (60 cm) long. Stalk to 36″ (90 cm).

A. lowii. Mexico. Compact small plant with 7 narrowly lanceshaped segments. Middle lobe has two subsidiary lobes and basal lobes one extra lobe each.

A. palmatum (*fissum*). Segments 7–11, very narrow spoonshaped, 18 × 3″ (45 × 7½ cm). Stalks to 36″ (90 cm).

A. pedatoradiatum. Mexico. Segments narrowly elliptic, 12 × 3″ (30 × 7½ cm). Two basal segments with 3 widespread lobes each. Stalks to 30″ (75 cm).

A. podophyllum (*polytomum*). Mexico. Footleaf Anthurium. Leaf diameter to 36″ (90 cm). 5–11 segments, all but 2 divided into 2–5 very long, narrow lobes. Two basal lobes divided into 5–6 very narrow lobes. Stalks to 24″ (60 cm). A beautiful species, especially attractive as a juvenile plant.

A. polyschistum. 'Putumayo'. Low-elevation Colombia. Little climber to 6′ (1.80 m), the leaves 3–4″ (7.5–10 cm) apart, compound, forming a half circle of 9–15 narrowly elliptic leaflets, 6 × ¾″ (15 cm × 19mm), 3-veined, satiny green. Stalks to 5″ (12.5 cm). An exquisite small plant easily trained on a trellis or tree-fern pole. Cuttings propagate in water. It offsets frequently. Dormant for a short period in late summer. Subject to fungus disease.

Heartshaped

A large number of Anthuriums other than the silver-veined types are broad or long heartshaped, bordering on halberd and arrowshaped. The heartshaped leaves usually have a narrower space between the basal lobes. They are usually leathery in texture and lighter colored beneath.

A. araliifolium (?). Brazil. The oddest of Anthuriums—if it is one. It has the 2 basal lobes and a squared notch instead of a pointed or curved one between them. Furthermore the middle lobe has three short-pointed lobes. Diameter 8″ (20 cm). Stalke 12″ (30 cm).

A. berriozabalense. Guatemala. Basal lobes long and crossed over each other. 9½ × 7½″ (25 × 18½ cm). Usually narrower. Stalk to 16″ (40 cm). Complex veined, and with a vein along edge.

A. cordifolium (*polyrrhizum? caribaeum?*) 22 × 12″ (55 × 30 cm) Veins raised, paler. Bluish green surface. Stalk grooved to 24″ (60 cm).

A. corrugatum (*papilionense,* in horticulture). Colombia. Gorgeous, most unusual leaf with wide notch, light green, leathery. 25 × 16″ (60 × 40 cm). Covered with a network of exceedingly fine, vertical and horizontal depressed veins, causing tiny raised rectangles. Soft, matte green.

A. fraternum. C. America. 16 × 8″ (40 × 20 cm). Stalks 16″ (40 cm). Appears to be confused with *Spathiphyllum cordatum.*

A. hoffmannii. Costa Rica. Silky, emerald green. Veins distinctly lighter. 14 × 7″ (35 × 17½ cm). A handsome species.

A. huegelii (*andicola*) Trinidad and Venezuela. Lobes short, spreading. Surface shiny, dark green. Texture thin, hard. Both surfaces black dotted. 12 × 7″ (30 × 17½ cm). Stalks red.

A. kyburzii. S. Colombia. Long heartshaped. 24 × 8″ (60 × 20 cm). Veins deeply depressed. Corrugated. Stalks to 30″ (75 cm).

A. lindenianum. Colombia. *Spathiphyllum cordatum* in trade. Also confused with *A. ornatum* but has longer middle lobe and a white spathe tipped with green. Leaves 10 × 5″ (25 × 12½ cm). Thin stalks 14″ (35 cm).

A. macdougalii. So. Mexico. Blade 8 × 7″ (20 × 17½ cm). Lobes spread, edges undulate. Leaves carried horizontally. Stalks 12″ (30 cm) or more.

A. × macrolobum (leuconeurum × pedato-radiatum). This cross produces large, heart-shaped leaves, 8 deeply cut lobes, the lobes lanceshaped; less leathery than *leuconeurum.*

A. × mortefontanense (veitchii × andreanum). Leaf about half as long as *A. veitchii,* more definitely heartshaped and broader but with deeply depressed horizontal veins, causing corrugation. 18 × 8″ (45 × 20 cm).

A. ornatum. Venezuela. Leaves reflexed, notch narrow. 10 × 7″ (25 × 17½ cm). Stalks to 24″ (60 cm). Spathe small, white. Stems covered with brown scale leaves.

A. 'Negrito' (cabrerense?). Colombia. Long pointed with rounded basal lobes. Leathery. Dark green.

A. radicans. S. Brazil. Small creeper. Blade 6″ (15 cm) long, reflexed and heavily quilted. Veins curved upward. Stalks short.

A. quindiuense. Colombia. Rosette of short leaves, fleshy, on wiry stems. Blades 6–8″ (15–20 cm) long.

A. regale. W. Brazil, E. Peru. Royal Anthurium. Incurving short, rounded lobes and lighter simple veining. Leathery. Dark olive green, pale beneath.

A. sanguineum. Colombia. From high altitude. Long, narrow. Satiny, bluish green. Leathery on a stout stalk. 15 × 4″ (37½ × 10 cm).

A. splendidum. Almost as broad as long. 12 × 11″ (30 × 27½ cm). Curved veining deeply depressed. Blade reflexed. Narrowly notched. Spathe pinkish.

A. variegatum. Ecuador. Long, pointed with red-purple small spathe.

A. wildenovii brevifolium. S. Brazil. 7 × 5″ (17½ × 12½ cm). Fleshy. Stalk thick.

A. wullschlaegeli. W. Indies. 14 × 9″ (35 × 22½ cm). Bright green above and below. Stalks to 15″ (37½ cm).

Rosette Plants

Stemless or nearly stemless plants with very short leaf stalks, arranged in a relatively loose rosette and often arising from a mound of exposed fibrous roots, called birdsnests. Most are epiphytic. The leaves are mostly coarse, fleshy, much like small or large culinary greens. Denizens of humid, warm forests. Suitable for pot culture especially as juveniles.

A. acaule. W. Indies. Leaves very long spoonshaped, leathery. 24 × 5″ (60 × 12½ cm). Stalks angled, 4–5″ (10–12½ cm).

A. affine. Brazil, Paraguay. Long, moderately wide, wavy edged, elliptic leaves. Fleshy.

A. bellum. S. Brazil. Tightly clustered, lanceshaped leaves, with veins deeply indented. 6–10 × 2–3″ (14–25 × 5–8 cm). Stalks 3 angled. Leathery.

A. comtum. S. Brazil. Spreading, leathery, dark green, long lanceshaped leaves. Blade 12″ (30 cm) long.

A. crassinervium. Panama-Venezuela. Broad spoonshaped leaves, 40″ (100 cm) long. Like a big vegetable. Fleshy.

A. crispimarginatum. N. Brazil. Dark, shiny green leaves with very wavy margins. 24 × 4″ (60 × 10 cm). Clustered, stiff, upright. Very attractive.

A. cubense. W. Indies. Big spoonshaped leaves like *A. recusatum.* 24 × 8″ (60 × 20 cm). Bird'snest.

A. haçumense. Costa Rica. 24 × 30″ (60–75 cm) long. Spoonshaped. The thick midvein lighter in color. Coarse, heavy texture. Bird'snest.

A. hookeri (huegelii) Guiana. Bird'snest Anthurium. Leaves 24 × 10″ (60 × 25 cm).

A. imperiale. (schlechtendalii) Tropical America. Leaves spoonshaped to 36″ (90 cm) or more. Leathery, corrugated, with very thick, short-angled stalks. Bird'snest.

A. maximum. Colombia. High-rain-forest plant. Bird'snest. Leaves spreading, spoonshaped, corrugated, 32″ (80 cm) long or more.

A. oblanceolatum. Tropical America. 42″ (60 cm) long, 8–10″ (20–25 cm) wide near top. Narrowing gradually to the base.

A. recusatum. Cuba. Bird'snest. Spoonshaped, leathery leaves difficult to differentiate from *A. cubense.*

A. salviniae. Guatemala. 24″ × 5″ (60 × 12½ cm). Shiny, corrugated, quilted, with flattened edges.

A. tetragonum. (Schlechtendalii) Costa Rica. Spoonshaped leaves, wide at top and narrowing gradually. 15–30″ (40–80 cm) long. Wavy margins. Very similar to *A. hookeri.*

A. venosum. Cuba. Lanceshaped, smooth, shiny, leathery leaves. 12″ (30 cm) long. Stalks 2″ (5 cm).

Strapshaped

Mostly epiphytic or growing on moist rocks. All are leathery and veining is simple. Most are very similar in appearance.

A. bakeri. Costa Rica. 24 × 3″ (60 × 7½ cm). Stalks to 10″ (25 cm).

A. coriaceum. S. Brazil. 36 × 4″ (90 × 10 cm). Epiphytic.

A. gladifolium. Venezuela to Brazil. Long pointed. 36 × 4″ (90 × 10 cm).

A. gracile. Costa Rica to Peru. A smaller plant. 12–15 × 1″ (30–37½ × 2½ cm).

A. pendulifolium. Colombia. 40 × 4″ (100 × 10 cm). Long stalked, pendant. Var. 'aureo-variegatum', beautifully variegated with yellow spotting.

A. spathiphyllum. Very similar to *A. bakeri.* Somewhat spoonshaped, 1½″ (3–¾ cm) wide.

A. veitchii. Colombia. King Anthurium. Broad strapshaped. Pendant. To 40 × 8″ (100 × 20 cm). Veins parallel, horizontal, deeply depressed, hence corrugated. Reflexed margins. Spectacular leaves for a high position.

Tridentleaved

A. arisaemoides. Ecuador. With 3 elliptic leaflets, each 6″ (15 cm) long. Three strong vertical veins. Stalks 12″ (30 cm).

A. insigne. (trilobum) Colombia. Leaflets long elliptic, glossy green, thin. Stalk thin, long.

A. trilobum (trifidum). Colombia, Ecuador. Three almost equal segments, 6–8 (15–20 cm) long. Elliptic. Stalks reddish. The best looking of this lot.

Vines

The vines not only have weak stems but depend for nourishment on attachment to moistened surfaces. However they are slow growing. Many have handshaped leaves of great beauty. Mostly untested, some may prove satisfactory for pot culture, especially as juveniles.

A. aemulum. (pentaphyllum bombacifolium) C. America. Handshaped, 18" (45 cm) in diameter. Leaflets 5–9, soft textured, spoonshaped, 9 × 3" (22½ × 7½ cm). Stalks to 18" (45 cm). Stems thin. Nodes of stem widely spaced.

A. angustisectum. Colombia. Handshaped, pendant. Segments long and narrow, almost cut to the base, 15 × 3½" (37½ × 7 cm). Stalks 20" (50 cm). Requires high humidity.

A. calense. Colombia. Halberdshaped, with long terminal lobe and roundish basals. Papery. Fresh green.

A. clavigerum. Colombia to Peru. Big vine with gorgeous, handshaped leaves 36" (90 cm) in diameter. Segments up to 9, segmented again and lobed.

A. digitatum. (A. pentaphyllum digitatum) Venezuela. Handshaped to 24" (60 cm) diameter. Leaflets 7, spoonshaped, shiny, leathery. Elliptic to 12 × 3½" (30 × 8½ cm). Leaves clustered at the nodes.

A. dussii. W. Indies. Big plant. Leaves 14" (35 cm) long heartshaped. Bright green.

A. enneaphyllum (variabile). Brazil. Like *digitatum*, but leaflets narrower, therefore more strapshaped. Measurements similar.

A. guildingii. (A. ravenii) Guadeloupe. Same as *dussii?*). More halberdshaped. Satiny. Corrugated. Margins undulate.

A. gymnopus. Cuba. Heartshaped, broad, cupped, nearly round, on thin stems.

A. kalbreyeri (A. clavigerum) (araliifolium in horticulture). Similar to *aemulum,* but leaflets broader, more spoonshaped, heavier textured; and leaf stalk very short.

A. latihastatum. Costa Rica. Tridentshaped. Segments narrow. Middle lobe 12 × 3½" (30 × 8¼ cm). Basal lobes somewhat shorter. Stalks to 12" (30 cm). Descriptions vary.

A. myosuroides. Costa Rica to Colombia in rain forest. Thin climber with small, long-heartshaped leaves, papery on thin stalks.

A. panduratum. (A. clavigerum) N. Brazil. Handshaped to 36" (90 cm) diameter. 7 leaflets, deeply lobed, drooping.

A. 'Patulum'. Ecuador. Halberdshaped. Smooth surfaced, shiny green. Basal lobes oval.

A. pentaphyllum. (longissimum?) Colombia to Brazil. Heartshaped. 5–7 narrowly elliptic segments. Basal lobes each with small attached lobe. Stalk grooved.

A. scandens. W. Indies, C. America to Ecuador. Pearl Anthurium. Dwarf creeper-climber. Leaves 3–7" (7½–17½ cm). Thin stem with brown scales.

A. undatum. W. Brazil and E. Peru. Tridentleaved. Leaflets arranged in a triangle. Spoonshaped. 10 × 4" (25 × 10 cm).

Aphelandra **Acanthaceae.** American tropics. Filtered to partial sun. 400–800 fc. Temperature min. 60°F (16°C). Humidity min. 50%. Houseplant Mix #2. Propagated from seeds and cuttings. Not easy as a houseplant. 80 species of which 4 or 5 grown indoors.

One species, *A. squarrosa,* is common in the shops; the others but rarely. Most of the genus is like a dwarf form of the tropical Justicias, therefore rather better suited to medium-sized pots. A few species are grown for their flowers alone.

A. bahiensis. Brazil. The leaves elliptical, 4" (10 cm) long; green above and purple beneath. Flowers 1" (2.5 cm) long, tubeshaped with colored bracts; both yellow. Beautiful foliage plant but rarely grown.

A. chamissoniana. Brazil. Shrubby, with narrowly elliptic leaves to 5" (12.5 cm). Veins, spreading, whitish. Spikes of 2" (5 cm) flowers.

A. ignea. To 6" (15 cm) high, spreading. Leaves, cleft at base, 4" (10 cm) long. Flowers 1½" (3.8 cm) long, yellow. Sometimes confused with *Xantheranthemum igneum.* Better for bloom than foliage.

A. squarrosa. Zebra Plant. Brazil. By far the most popular species. A split personality as it is usually sold in bloom and also has attractive, shiny, white-veined leaves.

A well-known houseplant nurseryman used to give his *A. squarrosa* plants a disapproving kick every time he passed them. This was not quite fair, because the difficulties are not so much in the production as in keeping them happy indoors. They are a favorite impulse purchase because of their showy leaves, rather than the flowers. But we have rarely seen them survive for long in good condition indoors. They can be recommended, nevertheless, for low mass plantings in large landscaped interior gardens where they receive professional attention.

Virtually all the plants now grown for market are compact cultivars that are sold when no more than 15" (37.5 cm) high, though they grow taller. All are single stemmed. Leaves are 6–8" (15–20 cm) long, broadly oval-pointed. In the species, if it still exists in cultivation, they can reach 12" (30 cm) in length. Veins are broad and deeply imbedded, white, forming quilts, the side veins vertical to the broad midrib. Flowers in short, square-sided spikes, are yellow.

For best growth keep in filtered sunlight at a humidity level above 50%. Do not water until the soil is quite dry. Overwatering can produce leaf and stem rot. Maintain moderate summer temperature and good ventilation. It is difficult to trim the plants. Usually they begin to deteriorate after reaching flowering size. It is, therefore, best to take cuttings with a leaf attached and propagate under a transparent cover and over bottom heat.

The principal cultivars have been 'Dania', 'Louisiae compacta' and the smaller 'Uniflora Beauty'. There is also 'Apollo', which is heavily gray felted and most spectacular. We are not aware of its origin. It was available for a while but has not appeared to our knowledge recently. It resembles a young loquat plant, but growers must have had difficulties.

A. tetragona. A shrub mainly grown for scarlet flowers, as are some well-known species that we have not included here.

Araucaria. **Araucariaceae.** So. S. America, Australia, Norfolk Island. Evergreen Tree. Partial to full sun. Min. 45°F (7°C). Humidity 50%. Cactus & Succulent mix #2 without lime. Propagation from seed. Difficult. 15 species of which one grown indoors.

These are evergreen trees that are grown in full sunshine mostly in the subtropics. They were common as juvenile pot plants, to 10' (3 m) in height, during the 1970s and recommended for indoor display. Recently they have been less in evidence. They are very fast growers from seed and therefore favored by nurserymen. But their ability to tolerate low light levels has been exaggerated. Without full sunlight, one set of branches after another turn brown. We believe that the survival rate indoors is poor. They may do better in the south.

A. heterophylla (excelsa). Norfolk Island Pine. The trunk is perfectly straight; branches are concentrated around widely separated joints and grow out horizontally—about 7 to each. The branches of this unusually symmetrical tree are divided into many branchlets forming a long, wide triangle clothed in numerous, short needles. The tree reaches a maximum height of 200 feet (60 m) in nature. Potted plants are usually 3–6" (90 cm–1.80 m) high, with 3–5 sets of branches.

'Gracilis'. Needles more densely packed along the branchlets. 'Glauca' carries its branchlets curving upward.

A. heterophylla prefers a soil with a pH of 5.5–6.5 and may need acidifying applications with the soil mix. Feed with high nitrate fertilizer. Water when soil is dry. The trees are sensitive to polluted air.

The very large seeds soon germinate when laid on moist soil in a warm environment. But without very bright light the distance between joints will become excessive; we have seen this phenomenon frequently in nursery-grown plants. Do not trim this tree except to encourage suckers around the base of the trunk. The symmetry will be spoiled for good, but you may secure a good harvest of plants to propagate.

The other species, including the famous Monkey Puzzle Tree, *A. araucana*, from Chile, are not suited to indoor culture. *A. columnaris*, the New Caledonia Pine, is much like *A. heterophylla*, but the distance between the joints is shorter. We have not seen it at nurseries or florists recently.

Ardisia. **Myrsinaceae.** Nearly worldwide warm temperate and subtropics. Shrubs and trees. Filtered to partial sun. 400–800 fc 14 hours daily. Temperature 40–80°F (4–27°C). Medium 3 parts sterilized garden soil to 1 part sphagnum peat. Houseplant Mix #2. Propagation from seed and cuttings. Moderately difficult. 250 species of which possibly 4 are grown indoors.

The Ardisias belong to the group of woody plants that do much better, even indoors, in the Northwest of the U.S.A. or in England than elsewhere because of their need for cool temperatures in summer. Some may be hardy in winter. Except for the well-known *A. crenata* we list nursery catalog plants with which we are not familiar but which we suspect require even cooler conditions and, very possibly, more light. The general shape of these shrubs is columnar and they make, when tall, good architectural plants.

A. crassifolia(?). Described as having narrowly elliptic leaves.

A. crenata. (Not *crenulata. A. crispa* in horticulture.) Coralberry. A plant much grown in greenhouses and indoors. India to Japan. A woody shrub that grows to 6' (1.80 m) outdoors but usually no more than 2–3' (60–90 cm) indoors. The leaves are leathery, shiny dark green, elliptic, shallowly and closely undulating; up to 4" (10 cm) long. It produces clusters of small white flowers followed by long-lasting, showy red berries. These are its chief attraction. It is a handsome shrub that is slow growing and long-lived when well established.

It requires filtered sunlight for maintenance and partial sun for flowers and berries. Even moisture. Fertilize every 2 months with 30-10-10. Treat with chelated iron (Sequestrene or other) twice a year. Provide very good ventilation with night in winter down to 50–55°F (10–13°C).

A. crispa. Japan. The true species. Differs from *crenata* principally in having smooth-edged leaves. Rarely grown indoors.

A. japonica. A semihardy small shrub to 1½' (45 cm). Extremely slow growing and frequently dwarfed and trained as bonsai. Leaves elliptic to 4" (10 cm) long. There are a number of cultivars which are variegated with different patterns, namely, 'Hakubotan', 'Hinotsukasa', 'Maculata', 'Marginata' and 'Matsu-Shima'. They should be tried for cool windowsill culture.

Arundinaria. (*Sasa*). **Graminiae.** Bamboo Cane. Asia. Woody grass. Filtered sun. Min. 400 fc. Temperature min. 40°F (4°C). Houseplant Mix #2 with sand. Propagation by division. Easy. 30 species of which 2 are grown indoors.

Small and giant grasses that include Tonkin Cane, growing to 40' (12 m). Formerly the premium bamboo for fly fishing rods.

A. fortunei (*Sasa fortunei*) = *A. variegata*, see below.

A. pygmaea. (*Sasa pygmaea*). Pygmy Bamboo. Offsetting tufts of erect grassy stems to 8" (30 cm) high, bearing 6–10 alternate, strapshaped pointed leaflets ¾ × ½" (18.6 × 12.5 mm) with very short stalks. Keep moderately moist. Fertilize sparingly with a balanced formula. Trim dead leaves and brown leaf tips. Colonizes and is easy to divide. Excellent for dish gardens and other small displays. Host to mites.

A. variegata (*fortunei*). Dwarf Variegated Bamboo. Offsetting, with stems to 3' (90 cm). Leaves alternate, 5 × ¾" (12.5 cm × 18.6 mm), vertically striped with white. An undisciplined but colorful plant. Pot-bind to keep small. Divide to propagate.

145

Asparagus. **Liliaceae.** Asparagus Fern. S. Africa.

Fine-leaved vines or canes from tuberous roots. Filtered to partial sun. 300–800 fc. Min. 50°F (10°C). Medium; 1 part humus, 1 part sterilized garden soil, 1 part sand. Or Cactus and Succulent Mix #2. Easy. Propagation from cuttings, division and seeds. Possibly 300 species of which a half dozen grown indoors.

These horticultural relatives of the common vegetable, Asparagus, are known as Asparagus Ferns because of their needlelike leaves or cladophylls. They are easy to grow in either relatively low light or moderate to full sunlight. *A. setaceous,* the original Asparagus Fern, has adapted to our seasons and is to be kept moist in summer and rather dry in winter. But some of the others still follow reverse seasons and are partially dormant in summer. When they stop growing after May, water sparingly until October when they usually resume growth.

Fertilize heavily during the growing months with a balanced formula. Roots are large. To keep the plants under control they should be divided and repotted yearly. They are occasionally attacked by spider mites (red). Overwatering causes root rot during cool periods or dormancy.

A. asparagoides. The Smilax of the florists, rarely grown by indoor gardeners. It is a vigorous, tuberous-rooted, branching vine with elliptic to lanceshaped leaves, 2″ × 1″ (2.5 × 1 cm), spaced 1–4″ (2.5–10 cm) apart.

'Myrtifolius'. The leaves are half size and closer together. This cultivar deserves more attention as it is useful in covering trellised walls. Trimmed, it makes a quite presentable pot plant that is long-lived and easy.

A. densiflorus. It is said that the true species is probably not in cultivation, and the identity of the cultivars is in dispute. However, the visible differences are so obvious that there is no problem for the amateur.

'Myers' ('Myersii', 'Meyer's) is a tuberous rooted, stemless plant that produces closely bunched, erect canes to a length of 2′ (60 cm). Innumerable clusters of needlelike leaves on branchlets form a gradually tapering tube or foxtail, an appearance unique among foliage plants. This is among the most dramatic of pot or basket plants. The symmetrical cloud of greenery, bright light green, can be displayed effectively as a specimen or the plants massed architecturally.

It appears on the market in quantity only in years when there is a good crop of seed. Indoors, propagation is usually by division. Do not allow to become pot-bound but divide frequently as needed; at least once a year for a vigorous plant. This is the most temperamental of the Asparagus Ferns and not at all easy to keep in top condition. High humidity and frequent misting are advisable. Fertilize sparingly.

'Myriocladus' (*A. myriocladus*) has long, ¼–½″ (6.25–12.5 mm) thick, whitish tubers and flexible, prickly canes up to 4′ (1.20 m) long. The needlelike leaves are clustered at the joints. This is a rather rank and unruly pot plant, but when half grown canes are trimmed back they will branch, and it becomes possible to maintain a more dense, compact, shrubby appearance that is quite attractive. As it produces an excess of tubers, decant once a year, remove dead tubers and trim about half of the remainder before repotting.

'Pyramidalis'. The canes are weak and hang over the sides of the pots or baskets dangling branches densely covered with soft, very dark green, needlelike leaves. The effect is odd, impressive and rather disorderly.

'Retrofractus' (*A. retrofractus*). Considered possibly a cultivar of *A. macowanii.* Quite similar to 'Myriocladus' except that the canes are much stiffer and the clusters of leaves are located at widely separated joints.

'Sprengeri' is widely used as a basket plant in restaurants and stores because of its tolerance of neglect and resistance to pollution. It also makes a fine pot or tub plant when supported on a pedestal. The flexible 2½′ (75 cm) canes bear longer, coarser, less numerous needles than 'Myers'. It tolerates bright shade but does better in partial sun. More drought resistant than 'Myers'; a drying out for 2–3 days is rarely harmful. There are several forms of 'Sprengeri', some with coarser leaves, more bluish-green color or shorter canes. In very low-light situations leaves will brown.

A. falcatus. Sickle Thorn. A robust, woody vine with a spiny stem and narrow, strapshaped leaves 2–3″ (5–7.5 cm) long. They are virtually stalkless and appear in groups of threes from the joints. It has little merit as a pot or vining plant.

A. scandens. A weak-stemmed, climbing vine to 10′ (3 m) or more with blue-green needle leaves in clusters of threes. The Var. *deflexus* is somewhat shorter, the needle leaves very numerous and distinctly metallic blue. A good sprawler in the greenhouse among other foliage plants. But we think that it can be trimmed and should be grown in pots more often as it is very fluffy and possesses a seductive charm wherever we have seen it. Excellent for a filtered sun situation.

The vines are attractive twined around pillars or trained on trellises as screens. The upright plants, massed in troughs, are an exotic way to create passages and can be used on low walls and dividers.

Aspidistra. **Liliaceae.** Cast-Iron Plant. Asia. Stemless herb to 2′ (60 cm). Shade to full sun. Min. 40°F (4°C). Houseplant Mix #2 or Sterilized Garden Soil. Propagation by division. Easy. 8 species; 1 grown indoors.

A. elatior. A legendary plant from Victorian times, this *Aspidistra* almost dropped out of sight and is still relatively rare because of its extremely slow growth which has made it an uneconomic crop. Recently tropical nurseries have been able to speed up the process. So a revival is taking place.

Leaves grow from a thick stem that crawls, partly buried on the surface of the soil. Blades are long, elliptic, 16–18″ × 4–5″ (40–45 × 10–12.5 cm). Stalk 6″ (15 cm). Flourishes in a north window or under 50 fc.

146

Prefers to be kept moist but tolerates neglect. Fertilize 4 times a year with a balanced formula. Disease and pest resistant. Sections are easily divided for propagation. Sprouts new leaves more readily when the rhizome is buried in the soil.

Ideal foliage plants for low-light situations anywhere, being even less troublesome and vulnerable than Dracaenas. Ideal for the lazy indoor gardener but also very handsome as decoration.

'Milky Way' and 'Minor'. Leaves are narrow, lighter green, less shiny and dusted with white spots.

'Variegata'. Wide leaves vertically banded with alternate white and green stripes. Shiny surfaced.

The Japanese have developed a number of other named cultivars with unusual variegation patterns, but these are still rarely available.

Aucuba. Cornaceae. Gold Dust Tree. Eastern Asia and Japan. Filtered sun or 300 fc. (12 hrs) daily. Temperature min. 40°F (4°C). Houseplant Mix #3 or Sterilized Garden soil with peat added. Large shrub. Propagated by cuttings. Difficult indoors. 3–7 species; 1 occasionally grown indoors.

Aucuba is a shrub with coarse, thick, but colorfully spotted leaves. Though often described as merely cool growing it is actually hardy. Use in cool, low-light situations and do not expose to summer heat. Excellent for massplantings. Very resistant to aerial pollution. Pot in acid (5.5–6.5 pH) garden soil. Keep constantly moist. Fertilize with high nitrate formula and add micronized or chelated iron yearly. As pot plants the dwarf cultivars are preferable. *Dracaena surculosa (godseffiana)* which has similar spotting is a smaller plant but more adaptable to a variety of conditions.

A. japonica is the most cultivated species. Woody and branched, with a habit like that of *Rhododendron*. Leaves are stiff, elliptic, toothed, to 7" (17.5 cm) long, shiny and most often splashed with yellow spots. There are many cultivars. 'Maculata' (or 'Variegata') is the typical Gold Dust Tree. There is also a gamut of varieties with narrower, longer or shorter leaves. A compact one is 'Nana'. Others are 'Crotonifolia', white spotted; 'Fructu Alba', with silver variegation; 'Goldieana', almost entirely yellow.

Ballota. Labiatae. Western Mediterranean. Herb. Partial sun. 500–600 fc. 12 hours daily. Sterilized Garden soil with lime or Houseplant Mix #1 with lime. Propagation by cuttings and seeds. Easy. 35 species of which 2 are frequently cultivated indoors.

One of the herbs is called Horehound, but the Black Horehound, *B. nigra*, is too large and much less interesting than the following 2 species for growing indoors. Leaves aromatic.

Both species prefer close to 50°F (10°C) at night in winter. Should dry out completely for a full day between waterings. Fertilize with a formula high in phosphate and potash. These are interesting and oddly attractive curiosities.

B. acepabalosa. Shrubby to 15" (37.5 cm), erect: so heavily white-woolly that the branches look like pipe cleaners. Leaves short, arrowshaped, heavily felted,

gray-green, 1" (2.5 cm) long on ½" (12.5 mm) stalks, paired-alternate. Tiny, white, woolly flowers at the joints.

B. pseudodictamnus. Similar growth habit with woolly-silvery leaves, apple green when young. Clusters of tiny silvery mauve flowers.

Bambusa. Graminiae. Tropical and subtropical Asia and the Americas. Mostly shrubby to treelike grasses. Filtered to partial sun. 400–700 fc. 12 hours daily. Temperature min. 45°F (7°C). Houseplant Mix #3 with sand. Humidity min. 40%. Propagation by division. Fairly easy. 100 species of which a few have been grown indoors.

Of the tall and woody grasses commonly called Bamboos, some produce offsets close to the base of the stems, others colonize by means of extensive underground runners. There are tropical and hardy species. Not much is known about the behavior indoors of these graceful, screening plants that, from a decorative standpoint, should have many uses.

We confess, because of our lack of experience with these plants, to treating the Bamboos very superficially, and we have seen no immediate need to describe all the principal cultivated species without having adequate information as to their relative potentials for indoor decorative use. We have chosen a dwarf *Arundinaria* with which we have had experience, a shrubby medium-sized *Bambusa* and a tall, thick-stemmed *Phyllostachys*. Other genera that might be considered are: *Chimonobambusa*, E. & S. Asia; *Pseudosasa*, Japan; *Sasa*, Japan; and *Semiarundinaria*, Japan.

Recently one firm has been supplying 50–70' (15–21 m) stems grown in the open in North Carolina. They have been very handsome decorations for the atrium of the IBM building in New York City, where they are planted in irrigated troughs a sufficient distance apart under a high glass roof. They have done well under natural sunlight until a new adjacent building obstructed part of the illumination thus requiring the installation of powerful lamps to extend the day length. They are probably a *Phyllostachys* species.

As Bamboos come in many sizes, such complex installations as that at IBM are not necessary. They should be very useful in smaller plantings. The dwarfs fit in 4–10" (10–25 cm) diameter pots. There is no reason why medium sizes cannot be grown in homes near sunny windows in tubs. Southern indoor gardeners should have few problems maintaining them.

B. glaucescens. A shrubby bamboo to 10' × 1½' (3 m × 3.75 cm), green leaved, later yellowish. Blades narrowly lanceshaped to 4" (10 cm).

Members of the genus are much used as garden ornamentals in subtropical conditions, and many named cultivars have been developed. These differ in height from dwarfs to 40' (12 m), and blades are striped with yellow, silver or white. To a number of these, botanists have ascribed individual species names, with what justification they themselves must eventually decide. Thus the genus includes a wide range of material in which the adaptability of different clones to indoor culture is uncertain.

Beaucarnea. **Agavaceae.** Ponytail Plant. Texas and Mexico. Succulent trees. Shade to full sun. Temperature min. 45°F (7°C). Houseplant Mix #1 or #2 with sand. Propagation by seed and offsets. Cast Iron. 6 species; 1 grown indoors.

B. recurvata. A superb sculptural plant tolerant of different environments and almost any amount of abuse. Outdoors it grows with a single stem, sometimes short branched at the top, to max. 30' (9 m). The base is an impressive, brown, woody cone (caudex). Indoor specimens are occasionally to 10' (3 m) while pot size ranges from a few inches to 5' (1.50 m).

Growing in tight spirals only on the tops of stems and branches, the leaves are very numerous, tough, max. ½" (12.5 mm) wide and up to 6' (1.80 m) long, hanging vertically. The var. *intermedia,* which is half as tall, is frequently grown.

Once the base has formed, even if only 1–2" (2.5–5 cm) across, the plants need a minimum of attention. North light or 50 fc. is ample. One can water them regularly or keep dry for a month or two at a time. Indoor temperatures matter little. Fertilizing with a balanced formula 2–3 times a year is ample.

Our own *Beaucarnea* is 4½' (1.35 m) tall, rather pot-bound in an 8" (20 cm) diameter pot. Single stemmed, the leaves reach almost to soil level. It is at least 30 years old. Such a plant grows twice as fast if given a larger pot and watered frequently.

The trimmed plants, usually no more than 2' (60 cm) tall and bearing several tufts of leaves are, in our opinion, mutilated and ugly. Nurserymen have used some of the tufts for propagation. The proper and decorative way to grow is with a single stem. The great number of leaves sinuously cascading down is a sight unique among foliage plants.

Begonia. **Begoniaceae.** Worldwide subtropics and tropics. Fleshy, leafy herbs. Filtered to partial sun. 300–800 fc. Temperature (for most) 57–75°F (23–30°C). Humidity min. 40%. Houseplant Mix #1, #2 or #3 with lime. Propagation from leaf or stem cuttings or seeds. Rather difficult. Over 1,000 species and 10,000 cultivars.

We confess to having had more difficulty writing about this genus than any other and suspect that our text reflects this. One cause is the huge number of species and cultivars that are being grown primarily for foliage by hobbyists, and the continuous introduction of new species and hybrids. Another is the excessive enthusiasm exhibited by their devotees who minimize the difficulties encountered in growing them indoors. This is understandable because no plant in this list exhibits greater diversity and beauty of foliage. In size Begonias are just right for pot culture in the home. They are relatively free of pests. Their cultural requirements seem to be simple. Novice indoor gardeners are naturally attracted to them.

But note the following:

1. The majority of species and cultivars are grown with ease in greenhouses or indoors where temperatures are moderate, the nights cool and the plants can be summered out-of-doors. The Pacific Coast offers those conditions.

2. But, in the rest of the country and especially in cities, Begonias do poorly indoors. Some manage very well in warm terrariums with high humidity. The majority succumb to summer and winter temperatures indoors, falling prey to fungal diseases. Under adverse conditions watering that simultaneously promotes growth and does not expose the plants to disease demands a refinement of technique and knowledge that few growers possess. Some of the best houseplant specialists we know have given them up. The successful ones have created special environments for their plants with considerable cost and effort.

3. Finally, the number of species that are reasonably tolerant of indoor environments is quite small while their look-alike cultivars are legion.

Thus it has been a real problem to decide how to organize the vast plant material and to decide which species or cultivars to mention. We have limited ourselves to a general survey of types and a very few specific plants. Our remarks are the result of lengthy experience with the genus and continuous observation of actual results achieved by the many Begonia growers we have known.

We believe that the craving for novelty has impeded development of more adaptable plants as it has for so many other far less interesting genera. Whenever the popularity of a plant depends on newness rather than improvement, fewer worthwhile ones remain available as they are superseded by others with untried characteristics. The potential for use remains great which is the reason that we give space to this maddeningly complex and unpredictable subject.

As pot plants they are rarely used as more than temporary displays in commercial situations. Basket plants fluctuate in popularity as decoration for restaurants. Florists in the eastern U.S.A. carried many foliage Begonias a few years ago but recently they have become scarce, probably for the reasons we have mentioned.

Although justly famous for their shapely, colorful foliage it has been the more floriferous plants that have stood up best in public esteem: Semperflorens or Wax Begonias as reliable bedding plants; the spring-flowering, tuberous Begonias for large and gorgeously colored flowers; the × Hiemalis and × Cheimanthes for more numerous smaller ones in winter. Also a number of the cane types are grown by hobbyists for their large, pendant clusters of white or pink blooms. However, the Begonias that concern us here are those with few or less attractive flowers but handsome leaves. We omit mention of semivining plants and confine ourselves to pot, basket and terrarium plants that typically are, useful for amateur indoor gardeners and may serve the purposes of plantscapers.

The great variety of leaf forms accompanied by decorative surface textures and colorings would lead one to expect Begonias to be among the most popular of indoor plants. That is not the case because the range of the cultural tolerance of individual species and cultivars is rather narrow and their usable life comparatively short. We believe that selected species or cultivars could be grown more widely by amateurs and be useful to indoor landscapers. However, practicality has not been the deciding principle either in collecting or hybridizing. As in so many of the variable plant genera, sheer novelty has taken over and adaptability neglected. Although we have a fairly wide experience growing the plants, we find it difficult to pinpoint any but a few species and their cultivars that possess sufficient tolerance of varied environments and treatments to recommend them to the average amateur any more than the professional plantscaper.

Our West Coast climate is particularly suited to a large number of species and cultivars. Heat is moderate by day and drops sharply for much of the year at night. Many others require high humidity accompanied by tropical temperatures, conditions best achieved in a greenhouse or terrarium. The difficulties experienced by most urban growers is therefore understandable. Summer day temperatures are much too high and the drop at night is insufficient. The plants are sensitive to aerial pollution. Overwatering is a common cause of loss. Fungus infections are frequent and so persistent that commercial growers have experienced great difficulty in coping with them.

Nomenclature. The number of species and, especially, cultivars is so great that there is no publication in print providing precise descriptions of habit and foliage necessary to differentiate them. Among the cultivars there is a considerable number of look-alikes that only devoted experts can tell apart. We, therefore, advise amateurs and professionals to refer to *Begonias* by Mildred L. and Edward I. Thompson, Times Books, 1981, for detailed categorizing, listing and illustrations, plus extensive authoritative cultural directions. For descriptions of the plants one must refer to the several catalogs of major Begonia nurseries. All we can do here is to provide general information based on our own experience.

Light. Light requirements cover a wide range. By and large, best results are achieved with partial to nearly full sun but most Begonias can also be grown in filtered sun. They are not shade-loving plants. Cane-type Begonias are the most demanding in respect to bright illumination. Many plants do very well under fluorescent light for 10–12 hours daily. Poor light causes lengthening of plants and encourages fungus infections.

Temperature. Some texts would lead us to believe that the plants will tolerate a wide range of temperature. This is true only of selected species and cultivars. The vast majority are cool growing, preferring the range between 58° and 72°F (14.5°–23°C), which is narrow inded. It is true that many plants will survive above and below this range for a time, but also that they are subject to disease at both extremes. Experienced growers know that Begonias collapse in northern Julys and Augusts when the temperature rises above 80°F (27°C). They are happiest on our West Coast where, even when the midday temperature is high, there is a sharp drop at night. As a type Rex Begonias are the principal exception, but they require a minimum temperature even higher than most tropical plants, namely 70°F (22°C) yet suffer when the thermometer rises above 85°F (29.5°C). This hardly allows, in both instances, for a wide range of tolerance. In northern urban centers many plants will do well in air conditioned rooms, but only those tolerant of relatively low humidity.

These requirement are a sufficient indication of how important it is to choose plants that suit your environmental conditions. That is not made any easier by the fact that most nurseries and florists have only the most rudimentary knowledge of the indoor cultural needs of the plants they sell.

Humidity. Very few Begonias thrive in low humidity. The medium range is 40–60%, but whereas many tropical genera can do very well with less than the optimum, Begonias do require the minimum or leaves will brown and growth be stunted. Rhizomatous and Shrubby Begonias both prefer 60% or higher, and a large number must be grown in terrariums to maintain humidity at proper levels. Rex Begonias must have 50% or higher.

Watering. Begonias are extremely sensitive to improper watering. Overwatering is especially pernicious although the plants are not at all drought resistant. The perfect condition is one of an absolutely even, just damp moisture level in very well-aerated medium. We often speak of "even moisture" which is never quite attainable except in a terrarium. This is close to being necessary for Begonias. So touchy is this matter that we have known specialists who consistently allowed their plants to reach the point of drooping before giving them a thorough dousing. It is a method that works very well as long as one is always present to note the symptoms. For the above reasons it is not usually advisable to grow Begonias on capillary matting. If the temperature is too cool or too warm excess watering will cause fungus infections. It need not be stressed that water should always be room temperature.

Fertilizing. Not a specially difficult matter with Begonias. Apply a balanced formula (20-20-20 for instance) every 3 weeks in summer and 5–6 weeks in winter.

Medium. In addition to those listed in our heading, many growers use a mix of approximately 2 parts sterilized garden soil, preferably somewhat clayey, 1 part sphagnum peat moss, 1 part perlite and 1 part Houseplant Mix. Add 1 tbsp. dolomite lime to the quart unless your water is hard. Use Houseplant Mix #1 for cuttings and for seeding. Cuttings also do well in live or long-fiber sphagnum moss.

Ventilation. Good aeration is important. Pollution-free air, open windows, fans, all help to maintain healthy plants.

Propagation. By leaf cuttings and stem cuttings. Leaf blades are sometimes cut in half horizontally, furled and stuck into the medium after a dusting of rooting hormone. Keep covered and at 70–75°F (22–24.5°C) in bright, indirect light. Leaves are also pinned to the medium surface and the principal veins cut with a razor. Plantlets develop at the cuts. Some species and cultivars will root if leaf blades and stalks are partially submerged in water. Cuttings, following the development of roots, should be transplanted to Houseplant Mix #1.

Potting. Nothing much to be said here except that shallow rooting calls for shallow pots, and that those plants that have spreading branches look superb in a basket.

Diseases and Pests. As we have stated elsewhere, we are not especially knowledgeable regarding diseases of plants. Neither amateurs in general nor plantscapers require any information in depth on this subject because they are both consumers and usually have neither the facilities nor the time to spend on the problem unless the circumstances are unusual. That is more the business of commercial growers. Differentiating between diseases is, therefore, not a prime necessity.

Begonias are more subject than most tropical plants to a variety of fungus and other diseases. Powdery mildew is one that is easily recognized and for which there are numerous sprays on the market. Root and stem rot are something else. But once the plant is attacked, analysis of the cause requires instant action and that is almost impossible for both categories of growers. The general advice of experienced Begonia growers is to spray the plants with a general fungicide at least every couple of weeks. This advice indicates the prevalence of the problem. And that is the only advice we can give. Any nursery supply company can suggest a combination of sprays that will provide some protection. The best course is prevention—good cultural procedures.

Leaves. The majority of Begonia leaves are asymmetrical; one side of the blade is narrower or shorter than the other. Thus a lanceleaf takes on an angelwing shape, the base of one side being attached at the level of the stalk, the other side projecting beyond the attachment of the stalk. Frequently the stalk is attached inside the edge of the blade or even at or near its center (peltate). Variations in this feature are responsible for much of the variety of leaf pattern.

Surface textures are extraordinarily varied, being oily shiny, hairy dull, quilted, puckered (bullate), etc. Edges are even, toothed, jagged, segmented, even divided into leaflets.

Coloring can occur in zones, spots and splashes or lines. Deep green, light green, chartreuse, brown, black, white, red, purple, appear on different species and cultivars. Metallic silver as a solid background, along veining or in spots is of frequent occurrence. The undersides range from green to brilliant red.

In short, it is impossible to categorize coloring except that the tints generally are fairly muted and

more evident when observing a single plant than when a great number is massed together, which produces a rather gloomy effect.

Stalks are long or short according to the species, but always fleshy and green to pink in coloration.

Rhizomatous Begonias. Rhizomes are thickened rootstocks; very fleshy in the case of Begonia. They creep just below or on the surface of the soil, may rise upright or bend over the edge of a pot or basket as they grow. The leaves grow from the joints of these roots. Thus the shape of the plants is very much determined by the meanderings of the root. If there is much branching the plant will be bushy; if not it may just wander. To some extent this can be controlled by confining the root and pushing it in a direction with inverted V-shaped wires pinning it down. Flowers are usually on long stalks, fairly numerous, 4-petalled, watery, pink or white. However the leaves are the main attraction. Unless given perfect culture most of these plants will go into dormancy, usually in winter, losing some leaves and ceasing to grow. Watering must be very sparing at such times, as the slightest excess can be fatal. Wait until the surface is thoroughly dry.

Miniatures with Leaves Max. 3″ (7.5 cm)

Unless the indoor environment is very humid and the temperature perfectly controlled these plants should be grown in terrariums where they thrive, being among the finest plants for this use. They are generally compact and rounded.

A large number of cultivars are derived by breeding or selection from B. bowerae (Mexico), the Stitchleaf Begonia. Blades are short angelwing shape, bright green with black check marks along the edge. Var. nigramarga has even smaller leaves with black veins and hairy edges. 'Chantilly Lace' is a popular member of this group. Black markings are a feature of a very large number of the cultivars.

Another set is roundish leaved with a central red spot.

B. prismatocarpa is a tiny-leaved plant with relatively large, 2-petalled, yellow flowers, grown for these alone. But a white-variegated variety is also pretty as a foliage plant.

All of these plants are best grown in terrarium conditions.

Medium-leaved Plants (3–6″, 7.5–15 cm)

Included are many larger versions of the B. bowerae type with various black markings. Also starshaped leaves having triangular lobes, similarly black marked. An old favorite is B. 'Cleopatra', with starshaped, yellow-green leaves spotted with chocolate. B. 'Gaystar' is even darker. Here also the red spot in the center appears. The whole group shows evidence of the constant interbreeding of similar plants.

Large-leaved Plants, (6–12″, 15–30 cm).

Very heavy-leaved plants in much the same vein as the previous sizes but with more oval or roundish blades, crested or ruffled. Huge star shapes occur. There are even leaves greater in diameter than 12″ (30 cm) including some with upright thickened stems. The leaves consist of several narrow leaflets and are described as palmlike.

Distinctive Foliage. In addition to these interrelated plants there are various categories of plants with unusual foliage. For instance there are the plants derived from *B. imperialis,* called the pustular type, with very low, grainy puckering, causing metallic reflections. *B. imperialis* is reddish brown and lime green. *B. pustulata* is yellow-green with darker areas and a red border. Here, too, are some of the silver and green cultivars such as *B.* 'Silver Jewell'.

Among the small-leaved plants are *B. versicolor,* with rounded blades bearing a network of silver and maroon veins. On *B.* 'It' the green leaves are splashed with silver.

The large-leaved species and cultivars include *B. masoniana,* formerly a favorite florist plant. The 'Iron Cross' Begonia has heartshaped yellow to apple green leaves with broad radiating bands of chocolate brown in the center. The surface is uniformly and deeply puckered (bullate). It requires Rex Begonia treatment. There is also a whole series of lanceshaped glossy-leaved plants.

Rex Cultorum. This is the horticultural name for an immense list of cultivars that, as noted, require higher minimum temperatures. They have the thickened stems of the Rhizomatous Begonias, but the flowers are few, unattractive and borne on short stalks close to the base. The leaves are generally broad, angelwing shape, some with toothed edges and others heavily lobed. A typical pattern is a colorful or dark area above the attachment of the stalk, a lighter outer area all the way to the edge or with the edge also colored. The colorings are the finest in the whole family. There are magnificent silver types, concentric colorful zonings, and all kinds of spottings and veinings. Also prevalent are blades curled in a helix; that is to say that the larger side of the blade is curved around the attachment of the stalk forming a fascinatingly shaped vortex.

The size of leaves ranges from a few inches to a foot or more, and well-grown plants have no peers for splendor in the whole foliage world. Maintaining perfect form, however, is impossible except on a temporary basis, the stems soon growing outward and old leaves dying off, so that it is essential to propagate leaves and grow on new specimen plants. They are strictly for temporary display. Naturally the choice of cultivars must be left to each individual or rest on availability from nurseries. They make splendid temporary massed displays.

Fibrous-Rooted Begonias. This is the other larger category. The roots of these plants are normal, consisting of a few branches and many fine branchlets. They reach down somewhat further into the medium but must still be rated as shallow. The percentage of long angelwing-shaped leaves is very great and the form usually narrow. Flowers dangle in trusses from the branches. Surface textures tend to be smooth or velvety.

Canelike Plants Including Shrubby Types

The description covers most of the plants in this category. Specifically canelike are those with erect, tall stems plus some with stems that grow out more or less horizontally. Shrubby plants just have more and shorter canes lending them a rounder profile.

The really tall canes belong to the Superba type and it is among these that *B. aconitifolia* is usually listed. We pay special attention to this plant because it is the only one we have so far found that we can recommend unconditionally to the average indoor gardener.

B. aconitifolia. The canes are few, slender and reaching a height of 3' (90 cm) or more. The shiny green leaves are divided into a number of very jagged segments but are almost as broad as long, approximately 6" (15 cm) in diameter when well grown. Veins are depressed resulting in quilting. The surface is richly patterned with silver spots of various sizes and shapes. The underside is pinkish as are the stalks. In good condition the leaves should overlap forming a solid column of greenery.

The cultural characteristics are unusual among Begonias. Minimum temperature is about 50°F (10°C), but exposure for long periods above 85°F (29.5°C) do it no harm. It flourishes in filtered sun and a minimum of 200 fc. It benefits from high humidity but does not suffer at 40%. Although it should not stand in water, it is not sensitive to normal watering procedures at any time of year. It does not go dormant. We have never had a plant that was attacked by insects or by disease. Any houseplant medium seems to suit it equally well. Except for the factor of temperature we rate it as Cast Iron. Flowers are few, white and pink tinted. Our plants have never flowered. Propagation success is almost 100% even when the leaves with an inch or two of branch or stem are planted in moist houseplant mix. Root formation is rapid.

The canes can be trimmed when young, whereupon they will branch and thicken. By repeating the process a very thick trunk is formed and offsets come up around it forming a tuberous base. With time leaves decline in size and are covered with an even dusting of silver spots. The plant in this state can be maintained in a small pot as a most sculptural pseudo-bonsai. It can be maintained for a number of years. The ability to renew itself and to put out new growth on old wood is extraordinary.

We expatiate on this plant for two additional reasons. We have distributed many hundreds to indoor gardeners who have had similar results. In fact it has become known as the Elbert Begonia, and nurseries receive inquiries for it. Yet to date we have not noticed a spark of interest in the community of Begonia hobbyists or for that matter in professional circles. It is no wonder that the popularity of Begonias, at least in parts of our country, has declined when such plants are neglected in favor of pretty novelties that present all kinds of difficulties for the grower.

We do not know whether our clone of *B. aconitifolia* is typical. Others may not come up to scratch. But this clone still exists and could well serve as a model for future breeding programs.

B. 'Sophie Cecile'. An old favorite; very tall growing, strong with great angelwing-shaped leaves spotted with silver and a good bloomer too, with heavy trusses of pink flowers. It likes plenty of sun. Were this plant more compact it might well be superior to *B. aconitifolia,* in possessing the additional flowering capability.

Typical of the horizontal-growing canes is *B.* 'Lenore Olivier' bred by the same grower as *B.* 'Sophie Cecile', Belva Kusler, who has had to her credit a number of the best modern Begonias. The leaves are thick, dark green, lustrous, deep red beneath. It blooms heavily. Many of these plants, in fact, are more attractive for their flowers than their leaves, but the public will never become really attached to the flowers. The potential is in producing sound foliage plants.

Among the bushy cane types are such plants as *B. foliosa,* which has very small, toothed angelwing leaves on graceful branches. Much the same can be said for *B. cubensis,* whose leaves are satiny and silvery green. *B. serratipetala,* likewise with small leaves, is notable for the deep dentation of the leaves, their dark green color and the red spots that cover the surface. *B. listada (listida)* has medium-sized pendant angelwing leaves with smooth edges, velvety with a light stripe down the center.

Also included in this group are two absolutely gorgeous small plants that require terrarium culture. *B.* "ex Kew species" (a temporary name) is from Sarawak. The light but brilliantly green leaves are covered with large, greenish yellow spots. Really like nothing else in the plant world—and devilishly difficult.

B. exotica (a temporary horticultural name) has large oval leaves that are carried horizontally. The plant spreads, forming mats of leaves no more than a few inches high. The blades are light olive green with radiating bands of rich pink. Somewhat easier than the previous species but nevertheless requiring a terrarium.

Semituberous Begonias

These are smallish plants with small leaves. They grow from tubers which, in some, form a broad surface that is very decorative when exposed. The small flowers are white or pink. *B.* 'Maxwelton' and *B.* 'Weltoniensis' have green leaves and make excellent semi-bonsai, shallow-pot plants. However, they, too, require terrarium or greenhouse conditions.

Summary

We have emphasized the difficulties growing Begonias indoors because, in our opinion, some very false expectatons have been disseminated regarding the culture of the genus. But we must also register our admiration for this truly marvellous repertory that offers endless vistas of unsurpassed foliage. What is required is a little extra effort such as, for instance, is required for orchid culture. We are hopeful that, in the future, more attention will be focused on breeding for ease of culture rather than mere novelty.

Bertolonia. **Melastomataceae.** Brazil. Creeping herbs. Filtered sun. 200–400 fc. Temperature min. 65°F (18.5°C). Humidity min. 50%. Terrarium culture. Packaged Houseplant Medium or Houseplant Mix #1. Propagation from cuttings. Difficult. 14 species of which half are grown indoors.

These hairy-leaved, creeping plants are strictly greenhouse or terrarium subjects. Difficult to grow in large quantities, they will likely remain plants for expert amateurs. Besides hairiness, their leaves are characterized by quilting, the result of the principal veins being depressed. All the blades are broadly elliptic with a narrow, shallow notch at the base. The delicate root system is shallow. Flowers 4-petalled, not often seen indoors. But an attractive foliage pot plant.

B. hirsuta. Clustered 3″ (7.5 cm) leaves with a silvery midvein.

B. × 'Houtteana' (*B. houtteana*). Blades 5–7″ (12.5–17.5 cm) long, sparsely hairy, yellowish green with veins bright pink. Spotted with lighter green.

B. maculata. Leaves to 3′ (7.5 cm) long, emerald green, heavily felted; veins purple. Flowers ¾″ (18.6 mm) across, rose.

'Wentii'. Exquisite branching vein pattern.

B. marmorata. Blades with crisply upturned edges and whitish veins. Flowers 1″ (2.5 cm) across, purple.

'Sanderana'. Veins silvery.

B. mosaica. Like *B. marmorata* but with a broader band of white on principal veins.

B. pustulata. Somewhat hairy; very quilted.

B. sanguinea. Velvety. Veins silver and dark pink.

The accuracy of the names of the last 3 species listed in catalogs is open to question.

For maintenance Bertolonias need very high humidity, 60–70% being preferred, constant warmth, though not above 85°F (34°C), constant moisture without sogginess and very sparing use of a balanced or high phosphate/potash fertilizer. Terrarium culture is virtually mandatory. Propagation is from stem cuttings in live or long-fiber sphagnum moss in a clear, covered container at 75°F (30°C).

Bignonia. **Bignoniaceae.** Brazil. Tropical vines. Partial sun. Min. 500 fc. 14 hours daily. Temperature min. 65°F (18.5°C). Humidity min. 50%. Packaged Houseplant Medium. Propagation from stem cuttings easy. 1 species (?), see below.

Except for *B. capreolata,* the familiar, rampant southern vine with large, deep orange-red trumpet flowers, all species formerly attributed to *Bignonia* have been assigned to a number of other genera. Nevertheless, species unlisted in *Hortus Third* are occasionally offered by nurseries as Bignonias. They are tender vines grown not for their flowers but for pretty colored foliage, usually on a trellis to 6′ (1.80 m). They require even moisture and high nitrate fertilizer.

B. argyraea. Silver Trumpet Vine. Deep green 3″ (7.5 cm) heartshaped leaves with a small notch at the base; veined silver.

Begonia Rex

Begonia versicolor with *Selaginella uncinata*

Begonia heracleifolia

Begonia masoniana. Iron Cross Begonia

PLATE 17

Begonia richardsoniana

Bertolonia sanguinea

Blakea trinervia

Bombax ellipticum. Shaving Brush Tree

PLATE 18

Bowiea volubilis. Climbing Onion

Brachychiton acerifolium

Brassaia (Schefflera) arboricola

Breynia disticha roseo-picta. Snow Bush

PLATE 19

Bucida spinosa. Black Olive

Bursera microphylla. Elephant Tree

Buxus microphylla 'Kingsville Box'

Caladium cv. (red)

PLATE 20

Caladium cv. (white)

Caladium humboldtii

Calathea makoyana

Calathea zebrina

PLATE 21

Calathea rotundifolia

Calathea ornata sanderana

Calibanus hookeri

Callisia congesta variegata

PLATE 22

Callisia elegans

Campelia zanonia

Carex morrowii

Carica papaya. Papaya

PLATE 23

Carissa 'Bonsai'

Carissa humphreyii variegata

Carludovica palmata. Panama Hat Plant.

Chamaecyparis pisifera 'Boulevard'

PLATE 24

B. argyreo-violascens. Leaf blades violet with silver-white veins.

B. villosa. Blades 4–5" (10–12.5 cm) long, dark green, veined with silver. Looks like *argyraea* and vice versa.

Blakea. Melastomataceae. Central and South American tropics. Shrubs. Filtered to partial sun. 400–800 fc. Temperature min. 60°F (16°C). Humidity min. 50%. Houseplant Mix #2 or #3. Propagation from cuttings. Somewhat difficult.

Blakea belongs to that widespread group of Melastoma Family species that inevitably attracts the attention of visitors to the forests of Central America and the Caribbean. They are diffuse shrubs of large size but usually not woody, with large, vertically set, broadly elliptical or lanceshaped leaves. The distinguishing feature is a set of 3 deeply set principal veins extending from the base to the apex of the leaf. Attempts to domesticate these plants have usually been abortive. *Blakea* is an exception though not an easy plant, for it requires virtual greenhouse conditions and succumbs readily to fungus.

B. gracilis. Spreading shrub, the leaves 6" (15 cm) long, shiny, lanceshaped. The 2" (5 cm), 6-petalled, white flowers, rarely appear on indoor-grown plants.

B. trinervia (or *trinervula?*). Leaves opposite to 8" (20 cm), elliptical, cupped, small-notched at base, deeply 3-veined with innumerable parallel transverse veins. Stalks 2" (5 cm) long. Stems and branches round and green. Purplish flowers are rare.

Boerlagiodendron. Araliaceae. S.E. Asia and W. Pacific. islands. Trees and shrubs. Filtered to partial sun. 400–800 fc. Temperature min. 55°F (13°C). Humidity min. 65%. Houseplant Mix #2 or #3. Propagation from cuttings. Rather difficult. 40 species of which one occasionally grown indoors.

B. eminens. Tree to 40' (12 m). Blades handshaped, 2' (60 cm) in diameter, cut into as many as 20, closely set, narrow, toothed and jagged segments, 6–12" (15–30 cm) long. Bright green. Stalks to 30" (75 cm), somewhat pendant. Grown as a juvenile pot or tub plant with a spread of 2–5' (60 cm–1.5 m). A superb plant but too diffuse in habit to be of much use indoors. Grown only as a juvenile in pot.

Bowiea. Liliaceae. Climbing Onion. S. Africa. Partial to full sun. Min. 500 fc. Temperature min. 50°F (10°C). Houseplant mix #2 with sand. Cactus & Succulent mix #1. Propagation from seed or offsets. Easy. 2 species, 1 grown indoors.

B. volubilis. This curious and amusing plant has large, shiny green bulbs that sit on top of the soil and put forth in winter a leafless vine with many fine, airy little branches rising in a cloud of greenery. Train on a pot trellis. Globular bulbs of various sizes are sold, from 1" (2.5 cm) or less to 7" (17.5 cm) in diameter. In fine specimens as many as 5 bulbs are piled on top of each other in an impressive mound. Carefully trained the plant becomes a beautiful combination of sculptural and screening decor. The vine is, at most 10' (3m) long, very thin and flexible; grass green.

Keep moderately moist from late October to late April or, to be more precise, from the time the bulb puts up a shoot until the greenery dies down. Do not water during the warm months. Fertilize once every 2 months during growth with a high nitrate formula. The easiest way to propagate is by separation of offsets. Specimens with several large bulbs, like shiny bald heads, invariably attract attention and amusement. When greenery is fully developed and properly trained, few foliage plants are more ornamental.

Brachychiton. Sterculiaceae. Bottle Tree. Australia. Shrubs and trees. Partial to full Sun. 800+ fc 15 hours daily. Temperature min. 60°F (16°C). Houseplant Mix #2 or Succulent Mix #1. Propagation by seed or cuttings. Moderately difficult. 12 species of which 2 are grown indoors.

The Brachychitons are semisucculent shrubs are trees with swollen trunks grown as ornamentals on the West Coast. A number may make attractive pot plants. At present only the following 2 are being grown indoors.

B. acerifolium. Flame Tree. To 40' (12m) in cultivation but grown indoors to no more than 3' (90 cm). Stem very thick at the base, with erect branches bearing 3-segmented leaves, each segment narrowly lanceshaped, to 6" (15 cm) long, leathery. Slow growing. Should be kept partly potbound. Allow to dry out between watering. A very attractive, sculptural plant.

B. paradoxus. (B. ramiflorus). A woody shrub with felted leaves that are nearly round and gently lobed up to 6" (15 cm) in diameter.

B. populneus. Very woody shrub with a thick base and dry, leathery, halberdshaped leaves to 5" (12.5 cm). The thin white veining is complex and decorative. A fine plant for a bonsai pot when small. Keep pot bound and moist.

Brassaia (Schefflera). Araliaceae. India to Australia. Trees. Filtered to partial sum. 400—600 fc. Temperature min. 50°F (10°C). Humidity min. 40%. Packaged Houseplant medium. Propagation by seed and branch cuttings. Easy. 40 species of which 2 grown indoors.

B. actinophylla. Queensland Umbrella Tree. To 30 or 40' (9 to 12 m) high in the tropics, topped by a mass of handshaped leaves with 12–16 leaflets, each one elliptical, leathery, to 12" (30 cm) long. Stalks to 18" (45 cm). Indoors it is a loosely branching shrub with fewer leaflets (7–9), no more than 12' (3.6 m) high. The few branches, the result of early trimming, give it a diameter of 7' (2.10 m) or more.

During a considerable stretch of time *B. actinophylla* enjoyed a vogue as the leading big plant for lobbies and atria. Culture is as indicated above. Well-grown plants, prepared for indoor conditions by subjection to a period of low light, did very well in competition with Fiddleleaf Figs, *Dracaena marginata*, palms and a few other plants considered close to Cast Iron. But its ability to grow in poor light was overestimated by buyers. They were often placed in positions where no large plant could be expected to survive.

Other factors started to take their toll. Market demand tempted nurseries to force them and to evade acclimatization procedures. Their branches become weaker and the leaves thinner. The whole appearance deteriorates, accompanied by an inability of the underdeveloped roots to cope with the demands of the heavy top growth. That is why *B. actinophylla* gradually has dropped from favor and joined a growing list of good plants that have been discarded because of poor cultural practices. It is true that new plants have entered the market, but those that have demonstrated their worth are not easily replaced.

B. arboricola. This closely related plant has stood up very well. It is much smaller, rarely growing over 6' (1.80 m) high indoors, naturally and profusely branched, the leaves with half the number of leaflets and growing to no more than about 6" (15 cm) in diameter. It is small enough to plant more than one stem in a large pot or tub. Thus, it develops much thicker clusterings of foliage and remains considerably more compact. It is an excellent living-room-size plant but too small for large spaces. At present we can rate it as Cast Iron as it seems to be quite free of pests and diseases unless severely abused.

Breynia. **Euphorbiaceae.** Asia and Western Pacific. Shrub. Filtered to partial sun. 600–800 fc 14 hours daily. Temperature min. 60°F (16°C). Humidity 50%. Houseplant Mix #2 with sand. Propagation from stem cuttings. Moderately easy. 30 species of which 1 is grown indoors.

B. disticha (nivosa). Shrub to 4' (1.20 m) with angular red branches and stalks. Leaves green to 2" × 1" (5 × 2.5 cm), lanceshaped, arranged alternate-opposite on the branches. Stalks very short.

'Atropurpurea'. Leaves purplish.

'Roseo-picta'. Green splotches and pink and red.

The coloration appears only in partial sun. Keep evenly moist and fertilize 6 times a year with high nitrate formula.

An attractive but diffuse, woody shrub that can be maintained in filtered sun but displays color only when exposed to partial sun or more. Subsidiary branches spreading and plant is difficult to keep compact. Best for pot culture as a colorful, and different, addition to the indoor garden.

Bucida. **Combretaceae.** Black Olive. Central America and West Indies. Partial sun. 600–800 fc. Temperature min. 50°F (10°C). Houseplant Mix #2 with sand and lime. Propagated from cuttings or seed. Easy. 6 species; 1 grown indoors.

B. buceras. Oxhorn Bucida. Versatile, small-leaved tree to 60' (18 m), horizontally branched and leafy.

Trunks irregularly spiny. Leaves alternate, spoonshaped, to 3½ × 1" (8.75 × 2.5 cm), shiny, dark green. Stalks to 1" (2.5 cm).

B. spinosa. The usual species (?) in horticulture. Trunks and branches more regularly spiny.

Keep moderately moist and fertilize with balanced formula 6 times a year. Provide 15 hours artificial light daily. Underpot. Subject to spider mites.

This is a fine plantscaping tree, easily trimmed to a neat round form. Available from nurseries in sizes from 10' (3 m) for plantscaping. *Bucida* has attracted attention lately for southern, indoor locations. It is slow growing and therefore expensive in large sizes, but tough and long lasting.

Train pot size plants to make decorative, formal shapes in artistic containers.

Buxus. **Buxaceae.** Box. Temperate zone worldwide. Small shrub. Partial to full sun. Minimum 600 fc. Hardy at 32°F (0°C). Sterilized (acid) garden soil. Houseplant Mix #2 or #3 with sand. Propagation from stem cuttings. Moderately difficult. 30 species of which one is grown indoors.

Buxus belongs to a small group of temperate zone bonsai plants that we list hesitantly as houseplants although we have not encountered special difficulties growing them on windowsills for coolness in winter. Three other genera that are similar in their requirements are *Chamaecyparis, Cupressus* and *Juniperus.* All have a wide range of habitat that includes species possessing more southerly habitats.

Box is a hardy to half-hardy shrub principally grown outdoors for dense, low garden hedges or as trained clumps. Notoriously slow growing, tiny leaved and responds well to continuous pruning. Only a few dwarfs of one species should be attempted indoors where they are trained as bonsai. With care they may well last for many years. Only recently have indoor gardeners become aware that they can be grown at all indoors.

Fertilize no more than 6 times a year with high nitrate formula. An application of iron (Sequestrene or micronized iron) twice a year is beneficial. Keep moist.

B. microphylla. Charming dwarf that grows to a maximum of 8" (20 cm) and very slowly. The plants are woody, with a bare trunk, and have close-set oval, shiny, ½" (1.25 cm) leaves closely attached to the numerous twisting and spreading branches.

'Compacta' (Kingsville Box) is a favorite of bonsai growers. Other cultivars are 'Baby Boxwood', 'Green Beauty' and 'Morris Dwarf'. Each has a slightly different growth habit. They usually grow no more than 6" (15 cm) high. Clones vary in their ability to withstand summer temperatures at a window.

Pot close, trimming top growth and roots. In the summer try to maintain the temperature below 85°F (29.5°C) and provide constant air movement. In winter set plants close to a window where the maximum temperature is 72°F (23°C) by day and lower at night. At that time of year they can be maintained in a north window.

Caladium. **Araceae.** Tropical America. Stemless, tuberous herbs. Partial sun. Min. 500 fc for 12 hours daily. Min. 65°F (18.5°C). Humidity min. 40%. Houseplant Mix #2 or Packaged Houseplant Medium. Winter dormant. Propagated by division.

There are about 15 species in this very popular genu. Almost all those in horticulture are cultivars assigned the grab-bag name *C. xhortulanum,* indicating their uncertain parentage. Only *C. humboldtii* is a frequently grown species. Other species are of purely botanical interest at present.

C. xhortulanum. The leaf blades display an extraordinary variety of color patterns. Simple or very complex veining in green, white, red and purple appear in contrast with the same background colors which occur as solids or as splotches, spots and zones in innumerable combinations. The blades are thin, translucent and borne vertically on long, semierect stalks. Shapes are generally heartleaved, from almost as broad as long to forms with a long triangular outline and attenuated tips. Edges are smooth to very undulating and crisped or frilled. In some only the principal veins are prominent; in others there is a network of connecting veins.

These cultivars can be divided roughly into two groups. The more popular plants are large leaved, max. 12 × 8″ (30 × 20 cm), with 12″ (30 cm) stalks. The other, with fewer cultivars, is characterized by more discrete marking and zonings running to velvety rose, red, gray and white zones with contrasting vertical veining and, usually, a green border. The blades are typically 8 × 3″ (20 × 7.5 cm), lanceshaped though notched and with more attenuated tips than the larger plants. There are some true dwarfs in this group. Some of the blades are curiously frilled and distorted, mottled in shining red and green. They have become comparatively rare although exquisite and elegant to a degree that makes their big relatives seem gross by comparison. They are splendid for dish gardens, terrariums and for display in decorative potting.

The larger-leaved plants are vigorous and need relatively little attention except watering when the soil is dry in summer. Fertilize with high nitrate formula every 2 weeks during the growing season to promote offsetting tubers. Avoid prolonged exposure to temperatures over 82°F (28°C). Excessive moisture accompanied by low temperatures can induce rot in tubers. Avoid long hours of intense sunlight as leaves will brown. Also watch for spider mites and mealybugs. Prevent or treat with systemic pesticides rather than sprays.

The smaller-leaved plants generally need higher humidity of min. 50% or can be grown in terrariums. In other respects treatment is the same.

Start with mature plants chosen at florists or nurseries, the leaves displaying their sizes, colors and shapes so that you can make a choice. However, seedsmen sell some of the more common cultivars as dormant tubers with descriptions. These should be planted just below the surface of the soil in the spring and kept at 70°F (22°C) until the leaves appear. In the fall withdraw water and store the pots at over 60°F (16°C) until the following spring when they sprout. Or the tubers may be removed from pots, dried, the pups separated and all of each cultivar stored in separate, sealed and labeled plastic bags.

Nothing is to be gained by describing the many cultivars of *C. xhortulanum. Exotica 4* illustrates and describes over 130, and new ones are constantly being introduced. However, it should be noted that many of the finest old cultivars, especially the very choice smaller plants, are disappearing and may be lost entirely unless amateurs and professionals alike support their production by being more discriminating in their choices. The few cultivars that dominate the market tend to drive the others out.

As a houseplant the large Caladiums make splendid displays but are not easy to keep in good shape because the leaves, facing vertically in all directions, soon lose symmetry of position if grown on a windowsill without almost daily turning to face the sun. The smaller plants are more satisfactory and can be grown under fluorescent light with 400 fc for 12–14 hours a day, while dwarf varieties can fit into a terrarium.

Caladiums are frequently used as massed temporary displays in public places. In the north a month is about as long as one can expect the plants to be in first-class condition because of dry air, drafts and continuous traffic, the leaves being thin and sensitive. In the South they last longer and can even be carried through the summer, at least where traffic is not heavy. They should be in pots plunged into whatever medium is available.

Species such as *C. bicolor,* probably the principal parent of many *C. xhortulanum* plants, *C. marmoratum, C. picturatum,* and *C. schomburgkii,* all display some variegation but are mainly of botanical interest.

C. humboldtii is the notable exception. It is a miniature plant with heartshaped leaves max. 4 × 2″ (10 × 5 cm) on thin, watery stalks to 2 × 3″ (7.5 cm). The blades are a rich, deep green, splotched on either side of the midrib with white. It spreads more quickly than other species, sending up new tufts of leaves from tuberous pups. Its requirements are nearly the same as those of other Caladiums, but it demands warmer temperatures, constant moisture and humidity. In short, it prefers terrarium conditions though it will survive very well under fluorescent light at 400 fc on a 12-hour day. In stable environments it will go dormant either not at all in winter or for only a few weeks. It is a superb miniature that deserves more attention.

Calathea. **Marantaceae.** Tropical America. Spreading, stemless herbs. Shade to filtered sun. 200–500 fc 12 hours daily. Temperature min. 65°F, max. 85°F (18.5–19.5°C). Humidity min. 50% Houseplant Mix #3 or long-fiber sphagnum moss. Propagation by cuttings, divisions and tubers. Difficulty: partial dormancy in winter. Over 100 species, at least 30 grown indoors.

The genus is notable for foliage of outstanding elegance with sober coloring but startling, contrasting surface patterns. Also see *Ctenanthe* and *Stromanthe*.

They are the joy of greenhouse growers and indoor gardening enthusiasts but are far from easy. Attempts to introduce them into the mass market have, thus far, failed. This is understandable as they are highly temperamental, prone to dormancy in winter, and the causes of frequent failure have been difficult to determine. In the past their irresistible attraction for spider mites has been the despair of growers. Now that we have more effective pesticides, this is no longer a serious drawback in the house. Mites continue to be a problem in public plantings.

Total height indoors is rarely more than 3' (90 cm). Some are entirely fibrous rooted while others bear tubers on the root branches or at their tips. Discovering these fleshy, oval growths has caused some owners to toss out the plants, believing them to have been attacked by some malignant disease. In some plants the leaves grow directly from the roots; in others from fleshy, short pseudo-stems like those of the Prayer Plants (Marantas) and bearing 2–6 opposite sheathed leaves. Blades are mostly simple, lanceshaped, ranging in size from 3–20" (7.6 to 50 cm) on thin, round stalks of various lengths. The joint of blade and stalk is a thickened elbow which permits it to fold up or down, depending upon species, at night.

The difficulties in maintaining Calatheas have to do with providing a very stable environment. Use a medium that is fibrous, porous, well aerated, rather loose in the pot but without air holes. Keep the temperature within the range indicated. Humidity above 50% is beneficial. Even moisture—soil that is not soaking wet—is an imperative. They are relatively slow growers and small drinkers. Drying out for a day or two is not harmful to the tuberous species but risky with the fibrous one. The conditions necessary are more those of a greenhouse, yet many amateurs do grow them successfully in the home. Fertilize very sparingly with high phosphate/potash formulas. Excess fertilizer or an accumulation of salts can be lethal. Leach thoroughly at least 3 times a year.

As the roots spread and throw up tufts of leaves, division is easy. During dormancy the plants should be kept warm and slightly moist at all times.

Species identifications are so confused that new studies are in progress to bring some order into the genus. To make recognition a little easier we have organized the plants roughly according to leaf patterns. When a question mark follows the species name or it is enclosed in single quotes it indicates a dubious identification used in horticulture.

Leaves Decorated with Narrow Stripes

C. ornata. Blades erect, elliptic, 12 × 4" (30 × 10 cm); stalks 12–15" (30–37.5 cm).

'Roseo-lineata'. In juvenile plants the lines, paired on either side of the upcurving veins, are a powdery pink and white. Purple beneath.

'Sanderana' has broader, shorter, oval leaves with fewer prominent veins but from 2–5 colored lines in alternating colors on either side of each. Very handsome.

Both cultivars lose their coloring as they mature.

C. vittata. Leaves spreading symmetrically, giving the effect of a large rosetta. Blades lanceshaped, 10 × 3" (25 × 7.5 cm). The upward-curving veins are bordered in white reducing the green to still narrower stripes. The texture is curiously like fine-woven fabric, the finish being decidedly matte. It is quite different in this respect from other Calatheas, being more tailored, cool and aristocratic. A vigorous grower, it is easier to maintain than most and should have commercial potential. Still rare, it deserves far more attention.

Leaves Decorated with a Distinct Leaf Pattern

In these unique plants the color of the leaf blade is light green, yellowish green, gray and sometimes translucent. On this background, seemingly imprinted, is a darker pattern of a straight branch bearing opposite or alternate leaflets. The more common type has more or less equal leaflets in the pattern whereas in a few, there is a pair of smaller leaflets between each pair of larger ones.

Botanies often list maximum leaf sizes larger than occur on plants grown indoors.

C. argyraeia. Blades lanceshaped, to 5 × 2" (12.5 × 5 cm). Stalks 3" (7.5 cm). Background silvery gray; the leaf pattern dark green, not reaching to the edge.

C. clossonii (?) Blades 9 × 3" (22.5 × 7.5 cm). Stalks 5" (12.5 cm). Yellow-green with short, irregular-sized, darker green leaflet pattern.

C. concinna. Blades 8 × 3" (20 × 7.5 cm). Stalks 3–4" (7.5–10 cm). Broad lanceshaped, yellow-green with pattern of dark green; narrow leaflets, curving to the edge.

C. eximia. Tuberous. Blades oval pointed, 6–10" (15–25 cm). × 3½" (9 cm). Stalks 4" (10 cm). Silvery gray; leaflet pattern olive green, narrow and pointed, not reaching the edge.

C. kegeliana (*C. kegeljani* (?), *C. bella* (?), *C. bachemiana* variant (?). Leaf blades leathery, broadly lanceshaped but notched at base; 12 × 4" (30 × 10 cm) on wiry stalks to 12" (30 cm). Silvery gray with leaf pattern closely set, narrow, now reaching edge.

C. leopardina (?) Blades to 6 × 2½ (15 × 6.5 cm). Nile green, overlaid by a very distinct, short, broad, alternate, leaflet pattern in a darker tone. Stalks to 10" (25 cm).

C. makoyana. Peacock Plant. Tuberous. Superb plant that fully deserves the common name for its exquisite color and pattern. Blade thin but tough, 10 × 4" (25 × 10 cm), with thin, wiry stalks to 10" (25 cm); broadly lanceshaped. Translucent chartreuse, the maroon underside glowing through, finely netted with veins. The overlay pattern is darkest green, alternating large and small, curved leaflets, major veins very narrow and continuing to the edges which are likewise narrowly bordered with green. It is as if a branch had been laid over delicately stained glass with the finest of network patterns. Usually dormant in winter when it should be kept quite dry.

C. stromata (?) 'Burle Marx'. This questionable name has been applied to plants with definitely oblong leaves with rounded corners ranging in size from 3–4 × 1½" (7.5–10 × 4 cm) to 8–10 × 2–3" (20–25 × 5–7.5 cm). Stalks 4–10" (10–25 cm). Several leaves per pseudostem. Obviously there is much variability between clones at least as they have appeared on the market.

The background color is a delicate, very light green, and the alternate leaflets of the pattern are thick, then attenuated in an upward curve to the very narrow dark green edge. The blades are carried horizontally so that the height of the plant is rarely more than 1' (30 cm).

Large numbers of these plants were offered in the shops a few years ago, and they continue to surface from time to time. They are more resistant to spider mite than most, and the winter dormancy is short, the leaves rarely dying down. They are also tolerant of temperatures to 50°F (10°C) or lower and are not demanding in regard to humidity. Very showy when well grown. We hope that interest in them will revive.

C. wiotii. Small plant with thin, oval-pointed blades 4 × 2" (10 × 5 cm). Stalks 3–4" (7.5–10 cm). Surface light green, the pattern leaflets dark, alternate, short, oval. The reverse gray-green. It has been described as dormancy free, but this is not our experience.

Leaf Pattern as Curved Brush Strokes

This is a variation of the leaf pattern in which the "leaflets" have become broad, upcurved bands, attached at one end to the midrib and, at the other, to the margin of the blade.

C. lietzei. Blade nearly oval, 8 × 3" (20 × 7.5 cm), dark green overlaid with broad bands of silver-green. Pseudo-stems bear 3 to 5 leaves. Erect runners produce leaves and roots in the manner of *Chlorophytum*. These can be separated and potted up. Blade purple beneath. Stalks 3" (7.5 cm). It grows somewhat taller than most.

C. louisiae. Leaves clustered, the blades 10 × 4" (25 × 10 cm), oval-pointed, concave, dark green, with broad, short yellowish green brush stroke pattern. Purple beneath.

C. rotundifolia. The blades are leathery, thick, nearly round, to 10" (25 cm) in diameter, with the edges turned down. The thick, brownish stalks are 3–4" (7.5–10cm) long. The background is dark green; the curving bands nearly white. Grayish beneath. This superb plant is rare because of slow growth and difficulty in propagation. It requires little light but plenty of warmth and humidity. Terrarium culture is best.

'Fasciata'. The white bands are more silvery.

C. warscewiczii. Leaves clustered. Blades 12 × 5" (30 × 12.5 cm), elliptical, convex. Velvety yellowish green with broad, closely set brush strokes in dark green. Red beneath.

C. zebrina. Largest of the genus in cultivation. Leaf blades to 18" (45 cm) or more, with the shape and color pattern of *C. warscewiczii* but the brush strokes shorter, more separated and splitting at the tips. Stalks to 12" (30 cm).

'Binottii'. Bands reach only half way to the margin.

'Humilior'. Leaves half as long or less. Brush strokes reach to the margins.

Leaves with Vertical Striping

C. aemula. Blade broadly oval, to 6" (15 cm) long on 4" (10 cm) stalk. Medium green with distinct, broad, lighter green, translucent, notched stripe down the middle. The notchings are like an inverted triangle. Gray-green below.

C. medio-picta. Blades broadly elliptic, 8 × 3" (20 × 7.5 cm), edge turned down, veins depressed. Stalks to 10" (25 cm). Dark green with narrow white feather down the middle. Purple beneath.

C. micans. Leaves narrowly elliptical, 5 × 1½" (12.5 × 4 cm). Blade horizontal on 3" (7.5 cm) stalks. Broad white, feathered band down the middle.

C. princeps. Blades lanceshaped to 12 × 4" (30 × 10 cm) on 15" (37.5 cm) wiry stalks. Very rich, burnished yellow-green background. Blackish green feathering along midrib. Veins thin, dark. Dark narrow edge. Keep warm and humid. Another unusual beauty.

Leaves with Vertical Striping and Feathering

A most complicated pattern with a vertical stripe down the center and one or more curving, feathery stripes on either side of the midrib.

C. lindeniana. Blades broadly elliptic to 12" (30 cm) or more by 5" (12.5 cm). Stalks to 12" (30 cm). Dark green, a yellow-green stripe down the midrib and just in from the margins. Yellowish green beneath with purple along the midrib and near the edge.

C. luciani. ('Tuxtla' in hort.). Leaves tufted. Blade oval-pointed, to 12" (30 cm) long; stalks the same length. Dark green with a metallic sheen. Broad silvery white strip along the midrib and feathered stripes near the edges. Grayish beneath. More mature plants lack the outer stripes.

C. metallica (?) Similar to *C. picturata*.

'Vandenheckei'. See below.

C. picturata. 'Vandenheckei'. Leaf blades elliptic to 6 × 3" (15 × 7.5 cm). Stalks 6–8" (15 to 20 cm). Dark green with broad, feathered, white stripe down the midrib and a narrow feathering near the edge. This is a relatively popular commercial plant of great elegance. 'Argentea', the juvenile form, has leaves half the size with a solid gray center bordered by dark green. Purple beneath.

C. roseo-picta. Exquisite plant. Blades broadly oval to 9 × 6" (22.5 × 15 cm), deep sheeny green with pink toned midrib and thin, feathered white line in from the edges. Stalks to 6" (15 cm). The blade also bears a short pointed tip. Sometimes the leaves have a reddish border paling toward the middle.

C. veitchiana. Peacock Plant. Markings quite as extraordinary as those of *C. makoyana*. On short stalks, the blades are very broadly oval to 10 × 6" (25 × 15 cm). A series of featherings of different widths appear in 4 shades of green, creating a pattern of a jagged variegated leaf against the dark green edging. Warm and humid growing.

Among the numerous other species and cultivars the following are also outstanding.

C. musaica. Blades long-heartshaped to 6" (15 cm). Stalks 4" (10 cm). The yellowish green leaves are netted with translucent yellow veins in a network of tiny rectangles. Unusual and beautiful.

C. rufibarba. Unusual in being covered with short hairs. Blade 7" (17.5 cm) or more long by 2" (5 cm), erect, the edges undulating, velvety, green above and purple beneath. Requires very little light (100 fc).

Calibanus. **Agavaceae.** Mexico. Succulent with thickened stem (caudex). Partial sun. 600 fc for 14 hours daily. Temperature min. 50°F (10°C). Cactus and Succulent Mix #2. Or Houseplant Mix #1 with sand. Propagation by seed or rooting offsets of the stem. Cast Iron.

C. hookeri is the only species in cultivation. It might well be described as a dwarf relative of *Beaucarnea recurvata* with its hemispherical thickened base, max. 16" (40 cm) across and 10" (25 cm) high, with a thick bark, splitting when mature. On this short plant the 10–20 leaves emerge in a bundle from the top of the stem and are tough, dark green, up to 2½ (75 cm) long and about 2/5" (1 cm) wide. As a result they sprawl all around the plant.

Extremely slow growing, *Calibanus* needs little attention. It can be watered regularly or allowed to dry out for a month or two without visible damage. Indoors it takes years to reach maturity. Fertilize no more than 2–3 times a year with a balanced formula. With time the thickened base (caudex) usually grows offsets above soil level on its body.

This is an interesting curiosity for the hobbyist and collector.

Callisia. **(Spironema) Commelinaceae.** Inch Plant. Tropical America. Trailing basket plant. Partial sun. 500–600 fc 12 hours daily. Temperature min. 60°F (16°C). Humidity minimum 40%. Packaged Houseplant Medium. Propagation by cuttings. Easy. 8 species; 5 grown indoors.

Waxy, fleshy-leaved basket plants with short blades and trailing stems. They require constant moisture and fertilizing with a balanced formula once a month at most. Stem cuttings will root in water or moist vermiculite under cover. Leaves clasp stem, are spiraled and, at the tips of branches, look like rosettes. The spread of the baskets is 2–3' (60–90 cm).

Lower leaves on the stems brown rather quickly and unless constantly pruned the growth becomes straggly. The plant grows from tufts of root which colonize. These last no more than a year, but replacement from rooted cuttings is easy.

C. congesta. Mature leaves are broadly lanceshaped to 2" (5 cm) long. New leaves are purplish.

'Variegata', violet with longitudinal white stripes.

C. elegans. (Setcreasia striata). Pinstriped Inch Plant. Grayish to olive leaves 2 × 1" (5 × 2.5 cm). Stems trail to 2' (60 cm). Dark green with fine white stripings; purple beneath.

C. fragrans. Leaves narrow, lanceshaped, 8 × 1½" (20 × 4 cm). Green.

'Melnikoff', striped with white or cream in varying widths. Stems to 3' (90 cm).

C. repens. The most common plant in the shops. Leaves 1–1½" (2.5–4 cm × 12.5 cm), striped like *C. elegans* of which it is probably a dwarf form. Stems shorter. New leaves pinkish in the sun.

C. tehuantepecana. 1" (2.5 cm) bright green leaves, closely packed, spiraling on long, vertically pendant stems to 3' (90 cm). Will grow in a north window with 200–250 fc light.

Campelia. **Commelinaceae.** Mexican Flag. Mexico to Brazil. Tall, fleshy herb. Partial sun. 500–700 fc. Temperature min. 60°F (16°C). Humidity min. 50%. Houseplant mix #2. Propagation from stem cuttings and offsets. Moderately difficult. 1 species.

Campelia zanonia grows to a maximum of 6' (1.80 m), the leaves spiraled and clasping the weak, fleshy stem. Leaf blades elliptic, pointed at tip, narrowing to a broad, short stalk. Max. 10 × 3" (25 × 7.5 cm).

'Mexican Flag'. Boldly striped vertically with green and white; the edges pink.

To keep short the plant can be potbound. Fertilize only 3 or 4 times a year with high phosphate and potash formula. Maintain uniformly moist. As it is subject to stem rot, spray frequently with a general fungicide. Can be grown in the South as an indoor bedding display. The most striking of the cultivated *Commelinaceae* but something of a problem child.

Canistrum. **Bromeliaceae.** Brazil. Intermediate-sized fleshy, rosette plants. 7 species. See *Aechmea* for culture.

C. fosteranum. Tubular rosette with scurfy scales; green, mottled chocolate brown.

C. lindenii (Nidularium lindenii). Leaves 2' × 3" (60 × 7.5 cm), finely toothed, green spotted with darker green.

'Exiguum fosteranum' (?). Upright vase shape. Leaves bright green with darker mottlings and ivory stripes.

'Roseum'. Open rosette, the leaves broader, yellow-green with darker mottlings. Underside with wine red bands and lines. Soft teeth on the margin.

Carex. **Cyperaceae.** Sedge. Temperate circumglobal. Grassy herb. Full sun. 40°F (4°C) minimum. Sterilized Garden Soil or Cactus and Succulent Mix #2. Propagation by division.

There are over 2,000 *Carex* species of which only a handful are used as ornamentals. The Japanese, typically, have selected dwarf evergreen species and variegated cultivars for display in their bonsai pots and dish gardens. Though cool growing they are small enough for amateurs to devise ways of keeping them from extreme heat.

The main requirements are plenty of sun, excellent drainage, good ventilation summer and winter, *constant wetness* and high nitrate fertilizer a couple of times a year. In winter place them close to the window where they will be cool. In summer ventilate with fans. They will also benefit from air conditioning at that time. They are very slow growing.

C. buchanani. A reddish brown grass about 1' (30 cm) high in tufts. It is curiosity that looks dried out at all times but is both a curiosity and very beautiful in a complementary setting.

C. foliosissima 'Albo-mediana.' Erect 5" (12.5 cm) tufts of bright green blades edged with a white stripe.

C. morrowii. Japanese Sedge Grass. Only the variegated cultivars are grown.

C. morrowii variegata. Leaves 4" (10 cm), curved. Almost entirely white with a narrow stripe of green. There are several other cultivars with reverse decoration and small differences in size. Although doted on by collectors this is a difficult plant requiring constant moisture, full sun, clean air and plenty of ventilation.

Carica. **Caricaceae.** Papaya. Tropical America. Partial to full sun. Min. 65°F (18.5°C). Min. 50% humidty. Houseplant Mix #2 with sand. Propagation from seed. Easy. 25 species; 1 grown indoors.

A short-lived fast-growing tree, it is decorative as a juvenile foliage plant; good for 2 years at most indoors.

C. papaya. Leaves handshaped, nearly circular, with 7 deeply toothed segments on long stalks. Indoors the blades usually 12" (30 cm) in diameter on stalks to 12" (30 cm); giving it a spread of 2' (60 cm). The stem is thick and pulpy. Although it should be kept moderately moist, it can be allowed to dry out for a few days if necessary. Fertilize with a low concentration of high nitrate formula with every watering. It drinks heavily. Seed germinates and grows rapidly. A pretty curiosity for the hobbyist.

Carissa. **Apocynaceae.** Old World Tropics. Shrub. Partial sun. 500–800 fc 12 hours daily. Temperature min. 50°F (10°C). Humidity 50%. Houseplant Mix #2 with sand. Propagation from stem cuttings. Moderately easy. Over 35 species of which only 1 is widely cultivated indoors.

C. grandiflora. Natal Plum. South Africa. Large, woody shrub to 15' (4.5 m), with oval, dark green, virtually stalkless, leaves, paired-alternate to 3 × 2" (7.5 × 5 cm). The many branches zigzag and are armed with forked flowers followed by 2", oval, red fruits. Widely planted as a hedge in Florida and elsewhere. Without full sun, flower and fruit are rare.

Most indoor gardeners prefer the dwarf cultivars. These are slow growing and amenable to frequent pruning so that they can be trained as bonsai. Some lack the spines of the species.

The following cultivars can to grown in a partially sunny window or with a minimum of 500 fc. In small pots they require constant moisture. Fertilize monthly with 30-10-10. During the heat of summer provide a drop in temperature at night of at least 10°F (5°C). They are usually sold as 4–6" (10–15 cm) rooted cuttings.

'Bonsai'. Multibranching dwarf with dull green leaves 1" (2.5 cm) long. Upright; much branched.

'Boxwood Beauty'. Leaves shiny green. Thornless. Otherwise like 'Bonsai'.

'Green Carpet'. Branches pendant. Leaves ½" (1.25 cm) long.

'Horizontalis'. Branches prostrate. Leaves 1" (2.5 cm).

'Petit Point'. Tiny, extremely slow-growing shrub with wedgeshaped leaves max. ½" (1.25 cm).

'Ruby Point'. Upright, the branches thicker. Young leaves pinkish.

C. humphreyii variegata (?) Upright plant to 6" (15 cm). Blades nearly round with narrow, creamy edge.

Other cultivar names have been applied to similar plants. They are fine for dish gardens and terrariums.

Carludovica. **Cyclanthaceae.** Ecuador. Stemless palmlike plants. Filtered sun or 300 fc 12 hours daily. Min. 65°F (18.5°C). Humidity min. 60%. Sphagnum moss. Propagation by division or seed. difficult. 3 species.

C. palmata. Panama Hat Plant. Spreading leaves directly from roots are like those of a fan palm; orbicular, up to 3' (90 cm) in diameter, divided into 3–5 broad, deeply cut segments. Spread 5' (1.5 m) or more. Requires high humidity, warmth, a drop of 10°F (5°C) at night and almost aquatic conditions. Never let the medium dry out. Seedlings grow more rapidly than palms, the leaves becoming fanshaped immediately. Thus the plants can be depended upon to be more ornamental in a shorter time than any species of palm. They are liable to occasional mealybug infestation.

The genera *Cyclanthus* with 1 species, *C. bipartitus* and *Dicranopygium*, with 44 species, are smaller plants, the blades often divided into only two segments and some with long, narrow leaflets. We have seen plants in the tropics always growing in deep shade in very wet locations. They are very attractive in semiaquatic plantings.

Ceratozamia. **Zamiaceae.** Mexico. For culture see *Zamia.*

The two species are difficult to distinguish from *Zamia* except by detail of the cones.

C. kuesteriana. Low, rounded trunk, said to branch from the base (?). Leaves not numerous, to 4' (1.20 m) in length. Leaflets alternate, leathery, 6–10" (15–25 cm) long, lanceshaped with edges turned downward.

C. mexicana. Trunk to 4' (1.20 m). Leaves 3–9' (90 cm–2.70 m). Leaflets 6–15 × 1–3" (15–37.5 × 2.5–7.5 cm), lanceshaped.

Vars. *latifolia, longifolia* and *miqueliana* display minor differences in leaf shape and size only observable when plants are closely compared.

Principally of interest as specimen plants in exotic indoor settings.

Chamaecyparis. **Cupressaceae.** False Cypress. Mostly temperate N. America and Asia. Large trees. Partial to full sun. Min. 700 fc, 15 hours daily. Temperature: Hardy to subtropical; see below. Sterilized acid Garden Soil or Houseplant Mix #3 with sand. Propagation from cuttings. 8 species of which 2 are occasionally grown indoors.

C. obtusa. Hinoki Cypress. Japan. Dwarf cultivars have whorls of short, needlelike leaves that become spatulate only on mature plants. This species is probably cooler growing than *C. pisifera.* Cultivars from Taiwan, of which there are many, occasionally are maintained well in sunny windows that are cool (max. 50°F, 10°C) at night in winter. Keep moist at all times and rather pot bound.

Popular cultivars include 'Nana', 'Nana aurea' and 'Reiss'.

C. pisifera. Similar to but more tender than the above. Leaves are more triangular, being broader at the base. Twigs short and woody. There are many dwarf cultivars of which the most famous is 'Boulevard' which is tolerant of window exposures and is very slow growing when maintained in small pots.

Chamaeranthemum. Acanthaceae. Tropical America. Creeping herbs. Filtered sun or 150 fc for 14 hours daily. Temperature 65°F (18.5°C). Humidity min. 40%. Houseplant Mix #1 with lime. Moderately easy. Propagation from cuttings.

C. gaudichaudii. Short, branching, creeping stems. Leaves broad lanceshaped, 3″ × 2″ (7.5 × 5 cm) on ½″ stalks, opposite-alternate with short internodes. Green with grayish, broad midvein.

C. venosum. India Plant. The wide, oval leaves are richly marked with complex silver veining on bright green background covering the whole surface. It prefers a situation with more air movement than *C. gaudichaudii.*

Fertilize with high-middle-number formula. Maintain even moisture. Flowers small, white.

These are attractive small pot and terrarium plants.

Chirita. Gesneriaceae. Tropical Asia. Low, stemless herbs. Bright shade to filtered sun. 150–500 fc 14 hours daily. Temperature min. 50°F (10°C). Max. 80°F (27.5°C). Humidity min. 40%. Houseplant Mix #2 with lime. Propagation from leaf cuttings. Moderately difficult.

There are over 100 species of which many are annuals, easily grown indoors for their small, pretty flowers.

C. sinensis. Hong Kong. Perennial. Leaves grow in a flat rosette; elliptic to 6 × 2″ (15 × 5 cm) with narrowing to thick 2″ (5 cm) stalks. Spread 15″ (37.5 cm). Leaves are thin and brittle, but with the edges turned down they appear to be unusually thick. Veining is complex and covers the entire surface. There are two forms, one simply dark green with lighter green veins, the other, far more striking; veins, broadly bordered with bright silver, give the effect of metal embossed leather. This form has recently been dubbed 'Silver Leaf' in catalogs. It is a plant of truly startling beauty.

The stalked flowers are pale pink; nodding, unimpressive.

Water sparingly. Allow the soil to dry out for a day or two between. Spray the leaves daily summer and winter. Provide excellent ventilation in summer and coolish night temperatures. Fertilize no more than once a month with a high potash formula. Mealybugs and spider mites attack the leaves.

To propagate, cut leaves at the base, dust with hormone powder and plant tips in barely moist vermiculite under clear plastic or glass cover at 72–75°F (23–24.5°C).

Chlorophytum. Liliaceae. Spider Lily. Worldwide tropical except N. America and Europe. Stemless herb for basket culture. Shade. 200 fc 12 hours daily. Min. 50°F (10°C.). Houseplant Mix #1 or 2 with lime. Propagation from tips of runners or by division. Cast Iron.

Among the many foliage plants with white and green variegation, Chlorophytums are so common and carefree that hobbyists often consider it beneath them to own a plant. Striking in color, symmetrical in growth habit, they deserve a place in every collection. Their wide use as basket plants in public places confirm their adaptability. There are over 200 species of which only a few are cultivated.

C. comosum. Spider or Airplane Plant, is the one commonly sold in nurseries and shops. The species is green leaved, stemless, extending its territory by shallow roots which give rise to tufts of spiraling leaves 18 × ½–¾″ (45 × 1.5–2.2 cm). Throughout the year stiff, stemlike runners longer than the leaves, grow out from the plant bearing clusters of small white flowers followed by tufts of young leaves and incipient roots. This tip can be detached and planted. The runners develop most profusely in low (north) light. A few are pleasant and useful for propagation, but a great number at one time give a disorderly appearance to an otherwise neat plant. We suggest that most of them be removed at the early stage.

The plant thrives best in bright shade and requires only the simplest of soils—even poor garden soil will do if fertilized. It benefits from constant moisture but is tolerant of being completely dried out for several days. Fertilize, at most, once a month with a balanced formula.

Pests and diseases rarely bother it. The only problem is the browning leaves, due to pot-binding, and, of course, age—a cause gardeners have a way of overlooking. The offending leaves are easily trimmed or, if dead, pulled out.

Although green plants are attractive, too, they have been superseded by a host of variegated cultivars. In nurseries and shops you will rarely, if ever, find cultivar labels on the plants and new, unlisted introductions are constantly appearing. The differences are in the length of leaves, their width, the amount of white or ivory striping and the quantities of stems bearing plantlets and flowers. One should examine plants closely at nurseries and florist before making choices. Being on the spot is better than depending upon descriptions.

'Mandaianum'. This is only one of the fine foliage cultivars developed by members of the Manda family at its greenhouses in New Jersey, dating back many years. It has not been seen often for some time, but we believe it is the same plant that has surfaced recently in the trade. It is the only clone that, in our opinion, is an exception to our criticism of plants with an excess of stalks bearing flowers and plantlets.

The leaves are a little over a quarter of an inch (6.25 mm) wide, and half as long as most cultivars. The darkish green is split down in the middle by a narrow, clean, ivory or white stripe. The plant produces great numbers of the additional long stems. These are sometimes branched, and each bears a tight cluster of upstanding leaves. Longer than most, the stems hang to as much as 3' (90cm) below the basket. The effect is imposing and highly decorative. This is an especially desirable plant, and its use should be encouraged wherever basket plants are required.

'Picturatum'. Leaves 12″ (30 cm) long with a yellowish stripe.

'Variegatum'. Leaves 18″ (45 cm) with white border.

'Vittatum'. Leaves 18″ (45 cm) long, with a white stripe down the middle.

C. bichetti. Leaves 8″ (20 cm) high, colonizing and growing as a solid mat of foliage. Both green and white-striped plants are available. It looks better in a pot than a basket. Peat resistant.

Chorisia. **Bombaceae.** Floss Silk Tree. South America. Partial to full sun. 600–1,000 fc. Temperature min. 45°F (7°C). Sterilized Garden Soil with peat. Propagation from cuttings. Difficult. 3 species, two occasionally grown indoors.

The Chorisias have remarkable bottleshaped trunks studded with corky, conical spines. At maturity large, colorful, lilyshaped flowers appear followed by puffs of white silk containing the seed. Little grown indoors but with some potential as foliage pot plants because branching is quite symmetrical and the trunk is sculptural.

C. insignis. Peru. Leaves compound, with 5–7 drooping, spoonshaped leaflets 5″ (12.5 cm) long.

C. speciosa. Brazil and Argentina. Leaves compound, leaflets lanceshaped, drooping to 5″ (12.5 cm) long.

Of interest only as juveniles. Both trees have a dry dormancy period following leaf loss.

Leaves are attractive to spider mites and subject to fungus. Spray with a general fungicide weekly. Maintain low humidity for best results.

Note: *Ceiba pentandra,* the Kapok Tree, which is closely related and common in the American tropics, is very occasionally grown indoors as a juvenile.

Cissus. **Vitaceae.** Worldwide tropics and subtropics. Vines used mostly as basket plants. Propagation from stem cuttings. Easy to difficult. For other cultural details see below.

There are 350 or more species of *Cissus* originating in the warmer parts of the world. Their flowers are insignificant, and the foliage, often reminding us of the close relationship to the grape vine, is unspectacu-

lar. Of those that are cultivated, one, *C. rhombifolia,* is a versatile basket plant of easy culture and fully adapted to growing indoors. It is widely used in the decoration of public places.

Although the horticultural *Cissus* species are few in number, their culture differs sufficiently to recognize three divisions.

Species Adapting to Normal Humidity.
C. adenopoda. Central Africa. Pink Cissus. Filtered sun. Temperature min. 55°F (13°C). Humidity 40%+. Houseplant Mix #2. Easy.

A fast-growing vine from tuberous roots. Leaves consisting of 3 leaflets to 6″ (15 cm) long, alternate oval-pointed, green, covered with purple hairs. Red beneath. Juvenile plants are compact but soon develop wide distances between the joints as they grow. Keep evenly moist, but due to the tubers, the plants can go for some time without watering. Fertilize monthly with a balanced formula. Sections of stem will root in water or moist vermiculite. Subject to the attacks of spider mites as are all these species.

To maintain in baskets the stems must be constantly trimmed back. Confining the roots reduces growth and size of leaves.

Besides use as basket decorations the vines can cover interior walls and pillars when trained on trellises.

C. antarctica. Australia. Kangaroo Vine. Leaves lanceshaped, dark, oily green, toothed, to 4″ (10 cm) long. Baskets spread to 2½' (75 cm) or more. Famous for its vigor and requires constant trimming. Same culture as *C. adenopoda.*

C. gongylodes. Brazil/Paraguay. Occasionally sold in baskets where the spread is to 3' (90 cm) or more. Leaves have 3 leaflets, green/grayish felted, to 7″ (17.5 cm) long. Stems develop long, red aerial roots like a fringe. Aerial tubers grow at tips of branches which drop to the ground or can be removed to produce new plants. Even moisture at all times.

C. rhombifolia. Grape Ivy. Mexico to Colombia. The vine has hairy stems and forked tendrils which make it an even more efficient climber than *C. antarctica.* The leaves are 3 compound, with the blades smooth edged below the middle and toothed above, 1–4″ (2.5–10 cm) long. The middle leaflet is diamond-rhombic shaped, the lower two narrower on the inner side. Culture as for *C. adenopoda. C. rhombifolia* is preferred because the leaves are shiny and the shape more ornamental. It is also somewhat easier to keep under control through pruning. Only the cultivars are widely grown.

'Ellen Danica'. Currently the most popular cultivar. With 5 leaflets, the whole leaf to 5″ (12.5 cm) in diameter. Leaflets narrow with deep teeth. A very graceful plant but excessively fast growing with long spaces between joints and therefore requiring heavy pruning. Young plants are shapely, but they soon become straggly, the thin stems hanging well below the basket or pot.

'Fionia'. By far the best cultivar at present, being a slower-growing and more compact plant. Leaves are divided into 3 leaflets, usually no more than 2" (5 cm) long and somewhat broader than other cultivars. They are more deeply and crisply notched and the green color is brighter. Not as frequent in the shops as, for instance, 'Ellen Danica' because nurserymen object to its relative slowness.

'Mandaiana'. Leaves with 3 leaflets that are dark green. Similar to 'Fionia' but it grows faster and spaces between joints become wide as it elongates.

C. striata. S. Brazil and Chile. Miniature Grape Ivy. Stiff, branching little vine with 5-parted leaves, shaped somewhat like those of 'Ellen Danica'. Stems reddish, hairy, Leaves bronze green, reddish brown beneath. It has a semidormant period in winter when it should be watered only after the soil has dried out. Otherwise, the same culture for *C. adenopoda.*

Vines requiring high humidity.

These species require 50% or higher humidity and temperatures of 65°F (18.5°C) or higher. Houseplant Mix #3. For lighting see in the following. Difficult plants indoors. Fertilize weekly with a mild solution of high nitrate formula.

C. amazonica? Brazil. Very tender vine with thin, flexible stems, tendrils and aerial roots. Leaves alternate, lanceshaped, 3 × 1" (7.5 × 2.5 cm). Color variable from gray-green to gray with silver side veins and brown midrib. Purplish beneath. Filtered Sun or 500 fc 14 hours daily.

C. discolor. Rex Begonia Vine. A gorgeously leaved vine requiring partial sun or 800 fc for 12 hours daily. Humidity min. 60%. Stems thin, red, stretching to 20' (6 m) or more. Can be grown in a basket with constant trimming. Leaves opposite, narrowly heartshaped, to 6" (15 cm) long.

The vines are sunken producing a quilted surface. Veins green, the quilting bright silver and a broad stripe down the middle of velvety red-purple.

C. sicyodes. Princess Vine. Brazil. Probably should not be included here as it requires 65% humidity or more and constant moisture. Leaves broad, heartshaped, 4" (10 cm) long.

Succulent species.

These very different plants require partial sun or 800 fc for 14 hours daily. Temperature min. 45°F (7°C). Succulent Mix #1. Water after thorough drying out of the soil. Fertilize with a balanced formula every month.

C. quadrangularis. S. Africa. Clambering vines with thick, square, winged stems and single leaves at the joints, 5" (12.5 cm) apart, deep green, mapleleaf-shape and 1" (2.5 cm) broad and long. Rather decorative, hanging in several strands from a hanging-basket pot. Needs very little attention. There are a number of species (or forms) with differently angled and winged stems that look and behave much the same.

C. rotundifolia. East Africa and Arabia. Stems 4-angled, velvety. Leaves almost round, 3" (7.5 cm) in diameter, thick, slightly toothed. Makes a good basket plant. It appeared in the shops for a while but is seen no longer. Very easy and adaptable.

Citrus. **Rutaceae.** Orange, Lemon, etc. S.E. Asia. Fruit trees. Full sun. 800–1,00 fc 15 hours daily. Temperature min. 40°F (4°C). Max. 85°F (29.5°C). Humidity min. 50%. Houseplant mix #2 with sand. Propagation from seed or cuttings. Rather difficult.

There are about 20 species and innumerable cultivars, the latter usually resulting from selection for best fruiting quality and/or suitability for growing in different subtropical environments. Notice the difference, for instance, between California and Florida oranges.

Indoor gardeners often plant seed from commercial fruit. Germination is rapid, and it is possible to grow a bushy shrub, but the plants, almost invariably, deteriorate with time.

However there are a few dwarf cultivars that have "stood the test of time" and make acceptable houseplants, even flowering and fruiting yearly if conditions are right. It might be argued that they do not belong here as their cheif decorative value resides in their colorful fruit. But with successful culture, these are also fine foliage plants, handsome even when unproductive. They are usually sold at nurseries and florists from the fall on, bearing fruit which makes them very colorful. The fruit lasts for months. Repeat flowering and fruiting is another matter, as innumerable buyers have discovered. It is by no means easy. Incidentally the orange, lemons and tangerines borne by these cultivars are anything but sweet; best for preserves if you have enough of them.

The small potted trees are very much alike, being bushy and 2–3' (60–90 cm) in height and breadth. Branches are numerous, zigzag and usually spiny. The leaves are shiny, dark green, elliptic, 2–6" (5–15 cm) long on very short stalks. Full sun is imperative along with regular moisture and feeding with high nitrate fertilizer every 2 weeks. Trace elements should be included in the formula. Although subtropical orchards suggest constant warmth, all the citrus (but one to be mentioned) require rather cool growing conditions. Avoidance of excessive summer heat and provision for very good ventilation accompanied by a sharp drop in temperature at night are necessities. Flowering starts in early sprint.

Nursery-grown plants frequently harbor scale insects. Whitefly is a common scourge. Both multiply when the humidity is low. The trees branch naturally when quite young and need little trimming at first. Growth is quite slow indoors.

C. aurantiifolia. Lime. The limes are tropical trees whose cultivars are usually labeled by their place of origin. The best two in our experience are the Key Lime from southern Florida and the Mexican Lime. The latter has leaves that are intensely fragrant. Most people will find them easier to grow and maintain for a longer time than, for example, *C. limon* and its hybrids, because they are warm growing, preferring a temperature of min. 50°F (10°C) and are less subject to root diseases. On the other hand, without nearly full sun they will neither bloom nor fruit.

The plants have green zigzag stems with long

spines and typical citrus leaves, 1½" (3.75 cm) long. They should be kept pot bound to some extent and rather dry in the fall. Resume regular watering and feeding no earlier than December.

Trimmed and trained as they increase in size, they become shapely pot plants up to 3' (90 cm) tall.

C. × Citrofortunella mitis. Calamondin Orange. With few spines, leaves 2–4" (5–10cm) long. Branches stiff, rather erect with fruit carried on the tips. Fruit a little over 1" (2.5 cm) diameter, bright orange. Fall-bearing, very acid.

C. hystrix. Thailand. Makrut or Makrood. Leaf blade to 6" (15 cm) long, divided into an upper and lower segment. Spines 1" (2.5 cm). Glossy dark green. Bears up very well in hot weather. We have not seen the fruit, whose rind is dried and used in Thai cooking. A very handsome plant and worthy of more attention as a pot plant and, eventually, in larger sizes as suitable for plantscaping. Very resistant to disease and insects.

C. limon. 'Meyer'. Dwarf Lemon. Small shrub with leaves 2" (5 cm) long. Fruit to 3" (7.5 cm), thin skinned, smooth.

C. limon. 'Ponderosa'. Ponderosa Lemon. Old favorite. With few thorns and not many branches. Bears when no more than 2½' (75 cm) high. Leaves 4–5" (10–12.5 cm) long, dull green. The yellow fruits about 4" (10 cm) in diameter, have a very thick, bumpy rind. Tub plants reach 6' (90 cm) or more in height.

C. × limonia (taitensis). Otaheite Orange. The name is a corruption of Tahiti. A bush lacking thorns. Fruit deep yellow, 2" (5 cm) in diameter. Insipid. Usually grows to 2½' (75 cm) at most indoors.

C. reticulata. 'Dancy Tangerine'. A spiny bush requiring higher humidity than the others. Leaves 1" (2.5 cm). Very well branched and gracefully flexible. The 2" (5 cm) red fruits grow at various levels. Fruiting December/January. A more decorative plant than the others and less sensitive to temperature changes.

Cleyera (Eurya). **Theaceae.** Asia and Japan. Shrubs and small trees. Shade to filtered sun. 300–500 fc 14 hours daily. Temperature min. 45°F (7°C). Houseplant Mix #3. Propagation from stem cuttings. Moderately easy but cool. 17 species; one grown indoors.

C. japonica (Eurya ochnacea). Also confused with *Eurya japonica,* but the leaves are longer and narrower, being elliptic to 6 × 1½" (15 × 3.75 cm). The tip is rounded. Fragrant, creamy white flowers.

It needs good air movement; summer temperatures below 90°F (33°C) and to be kept cool in winter. Constantly moist. Fertilize monthly with high nitrate formula. Apply chelated iron once or twice yearly. Difficult to establish and slow growing but highly decorative when carefully trimmed. Maximum height about 15' (4.5 m) but best kept to a maximum of 2' (60 cm) indoors.

'Tricolor'. Leaves dark green with lighter zones, variegated with yellow splotches and with pinkish edges. This is the plant most frequently grown.

Clusia. **Guttiferae.** W. Indies and tropical S. America. Strangling, climbing trees. Filtered to partial sun. 500–800 fc. Temperature min. 60°F (16°C). Humidity min. 40%. Houseplant Mix #3 with sand and lime. Propagation from cuttings. Easy. 145 species of which 1 grown for foliage indoors. Easy.

C. rosea. Scotch Attorney. A strangling tree, like some *Ficus,* from 20–50' (6–15 m) in height. Leaves extremely thick, definitely spoonshaped, the tips frequently squared off, to 8 × 4" (20 × 10 cm) long, carried horizontally. Stalks 1" (2.5 cm). Flowers pink or white, 2" (5 cm) in diameter but rare indoors.

'Aureo-variegata'. Marked with angled, irregularly thick stripes of yellow and cream, often interspersed with green brushings and spots.

'Marginata'. Green leaves edged with yellow.

There are 3–4 different, not clearly identified, plants being offered in the trade that are probably other species, with narrow or very wide leaves. Also a dwarf with 4" (10 cm) long leaf blades.

An easy, not overly attractive pot plant that requires plenty of root space. It is best grown to a height of 2' (60 cm) or less so that the leaves are seen from above.

Coccoloba. **Polygonaceae.** Florida, W. Indies and C. America. Trees. Partial to full sun. Temperature min. 50°F (10°C). Humidity min. 50%. Equal parts peat and gritty sand plus 1 tbsp. dolomite lime to the quart. Propagation by seed and cuttings. Moderately difficult. Of the 150 species possibly 3 grown indoors.

Large limbed, spreading trees 20–80' (6–24 m) tall. Fertilize once a month in summer with a balanced formula. Leaves are dropped seasonally, frequently Jan/Feb, at which time reduce watering. Keep evenly moist when leaves return after only a short delay. Subject to mealybug infestation.

C. diversifolia (floridana, laurifolia). Pigeon Plum. Blades on short, thick stalks, broadly oval to oblong, 4" (10 cm) long. A small tree to 20' (6 m). Young plants do well in an 8" (20 cm) wide pot for a while.

C. pubescens (grandifolia). Outdoors the tree reaches 80' (24 m). Branches reddish velvety. Leaves round, thick, to 3' (90 cm) ! across, notched at base, undulating edged, dark green. Branches are few and the enormous leaves likewise. Large (15'–4.5 m) specimens are spectacular in exotic plantings.

C. uvifera. **Sea Grape.** A common tree of southern beaches. To 20' (6 m) with thick, spreading and nearly prostrate branches. Leaves olive green, the veins red, shape almost round, with or without a notch at the base, 8" (20 cm) across. Tending to straggle even as a juvenile but an interesting curiosity in a large pot or small tub. Rarely last for very long indoors.

'Aurea' or 'Variegata'. Heavily and irregularly variegated with creamy areas. A striking decorative plant and well worth some effort to maintain.

Cuttings root readily in moist sand under a transparent cover at 75°F (24.5°C).

Coccolobas 15' (4.5 m) tall and with a spread as great can be maintained in large southern indoor display gardens. In the North, indoors, they make good pot plants 2–3' (60–90 cm) high.

Codiaeum. **Euphorbiaceae.** Croton. Western Pacific. Partial to full sun. Min. 800 fc. Temperature Min. 50°F (10°C). Garden topsoil or Houseplant Mix #1. Propagated by cuttings. Not easy indoors. Plants in cultivation are all designated as one species.

C. variegatum. The sole species, consisting in fact of a horde of differing cultivars. Plants are single stemmed but offsetting, ranging in size from 12" to 8' (30 cm–2.5 m). Leaves variable in width, length and shape; frequently irregularly shaped and lobed. The texture is thick and the surface oily in appearance. Colors vary endlessly with dots and splotches of yellows, oranges, reds and purples on green.

If anything, Crotons prefer a rather sterile, non-fibrous soil like Pelargonixums. Color and condition is improved in very high light and excellent ventilation is a necessity. Low light and cold are a combination sure to bring on fungal infections. Fertilize no more than 4 times a year with a balanced formula. Water only when soil is dry. The plants are subject to mite and mealybug infestations. Leaves are not damaged by most recommended pesticides. Propagation outside nursery conditions is difficult.

The taller Crotons are used more in outdoor gardens as backgrounds. Their major popularity indoors is as 1–2 (30–60 cm) bedding plants or in individual pots. The type of coloration is better suited to massing along in beds or in relation to annual or perennial flowering plants selected for color. When planted among other foliage plants they tend to clash. For pots one chooses the sizes and colors preferred. Despite there being so many cultivars and that these are propagated vegetatively, it is advisable to see plants themselves before buying. Crops of known cultivars can differ because of culture and other factors.

As one can never predict which of the older cultivars will be on the market at any given time and new variations, usually unlabeled, appear regularly in the shops, we do not list the names here. Readers are referred to *Exotica, Series 4,* for illustrations of some of the plants and the individual leaves. Refer also to current seed and plant catalogs.

Coffeea. **Rubiaceae.** Coffee. Old World tropics. Small trees. Filtered sun. 400–500 fc. Temperature min. 40°F (10°C). Humidity min. 40%. Houseplant Mix #2 with sand. Propagation by stem cuttings. Easy. 40 species. Of the 3 that produce highgrade coffee beans there are many cultivars of Arabian coffee.

C. arabica. Small tree, to 15' (4.5 m), but is usually grown indoors to no more than 3' (90 cm). Leaves opposite, elliptic, to 6" (15 cm) long, crinkled, the edges scalloped, the veins depressed. The surface is dark, oily green.

Shrubby, much branched in a pot or tub. Do not expose to full sun or to temperatures over 85°F (29.5°C). Keep moist and fertilize with high nitrate formula every 2 weeks in summer. Growth is rapid and pruning is suggested indoors. As propagation is not easy, it is better to purchase a plant.

It is a reliable foliage houseplant and is occasionally used in plantings as a nearly columnar, architectural feature. In a dry atmosphere it will lose leaves, especially in summer.

Coleus. **Labiatae.** Old World tropics. Pot and basket herbs. Partial sun. 500–800 fc 14 hours daily. Temperature min. 60°F (16°C). min. humidity 40%. Sterilized garden soil or Houseplant Mix #2 with sand and lime. Propagation by stem cuttings or seed. Easy. 150 species; 1 species and innumerable cultivars grown indoors.

Coleus competes with Croton and Caladium for the prize as the most colorful of foliage plants. A large number of species may have been involved in the immense population of modern cultivars. New ones with different colors and leaf forms appear regularly in catalogs every year. Many strains of hybrid seed are unpredictable so that anybody may have the luck to find a new, gorgeous leaf in the crop and propagate it.

Attempts to organize this chaotic mass of material having proved hopeless, it is now roughly sorted out into 3 major categories. *C. blumei,* an upright plant with square stems and large leaves which has played a role in many cultivars, has been selected as the grab bag for most of the old varieties. New ones are designated as *C. xhybridus,* a meaningless term equivalent to the world cultivar. Those with a creeping, trailing habit and smaller leaves in darker colors, best for basket culture, are bunched under *C. pumilus.* One true species is grown as a herb. Seedsmen apply fanciful names to various strains with recognizably different leaves in all three categories.

Coleus prefer filtered sunlight in the garden but indoors require at least partial sun if they are to remain compact and display their brightest coloring. The erect plants are fast growers that do not react well to pruning. The trailing basket plants are equally quick but more amenable to trimming. Both can be kept in check by pot-binding, letting them dry out well between waterings and fertilizing with a balanced formula only once or twice a season. But note that they are heavy drinkers and the soil dries out fast. They are all very subject to mealybug and whitefly infestations.

The genus consists of both annuals and perennials. *C. blumei* is commonly treated as an annual, usually deteriorating before a year is out. *C. pumilus* is perennial.

Seed is quick to germinate. However, if you wish to perpetuate a plant with an especially pleasing color, you can do it easily by means of stem cuttings in moist medium at a temperature of 72–80°F (23–27°C). The cuttings from annual-type plants roots as quickly as the perennials.

C. amboinicus. Spanish Thyme. S.E. Asia. A kitchen herb widely used in the Caribbean with a powerful aromatic scent akin to oregono. Finely velvet-textured, round, branched stems to 3' (90 cm). Takes pruning and branches well. Leaves broadly lanceshaped, with scalloped edge, the veins depressed. Rich dark green. There is a variegated cultivar with dark green center surrounded irregular by lighter green and edged with a broad band of white. A most ornamental and useful plant. Tolerant of north light or 200 fc, but the tricoloring of the leaves develops only under more intense illumination. An excellent fluorescent-light plant. Perennial, long lasting and easy.

C. blumei and *C. xhybridus.* The common, large-leaved plants of gardens and shops, cultivars all, of mixed parentage.

Square stems and branches to 6' (1.80 m) but usually no more than 15" (37.5 cm) indoors. Leaves paired alternate; short spaces between joints; short stalks. Blades broadly lanceshaped to 6" (15 cm) long. Edges symmetrically scalloped or toothed. But there are many varieties that are narrower with deeper lobing or frilling and with a felted surface. Colored in various combinations, of concentric stripings, blotchings and specklings of white, yellow, orange, red, purple and green.

C. pumilus (C. rehnaltianus). Trailing plant with many weak, thin stems and branches. Leaves to 3" (7.5 cm) on 1½–2" (3.75–5 cm) stalks. Lanceshaped, scalloped or toothed, zoned in white or green with purple and darker shades of pink and red. However, some of the new cultivars have lobed and slashed leaves in light green and a more upright habit, better suited to pot culture. These may require a different designation. The basket types are perennial and long-lived. Will tolerate short periods of total dryness.

C. spicatas (?) India. The plant which has appeared in the trade and is described below may be the above species. It is felted all over; with thickish, straggling stems to 18" (34 cm). Leaves thick, to 1½" (3.75 cm) long, broadly spoonshaped with 4 to 6 low scallops at the tip. Minty aromatic. Requires a sunny window or 600 fc 15 hours daily. Dry between watering.

A very leafy and sturdy basket plant of easiest culture.

Note that we recommend none of the many cultivars because they are constantly changing. Although they may differ slightly in culture, no tests have been made indoors that confirm the superiority of any one or more plants over others.

Colocasia. **Araceae.** Taro. Worldwide tropics. Semiaquatic, tuberous, stemless herb. Filtered sun. Temperature min. 65°F (18.5°C). Humidity min. 50%. Cactus & Succulent Mix #2 without lime. Propagation from tubers. Easy. 6 species; 1 grown indoors. Dormant in winter.

C. esculenta. Elephant's Ear. Dasheen. The latter common name is a corruption of the French, *de Chine*, from China.

The round tubers are 3–4" (5–7.5 cm) deep in the spring. Leaves are broadly heartshaped with prominently raised veins, the edges turned downward; 2–3' (90 cm), attached to the blade above the shallow basal cleft (peltate).

Provide a substantial tub for the large roots and feed with high nitrate fertilizer with every watering. Keep very moist; in fact the tubers can be planted in soil below 2–3" (5–7.5 cm) of water.

These very large plants are those most available and used for temporary displays in exotic plantings or as single decorative plants. There are a number of smaller-leaved and stalked cultivars that are more rarely seen; similar to large-leaved Alocasias or Anthuriums, with purplish leaves and stalks. An easy plant for a lush show of foliage.

The leaves die down in the fall. Dig up the tubers, dry them and store at min. 60°F (16°C) until early spring.

Coprosma. **Rubiaceae.** New Zealand, Australia and Western Pacific. Shrubs and small trees. Partial sun. 500–800 fc, 14 hours daily. Temperature min. 45°F (7°C). Houseplant Mix #1. Propagation from stem cuttings. Moderately difficult. 90 species, 1 grown indoors.

Coprosmas are popular outdoor shrubs in relatively cool subtropical regions. There are many, nearly indistinguishable cultivars, any of which might prove eventually to be indoor gardening material where protected from excessive heat.

As their habitat indicates, Coprosmas are rather cool growing, not tolerating over 85°F (29.5°C) in summer and preferring a location near a window in winter. Constant air movement is also important. Keep evenly moist and fertilize with high nitrate formula monthly. Slow growing.

Woody, branching, semiprostrate shrubs to 20' (60 cm) high and wide.

Leaves opposite, paired, broadly elliptic to broadly oblong; very thick and leathery; to 3" (7.5 cm) long on short stalks. Usually only the cultivars are grown.

'Argentea'. Leaves variegated with white, silver and pink.

'Beatson Gold'. Leaves 1" (2.5 cm) or less. Green, edged with gold. An excellent bonsai plant.

'Variegata'. Mirror Plant. Leaves shiny green with an ochre yellow flame design in the center.

Cordyline. *(Dracaena).* **Agavaceae.** India, Australia and New Zealand. Herbaceous shrubs or trees. Shade to filtered sun. Min. 50 fc 12 hours daily. Temperature min. 45°F (7°C). Packaged Houseplant medium. Propagation by stem cuttings. Easy to Cast Iron. 20 species of which 5 much grown indoors.

Cordyline, Dracaena and *Pleomele* originally belonged to the **Liliaceae.** Not long ago all 3 were assigned to the family **Agavaceae.** At the same time some Dracaenas were moved to *Cordyline,* which now has 20 species augmented by the whole of *Pleomele* which has disappeared. Rather than attempt to convert the public to the new names, nurserymen and shops usually adhere to the old ones. This has, understandably, led to confusion in the trade. It has happened recently in other instances when botanists have changed popular established names, where reason might suggest a less didactic approach, especially as there is so much controversy as to nomenclature in professional circles.

Both *Cordyline* and *Dracaena* are usually single stemmed as young plants as well as in the smaller species, branching when they reach tree size. However the branches of this type of tree continue to behave like single stems, producing their leaves as closely spiraled tufts at the tips. Thus branches removed from *C. australis* or *Dracaena draco* and rooted are very much alike, and culture is almost identical. Both genera supply some of the most frequently used plants for commercial and amateur indoor decoration, principally because of their sizes and tolerance of low light levels.

Indoors Cordylines are comparatively thin stemmed and unbranched unless the growing tips are removed. The long leaves are virtually without stalks or possess them in various lengths. They are slow growing, the leaves overlapping in tight spirals. As the lower leaves die, bare stems are left behind marked with raised rings at the joints. The green-leaved species are usually Cast Iron in culture, equally indifferent to heat or considerable coolness and quite satisfied with a north window or low artificial light levels. Low humidity also does not bother them, and failure to water for a week or more when thoroughly dry causes little or no damage. Insects and disease rarely attack them, though mites can be a problem. Cultivars, especially those with white, purple or red zones are more demanding. They should have filtered sun or 400 fc and humidity of 50%. They are subject to fungal infections especially at lower temperatures and above 85°F (29.5°C). They should be sprayed with anti-damp fungicides frequently. Both types need fertilizing no more than 4 times a year with a balanced formula so that elongated growth will not be encouraged by excessive feeding.

Cuttings root and grow in water as well as moist, sterilized mixes. Tall plants can be air layered. Stems can be cut in lengths on 1–3 joints, preferably with leaves, and buried horizontally in sterile medium such as sand. Provide a soil temperature of 75–80°F (24.5–27°C). The remaining stump will eventually produce a stem or an offshoot from the base.

C australis. A 40' (12 m) tree. Grown in pots with single stems to a height of max. 6' (1.80 m). Leaves dark green, strapshaped to 3' × 1–3" (90 × 2.5–7.5 cm), rather stiff and thick, without stalks.

Note: The custom of planting several rooted cuttings to a pot is so general that the old rule of single stems is beginning to disappear. These clusters of smaller cuttings accelerate the production of very leafy plants but often debilitate them all, affecting the longevity of the display.

'Aureo-striata'. With creamy yellow stripes.

'Cuprea'. Blade reddish brown. Rather a dull, dark shade.

'Doucetii'. Cream and white vertical stripes; edges pink.

'Marginata'. Not to be confused with *Dracaena marginata*. Green with cream-striped edge.

C. indivisa. (Dracaena indivisa). The two names are constantly confused. This is the commercial plant par excellence. Quite an indestructible plant, widely used in plantscaping. Single stemmed to 25' (7.5 m) tall with 6' (1.80 m) leaves. Indoors to 6 or 8' (1.80–2.40 m), the leaves swordshaped to 3' × 6" (90 × 15 cm). Often sold without a visible stem in pots as a low fountain of foliage. Dark green.

'Bruantii'. Tall growing, to 15' (4.5 m). Leaves narrow and erect. Reverse red.

'Purpurea'. Woody stemmed, the leaves forming a spiky globe at the top, being stiffer and more erect. Surface of blade metallic purple.

'Rubra'. Leaves spreading, bronzy green. *C stricta. (Dracaena stricta).* Grows to 12' (3.60 m). Leaves swordshaped, 2' × 2" (60 × 5 cm) but often broader. Narrowing at the base but not to a true stalk. There are some rare cultivars with colored leaves.

C. terminalis (Dracaena terminalis) Ti Plant. E. Asia. Some of the species and cultivars were introduced a long time ago from Hawaii as Ti Plants and listed botanically as Dracaenas. Most originated in S.E. Asia and the western Pacific. For a while they were very popular in this country, but being warmer grower then other Cordylines, they were unhappy in cool houses, needed higher humidity and there was trouble with fungus. So they were gradually superseded by the plainer but more carefree *C indivisa* and the more adaptable of the Dracaenas. Recently they have made a partial comeback, probably because of the development of more effective fungicides and more versatile clones.

They grow outdoors to 10' (3 m), the bare stem marked with leaf scars and the leaves a massed tuft at the top. Blades are elliptic to swordshaped, 12–15 × 2½–5" (30–37.5 cm × 6.75–12.5 cm), the stalks thin, channeled and half the length of the blade. The dwarf cultivars are about half size. The arrangement of the leaves is in a spiral but often less tight than the other species, and they are borne more erectly, less spreading.

Offsetting by runners near the soil surface is more common in this species, and the runners are easily separated at root level. By and large the dwarf cultivars are the most attractive and easiest to handle in the house.

Note: The bare stems of the Cordylines are without grace. In mixed foliage beds they should be surrounded by heavier, lower-growing foliage.

Cultivars are numerous and increase yearly so that old ones rapidly become obsolescent. We list the following to indicate the colors that can be expected.

'Amabilis'. Metallic green edged, pinky cream.

'Baptisii'. Coppery green, edged red.

Note: The red and purple shades are rich but dark; they attract the eye far more when seen close up than at some distance in a mixed planting.

'Baby Ti'. Compact plant; leaves to 15" (37.5 cm). Green with zones of pink.

'Bicolor'. Metallic green suffused with pink and with a pink margin.

'Calypso King'. Dwarf. Tufted growth. Wide, bronzy purple leaves.

'Calypso Queen'. Dwarf. Bronzy red with a flush of purple at the center.

'Firebrand'. Leaves purplish. Young foliage crimson.

'General Pershing'. Blades 12 × 4" (30 × 10 cm). Pink and red lengthwise variegation.

'Mme. Eugene Andre'. Green with red border.

'Margaret Storey'. Emerald green, bordered pink. Leaves 20" × 6" (50 × 15 cm).

'Negri'. Leaves 20 × 4" (75 × 10 cm). Very dark green.

'Tricolor'. Blades broad, erect, tip attenuated; streaked with white, pink and red rather irregularly.

Corynocarpus. **Corynocarpaceae.** New Zealand. Trees. Partial to full sun. 600–1,000 fc. Temperature min. 45°F (7°C). Houseplant mix #3. Propagation from seeds and cuttings. Moderately difficult. 4 species of which 1 occasionally grown as juvenile indoors.

C. laevigata. Tree to 50' (15 m). Leaves spoonshaped to 8 × 3" (20 × 7.5 cm), leathery, shiny dark green, arranged alternately. Very leafy and branched. Slow growing. Trains well. Best at 2–4' (60 cm–1.2 m). Keep evenly moist. Feed with high nitrate fertilizer 4 times a year. Add supplementary iron.

As with other New Zealand plants a temperature under 85°F (29.5°C) in summer and 72°F (23°C) in winter, along with plenty of ventilation, is advisable.

Crassula. **Crassulaceae.** Mostly S. Africa. Leaf succulents. Partial to full sun. Min. 600 fc 14–16 hours daily. Temperature min. 50°F (10°C). Cactus & Succulent Mix #1 or 2 with lime. Propagation from leaf cuttings. Easy to difficult. Over 300 species; at least 50 cultivated indoors.

Crassulaceae is the premier leaf succulent family and *Crassula* its largest genus. Mostly from the arid South African deserts, they are with few exceptions rather difficult to grow indoors due to the unavoidable special problem of watering frequency, the shortage of sunlight and the problem of keeping them rather cool in winter. Stems and leaves are rubbery and the latter often extraordinarily thick. A frequent feature is the subtle waxy finish of the leaves or their dusting with a bluish or grayish powder. A few species grow from 2–10' (30 cm–3 m) high, but the rest to less than 15" (37.5 cm). Their attraction resides in the fantastic sculptural shapes into which harsh natural conditions have forced them in order to survive.

Basically the culture is simple. Do not overpot. Make certain that the medium is gritty and drains perfectly. Keep in a sunny window and in a position where they receive maximum light or close to and under the center of fluorescent fixtures. See Watering Succulents (p. 000) and follow the advice the section

contains. Fertilize with balanced formula at #18 recommended strength and with each watering. The difficulty is in the need for constant observation of behavior of the plants and attention to its needs.

All Crassulaceae are sensitive to pesticide and fungicide sprays, especially Malathion, which is lethal. Before using any spray, test a leaf. Spread the spray liquid on the surface of the leaf. Any damage, a pronounced shrivelling, usually will occur within 24 hours.

Some species offset, permitting the removal of rooted pups and transplanting to separate pots. But the best way to propagate is by means of the lower leaves, removed during the growing season and laid on sterilized sand at a temperature of 75–85°F (24.5–29,5°C) in bright filtered sun and misted once every day. Roots will appear from the base. The cuttings can be potted up after small new leaves appear. In the early stages of growth after transplanting they can be watered when dry. Note that the leaves of leaf succulents break off very easily. This is a convenience when taking cuttings but requires the greatest care in handling the plants so that they are not disfigured.

In botanies the genus has been divided into sections that are difficult to correlate with the visual appearance of the plants. We have arranged them according to our own system which, we hope, has at least the merit of convenience.

Tree type. *C. arborescens.* A spreading, round-topped, dwarf, shrubby tree, usually max. 24 × 24" (60 × 60 cm) but capable of growing to 10' (3 m). Stem and branches thick. Leaves nearly round with a short-pointed tip, smooth surfaced, cupped, thickish, 1½–3" (3.5–7.5 cm) long and wide, quite glowing light gray decorated with red spots, the rim red. Var. *undulatifolia,* bluish gray, longer, twisted leaves. Var. *undulatifolia rubra,* leaves darker gray, edged with purple.

A decidedly more difficult plant to grow than *C argentea.* Very succulent and slow growing. Maximum sun and a long dormancy that must not be interrupted. A most beautiful plant. But fine specimens are rarely seen.

C. argentea (portulacea, ovata). A singularly inappropriate and confusing name since the leaves are green whereas those of *C. arborescens* are gray. Furthermore, it is easily confused with *C. portulacea* which is described in Jacobsen's *Lexicon* as very similar. The result is that some of the cultivars are listed as *C. × portulacea. C. ovata,* a more recent designation for *C. argentea,* is yet to establish itself fully. It matters little to either amateur or decorator as all are essentially what we recognize as the traditional Jade Tree.

The Jade Tree has had a long history of popularity because of its tolerance of neglect and unusual rubbery, spreading growth that is very oriental in its sculptural appearance.

C. argentea grows to 10', (3 m) like *arborescens* but rarely reaches a height and spread indoors of more than 3' (90 cm) with a decidedly flat top. Stems and branches are brown, rubbery, thick. Branches zigzag horizontally.

Leaves spoonshaped, green thick, shiny, 1–2½" (2.5–6.25 cm) long, acquiring a red edge in bright sun.

Drought and neglect resistant. Water every 2 weeks in summer and once a month in winter in general. But do not water on cool or cloudy days and unless soil is bone dry. Fertilize no more than 3 or 4 times in summer with a balanced formula. The plant will stretch badly in low light.

'Aurea'. Leaves green with a tan cast.

'Pallida'. Gray toned.

'Rubra'. Trunk and leaves stained with purple.

'Sunset'. Edges bright yellow but only in full sun.

'Variegata'. Cream striped. Maximum sun. Hideous but rather spectacular.

Nurserymen have also segregated what is called the 'Obliqua' groups, with somewhat thinner leaves. These are faster growing and looser in habit. Best in small pots for florist sales.

(obliqua) 'Medio-variegata'. With yellow stripe down the center of the leaf.

(obliqua) 'Variegata'. Tricolor Jade. Leaves cupped, streaked with white and rose. Most popular of the cultivars.

C. × portulacea is the designation for a group of dwarf plants with ½" (1.25 cm) leaves. Much branched the plants grow to 12" (30 cm) high and wide with flat tops.

C. × portulacea. Mini Jade Tree. Leaves green.

C. × portulacea rubra. 'Crosby's Compact'. As above but with darker leaves, the edges red rimmed.

C. × portulacea convoluta. 'Collum' and 'Hobbit'. Tubular rolled leaves. Curiosities.

Columnar type. Plants from driest desert conditions, usually growing only a few inches high (10–15 cm) although a few cultivars exceed this. Single stemmed, occasionally branching. The stems completely hidden by the leaves which are short, broad, massively thick, geometrically complex, fitting together and overlapping like carefully shaped stones in masonry. Widths are mostly ¼–¾" (6.25–18.6 mm) outer edges straight or rounded. The columns are square or round.

Grown principally by hobbyists. Some of the species are C. alstonii, arta, columella, columnaris, cornuta, deceptrix, hottentotta, marnieriana, quadrangula, tecta, teres. Consult catalogs of succulent nurseries for illustrations.

C. lycopodioides and pseudolycopodioides. Leaves are thin and the columns narrow and straggling. The tiny dark green leaves, the tips turned upward, packed one above the other as if braided. Height to 6" (15 cm), colonizing rapidly.

C. pyramidalis. Arrangement and thin leaves same as above. But the column is erect, the leaves bigger. Attains 8" (20 cm) in height, square, the growing tip pyramidal. A splendid miniature when well grown.

Mounding type. The leaves, broader than long, with a rounded outer edge, overlap so tightly as to appear fused. The symmetrical mound is 1" (2.5 cm) or so high. Typical species are C. barbata (very gray hairy), hemisphaerica and orbicularis.

Loose erect columns. Leaves thin but similar in outline to the Columnar Type but with a wider spread between the joints. Shrubby in growth and up to 2' (60 cm) high, but very rarely. The leaves without stalks and frequently encircling the stem (perfoliate). Colonizing. Diffuse. Typical species are C. lactea, perforata, perfossa.

Long-leaved type. Consisting of plants with longer leaves than the other species. The outstanding example is:

C. falcata. The Airplane Plant. Single stemmed. Stalkless leaves opposite, to 7" × 1¼" (17.5 × 3.13 cm), powdery blue-gray, half twisted like an airplane propeller and overlapping at the base. Usually grows to a max of 1' (30 cm). Notable for a fine cluster of deep pink to red flowers which is rare indoors.

There are cultivars that are larger, smaller and with somewhat differently shaped leaves in all categories. See the bibliography for succulent references.

Cryptanthus. **Bromeliaceae.** Earth Stars. Brazil. Low, flat, spreading, rosette plants. Partial to full sun. 500–1,000 fc 16 hours daily. Temperature 55–90°F (13–33°C). Humidity 50%. Packaged Houseplant medium. Equal parts peat and gritty sand. 1 fir bark, 1 sand, 1 tree fern (fine). Propagation by offsets. Easy. 20 species; about 10 grown indoors. Many hybrids.

Cryptanthus are easiest and arguably the most colorful of bromeliads for indoor culture. Their stiff, somewhat abrasive, narrow to broadly triangular leaves, spreading outward in a flat rosette, are striped horizontally or vertically with brown, silver, purple, yellow, orange, pink, ivory or red in different combinations. The layer of moisture-absorbent scales on the leaves, typical of the family, reflect light, shimmering like those on a butterfly's wings.

The spread is 5–18" (12.5–45 cm).

Superbly colorful pot plants.

For indoor landscaping they are useful as massed border plantings in well-lighted situations.

Unlike those of most bromeliads, the roots are fully functional. Therefore use comparatively larger pots with room for expansion. Growers have been advised not to expose them to full sunlight as it is said to bleach out the colors. But this does not apply to window or fluorescent light culture. Leaves will develop a greenish hue if underlighted. They prefer even moisture in summer and drying out between waterings in winter. High humidity is not a necessity if they are misted at least once every 2 days with very dilute (1/8–1/16) strength balanced fertilizer. Fertilize soil at ¼ recommended strength every 6 weeks.

A plant lasts up to 2 years. After an insignificant blooming or without it the plant dies off having produced offsets from submerged runners. Cut these loose and pot up after development of a root system. They are rarely attacked by disease or pests.

In the following descriptions we have arranged the species together with their accepted cultivars into 3 natural and easily recognized categories: Plain-Leaved, Horizontally Banded and Vertically Striped.

Chamaeranthemum venosum 'India Plant'

Chirita sinensis

Chlorophytum comosum variegatum. Spider Plant

Chlorophytum bichettii

PLATE 25

Chorisia insignis. Floss Silk Tree

Cissus amazonica

Cissus rhombifolia 'Fionia'

Cissus discolor

PLATE 26

Citrus 'Dancy Tangerine'

Citrus hystrix. Makrut

Clusia rosea. Balsam Apple. Photo Gordon Courtright

Coccoloba uvifera. Sea Grape

PLATE 27

Codiaeum variegatum. Croton

Codiaeum cv.

Coleus amboinicus. Cuban Thyme

Colocasia esculenta. Elephant's Ear. Photo Pac. Trop. Bot. Gard•

PLATE 28

Cordyline terminalis. Ti Plant

Crassula argentea. Jade Plant

Crassula cornuta

Crassula pillansii

PLATE 29

Crassula falcata. Airplane Plant

Cryptanthus 'Pink Starlite'

Cryptanthus fosterianus 'Elaine'

Cryptanthus zonatus

PLATE 30

Ctenanthe oppenheimiana 'Tricolor'

Ctenanthe lubbersiana

Cupressus sempervirens 'Swane's Golden'

Cussonia paniculata. Cabbage Tree

PLATE 31

Cyanotis somaliensis

Cycas revoluta. Sago Palm

Cyperus alternifolius. Umbrella Plant

Cyrtosperma johnstonii

PLATE 32

A selection of the many cultivars whose parentage is not certain and some of which we have not seen ourselves, are arranged separately under the same headings.

Plain-Leaved Species

C. acaulis. Rosette consisting of 3-leaved alternate spirals. The broadly triangular green blades dusted with gray scales, the margins undulating and finely prickly, 4–6 × 1½" (10–15 × 4 cm). Gray beneath. Var. *argenteus* is more silvery.

'Ruber'. Pink Earth Star. Surface suffused with pink.

'Variegata' (?). Vertically striped with yellow. An exceptional plant.

C. bahianus. Rarely grown. Stem to 10" (30 cm). Leaves narrowly triangular to 10" × ½" (25 × 1.25 cm). Edges distinctly spiny; surface green or with a reddish cast (Var. *rubra*; silvery below).

C. beuckeri. Marbled Spoon. Leaves spiraled. Blades to 6 × 2" (15 × 5 cm), broad in the middle, attenuating toward the tip and rounded to the thick, 1–2" (2.5–5 cm) stalk. Green interspersed with indistinct clouds of brown or yellow.

Horizontally Banded Leaves

These are plants with longer, narrower leaves and often symmetrical undulating edges. The predominant colors are green, tan and silver in narrow to broad horizontal striped, the latter frequently like pictures of sound waves.

C. fosteranus. Flat rosettes. The leaves narrowly triangular to 7" (17.5 cm) or more. Narrow or broad, wavy banding alternately light green and tan with a reddish hue.

'Elaine'. Edges deep pink.

C. zonatus. Zebra Plant. Flat rosettes of narrow triangular leaves, to 9" (22.5 cm) long, the edges crinkled. Marked with broad, wavy, horizontal bands of brown and silver. These are the largest plants and the easiest to maintain.

'Brahmer'. Pink toned with suffusion of olive down the center.

'Fuscus'. Brown bands alternate with reddish tan. No silver.

'Jamie'. Shimmering silver bands very broad; brown bands narrower.

'Zebrinus'. Maximum size, the leaves 10" (25 cm) or more. Quite reddish with silver bands.

Vertically Striped Leaves

C. bivittatus. Flat rosettes with short stems. Leaves triangular, narrow, the tips frequently much attenuated, edges undulating; 5" (12.5 cm) or more in length. Greenish brown with two pink or red vertical stripes. Var. *major*, leaves to 8" (26 cm). Var. *minor*, leaves 4" (10 cm). Also listed as *C. roseo-pictus*.

'Pink Starlite'. Spreading 6–7" (15–17.5 cm). Central stripe of green or brownish green enclosed in broad stripes of brilliant pink. One of the most colorful of houseplants.

C. bromelioides. Giant Earth Star. Leaves stemless, narrowly triangular, more erect than other species, tips attenuated, to 8 × 1½" (20 × 3.75 cm), olive green, the reverse silver.

'Tricolor'. Vertically striped with narrow lines of metallic green on white. Handsome.

Plain-Leaved Cultivars.

'Autumn'. Leaves narrow. Pink dusted with copper.

'Black Prince'. Toned with purple and mahogany.

'Brown Turkey'. Small, tan.

'Carnival'. Salmon and pink toned.

'Cascade'. Bronzy red. Long-stemmed, trailing offsets. Like *C. pseudoscposus* (?)

'Cherry Sundae. Unusually wide leaves.

'Morgenrot'. Leaves broad. Pale green with reddish stripe. Turns glowing red in strong sun.

'Old Gold'. Flat, with wide leaves. Golden green with silver scales.

'Sunburst'. Olive green with zones of pink and pale orange.

'Sunrise'. Orange-pink with silver scales.

Ctenanthe. **Marantaceae.** Brazil. Spreading, clustered-leaved herbs. North light to filtered sun. 200–500 fc 12 hours daily. Temperature min. 65°F (18.5°C). Humidity min. 60%. Houseplant Mix #3 or long-fiber sphagnum moss. Propagation by cuttings, division and tubers. Difficult. 9 species of which 6 are grown by hobbyists. See *Calathea* for other details.

C. compressa. Leaf blades oblong, green, 12" × 4" (30 × 10 cm) on 10" stalks.

C. glabra. (*Calathea glabra* Hort.) Spreading by runners. Dimensions are for *C. compressa*, but shape more oval and upcurving, veins more noticeable being darker.

C. kummeriana. Leaf blades broadly elliptic, 6 × 2½" (15 × 6.25 cm), base color light green, veins upcurving to edges, bordered dark green. Stalks to 8" (20 cm). Purple reverse. A showy species.

C lubbersiana. Blades oblong 8" × 2½" (20 × 6.25 cm), the whole marbled with yellow, light and dark green. Stalks to 12" (30 cm).

C. oppenheimiana. Blades elliptical to 15 × 4» (37.5 × 10 cm) with gray sickleshaped marking to the edge. Stalks to 15" (37.5 cm).

'Tricolor'. With large zones of yellow and smaller areas of soft green, gray and pink. A magnificent plant. Rare and slow growing. It does well in long-fiber sphagnum moss, lightly packed. Terrarium culture.

C. setosa. Blades elliptic to 12 × 4" (30 × 10 cm). Green above and below. Stalk to 12" (30 cm), hairy.

'Burle Marx'. Half the size of the species. Blade silvery gray with upcurving green stripes to the edges.

'Hummel's Black Wart'. Blades marked with very dark and lighter green.

Cupressus. **Cupressaceae.** Cypress. N. America, Europe, Asia. Large trees. Partial to full sun. Min. 800 fc, 16 hours daily. Temperature min. 50°F (10°C) for the tropical and subtropical species. Houseplant Mix #3 with sand. Propagation from cuttings. 22 species of which at least 2 are grown indoors.

Some of the true Cypress are warm-climate plants that do well in tropical settings. It is surprising that they have been so little used as large trees for indoor plantings. Juvenile trees are favored for bonsai and are also attractive when allowed to grow without training.

Their only major demands are moisture and rather bright light. They do well in a sunny south window.

C. lusitanica. Portuguese Cypress. Actually native to Central America. Juvenile leaves very short, whorled and triangular. Branches drooping. Little-grown in this country probably because they are too tender even for much of California. They are, therefore, also not readily available. They have substantial potential as a house and atrium tree. Good air movement is a must.

C. sempervirens. Italian Cypress. Less tropical then *C. lusitanica* and more popular. Must be grown with max. night temperature of 60°F (16°C) in winter. Keep on a windowsill in full sun or under fluorescent light at max. 75°F (24.5°C) in winter.

'Swane's Golden'. Beautiful golden green foliage. It trains well and matures as a columnar shape. Slow growing and sturdy. Patented cultivar.

Cussonia. **Araliaceae.** Tropical Africa. Small succulent trees. Partial to full sun. 600–1,000 fc 12–14 hours daily. Temperature min. 55°F (13°C). Houseplant Mix #2 with sand. Branch and stem cuttings. Rather difficult. 25 species of which 2 or 3 cultivated indoors.

Growing to 15' (4.5 m) in nature, these decoratively leaved trees attain max. 5' (1.5 m) indoors. Dormant in summer. Growth is mostly between November and May.

During the growing season water as soon as soil is dry. Fertilize monthly with high potash formula (for instance, Hyponex 7-8-19). In summer leaves may drop completely but watering once a month may retain them until new growth starts. Leaves are attacked by spider mites.

Propagate during the growing season from section of the pulpy stem or branches planted upright in moist, sterile sand and maintained at 75°F (24.5°C) or higher. The shoot rises from the center of the cut.

Dormancy makes them unsuitable for plantscaping, but they are an interesting and challenging plant for indoor gardeners.

C. paniculata. Cabbage Tree. Handshaped leaves to 12" (30 cm) in diameter or more. The number of leaflets increases as the plant matures from 5 to 12. Leaflets 6" (15 cm) long, jaggedly cut into 5 lobes. Thin stalks to 8" (20 cm). Spectacular.

C spicata. Cabbage Tree. Similar to the above. Leaflets more narrow and divided into jagged spoonshaped subleaflets, creating a snowflake design. This is a warmer-growing species and should have a minimum temperature of 65°F (18.5°C). It also remains leafy more frequently in summer.

C. thyrsiflora. Handshaped leaves, the segments spoonshaped to 3" (7.5 cm) long.

Cyanastrum. **Cyanastraceae.** Nigeria. Tuberous stemless herb. Shade to filtered sun. 300–500 fc 14 hours daily. Temperature min. 60°F (16°C). Humidity 50%. Houseplant Mix #1. Propagation from tuber offsets. Easy. 7 species. 1 cultivated indoors.

C. cordifolium compactum, has 8" (20 cm) long, broadly heartshaped, leaves with deeply set veins giving a corduroy effect. Stalks of the same length. Blue fragrant flowers on short spikes directly from the soil. Requires constant moisture in summer and high-middle number (phosphoric) fertilizer every 2 weeks. Partial dormancy occurs in winter, and soil should be allowed to dry out except for light watering once a week.

Cyanotis. **Commelinaceae.** Tropical Asia and Africa. Creeping, semisucculent herbs. Partial to full sun. 500–800 fc 14 hours daily. Temperature min. 50°F (10°C). Cactus & Succulent Mix #2. Propagation from offsets. Easy. 50 species of which only 2 much grown indoors.

The two houseplant species are so similar that labels are often switched. They are thin stemmed, with hairy, clasping leaves that look well in hanging pots or small baskets. Water when soil is dry in summer and spray well once a week in winter unless leaves start to shrivel, in which case water lightly. Trim back lanky stems. If fertilized at all use 15-30-15.

C. kewensis. Teddy Bear Plant. India. Main stem short, to 4" (10 cm) high, reddish hairy; the opposite-alternate, swordshaped leaves, crowded and overlapping at the base; 1–1½" (2.5–3.75 cm) long, hairy, green, red tipped. Flowering stems pendant, the leaves half size and wider spaced. Small reddish flowers.

C. somaliensis. Pussy Ears. Africa. Narrowly triangular leaves of the same length as above, but edging hairs are longer. Flowers blue.

Cycas. **Cycadaceae.** Bread Palm. Old World tropics and Australia. Small, palmlike trees. Partial to full sun. Temperature min. 50°F (10°C). Humidity min. 50%. Houseplant Mix #2 with perlite and sand, not vermiculite. Propagation from suckers on the trunk or from the base. Rather difficult. 20 species of which 2 are grown indoors.

Note: Other genera formerly belonging to **Cycadaceae** have been assigned to **Zamiaceae** based on the pattern of the leaflet veins, except one to Stangeriaceae. See *Ceratozamia, Dioon, Encephalartos* and *Zamia.*

Cycas and the other genera listed above can take the place of palms indoors where narrower and/or somewhat shorter foliage is more appropriate.

Though *Cycas* species grow 10–20' (3–6 m) high in nature they are usually no more than 5' (1.5 m) with a spread of 4–6' (1.20–1.80 m) indoors.

They are very slow growing, long lasting and drought resistant. They make fine pot and small tub plants for the house provided they have sufficient sun.

If they are not used more in commercial plantings

it is probably due to the cost of fine specimens, for which their slow growth is responsible. Proportions are better suited to most plantings than palms, and they are less subject to infestation by pests.

The plants start as beautiful, brown, furry cones with a few leaves. As the cone grows slowly into a trunk, the leaves accumulate in number and increase in length. Later on the trunk is bare except for the leaf scars, and the foliage is concentrated in a cluster at the top much as with palms.

Leaves grow to max. 5' (1.5 m), erect, then curving downward at the tips. The rib is lined on either side by numerous narrow, stiff, curving, dark lacquered green leaflets to 10" (25 cm) in length. Without strong sun new leaves will degenerate and die off. In a window the plant must be given a quarter turn weekly to preserve the symmetry. Keep moist during the spring and summer growing season but allow to dry out well between waterings during the winter months when they are dormant. Fertilize no more than 4 times during the growth period with high nitrate formula. If suckers appear they can be removed and rooted in moist sand maintained at 85°F (29.5°C). Amateurs are well advised to buy rooted plants.

C. circinalis. The Sago Palm. Leaflets from ½–1" (1.25–2.50 cm) wide. Temperature min. 60°F (16°C). Warmer growing than *C. revoluta.*

C. revoluta. Leaflets ¼–½" (6.25–12.5 mm) wide, very closely set. The leaf is more feathery in appearance. It tolerates 50°F (10°C). Tolerates high temperatures. The easier to maintain of the two.

Cyperus. **Cyperaceae.** Umbrella Sedge. Worldwide tropics. Grasslike aquatic herb. Filtered to full sun. 400–1,000 fc 14 hours daily. Temperature min. 60°F (16°C). Humidity min. 60%. Houseplant Mix #2 with sand. Propagation by division or top of stalk. Easy if special conditions are met. 600 species of which 4 grown indoors.

The cultivated Cyperus are easily recognized by their thin, straight, erect stalks topped by a flat pinwheel consisting of a tight, short spiral of stalkless, long, pointed, strapshaped leaflets, short and straight or long and curving gracefully downward at the tips.

All grow in marshy, shallow water. Submerge pots or troughs or keep soil in pots with soil constantly wet. For safety's sake keep pots in water-filled saucers. Fertilize 2 or 3 times a year with a balanced formula. Plants spread by subsoil runners that can be severed and potted up. To propagate the tops, remove any flowers, cut leaflets in half; cut stalk 3" (7.5 cm) below the leaflets. Plant up to leaf cluster in moist sand. Maintain 80°F (27°C) soil temperature.

These are graceful plants for a pot in a sunny window. The smaller varieties fit under lights as juveniles. They have been used effectively in indoor pools. Little attention is required as long as there is sufficient light.

C. albostriatus (diffusus). Dwarf Umbrella Sedge. W. Pacific islands. Best for pot culture. Less demanding in regard to moisture and light. Filtered sun is sufficient. Stalks 8–20" (20–50 cm) tall. Leaflets 8–16, 8 × ½" (20 × 1.25 cm). Compact and bushy.

'Variegatus' is striped with white on stems and leaflets.

C. alternifolius. The Umbrella Plant. Madagascar. 2–3' (60–90 cm). Stems bluntly triangular. Leaflets 12–40. To 12 × ½" (30 × 1.25 cm), drooping at the tips. Requires constant warmth, high humidity and complete wetness. Stems grow to various heights on the same plant.

'Gracilis'. Dwarf, usually less than 1' (30 cm) high. Leaflets fewer, shorter, very narrow and straight, angled upward.

'Variegatus'. Creamy bands on leaflets and stalks.

C. isocladus. Miniature Papyrus. Africa and W. Pacific islands. Stalks triangular to 2' (60 cm). Tufts of very numerous leaflets, short, threadlike. Warm growing, requiring high light and constant moisture.

C. papyrus. Papyrus. The most imposing member of this huge family. 4–10' (1.20–3 m). Leaflets in a fantastic cloud of hundreds. Threadlike, 12" (30 cm) or more long.

Much too big for house culture but superb massed in sunny aquatic plantings.

Cyrtosperma (Alocasia). **Araceae.** Copper Cobra. Old and New World tropics. Filtered sun. 300–500 fc 12 hours daily. Temperature min. 65°F. (18.5°C). Humidity min. 50%. Long-fiber sphagnum moss or Houseplant Mix #3. Propagation by division. Moderately difficult. 15 species of which one presently in cultivation.

C. johnstonii (Alocasia johnstonii). Cobra Plant. Solomon Islands. Mature plants grow to 2½' (75 cm) indoors. Leaf blades arrowshaped and deeply cleft, to 18 × 8" (45 × 20 cm), the basal lobes to 5" (12.5 cm) long. The attitude of the blade is the reverse of most aroids, the tip being held upright above the basal lobes, hence the common name. The surface is bright, oily green, covered with a network of veins in blood red. The stalks 2' (60 cm) or more long, brown spotted, spiny.

Keep soaking wet during spring and summer but allow to dry out before watering in winter. Fertilize with high nitrate formula every 3 weeks in summer.

Dianella. **Liliaceae.** Flax Lilly. Southwestern Pacific. Filtered to partial sun. 400–600 fc 12 hours daily. Temperature min. 50°F (10°C). Humidity min. 40%. Houseplant Mix #3. Propagation by division. Easy. 25 species, mostly too cool growing, 2 suitable for the house.

D. caerulea. New South Wales. Plants grow in narrow tufts, the stemless leaves opposite and superimposed, iris fashion, but gracefully curved. 18 × 1" (45 × 2.5 cm), the edges rasping. Medium green. The blue flowers on long stems are rare indoors.

'Variegata'. Leaves longitudinally striped with gold, turning yellowish green with age.

Keep constantly moist and fertilize with a balanced formula once a month. Does well under fluorescent light. The variegated plant is distinctive and elegant. Easily propagated by cutting the root connecting the tufts and potting up. Should be grown more often.

D. ensifolia (Dracaena ensifolia). Umbrella Dracaena. Much like a *Dracaena,* the stem to 6' (1.80 m), marked with leaf scars. Leaves swordshaped to 12 × 2" (30 × 5 cm), dark green, spiraled. Tolerant of low light. But there are other, more attractive plants of the type.

Dichondra. **Convolvulaceae.** Central America and Western Pacific. Creeping vine. Partial to full sun. 500–1,000 fc 12 hours daily. Min. 55°F (13°C). Sterilized garden soil with peat. Propagation by runners. Rather difficult indoors. Nine species of which one sufficiently warm for the indoors.

D. micrantha. (repens). Thin-stemmed trailer for small baskets, with hoofshaped leaves ½" (1.25 cm) across. Keep just moist and fertilize 2–3 times a year with a high-middle- and third-number formula (phosphorus and potash). Peat is added to the medium to increase water retention. Difficult to establish well.

Dichorisandra. **Commelinaceae.** Peru and Brazil. Fleshy herb. Filtered sun. 300–400 fc 12 hours daily. Temperature min. 60°F (16°C). Humidity min. 50%. Packaged Houseplant Medium or Houseplant Mix #3 with lime. Propagation by cuttings in long-fiber sphagnum moss and by division. Moderately difficult. 30 species of which 3 grown indoors and in greenhouses.

D. reginae. A very decorative pot plant requiring continuous moisture, warmth and high humidity. Subject to fungus diseases. Fertilize once a month with a high phosphate/potash formula.

Height to 12' (60 cm) indoors. Leaves clasping the stem in alternate pairs, lanceshaped, thick, juicy, to 4" (10 cm) long; brilliantly striped with green, purple and silver.

A gorgeous plant when well grown but exceedingly temperamental.

C. thrysiflora. Leaves green, to 6" (15 cm) long. Grown more for its blue flowers.

'Variegata'. Leaves striped with silver.

C. warscewicziana. Leaves to 5" (12.5 cm) with silver stripe down the center.

Dieffenbachia. **Araceae.** Dumb Cane. Tropical America. Large-leaved, stemmed herb. Filtered to partial sun. 300–800 fc. Temperature min. 60°F (16°C). Humidity 40–50%. Houseplant Mix 1,2 or 3 with lime. Propagation from stem cuttings or air layering. Easy to difficult. 30 species or more of which at least 20 are grown indoors.

Dieffenbachias have fleshy, thick, unbranched stems and spiraled, long-stalked leaves displayed horizontally or curving downwards at the tips. As old leaves die off the bare stem is revealed. The common name is due to calcium oxalate in the sap which causes temporary numbing of the tongue and vocal chords if anyone is so over-curious as to chew a piece.

They are magnificent plants that display large, shapely leaves with an unusual degree of natural variegation. Selection and hybridizing have brought forth a host of cultivars that compete for attention.

In the last few years variegation types have constantly changed in the shops. Leaves are seen with markings of 3, 4 and 5 different shades of white to dark green. Deriving from *D.* × *bausei* and their ilk, they make a more decorative impression at first sight than the simpler-patterned earlier species and cultivars. No doubt the attraction for the impulse buyer is strong. But without distinct patterning they are unesthetic and dull so that the novelty soon wears off, and it is realized that they are a hash of minor color changes that cancel each other out. The plants themselves are also becoming less vigorous and more vulnerable to disease, hence some reduction in their popularity. Other species and cultivars are still around and are usually both more attractive and easier to maintain.

Light requirement varies between low and high according to the species or cultivar. Stem rot can occur if over-watering is continued. Fertilize no more than once a month with high nitrate formula. The plants are subject to scale, mite and mealybug infestation. The first, because of the large leaf size, is easy to swab off. The young of the two others take refuge in the interstices of the stem-clasping stalks. A number of thorough dousings with pesticide are needed to get rid of them.

Watering for Dieffenbachias is crucial. Despite their fleshy appearance they must not be kept continuously moist but allowed to dry out between waterings. Signs of excess moisture are wider spaces between the joints, thinner and smaller leaves, and dripping from the tip of the leaf. Lower leaves will begin to droop if the need for moisture is real. High humidity or frequent mistings also increase the size of leaves.

A major decorative problem is fast growth of the stem. It can be inhibited by tight potting and minimal watering. Eventually it becomes too tall—to 10' (3 m). Heel cuttings with leaves attached will root in sphagnum or peat moss. But the simplest method is air layering, just below the lowest healthy leaf of the crown. Sections of stem laid on or in moist, sterilized medium will root and sprout if kept in bright shade with 75°F (24.5°C) bottom heat.

Usually Dieffenbachias displayed in the shops are large leaved, requiring a position near a sunny window and plenty of room, as the spread is 3' (90 cm) or more. Turn weekly.

Interior plantscapers have not taken to them as much as one might expect. This may be attributable to the greater adaptability of competing plants. Light needs are, in practice, usually higher than expected. If they have to be replaced, it is more difficult to restore them. Nevertheless their showiness is incontestable, and attrition of the market will induce nurseries to be more careful to grow the reliable and more decorative plants. They are fine for temporary displays. In the South they have been used somewhat more freely in permanent plantings.

D. acuminata. Broad, elliptical blades, 15 × 6" (37.5 × 12.5 cm), the veins sunken; surface sprinkled with bright yellow dots.

D. amoena. Hortus Third describes the popular plant that goes by this name but asserts that it is not in cultivation, posing an enigma without supplying a solution. It continues to be our favorite. We have never known it to be listed or sold under any other name. It is certainly the most vigorous and reliable of the larger plants.

With a stem that can grow to more than 10′ (3 m) and 3" (7.5 cm) in diameter, it is very imposing indeed. the blades are elliptical, 20 × 8" (50 × 20 cm) on stalks to 12" (30 cm). Dark green with irregular splashes of white or cream following the veins part way to the edges.

'Golden Snow', 'Snow Leaf' and 'Tropic Snow' are among those having broader jagged white stripes.

'Tropic Snow' is most in vogue at present and, though requiring somewhat more light, is certainly superior to many of the novelties.

D. × bausei. This is an old (1890?) hybrid that has regained popularity. To 6′ (1.80 m) tall. Blades lanceshaped to 15 × 4" (37.5 × 10 cm), the tip coming to a long point. Surface scrambled with chartreuse, green and cream. Its temporary popularity has spawned a number of related cultivars.

C chelsonii. Leaves broadly lanceshaped, 15 × 7" (37.5 × 17.5 cm) with a horizontally feathered gray stripe down the midrib. Grows to 5′ (1.50 m).

D. daguensis. To 5′ (1.50 m). Blades elliptical on very thick stalks to 15" (37.5 cm). Green.

'Ripple Leaf'. Veins depressed. Rich jade green.

D. delecta. Stems weak, the leaf blades pendant, narrowly elliptic, 12" × 2½" (30 × 6.25 cm). Yellow feathering along the midrib. Humidity 60%+. Temperature 65°F+ (18.5°C) Rare and difficult.

D. exotica (?) 'Arvida'. To 3′ (90 cm). Leaves lanceshaped, 10 × 4" (25 × 10 cm). The green brilliantly splashed with white. Filtered sun. 400 fc 12 hours daily. Humidity 65%+. A very tender and difficult plant but an incomparable eye catcher.

D. fournieri. Large lanceshaped leaves on thin, tough stalks. Blade to 15" (37.5 cm) splashed with ivory; held upright.

D. hoffmannii. Somewhat bigger edition of *D. exotica* 'Arvida' but variegation more irregular and less brilliant.

D. imperialis. Leaves oval, borne erect, to 20" (50 cm), irregularly splashed with yellow. A form with a narrow leaf also bears this name in the trade. Has creamy splotches.

D. leonii (?) Blades lanceshaped, 10 × 3" (25 × 7.5 cm) Satin surfaced, dark green, massively blotched with yellowish green to white.

D. leopoldii. To 3′ (90 cm). Blades oval with narrowed tip, 14 × 6" (35 × 15 cm). Velvety green with prominent midrib. 55% or more humidity.

D. longispatha. Leaves erect with thick, short stalks.

Lanceshaped to 20 × 6" (50 × 15 cm). Leathery. Veins depressed creating a corrugated surface. High humidity.

D. maculata (D. picta). A grab bag for various medium-sized plants whose leaves are covered with various degrees of white splotchings. Leaves lanceshaped, mostly to 15" (37.5 cm) long. Height 4′ (1.20 m). Sturdy plants requiring only filtered light and moderate humidity of min. 40%. Our listing of cultivars is by no means exhaustive.

D. maculata angustior lancifolia. Leaves somewhat narrower to 6" (15 cm), held upright; variegated with ivory spots and streaks.

'Barraquiniana'. Blade with a pointed tip, white midrib and scattered creamy dots. Stalk white.

D. 'Camille'. Popular dwarf to 2′ (60 cm), the leaves clustered, marked with a broad area of greenish ivory down the center.

'Compacta'. The size of 'Camille' but with ivory to white spotting. ('Exotica Compacta' and 'Perfection Compacta' are other good dwarfs.)

'Janet Weidner'. Leaf 15 × 6" (37.5 × 15 cm) with yellow swathe down the midrib.

'Jenmanii'. Markings more related to *D. amoena*. Grows to 3′ (90 cm). Good, reliable and pretty plant dwarf.

'Lancifolium'. Narrowly elliptical, 10 × 2" (25 × 5 cm), profusely white spotted. Stalks reddish.

'Lucy Small'. To 3′ (90 cm). Blades 10" (25 cm) long, speckled with yellow.

'Marianne'. Blades to 15" (37.5 cm) have greenish cream center turning to green with maturity.

'Mary Weidner'. Blades to 20" (50 cm) long, thick, splotched with white. Stalks marked with brown.

'Rudolph Roehrs'. The famous and popular cultivar. Leaves to 24" × 5" (60 × 12.5 cm), spreading on long stalks. Blade chartreuse with green midrib and margins. Requires higher light and humidity.

'Shuttleworthii'. Blades narrowly lanceshaped, to 15" (37.5 cm). Midrib white bordered by whitish band.

'Superba'. Leaves heavily blotched with white, the edges green.

'Viridis'. Leaves green, corrugated.

C. meleagris(?) Very dark leaves with cream spots, the stalks spotted with reddish brown.

D. × memoria-corsii. A distinctive, popular species-cultivar (or vice versa). Leaves narrowly elliptic 18 × 4" (45 × 10 cm). Stalks 5" (12.5 cm). Gray-green blade, dark veined, mottled with greenish cream and ivory. Light along midrib. Variable.

D. oerstedii. To 3′ (90 cm), blades 10" (25 cm) long with unequal halves. Stalks erect.

'Variegata'. Midrib broad and white.

D. pittieri. The species is variable, so one wonders which description is accurate. Grows to 3′ (100 cm) Blades elliptic, 12–18 × 3–5" (30–45 × 7.5–12.5 cm). Stalks thick, winged, 5–7" (12.5–17.5 cm). Corrugated, emerald green, irregularly spotted with cream and yellow.

D. seguine. Mother-In-Law Plant. As big as *D. amoena*, the blades broadly lanceshaped to 20" × 5"

(50 × 12.5 cm). Of very heavy texture, with thick, fleshy stalks.

'Liturata'. With thick, white midrib.

'Wilson's Delight'. With white midrib and white lateral veins. Superb looking but requiring somewhat cooler conditions, not over 80°F (27°C) and humidity 60% or higher. Very subject to fungal diseases of the stem. Keep rather dry.

D. xsplendens. Blades broadly elliptic to 12 × 5½″ (30 × 13.75 cm), but usually smaller. Spotted irregularly with lime green.

Dioon. **Zamiaceae.** Mexico and Central America. Small palmlike trees. Handsome and easy. See *Cycas* for culture. There are approximately 4 species.

Note: The leaflets of the **Zamiaceae** have a number of longitudinal veins but no midrib as do the **Cycadaceae.**

D. edule. Chestnut Dioon. Very similar in appearance to *Cycas circinalis.* Grows to 6′ (1.80 m). Leaves 3–6′ (90 cm–1.80 m). The leaflets narrow and close together. Especially feathery and graceful when large. Filtered sun.

D. purpusii. With a short trunk. Leaves partly erect. Leaflets 4″ (10 cm), very numerous and narrow. A good cycad for the house.

D. spinulosum. Leaves to 6′ (1.80 m), the leaflets spiny. Grows to 20′ (6 m)!

Dioscorea. **Dioscoreaceae.** Yam. Worldwide. Vines with tuberous roots. Partial to full sun. 500–1,000 fc 14 hours daily. Temperature min. 45°F (7°C). Sterilized Garden Soil with Peat or Houseplant Mix #2. Propagation from underground or aerial tubers or stem cuttings. Easy. 500 species of which 8–12 tropical species are of interest indoors.

The Dioscoreas are remarkable for both their foliage and tubers. But they are dormant for an extended period, varying according to the species. As such they are of interest only to indoor gardeners unless plantscapers are able to use them for temporary displays.

The true yams should not be confused with sweet potatoes which are sometimes called yams in the South but belong to the Family **Convolvulaceae.**

The Elephant-Foot Type

D. elephantipes (Testudinaria). Elephant Foot. Hottentot Bread. South Africa. Extremely succulent. The tuber, mostly above ground, attains a diameter of 3′ (90 cm) and is humped like the carapace of a tortoise to a height of max. 8″ (20 cm). It is covered with 5–7 sided, inch (2.5 cm) high protuberances, carrying the resemblance further. The substance is brown-corky packed in thin layers. Certainly the most sculptural form of its type in nature.

A thick, strong stem rises from near the center and can travel 30′ (9 m) or more. Leaves are kidneyshaped to 2″ wide. Flowers insignificant on a little tassel.

Roots extend down from under the plate of the tuber during the growth period and die off during dormancy. The season usually extends from early spring to late fall, but indoors it is uncertain. If and when leaves start to turn yellow withhold water completely and store dry until the tuber sprouts again. Storage temperature should be at max. 55°F (13°C).

Roots do not dig deep. Pot small tubers like other plants. Large ones need ample, shallow tubs. When growth resumes water thoroughly and then allow to dry out nearly completely before repeating. Fertilize during growth with each watering, using 20-20-20 at recommended strength. Small-tubered plants can grow with their stems on pot trellises; large ones need a full window trellis.

Leaves are subject to spider mite. A fungicide soil drench is recommended along with the first watering.

Large tubers have become rare because they are now environmentally protected, but small ones, grown from seed or cuttings, are available and grow relatively fast. Cuttings taken in late spring or summer root readily in moist medium.

D. macrostachya. Western Mexico. Very similar to the above. Leaves heartshaped to 5″ (12.5 cm) long. Tubers not so geometrically plated. Culture the same.

It is something of a botanical marvel that these two species that are so nearly identical live at such a great distance apart. No similar example of oceanic and continental leapfrogging comes to mind. I refer especially to the Mexican species being found only on the Pacific side.

Dioscoreas with Other Surface Tubers

D. hemicrypta. A delicate vine with heartshaped, blue-green leaves to 3″ (7.5 cm) long. The smooth brown tuber is conical. We do not know the eventual size.

D. sylvatica. Tuber mounded, smooth, to 2′ (60 cm) in diameter. The thin stems trail. Leave are very broadly triangular, 1″ (2.5 cm) long and 1½″ (3.75 cm) broad. Blue-green. Several varieties are listed with unimportant differences in tuber and leaf size.

Culture of both is much the same as for *D. elephantipes.*

Large-leaved Species

The two species below belong to the community of edible yams of which there are any number of species and cultivars. They produce large underground tubers and beautifully shaped leaves. We have not tested the tubers for edibility. If bland in flavor when boiled, they are, presumably, safe to eat; if bitter, probably not. Both are rampant vines for a large trellised window.

D. trifida. Cush-Cush or Yampee. W. Indies and S. America. vine to 20′ (6 m), 3-angled, winged, spotted with red, twining. Stalked blades with 3 triangular segments, the central one twice the size of the two others. They grow to 10″ (25 cm) long and wide. Tuber large, submerged in the soil.

D. zanzibarensis (sansibarensis). Zanzibar. Closely related to *D. batatas,* the Chinese Yam, from more temperate parts of E. Asia. Spectacular.

Vine to 40′ (12 m), twining, bearing shiny brown

yamlets the the joints of the leaves which can be planted. Stalked leaf blades light green, 10" (25 cm) long and usually broader still. There are three lobes, the middle one a little longer, broader and pointed, the two side ones narrower, curved upward at the tip. A superb vein pattern is visible when light shines through it. Magnificently suggestive of a flying bat of large size.

The underground tuber grows to 2 pounds or more in a single season and is white in and out. We have grown them to this size in a sunny south window.

Plant small aerial or ground-grown tubers 2–3" (5–7.5 cm) deep in Houseplant Mix #2 or 3 as soon as they start to sprout in the spring. The pots should be at least 8" (20 cm) in diameter. Set in maximum sun and keep constantly moist. Fertilize with high nitrate formula with every watering. Maintain temperature above 60°F (16°C).

Tropical Heartleaved Dioscoreas

D. bulbifera. The Air Potato. Tropical East Asia. Interesting for its prodigal production of small, aerial potatoes in the joints. Twining vine with heartshaped leaves to 6" (16 cm) long and wide. Grow in a window with partial sun or under fluorescent lights on a small trellis. A 5" (12.5 cm) pot is ample. Houseplant Mix #3 or Packaged Houseplant Medium. Temperature min. 60°F (16°C). Keep evenly moist and fertilize with every watering with high nitrate formula at ¼ recommended strength. When leaves start to turn yellow remove aerial tubers and store dry until they sprout the following spring.

D. discolor. Designation for a number of vines with heartshaped leaves colored purplish, brown and silver, including *D. dodecaneura* (?) and *D. multicolor* (?). Blades are variable in shape but usually heartshaped. *D. discolor* blades are olive green streaked with lighter green and silvery gray; the veins, which follow the line of the edge, reddish to silver; the reverse purple. Most of these plants have an attractive velvety sheen. Some produce aerial tubers, some not. Culture the same as for *D. bulbifera.*

Dizygotheca (Aralia). **Araliaceae.** False Aralia. New Caledonia and Polynesia. Small trees. Filtered to partial sun. 500–700 fc. Min. 50°F (10°C). Humidity min. 50%. Houseplant Mix #3 with sand. Propagation by stem cuttings. Moderately difficult.

There are 15 species of which 3 are grown indoors as juveniles, one in particular being popular for its brown, spidery, pinwheel leaves, although it is neither easy nor long lasting in terms of display value. The stems are really slender canes bearing the long-stalked leaves in a spiral. Lower leaves are not long lasting, and plants that have been forced under greenhouse conditions disappoint by soon losing them. However, tip cuttings root easily in moist sphagnum moss in moderate light at 70°F (22°C) with 60% humidity. Cut the rest of the cane close to the soil, and one or more new canes will appear in due course.

Maintain even moisture and fertilize with high nitrate formula at ¼ strength. The plants are subject to scale, mite and mealybug infestation.

It is best to start with plants no taller than 1½' (45 cm) or with a number of canes in a larger pot.

Large specimens, either one or more planted to the pot or tub, are imposing sculptural as well as screening plants but must be replaced relatively frequently.

The descriptions below apply to juvenile plants as they are grown for sale.

D. elegantissima. Rarely branching canes to 5' (1.50 m) or more. Leaves compound, handshaped, on 4–6" (10–15 cm) brown stalks, marbled with white. Leaflets dark, reddish brown, 6–10 arranged in a circle, 5–10 × ½–1" (12.5–25 × 1.25–2.50 cm), strongly and regularly triangular sawtoothed.

Balanced off center on the thin, almost erect, spiraled stalks, the spiky leaflets form a near circle, graduating from the short to the long. The result is like an elegant fabric design, and, in practice, the plants are ideal for screening and for shadow play with lights. One of the most beautiful of all foliage plants. Such cultivars as exist have broader leaves and a more prosaic appearance.

D. kerchoveana. A similar plant except that leaflets are green, or spoonshaped, broader, more conventionally toothed, and concave-upcurving.

D. veitchii. Similar but edges of the leaflets merely undulating; green above, reddish below.

Dorstenia. **Moraceae.** Africa, America and Asia. Small to medium-sized herb. Filtered sun. 300 fc 12 hours daily. Temperature min. 65°F (18.5°C). Humdity 40%. min. Packaged Houseplant Medium. Propagation from seed. Easy. 170 species of which a large number are African succulents requiring much higher light. Only 2 species can be considered properly as foliage display plants.

D. contrajerva. Torus Herb. Leaves attached to a thick, fleshy stem that grows very slowly, covered with the leaf scars and eventually becoming unsightly. But this takes a long time, and the leaves themselves are most attractive, of very thin substance, hairy all over, divided into 7 deeply cut jagged segments, dark green mottled with areas of silver green. Length is about 5" (12.5 cm) and width is nearly as great. Stalks reach 6" (15 cm). The spread of the plant is about 12" (30 cm) and the height rarely more. The production of flower receptacles, typical of the genus, consisting of an oblong surface with a crimped rim bearing innumerable nearly microscopic flowers, is continuous. Viable white seed, visible on the surface, is propelled into other pots or can be removed by hand, permitting the easy reproduction of this beautiful plant.

Even more attractive in our opinion is *D. contrajerva* var. *amplifolia,* a natural variety, with leaves to 8" (20 cm) in length.

A beautiful plant for display below eye level. We have never encountered pests on this plant. It will grow even in a north window.

Less attractive in our opinion is *D. contrajerva* var.

amplifolia which has smaller leaves with narrower segments.

This is a splendid, long-lasting, houseplant of easiest culture but of interest only to the amateur. There would be no problem producing it commercially, but it is not of a type that attracts the attention of impulse plant shoppers.

D. turnerafolia. Bearing up to 10" (25 cm) lanceshaped, dark green, oily-surfaced leaves. The receptacles are purple on long maroon stalks. Culture the same as *D. contrajerva.* An excellent, leafy houseplant.

Succulent types. there exists a host of African succulent species of small size, with thickened stems (caudices) and flower receptacles that assume fantastic shapes. Easy to grow and maintain. Seed is produced quite spontaneously even under fluorescent light. But we cannot, legitimately, include them here as primarily foliage plants.

Dracaena (including *Pleomele*). Old World tropics. Shrubs and single-stemmed, leafy herbs. Shade to filtered sun. 50–300 fc. Mostly min. 50°F (10°C). Packaged Houseplant Medium. Propagation by cuttings. and offsets. Easy to Cast Iron. 40 or more species of which approximately 10 are cultivated indoors.

Dracaena is probably the most important commercial foliage genus at the present time, offering a number of nearly or fully Cast-Iron species and cultivars plus ornamental varities for the collecting amateur and horticulturist. With some exceptions they have fleshy or pulpy stems crowned by leaves arranged in a more or less tight spiral. Blades are generally long, narrow, elliptical or lanceshaped with tough to fleshy stalks. They are occasional bloomers at night, the foxtails of tiny white flowers intensely and insipidly perfumed.

Its popularity is due to easy and quick growth in tropical Central America, where most of the commercial production is located, generally slow growth indoors, long-lasting leaves, tolerance of both high temperatures and moderately cool ones, endurance of underwatering if not excessively protracted, a very low light requirement and hardly any fertilizer. To maintain bright leaves even moisture is recommended along with monthly feeding of a balanced formula at ¼ recommended strenth.

We have divided the genus into three types of plants.

Trees
D. Americana. Central America. 30' (9 m).

D. arborea. West tropical Africa. 40' (12 m).

D. draco. The Dragon Tree. Canary Islands. 70' (21 m).

Three trees with quite similar habit. Stems bare, branches few and equally bare except for the tips, hidden by a thick crown of stiff, pointed, strapshaped leaves 2–3' × 2–3" (60–90 × 5–7.5 cm). *D draco* is the most cold tolerant. All are drought resistant, slow growing. Light requirement, however, is at least partial sun.

Not recommended for pot culture except as juveniles, 2–3' (60–90 cm) high.

When they are available, which is not often, tall specimens, especially branched ones, are ideal for big exotic plantings.

D. (Pleomele) reflexa. Madagascar. Shrubby tree to 30' (9 m). Available only as young plants. The typical appearance of this strange plant is of 3 or more unbranched canes in a tub or pot. The stems weak and untidily twisted to 10' (3 m) or more and completely covered from bottom to top with very dark green, spiraled, strapshaped leaves to 15 × 1" (37.5 × 2.5 cm) but usually shorter. The lower leaves seem to stay on forever, and the tolerance of the plant to abuse is unbelievable.

The undisciplined but striking mass of foliage can be most useful as an architectural plant near stairs or in corners where it breaks the architectural line, but a wall acts as a visually steadying influence. It is totally ineffective as the center of attention.

'Gracilis'. Strapleaved to 15" (37.5 cm) Dark green.

'Song of India' (Sri Lanka). What a beauty! It is hard to believe that it is a cultivar of *D. reflexa.* Thin stemmed, the 6 × 1½" (15 × 3.75 cm) swordshaped leaves, light green in the middle with wide, brilliant golden margins. Lovely in pots to 3' (90 cm) high. It can grow as tall as the species but then loses all charm for it should be seen only from above. Not easy, requiring warmth and high humidity. Filtered sun. Very tender. Spray with fungicide regularly to prevent leaf and stem rot.

'Song of Jamaica'. The golden stripe is down the center of the leaf. Culture as for the above.

Shrubs
D. marginata. It might be called the Bank Plant, so frequently has it been used in their august premises.

One to several leaf-scarred stems grow from soil level to 8' (2.40 m) or more. If pruned a stem rarely produces more than a couple of branches. The peculiarity of these stems, and their charm, is that they support themselves but never grow straight. They are naked to the top, which is crowned with short, closely spiraled leaves 2' × 1" (60 × 2.5 cm), dark green with a narrow margin.

Older plants with curiously distorted stems are highly prized and nurserymen do their bit to train them that way. Smaller plants on short stalks have a more ordinary appearance. The plant is Cast Iron in culture; tolerant of 50 fc and considerable neglect.

'Tricolor'. The leaves are vertically decorated with parallel stripes of pink, cream and, in some clones, green.

Splendid as a low display plant to be seen from above. It becomes rather unsightly when over 2' (60 cm) unless placed where it can be looked down upon. It requires filtered sun or 500 fc.

D. surculosa (godseffiana). Gold Dust Dracaena. A branching shrub to 3' (90 cm) but normally grown much shorter indoors. Leaves elliptical, shiny, thick, to 4 × 1½" (10 × 3.75 cm) with an attenuated tip; dark green, profusely spotted with ivory or yellow.

D. surculosa punctulata (?). Leaves to $8 \times 2''$ (20×5 cm), sparingly spotted with yellow.

Keep evenly moist and feed regularly with high nitrate formula. Cuttings root quickly in Jiffy-7s.

'Florida Beauty'. Almost completely covered with rounded cream spots.

'Friedmannii' ('Friedman', Milky Way). Broad white center stripe surrounded by fine white dots.

'Kelleri'. Leaves thicker, somewhat longer and narrower, with ivory blotchings.

This colorful plant might be more popular were it not for the poor growth habit. Branches lengthen unpredictably and do not respond well to pruning. Very pretty when small in 4–6'' (10–15 cm) pots.

Colonizing Single-Stemmed Herbs

These spread by underground runners.

D. (Pleomele) angustifolia honoriae (variegata). Stem weak; leaves strapshaped pointed, spiraled to $15 \times 3''$ (37.5×7.5 cm) or longer. Green with creamy margin. Shade tolerant but requires humidity of 50%. Tall plants must be supported. Best when short.

D. deremensis. Tropical Africa. Fine and popular plants displayed singly or in clusters. They become unsightly, however, as soon as there is much length of bare stem.

Stems grow to 15' (4.5 m) but are rarely over 5' (1.5 m) indoors. Leaves narrowly swordshaped to $2 \times 3''$ (60×7.5 cm), spiraled and overlapping at the base. Min. 60°F (16°C) and 50% humidity. At lower temperature and humidity leaves tend to brown. Keep evenly moist and fertilize monthly with a balanced formula. Plants in the shops are often inadequately rooted, having been forced excessively. Spray with fungicide and water more sparingly to save them. Poor soil must be replaced. Once well established they are more tolerant. Slow growing.

'Bauei'. Gray-green, striped down the center with broad panels of white reaching to the margin on either side.

'Janet Craig', a sport of 'Warneckei'. A more vigorous plant than the species. Leaves dark green with a wavy edge, $20 \times 4''$ (50×10 cm); of solid substance, curving over at the tip. A Cast-Iron plant and an important commercial variety. North light.

'Janet Craig Compacta'. An extremely compact form with the $6 \times 3''$ (15×7.5 cm) almost black-green, vertically ribbed leaves, angled upward and closely overlapping. Maddeningly slow growing but undemanding. Tolerates 45 fc and extreme abuse. No beauty but ideal greenery for a lazy gardener. Usually sold singly from 1' (30 cm) to 3' (90 cm).

'Longi'. Very dark green, strapshaped, pointed leaves with clean white stripes down the middle.

'Warneckei'. Leaves striped with white, brown-gold and gray-green. Surprisingly tolerant of low light. The plant has been so popular that its variability has been used to develop many more varieties than we list.

'Warneckei Compacta'. A dwarf of very compacted form with the same coloring.

'Warneckei Gold King'. Widely banded with green-gold.

'Warneckei Lemondrop'. Tannish yellow stripes.

'Warneckei Roehrs Gold'. Center stripe cream, white stripes and green margin.

'Warneckei Snow Queen'. Intensely white broad stripes.

D. fragrans. The Corn Plant. Canes grow to 20' (6 m) but usually not over 10' (3 m) indoors. Stem thick and woody. Strapshaped leaves to $3' \times 4''$ (90×10 cm), curving, dark green, firm. This is the most frequently used plant for offices and other public places as well as in the home.

The plants are Cast Iron, accepting light as low as any indoor foliage, usually disease free, rarely attacked by pests, tolerant of pollution and neglect. They are sold in tubs with 3 or 4 canes 2'' (5 cm) thick with the tops cut and the leaves growing from 1–3 sideshoots. Mutilated, ugly, but cheap for their size and virtually carefree.

In the tropics the canes are grown relatively quickly to a considerable height in vast numbers. They are then cut into sections, the bottom end wrapped in moist moss and stacked until roots form. This accounts for their low cost, but, unfortunately, they are often also inadequately rooted. We find that it takes up to a year to establish them well indoors unless a U.S. nursery has held them for a while before selling. Further, they are often sold potted in Florida muck with a top dressing of bark and peat moss. Such plants should be repotted in Houseplant Mix #2 or a good packaged houseplant medium. Once well established they are virtually permanent.

'Lindenii'. Leaves bordered with yellow.

'Massangeana'. The most commonly grown cultivar. With a broad yellow band down the center of the leaf

'Rothiana'. With white edges.

'Victoriae.' Magnificent! Broad stripes of cream and yellow. Rare because the propagated plants do not reliably carry on the true color.

D. sanderana. Ribbon Plant. As the spirals are looser the leaves are further apart, to $9 \times 2''$ (22.5×5 cm), the tips very drawn out. Light green with a broad white margin. Weak stemmed. Those above 2½' (75 cm) must be staked. Undecorative once the naked stems are tall. Fast growing and rather short lived.

'Borinquensis'. Centered with light green; bordered by a thin line of white and framed by a broad, dark green margin.

'Celes'. Stiff, upright leaves, coming to a sharp point. Dark green with white margins.

'Margaret Berkery'. Ascending spiral leaves $9 \times 3''$ (22.5×7.5 cm). Dark green with white stripe down the middle. White stripe still broader on the reverse giving the effect of a brilliantly variegated stem as long as it is covered.

Usually planted 3 or 4 to a pot. The effect is rather dun. Plants purchased in the shops are usually badly rooted.

D. thalioides (Pleomele). Shrubby, multistemmed growth to 2½' (75 cm). Stiff leaves with vertical depressed veins, swordshaped, $15 \times 3''$ (37.5×7.5 cm). Very leafy. Cast Iron.

Dyckia. **Bromeliaceae.** Southern S. America. Low, colonizing, succulent herbs. Partial sun. 500–800 fc 14 hours daily. Temperature min. 45°F (7°C). Houseplant Mix #2 with sand. Propagation from offshoots. Easy. 100 species of which about 12 are grown indoors.

Dyckias are rosette plants with long, narrow, spreading, stiff, rough-surfaced and spiny-edged leaves. Water only when complete dry and mist leaves from time to time. Fertilize with 1/8 strength high nitrate formula from May to October with every watering. The plants may retain their reverse growth cycle, active in winter rather than summer. They spread by underground runners. Excellent pot plants needing little attention.

D. altissima. Leaves to 18 × 1″ (45 × 2.5 cm). Very attenuated, horizontal, spiny edged.

D. brevifolia. A compact species. Leaves very numerous, bright green, spiny, 8″ (20 cm) long.

'Yellow Gold'. Yellowish leaves.

D. cabrarae. Rosettes of tightly packed leaves.

'Carlsbad'. Leaves thicker, to 12″ (30 cm) long.

D. encholirioides. Gray leaves with hooked tips.

D. fosterana. Fabulous sprays of whitish, formidable-looking leaves armed with swordfish teeth. 15 × 1″ (35 × 2.5 cm).

'Lad Cutak'. Leaves purplish and swirled. Heavily toothed.

D. platyphylla. Leaves to 18″ (45 cm). Deep green and glossy.

Ehretia. *(Carmona).* **Boraginaceae.** Worldwide tropics and subtropics. Shrubs and trees. Filtered to partial sun. 250–800 fc. Min. 60°F (16°C). Houseplant Mix #3, or 4 parts peat to 1 perlite. Cast Iron. Propagation by seed and cuttings. 50 species of which one presently grown indoors.

E. microphylla. Phillipine Tea. A most unusual borage; a fine little shrub for pot culture and one of the easiest for pseudo-bonsai training. Maximum height 12′ (3.60 m). Woody and very much branched; the joints corky; the almost stalkless leaves to 1″ (2.5 cm) long, shiny dark green, finely blistered, spoonshaped with a few shallow lobes near the tip. Very small, white flowers are produced throughout the year followed by red berries that soon drop. The seed is viable. Long-lived.

Ehretia can grow in a north window or under 2-tube fluorescent light. Even moisture. Fertilize with a high nitrate formula with every other watering. Treat with micronized or chelated iron twice a year. Very adaptable to trimming and training. When not pruned it grows with surprising speed. Seed germinates promptly. Occasionally subject to mealybug which is difficult to eradicate as the young take refuge in the joints.

Other Ehretias might well be tested as possible houseplants.

Elaeagnus. **Elaeagnaceae.** Europe and Asia. Shrubs. Partial to full sun. 500–1200 fc. Temperature min. 40°F (4°C). Sterilized Garden soil or Houseplant Mix #3 with sand. Difficult. Propagation by cuttings and soil layering. 40 species of which 2 occasionally grown indoors.

E. angustifolia. Russian Olive. Hardy and deciduous. Grown for the small, fragrant flowers. Not properly a houseplant, but those with cool homes and good light occasionally try it.

E. pungens. Arbutus Shrub. China and Japan. Evergreen and possible in a house that is cool summer and winter. Shrub to 15′ (4.5 m), the branches erect, usually thorny. Leaves green, the surface dotted with minute tufts of white hairs. Gray beneath with brown scales. Elliptical with wavy margins to 3″ (7.5 cm) long. In spiral clusters 1½″ (3.75 cm) apart or more. Keep cool and well aerated, barely moist and fertilized every 2 weeks with a balanced formula.

Not recommended, as being too cool growing for most. Only the following dwarf cultivars are grown indoors.

'Aurea'. Leaves yellow edged.

'Compacta'. Shrubby to max. 3′ (90cm).

× ebbingei. Compact, thornless. Leaves green with silver scales.

× ebbingei 'Gilt Edge'. Striped with yellow.

'Fruitlandii'. Blades more rounded, with wavy edges and larger.

'Marginata'. Normal size but leaves silver edged.

'Nana'. Dwarf to 2′ (60 cm).

'Variegata'. Normal size but leaves silver edged.

Encephalartos. **Zamiaceae.** Central and South Africa. Palmlike plants with or without trunks. Partial to full sun. 600–1000 fc 14 hours daily. Temperature min. 45°F (7°C). Humidity 40%. Houseplant Mix #2 with sand or Cactus and Succulent Mix #1. Propagation by offsets from stem or from seeds. Difficult. 20 species mostly in cultivation. See Cycas.

We do not detail the appearance of these plants, descriptions of which can be found in standard references and catalogs.

We do not recommend them for the house for the following reasons. They need plenty of room because of the length of the leaves (6′—1.80 m) or more, and the stiff spininess of the leaflets and stalks. They are also cool growing summer and winter; need unpolluted air and plenty of light. Small plants are not very attractive. Other Cycads are certainly preferable.

Of value to plantscapers as mature plants for the magnificence of the great leaves and the forked, twisted, lacquered shapes. They must be segregated from traffic because of the sharpness of the tips. Large specimens are very costly. If light is inadequate they must be replaced and restored periodically or new leaves will abort.

Epipremnum (Scindapsus, also Raphidophora). **Araceae.** S.E. Asia and Western Pacific. Pothos (in part). Tropical vines. North light to filtered sun. 200–400 fc 12 hours daily (for young plants). Temperature min. 65°F (18.5°C). Humidity 50%. Packaged

Houseplant Medium. Propagation from stem cuttings. Easy. 10 species of which 3 cultivated indoors.

One species (Pothos) is a most popular pot and basket plant. Leaves are alternate on thin stalks. They should be kept evenly moist and fertilized no more than once every 2 months with a balanced formula. All three species are houseplants with small leaves when young. Adults have very large ones.

E. aureum (Scindapsus aureus). Pothos. A rampant vine with 30″ (90cm) long, heartshaped leaves, split horizontally into a number of narrow segments on either side of the midrib. Green or splotched with yellow and white.

Adult plants are splendid wall coverings or tree climbers in permanent southern plantings, outdoors or in. Adult plants need more sun than young ones.

As juveniles the leaves are 3–4″ (7.5–10 cm) long, unsplit. Kept in a basket they are easily controlled by pruning. The old-fashioned florists' Pothos has rather irregular yellow streaking.

'Marble Queen'. Extremely popular and nearly Cast Iron. Yellow variegation is much more consistent though occasionally reverting to green. Remove green-leaved stems.

'Tricolor' is more profusely streaked with yellow, cream and light green. It also reverts occasionally.

Nurseries attach their own names to various sports with only small changes in variegation.

E. falcifolium. A quite different plant. Initial growth is rapid and trailing. Leaves are elliptic with attenuated tips, to 12 × 2½″ (30 × 6.25 cm), much bigger in mature plants (2′ × 5″, 60 × 12.5 cm), the numerous upward-angled veins dark green, lighter silvery green between.

E. pinnatum (Raphidophora pinnata) (Monstera nechodomii). Leaves also attaining great length, to 3′ (100 cm) in maturity. Juvenile leaves segmented alternately on each side of the midrib; segments broadly based, swordshaped, to 6 × ½′ (15 × 1.25 cm) with 1–3 vertical veins. A very unusual and beautiful form.

All 3 species can be propagated in water from stem cuttings.

Episcia. **Gesneriaceae.** Tropical America. Creeping and trailing herbs. Filtered sun. 500–800 fc 14 hours daily. Houseplant Mix #1 or 2 with lime. Sphagnum moss. Temperature min. 65°F (18.5°C). Humidity min. 50%. Propagation by stem cuttings. Moderately easy to difficult. 10 or more species of which 3 and many cultivars grown indoors for foliage.

Episcias have small but brilliant flowers in bluish, yellow, orange or red; however, many are shy bloomers indoors and are grown primarily for the extraordinarily rich texture and coloration of the foliage.

These are warmth-loving plants equipped with thick, juicy, crawling stems that put down fine, shallow roots where joints touch the soil. The elliptical leaves range from 1″ (2.5 cm) to 6″ (15 cm) in length, and half as much in width. They are very thin and veined in a complex pattern, but a prominent quilting frequently combined with heavy felting

often gives them a very thick appearance. Veins protrude on the undersides forming shallow cells. Base colors of the blades are bright to very dark green and light to dark brown. The tracery is often broadly silvery. Silver, pink or white zones and blotchings are common. The stalks are thick, fleshy and usually no more than half the length of the blades.

They are superb for small pots, for medium-large baskets and terrariums; far more decorative than most of the low-growing foliage plants for these purposes and less temperamental than some. Still, to appear at their colorful best they require a considerable amount of attention, more so in the North than the South where normal temperature and humidity are closer to their needs.

Not good commercial plants. Greenhouse production is easy, but they do poorly in shop and commercial locations as well as homes where they are not constantly serviced. Low humidity, drafts, carelessness in watering cause rapid deterioration.

Episcias have frequently been recommended as low-light plants but growth is inhibited and color is muted when they receive less than filtered to partial sun. Direct sun, on the other hand, can be damaging. Temperatures over 80°F (27°C) do harm if protracted.

They are to be kept barely moist in medium that is loose so that aeration is constant and the delicate roots can penetrate the soil. Azalea-type pots are sufficiently deep. Fertilize with 15-30-15 at ⅛ recommended strength with every watering. Leach well at least twice a year. They flourish in closed terrariums. Stems are very brittle and must be handled carefully. Prune them regularly to prevent their hanging far over the sides of baskets or pots.

To propagate make stem cuttings with two joints and a whorl of leaves at the tip. Dust cut end with hormone powder and plant one joint deep in moist vermiculite, perlite or sphagnum moss. Cover with glass or plastic. Keep warm in bright indirect light. Episcias also grow suckers tipped by a cluster of leaves. Pin the tips down with hairpins in the same pot if there is sufficient room; or surround the main pot with small ones filled with moist medium and pin a sucker into each of them.

Mealybug infestation is common and difficult to eradicate. We have use Safer's with rubbing alcohol as a spray but wash the leaves well with clear water a couple of hours after treatment. Excessive heat or cold beyond the limits we have set frequently causes stem rot.

The majority of modern Episcias are cultivars of two species, *E. reptans* and *E. cupreata*, silver variegation coming from *E. reptans* and green from *E. cupreata* var. *viridifolia.* Both species are so variable that where actual hybridization has played a role and where not is largely unknown. The browns are shared by both, and other colors result from spontaneous appearance in large plantings. The number of cultivars is legion with many look-alikes, some of which revert to variations in one or the other species. The best way to pick out Episcias is to visit specialized gesneriad nurseries. Growers of African Violets or Gloxinias usually carry some Episcias.

'Chocolate Soldier'. An old and reliable plant, the leaves large, brown, veined with silver.

'Cleopatra'. By many considered the prize among terrarium foliage plants. 'Pink Brocade' is very similar but 'Cleopatra' has the sharper color pattern. Leaves are large, quilted, pale green down the midvein, this enclosed in pure white and the border broad, in pure pink. The edge is scalloped. Livelier and fresher coloring cannot be imagined. It is, of course, a freak, but most extraordinary. The plant grows as a completely circular, flat rosette and should therefore be in a round, domed terrarium. The ideal medium is long-fiber sphagnum moss that is barely moist. Feed no more than 2–3 times a year. There is no special difficulty propagating leaves with an inch of stalk in sphagnum moss under cover.

'Ember Lace'. Medium-sized (3", 7.5 cm) brown leaves splashed with bright pink. A trailer with many suckers.

'Moss Agate'. Large, quilted green leaves with silver veining. Spectacular and easy.

'Shimmer' and 'Silver Sheen'. Silver-centered leaves with brown margins. Fairly reliable.

Miniatures. The latest development has been a whole series of miniature cultivars with ½–1" (1.25–2.50 cm) leaves. Neat little plants for shallow pots.

E. lilacina. More erect plants with 6" (15 cm) leaves and larger, bluish flowers.

'Quilted Beautry' and 'Shaw's Gardens' are among the cultivars that display the heavy towelling effect unique to this species. Grow in moist sphagnum moss and 600–800 fc.

Equisetum. **Equisetaceae.** Horsetail. Scouring Rush. Worldwide except Australia and New Zealand. Aquatic herbs. Shade to filtered sun. 200–300 fc, 15 hours daily. Temperature: hardy. Medium-wet sphagnum moss. Propagation by division. Difficult. 35 species of which only dwarf varieties have been grown indoors.

These very ancient and primitive plants are usually hardy and have, until recently, been cultivated only by the Japanese who have selected a number of cultivars. Some species extend their range to areas where frosts are rare, and 2 varieties are worth trying as charming oddities.

They grow as short, jointed, green canes with horizontal to drooping, split pinwheel branches, looking like tiny groves from the age of reptiles and spreading by their roots. The dwarfs reach a height of max. 10" (25 cm). They should be grown in long-fiber or live sphagnum moss kept constantly wet and wintered close to the window panes where they are cool. Use water that has been allowed to stand for a day and do not fertilize.

E. diffusum. To 6" (15 cm), growing in tufts and colonizing by means of runners.

E. scirpoides (E. variegatum, Hort.?). Threadlike stems unbranched to 3" (7.5 cm) high.

E. 'Variegatum' (?). A doubtful catalog labeling.

Stems stiff, erect, to 6" (15 cm) high; joints brown.

Eriobotrya. **Rosaceae.** Loquat. East Asia. Small tree. Partial sun. 500–800 fc. Temperature min. 45°F (7°C). Sterilized Garden Soil or Houseplant Mix #2. Propagation by seed and branch cuttings. Easy. About 6 species of which 2 occasionally grown indoors.

The trees are common around the Mediterranean where they are grown for their small golden fruits and large, rusty brown, scarfy leaves. Seed large. Plant just below the surface.

E. deflexa. Leaves elliptic to 10" (25 cm). Edges saw-toothed. Texture very dry and thin. Surface fuzzy-rusty. Gray beneath. Somewhat warmer growing than the following.

E. japonica. Loquat. Very similar leaves to the above.

Both are grown as juveniles in pots or tubs to a height of max. 4–5' (1.20–1.50 m).

Allow to dry between waterings. Fertilize once a month with high nitrate formula. Subject to considerable leaf wilt, and leaves drop for a short period in summer.

Large specimens might make a good show as permanent plants in southern locations.

Eugenia. **Myrtaceae.** Mostly American tropics. Shrubs and trees. Filtered to partial sun. 500–800 fc 14 hours daily. Temperature min. 65°F (18.5°C). Humidity min. 40%. Houseplant Mix #3. Propagation from seeds and cuttings. Easy. Over 1,000 species of which 2 suitable for the indoors.

E. pitanga. Pitanga. A much branched shrub with stiff, shiny, elliptic leaves 3" (7.5 cm) long. Young branches and leaves finely red-hairy. Cooler growing than E. uniflora.

E. uniflora. Surinam Cherry. Leaves to 2½" (6.25 cm), the veins depressed. Stalks short. New leaves red.

Keep evenly moist and fertilize regularly with a balanced formula. Dose with iron chelate or micronized iron twice yearly.

Both make fine pot and, eventually, tub plants to 3 or 4' (90 to 1.20 cm). Spread 2½' (75 cm).

Euonymus. **Celastraceae.** Mostly Asia. Shrubs and small trees. Partial to full sun. Most species are hardy. Sterilized Garden Soil. Propagation by seed and cuttings. Difficult. 170 species of which two are grown indoors.

Euonymus belongs to that group of cool-growing evergreens which we hesitate to recommend to either amateurs or professional plantscapers. The fresh, outdoorsy greenery, somewhat akin to privet but offering much more variety of coloring and shape, is very refreshing. The plants have been florists' favorites for dish gardens, but we are inclined to attribute part of the decline in the popularity of these plantings to their inclusion. They look very pretty but under indoor conditions grow rapidly which is what no good dish-garden plant should do. Once they are moved to larger pots they can become large-sized shrubs unless roots and branches are trimmed. They will deteriorate without plenty of sun and protection against temperatures much over 80°F (27°C). The natural speed of growth therefore makes them rather short-lived indoors. As we have pointed out sufficiently, the virtues of a good crop plant are handicaps under a roof. With these reservations we describe the plants below.

Euonymus grows best, then, in bright sun and in ordinary mildly acid garden soil. Keep the soil moist but not soaking and fertilize regularly with high nitrate formula, adding an iron supplement twice a year. Good ventilation is a must as leaves will succumb rapidly to mildew if light is too low accompanied by warm temperatures and high humidity. They are not plants that love confinement. We do not recommend them for dish gardens abut rather for good-sized pots deep enough for the taproot system. As they are handsome they can provide considerable pleasure but should not be recommended for situations that do not meet the required conditions. As indoor plantscaping material we should think that they would be difficult to maintain in most situations.

E. fortunei. China. This is the less frequently used of the 2 species as it is a large, trailing and climbing shrub colonizing by means of rootlets at the joints. Max. length 20' (6 m). Leaves are shiny green, elliptic to spoonshaped with blunt-toothed edges, to 2' (5 cm) long. Var. *acuta* has half-sized leaves, and the toothing is more pointed. There are numerous variegated and dwarf cultivars which can be trained.

'Aureo-variegata'. Japanese cultivar with bright yellow variegation.

'Minima'. Trailing stems. Leaves deep green with a pattern of lighter-colored veins.

'Variegatus'. A dwarf with yellow variegation.

With care they can be maintained in small pots. Plenty of light and air.

E. japonica. Spindle Tree. Japan. Much planted as hedging or clumps in the South. There are a very large number of attractive named cultivars, but the indoor growing qualities have been poorly tested. Among the choices may be several more suitable than those we list.

These are shrubs to 15' (4.5 m). They are erect and much branched, the branches rising and the leaves closely rowed. Blades 1–1½" (2.5–3.75 cm) long, shiny, narrow, bluntly toothed. Texture is generally quite thick.

'Albo-variegata'. Blades edged with white and also dotted or blotched.

'Aureo-variegata' ('Yellow Queen'). Blades broader, oval, marked with yellow.

'Medio-pictus'. Leaves have yellow centers. Upright growth.

'Microphyllus'. Dwarf with the stems clustered. Leaves glossy.

'Microphyllus variegatus'. Leaves very small, edged with white. A true miniature.

'Silver Queen'. Leaves thick, with broad white edging.

Euphorbia. **Euphorbiaceae.** Spurge. Worldwide. Herbs and shrubs. Partial to full sun. 600–1,000 fc, 16 hours daily. Temperature min. 45°F (7°C). Mostly Succulent Mix #1 or #2. Propagation from seeds or cuttings. Easy to difficult. Over 1600 species of which more than 250 are grown indoors.

The large number of *Euphorbia* houseplants consists mainly of stem succulents, a majority of which come from the deserts of South Africa. They are superbly sculptural, but most have only tiny leaves. Of those that display more attractive foliage we list a few typical species. We also include the curious *E. tirucalli* as the most popular representative of the leafless stem succulent species that possess the decorative quality of foliage plants.

Most of these plants are active from late spring to late fall and dormant from November to May. But the safest way to judge whether it is time to water is by the behavior of the plants. Water thoroughly after a complete drying as long as new leaves or branches are growing. Cease when leaves turn yellow rapidly. Spray weekly from then on. Resume watering when new leaves appear. Fertilize no more than 3 times during active growth with 20-20-20 at ¼ strength indicated on the label. Watch out for mealybugs and mites.

Propagation from cuttings is not easy. When cut, the stems bleed a quantity of the white sap. Wash this off and dry out the cutting for a few hours before planting in sterile medium. Either sand, vermiculite or sphagnum can be used. Do not water completely but spray every 3 days. Also spray the soil with Banrot or some other fungicide effective against damping off. Place in filtered sun or under artificial light in a temperature of 75°F (24.5°C). Bottom heat encourages rooting.

Leafy Plants

E. anchoreta. Canary Islands. Shrublet, 12–14" (30–35 cm) high, with thick stem and white bark. Leaves elliptical, 2" (5 cm) long in rosettes at branch tips; stalkless, whitish powdered. Requires good air movement and coolness in winter, 45–70°F (7–22°C). Allow to dry between waterings. This culture applies to other Canary Island species.

E. angrae. S.W. Africa. Small, branching shrub with very small, elliptical leaves, somewhat thick and velvety.

E. berthlolotti. Canary Islands. Shrub to 6' (1.80 m), very broad at the top. Branches gray. Leaves stalkless, elliptical, 2" (5 cm) long, gray-green. Usable as a juvenile pot plant.

E. bravoana. Canary Islands. Stem to 3' (90 cm) or more, spreading, with few branches at top. Bark greenish yellow becoming black with age. Leaves stalkless, elliptical, bluish, with white edges.

E. cap-saintemariensis. Madagascar. Branching little plant to 12" (30 cm) high but usually shorter. Branches, round, smooth with grayish bark. Leaves in rosettes at tips; 1 × ⅜" (2.5 cm × 9.37 mm), elliptical, very stiff, edges curved upward and regularly crimped; reddish green. Grows by offsetting. A very attractive little pot plant with tiny, cupped yellow flowers. Will accept moisture throughout the year but should be kept relatively dry in winter.

E. cotinifolia. Central and South America. Shrub to 8' (2.40 m) much used in tropical America for hedges. Very upright branching, the leaves 3–5" (7.5–12.5 cm) long, lanceshaped, stalks 2–3" (5–7.5 cm). The color is normally a deep maroon, the flowers yellow and very small. Easily grown, these attractive plants deserve more attention as they make excellent houseplants if kept trimmed. They like a sunny position and Houseplant Mix #2 with sand. Temperature min. 65°F (18.5°C).

E. decaryi. Madagascar. Leaves and growth habit much like *E. cap-saintemariensis* but somewhat more trailing. Stems are very thick, square, short and the angles have close-set, harmless spines. Grayish tan. A collector's delight and splendid for dish gardens. It tolerates moisture throughout the year but should be kept relatively dry in the fall. Spreads by offsets and can be divided. Prefers partial sun but will grow under 600 fc fluorescent light. The leaves turn a rich bronze-red in bright sun.

E. dendroides. Mediterranean. Shrub to 6' (1.80 m) but grown much smaller indoors. Branching, the leaves stalkless, narrow to 2" (5 cm). A cool grower.

E. francoisii. Resembles *E. cap-saintemariensis* and *E. decaryii.* Branches creeping and offsetting. Leaves on short stalks, narrow, to 2" (5 cm) long, edges undulating, veining prominent.

E. lambii. Canary Islands. Shrub with opposite branches on the stem. To 3' (90 cm) or more. Bark brown, splitting. Leaves in rosettes at branch tips, stalkless, narrowly elliptical, bluish. Cool in winter.

E. leuconeura. Madagascar. Stem to 15" (37.5 cm), 4-angled, the angles decorated for their entire lengths with a thick fringe of red hairs, the green areas between being marked by oval, white leaf scars. Unbranched. The leaves in a rosette at the tip, elliptical, to 4" (10 cm) long. A lovely plant that blooms easily and inconspicuously but produces viable seed spontaneously. Water May to September. Spray plants only in winter. Seed can be started at any time of year. Short-lived, behaving almost like an annual but easily replaced and, when well grown, quite spectacular for its size.

E. neohumbertii is similar but stem 5-angled, green with lighter stripes. Relatively rare.

E. primulifolia. Madagascar. With a corky, thickened base and a short stem tipped with a rosette of oval, undulating, dull green leaves. The stalks are flat.

E. quadrata. S. Africa. Shrublet to 2' (60 cm), with a few reddish purple branchlets. Leaves in a rosette, leathery, green, broadly oval to 2 × 1" (5 × 2.5 cm), with broad stalks 2" (5 cm) long, the edges red.

E. viguieri. Stem to 36" (90 cm) but usually shorter indoors; 6-angled and covered with leaf scars and short clustered thorns. Leaves spoonshaped in a close spiral at the tip, to 20" (50 cm) long but usually half that length and 1½" (3.75 cm) wide. Veins white. Base of leaves turns red in some varieties when the plant is in bloom. Flowers red or yellow.

Treat like *E. leuconeura.* This is a robuster and larger plant.

Virtually Leafless Shrubs

E. tirucalli. Milk Bush. This is the most common in cultivation of a large number of species that have green to powdery blue, usually cylindrical, branches in large, more or less upright, clusters. The common name refers to the white, milky sap that characterizes the **Euphorbiaceae** in general. Tiny leaves are very short-lived, but the mass of branches and twigs has the decorative value of foliage. Branches break off spontaneously at the joints from time to time but are soon replaced. *E. tirucalli* has attracted considerable attention because of its curious and decorative form. It is frequently seen in better plant shops where it is altogether unique among the taller plants.

In the wild it may grow to 30' (9 m) with a woody-appearing trunk. But, for indoor decor, they are usually sold in small or large tubs, attaining a height of 5' (1.5 m) and a spread of at least 3' (90 cm), sometimes considerably more.

E. tirucalli requires partial to full sun and is not recommended for fluorescent light culture. Keep moist from May to September, dry December and January, slowly increasing moisture from February to May and decreasing during October and November. Houseplant Mix #1 or 2 with lime. The culture of the other species of this type (*see* Jacobsen) is much the same.

They are excellent sculptural or screening subjects in succulent arrangements where sunlight is available. They may do well in a sunny south window.

Evodia. **Rutaceae.** Madagascar to Polynesia. Shrubs and small trees. Filtered sun. 350–500 fc 12 hours daily. Temperature min. 60°F (16°C). Humidity min. 40%. Houseplant Mix #1 or 2. Propagation from tip cuttings and seed. Easy. 50 species. 1 grown indoors.

E. hortensis (?) Material offered may be *E. lepta* from S.E. Asia. Lacy Lady. An unusual little shrub with trident leaves, the leaflets 5 × ½" (12.5 × 1.25 cm); sides of midrib unevenly wide and undulating. Stalks to 2" (5 cm). Adapts well to pruning. Tiny white flowers in winter followed by viable seed in clusters. Keep evenly moist and fertilize once a month with ¼ strength balanced formula. Probably reaches a height of 2' (60 cm) indoors. A very pretty and different shrub.

Excoecharia. **Euphorbiaceae.** S.E. Asia. Shrubs. Partial sun. 350–800 fc 14 hours daily. Temperature min. 60°F (10°C). Humidity min. 40%. Propagation from cuttings. Easy. 2 species occasionally grown indoors.

E. bicolor. 'Picara'. Viet Nam. Shrub to 15' (4.5 m). Branches thin, whiplike, closely packed with paired, opposite lanceshaped leaves to 4" (10 cm) long. Requires constant moisture. The milky sap is used as a fish poison. Rarely grown.

E. cochinchinensis. Blindness Tree. The common name probably refers to the poisonous sap. Nevertheless, this is a delightful, lovely shrub of easy culture, and we recommend it highly.

Woody shrub, the bark a rich cinnamon. Leaves alternate, somewhat spoonshaped, to 4" (10 cm) long; veins depressed, quilted between; surface oily-shiny. Reverse rich cordovan red which gives a bronzy sheen to the green upper surface of the blade.

Culture is very easy being merely a matter of keeping the soil moist and feeding occasionally with a balanced formula. It occasionally is attacked by mealybug, but the infestation is easy to eradicate. Leaves hold well, growth is slow. Cuttings of young growth root quickly in moist houseplant mix.

This is an excellent pot or basket plant, and larger specimens should do well in commercial plantings. Plants should be raised to near eye level or above to show the color to best advantage.

× *Fatshedera.* **Araliaceae.** Hybrid between *Fatsia* and *Hedera.* Cool-growing houseplant. Shade to filtered sun. 50–500 fc. Temperature min. 45°F (7°C). Houseplant Mix #3. Propagation from cuttings. Moderately easy.

× *F. lizei.* Like a giant, shiny green ivy, growing to 8' (2.40 m) or more. Leaves 8 × 12" (20 × 30 cm), with 3–5 deep-cut triangular lobes to 6" (15 cm) long, glossy, leathery. They spiral the weak stem that requires support by a trellis or stake. Keeping it under control is a matter of underpotting and some pruning. Usually the plant is grown no taller than 5' (1.50 m).

Keep evenly moist and fertilize monthly with high nitrate formula unless no growth is desired, in which case it can be withheld. Treat with iron chelate or micronized iron twice a year. Very subject to mite infestation. Like most plants of Japanese origin it requires cool summers and is likely to succumb if the temperature continues above 85°F (29.5°C) for long. After a year roots and top growth should be trimmed and the soil changed.

Not an ideal houseplant though it will do better in our Pacific Northwest than most of the rest of the country. Temperamental and difficult to maintain in good condition for long.

Used in commercial locations occasionally for its ability to withstand drafts, cool temperatures and low light, but requires constant moisture. Needs frequent replacement.

'Dwarf'. Much more compact and shrubby; the best for pot culture.

'Medio-picta' ('Aurea'). Center of leaf covered with yellow-tan variegation.

'Variegata'. Wide cream margin.

'Variegata Monstrosa'. Small, 3-lobed leaves, 3–4" (7.5–10 cm), broader than long, dull green with lighter mottling. Some leaves distorted. Can be grown in 5" (12.5 cm) pots. Unreliable in our opinion.

Fatsia. **Araliaceae.** Paper Plant. Japan. Large, cool growing house shrub. Shade to partial sun. 100–600 fc. Min. 40°F (4°C). Humidity 40%. Houseplant Mix #3. Propagation by cuttings. Not easy. 1 species.

F. japonica. A shapely shrub that grows to 20' (6 m) but rarely over 8' (2.4 m) indoors. Leaves hand-shaped to 12" (30 cm) in diameter, divided into 7–11 spoonshaped segments. Shiny dark green.

'Moseri' is more compact and the usual plant cultivated. Requires coolish growing conditions, even moisture and high nitrate fertilizer. It is a plant better suited to a cool greenhouse than to normal indoor conditions. It is subject to fungal diseases if too warm, above 85°F (29.5°C), needs plenty of ventilation and is sensitive to pollution. Also very subject to spider mite infestation.

Ficus. **Moraceae.** Mostly Old World tropics. Vines, shrubs and trees. Shade to partial sun. 100–800 fc. Temperature min. 55°F (13°C). Humidity min. 40%. Packaged Houseplant Medium or Houseplant Mix #1, 2 or 3. Propagation by cuttings, air layering and division. Mostly easy. 800 species of which at least 30 grown indoors.

Because of their adaptability, versatility and resistance to disease and pests, fig species will always be an important resource for the amateur or professional indoor gardener. However, the recent history of some cultivars demonstrates the degree to which excessive price competition can be responsible for their deterioration and a reduction in their use. *Ficus elastica,* the Rubber Tree, has been one of the oldest and most reliable of houseplants. Even 10 years ago it was still very popular, indeed perhaps the most common large-leaved plant for indoor decoration. But competition in the market became so fierce that growers selected stock for a quick return on investment rather than merit and then proceeded to force them to saleable size at too rapid a pace.

The new plants had poor root systems and were potted in wretched soils. Instead of displaying compact shapes they had long gaps between joints; texture of foliage became soft; they had acquired viruses and were less resistant to fungal disorders. The public and professional contractors, discovering that they no longer lived up to their reputation as Cast Iron plants, gradually learned to avoid them.

Fortunately, the Fig genus offers so many alternatives that acceptable plants for most environments are available, and new introductions have filled the gaps. *F. elastica,* too, will make a comeback once inferior stock is no longer worth growing and good cultural methods are again employed.

We divide the genus into vines, shrubs, trees and succulents. But note that there are so many species similar to those we list that they constitute an almost inexhaustible source for potential new indoor plants.

Vines

F. pumila (F. repens). Eastern Asia. Creeping Fig. A creeper whose stems attach themselves to walls, cedar slabs or soil by rootlets wherever the joints come into contact with the surface. Leaves virtually stalkless, thin, 1" (2.5 cm) long, lanceshaped. New leaves are light green becoming darker with age.

It will manage with 100 fc 12 hours daily. Best temperature range 50–80°F (10–27°C). Keep soil evenly moist. Fertilize no more than 2 or 3 times a year with a balanced formula. Maintain at least 50%

humidity or spray plants daily.

This most adaptable of creepers where tropical conditions are maintained has many uses. Plant in baskets lined with moss or in small hanging pots. Use in terrariums as a groundcover. This is the major plant for wire topiary and for wreaths, the forms filled with sphagnum moss into which cuttings are inserted. Constant moisture must be maintained.

Use as a wall covering where there is sufficient humidity or the possibility of applying frequent sprayings. When properly maintained, the creeper will eventually cover large surfaces with a thin but solid mantle of foliage.

F. pumila minima. Quilted Fig. ½" (1.25 cm) leaves, quilted between the veins. Preferred for smaller topiary and terrariums.

F. pumila quercifolia. Miniature Oakleaf Fig. Blades ½" (1.25 cm), quilted, with a few blunt lobes at the upper end. Same purposes as above.

F. sagitata (radicans). Trailing Fig. E. Asia and Western Pacific. Stems thin, wiry, creeping. Leaf blades quilted, narrow, lanceshaped, 2–4" (5–10 cm) long.

'Variegata'. Leaves grayish green, the edges irregularly blotched with white. The form usually sold.

Stems are sufficiently strong to extend beyond a basket without becoming pendant. For adequate maintenance min. 55°F (13°C) is required and min. humidity of 50%. Apply frequent sprayings. Filtered sun. Long exposure to full sunlight produces leaf spots.

Shrubs

F. aspera (parcelli) W. Pacific. Clown Fig. Small, diffusely branched tree. Leaves elliptic, 8 × 2½" (20 × 6.25 cm) with toothed edges. Very thin, dry, the upper surface rough to the touch. Liberally streaked and spotted with ivory. Vulnerable to mites. Does best in at least partial sun and requires less humidity (40%) than others. But leaves are easily spotted and not long-lived, being replaced relatively promptly from the joints. Use Houseplant Mix #2 with sand and do not overwater. A very showy plant but difficult to keep in good condition.

F. deltoidea (diversifolia). Mistletoe Fig. Malay Archipelago. Shrub to 6' (1.80 m), woody, with twisted, spreading branches. Leaves thick, leathery, dark green, 2" (5 cm) long, the forms definitely oval or wedgeshaped. It freely produces little, round fruits that gradually turn red. Shade to filtered sun. Easy under 400 fc fluorescent light. Usually grown to max. 2' (60 cm). Supply even moisture. Min. 60°F (16°C). Responds to limited training.

'Variegata'. Leaf blades mottled stark white. Not often grown.

F. montana (quercifolia). S.E. Asia. Oak Leaf Fig. Woody shrub; leaves rough surfaced to 5" (12.5 cm) long with 5 curving lobes. Produces acornshaped fruit. Grows in ·north light. A good-looking pot plant.

F. perforata (jacquinifolia). West Indian Laurel. Large shrub to 15' (4.5 m). The thin, upturned branches bear leaves near their tips. Blades 3 × 1" (7.5 × 2.5 cm), elliptical to spoonshaped, edges turned down, dry textured. Makes a compact little 2–3' (60–90 cm) potted tree but requires partial sun. Tolerant of drying out between waterings. Fertilize only 2–3 times a year.

F. pseudopalma. Phillipine Fig. Stems arise from the base reaching max. 15' (4.5 m); covered with fiber. Leaves in upright tufts at the tips of stems. Blades thin textured, wavy edged, spoonshaped, toothed, to 30" (75 cm) long.

Not a good houseplant.

This unusual looking fig is a good specimen for partly sunny plantings as it shows its leaves without crowding out other plants.

F. subulata. (salicifolia). S.E. Asia, W. Pacific. Stem and branches thin. Leaves lanceshaped, 4–10" (10–25 cm) long, narrow, on a short stalk. Similar to *F. longifolia*.

Trees

A number of fig trees start life from seed deposited by birds on the limbs of tropical forest trees. After rooting in the debris there, they let down long filaments that reach the ground and root. The true trunk then grows, gradually envelopes and finally strangles the host tree. Others attain their huge spread by letting down stilt roots from their horizontal branches. Despite their great size at maturity, most are very adaptable plants for the indoor garden or plantscape. They are easy to propagate from stem or branch cuttings in moist peat or sand. They can be trimmed to maintain small size or they may be allowed to grow into shapely small trees. Virtually all tolerate shade or filtered sun. Keep evenly moist and fertilize no more than 4 times yearly with a balanced formula. Subject to spider mites; the leathery leaves do not suffer damage from most of the standard sprays.

F. benghalensis. Banyan. Covering large areas by means of its stilts. Leaves thick, elliptic, to 8" (20 cm) long.

'Krishnae'. Leaves are cupped and crimped on the edges.

Both the species and several other cultivars are suitable for pot or tub culture and can be kept trimmed to shape. They prefer humidity above 50%.

F. benjamina. Weeping Fig. Western Pacific. Currently the most popular small foliage tree. More than most tropical trees its branching and small leaves resemble the customary appearance of trees in the temperate zone. Economy of production, tolerance of low light, slow growth indoors and few maintenance problems are also recommendations.

Branches numerous, thin and drooping. Leaves alternate, broadly elliptic, much like Poplar leaves, to 5 × 2½" (12.5 × 6.25 cm) long but usually much shorter (3 × 1½" (6.50 × 3.25 cm); smooth, shiny. Branches are strengthened by trimming. Filtered sun. Rather indifferent to the medium and tolerant of some neglect in watering. Occasionally subject to spider mites. Transportation or, indeed, any displacement usually results in leaf loss, though only

Dianella caerulea variegata

Dieffenbachia amoena. Dumb Cane

Dieffenbachia 'Arvida'

Dieffenbachia seguine 'Liturata Wilson's Delight'

PLATE 33

Dieffenbachia maculata 'Rudolph Roehrs'

Dioon edule

Dioscorea macrostachya

Dioscorea discolor

PLATE 34

Dioscorea trifida

Dizygotheca elegantissima

Dorstenia contrajerva. Torus Herb

Dorstenia foetida (complex)

PLATE 35

Dracaena fragrans 'Victoriae'

Dracaena fragrans 'Massangeana'

Dracaena godseffiana 'Friedman'

Dracaena goldeiana

PLATE 36

Dracaena 'Totem'

Dracaena 'Tricolor'

Dracaena deremensis 'Longii'

Dracaena 'Song of India'

PLATE 37

Dyckia fosteriana

Ehretia microphylla. Phillipine Tea

Encephalartos altensteinii

Encephalartos horridus. Photo John Jocius, Glasshouse Works

PLATE 38

Epipremnum falcifolium

Epipremnum 'Marble Queen'

Episcia 'Cleopatra'

Episcia lilacina

PLATE 39

Equisetum trisenales. Horsetail

Eriobotrya japonica. Loquat

Euphorbia cotinifolia

Euphorbia decaryii

PLATE 40

Euphorbia viguieri

Euphorbia brachiata

Euphorbia 'Flame Leaf'

Euphorbia leuconeura

PLATE 41

Evodia hortensis

Excoecharia cochinchinensis

×Fatshedera lizei

Ficus (diversifolia) deltoidea. Mistletoe Fig

PLATE 42

Ficus elastica 'Tricolor'

Ficus sagittata variegata

Ficus palmieri

Ficus benjamina. Bonsaied

PLATE 43

Ficus parcelli. Clown Fig

F. benghalensis. Banyan. Photo Gregory A. Koob

Fittonia verschaffeltii argyroneura 'Nana'

Fittonia verschaffeltii argyroneura variegata

PLATE 44

Fittonia verschaffeltii

Furcraea foetida medio-picta

Gasteria sp.

Gasteria sp.

PLATE 45

Geogenanthus undatus

Gasteria sp.

Graptophyllum pictum aureo-medium

Graptophyllum pictum

PLATE 46

Grevillea robusta. Silk Oak

Gynura aurantiaca. Velvet Plant

Haemaria discolor var. *Dawsoniana* with *Selaginella uncinata*

Haworthia truncata

PLATE 47

Haworthia limifolia

Haworthia setata

Haworthia margaritifera

Haworthia sp. Clockwise from upper left *H.limifolia, H.* sp., *H. fasciata, H. retusa, H. set*

PLATE 48

temporarily. They like to stay in one place.

10–20' (3–6 m) trees are supplied for large indoor plantings. To speed up production of large pot or tub sized plants, nurseries have been forcing growth, resulting in weak, elongated stems. Then, very ingeniously, they have braided 3 or more together so that they support each other and make a neat standard. Once the roots are well established and the tops fill out, the stems fuse forming a patterned solid trunk that is an attractive feature. However we have observed that some of these composite plants are not very long lasting.

'Exotica'. The leaves are only 2" (5 cm) long and the branches even thinner and "weeping".

'Nuda' (*F. nuda*). Lighter colored but thicker green foliage. Large specimens bear up particularly well indoors.

F. buxifolia. Boxwood Fig. Grows to a medium-sized tree, but is excellent for pot culture and training. Leaves wedgeshaped-triangular to 1½" (3.75 cm) long. Stems brown, woody. Tolerant of low humidity and light. Prefers Houseplant Mix #2 with sand. Temporarily loses leaves in late winter but breaks out anew almost immediately.

F. capensis. Tropical to South Africa. To 60' (18 m). Leaf blades nearly round or broadly spoonshaped, to 7" (17.5 cm) long. Trunk gray.

F. carica. Edible Fig. Mediterranean. Winter-dormant small tree with grape-leaf-shaped blades. Recommended only for greenhouse culture. Temperature tolerance to 40°F (4°C).

F. elastica. Rubber Tree. Northern India. Large tree with thick, oblong leaves to 12" (30 cm) long. A traditional houseplant very tolerant of low temperatures and poor light. One of the classical Cast-Iron plants. It can be pruned and trained. We have, for instance, seen a magnificent room divider screen made of a series of the plants in small tubs, their branches trained on a wood trellis like espalier. Specimens for large plantings are grown to a height of over 15' (4.5 m), especially in the South. See remarks p. 000.

F. elastica has always been tolerant of coolness. Newer cultivars have been chosen for situations in warmer modern homes and public buildings. The cultivars in the trade are, themselves, extremely variable, not so much in appearance as in the ability of clones to adapt to different environments.

'Congesta'. Leaves more closely set on the stem and branches with shorter distances between joints.

'Decora'. Leaves on average, longer and wider. Very vigorous.

'Doescheri'. Showing a wide range of spectacular variegation; irregular zones of greens, gray, white and cream. Stalks and midribs pink. A stunner but requires 50% humidity and temperature of min. 60°F (16°C). Houseplant Mix #3. Even moisture. Spray with a general fungicide. Filtered to partial sun.

'Honduras'. Leaves broadly oval with tiny pointed tip; thick texture, shiny. Midvein white and surface irregularly marked with white streaks following the leaf pattern.

'Purpurea'. Leaves and stalks purple toned.

'Robusta'. Leaves very cupped, heavy textured, shiny.

'Rubra'. The long leaf is pink or red.

'Schrieverii' or 'Schryveriana'. Leaves dark green, grayish in the center, surrounded by two lighter shades of green and an irregular cream margin.

'Tricolor Asahi' or simply 'Asahi'. Variegation similar to 'Doescheri' but even brighter. Fast growing but very tender and temperamental.

These cultivars are usually sold at least 4' (1.20 m) high. Much of the material on the market is poorly established as the result of excessive forcing. All kinds of mongrels also turn up in this group.

F. lyrata. (pandurata). Fiddleleaf Fig. A large tree that is usually marketed 6–15' (1.80 to 4.5 m) tall for commercial locations. A houseplant only in a tub for large rooms. The leaves are variable, 10–15 × 5–7" (25–37.5 × 12.5–17.5 cm). The blades are irregularly fiddle to wedgeshaped, broadly undulating, very thick and leathery; dark green. Among the most sculptural of leaves. Arranged rather haphazardly on the few branches, adding to its sculptural impact. It stands up well in low-light locations indoors and tolerates considerable abuse.

'Phyllis Craig' is a dwarf with 6" (15 cm) leaves. Superior as a pot plant but rather rare.

F. microcarpa. Green Island Fig. Broad, oval leaves, 3 × 2" (7.5 × 5 cm), thick, dark green. Branches pendant. Prunes well for pseudo-bonsai.

F. mysorensis. A 30' (9 m) tree. Young stems and branches brown-hairy. Leaves elliptic, to 8" (20 cm). Requires warmth and high humidity. Grown as 10–15' (3–4.5 m) small trees for indoor display with some sun.

F. nekbudu. Tropical Africa. Kaffir Fig. A 70' (21 m) tree. Leaves oblong, distinctly veined, to 12" (30 cm).

F. nitida. See *F. benjamina*, of which this is only a variety.

F. retusa. So. China, Western Pacific. Chinese Banyan. Branches pendant. Very popular as a pot plant and as a specimen for large displays because of its dense, small, deep green foliage. Tolerant of shade and undemanding in respect to humidity.

F. rubiginosa (microphylla). Little Leaf or Rusty Fig. Branches and twigs rusty, scurfy. Leaves elliptic to 4" (10 cm) long, rusty beneath.

'Variegata'. With uneven band of ivory along the edge.

F. stricta. Western Pacific. Leaves elliptic, 6" (15 cm) long. Branches, thin and pendant.

F. traingularis (?) Leaves to 3" (7.5 cm), wedgeshaped-triangular, the corners rounded. Prolific producer of tiny figs.

'Variegata'. Beautifully variegated with cream areas. A superb display piece usually sold as a 5–8' (1.5–2.4 m) tree. Also fine as a juvenile pot plant but by no means common.

F. wildemanniana (cyathistipula), West Africa. Very long, somewhat fiddleshaped leaves, ultimately 28 × 10" (70 × 25 cm) but slow growing and an excellent plant for a pot or tub. Min. 65°F (18.5°C). Min. 50% humidity. Filtered sun.

Succulents

F. palmeri. Baja California. Succulent tree to 65' (20 m). It forms a bottleshaped trunk when no more than 6" (15 cm) high. Leaves gray-green, heartshaped, to 6" (15 cm) long with ivory midvein. Dormant in August–September.

F. petiolaris. Mexico. To 5½' (1.75 m). Leaves heartshaped to 5" (12.5 cm) long with an extended tip. Veins pink to red in bright light. The woody, thickened trunk develops very early. Dormant in September.

Grow both plants in Cactus & Succulent Mix #2. They thrive in filtered to full sun but also do well in artificial light as low as 500 fc for 14 hours daily. Fertilize with balanced formula 2 or 3 times in summer. Do not water during dormancy.

Both plants branch well at the top of the trunk but remain compact. Cuttings root in moist sand.

Fittonia. **Acanthaceae.** Mosaic Plant. Colombia and Peru. Warm house, creeping herb. Shade to filtered sun. 100–500 fc 12 hours daily. Temperature min. 60°F (16°C). Humidity min. 55%. Houseplant Mix #1 or 2 with lime. Propagation from stem cuttings. Moderately easy. 2 species; 1 in active cultivation.

A most lovely creeper, suitable for pots and small baskets but happiest in a terrarium.

F. verschaffeltii var. *verschaffeltii.* The leaves are broadly elliptic, 3–4" (7.5–10 cm) long, covered with a filigree network of red veins. They lie very flat and the fleshy stems root at the joints.

Var. *argyroneura minor.* Leaves 1–2" (2.5–5 cm) long, the veins white.

Var. *argyroneura variegata.* Blades with ivory patches.

Var. *pearcei* ('Pearcei'). Veins pink, less prominent; surface puffed, edges turned down.

Keep evenly moist. Fertilize no more than monthly with a balanced formula. Beware of fungus during the hot days of July and August.

Note: It is a peculiarity of this and other tropical creepers with leaves close to the soil that, as they colonize, their older parts die off leaving empty patches. These bare spots can be replanted with rooted cuttings. At the same time, the soil surface should be renewed and stirred to permit aeration. The gradual packing of the soil surface causing resistance to the fine roots is a frequent cause of deterioration. This is less noticeable in a terrarium.

Difficult to maintain in commercial plantings.

Fortunella. **Rutaceae.** Kumquat. China to the Malay Peninsula. 4 or 5 species of which 2 grown indoors. See *Citrus* for culture.

F. japonica. Spiny, much-branched shrub with 3" (7.5 cm) elliptic, shiny green leaves. Usually grows to max. 10' (3 m).

F. margarita (F. hindsi?). Usually almost thornless. Leaves lanceshaped to 4" (10 cm) long.

Both plants look like small orange trees. The fruit

rarely grows indoors. As juveniles they make nice leafy, shrubby plants but require very cool conditions, especially in summer.

Gasteria. **Liliaceae.** South Africa. Succulent herbs. Partial sun. 500–800 fc 14 hours daily. Temperature min. 40°F (4°C). Cactus & Succulent Mix #1 or 2. Propagation from seeds and offsets. Easy. 50 species; most of them grown indoors.

Gasterias are stemless succulents with thick, strap or long-triangular leaves, either spiraled or opposite-layered. Mostly 2–6" (5–15 cm) long but, in some variations, up to 1' (30 cm). Plain dull or shiny green, or spotted with raised whitish dots or beads. Often rough surfaced. Frequently triangular in cross-section.

They are drought resistant, enduring a month or more without watering. They can be kept moist during the growth period but dry dormancy, usually in winter. If not supplied with plenty of sun allow to dry out between waterings. They prefer tight potting. Fertilize with a high-middle-number formula no more than 4 times a year.

The flowering is similar to *Aloe* but less colorful. The plants offset freely, and pups are easily removed when rooted and potted up. Variegated cultivars are popular. Among the easiest of succulents.

Because of the great number of species and cultivars marked by rather small differences of serious concern only to specialists, we are not listing them. Consult Jacobsen.

× *Gastrolea* (Gasteria × Aloe). **Liliaceae.** Succulent herbs. Culture as for *Gasteria.*

Aloes have been hybridized with Gasterias, resulting in the aloes' transmitting their rosette leaf arrangements. There are several of these, of which × *Gastrolea beguinii,* having triangular leaves to 4 × 1" (10 × 2.5 cm) is the most popular. Surface prettily marked with pearly bumps.

Geogenanthus. **Commelinaceae.** Seersucker Plant. Brazil and Peru. Creeping herb. Shade to filtered sun. 100–400 fc. Temperature min. 65°F (18.5°C). Humidity min. 50%. Houseplant Mix #3. Propagation from stem cuttings. Difficult. 3 species; one grown indoors.

G. undatus. Beautiful creeping pot plant with fleshy stems to 10" (25 cm) rooting at the joints. Leaves paired, very short stalked, broad, lanceshaped, 4 × 2" (10 × 5 cm). The silky ruffled surface is green with symmetrical, silvery stripes. Red beneath. Best kept in a terrarium as it is very sensitive to sudden temperature changes and low aerial humidity. The display must be frequently repaired by means of planted cuttings, as older parts die out.

Graptophyllum. **Acanthaceae.** Caricature Plant. W. Pacific. Shrubs. Partial sun. 500–800 fc. Temperature min. 65°F (18.5°C). Humidity min. 50%. Sterilized sandy garden soil with lime or Houseplant Mix #1 with lime. Propagation by cuttings. Moderately difficult. 10 species of which one is cultivated indoors.

G. pictum. In the West Indies it is used, along with *Pseuderanthemum atropurpureum,* as a colorful, leafy hedge plant to 6' (1.80 m). The 2 are so similar as to be almost indistinguishable. However the Graptophyllums are brighter colored and the flower is a narrow, red-purple tube with little flare, while that of *Pseuderanthemum* is open faced and white, spotted with purple. *Graptophyllum* is the better houseplant but, in pot, grows as a fleshy, small herb for some time before producing offsets and becoming more woody. Pruning assists the process.

Stems pink, the elliptic leaves thin, 5" (12.5 cm) long, the surface irregularly divided into patches of purple, pink and cream or yellow.

'Aureo-marginata'. Green with yellow edge of irregular width.

'Tricolor aureo-medium'. Leaves green with deep yellow and cream zone in the center.

But the species is variable, and various combinations appear. Often the new leaves have patches of burnt orange.

Fertilize 2 or 3 times a year with high-middle-number formula. Young branch tips root quickly in moist vermiculite or sphagnum moss in a closed, transparent container. Keep evenly moist until well established, whereupon it is able to endure several days of complete dryness. Disease and insect resistant.

Grevillea. **Proteaceae.** Spider Flower. Australia. Shrubs & trees. Partial to full sun. 500–1,000 fc. Temperature min. 50°F (10°C). Houseplant Mix #3 or Sterilized Garden Soil with peat. Propagation by seed. Moderately difficult. 250 species of which one grown frequently indoors.

Grevilleas are popular on our West Coast as outdoor groundcovers, shrubs and trees for their fine cut foliage and spring flowering. They are fast growing, germinating quickly from seed. The taller ones do not take kindly to trimming and branch properly only in full sunlight. Watch closely for spider mite infestations. Spray undersides of leaves with water. Test pesticides on sample leaves before using. Allow soil to dry between waterings; they are heavy drinkers. Fertilize with high nitrate formula once a month.

The only species much grown indoors is *G. robusta,* but others should receive more attention.

They are graceful screening plants for partially sunny locations. Tall specimens may prove very useful. As a houseplant we prefer *Jacaranda* which has a very similar appearance.

G. banksii. Tree to 20' (6 m). Hairy leaves compound, the leaflets narrowly strapshaped to 10" (25 cm) long, white haired below.

G. mimosoides. N. Australia. Tree with leaves 10 × 1" (25 × 2.5 cm).

G. paniculata. 8' (2.4 m) shrub. Leaves needlelike.

G. polystachya. Tree to 30' (9 m). Leaves 10" (25 cm) with 2–6 narrow leaflets.

G. robusta. Silk Oak. The most frequently grown indoors. Tree to 150' (45 m). Seeds large. Single

stemmed as a juvenile. Ferny foliage of many leaflets. Grows 3' (90 cm) in a year from seed.

G. thelemanniana. Humming Bird Bush. Shrub to 5' (1.5 m). Bluish, ferny leaves, 2" (5 cm) long with needlelike leaflets. Forms an attractive, dense mass of fine foliage.

Also worth trying are *G. lanigera,* with minute hairy leaves forming mounds and 'Noell', a branching shrublet with needlelike foliage.

Guaiacum. **Zygophyllaceae.** Lignum-vitae. Tropical and Subtropical America. Trees and Shrubs. Partial to full sun. 500–1,000 fc. Temperature min. 60°F (16°C). Houseplant Mix #2 with sand. Propagation from seed and cuttings. Easy. 6 species of which one occasionally grown indoors.

G. officinale. Source of an extremely hard wood and a commercial gum. To 30' (9 m), much branched and very leafy. Leaves compound, with 2 or 3 pairs of leaflets 1¼" (3.75 cm) long, elliptical, shiny, hard, thin.

A drought-resistant tree with a round profile that makes an excellent pot plant for training. Fertilize every 6 weeks in summer with a balanced formula. Reported to be fast growing but is not so indoors.

Guzmania. **Bromeliaceae.** Tropical America. Warm-growing, vase-type rosette plants. Partial sun. 500–800 fc. See *Aechmea* for culture. Moderately difficult. 40 species of which a few grown for foliage rather than flowers.

Guzmanias, because of colorful and long-lasting flowering stalks, are among the more popular bromeliad gift plants. The three species listed below are notable for the patterning of their leaves.

Like *Aechmea,* etc., the old plant dies off after producing pups that develop slowly indoors. Near-mature plants last a year or more, but it is best to replace them with nursery-grown plants.

Showy in low, mass display plantings.

G. lindenii. Leaves stiff, erect to spreading, to 24" (60 cm) long, green streaked horizontally with light green and ivory or even pink in rippling lines. Common name: Large Snake Vase.

G. musaica. Mosaic Vase. Rosette with leaves to 2½' (75 cm) × 3" (7.5 cm); dark green, closely patterned with light on dark green marbling or the lighter color in separated broad bands. Reddish dotted below. Variable.

G. vittata. Snake Vase. Leaves 2' × 2" (60 × 5 cm), very erect, neatly banded with silvery scales over dark green above and below.

Gynura. **Compositae.** Java to Phillipines. Trailing basket plant or vine. Partial sun. 500–800 fc. Temperature min. 60°F (16°C). Sterilized Garden Soil or Houseplant Mix #1 with lime. Propagation from stem cuttings. Easy. 100 species. 3 grown indoors.

G. aurantiaca. Velvet Plant. A favorite basket plant of the shops. Stems, stalks and leaves green covered with a felt of red-purple hairs. Stems spreading to 3' (90 cm) or more, eventually trailing. Leaves broadly elliptic, coarsely lobed, to 6 × 4″ (15 × 10 cm).

'Sarmentosa' (*G. sarmentosa*). Purple Passion Vine. The variety usually grown. Leaves narrower and a richer purple. More trailing stems. An excellent basket plant.

'Sarmentosa aurea-variegata'. Leaves splashed with cream and yellow. A not particularly esthetically pleasing type of variegation.

G. bicolor. Low, branching plant to 2′ (60 cm), with leaves radially clustered at the tips. Leaves 6 × 1½″ (15 × 3.75 cm) with 7 angular, coarse teeth or lobes, purplish green above, purple beneath.

G. procumbens. Stems, branches and leaves purple. Trailing. Leaves 5 × 2″ (12.5 × 5 cm) with few teeth; green with purple midvein.

Showy basket plants for a sunny window. The flowers are burnt yellow but not prolific.

All but *G. bicolor* can be used as climbing vines. Suitable for baskets only in sunny locations.

Haemaria. **Orchidaceae.** Malaysia. Creeping herbs. Shade. 300 fc 12 hours daily. Temperature min. 55°F (13°C). Humidity min. 50%. Medium a mix of 1 part fine size fir bark, 1 part peat, 1 part sand or perlite. Propagation from stem cuttings. Moderately difficult. 1 species.

Haemaria (Ludisia) discolor, var. *dawsoniana*. Plants are usually labeled the variety even though they may be closer to the species; there is considerable variation between clones. This extraordinary plant belongs to a small group of species that are the exceptions to the rule that orchid foliage is, to say the least, uninteresting. Its spikes of little, white flowers are pretty, but it is appreciated primarily for leaves that should have earned it the name "Black Orchid."

It is a creeper-trailer, the reddish stems very thick and juicy, rooting shallowly at the joints and becoming erect at the tips. The lanceshaped, spiraled leaves are 3½″ (8.75 cm) long with short stalks that envelope the stem. Leaves are green-black to brown-black, velvety, with none or a few lighter veins. The variety, however, is brown or green-black with a gorgeous network of neon bright, burnt orange veins.

The plant needs only shallow potting but a broad surface to roam over. Supply high nitrate fertilizer at ⅛ the suggested strength once a month in spring. Maintain even moisture but do not soak. Light, well-aerated medium is a must. Terrarium conditions, therefore, with a temperature ranging from 60–80°F (16–27°C), are ideal. Cuttings placed in water quickly put out the knobby beginnings of roots. They can also be rooted in sphagnum peat moss and other fibrous mediums. As soon as roots appear the cuttings can be potted up but with great care not to damage the delicate, very watery, root points.

Harpephyllum. **Anacardiaceae.** Kaffir Plum. S. Africa. Tree. Partial sun. 500–700 fc. Temperature min. 50°F (10°C). Sterilized Garden Soil with peat or Packaged Houseplant Medium. Propagation from seed or cuttings. Moderately easy. 1 species.

H. caffrum. Tree to 30′ (9 m). Leaves compound; leaflets 5, 2 pairs opposite, fifth at top; lanceshaped, 3″ (7.5 cm) long, shiny, hard, edges undulating.

Needs cool temperatures in summer and plenty of ventilation. Slow growing. It makes a neat pot plant for a year or two.

Haworthia. **Liliaceae.** South Africa. Small rosette succulents. Filtered to partial sun. 300–800 fc 14 hours daily. Temperature min. 50°F (10°C). Houseplant Mix #2 with sand or Cactus & Succulent Mix #2. Propagation by offsets or seed. Easy to difficult. Over 160 species and many cultivars of which a large number are grown by collectors.

Haworthias are rarely taller or broader than 5″ (12.5 cm). Variation is very great, hence they are ideal subjects for collection by those who have little space to grow. In potting they like a tight fit which also inhibits excessive watering. In summer water once a week and in winter once a month or a weekly spraying is sufficient. Treatment with very much diluted balanced fertilizer 2 or 3 times during the warm season is sufficient. Insect infestation is rare. Fungal diseases occur only if the plants are kept too moist.

Most of the plants offset, producing a number of pups yearly. Allow the colony to spread or remove the offsets when they have grown their own roots and pot them up separately.

The leaves are thick, wedgeshaped or long-triangular. Textures vary from juicy smooth to hard and rough, colors from bluish to darkest green. The surface may be beaded, channeled or streaked.

Some species even possess the feature of "windows," which occur in other South African succulent genera. In *Haworthia* it is confined to the fleshy-leaved rosettes. A section of the tip of each leaf is lacking in chlorophyll, and though it may be very thick, light passes right through. This is a device for reducing the metabolic activity resulting from excess sunlight in desert conditions where growth must be restricted so as not to outstrip the water supply. When these Haworthias are exposed to a lengthy period of bright sun, they become entirely translucent and some acquire a pinkish tinge.

Because of the complexity of the genus and the great number of variations, we must limit our descriptions to a few species that are typical. Consult Jacobsen for others. Amateurs will find numerous plants offered by mail order succulent nurseries. Also, in order to avoid repetition it should be noted that the species we list and others often have 5 to 15 different distinct variations of interest mainly to collectors.

H. cymbiformis var. *cymbiformis*. Stemless rosette to 4″ (10 cm) broad, cusped with numerous thick, juicy leaves, concave above and boatshaped below, grayish green, the upper third of the leaf translucent. Dry out well between waterings. The whole *cymbiformis* complex needs more light than other species and is subject to fungal diseases when overwatered.

H. fasciata. Leafy rosette to 3″ (7.5 cm) high and

across. Leaves narrow-triangular, rough surfaced, hard, flattish on top and boatshaped below. Decorated with neat transverse rows of round white raised spots. Some varieties have leaves to 4" (10 cm) long. The most popular and common species.

H. limifolia. A superbly beautiful little plant and one of the easiest to grow. Rosette of a few very thick, long-triangular leaves. These are darkest green, giving the impression of being as hard as jade, concave above and rounded below. The whole surface is sculptured with closely packed transverse ribs. They curve in the direction of growth, accenting the spiral arrangement. Produces many pups. It merits greater popularity.

H. margaritifera var. *margaritifera.* Occasionally attaining 6" (15cm) in diameter. Leaves broadly triangular to 3 × 1" (7.5 × 2.5 cm), extremely thick; flat above and boatshaped below. Dark green with large, raised, pearly white beads distributed evenly top and bottom. Probably the largest growing of the Haworthias.

H. reinwardtii var. *reinwardtii.* The rosette is extended into a columnar stem with the leaves spiraling closely around it, incurved and overlapping. Blades 1–2 × ½" (2.5–5 × 1.25 cm) long-lanceshaped with narrowing tip; the underside rounded and liberally sprinkled with white beading. Grows to 4" (10 cm).

H. setata. Many-leaved, stemless rosette to 5" (12.5 cm) across. Leaves light green to 2 × ½" (5 × 1.25 cm), lanceshaped, ending in a soft, translucent bristle. Underside double convex. Edges and convexities lined with long white bristles. A very showy plant for its size.

H. truncata. A most curious, very succulent plant. The leaves, attached to an underground stem, grow upward in a straight line. The tip, the broadest part, is rectangular and windowed. Below it is convex on the inner surface and rounded on the outer. Very dark green to ¾" (18.6 mm) long, ½" (1.25 cm) wide and ¼" (6.25 mm) thick. In nature only the rectangular tip shows above soil level. In cultivation the leaves are usually raised above the soil as they are thus less likely to rot from overwatering. Water when the leaves show a first sign of shrivel. The row of leaves sometimes extends to 12 in a pot, and side branches produce their own roots that can be severed and potted up separately. It requires partial sun and will not suffer in full sun. Use a very sandy mix. the similar *H. maughamii* with much shorter leaves is also rarer.

Hechtia. Bromeliaceae. SW. U.S. to Central America. See *Dyckia* for culture.

Longer-leaved succulent cousins of *Dyckia* and to be treated in the same way. Leaves over a foot in length (30 cm) by 1" (2.5 cm) wide, spiny, silvery. Most attractive as juvenile plants. Propagation from offsets.

Some species of interest are: *H. argentea, glabra, glomerata, marnier-lapostollei.* Plants from our Southwest are cold tolerant.

Hedera. **Araliaceae.** Ivy. Temperate Old World. Woody vines. Filtered to partial sun. 300–750 fc for 12 hours daily. Temperature min. 40°F (4°C). Houseplant Mix #3. Propagation by cuttings and soil layering. Easy to moderately difficult. 5 species, all in cultivation.

Indoors, ivies can be used as groundcovers, wall coverings and for growing on topiary forms. The general conception that they are always easy is derived from the fact that a number of hardy cultivars are virtually indestructible out-of-doors. Indoors they are frequently by no means ideal. Almost all prefer a very cool house.

For one thing, the most popular cultivars are less adapted to shade than they are reputed to be. Without bright light many lose their good green color, and variegated ones cease to grow actively. Moisture should be even and the fertilizer high in nitrate (first number) applied no more than once a month at ⅛ the dilution indicated on the label. A real problem is insects, for ivy persistently attracts aphis, which are easy to eradicate indoors, and all kinds of spider mites and mealybugs that, because of the many small leaves and joints, are not. Constant washing with water or spraying with appropriate pesticides will keep the situation under control.

Propagation is easy, as the joints of the creeping or trailing stems put out roots. Pin them to the soil and separate after they have rooted. Shallow potting is adequate since the roots are short.

H. canariensis. Algerian Ivy. Stems and stalks red. Juvenile leaves diamondshaped to 4" (10 cm) long; usually shorter.

'Variegata'. The blades edged white. A relatively stable species.

H. colchica. Persian Ivy. The 3–6" (7.5–15 cm) long blades, are very broadly lanceshaped.

'Dentato-variegata' has edges irregularly marked with cream.

'Gloire de Marengo' is similar. An excellent clone, easier to maintain.

H. helix. English Ivy. Most ivies of the shops and nurseries belong to this species. It is most unstable, resulting in endless numbers of cultivars of different leaf forms and variegation. The catch is that some decorative forms only occur in the juvenile stage and are prone to revert to plain leaves as they grow older, the variegated ones more than the solid green-leaved. Maintenance of many of these cultivars is dependent on enthusiasts who take cuttings of typical juvenile branches and grow them on. The availability of any one commercial cultivar depends on nurserymen's keeping a good stock for propagation. It follows that what can be found in shops or nurseries in quantity at any one time is very much of a gamble.

Leaves are heartshaped, diamondshaped, 3–5 triangular lobed, narrow to broader than long. Some plants are called self-heading, meaning that they are thicker stemmed and more branching than others, thus more compact. Others extend and trail. A few have tiny leaves, plain or frilled, in tight ranks.

The most popular cultivars for indoor culture in

this country are generally less hardy than those favored by English growers, but nearly all require a cool house and excellent ventilation. A few of the miniatures can live in terrariums. Not only are the clones great in number, many are sold under two to four different names added to which nurseries are constantly marketing plants under their own labels. Some of the latter may be really something new, others only repeats of some rare cultivars. Except where the cultivar is a distinct and stable type, it is best to pick out plants personally at shops or nurseries. For these reasons we give only a listing of some popular cultivars according to type. Specialists tend to have their own favorites.

Large Green-leaved. 'Conglomerata', 'Flamenco', 'Fluffy Ruffles', 'Garland', 'Helvetica', 'Manda's Crested', 'Pedata', 'Pin Oak Improved', 'Plume d'Or', 'Ralf', 'Shamrock', 'Spear Point', 'Wilson'.

Miniature Green-leaved. 'Gnome', 'Green Finger', 'Irish Lace', 'La Plata', 'Merion Beauty', 'Needle Point', 'Spinosa', 'Tobler'.

Variegated-leaved. 'Cavendish', 'Bruder Ingobert', 'Conglomerata erecta', 'Discolor', 'Eva', 'Glacier', 'Gold Dust', 'Gold Heart', 'Heise Denmark #1 & #2', 'Hahn's Variegated', 'Harold', 'Itsy-Bitsy', 'Jubilee', 'Maculata', 'Plume d'Or Glasshouse', 'Tricolor'.

H. nepalensis. Blades soft moss green with prominent gray veining. 2½" (6.25 cm) long, notched at the base, with two curving shallow lobes and straight sides, coming to a point. This is a comparatively rare species of considerable beauty. Cool growing.

'Marbled Dragon'. Leaves to 3" (7.5 cm); veins light gray.

'Sinensis' had a deeper notch and larger basal lobes.

'Suzanne'. Trailing plant with finely hairy leaves.

H. rhombea. Japan. Blades heartshaped, attached to long, trailing stems. More tolerant of higher temperatures.

Helichrysum. **Compositae.** Old World subtropics. Small shrub. Partial to full sun. 500–1,000 fc 14 hours daily. Temperature min. 45°F (7°C). Sterilized sandy garden soil with lime or Houseplant Mix # 2 with lime. Propagation by seed or cuttings. Moderately difficult. At least 400 species of which only 2 grown indoors.

H. angustifolium. Curry Plant. Mediterranean. The leaves smell like an Indian curry mixture but are not used in cooking, nor is this the source of curry leaves, which is *Murraya koenigii.* However, it is a very handsome little shrub capable of being trimmed to a round shape.

To 1' (30 cm) or more. Leaves narrowly oblong to 1½" (3.75 cm), surface gray woolly.

H. petiolatum. Licorice Plant. S. Africa. Shrub to 4', (1.20 m). Leaf to 1" (2.5 cm) broadly lanceshaped, white woolly above and below; stems the same. With a spreading-trailing habit suitable for baskets. Not a source of licorice.

Lovely little shrubs with the leaves clustered in the joints on very short stalks, and facing upward. Excel-

lent for training. Dry between waterings. Fertilize no more than 3–4 times a year with high-middle-number fertilizer.

Hemigraphis. **Acanthaceae.** Southeast Asia. Trailing pot or basket plant. Filtered sun. 300–500 fc. Temperature min. 60°F (16°C). Humidity min. 50%. Houseplant Mix #2 with sand or Packaged Houseplant Medium. Propagation from cuttings. Moderately easy. 60 species; 2 grown indoors.

H. angustifolia. Stems to 10" (25 cm), curving over, purple. Leaves 2–3" (5–7.5 cm) long, lanceshaped, notched at base, blue-green.

H. colorata (alternata). Flame Ivy. Low, spreading plant, rooting at the joints. Stems thin, branched, broadly heartshaped, 2–4" (5–10 cm) long, surface puckered, edges finely toothed, metallic violet above, reddish purple beneath.

'Exotica'. Waffle Plant. Very puckered maroon leaves.

'Exotica Variegata'. Variegated with yellow splotches.

(sp. ?) 'Esmeralda'. Creeper with roundish leaves and tan veining.

(sp. ?) 'Red Equator'. Miniature creeping plant. Much branched, with ½" (1.25 cm) oval, purple leaves.

Better suited to ground covering than to pots. Grows into neat mats of foliage.

Hibiscus. **Malvaceae.** Worldwide. Herbs, shrubs and trees. Partial to full sun. 600–800 fc 15 hours daily. Temperature min. 50°F (10°C). Humidity min. 50%. Houseplant Mix #2 with sand and lime. Propagation from cuttings. Easy. 250 species of which a few grown indoors.

H. rosa-sinensis, the Chinese Hibiscus, is widely grown outdoors in the South and indoors as a gift plant for its large, colorful flowers. There are also cultivars with white-variegated leaves but these, too, are grown for flowers. The leaves are thin and subject to both mite and mealybug infestations. The following 2 tree species are typical of a number that should be about equally adaptable to indoor culture as juvenile pot plants.

H. alatus. Mahoe. Caribbean. Tree to 80' (24 m) but usually much smaller. Leaves broad heartshaped to 4" (10 cm) long. Dry soil between waterings. Fertilize with high-middle-number formula once a month. Keep pot-bound to prevent rapid growth. Trim to branch. The similar *H. tiliaceus* should do as well.

H. newhousei (?). Shrub or tree. Leaves elliptical with pointed tip; firm textured, dark shiny green. Same culture as above.

Both of these are sturdy, handsome foliage plants amenable to trimming. They might make suitable trees for large plantings. Both are pest resistant.

Hoffmannia. **Rubiaceae.** Taffeta Plant. Tropical S. America. Filtered sun. 300–500 fc for 12 hours daily. Temperature 65–85°F (18.5–29.5°C). Humidity min. 55%. Houseplant Mix #1 or 2 with lime. Propagated from cuttings. Difficult. 100 species of which 3 grown indoors.

These very tender pot plants are unmistakable because of the large size of the thin leaves on short stems, the velvety iridescent color, the brightly contrasting midvein and very symmetrical lateral veining that results in a prominent corrugation of the surface. The shapes are long-elliptical or spoonshaped. During summer they can be kept evenly moist and fertilized once a month with ¼-strength balanced formula. In winter they may become dormant and should then be kept quite dry except for occasional sprayings until the stem begins to sprout again. They can usually be accommodated in 4 to 5″ (10–12.5 cm) pots.

Their large leaves make them difficult to handle for they are also very thin and develop dead spots when humidity or temperature declines or they are attacked by spider mites, to which they are prone. Very aristocratic plants, they are a constant challenge better suited to straight greenhouse treatment than the home. They do best in partly or completely closed terrariums.

H. giesbreghtii. Velvety green leaves, rose colored beneath. Stems 4-angled to 2′ (60 cm) but usually kept to 1′ (30 cm). Leaves 10 × 4″ (25 × 10 cm), lanceshaped.

'Variegata'. Overall mottling of pink over bronzy green and very velvety.

H. refulgens. Low, spreading. Leaf blades spoonshaped to 6″ (15 cm) long; dark velvety green, reddish beneath. Far and away the most manageable plant.

'Vittata'. Silver veined.

'Fantasia'. A hybrid. Satiny greenish copper surface.

Cv. or sp. 'Nana'. Shrublet with much smaller leaves, corrugated, coppery green.

Homalocladium. **Polygonaceae.** Ribbon or Tapeworm Plant. solomon Islands. Herb. Shade. 100 fc. Min. 55°F (13°C). Sterilized Garden Soil or Houseplant Mix #1. Propagation by division or cuttings. Cast Iron. 1 species.

H. platycladum. A most curious plant and one of the easiest of all to grow indoors. The lower parts of the stems are round and tough, branching into continuations that are dark green, fibrous, thin and flat, ½″ (1.25 cm) wide and marked at intervals of 1–2″ (2.5–5 cm) by joints to which thin leaves are attached. These latter are 1–1½″ (2.5–3.75 cm) long, narrow, pointed, elliptical, attached singly or as pairs. Stems and ribbons may grow to 2′ (60 cm) or more, providing a tangle of greenery until leaves disappear as they do in winter.

Grow in north light or even under 50 fc of artificial light. The plants are quite drought resistant and need virtually no fertilizer. The only weakness appears to be a tendency to acquire a mildew fungus if low light is accompanied by minimum temperature. As it puts up several stems from the base, it is easy to divide for propagation.

H. platycladum has been used in light conditions that are so low as to make it a miracle that the plant can survive—in restaurants and hotel lobbies for instance. A remarkable plant for the difficult spot.

Homalomena. **Araceae.** Tropical America and Asia. Herb. Shade to filtered sun. 100–500 fc. Temperature min. 65°F (18.5°C). Humidity min. 50%. Houseplant Mix #1 or 2. Propagation from cuttings or division. Difficult. 130 species of which about 10 cultivated indoors.

Homalomena belongs to a group of aroids that have been insufficiently studied and are sometimes confused with *Alocasia* and *Schismatoglottis.* They are handsome plants but difficult indoors.

They require the equivalent of terrarium conditions but are not light demanding. Keep evenly moist and protected from drafts. Only *H. wallisii* is frequently grown. They are of two types, those with larger leaves, the others much more compact and short with smaller leaves.

H. humilis. Malay Peninsula. Blades broadly elliptic to 5 × 2″ (12.5 × 5 cm), the edges irregularly toothed, velvety green; veins curved upward, depressed. Stalks purple, to 6″ (15 cm).

H. lindenii (Alocasia?). Broadly heartshaped blades to 16 × 10″ (40 × 25 cm), the midrib and veins yellow, edges undulating and curved under. Stalks to 20″ (50 cm).

H. novoguinensis. Blades oblong, the halves noticeably uneven, 5 × 2″ (12.5 × 5 cm). Side veins paired.

H. pendula. To 2″ (60 cm) or more high. Leaves "honey green."

H. picturata. Long arrowshaped leaves; midribs feathered with silver. Less demanding of high humidity.

H. pygmaea. To 12″ (30 cm). Leaves elliptic, 4 × 1½″ (10 × 3.75 cm). Halves of blade unequal, undulating. Veins purplish below. Stalks 4″ (10 cm).

H. roezlii. Like *H. wallisii* but with larger leaves. See in the following.

H. rubescens. To 2½′ (75 cm) with a strong stem. Blades broadly heartshaped with many ascending veins, 14 × 9″ (35 × 22.5 cm). Shiny green with pink to red veins. Juvenile leaves metallic rose. Stalks purplish, to 20″ (50 cm).

H. sulcata. Leaf blades long lanceshaped, shallowly notched, 8 × 4″ (20 × 10 cm), green, copper colored beneath. Stalks 15″ (37.5 cm). To 2½′ (75 cm).

H. wallisii. Leaf blades elliptic, leathery, to 8 × 3″ (20 × 7.5 cm) spreading. Green mottled with yellow. Stalks 3–4″ (7.5–10 cm). Slow growing.

'Mauro'. Almost black-green with brilliant gold splotchings. An outstanding display plant when well grown.

Hoya. **Asclepiadaceae.** S. Asia and W. Pacific. Tropical vines. Partial to full sun. 600–1,000 fc. Temperature min. 65°F (18.5°C). Houseplant Mix #2. Propagation by cuttings. Moderately difficult. 200 species of which only one grown for foliage.

H. carnosa. The Wax Plant. Numerous *Hoya* species bear pendant clusters of exquisite glassy flowers, but only after they have been grown from rooted cuttings for at least 3 years. The thick, waxy, variegated or curiously distorted leaves of *H. carnosa* cultivars are the exceptions, responsible for their being commonly sold, even in variety stores. This is somewhat deceptive as it suggests that they are carefree, which is by no means the case. The thickness of the leaves is the giveaway that they are essentially succulent vines requiring bright light and dormancy in winter. At that time water only when lowest leaves show signs of shrivelling, otherwise root rot will set in. Fertilize only when in active growth once a month with a balanced formula at ¼ the recommended dilution. Root cuttings only in summer. If flowers do develop be careful not to remove the stalks that support the cluster as it is from these that they continue to bloom.

H. carnosa is a trailer or climber with thick, waxy, green, elliptic leaves to 3″ (7.5 cm) long, borne on short, thick stalks. Both the species and cultivars must be supported on a trellis or stake or be grown in baskets.

'Compacta' The Hindu Rope Plant. An odd and quite hideous monstrosity that is very popular. Long strands of overlapping, distorted and curled green leaves.

'Compacta Variegata'. Blades with cream edges.

'Krimson Princess'. Cream centers and reddish edges.

'Krinkle Curl'. Very small, puckered leaves on a short vine. Good for small pots.

'Krinkles 8'. Leaves dark green, puckered. Pink flowers.

'Krinkles 8 Variegata'. Puckered leaves bordered in white.

'Mauna Loa'. Blades have gold variegation in the center.

'Red Buttons'. Leaves turning red in bright light.

'Rubra'. Leaves variegated with red.

'Variegata'. Leaves marked with pink and cream.

'Verna Jeanette'. With silver frosted surface and broad white edge.

The coloring of the variegated cultivars is different on almost every plant. New leaves may be bright pink and then turn half green/half white, and the variegation of others will vary in degree depending on soil, feeding and light intensity without there being any clear rule to follow in controlling it.

Hypoestes. **Acanthaceae.** Polka-Dot Plant. Madagascar. Herb. Filtered sun. 300–500 fc. Temperature min. 55°F (13°C). Houseplant Mix #1 with lime. Propagation from seed and cuttings. Easy. 40 species; 1 grown for foliage.

H. phyllostachya (sanguinolenta). Branching plant to 20″ (50 cm), notable for its 2″ (5 cm) long, thin, elliptical, dark green leaves, liberally sprinkled with pink spots. There are numerous named and unnamed cultivars differing primarily in the amount of pink spotting.

Until recently even the best of the cultivars have reverted to green after a while when grown indoors. However Claude Hope of Linda Vista, S.A. in Costa Rica has been developing superior stable strains that are very richly colored. Seed is available of plants with white spotting as well. 'Pink Splash' is one of the improved pink ones.

These are fast-growing plants that require pruning and are at their peak during a single year and should then be replaced. They are most grown to a height of 12″ (30 cm) at most. A 5″ (12.5 cm) pot is usually adequate. Supply even moisture. They are heavy drinkers requiring frequent watering. Fertilize with ¼-strength balanced formula with every fourth watering. Color develops better in partial to full sun. Subject to mealybug and white fly. Test leaves before using a pesticide.

Ilex. **Aquifoliaceae.** Holly, Asia and the Americas. Hardy to subtropical shrubs and trees. Partial to full sun. 600–1,000 fc. Temperature min. 45°F (7°C). Sterilized garden soil. Packaged Houseplant Medium with some sand added. Propagation from cuttings. Moderately easy. 400 species and innumerable cultivars. Only a few suitable indoors.

Hollies have not been considered houseplants as almost all the species and cultivars derive from temperate to cold climates. A few that come to us from warmer habitats may be suitable for the indoors. Unfortunately, only one of these has leaves with the prickly lobes that are such an attraction.

They all grow on the cool side and must be protected from protracted temperatures over 80°F (27°C) in summer. Good ventilation is essential. Fertilize with high nitrate formula and dose with chelated or micronized iron once a year. Keep evenly moist but avoid sogginess, which can be lethal. Trim to produce more compact, branching plants. Propagate young wood in Jiffy-7s.

I. cinerea. China. Large shrub. Leaves almost stalkless, lanceshaped, 5 × 1½″ (12.5 × 3.75 cm); teeth tipped with black. Berry red.

I. dimorphophylla. Okinawa. Woody shrub with 1″ (2.5 cm), sparkling light green, very spiny leaves. A perfect holly type that fills a gap in the foliage houseplant repertory. Berry red.

I. hanceana. Hong Kong. Little shrub with 1″ (2.5 cm) leathery leaves, spoonshaped. Not spiny. Berry red.

I. paraguariensis. Yerba Mate. Tree to 20′ (6 m). Leaves dark green, 5 × 2½″ (12.5 × 6.25 cm), elliptic, margins scalloped. Berry red.

I. pubescens. Taiwan. 10′ (3 m) shrub with 4-angled branches. Leaves olive green, spoonshaped, to 2″ (5 cm) long, partly toothed. Berry red.

Iresine. *(Achyranthes)*. **Amaranthaceae.** Bloodleaf. S. American tropics. Herb. Full to partial sun. 600–800 fc 14 hours daily. Temperature min. 50°F (10°C). Sterilized garden soil with humus or peat. Propagation by seed or cuttings. Moderately difficult. 70 species of which 2 grow indoors.

Colorful, weak, fleshy-stemmed, little herbs to be

treated as annuals, replacing plants with cuttings rooted in fall and spring. A sunny situation brings out the brilliant color. Very subject to spider mite infestation and fungal infections if subjected to long stretches of low light and low temperatures. Sensitive to aerial pollution.

I. herbstii. Blood Leaf. Usually grown to less than 2' (60 cm). Stem pink, branching. Leaves opposite-alternate, nearly round to broadly oval, to 2" (5 cm) in diameter, with a notch at the tip. Bright, purplish red.

'Acuminata'. Leaves lanceshaped.

'Aureo-reticulata'. Chicken Gizzard Plant. Green to purplish red with broad yellow, ascending veins and midrib.

I. lindenii formosa (possibly a form of 'Acuminata' above). Leaves lanceshaped; red or green with yellow veining.

Plants are variable in details of leaf and vein coloring. Quite showy when well grown.

Jacaranda. **Bignoniaceae.** Mostly South America. Small trees. Partial sun. Temperature min. 40°F (4°C). Propagation from seed or cuttings. Houseplant Mix #2. Easy. 50 species of which no more than 2 grown indoors.

Without direct comparison of different plants of the genus it is difficult to decide which species of *Jacaranda* indoor gardeners are growing. The distinguishing feature of juvenile trees is the multipaired leaflets, ½' (12.5 mm) long on the multipaired 8"–2' (20–60 cm) leaves. *J. acutifolia* 10' (3 m), from Peru is described as having "linear-lanceolate" leaflets; *J. mimosifolia* (*J. ovalifolia?*) 50' (15 m), from N. Argentina has "oblong rhomboid" leaflets. The plants we have been growing have elliptic-pointed leaflets. They probably act pretty much alike as juveniles.

The trees are admired in the Mediterranean and more southern climes for their masses of blue flowers. Indoors we have only the foliage. Useful for small-scale screening, it is also a graceful, potted, specimen plant if carefully trained.

A notable feature is the fast growth which is a drawback in some ways. Leaves are deciduous for a short time which creates a good deal of debris and disfigures the tree temporarily. It is also host to whitefly. Nevertheless, it has attractions because most of the other feathery leaved plants, especially the leguminous ones, are slow growing and require great patience. With *Jacaranda* we have quick results.

It can be grown best in a maximum 6" (15 cm) pot until its roots are hopelessly potbound. Use Houseplant Mix #2. Water regularly and fertilize in summer with a high-middle-number formula. One can control growth in two ways. Either let the stem grow to the height you prefer, then trim it, removing lower branches, thus creating a standard. Or clip early and often, encouraging branching. Cuttings will sprout roots in water. *Jacaranda* prefers a sunny exposure but survives in a bright northern window. We find it not very practical but decorative and amusing.

Kaempferia. **Zingiberaceae.** S. Asia and W. Pacific. Stemless herbs. Filtered sun. 300–500 fc. Temperature min. 65°F (18.5 °C). Humidity min. 50% Houseplant Mix #3 or Sphagnum moss. Winter dormant. Propagation by division. Easy. 50 species; 7 grown for foliage.

These gingers are greenhouse and house pot plants with attractive foliage and 1" (2.5 cm) white, yellow or bluish, 4-petalled flowers, arising from the base of the leaves and extruded from a tubular sheath one after another like Roman-candle fireworks. The pseudo-stems consist of 2 or 5 sheathed leaves. During the warm months keep the soil constantly wet and fertilize once every 2 weeks with a weak solution of high phosphate fertilizer.

In November dry out the soil and store the pot until April, then water well to induce sprouting. They can be kept green through winter but will be severely weakened. The thick roots may also be decanted and stored in a warm place until they show growth. The roots spread, sending up the leaves in a widening circle. Hence it is easy to divide the plants.

Although highly touted for the iridescent patterning of the leaves we have observed that in most plants the decorations are unreliable and weak. However the shape and the veining and pleating of the leaves is pleasant.

K. decora. Described as having large, pale yellow, pleated leaves. Flowers yellow.

K. atrovirens. Peacock Plant. Borneo. 4–5 leaves to a pseudo-stem, each to 6 × 3 (15 × 7.5 cm) long, dark green, iridescent and with feathered design.

K. elegans. Dwarf species with small, green leaves.

K. galanga. Leaves two, 5 × 3½" (12.5 × 6.25 cm), broadly oval, pleated.

K. gilbertii India. Leaves oblong to 4" (10 cm) long, the edges white.

K. masonii (hort.) Possibly *K. galanga* or vice versa. Leaves Narrow(?). "Iridescent bluish green, zoned in emerald."

K. pulchra. Resurrection Lily. S.E. Asia. 1 or 2 leaves to the pseudo-stem, 5 × 3½" (12.5 × 6.25 cm), broadly oval. Pleated. Dark green with lighter feathering. Flowers white(?).

K. roscoeana (hort.). Peacock Ginger. Much confused with *K. pulchra*. Leaves pleated, iridescent green with bronze feathering. Lavender flowers with white eye.

It is evident that there is much confusion between clones of these plants and that the color of the flowers is not a definitive difference at least in horticulture. All have similar iridescence and feathering. This seems to vary not only according to the cultivar but culture.

Kalanchoe. **Crassulaceae.** Africa and Madagascar. Leaf succulents. Partial to full sun. 500–1,000 fc. Temperature min. 40°F (4°C). 2 parts Houseplant Medium to 1 part gritty sand or Houseplant Mix #2 with sand. Add lime to both. Propagation from leaf and stem cuttings. Moderately difficult. 125 species of which 8 or 10 are grown indoors.

Long-lasting upfacing clusters of 4-petaled white, yellow, pink or red flowers have secured *K. blossfeldiana* cultivars a firm place among the popular gift plants. Once the flowers are gone, however, it is difficult to bloom them again. Being short-day plants, buds will not set unless they are subjected to artificially long nights, a requirement most amateurs cannot cope with.

Some Kalanchoes are appreciated for colorful leaves or are interesting for their curious ability to produce plantlets. These are the ones we list. All are pot or basket plants.

All need bright light to flourish. Short-day treatment is not necessary unless flowering is desired. Water at least weekly from May through September, monthly October through December, not at all during January and February. Then resume weekly watering in March and April. A method of avoiding overwatering at any time is to wait until bottom leaves on stems show signs of shrivel. Fertilize with a balanced formula no more than once a month in spring and summer.

Leaf or stem cuttings root in sand at 75°F (24.5°C) when misted daily under bright light. Plants also root where joints come into contact with moist soil. Cut sections free and pot up separately. In addition there are the plantlets that grow out from some of the succulent leaves. They eventually drop to the ground, and, after they have anchored themselves, they can be potted up.

Plants with Plantlets on Leaves

K. daigremontiana. Mother of Thousands. Madagascar. Single-stemmed, fleshy plant with spiraling, elliptic leaves up to 3" (7.5 cm) long with toothed margins; very thick; spotted with purple beneath. Stalks thick and short. Plantlets with roots showing produced close together near the tips. Dry well between waterings. Fertilizer generally unnecessary. Plantlets drop and root spontaneously.

K. fedtschenkoi. South American Air Plant. Madagascar. To 2' (60 cm) high but usually grown and sold as basket plants with trailing stems. Leaves, wide, spoonshaped, to 2" (5 cm) long, with a powdery, bluish purple surface. The scalloped upper half of the leaf produces plantlets. Leaf drop on the lower parts is frequent and disfiguring. Trimming the tips of branches encourages branching near the base and renews the leafy appearance.

K. fedtschenkoi marginata. Aurora Borealis Plant. The most colorful of the Kalanchoes and the one usually seen as a foliage plant in shops. Leaves light green bordered with pink and cream.

K. fedtschenkoi variegata. Centered with cream and bluish areas.

K. pinnata. Hawaiian Air Plant. Leaves often offered as a mail order novelty. Pinned to a curtain they produce plantlets. The leaves are thick, rubbery, broadly elliptic and scalloped, to 5" (12.5 cm) long on round stalks. Pot up the plantlets and you will have a rubbery green plant with a thick but weak stem. No beauty.

K. tubiflora. Chandelier Plant. Madagascar. Single stemmed, growing to 2' (60 cm) indoors. Unbranched. Spiraled leaves 2–5" (5–12.5 cm) long, spotted brown and white or simply greenish brown; very narrowly tubular, the plantlets in tiny clusters on the tips. Stems and leaves spotted purplish brown. Quite drought resistant even in summer.

Other Foliage Kalanchoes

K. beharensis. Velvet Leaf. Madagascar. A most imposing, sculptural plant; the most impressive of Kalanchoes and unique among succulents. The single stem is thick and pulpy but sturdy, to 12' (3.6 m). The few leaves on shortish stalks are long-heartshaped to 15" (37.5 cm) long and sometimes almost as wide at the base. The edges undulate so broadly and deeply that they give the impression of being lobes. The surface is usually deeply concave. The leaves face outward with the base at the top.

The whole plant is covered with a hard, tight, short-haired surface. But the covering of the brown leaves is remarkable, like rep fabric, and the hairs are so closely packed and stiff that they provide a strange sensation when touched. The underside is uniformly gray. The texture of the leaf is thick, stiff, extremely brittle and dry.

The plant cannot be recommended for commercial plantings except for use in providing an exotic note. But it is quite manageable as a houseplant. Grow it to 2 or 3' (60 or 90 cm) in a 8–10" (20–25 cm) pot. Use a small and then a larger tub for a taller plant. The roots are not large. We, ourselves, grew an 8-footer (2.40 m) without problems, though placed 4' (1.20 m) back from a normal south-facing window.

'Fernleaf'. The leaves irregularly toothed.

'Oakleaf'. With 7–9 very deep, jagged lobes. A beautiful form.

'Roseleaf'. A dwarf with 2" (5 cm) long diamond-shaped, gray-felted leaves with scalloped margins. Grows to one foot: branching and suckering. This may be considered a quite different species, attractive as a small pot plant.

The larger-leaved plants make good juvenile pot plants and are easily grown to large size. Among leaf succulents they are uniquely handsome.

K. marmorata. Ethiopia, Somalia. Penwiper Plant. Compact, many-leaved succulent shrub with wide, spoonshaped leaves, scalloped at the tips and with prominent purple spots on a grayish surface. Water sparingly. Keep cool in winter.

K. millotti. Madagascar. Small branching plant with opposite-alternate closely packed leaves, the upper halves broadly rounded and bluntly toothed, narrowing below abruptly to the short stalk. The whole plant is short felted like *K. beharensis.*

K. rhombopilosa. Madagascar. Shrub to 5" (15 cm) with odd 1"-long, broadly wedgeshaped leaves, finely hairy, shallowly 3-lobed at the blunt tips; the whole somewhat cupped, streaked and spotted maroon. Leaves produce roots.

K. tomentosa. The Panda Plant. Madagascar. Popular commercial pot plant. The thick, shallow, boatshaped, bluntly elliptic leaves, 1½–3" (3.75–7.5 cm). Densely felted, silvery, with brown spots on margins. Not al all easy to maintain, with long dormant period. Leaves root quickly.

Laurus. **Lauraceae.** Laurel. Mediterranean. Shrub. Partial to full sun. 800–1,000 fc 15 hours daily. Half hardy. Sterilized Garden Soil or Houseplant Mix #3. Propagation by cuttings. Difficult. 2 species; 1 grown indoors.

Laurus nobilis. The classical Laurel of antiquity and an important culinary herb. The leaves are pleasantly aromatic. Tree to 40′ (12 m) but usually grown outdoors to no more than 8′ (2.40 m) and not over 3′ (90 cm) indoors as the roots are large. Leaves elliptic to 4″ (10 cm) long; hard, shiny and brittle.

An attractive shrub when trained. The principal requirements are ample sun and constant watering. Keep somewhat pot-bound. Fertilize with high nitrate formula. Keep cool in winter. Subject to scale.

Lavandula. **Labiatae.** Lavender. Mediterranean. Herb. Filtered sun, 300–500 fc 14 hours daily. Temperature min. 55°F (13°C). Houseplant Mix #2 with lime. Easy. 20 species; 1 suitable for indoors.

The above information applies only for the one warm-growing species. The standard English lavenders require much cooler conditions and, both in respect to manner of growth and appearance, are unsuitable as houseplants.

L. dentata. French Lavender. Much-branched herb to 2′ (60 cm), the branches thin, sweeping upward and forming a cone shape. Leaves 1–1½ × ¼″ (2.5–3.75 × 6 mm), finely and evenly segmented into many bluish green leaflets. Deliciously perfumed when stroked. It should be treated as an annual and cuttings rooted in water, moist vermiculite or sphagnum moss. Use high-middle-number fertilizer. This beautiful plant is one of the few culinary herbs that do really well indoors.

Leea. **Leeaceae (Vitaceae).** Tropical Asia and Africa. Shrubs. Shade to partial sun. 100–800 fc 14 hours daily. Temperature min. 55°F (13°C). Humidity min. 50%. Houseplant Mix #2 with sand and lime. Propagation from cuttings. Easy. 70 species. Some 8 currently grown indoors.

L. aculeata. Malaysia. Shrub with trident leaves on long stalks. Leaflets elliptic, 3–6″ (7.5–15 cm) long, toothed.

L. amabilis. Borneo. Leaves compound, 2′ (60 cm) long. Leaflets 9, paired-opposite, elliptical, 4″ (10 cm) long, with short point at tip; velvety bronze-green with midrib bordered by a broad white stripe.

'Splendens'. More reddish in tone.

L. coccinea. West Indian Holly. Shrub to 8′ (2.40 m). Paired-opposite leaflets, either single or consisting of 3 subleaflets each 3–4″ (7.5–10 cm) long, elliptical and toothed. Much used recently in commercial plantings.

L. rubra. Very similar, except that the leaves are dark red.

The two above species are widely planted as hedges in the West Indies. Excellent for 6–8″ (15–20 cm) pots. Fine decorative plants for warm, well-lighted locations. The thin leaves indicate their vulnerability to drafts, insect infestations and neglect. They are big drinkers but soil should be allowed to dry out before watering. Fertilize sparingly with a balanced formula.

L. sambucina. (roehrsiana). Handsome shrub with long-stalked compound leaves, 3′ (90 cm) long. Leaflets paired, opposite, 4″ (10 cm) long, deeply toothed. Surface corrugated, bronzy green, the veins rose colored in bright light.

In the past Leeas have been sold in large pots or tubs as 3′ (90 cm) or taller plants. Recently they have appeared on the market in 4″ (10 cm) pots and have become popular because of the delicate, thick covering of foliage.

Ligularia. **Compositae.** Europe and Asia. Low-growing herbs. Partial to full sun. 700–1,000 fc 14 hours daily. Temperature min. 40°F (4°C). Sterilized Garden Soil or Houseplant Mix #1 with sand. Propagation from seeds or division. Difficult. 100 or more species. Only one attempted indoors.

The spectacular shape, much broader than long, and the variegation of the leaves are a constant temptation to try it indoors. Unless you have a very cool house, an unheated sunporch or a really sunny window, maintenance is impossible. A temperature above 80°F (27°C) in summer is harmful and winter levels must not go over 60°F (16°C) dropping to a maximum of 55°F (13°C) at night. Keep constantly moist and fertilize no more than once a month during the warm season with a balanced formula. The plants are not long lasting indoors.

L. tussilaginea. Stemless, the few leaves arising from the base, green, leathery, kidneyshaped with a narrow cleft; much wider than long, 6 × 12″ (15 × 30 cm). Stalks to 12″ (30 cm).

L. tussilaginea argentea. 'Gingetsu'. Leaves edged in creamy white and gray.

L. tussilaginea aureo-maculata. Leopard Plant. The plant usually grown. Leaves covered with large yellow spots.

L. tussilaginea crispata. Green leaves fantastically curled and crisped.

'Glasshouse Gold'. Leaves splashed with yellow and gray.

Mangifera. **Anacardiaceae.** Mango. S. Asia. Tree. Filtered to partial sun. 800 fc. Temperature 65–95°F (18.5–34.5°C). Houseplant Mix #2 with sand and lime. Propagation from seed. Easy. 40 species. 1 grown.

Mangifera indica. Mango. Grown as a pot plant from seed of the fruit. Leaves elliptic to 12 × 2½″ (30 × 6.25 cm) long, on short, thick stalks; drooping. At first brown, lax, like thin rubber sheeting, gradually turning green and hard. Seed oval, 3″ (7.5 cm) long. After seed has dried for a few days, remove the outer skin. Plant in a 6″ (15 cm) pot at a depth of 1″ (2.5 cm) with the thicker edge up or laid on its side. Germination prompt, at most 10 days to 2 weeks indoors.

Supply even moisture. Fertilize weekly with a balanced formula. The treelet, which in nature grows to 40′ (12 m) or more, is reluctant to produce branches as a juvenile when trimmed. An easy pot plant but to be discarded when it grows too big.

There are so many cultivars that characteristics and details of culture may differ considerably. One usually plants the seed of whatever fruit is in the market. A variety from Belize has done best for us.

Manilkara. (Achras). **Sapotaceae.** Sapodilla. Large tree bearing edible fruit. Filtered to partial sun. Temperature min. 60°F (16°C). Humidity min. 40%. Sterilized sandy Garden Soil or Houseplant Mix #3 with sand. Propagation from seeds. 85 species of which one grown indoors.

Manilkara zapota (Achras sapota). A 100′ (30 m) tree that was the original source for chicle used in chewing gum. It also produces a round, reddish brown, edible fruit. It is one of a number of tropical trees that are grown by amateurs indoors because as more and more of the fruits enter our markets, the seeds become available. They are good pot plants that extend the limited repertory of foliage plants offered in the shops. Because they start life under the canopy of mature trees, they have moderate light requirements as juveniles.

The leaves are simple, oval, leathery; similar to many other tropical trees. They are 6″ (15 cm) long and nearly half as wide.

The medium-sized seeds have a hard covering. File a small section of the side until the flesh is revealed and soak overnight. Plant below soil level and keep moist at minimum 72°F (23°C). Prune to produce branching.

Other fruit trees of this family make good small houseplants.

Maranta. **Marantaceae.** Prayer Plant. Brazil. Creeping herb. Filtered sun. 200–500 fc. Temperature min. 55°F (13°C). Humidity min. 50%. Houseplant Mix #3 with lime. Propagation from cuttings. Fairly easy. 20 species; 2 grown indoors.

These fleshy, low foliage houseplants are known to all by their common name. Like other **Marantaceae** the leaves are arranged on the horizontal stems in the manner of an Iris: alternate, the stalks overlapping and clasping the stem. The common name arises from the upward folding of the blades at night rather than downward as in most plants with movable joints between stalk and leaf.

M. bicolor. Tuberous. Fleshy, jointed stems. Blades elliptic to oval, 5 × 2½″ (12.5 × 6.25 cm), the upper end rather blunt. A row of large brown spots are on both sides of the short-branched, broad, lighter midrib. Violet beneath. Small white flowers.

M. leuconeura. Prayer Plant. Without tubers. Stems creeping, pendant. Leaves 5½ × 3″ (13.75 × 7.5 cm), oval but somewhat flattened at the tip. Surface of blade lustrous green with gray or red lateral veins; blotched with purple beneath.

Var. *erythroneura.* Iridescent surface with light green wedges down the center and brilliant red lateral veins.

Var. *kerchoviana.* Light green with distinct, wedgeshaped, dark brown spots on either side of the lighter green midvein.

Var. *leuconeura.* The common Prayer Plant. Spotted with dark purple or brown on either side of lighter midrib area.

The nomenclature of these plants has become mixed up with time, and we are following that used by *Hortus Third.*

Both species are partially dormant in winter. They should be watered sparingly and kept in a humid environment until new growth starts. They will do better and last longer in a terrarium.

Melia. **Meliaceae.** Asia. Medium-sized tree. Partial sun. 600–800 fc 14 hours daily. Temperature min. 45°F (7°C). Houseplant Mix #2. Propagation from seeds or cuttings. Moderately easy. 10 species; one cultivated in tropics and subtropics.

Melia azedarach. Neem Tree. Grown indoors to max. 10′ (3 m). Leaves compound, leaflets short stalked, lanceshaped, the tip blunt, the edge feathery toothed. Flowers rare indoors, lavender in clusters, followed by poisonous yellow berries. The tree loses leaves for a short period in November. An extract from the tree is considered a promising general pesticide.

Keep evenly moist most of the year but allow to dry out between waterings in the late fall. Fertilize once a month with 20-20-20 at ¼ recommended solution. Will branch more if trimmed.

Meryta. **Araliaceae.** Western Pacific. Small trees. Filtered sun. 300–500 fc. Temperature min. 60°F (16°C). Houseplant Mix #3. Propagation from cuttings. Fairly easy. 15 species of which 1 grown indoors.

M. sinclairii. Tree to 25′ (7.5 m). Leaves numerous, shiny, closely spiraled on the stem, lanceshaped, 10–18 × 3–5″ (25–45 × 7.5–12.5 cm) on 6–10″ (15–25 cm) stalks borne horizontally. Usually grown to no more than 4 or 5′ (1.2–1.5 m). The principal veins of the blades are prominent, similar to some *Ficus.*

M. sinclairii has been promoted as a large, reliable houseplant but has not caught on as yet. The problem may be in the high cost of production.

Mimosa. **Leguminosae.** Tropical America. Shrubs and vines. Full sun. Min. 1,000 fc. Temperature min. 50°F (10°C). Cactus & Succulent Mix #2 without lime. Propagation by cuttings. Difficult. As many as 500 species but only 1 grown indoors.

The true Mimosas are common shrubs of the tropics, usually growing in relatively dry areas and sunny positions. Their compound leaves consist of a large number of leaflets. Acacias, with the same leaf arrangements, acquired the common name of Mimosa which also applies to the powdery yellow spring flowers of the shops.

M. pudica. Sensitive Plant. Low-growing, weedy

plant with long, thin, spiny branches, rooting at the joints. Leaves bear 15–25 pairs of tiny leaflets that fold together temporarily whenever touched. Quickly spreading and intolerant of pruning, the plant is worth growing only as a curiosity. It is usually short-lived indoors, requiring very high light. Subject to spider mites.

Monolean. **Melastomataceae.** Colombia. Herb. Filtered sun. Temperature 60–90°F (16–33°C). Humidity min. 50%. Houseplant Mix #2 or Sphagnum Moss. Division of thickened stem. Difficult.

M. primulaeflora. Leaf stalks rise directly from a horizontal, partly buried stem to 3″ (7.5 cm) or more across. Stalks to 10″ (25 cm), green or reddish. Blade lance shaped 6 × 3–4″ (15 × 7.5–10 cm), 3-veined, heavily quilted, very dark, lustrous green. The pink flowering is attractive.

The plant grows best in a terrarium. There are several cultivars available from exotic plant nurseries having leaves with various degrees of metallic reddish sheen that is very striking. Winter dormant.

Monstera. **Araceae.** Window Leaf Vine. Tropical America. Large vines. Shade to partial sun. Temperature min. 65°F (18.5°C). Humidity min. 60%. Houseplant Mix #2 or 3. Propagation from cuttings. Difficult. 25 species of which most have been grown indoors.

Monsteras are vines with leaves that are not only usually outsized but possess the unique feature of windows. These are holes of various shapes in the blades. What their function is, if any, is a matter of speculation. Possibly they are a means of reducing the weight of water during torrential rains. In any event, they are strikingly decorative. One other characteristic of some is that blades are divided unequally on either side of the midrib. The deep lobe segments are rectangular or curved-pointed. Otherwise, for all practical purposes, they are very similar to large Philodendrons, and some are grown and used in the same ways.

Out-of-doors in the tropics they climb to the very tops of trees, creating a giant tapestry of overlapping leaves. Indoors they are being used to some extent in high-ceilinged, sunny and warm, principally southern-oriented displays. Whether they will continue to be is the question, for they are all rampant vines.

As a pot plant only the juvenile sizes can be considered. These have leaves smaller and simpler in shape than the mature ones, therefore less ornamental. So their usefulness will depend on the future availability of cultivars that can be induced to produce decorative leaves earlier in their development. This is not easy, as has been demonstrated sufficiently with Philodendrons. Also the growing of aroids on cedar slabs or cork bark is no longer in vogue and is not very likely to return for some time.

The fact that a few specialist nurseries are still growing a considerable number of species is due to the interest of botanical gardens and horticulturists with large greenhouses, rather than the public at large.

For details of culture, which are identical, see *Philodendron*. Note that mature leaf forms usually develop in partial sun while juvenile leaves can be maintained in the shade. Also we must warn that the mature leaves are developed only when the vine has a support on which to climb. Unsupported, they quickly revert to simple shapes. Cuttings root in water or moist mediums.

The variability of species is such that both botanical and horticultural names remain confused.

M. acuminata. Shingle Plant. Leaves widely spaced on thin stems, broadly lanceshaped; simple when young. Mature blades, developing in bright light, pierced by 3–6 oval windows; 10 × 5″ (25 × 12.5 cm) on thin stalks.

M. adansonii (M. pertusa and *jacquinii).* Juvenile blades simple. Mature blades 2–3′ (60–90 cm) long and 10″ (25 cm) wide, combining long, narrow, oval windows with long-pointed, curving lobes. Sheaths of the stalks reaching almost to the blades.

M. deliciosa (Philodendron pertusum). Ceriman. Swiss Cheese plant. *P. pertusum* is the name that has been applied to young plants which, earlier than most Monsteras, develop large, decorative, more or less heartshaped leaves with symmetrical, scimitarlike lobes, cut almost to the midrib. Older plants have, in addition, a row of small windows on either side of the midrib. The vine climbs to 30′ (9 m) or more. Blades to 3′ (90 cm) long and almost as wide. Stalks to 3′ (90 cm). Var. *borsigiana,* smaller leaves with fewer lobes and windows.

'Albo-variegata'. Leaves splashed with white. A slow grower.

'Marmorata'. Leaves and stalks marbled with varying intensities of off-white to yellow.

This is the most famous of the Monsteras, as much for its delicious edible fruit that looks like a corn cob as for the leaves. It has also proved, thus far, the easiest to adapt to pots and tubs. The method is to take sections of stem with mature leaves and root them, which is quick and easy, so that they can be attached to cedar or cork slabs by their aerial roots and then displayed for sale. Like the large Philodendrons, further growth requires taller supports. If these are not supplied, the stems will hang down and revert, becoming unsightly. Though *M. deliciosa* is quite slow growing indoors, the decorative look is of short duration, suitable only for temporary displays.

M. dubia. Young leaves are simple, silvery, with dark green veins. Stalks short, the blades clinging closely to the support. Quite manageable in the house. It requires high humidity. Older leaves are 4 × 2′ (1.20 m × 60 cm) with up to 20 pairs of strapshaped segments. Stalks 20″ (50 cm).

M. epipremnoides (M. leichtlinii). Costa Rica. A monstrous and magnificent plant, the leaves 36 × 22″ (90 × 55 cm) on long stalks; broadly lanceshaped and with rectangular segments, some of which are joined at the tips forming large, horizontal holes. A line of smaller holes borders the midrib. This description covers only some specimens. That none of the segments curve upward toward the tip appears to differentiate it from other Monsteras.

Young plants are designated as *M. leichtlinii* and *M. obliqua expilata*. They have much smaller, oval leaves with large-angled holes. Or they may well be *M. friedrichsthalii,* which they also resemble.

This is probably a typical instance of botanists collecting a plant in different stages of development and designating each as species.

M. friedrichsthalii. Heartshaped, thin leaves, 2' (60 cm) in length with large-angled, oval holes; almost skeletal in appearance.

M. karwinskyi. Hortus Third describes this plant in much the same terms as we have *M. epipremnoides.* We have not found it listed in catalogs, etc.

M. obliqua. See above. Mature leaves 8 × 4" (20 × 10 cm). Most of the blade pierced by elliptical, leafshaped holes.

M. pittieri is described as somewhat smaller than *obliqua.*

The above species are obviously well scrambled. Because of the holes they make a unique and rather wonderful show. One should choose plants according to their appearance rather then their labels.

M. punctulata is similar to *M. deliciosa,* but blades are longer and narrower and the stalks decorated with large dots.

M. standleyana. 2' (60 cm) long blades, leathery; half as wide. 'Variegata' is splashed with white.

Muehlenbeckia. **Polygonaceae.** Wire Plant. New Zealand and S. America. Full sun. Temperature 50–85°F (10–29.5°C). Sterilized Garden Soil or Houseplant Mix #3. Propagation from cuttings. Difficult. 20 species; 1 grown indoors.

M. complexa. Maidenhair Vine. Rapidly growing vine with stems like black threads, the widely spaced leaves thin, elliptic, ½–¾" (12.5–18.6 mm) long, deep green. Is a haze of greenery when trained on a trellis and can also be grown in a basket. Tiny greenish flowers followed by white berries. Often listed as a houseplant, but that is not our experience. It needs plenty of space, full sun and cool temperatures in summer as well as winter.

Murdannia. **Commelinaceae.** Herbs. Shade to filtered sun. 50–300 fc. Temperature min. 55°F (13°C). Packaged Houseplant Medium. Propagation by division or cuttings easy.

M. acutifolia variegata. Fleshy stems to 2½' (75 cm) with opposite 8 × ½" (20 × 1.25 cm) clasping leaves, striped thinly with white on lively green. Reddish joints. Strong, fast grower. Stem cuttings root quickly in water. Fertilize monthly with standard packaged formula. An easy pot plant, but the stems are weak and usually elongate more than desired. Hence it is necessary to produce new plants as soon as they have passed their peak.

Murraya. **Rutaceae.** Mock Orange. India and S.E. Asia. Shrub. Filtered sun. 500 fc 14 hours daily. Temperature min. 65°F (18.5°C). Houseplant Mix #2 with sand. Propagation from seed and cuttings. Easy. 4 species; 2 grown indoors.

Murraya is a small genus with considerable potential for indoor horticulture. Only 2 appear to be in cultivation. *M. alata,* which we have not seen listed, looks like an excellent prospect, but the flowering of rather large-petalled white blooms takes it out of our category of foliage plants. *M. koenigii,* however, also rarely if ever grown, belongs here and should be of interest.

M. exotica. Orange Jasmine. Woody, branching shrub to 3' (90 cm), the branches white. Leaves compound, the leaflets 5–11, alternate, spoonshaped to 1" (2.5 cm), glossy green like other citrus. Flowers small, white, very fragrant. Best bloomer.

M. koenigii. Curry Leaf. This is the true Curry Leaf, which is aromatic and much used in Southeast Asian cooking. It should not be confused with curry, which is a powdered mix of various spices.

This ia a small tree with compound leaves, the 11–21 leaflets lanceshaped. Should be as easy to grow as the other 2 species, but the longer leaves give it a wider spread in pot.

M. paniculata. Altogether like *M. alata* except that it grows to 10' (3 m). *Hortus Third* lists *M. alata* as identical with *M. paniculata.* We have seen the latter as a very large-spreading shrub with innumerable branches, whereas nurserymen assure us that *M. alata* is more compact. We believe that both (if they are really different) make excellent pot plants.

Keep constantly moist. A fast grower indoors but tolerates frequent pruning. The foliage is very long-lived. It is a heavy drinker. Fertilize with balanced formula once a month. Considering its origins it tolerance of low light is remarkable. Very insect and disease free.

This is the easiest Citrus Family plant for indoor gardening, a classic shrub that also can be shaped or trained to a standard. It should do very well in windowed and other moderately well-lighted commercial situations. Tub size there are few foliage plants to match *M. alata/ paniculata,* with white branches contrasting with the deep green shining leaves.

Musa. **Musaceae.** Banana. Tropical Asia and Western Pacific. Treelike herbs. Partial to full sun. Temperature min. 50°F (10°C). Humidity 50%. Sterilized Garden Soil with Peat or Houseplant Mix #3. Propagation from offsets. Difficult. 25 species; 1 or 2 grown indoors.

Despite their mature height of 10–20' (3–6 m) banana plants are herbs, not trees. The giant leaves spiral on clumps of pseudo-stems. At the end of their growth cycle they renew themselves from offsets. But indoors it is advisable to replace them with new young plants from the nursery. This limits their potential use both for amateurs and in commercial plantings.

Keep constantly moist and fertilize with a balanced formula 3 or 4 times a year. On display the oversize leaves must be given a protected position as they are easily damaged and become unsightly. They are also attacked by all types of insects and fungus infections. Nevertheless, if carefully tended, they can serve as handsome temporary displays.

In a home, place close to a sunny window. Underpotted they stay manageably small. Dwarf cultivars can be grown in pots for a year or two. Some have been touted as producing fruit indoors, but this is unrealistic without expert attention to an ideal environment—and some luck.

Mature banana plants, even with fruiting stems, are occasionally used as an exotic element in large indoor plantings, mostly in the South. Young variegated cultivars are attractive but for a period of no more than a year or two.

Ensete. 7 species, is a closely related genus, little if ever grown indoors.

M. acuminata (cavendishii). To 20' (6 m) with leaves 9 × 2' (2.70 m × 60 cm) Numerous cultivars.

'Dwarf Cavendish'. Much reduced in size and more suitable for indoor growth and display.

'Zebrina' ('Sumatrana'). Bloodleaf Banana. To 12' (3.6 m). Leaves bluish green variegated with blood red. Very tender.

M. xparadisiaca 'Vittata'. Leaves light green variegated with milky green and white. Midrib white and edges red. Will grow in filtered sun.

Myrciaria (Eugenia). **Myrtaceae.** Tropical America. Intermediate house shrub. Partial to full sun. 600–1,000 fc. Temperature min. 50°F (10°C). Houseplant Mix #2. Propagation from cuttings. Moderately easy. 40 species; 1 grown indoors.

M. myriophylla. Slow growing, very much branched little shrub. Leaves 1½–2" × ¼" (3.75–5 cm × 62 mm), pointed strapshaped, in opposite pairs.

A lovely, lacy-looking mound of branches and leaves for an 8–10" (20–25 cm) pot. Moisture loving. Fertilize monthly with high nitrate formula.

Myriophyllum. **Haloragaceae.** Water Milfoil. Worldwide temperate and tropical aquatic herb. Partial sun. 600 fc. Temperature min. 50°F (10°C). Cactus and Succulent Mix #2. Propagation by division. Easy. 45 species.

A type of plant that doesn't impress as being of interest or even possible indoors. Nevertheless, we include it because it has had its devotees among those who have installed indoor gardens with shallow pools. As more experience is acquired regarding the maintenance of pools, this, and other aquatic plants, may attract more attention.

M. aquaticum (brasiliense). Brazil and south. Parrot's Feather. Vigorous aquatic plant. The leaves simple, threadlike in tufts, yellowish green, in appearance like the most delicate of Asparagus Ferns but the stems limp, floating. Plant in shallow pots below surface of the water. It needs frequent trimming to prevent overcrowding. Colonizes and can be divided.

Myrsine. **Myrsinaceae.** Asia and Africa. Dwarf shrubs. Partial sun. Temperature min. 50°F (10°C). Sterilized Garden Soil or Houseplant Mix #2 with sand. Propagation from cuttings. Temperamental. 5 species; 2 grown indoors.

M. africana. African Boxwood. Woody shrub to max. 6' (1.8 m) but usually no more than 3' (80 cm) indoors. Leaves alternate, teardrop shaped, ½" (1.25 cm) long, on reddish brown branches. Makes a good pseudo-bonsai.

M. nummularia. Oval, nearly stalkless leaves to ¾" (18.6 mm) on wiry, creeping branches that root at the joints.

The plants suffer from temperatures over 85°F (29.5°C). Roots are shallow and require constant moisture. Feed with high nitrate fertilizer once a month. Treat with chelated or micronized iron once a year.

These are tempermental plants that seem to suffer from fungal root infections. Proper cultural methods have not yet been developed. They probably do best in places where temperatures in summer are relatively low. Pretty plants worth an effort.

Myrtus. **Myrtaceae.** Myrtle. Mediterranean. Shrubs. Shade to full sun. Min. 100 fc. Temperature min. 40°F (4°C). Houseplant Mix #3 with sand, or Sterilized Garden Soil with peat. Propagation by seed or cuttings. Moderately difficult. 16 species; 1 grown indoors.

M. communis. Woody shrub to 15' (4.5 m), but only the smaller cultivars are grown indoors. These are max. 2' (60 cm). Much branched with alternate pairs of opposite, elliptic leaves to 1½" (3.75 cm) long; shiny, dark green, hard. Aromatic when crushed. An excellent plant for trimming and will stay small if potbound.

There are many named compact and small-leaved (½" (1.25 cm)) cultivars, differing mostly in branching and closer to looser arrangement of leaves. Among these are 'Buxifolia', 'Compacta', 'Microphylla', 'Minima', 'Nana'. These names suggest how very much alike they are.

'Variegata' is most frequently grown. Tiny leaves edged in white. Good for bonsai.

Keep moist and fertilize 4 times a year with a high nitrate formula. Requires patience to establish well. Protect against temperatures over 80°F (27°C). Sensitive to aerial pollution and requires good ventilation.

Nandina. **Berberidaceae.** Heavenly Bamboo. India and E. Asia. Shrub. Filtered to full sun. 500–1,000 fc. Temperature min. 40°F (4°C). Sterilized Garden Soil with peat. Propagated by seeds and division. Difficult. 1 species.

N. domestica. Stems growing from the base, numerous, crowded, forming a dense mass; unbranched. Leaves numerous, compound. Leaflets opposite, odd numbered, elliptical, 2 × ½" (5 × 1.25 cm). Young foliage reddish. Usually not higher than 2' (60 cm) indoors. Larger plants are grown for commercial plantings in cool locations; to 8' (2.4 m).

This is a typical cold-tolerant plant requiring good ventilation and some rest in winter. Keep constantly moist and fertilize very sparingly with a balanced formula. There are several cultivars.

'Compacta'. To 3' (90 cm).

'Nana Harbour Dwarf'. To 2' (60 cm).

'Nana Purpurea'. Young foliage purple.

'Wood's Dwarf' is listed.

We have found this a difficult plant to grow, and we know nobody who has done well with it though it is constantly recommended. We suspect that it needs outdoor or greenhouse rather than indoor conditions.

Nautilocalyx. **Gesneriaceae.** Tropical America. Herbs. Filtered sun. 500 fc. 14 hours daily. Temperature min. 65°F (18.5°C). Humidity min. 50%. Houseplant Mix #3 with lime. Moderately easy. 15 species; 6 grown indoors.

Of the 6 species, 3 cannot be rated as foliage plants.

N. bullatus. Thick stemmed, hairy, to 2' (60 cm). Leaves paired, opposite-alternate, broadly elliptical, 5–9" (12.5–22.5 cm) long, short toothed; heavily veined and quilted. Dark green becoming olive with age.

N. forgettii. Growth habit like *bullatus* but leaves lanceshaped, 7 × 1½" (12.5 × 3.75 cm), shiny, metallic brown or silvery with redish veins in a prominent "tree" design. Reddish purple beneath.

N. lynchii. Leaves dark maroon, quilted, spoonshaped. Keep evenly moist and fertilize with a high phosphate formula at ⅛ recommended strength with each watering. As these plants grow taller, the stem deteriorates, hence they should be replaced yearly with new plants from cuttings which root easily in moist sterilized medium.

Richly toned pot plants. Possibly interesting for dense temporary plantings. They have been produced in quantity from time to time but have not gained much favor with the public. Difficult to maintain in shop.

Neoregelia. **Bromeliaceae.** Brazil. Fleshy rosette plants. 52 species of which about 6 are frequently grown. See *Aechmea* for culture.

At blooming time the inner leaves of some species become richly colored. This display may last for 6 months but occurs only once. Thus, to benefit from the spectacular coloration it is necessary to purchase plants when they are preparing to bloom. Other species and cultivars, however, are less dependent on this phenomenon for their attraction, being normally decorated with colored stripes, spots or blotches. These, then, can be depended upon for a longer display. However, flowering is followed, as in all bromeliads, by the development of pups and the eventual death of the mature plant. In practice, therefore, approximately one year is the useful life of these plants. As we point out for *Aechmea*, full maturity of the offshoots is achieved only under conditions difficult to attain indoors.

The following is a selection of showier species and cultivars. They are superb for massing in formal beds or with taller foliage as a background.

N. ampulacea. Small, narrow, erect, colonizing vases. Waxy leaves 6 × ½" (15 × 1.25 cm), rounded at the tip with brown splotches arranged in rows.

N. A. × compacta. Leaves to 8", dotted red.

'Brazil'. Green with brownish purple bands.

N. Carolinae (marechallii) Blushing Bromeliad. Low, spreading rosette. Leaves to 15 × 1½" (27.5 × 3.75 cm), green; inner leaves purplish red.

'Meyendorfii'. Leaves coppery olive green.

'Roseo-striata'. See 'Tricolor' below. Leaves suffused with pink.

'Tricolor'. Ivory stripes. Inner leaves brilliant red at flowering time. This is the popular cultivar.

Other variegated cultivars are also available occasionally.

N. marmorata. Leaves 15 × 2½" (27.5 × 6.25 cm). Light green with darker spots.

N. schultsiana. 'Fireball'. Colonizing, small, bright red vases in high light.

'Fireball Hybrid'. Vases "vivid purple".

N. spectabilis. Fingernail Plant. Leaves 15 × 1½" (27.5 × 3.25 cm). Upright vase, green with blunt tip reddened, striped with grey beneath. Inner leaves purple.

'Variegata'. Leaves mottled with purple and striped with gold.

Nephthytis. **Araceae.** W. Africa. Herbs. 4 species. See *Syngonium* for culture.

Nurserymen have persistently offered Syngoniums or unidentified aroids with more or less heartshaped to broadly arrowshaped leaves under the name of *Nephthytis*. This genus appears to provide no foliage plants of ornamental value. Nevertheless, the generic name keeps popping up on the labels of new introductions closely resembling Syngoniums already in the trade.

Nicodemia. **Loganiaceae.** Mauritius. Intermediate house shrub. Partial sun. 600 fc. Temperature min. 55°F (13°C). Sterilized Garden Soil or Houseplant Mix #2 or #3. Propagation from stem cuttings.

N. diversifolia. In *Hortus Third*, *Nicodemia* is referred to *Buddleia* (?), and the species *diversifolia* is not listed although the plant is popular with hobbyists. Leaves in opposite pairs, very much resembling those of an oak, deeply scalloped, to 4" (10 cm) long, with a metallic bluish tinge. Branching and fast growing. Ventilate well and keep cool in summer. Fertilize twice monthly with high nitrate formula in summer and once a month in winter. Maintain even moisture. A handsome indoor shrub to 3' (90 cm).

Ophiopogon. **Liliaceae.** Lilyturf. Mondo Grass. Small, grassleaved pot plants. Shade to filtered sun. 200–500 fc. Temperature min. 45°F (7°C). Houseplant Mix #1 or 2 with sand. Propagation from offsets. Fairly easy. 10 species.

These grassy members of the Lily family are half to

Hedera 'Mini Green'

Hedera 'Silver King'

Hedera cv.

Hedychium densiflorum variegatum

PLATE 49

Helichrysum angustifolium. Curry Plant

Hemigraphis colorata (alternata)

Hibiscus elatus. Mahoe

Hoffmannia refulgens

PLATE 50

Hoffmannia ghiesbrecktii variegata.

Homalocladium platycladum. Ribbon Plant. Photo Gordon Courtright

Homalomena sulcata

Homalomena wallisii 'Mauro'

PLATE 51

Homalomena 'Rangoon'

Hoya bella variegata

Hoya argentea picta

Hoya multiflora

PLATE 52

Hypoestes phyllostachya (sanguinolenta). Polka Dot Plant.

Hypoestes phyllostachya alba-variegata.

Ilex dimorphophylla.

Iresine herbstii

PLATE 53

Jacaranda mimosifolia

Kaempferia roscoeana.

Kalanchoe beharensis. Velvet Leaf

Kalanchoe 'Miyakae'

PLATE 54

Kalanchoe daigremontana. Devil's Backbone

Laurus nobilis. Laurel

Lavandula dentata. French Lace

Leea coccinea. West Indian Holly

PLATE 55

Ligularia tussilaginea aureo-maculata. Leopard Plant.

Mangifera indica. Mango

Maranta leuconeura 'Massangeana'

Mimosa pudica. Sensitive Plant.

PLATE 56

Monolena primulaefolia.

Monstera deliciosa. Photo Gordon Courtright.

Monstera pittieri

Muehlenbeckia complexa. Wire Plant.

PLATE 57

Murdannia acutifolia 'Variegata'

Murraya paniculata. Orange Jasmine

Myrsine africana. Cape Myrtle

Myrtus communis. Myrtle

PLATE 58

Nandina domestica. Heavenly Bamboo. Photo Gordon Courtright

Nautilocalyx picturatus

Neoregelia carolinae 'Tricolor'

Neoregelia meyendorfii variegata

PLATE 59

Nicodemia diversifolia

Ophiopogon japonicum variegatum

Ophiopogon 'Atakai'. Dwarf form.

Oplismenus hirtellus variegatus. Basket Grass

PLATE 60

Osmanthus heterophyllus variegatus

Osmanthus fragrans. Sweet Olive

Oxalis regnellii

Oxalis martiana aureo-reticulata

PLATE 61

Oxalis hedysaroides (alstonii) rubra. Firefern

Pachypodium geayii

Pachypodium lamerei

Pandanus veitchii variegatus

PLATE 62

Pedilanthes tithymaloides variegatus

Pelargonium carnosum. Photo W. Rauh

Pelargonium 'Dr. Livingstone'

Pelargonium 'Variegated Prince Rupert'

PLATE 63

Pelargonium 'Nutmeg'

Pelargonium 'Coconut'

Pellionia daveauana. Trailing Watermelon

Peperomia obtusifolia 'Green Cascade'

PLATE 64

fully hardy. The former can be maintained in the home with plenty of air circulation. Keep at an open window in summer and at 60°F (16°C) or less in winter. They are semiaquatic plants requiring constant moisture. Fertilize 4 times a year with 20-20-20. They are charming and unusual pot plants that colonize by underground runners and are easily separated for potting up. Ideal for the cool dish garden.

O. jaburan. Tight tufts of leaves to 18 × ¼″ (45 cm × 6.25 mm).

'Variegatum'. Leaves with thin, vertical, white stripes. A splendid, easy pot plant that deserves greater popularity. Excellent for massing.

O. japonicus (Mondo japonicum). Tufts of grassy leaves growing from tubers and putting out runners. Leaves to 10 × ⅛″ (25 cm × 3 mm), dark green, erect, curving at the tips. Very compact.

'Atakai'. Leaves 6″ (15 cm), striped white.

'Kyoto Dwarf'. 2″ (5 cm) high, vertically ribbed, black-green.

'Old Gold'. Leaves lax to 10″ (25 cm). Green stripes on ivory. Delicate and difficult indoors.

O. planiscapus var. *nigrescens,* 'Arabicus'. Black Mondo Grass. Leaves 15 × ¼″ (37.5 cm × 6 mm), curving over in a circle. The green of the leaves is so dark as to appear black. Frequently seen as a curiosity in English gardens and well worth growing indoors.

Oplismenus. **Graminiae.** Basket Grass. Southwest U.S., Central America, West Indies. Grassy basket plant. Partial to full sun. Temperature min. 50°F (10°C). Sterilized Garden Soil or Houseplant Mix #2 with sand. Easy. Propagation from stem cuttings. 20 or more species; 1 grown indoors.

O. hirtellus. Creeping, grass, rooting at the joints, with wiry stems to 2′ (60 cm) that are pendant when growing in baskets.

'Variegatus' (*Panicum variegatum*). This is the plant usually grown. Stems pinkish, the stalkless leaves, long lanceshaped, 4 × ½″ (10 × 1.25 cm), alternate, set an inch (2.5 cm) or more apart. Striped green and white vertically. With pink lines in bright light. Keep constantly moist and fertilize sparingly.

An airy, easily grown, screening basket plant. Needs frequent grooming as old leaves turn brown.

Osmanthus. **Oleaceae.** Temperate Asia and N. America. Shrubs and medium-sized trees. Partial to full sun. 500–1,000 fc. Temperature min. 40°F (4°C). Long-fiber sphagnum moss. Moderately difficult. Propagation from cuttings. 40 species; 2 occasionally grown indoors.

O. fragrans. Sweet Olive. A 30′ (9 m) tree outdoors. Grown indoors to max. 4′ (1.20 m). Leaves elliptic, hard, shiny, to 4″ (10 cm) long. Small, white, perfumed flowers. A very slow grower. Prefers warm temperatures, 55–85°F (13–29.5°C) and good air movement. Keep moist. Fertilize with high nitrate formula and trace elements. A splendid small shrub for a sunny window.

O. heterophyllus (aquifolium, illicifolius). Japan and Taiwan. Holly Olive. Woody, branching shrub to 20′ (6 m). Leaves shiny, broadly elliptic with spiny teeth; 2½″ (6.25 cm) long, in pairs, opposite and alternate. Cooler growing than *O. fragrans* and preferring full sun. Cultivars with yellow margins, such as 'Argenteo-marginatus' or yellow with some gray blotches such as 'Aureus' are colorful.

Very little grown indoors because they require low maximum temperatures in summer and 50°F (10°C) or lower at night in winter.

Oxalis. **Oxalidaceae.** Wood Sorrel. Worldwide. Herbs. Partial sun. 400–500 fc. for foliage. Temperature min. 40°F (4°C). Houseplant Mix #2. Propagated from pips and seeds. Easy. 850 species but only a few grown for foliage.

The large-flowered *Oxalis,* grown almost entirely as greenhouse and houseplants, are low herbs whose separate, fleshy flower and leaf stalks rise directly from little, colonizing pips. The leaves always have three segments which change position at night; those with a center vein folding upward while others drop down from a horizontal position. Flowers have five deeply cleft lobes in white, yellow, pink or red. They bloom profusely but suffer from the drawback of a rather short season indoors and long dormancy. *Oxalis* species grown for foliage also bloom, of course, but less prolifically and with smaller flowers. However they have the advantages of year-round activity indoors if kept warm, moist and well lighted and leaves that are more ornamental. They are very charming pot plants that deserve greater popularity.

Culture presents no special problems except mite infestations. Plants growing from pips must be cut down once they are infested. Wash off the pips and soak in a recommended pesticide. Allow to dry out for a week, then replant in fresh mix and keep the soil just barely moist. Sprouting is variable; sometimes very quick, occasionally delayed. Be patient. In general just keep the plants in moderate light; water when the soil approaches dryness and fertilize with a balanced formula. The small roots can be accommodated in azalea-style pots. Propagate by separating singles or clusters of pips. Fibrous-rooted, stem types are best propagated from seed.

O. corymbosa (O. martiana) aureo-reticulata. The plant grows into lovely mounds of foliage 6″ (15 cm) high, the leaf segments broadly heartshaped, widest at the top and intricately veined in pure gold. The pink flowers make an unsatisfactory color match. But the leaves are incomparable. Their size varies according to culture, reaching a diameter of 1½″ (3.75 cm) indoors. Among the most handsome of all small foliage plants. Spreading rhizomes eventually make pot plantings 6–8″ (15–20 cm) across.

O. hedysaroides 'Rubra'. Fire Fern. Ecuador. Fibrous rooted with branched stems to 15″ (37.5 cm) indoors. Leaflets deep red, to 1″ (2.5 cm) long, shallowly lobed. The leaflets raise or lower themselves individually during the day, responding to changes in light and air movement. At night they turn downward.

O. ortgiesii. Peru. Tree Oxalis. to 1½' (45 cm) with hairy, deeply lobed segmented leaves. Handsome. Cooler growing than the others. Protect against extreme summer temperatures. Allow to dry out between waterings. Can be trimmed and branches well.

O. regnellii. South America. The plant is being sold these days as "Real Shamrock" though it bears no resemblance to any clover of the Emerald Isle. Its attractions are inherent; superb, strictly triangular leaflets with 1" (2.5 cm) segments, maroon beneath, on 6" (15 cm) stalks; little white flowers always present held above the foliage; no dormancy; among the easiest of foliage or flowering plants to maintain in the house. It will accept almost any kind of soil, has small roots and propagates actively by means of little pips. It can be grown and flowered in a north window. A gem.

O. siliquosa. S. America. Somewhat succulent plant with red leaves and yellow flowers. Dormant period.

The only other genus of the *Oxalidaceae* actively grown as houseplant is *Biophytum. B. sensitivium* grows no more than 6" (15 cm) high, single stemmed, with a whorl of densely packed, compound leaves that give it the appearance of a miniature palm. Pink flowers. It is an annual but spontaneously develops viable seeds that can be collected and planted or that distribute themselves spontaneously among other pots in the house. As the roots are small this is no nuisance. A charming plant that needs minimum care.

Pachypodium. Apocynaceae. Mostly S. Africa and Madagascar. Complex succulents with caudices, thickened roots, widely ranging in size. Partial to full sun. 600–1,000 fc. Min. temperature 40°F (4°C). Houseplant Mix #1 or Succulent Mix. Add lime. Propagation mostly from seed. Easy to difficult. 15 or so species mostly in cultivation.

Pachypodium is a fascinating genus of curious succulents which bear showy yellow to red flowers. Strangely, it is omitted from *Hortus Third.* Those grown mainly for foliage are few but a number of variations are recognized. Indoors they should be kept at least slightly moist throughout the year and regularly watered during their most active growing period, in summer with us. Fertilize with high dilutions of high nitrate fertilizer in summer. The treelike plants must be moved to bigger pots as they grow, roots being rather large. The only training possible is tipping of the stem to produce three or four short branches. They are occasionally attacked by mealybugs but are not preferred hosts.

P. geayi. Madagascar. A 24' (8 m) swollen, thorny trunk topped by a crown of leaves to over 1' (30 cm) long and max. ⅔" (16 mm) across. Silvery beneath. Mature plants have a few short branches at the top. Indoor-grown plants are much shorter.

P. lamerei. Madagascar. The most popular species. To 18' (5.40 m) tall and max. 2' (60 cm) thick, but usually much smaller indoors. Spiny from top to bottom. Leaves similar to *P. geayi,* about the same length but broader, up to 3" (7.5 cm) across. Some clones are more branching than others but only after reaching to maximum height. Some branching can be induced in juveniles by lopping off the growing tip. The leaves are tightly whorled and form a solid bush at the top. Keep rather moist and in at least partial sun. This is a sculptural plant that does much better indoors than most large, cylindrical cacti and the leaves are an additional adornment.

P. lealii. Caudex broader at the bottom and tapering. Branches along the trunk grow vertically. Spines are further apart. Leaves broad, lanceshaped, to 3" (7.5 cm) long. This is much less attractive as a foliage plant.

There are a number of small and big similar species or variations but the above are best for foliage. They make very interesting sculptural, relatively carefree houseplants.

Pandanus. Pandanaceae. Screw Pine. Old World tropics. Small to large trees. Partial to full sun. 600–1,000 fc. Temperature tolerance varies. Min. 40°F (4°C). Sandy Garden Soil or Houseplant Mix #3 with sand. Propagation by offsets. 650 species of which 7–10 grown indoors. Except for the requirement of bright light, they can take Cast-Iron culture.

When mature these decorative trees have a few short, nearly horizontal branches that bear masses of spiraled, very long, narrow, stiff leaves, usually spiny and folded in a V. The name Screw Pine is apt because the foliage resembles a spiral staircase, the great number of leaves overlapping evenly with each turn around the trunk or branch. Even quite young trees raise themselves above soil level by means of a set of stiff, thick stilts.

As young pot plants they resemble Dracaenas. Later, before branching begins, the leaves become much longer and more numerous. A tub is required to hold the extensive root system.

Pandanus are currently appearing somewhat more frequently in shops. No doubt the slow rate of growth hinders production. If this were overcome there are still the objections that we list below to inhibit their popularity. However, there is no question that they possess a shining brightness of surface or beautiful variegation that attract attention. Culture is very simple and the plants are long lasting.

Young growths are handsome in 6–10" (15–25 cm) pots. Somewhat larger sizes in small tubs are fine decoration for sunny corners, but the long leaves take up a lot of room, a spread of 6' (1.80 m) not being unusual.

They can be permanent plantings wherever sufficient natural light is available. But many of the plants have sharply spined edges that are a hazard. There has never been much use for low-spreading plants of such size. Fan palms are an example. Plantscapers prefer bare stems behind lower foliage.

P. baptistii. New Britain Island. Leaves 3' × 2" (90 × 2.5 cm), spineless. Described as dark green or with white stripes down the middle.

'Aureus'. Blue-green with yellow stripes!

P. dubius. Western Pacific. A 60′ (18 m) tree, the leaves 12′ (!) long and 7″ wide (3.6 m × 25 cm). Cultivated apparently only as a juvenile labeled *Pandanus pacificus*. Leaves are broader than most on young plants, shiny green with the edges finely spiny. Underpotted it is manageable as a houseplant. Produces many offsets.

P. pristis. Madagascar. Very different from the others and cool tolerant. Leaves much twisted and spiny; strapshaped to 15″ (37.5 cm) long, forming a low rosette. It very much resembles a large *Cryptanthus*.

P. pygmaeus (polycephalus, gramminifolius). Miniature Screw Pine. Produces stilts when quite small. Leaves to 15 × ½″ (37.5 × 1.25 cm), shiny green. Most suitable for pot culture but not easily available.

P. sanderi. Leaves to 2′ × 2″ (60 × 5 cm), angled downward from the middle to the tip. Of easy culture but rather odd looking.

'Roehrsianus'. Brilliantly striped with yellow. Gorgeous, but a more temperamental plant.

P. utilis. Common Screw Pine. Madagascar. A most ornamental tree much grown in Florida and other subtropical and tropical regions. Branching, to 60′ (18m) with a smooth trunk. Leaves 6′ × 4″ (1.8 m × 10 cm); stiff, erect, with fine red spines along the edge. There are some named variegated cultivars.

P. veitchii. Polynesia. Most cold tolerant and adaptable to indoor culture. Leaves to 3′ × 3″ (90 × 7.5 cm), light green with vertical cream lines and fine spines along the edges.

'Compactus'. A dwarf with very pure white lines.

'Verde'. New growth white changing to green. Notable for the extraordinary brilliance of the leaves and the vigorous growth.

The soil should be sandy but also rich in organic matter. In the house it is advisable to grow all the Pandanus at a minimum temperature of 55°F (22°C) although *P. veitchii* can be trusted at much lower levels. Constant moisture is essential. Fertilize with 20-20-20 or other balanced formula. To slow growth feed only every other month and allow the plants to become pot-bound. Insect attacks are of rare occurrence. Pups appear with time around the parent plant. These can be cut free, carefully dug up and transplanted after they have developed their own root systems.

Pedilanthes. **Euphorbiaceae.** Mexico and Caribbean islands. Succulent shrub. Partial sun for foliage. Min. 400 fc, 12 hours daily. Temperature min. 50°F (10°C). Succulent Mix #2. Propagation mostly cuttings. Easy. 30 species of which one widely cultivated.

P. tithymaloides. Red Bird Cactus. The species is so variable that almost every geographical location shows different stems, leaf size and coloration. Basically the plant consists of rubbery stems, usually not much branched, with prominent nodes and alternate leaves that are stalkless. Elliptic in shape, the leaves range in size from ½″ to 5″ (1.25 cm to 12.5 cm). They are fleshy-waxy, shiny and range in color from darkest green to light green or heavy variegated with white. Habit varies from erect to sprawling. When bent over the branches readily produce roots at the prominent joints. Flowers are up to an inch long in clusters, tube shaped with a prominent beak.

P. tithymaloides will grow in just about any soil but prefers a succulent mix with a little extra peat and lime. Growing period is in the warm months during which time it should be watered once a week. In winter water should be partly withheld but not eliminated entirely. Cuttings root promptly in sand if sprayed daily.

The variegated forms are deservedly popular and grow into big pot plants. They could be used more than at present for landscaping where some overhang is required or a medium high transition plant for bedding.

Pelargonium. **Geraniaceae.** South Africa. Leafy herbs. Filtered to full sun. 400–1000 fc for 14 hours daily. Temperature min. 40°F (14°C). Sterilized Garden Soil. Propagation from cuttings. Moderately difficult to easy. 280 species of which about 20 grown for foliage.

Pelargoniums can be divided into categories of: hardy, single-flowered garden plants; showy single- and double-flowered, half-hardy plants; stem succulents with long dormancies; and plants with small single flowers and scented leaves. Only the last are grown essentially for their foliage.

The Scented Geraniums grow 1–3′ (30–90 cm) high on weak, zigzag stems that tend to flop over when tall, yet become somewhat woody with age. At normal house temperatures the variously shaped, usually hairy, leaves are borne throughout the year. Dormancy will intervene only if the temperature is too low or water is withheld. After 2 years at most, as the stems harden and become woody, it is advisable to replace the old with new plants raised from cuttings.

Geraniums thrive in ordinary soil and, having small roots, in small pots. This has an influence on watering. Semisucculent as most of them are, the principal risk is overwatering. The risk is much reduced by using a minimum of soil for the roots. For a change, clay pots are superior to plastic as they dry out more rapidly. Nevertheless, the plants should be thoroughly watered as soon as the soil dries out or the leaves will turn yellow. Incidentally, plants sent through the mail usually arrive with yellow leaves but recover rapidly. If good garden soil is not handy, Houseplant Mix #1 or 2 with sand will do.

To flower they need full sun, but for foliage any exposure except north is satisfactory. Long day length under artificial light insures against dormancy in winter.

Heavy fertilizing only causes them to grow long spaces between joints and weakens their resistance to disease. Treat with a weak solution of a balanced formula no more than once a month in summer and not at all in winter. Insects do not bother them indoors so far as we are aware. Lower leaf drop is common and contributes to the unsightliness of taller plants. Remove dried leaves. Pruning results in branching and makes the bare lower parts of stems less obvious. However, only some of the species and cultivars respond well.

To propagate, take branch tip cuttings with healthy leaves and at least two bare joints. In the summer these often root in plain water. If unsuccessful, try the Texas method (see Propagation p. 000)

P. abrotanifolium. Southernwood Pelargonium. Shrubby. Branches thin and clustered leaves small; cut into narrow segments giving an airy, lacy effect. Similar in appearance and scent to *Artemisia abrotanum,* true Southernwood, an herb.

P. capitatum. Diffuse growth. Leaves almost round; shallowly lobed and crisped. Rose scented.

'Attar of Roses' is assigned to this species but looks more like *P. graveolens;* 5 parted with deeply toothed lobes. Scent intense and pure.

P. citriodorum. Doubtfully a species. Also called "Prince of Orange." Blades with 3 rounded, shallowly toothed lobes. "Prince of Orange Variegated" has a white edge. *P.* × *citrosum* may be only a variation of "Prince of Orange". Orange scented.

P. × *concolor (P. capitatum* × *ignescens).* More deeply lobed than *P. capitatum;* red flowers.

'Concolor lace' and 'Filbert' have leaves more deeply divided.

P. crispum. The most lemon scented. Leaves are generally small in tufts at joints; 3-parted with sharp, shallow teeth and much ruffled. Leaves of the species are about 1" across (2.5 cm) *P. crispum minor* has even smaller leaves. Keep cool in summer.

'Prince Rupert'. Blades larger, to 1½" (3.75 cm).

'Variegated Prince Rupert'. Blades variegated with white. A very popular variety much used for training into wreath forms, etc.

P. crispum hybrids. Two of these are 'French Lace' and 'Lady Mary'. Small differences in form.

P. denticulatum. Peppermint scented. Large plant, to 3' (90 cm) with up to 4" (10 cm) or larger, grayish, velvety leaves divided into 5 major segments, the two lower ones split into two. The segments very narrow and multilobed.

P. denticulatum filicifolium. The Fernleaf Pelargonium. Even more finely cut blades than the above.

P. × *fragrans.* Nutmeg Geranium. Leaves 3-lobed and ruffled, similar to *P. odoratissimum.*

Var. *variegatum.* Variegated with white.

P. fragrans × *odoratissimum* is more compact.

'Logeei Old Spice' has small, grayish green leaves on long stalks. Very delicate aroma and a unique, smooth, velvety texture that is enchanting to see and feel.

P. graveolens. Rose Geranium. Woody shrub to 3' (90 cm). Source of the best rose-scented plants. Leaves 5–7 lobed, finely cut but not as narrowly as *P. denticulatum.*

'Dr Livingstone'. Skeleton Leaf Rose. Lacy leaves like *P. denticulatum.* The spiraled leaves are very

closely set. Perfect for training; remove the cluster of leaf buds at the tip and short branches will grow, topped by tight spirals of stalks to 4" (10 cm) and 2–3" (5–7.5 cm) leaves. Rapidly becomes a standard to 2' (60 cm) with a very symmetrical crown of lacy leaves. Long lasting but rarely blooming indoors. Cuttings root readily in water.

'Lady Plymouth'. Leaf unevenly lobed. Variegated.

'Grey Lady Plymouth'. Leaves regular but with a silvery tint.

P. × *blandfordianum* = *P. echinatum* × *graveolens.* Rose scent.

'Camphor Rose'. Camphor scented.

'Minor'. Leaves smaller.

'Rober's Lemon Rose (*P.graveolens* × *tomentosum*) Lemon rose scent. Leaves irregular in shape.

'Variegatum'. Mildly mint scented.

P. grossularioides. Gooseberry Geranium. Coconut Scented. Often listed as *P. parvilflorum.* Leaves 1 ½" (3.75 cm) in diameter, varying in lobing and segments.

P. × *melissimum. (P. crispum* × *graveolens).* Lemon Scented.

P. × *nervosum.* Lime Geranium. leaves 1" (2.5 cm) long and wide; almost round, not lobed but deeply toothed and hairy.

'Toronto' (*P. torento*), Ginger Geranium, seems to belong here. Lavender flowers.

P. odoratissimum. Apple Geranium. Roundish, small leaf with three, shallowly toothed, almost equal lobes.

P. quercifolium. Oak Leaf Geranium. Aromatic herbal scent. The plant has a trailing habit suitable for basket culture and behaves well indoors, enduring the highest summer heat and blooming prettily with single white, purple-spotted flowers.

The leaves are distinctive, being 2½" (6.25 cm) long, 5-lobed, the segments blunt, short and wide, minutely toothed; rather like some oak leaves.

'Beauty'. Blade with a dark splotch in the center. Flowers lavender.

'Fair Ellen'. Leaves 2" (5 cm) long. Probably the easiest to grow.

'Giant Oak'. 3–4" (7.5–10 cm) leaves. Light pink flowers.

'Pretty Polly'. Deeply lobed. Almond scented. Pink flowers.

'Skelton's Unique'. Lobes shorter. Very trailing stems.

'Village Hill Oak'. Small leaves, deeply lobed, the edges wavy.

P. radens. Similar to *P. denticulatum.* Small leaves, inricately cut. ('Dr. Livingstone' is considered by some to belong here. Leaves are larger.)

P. × *scabrum.* Apricot Geranium. Shrubby plant to 4' (1.20 m) Blades 1" (2.5 cm) long, deeply 3 lobed. Lower surface rough.

P. × *scarboroviae* = 'Countess of Scarborough'. Strawberry Pelargonium. Similar to *P. crispum* but more deeply toothed and not crisped.

P. tomentosum. Peppermint Geranium. Shrubby

plant with 3–4" (7.5–10 cm) blades with 3 irregular lobes, only slightly toothed. Soft hairy above but green, heavily white hairy below.

'Joy Lucille' and 'Joy Lucille Variegated' are possibly hybrids with *P. graveolens*.

P. vitifolium. Grape Leaved Geranium. Very similar to *P. capitatum* but hairier and growth more erect.

Pellionia. **Urticaceae.** East Asia and Western Pacific. Pot or basket trailers. Shade to filtered sun. Min. 100 fc 12 hours daily. Temperature min. 65°F (18.5°C). Humidity 50%. Houseplant mix #1 with lime. Fairly easy. Propagation from cuttings. 50 species of which 2 grown indoors.

P. daveauana. Fleshy, pinkish stems to 2' (60 cm), lined with short-stalked asymmetrical, oval to lanceshaped leaves 2" (5 cm) long, the edges rippled. The center pale green, margins dull purplish. Pink below. Var. *viridis (P. argentea)*. Leaves grayish green. Edges crisped. For a small basket or terrarium.

'Frosted', Jack Frost Vine. Trailer with closely set, puckered leaves. Veins frosty white extending to the crimped edges. Very showy.

'Satin Creeper'. Blades gray and olive with brownish umber markings.

P. pulchra. Watermelon Patch. Habit and leaf shape of *P. daveauana*. Blades green with black veins. Very dusky in appearance.

Good plants for terrariums or dish gardens. Keep on the dry side. When grown on shelf a thorough daily misting is beneficial. The plants are happy in a north window.

Peperomia. **Piperaceae.** Worldwide tropics and subtropics. Mostly trailing herbs; some succulents. Shade to filtered sun. 100–600 fc. Temperature mostly min. 55°F (13°C). Humidity 30–60%. Houseplant Mix #1, 2 or 3 with lime. Propagate from stem cuttings and by division. Easy to difficult. 1,000 species or more; 30–50 grown indoors; many more offered in catalogs.

New Peperomias are continuously being discovered and imported by travellers and botanical explorers. But, except for a few dozen well-researched species, the genus is a prime example of utter taxonomic confusion; a great many plants are listed in catalogs according to collection numbers or under arbitrarily applied names. Obviously this is an extremely variable genus, both in the wild and in cultivation, with small changes occurring frequently.

This is a further demonstration of our contention that, in very complex, variable genera with wide natural distribution and also many years of cultivation, the parameters of species and cultivars become confused. As usual, we treat variations as cultivars, because the odd plant with little or no chance of survival in nature, hardly merits the status of a natural variety; e.g., a Latin form or variety name tacked onto that of the true species.

Most Peperomias adapt well to indoor conditions and are undemanding. The variegated cultivars are colorful. More than any other of the smaller tropical foliage plants, they hold their leaves for a long time.

They propagate with ease. They have a large and devoted following among serious amateurs. How then can we account for the fact that no species has achieved great popularity with commercial growers or the public?

We are of the opinion that this is because they are rather small plants on the whole; the green-leaved species and cultivars have simple, rather unexciting foliage, and the variegated ones include many look-alikes. Plants of the *P. caperata* type are better greenhouse than indoor plants. Of the others only 2 species *P. obtusifolia* and *P. scandens* are suitable for large baskets, and neither is commercially produced in great numbers. The rest are smaller pot plants. It is true that they seem to be more popular in the South than the North, in the country than the big cities. We have tried to identify faults in the plants themselves but have not succeeded in discovering any that are provable.

A few cultural needs are shared by all but the succulent species.

1. They have relatively shallow roots. Use azalea-type pots and baskets.

... They like tight potting. Allow them to become quite pot-bound before moving to the next larger size.

3. The light requirement is from shade to filtered sun. In greenhouses thay are frequently grown under the benches. Indoors they are satisfied with a northern exposure. Variegated plants require somewhat more light.

4. They object to being soaking wet. To keep the soil just moist and well aerated use lightly packed fibrous or somewhat sandy soil. Underpotting contributes to a healthy condition. Allow to dry out well between waterings.

A more difficult matter for some is humidity which should be 50–65% for most species except the succulents. The *P. caperata* group is the most demanding. But for the rest, even our minimum is not an absolute necessity.

They suffer from very high temperatures if protracted. A 10°F (5°C) drop at night is very beneficial.

Insects are a rare problem. Diseases are contracted through overwatering and at excessively high and low temperatures.

Propagaton by means of leaves (of the thicker-leaved species), cuttings and division is successful in moist sphagnum moss, vermiculite or sand. A number grow roots in water.

Limitation of space allows us to describe only some of the more popular commercial plants, some collectors' favorites and a few succulents. The number of questionable species bearing provisional names is considerable. We divide the list into convenient categories.

Plants with Short, Watery Stems and Few Branches

P. argyreia. (sandersii). Watermelon Begonia. S. America. Usually less than 10" (25 cm) high, the crowded stalks alternate, erect, 6–8" (15–20 cm) long. Blades smooth, waxy, lanceshaped, cupped, the base rounded, 5 × 4" (12.5 × 10 cm), facing outward. The stalks attached to the lower third (peltate). Color green, decorated with broad gray stripes radiating from the attachment of the stalk.

P. arifolia. Little different from *P. argyreia* except that the blades are green and the base notched.

'Litoralis'. Blades wider and more waxy with broad, curving silver stripes. This may be a variation of *P. verschaffeltii*.

P. caperata. Emerald Ripple. Very compact, to 6" ((15 cm) high. The outfacing blades heartshaped, the clefts narrow and lobes overlapping. Corrugated and puckered between the veins.

'Argentea', "Silver Ripple." Surface silver-gray.

'Little Fantasy'. "Mini-Ripple." Green colored dwarf.

'Maculata'. Leaf surface decorated with cream spots.

'Tricolor'. "Cream Ripple." A central green core is surrounded by a broad, white margin.

P. gardneriana (?) Leaves lanceshaped with rounded base, the stalks attached to the lower third. Edges shallowly toothed. Veins depressed, quilted. To 8" (20 cm) high.

P. griseo-argentea (or *griseoargentea*) (*P. hederifolia*). Ivy Leaf Peperomia. 6–8" (15–20 cm) high, tufted. Blades heartshaped to 3" (7.5 cm) and almost as wide. Puckered between the darker, sunken veins. Pewter colored throughout. Stalks to 4" (10 cm) reddish.

'Blackie'. A popular cultivar with smooth, metallic, black leaves. Popular with amateurs.

'Nigra'. Dark, silverish, corrugated.

'Nana'. "Peruviana." Forms tight little mounds of foliage. Leaves 1" (2.5 cm) or less.

P. marmorata. Silver Heart. Blades similar to *P. caperata* but more pointed and to 5" (12.5 cm) long. Green with gray stripes between veins. Red veined below.

P. meridana. Like *P. gardneriana* but branched and leaves smaller, to 2" (5 cm), more puckered.

P. ornata. S. Venezuela. Stems very short and leaves in a compact spiral. Stalks to 5" (12.5 cm) high, erect, reddish. Blades nearly elliptic, smooth, to 5 × 2" (12.5 × 5 cm). Veins dark green against light green. Some clones have red midribs on the blades.

P. verschafeltii. Sweetheart Peperomia. Tufted to 6" (15 cm) high and very short stemmed. Blades heartshaped, 4 × 1½" (10 × 3.75 cm) but proportion of width to length varies. Blue-green with silvery stripes between the depressed veins. Hardly distinguishable from *P. arifolia* 'Litoralis'.

The above set of plants is easily recognizable by the compact, branched habit which suits all for growing, as the roots are shallow, in 4–6" (10–15 cm) azalea-type pots. They make a most compact and symmetrical display of interesting leaf shapes and stripings. In the spring narrow spikes of tiny white flowers are attractive.

Formerly a frequent sight in florist shops, they are less so now. The public has become more intolerant of plants requiring such high humidity and cool temperatures in summer. Without this care they are short-lived. There are, however, many amateur indoor gardeners who favor them and grow them successfully.

Thick-leaved Semi-upright Species

All the stems become prostrate as the stems elongate. In general they demand less humidity, 40% being sufficient. They also need somewhat lower light than the previous group. They also need tight potting and drying out between waterings. On the whole they are much easier to grow than the previous category.

P. bicolor (*velutina*?). Inca Princess. Stems at first erect, to 10" (25 cm), offsetting. The blades, on short stalks, oval, cupped, somewhat felted, 2 × 1" (5 × 2.5 cm) or wider. Metallic dark green, the broad midrib, veins and edge lighter green and lightly feathered. Red beneath.

P. clusiifolia. False Clusia. Red Edge Pepromia. To 1' (30 cm) high, the leaves spiraled, thick, spoonshaped to 4" (10 cm) long, the narrowed bases clasping the stems. Purplish green with reddish edges.

'Variegata'. Broad, irregular yellowish margin.

P. glabella (?) Wax Privet Peperomia. 6" (15 cm) high, offsetting. Leaves alternate, thick, broadly elliptic, 1¾" (4.36 cm) on short stalks. An easy, tough species.

'Variegata'. With cream variegation.

P. incana. Felted Peperomia. A semisucculent to 15" (37.5 cm) with thick stems. The whole plant is heavily white felted. Blades broadly heartshaped to 3" (7.5 cm) long on 1½" (3.75 cm) stalks. One of the most vigorous of Peperomias but usually available only from specialist nurseries.

P. magnoliifolia. To 10" (25 cm). Leaves alternate. Blades short stalked, spoonshaped to 4" (10 cm) long. Purple edged. Stalks brown. Similar to *P. obtusifolia* but veins more numerous and distinct.

P. obtusifolia. By far the most popular plant in this group. Plants are variable and there are numerous cultivars. Stalks thick and short. Blades oval to 5" long, quite thick and waxy. One of the easiest to grow in the genus and though listed as growing 6" (15 cm) high, stems and branches are often much longer. This is a prime example of our treating the varieties as cultivars, which they certainly are, even when discovered in the wild with variegation.

'Alba'. Blade ivory gradually fading to green.

'Albomarginata'. "Hummel White Cloud." The surface puckered and variegated with white.

'Clusiifolia'. Blades purple with reddish tips and shaped like *P. clusiifolia*. Probably a cultivar of that species.

'Gold Tip'. "Marble Peperomia". Edges streaked with ivory, yellow and chartreuse. The base green.

'Golden Gate'. Most spectacular of the cultivars. Blade abnormally wide, the center slate green, enclosed in an irregular zone of cream; the edges deep green. Note: These light-colored variegated plants require somewhat more light than the green-leaved forms.

'Green and Gold'. Edge rich yellow.

'Minima'. Dwarf plant with green leaves.

'Minima Variegata'. Slate green with ivory edge.

'Variegata'. Blades slate green, the margins ivory.

P. orba. "Princess Astrid." Dwarf, clumping plant with 1" (2.5 cm) green leaves. Spreads rapidly and is very vigorous.

'Variegata'. Blades flat, edged in deep cream.

P. pereskiifolia. Stems weak, reddish, to 10" (25 cm). Leaves in separated tight spirals. Blades to 2½" (6.25 cm), oval to spoonshaped.

P. rubella. Red Ivy Peperomia. A compact little plant to 6" (15 cm) with many hairy, branching stems bearing thick, elliptical leaves ½" (1.25 cm) long, in groups of three to five at a joint. Green above, red beneath; the stalks very short. Very similar to *P. verticillata*.

P. velutina. Stems zigzagging to 12" (30 cm). Blades broadly elliptic to 3" (7.5 cm) long; dark green, the midrib and veins silvery; dusty pink below with green veins.

P. verticillata (pulchella). Vigorous, somewhat hairy plant to 1' (30 cm). Leaves in sets of 4 at the joints; thickish, concave, 1" (2.5 cm) long. Neat. Nearly succulent. Offsetting.

Trailers

The manner of growth is horizontal to pendant. Some of the stems are juicy-succulent like the previous group, but others are wiry-stiff, the joints usually further apart. Branches grow longer, up to 15" (37.5 cm). Young plants do well in a pot while older plants are excellent for baskets.

P. cubensis. Creeping plant with alternate leaves broadly lanceshaped to 3 × 2" (7.5 × 5 cm). Stalks 2" (5 cm).

'Variegata'. The blades irregularly margained in cream.

P. dahlstedtii (fosteri). Stems tough, erect, then horizontal. Leaves tightly spiraled with very short stalks; leathery, elliptical, to 2" (5 cm) long with 3 depressed veins. Adapts to low humidity and moisture.

P. puteolata. Parallel Peperomia. Stiff, branching, wiry, horizontal stems, the joints widely separated. Leaves in 2s and 3s, narrowly lanceshaped, 4 × 1" (10 × 2.5 cm), velvety with 5, thin, distinct, lighter parallel veins. A very charming, easy species.

P. quadrangularis. Trailing, 4-angled, stiff stems; the leaves in opposite pairs, leathery, almost round, 1¼" (3.12 cm) long and nearly as wide. Veins parallel, yellow.

P. rotundifolia (nummulariifolia, prostrata). Creeping Buttons. The names suggest the plant. A creeper with delicate zigzag stems and alternate, round, slightly domed leaves. Joints root where they touch the soil.

'Pilosior'. Stems reddish. The surface of the blade appearing blistered, green decorated with branching silvery veins.

Lovely plant for a hanging pot or terrarium.

P. scandens (serpens). False Philodendron. According to some *P. scandens* is hairier and larger leaved than *P. serpens*. This is a typical example of problems with the naming of species. The two may well be separate, but the differences between them are of a kind very frequently listed, if noticed at all, as simple variation.

Vigorous, branching stems, the leaves thick, waxy, alternate; heartshaped to nearly round, up to 2½" (6.25 cm) in length.

'Variegata' has a broad cream edge.

The most commonly seen as a basket plant in the shops.

P. urocarpa. String of Coins. Much-branched creeper with the leaf blades broadly heartshaped, the cleft being curved and wide, 1½" (3.75 cm) long and wide. Quilted between the veins; finely hairy above and below. *P. trinervis* is similar but blades narrower and without a cleft.

Succulent Species

They require Cactus & Succulent Mix #1 or 2 and very careful watering with exposure to full sunlight. They can be grown under 800 fc fluorescent light for 15 hours daily. Water when bottom leaves show slight signs of shriveling. Imported plants will be active in winter, dormant in summer. U.S. propagated plants may follow our seasons.

P. columnella (columnaris). Peru. A most extraordinary plant, the stem erect, branching and the leaves solid, hoofshaped to ⅜" (9.37 mm) across, so closely attached and spiraled that they form a column. Powdery gray-green. Requires cool temperatures, excellent ventilation and bright light.

P. dolabriformis. Peru. Branching plant to 12" (30 cm) or more, the stalkless leaves sickleshaped, held vertically as the result of a folding and fusing of the 2 halves of the blade, leaving a translucent slit or window at the top. This is similar to the windows in South African succulents. To 1½" (3.75 cm) long, thick. A most curious plant but easy. Cuttings root in moist sandy mix. Filtered sun and 400 fc fluorescent light. Dry between waterings.

P. nivalis. Peru. Matforming plant with stems to 4" (10 cm). Leaves thickly covering stems, narrow, thick, boatshaped, ⅜" (9.37 mm) long.

Pereskia. Cactaceae. Tropical America. Shrubs and Vines. Partial sun. 500–800 fc. Temperature min. 50°F (10°C). Houseplant Mix #2 with sand. Propagation from cuttings. Easy. 20 species of which 1 grown indoors.

P. aculeata. Lemon Vine. A rampant vine to 30' (9 m). stems short spiny. Leaves elliptical, shiny green to 3" (7.5 cm) long. The species is grown for its fruit and yellow flowers.

'Godseffiana'. A beautiful pot and basket plant that is more shrubby, producing thick stems and many branchings. It is amenable to pruning and, therefore, can be grown as a pot or basket plant. The young clustered leaves at the tips of branches are vibrant pink in the spring, change to brilliant apricot and slowly become green. The display is spectacular. Active growth may cease from November to January, but leaves are retained. Charming as a rooted cutting in a small pot.

Keep evenly moist and fertilize with a balanced formula once a month from spring to late fall. Cuttings root rapidly in houseplant mix when planted in the spring. A very satisfactory and rather neglected houseplant.

Peristrophe. Acanthaceae. Old World tropics. Fleshy herbs. Partial sun. 500 fc. Temperature min. 65°F (18.5°C). Houseplant Mix #2 preferably with some sand. Propagation by cuttings and division. Easy. 15 species of which 1 grown indoors.

P. hyssopifolia (angustifolia). To 18" (45 cm) high, the angled, thin stems rising from the base. Leaves lanceshaped, narrow, to 3" (7.5 cm) long, alternate at the joints which are 1" (2.5 cm) apart; very thin textured. Violet, fragile flowers.

'Aureo-variegata', with leaves centered with yellow, is the usual plant grown. Fast growing with a diffuse habit. Lower leaves short-lived. Replace at least yearly. Branches root at the joints in water.

Persea. Lauraceae. Taiwan, Korea, Japan, Central America. Small to large trees. Partial to full sun. Temperature min. 65°F (18.5°C). Humidity min. 50%. Partial to full sun. Packaged Houseplant Medium. Propagation by seed. 150 species; 1 grown indoors.

P. americana. Avocado. This is a unique example of a plant widely grown by indoor gardeners yet not supplied by nurserymen for the ornamental trade. As a commercial plant it is unsatisfactory because of its rapid but very diffuse growth habit. Amateurs, however, discovered that the very large seeds from fruit bought in the market, sprout with ease and grow very well near a sunny window, attaining a height of 10' (3 m) and a spread of 5–6' (1.5–1.8 m).

The leaves are lanceshaped, thin, up to 8" (20 cm) long. The plants are grown from the seeds of ripe fruit. Suspend in a glass in contact with water or plant in moist soil with the upper, broader end exposed. Unless the lighting is very bright the first shoot will be a foot long or more. As soon as there are four real leaves the upper two should be removed in order to induce branching, and the branches must also be trimmed early on or the tree will become either too tall with long spaces between joints or impossibly broad. However, if this treatment is applied religiously an Avocado plant can be a large and attractive decoration for a few years.

As the tree grows, its large roots must be transferred to ever larger pots and, eventually, to a tub. Maintain even moisture and feed with a balanced fertilizer with every watering.

A number of species are listed from Taiwan. These are not fruitbearing but are sufficiently warm growing, with thicker textured leaves, to warrant consideration for commercial development as indoor landscape plants.

Philodendron. Araceae. Tropical America. Vines mostly rooted in trees. Filtered to partial sun. Temperature min. 60°F (16°C). Min. 50% humidity. Packaged Houseplant Medium or long-fiber sphagnum moss. Propagation from cuttings. Easy to difficult. 200 species, almost half have been cultivated indoors.

Most of the important tropical foliage vines are aroids. They include *Monstera, Epipremnum (Pothos), Scindapsus, Syngonium* and *Philodendron.* The last is by far the largest genus. Its history in the United States tells us something regarding the problems with such plants.

In the 1930s the little Heartleaf *Philodendron,* called at the time *P. cordatum* and now designated as *P. scandens* subspecies *oxycardium,* becme enormously popular. This tough little vine, grown as a trailer in small pots, was the first to invade offices. There was hardly a desk or windowsill without one. It was equally common in homes. Virtually indestructible, it fostered the impression that all Philodendrons shared the same toleration of abuse, poor light and insufficient nourishment. As the whole genus is very easy to propagate nurserymen judged it a good bet for the houseplant market. And so it proved. The much larger-leaved and more spectacular *P. domesticum,* called *hastatum* in the trade, and *P. panduraeform,* the Fiddle-leaved Philodendron, led the way. Grown in pots and attached to cedar slabs or tree fern stakes, they were sold everywhere as large foliage decorations for the house and office. It was a common sight to see them wrapped in gaudy red ribbon lined up in the windows of new restaurants and stores, the gifts of well-wishers.

Their vogue lasted a surprising length of time, primarily because they needed little light, then declined as rapidly as it had begun. They had been showy novelties with little competition but as soon as other foliage plants entered the market they faded away.

The fact is that all large vines are difficult to handle indoors, and Philodendrons share with other aroid vines a serious handicap. The showy leaves that make them desirable are preceded by juvenile leaves that are usually little different from those of the Heartleaf Philodendron. They change to large blades with complicated shapes only when they climb attached to a surface. Nurseries rooted lengths of vine with mature leaves and attached them to supports. But, once indoors, the vines had nowhere to go. New growths, extending upward and outward, produced juvenile leaves. It did no good to cut off these additional growths because the aging lower leaves died away. Low humidity in homes and offices contributed to the deterioration of the plants. What the environment began a variety of houseplant pests finished.

Nurserymen switched their efforts from the faster-growing vines to self-heading plants. Self-heading is nothing but jargon for a vine that is slow growing, has leaves arranged in a very tight spiral and a stem or trunk that is short and slow growing. It was hoped that these would make better pot plants.

There are two principal types. One distinguished by abnormally thick and broad clasping stalks and thick, horizontally held leaves, remains below 3' (90 cm) in height and with a spread of no more than 2' (60 cm) for a very long time. The other has a thick trunk marked by large leaf scars, long-spreading stalks and big, outfacing leaves. These can reach a height of 15'

(4.5 m) but can be treated so that the trunks remain under 1' (30 cm).

One after the other both types have been tried on the market, mostly with limited commercial success. But a few of the large-leaved, self-heading Philodendrons have proved very adaptable to indoor conditions and more will be discovered with time. The *Philodendron* story is by no means over.

Many Philodendrons are undemanding and our heading sufficiently indicates the needs of the more adaptable indoor species. However, there are numerous others from rain or cloud forests that require very high humidity, 65% being a minimum. These are quite impractical indoors. We have, nevertheless, listed a few to indicate the difference. Some of them are gorgeous and very tempting.

The growth rate and size of leaves of the larger plants can be controlled through a combination of tight potting, very little fertilizer and more intense light. Keeping the soil rather dry also helps to reduce size.

The vines all develop incipient tendrils at the joints. Wherever they exist, the section can be propagated by cutting off along with a leaf. If the blade is very large, slice it to a half or a quarter of the original size. Simply set the cutting in water and the tendrils will become roots. Some of the species develop long runners without joints by means of which plants growing in trees anchor themselves in the ground below. It is amusing to observe these tubular, rubbery growths that, even from a potted plant, may extend for yards. However, they serve no purpose indoors so cut them off at the base.

As we have already indicated, the vines cannot be effectively pruned for long. Self-heading types with thick stems may be shortened by means of air layering.

Eradicate the standard houseplant insects with pesticide sparays or systemics. Very little damage is done unless treatment is neglected.

In the following lists by categories there is the usual confusion where variable genera are concerned. Here, in addition, there is a new wrinkle. With their usual inconsistency horticulturists list a number of cultivars as if they were species, for instance, *P.* 'Burgundy', which is absurd. They are almost certainly cultivars by rights, but as we are unable to relate them to particular species, we are obliged to use their terminology.

Our categories are more than usually arbitrary but may be of some assistance in selecting plants to meet decorative needs.

Thick-stemmed, Tree Type, Selfheading

These plants have been categorized as "tree type" because, as they mature, the stem thickens into a more or less self-supporting trunk bearing a cluster of very large leaves at the tip. As young plants they are slow growing, attaining a spread of 8' (2.40 m) or more in a tub. They are magnificent decoration where there is room and the right setting for such big plants.

Though they have considerable low-light toler-ance, maintenance in good condition requires high humidity. In normal commercial-display situations they deteriorate and require restoration treatment in a greenhouse at 6-month intervals.

P. bipinnatifidum. Leaf blades max. 3' (90 cm); stalks the same. Blade outline more or less arrowshaped, to 15" (45 cm) wide, deeply cut into long segments; basal lobes narrowly segemented. Slow growing and now frequently seen in the shops.

'Seaside'. Segments lobed.

P. eichleri. Blades lanceshaped to 3' (90 cm). Edges with deep, broad, spaced, rounded lobes.

P. lundii. Rather like *P. bipinnatifidum;* somewhat shorter-broader and with broader segments.

P. mello-barretoanum. Grows very tall in nature. The stem thick. Almost circular in outline, the blade's three lobes are more nearly equal as are the lobed segments.

P. selloum. Still the most popular and satisfactory self-heading species. Similar to *P. bipinnatifidum* but segments usually broader and more distinctly lobed. Cultivars include dwarf forms and numerous hybrids. It is very sturdy, needs little humidity and is tolerant of underwatering. A plant we have grown for 15 years in a 10" (25 cm) pot is as vigorous as ever. The stem is only 8" (20 cm) high. It is badly pot-bound but has remained manageable. Filtered sun is quite sufficient.

P. tweedianum. Blades long-heartshaped, 18 × 10" (45 × 25 cm) with large, overlapping basal lobes and ruffled edges. Stalks erect.

P. undulatum. Similar to the above but basal lobes more widely spread, 22 × 15" (55 × 37.5 cm). The leaves of mature plants are larger.

P. williamsii. Striking plant, the blades 30 × 8" (75 × 20 cm), facing outward. Basal lobes to 6" (15 cm) or more. Margins very undulating.

Self-heading Shorter Plants

See introductory remarks for the previous group. The stems are less thick and require support but leaves are closely spiraled and growth is slow.

P. fragrantissimum. Considered self-heading but somewhat climbing when young. Mature leaves broad-heartshaped with many parallel, depressed veins spreading from the midrib that provide a fine, symmetrical corrugation. 10" (25 cm) long and almost as broad. A superb textured leaf. High humidity required.

P. 'Lynette' (*P. wendlandii* × *elaphoglossum*). Quilted Birdsnest. A definite rosette with 4" (10 cm) stalks and 12–18" (30–45 cm) long, elliptical blades with a squared base, corrugated by numerous, horizontal, parallel, depressed veins. A very different and hand-some plant but relatively rare.

P. melinonii. Red Bird'snest Philodendron. At maturity leaves reach 3' × 16" (90 × 40 cm). Best grown as a juvenile when a dense rosette is formed with blades 12–16" (30–50 cm) long and lanceshaped. Veins light. Purple beneath. Prefers high humidity.

P. pinnatifidum. Blades to 2' (60 cm) long, arrowshaped, the deep cut segments straight edged, not wavy.

P. wendlandii. Grows like *P.* 'Lynette' but leaves not corrugated; 30" (75 cm) long. An adaptable plant.

Small-leaved Vines

Leaves less than 10" (25 cm) long. The blades of many other species are similar when young. These are all vines that need support or are kept small and are allowed to trail from pots. They range from nearly Cast Iron to demanding of humidity so high that it is virtually unattainable indoors. We list a few of the latter for comparison.

'Burle Marx' 'Fantasy'. Distinctive but without a species name. The 3–4" (7.5–10 cm) long, lanceshaped blades are metallic-bluish green with a fine network of purple veins. It requires constant humidity of min. 65%. Not a houseplant.

P. frits-wentii. Shiny, heartshaped blades with broad, round basal lobes, on long stalks.

P. grazielae. Pigtail Philodendron. 3–4" (7.5–10 cm) heartshaped leaves, concave, with a long, curled tip.

P. longistilum. Narrow, spoonshaped blades to 7" (17.5 cm). Stalks very short. Makes a good juvenile pot plant but grows rapidly, with long spaces between joints.

P. melanochrysum (andreanum). Only young plants grown indoors. Leaves then are heartshaped, 3–4" (7.5–10 cm) long, velvety with a golden sheen. Some varieties almost black. A beauty, but it requires very high humidity and warmth.

P. microstictum (pittieri). Satin Sheen Plant. Like *P. melanochrysum* but blades have a reddish bronze sheen.

P. ornatum (soderoi). Blades to 2' (60 cm) long at maturity but when young are heartshaped and only 2–3" ((5–7.5 cm) long, the veins depressed, the surface splotched with silver. A very attractive vine but requiring warmth and high humidity.

P. scandens (P. oxycardium). Mature leaves are 1' (30 cm) long but young ones have 3–4" (7.5–10 cm) heartshaped leaves, narrower than *P. microstictum.* Cast-Iron culture. Nevertheless, these former favorites are out of style and less frequently seen. Useful in special situations, such as balconies, from which they can trail as a continuous green curtain. *Forma micans* is purple beneath. There are also variegated and chartreuse cultivars requiring higher humidity.

Broad, Heartshaped Leaves.

Grow large rooted cuttings from the nursery, with 3–6 leaves. These are as handsome as the great Alocasias and Anthuriums and grow slowly enough to make a spectacular show for a long time. Then take cuttings that root easily. Mist frequently.

P. gloriosum. Blades 15 × 12" (37.5 × 30 cm), edges turned downward, velvety green and principal veins nearly white. High humidity.

P. mamei. Shaped like the above though somewhat narrower. Surface blotched with lighter green.

P. verrucosum. Blades 24 × 15" (60 × 36.5 cm). Edges turned down and undulating. Rich metallic green sheen; principal and some side veins pale. Reddish beneath between veins. Stalk to 20" (50 cm), reddish. High humidity.

There are many other large, broader, heartshape leaved species that differ from each other only in minor details.

Long, Heartshaped Leaves.

Leaves narrower than those of the previous group and usually with straighter sides. Thus the shape is long-triangular except for the cleft at the base. Basal lobes are usually rounded.

P. 'Burgundy'. Leaves 1' (30 cm) long, rather straight sided, the lobes short and rounded. Surface shiny, deep green with a reddish tone; stalks red. Compact and slow growing. Less popular than one might expect, probably because the color is very dark.

P. cordatum. Blades 18 × 10" (45 × 25 cm). Basal lobes long and rounded. Stalks to 2' (60 cm). Joints widely spaced.

P. cruentum. Redleaf Philodendron. Blades 18×10" (45×25 cm). Edges very little angled so that the form is lanceshaped except for a narrow notch and short, rounded basal lobes. Brilliant red beneath. Stalks 12" (30 cm), winged for most of their length.

P. domesticum (hastatum). Blades 2' × 1' (60 × 30 cm); long heartshaped to triangular, edges undulating, basal lobes rounded. Stalks as long and with a central ridge. Cleft 4" (10 cm) deep. The species most frequently used for training on cedar slabs.

P. erubescens. Blades 12 × 7" (30 × 17.5 cm), the basal lobes very short. Coppery reddish beneath. Stalks reddish near base. Joints widely spaced.

'Golden Erubescens'. Blades golden yellow.

P. imbe. Blades 13 × 5" (32.5 × 12.5 cm). Cleft narrow. Stalks as long as the blades. Principal side veins distinct.

× 'Mandaianum'. A very early cross. (*P. domesticum* × *erubescens*). Blades reddish toned; stalks deep red.

P. 'New Yorker'. Compact, on erect stalks, the blades 12" (30 cm) long; lobes rounded, spreading; glossy, reddish toned reverting to green. Stalks red spotted.

P. sagittifolium. 2' × 1" (60 × 25 cm). Rather straight sided, the cleft deep and narrow and the lobes long-oblong. Weak stemmed.

P. variifolium. Blades heartshaped, the edges turned down, 11 × 5" (27.5 × 12.5 cm), light green between the principal veins.

Again, there are numerous other species and cultivars of the type.

Large Cutleaved Vines.

There is litle difference between these vines and the cut-leaved self-heading plants except that they are of litle use to the indoor gardener because of their rapid early growth. Future hybridization may overcome this handicap.

P. angustisectum (P. elegans). Blades 2' × 18" (60×45 cm), broadly triangular in outline with long, narrow segments on either side of the midrib. Tip lobe triangular, with 3 low, round lobes. Basal lobes each with 3 narrow segments.

P. distantilobum. Rampant vine requiring tropical conditions, the leaves with very long stalks; the segments long-elliptical; virtual leaflets as they are cut to the midrib but without stalks.

P. lacerum. A West Indian species with yard-long (90 cm) blades, almost as broad and with stalks the same length. Broad, lanceshaped in outline. Segments deep, narrow, somewhat spoonshaped. Basal lobes overlapping with shorter, more elliptical segments.

P. pinnatilobum. Fernleaf Philodendron. From the Amazon and requiring maximum humidity. Blades 2′ × 18″ (60 × 45 cm), rather like *P. distantilobum* but less coarse and more compact. The deep segments, narrowly elliptical. Stalks purple-spotted.

'Fernleaf'. Segments narrower, straightshaped-pointed.

Rooted cuttings of mature leaves make a fine show. The plant has recently gained in popularity. Indoors grow in sphagnum moss. Very tempermental.

P. radiatum (dubia). Similar to *P. angustisectum*, even to the tip and basal lobe forms, but 3′ (90 cm) long and nearly as broad. It is difficult to think of such plants as being really different species.

Leaves with 5 Segments or Lobes.

Leaves different in shapes from other aroids and very decorative. The vines are mostly rampant and suitable only for large trellis culture or temporary attachment to cedar slabs. With a greater popularity potential if growth can be retarded and the distance between joints reduced.

P. bipennifolium (P. panduriforme). Fiddleleaf Philodendron. Frequently grown on cedar slabs. Blades 18 × 8″ (45 × 20 cm) with edges turned downward. Tip lobe half the length of the blade or more, lance to spoonshaped; the middle lobes squarish with the tips curved upward; basal lobes shorter, squarish, with tips turned downward; cleft 1″ (2.5 cm) wide. Surface shiny, dark green. Stalks shorter than the blades. Joints widely separated.

P. pedatum (lacinatum?) Blades 30 × 12″ (75 × 30 cm) and even larger when fully mature. Divisions much more deeply cut than the above, therefore segmented. Upper segment elliptical; middle segements each divided into 2 scimitar-shaped lobes with tips curving upward; lower segments divided into 2 or 3 lobes pointing downward.

P. squamiferum. Blades to 24″ (60 cm) long, divided into 5 major segments. Upper segment broadly elliptical with a small tip; middle lobes scimitar shaped, tips curved upward; bottom lobes short, oval. Stalks to 30″ (75 cm) with red bristles.

The following cultivars are probably hybrids between *P. laciniatum* and *P. squamiferum*. The segments are more separated, the plants somewhat more compact or slow growing.

'Florida Beauty'. Frequently sold as *P. squamiferum*. The segments blunter. Stalks warty. Relatively easy. Filtered light.

'Florida Beauty Alba'. New leaves chartreuse with ivory veins. Ages to deep green.

'Florida Beauty Albo-variegatum'. Blades streaked with white.

'Florida Beauty Variegata'. Leaves deeply segmented and broadly streaked with yellow and deep cream.

'Florida Beauty-White Squamiferum'. New leaves gray-green with white feathering, they age to green. Compact.

Leaves with Channeled Stalks.

Clambering vines mostly with very prominent, channeled stalks and stiff, lanceshaped blades. Low-spreading pot plants when young. Very distinctive. Remove the center leaves of the rosette to prolong compact, leafy growth.

P. martianum (cannifolium). Tightly spiraled rosette. Leaves thick, stiff, glossy, lanceshaped, to 18 × 6″ (45 × 15 cm), midrib broad. Stalks 12″ (30 cm), deeply channeled in a V, fleshy, whitish.

P. ventricosum. Blades shorter, elliptical. Stalks even longer and more prominent than the above, thicker, the channel shallower.

P. warmingii. Blades like *P. martianum* but more triangular, the edges straighter.

'Weber's Selfheading'. Blades somewhat broader than the above and the tip narrower and longer.

All the above look like insignificant variations of the same plant.

Blades Spoonshaped.

Rosette plants when young with simple, long, distinctive, spoonshaped blades.

P. linnaei is virtually stalkless while *P. longistilum* has short, stiff stalks.

Blades Trident.

P. deflexum, fenzlii, trifoliatum, tripartitum and *trisectum* have blades divided into 3 segments, each 10″ (25 cm) or longer and elliptical-pointed. They are rampant, rapidly growing vines with thin stems and widely spaced joints; of little or no use indoors.

Phyllanthus. **Euphorbiaceae.** West Indies and Tropiical Asia. Shrubs and small trees. Filtered to partial sun. Min. 500 fc. Temperature min. 50°F (10°C). Packaged Houseplant Medium with lime or Houseplant Mix #2 with sand and lime. Propagated by cuttings, but difficult. Easy. 650 species of which only one currently grown indoors.

The genus not only has plants with normal leaves but a large number whose apparent leaves are really flattened branches or cladophylls, technically like those of the Asparagus Ferns but much more leaflike. They are long and narrow, with herringbone patterned veins each terminating in a notch, representing a joint. From these hang tiny pink flowers so that one has the impression of flowering leaves. Culture is simple; the only points to note are that most are lime loving (6–8 pH) and possess an inordinate thirst. As they must be kept constantly moist, at least in pot, watering is a daily chore. Fertilize with high-middle- and last-number (phosphate and potash) formulas.

P. acidus. A small tree with compound leaves widely grown in the tropics for its edible fruits. These are yellow, melon shaped and about 1″ (2.5 cm) in diameter. They grow in massive clusters on bare areas of trunks and branches. As a pot plant this night well be worthwhile growing indoors.

P. angustifolius. Foliage Flower. West Indies. A large shrub that makes a fine pot plant. The stem is round. The cladophylls are compound, about 4" (10 cm) long except the one at the tip which may reach 10" (25 cm). The little pink flowers appear on new growth at various times of year. The trunk is straight and the arrangement of branches very symmetrical.

P. arbuscula. Foliage Flower. Cladophylls shorter than the above. The tip cladophyll much shorter.

P. epiphyllanthus. Single stemmed, the cladophylls spiraled, to 5" (12.5 cm) long.

P. niruri. Stem opposite branched. The paired oblong leaves numerous, oblong, less than ½" (1.25 cm) long.

P. speciosus. A larger, branching plant with compound leaves, to 4" (10 cm), narrowly lanceshaped. Rare.

All these and others deserve the attention of indoor gardeners as decorative novelties. However, propagation is a difficulty that must be overcome.

Phyllostachys. Graminiae. Bamboo. China. Tall, woody grasses. For culture see *Bambusa.*

P. bambusoides. Japan. Spreading by underground runners. Stems to 70' × 6" (21 m × 15 cm). Blades to 7 × 1½" (17.5 × 3.75 cm). Probably hardy even indoors. There are a number of varieties and cultivars, all of them tall. They can be grown as juveniles in large pots or up to 50' (15 m) in atria.

Pilea. Urticaceae. Worldwide subtropics and tropics. Shrubby or creeping herbs. Shade to partial sun. Min. 500 fc. Temperature min. 60°F (16°C). Humidity min. 50%. Houseplant Mix #2 with sand or long-fiber sphagnum moss. Propagation by stem cuttings and division. Easy to difficult. 200 species of which about 20 grown indoors.

Some authorities claim that there are as many as 2,000 species. These are mostly fleshy, low-growing herbs, moisture and shade loving, in rather acid soil. Others are shrubs in partial or full sun, living on alkaline soils. Cuttings root readily in vermiculite under transparent cover. The flowers are insignificant, in flat-topped clusters.

P. bertertonia (mollis). Said to be from the W. Pacific. Erect, branching plant to 8" (20 cm) or more indoors. The leaves are opposite-alternate on closely set joints. Blades broadly lanceshaped, 2½ × 1½" (6.75 × 3.74 cm) with midrib and 2 prominent veins; the surface covered with heavy puckers like the Iron Cross Begonia (*B. masoniana*). Medium green. Stalks short.

'Moon Valley'. To 10" (25 cm) or more. Blades 4" (10 cm) long, zoned in yellow-green through tan. Bright and very striking. It was popular a few years ago.

Both plants require filtered sun and watering when dry. Humidity min. 50% with excellent ventilation. Some sand should be included in the mix.

Subject to mites. Succumbs to fungus diseases when temperatures are excessively high or low.

P. cadierei. Aluminum Plant. A standard, easy foliage houseplant. Leaves oval-pointed to 3" (7.5 cm) long, convex, with veins depressed, the quiltings prominently marked with bright silver. A fast-growing, offsetting plant to 18" (45 cm). Stems numerous, weak, 4-angled. Trimming strengthens the stems and induces some branching. Easy to divide. It grows well in a north window with constant moisture. One of the easiest of the medium-sized, herbaceous plants and very decorative.

'Minima' is shorter and branches more readily.

P. depressa. Shiny Creeping Charlie. A little creeper, rooting from the joints of stems and spreading by offsets. The leaves tiny, thick, broadly wedgeshaped and always shiny, wet looking. Shade- and moisture-loving plant; very tough and easy but undisciplined.

P. 'Ebony'. Plant of uncertain origin. A creeper with reddish wiry stems and small oval, widely toothed leaves, quilted like *P. cadierei* but almost black-green. Grow in sphagnum moss in a terrarium.

P. forgettii (?) Possibly the species sold in horticulture under the name of *P. spruceana* 'Norfolk'. Leaves tightly spiraled, opposite-alternate, almost stalkless on low, creeping stems. Blades 4 × 3" (10 × 7.5 cm) or proportionately broader, elliptical. Edges turned down; midrib and two principal curving veins depressed; many transverse veins with prominent quilting between. The quilting is silver on coppery bronze background; the effect spectacularly colorful.

Basket plants grown in greenhouses ae symmetrical and magnificent but are difficult to maintain for long as they require very high humidity, warmth and filtered sun. Small plants are very decorative and easy to grow in terrariums. Poor results with the larger plants indoors are responsible for their less frequent appearance in shops.

P. grandifolia. Maroon Bush. A species that grows in Jamaica to a large bush with 3–4 × 1½–2" (7.5–10 × 3.75–5 cm) pointed elliptical leaves, puckered; light green tinged with red. This is a plant that grows in partial to full sun on limestone. Add lime to the soil and feed with high phosphate/potash formula. It requires very good ventilation.

'Coral'. Blades pinkish bronze; very showy. Full sun.

P. involucrata. Panamiga. Friendship Plant. Growth and quilting like 'Norfolk' but leaves half as large, hairy, bronzy green, purple beneath. A good small pot plant that mats well, requiring little light. Keep moist and humid.

P. microphylla. Artillery Plant. An old favorite that is no longer in style. Weedy, much branched, shrubby-succulent, little plant with branches held out horizontally, covered with tiny, fleshy green leaves. *P. microphylla prostrata* is lower and more spreading. Grows in acid soil and requires high nitrate fertilizer at ¼ recommended strength monthly. Humidity 60% and constant moisture. Fine in a terrarium. Good in baskets if the cultural requirements can be met.

P. nummulariifolia. Hairy Creeping Charlie. Little plant with long, trailing branches and nearly round, finely hairy, short-stalked, toothed blades. Treat like *P. microphylla.*

P. pubescens liebmanii, 'Silver Cloud'. Leaves like *P. involucrata* but smooth, slightly hairy, undulating, silvery pink. Terrarium culture.

P. repens. Blackleaf Panamiga. Leaves hairy, to 1½" (3.75 cm) long, toothed. Dark brown-green. A weak little plant, difficult to maintain. Very high humidity. Terrarium.

P. serpyllacea. Similar to *P. microphylla* but stems and branches more erect and sturdier, the leaves nearly round, a little larger and very clustered. A much more shapely plant but not frequently seen. Makes a good size pot plant to 12" (30 cm).

P. 'Silver Tree'. To 8" (20 cm). Stems erect. Blades almost stalkless, lanceshaped, to 3 × 1" (7.5 × 2.5 cm) with scalloped edges. Brown with two broad vertical bands of silver. A pretty, but weak plant difficult to maintain outside of a terrarium.

Pimenta. Myrtaceae. Tropical America. Small trees. Partial to full sun. 800–1000 fc. Temperature min. 50°F (10°C). Humidity 50%. Sterilized Garden Soil. Houseplant Mix #2. Propagation by seeds or cuttings. Easy. Probably 2 species.

Of the two frequently cultivated species one produces Allspice and the other the leaves for Bay Rum. Both make good pot plants of easy culture. Fertilize with a balanced formula once a month during the warm season.

P. dioica. Allspice. Tree to 40' (12 m), much branched with leathery, elliptical, shiny leaves 6 × 2" (15 × 5 cm). Deliciously aromatic leaves.

P. racemosa. Bay Rum Tree. It is not common knowledge that the fresh or dried leaves possess a strong lemon flavor in cooking. Leaves like *P. dioica* but veins more netted.

Piper. Piperaceae. Worldwide tropics. Shrubs and clambering vines. Filtered to partial sun. 400–800 fc. Temperature min. 50 × 65°F (10 × 18.5°C) minimum. Humidity min. 50%. Houseplant Mix #3. Propagation by seed or cuttings. Easy to moderately difficult. 1,000 species of which about 10 are grown indoors.

The *Piper* genus is best known for *P. nigrum,* Black Pepper. Indoor gardeners grow *P. crocatum* and *ornatum* for their exotic foliage. Other species have been almost unknown until a number of them were introduced by Glasshouse Works. Though currently in vogue with amateur collectors, their future in public favor is difficult to predict. We list some that have been recommended.

P. aduncum. Shrub with arching branches on "bamboolike" stems. Leaves lanceshaped. Control size by underpotting.

P. auritum. False Sarsaparilla. Tall canes with swollen joints. "Thin, wide, heairy leaves" with scent of sarsaparilla.

P. crocatum. Pink Lacquer Vine. Often confused with *P. ornatum.* Note difference in measurements;

this leaf is narrower than *P. ornatum.* Wiry climber usually grown as a trailing pot or basket plant. Blades heartshaped, 4 × 1½" (10 × 3.75 cm), the tip attenuated. Dark olive green marbled silver or pink. Low quilting between veins. Purple beneath. Stalk attached just below the notch (peltate). Min. 65°F (18.5°C) and 65% humidity.

P. florencianum. Quilted Velour. Shrub with upright canes. Light-colored veins form a richly netted pattern on the partially folded, velvety surfaced blades. Stalks winged. Shade.

P. lanceaefolium. Bamboo Piper. Blades lanceshaped to 4" (10 cm) long; veins prominent; stalks olive green with dark spotting and swollen joints.

P. magnificum. Peru. Shrub to 3' (90 cm). Canes stout, corky, with fringed wings. Leaves heartshaped to 9 × 5" (22.5 × 12.5 cm), quilted betwen the veins, maroon beneath. Stalks winged and clasping the stem. Keep moist at all times. Control height by underpotting.

P. nigrum. Sri Lanka and S. India. A horticultural form of the black pepper vine. Leaves small, leathery, dark green, heartshaped. Low light, warmth and high humidity.

P. ornatum. Celebes Pepper. Beautiful heartshaped leaves 4 × 3" (10 × 7.5 cm) with stalk attached just below the cleft. Pinkish white marbling on light green; green beneath. Moist, warm, high humidity, low light.

P. porphyrophyllum. Malay Penninsula. Tall vine. Blades heartshaped, like *P. ornatum,* but 6 × 5" (15 × 12.5 cm), quilted between veins; olive green with pink spots along the veins. Stalks reddish.

P. sylvaticum. India, Burma. Creeping vine with leaves to 4" (10 cm), heartshaped, puffed between the 5 vertical veins.

Pisonia. *(Heimerliriodendron).* **Nyctaginaceae.** Subtropics and tropics. Shrubs and trees. Filtered to partial sun. 400–600 fc. Temperature min. 50°F (10°C). Humidity min. 50%. Houseplant Mix #2 with sand. Propagation from seeds or cuttings. Moderately difficult. 50 species of which 1 grown indoors.

P. umbellifera (*P. brunoiana, P. grandis ?, Heimerlieriodendron brunonianum*). Bird Catcher Tree. To 25' (7.5 m). Leaves elliptical to somewhat spoonshaped, max. 15 × 3½" (37.5 × 8.25 cm); somewhat leathery. Stalks 4" (10 cm). The variegated cultivar is usually grown.

'Variegata'. The background of the leaf is white or ivory with feathered, interlocking blotches of gray and green.

P. grandis. 'Tricolor'. This may be a different plant as the stalks seem to be longer, giving it a more spreading look. The markings are similar but there is less white or ivory.

Plants are usually sold as 6–8' (1.8–2.4 m) specimens. However, when underpotted and trimmed, they can be trained much smaller. Very decorative indoors.

Possibly valuable for large plantscapes with some coolness in winter. Leaves are subject to various diseases. Keep evenly moist and fertilize sparingly with high phosphate/potash formula.

Pistia. **Araceae.** Corn Lettuce. Worldwide tropics. Aquatic herb. Full sun. 1000 fc 15 hours daily. Water temperature min. 60°F (16°C). Humidity min. 50%. Sterilized Garden Soil or humus and sand. Propagation by offsets. 1 species.

P. stratiotes bears no obvious resemblance to other aroids. The short, broad wedgeshaped, stalkless leaves grow in a symmetrical rosette 60″ (15 cm) in diamter. The blades are fuzzy, vertically ribbed and the texture much thinner than it appears. They are a glowing gray to yellow-green in color. Like a lovely floating flower.

The plants must be bought from an aquatic plant nursery. Lay on the surface of the water 3–4″ (7.5–10 cm) deep. The thin roots reach to the soil below. Or plant in a wide, shallow pot and set with the rim at the water surface. Placed in a sunny window or under lights, they quickly produce offsets that are easy to separate. The crop is so large that one of the chores is weeding them out to allow a few of the rosettes room to grow to maturity.

Keep the water level up and fertilize every 2 months in summer with ⅛-strength balanced fertilizer to the gallon of water in the vessel. Change the water every 3 months to prevent buildup of salts. The presence of other aquatic herbs is beneficial.

The worst enemy is mealybug. If, by chance, they infest the plants, we see no way to get rid of them, except to throw everything out and start afresh.

Very decorative for plantscape pools.

Pithecellobium. **Leguminosae.** Circumglobal tropical. Trees and shrubs. Partial to full sun. 500–1,000 fc. Temperature min. 40°F (4°C). Houseplant Mix #1 with sand. Propagation from seed. Easy. Over 100 species of which one grown indoors.

P. flexicaule. Texas Ebony Tree. Grown primarily as pseudo-bonsai from 4–10″ (10–25 cm) in height. Slow growing. Leaves compound, consisting of 3–5 pairs of oblong leaves, max. ½″ (1.25 cm) long. When kept above 55°F (13°C) in winter, it remains green. It grows a naked stem and a branching flat top spontaneously. A fine plant for pseudo-bonsai.

Pittosporum. **Pittosporaceae.** Old World temperate zones and subtropics. Shrubs and trees. Partial to full sun. 500–1,000 fc. Temperature min. 40–90°F (4–33°C). Sterilized Garden Soil or Houseplant Mix #2 with sand. Propagation from seeds or cuttings. Fairly easy. 100 species of which only 1 widely grown indoors.

Only *P. tobira*, Tropical Mock Orange, has achieved some degree of popularity among indoor gardeners. The genus has wide distribution from the Himalayas to Taiwan and the Philippines with many species native to New Zealand. Most are cool growing. *P. tobira* flourishes in southern Italy and Spain where it is exposed to near freezing weather in winter and high temperatures in summer. It appears to be adaptable

to homes and other situations that are cool in winter and have excellent ventilation in summer.

They are handsome, medium-high, spreading, woody shrubs, to 10′ (3 m) with leathery leaves in symmetrical clusters; more compact and leafy but rather like *Rhododendron*. The yellow or white flower clusters are attractive and fragrant. Certainly the warmer-growing species deserve more attention as large pot plants in the house and as trimmed tub plants in airy commercial settings enjoying ample light. However, it should be noted that they are slow in growth. Propagation of cuttings from branches usually requires professional handling. Seed is easier but slow.

The following descriptions are short because, except for *P. tobira,* there is not much experience to draw on.

P. bicolor. S. Australia. Small tree with gray bark. Leaves leathery, oblong, 2½″ (6.25 cm) long; scurfy beneath. Cool.

P. crassifolium. New Zealand. Tree to 35′ (10.5 m). Leaves spoonshaped, to 3″ (7.50 cm) long, thick and leathery; edges turned down; scurfy beneath.

'Compactum'. Leaves gray-green, soft.

P. daphniphylloides. Taiwan. Shrub to 10′ (3 m), densely branched, the leaves in tight whorls or spirals, elliptic. Stalks to 1″ (2.5 cm). Warmer growing.

P. hawaiiense. Tree to 15′ (4.5 m) with a white trunk. Leaves spoonshaped, 8″ (20 cm) long, very thin, the veins very much depressed.

P. phyllyraeoides. Australia Willow-Leaved Pittosporum. Tree to 30′ (9 m). Leaves narrowly lanceshaped to 4″ (10 cm) long. Branches and leaves pendant. As reliable as *P. tobira,* but the growth is less sculptural-compact.

P. tobira. Japan. Tropical Mock Orange. Shrub to 18′ (5.4 m), very branched, flat topped and usually no more than 5′ (1.5 m) high outdoors. Usually to max. 3′ (90 cm) high and 2½′ (75 cm) broad indoors. Leaves spoonshaped, leathery, the tip blunt, arranged in close spirals facing upward so that the tips of branches seem to bear rosettes. Very neat.

'Compacta'. A dwarf form suitable for bonsai treatment.

'Variegata'. Blades irregularly edged in white over olive-green. The variety usually grown at present.

'Wheeler'. Similar to 'Compacta'. The leaves more oval. Best for pot culture.

Plectranthus. **Labiatae.** Swedish Ivy. Old World tropics. Mostly trailing herbs; some succulents. Shade to partial sun. 150–800 fc. Temperature min. 55°F (13°C). Houseplant Mix #2. Propagation from cuttings. Easy. 250 species of which 3 widely grown indoors.

The genus includes very tolerant basket plants widely used in private and commercial situations. They are often seen in the north-facing windows of restaurants. Not deeply rooted, they need regular watering before the soil dries. Fertilize every 2 weeks in summer with high nitrate formula. The stems root easily at the joints, and cuttings quickly put out roots in water.

As basket plants develop long branches they must be trimmed back, but further branching is limited. In aging the plants become woody, decline in vigor and must be replaced. Under adverse conditions of excessive heat, cold or pollution, leaf spotting and drop are common. Occasionally attacked by mealybug and white fly, they are best treated by spraying strongly with water as the thin leaves do not react well to pesticides. Nevertheless, two of the species have proved quite satisfactory in commercial situations.

P. australis. Short-hairy shrub with erect stems to 2' (60 cm). Blades broadly lanceshaped to 1½" (3.75 cm) long and coarsely toothed. Stalks to 1" (2.5 cm). Coolish.

P. coleoides. S. India. Compact, shrubby plant with closely clustered, branched, purple stems to 3' (90 cm). Leaves opposite-alternate, overlapping. Blades lanceshaped to 4 × 2½" (10 × 6.25 cm), velvety, the veins depressed; irregularly scalloped and/or toothed. Warm growing.

'Marginatus'. Blades green, mottled with light green and edged with white.

'Marginatus Minimus'. Branches trailing. Blades 1–1½" (2.5–3.75 cm) long, edges white. More popular as a basket plant.

'Variegatus'. Like the previous but veins more depressed, quilted, with irregular white border.

P. fruticosus (forsteri). S. Africa. Erect to 3' (90 cm). Leaves broadly lanceshaped and coarsely scalloped to 4" (10 cm) long. Stems 4-angled. Var. *marginata* is broadly edged in white. Can be trained to a standard.

P. madagascariensis aliciae. Busy Mint. Miniature trailer with tiny, crimped leaves. Veining complex, very depressed. Edges toothed.

P. nummularius. Watery-stemmed trailer with branches to 12" (30 cm). Leaves nearly round, to 2½" (6.25 cm) in diameter, coarsely toothed. Like *P. oertendahlii* but entirely green and more undisciplined.

'Freckles'. Leaves spotted with yellow.

'Variegatus' is irregularly blotched with white.

P. oertendahlii. Swedish Ivy. Finely hairy trailer, the branches to 18" (45 cm) long. Blades almost round, to 2½" (6.25 cm) in diameter; shallowly and broadly scalloped. Stalks to 1" (2.5 cm). The complex vein network white. A sturdy plant, fast growing and easily propagated. Tolerates shade and temperatures down to 50°F (10°C). A popular basket plant for every use.

P. prostratus. Pillow Plant. Tanzania. Finely hairy, mat forming plant with 2" (5 cm) branches, rooting at the joints. Leaves thick, ¾ × ½" (2.0 × 1.2 cm). Succulent culture. Full sun. Grow on surface of sand mixed with some finely milled sphagnum moss. In winter mist occasionally. In summer water weekly.

P. tomentosus. Woolly Swedish Ivy. S. Africa. White, woolly small shrub with leaves that are thick, almost round and 3½" (8.75 cm) in diameter. Edges scalloped. Succulent culture. Full sun.

Podocarpus. **Podocarpaceae.** Southern Hemisphere north to Japan and West Indies. Shrubs to tall trees. Filtered sun. 3 parts sandy, sterilized garden soil to 1 part peat. Propagation by seeds or cuttings. Easy to moderately difficult. 75 species of which a few grown indoors.

Podocarpus are mostly tall evergreen trees, among the few that are not hardy and can be grown successfully in large pots or tubs indoors. There are both warm- and cool-growing species. Only one, *P. macrophyllus,* has achieved wide acceptance. Almost all have narrow, straightsided, elliptical, shiny and firm-textured leaves, without stalks.

P. elongatus. Tropical Africa. Weeping Podocarpus. Often mislabeled *P. gracilior.* A 70' (21 m) tall tree that, as a young plant, is very graceful, branches being pendant like a Weeping Willow. The spaced leaves to 4 × ¼" (10 cm × 6.25 mm). Large specimens are splendid screening plants. Minimum 55°F (13°C).

P. gracilior. Tropical Africa. Fern Pine. Like *P. elongatus* but may differ in that the leaves are often black tipped, the branches more erect and the leaves much more numerous and closer set.

P. macrophyllus. China and Japan. Buddhist Pine. Tree to 45' (13.5 m). Leaves long elliptical to 4 × ⅜" (10 cm × 9.35 mm); dark above, lighter beneath, in crowded spirals. Var. *maki,* is the most commonly grown. The branches more erect. A columnar, architectural plant for low light, cool situations. Sometimes gets scale infestation. A very fine tub plant for mixed foliage plantings.

'Variegatus'. Leaves a little wider and speckled with white.

P. nagi. Broadleaf Podocarpus. Japan. Like *P. macrophyllus* but leaves wider, 3 × 1" (7.5 × 2.5 cm). Cool growing. Also impressive as a columnar specimen.

P. nivalis. False Yew. New Zealand. Shrub to 6' (1.8 m), with spreading branches. Leaves ¾" (19 mm) with blunt tips (strapshaped), thick. Minimum 45°F (7°C). For cool situations with partial sun.

'Aureus'. Young leaves golden, turning green.

Polyscias. **Araliaceae.** Western Pacific and Tropical Asia. Shrubs. Shade to partial sun. Min. 50 fc. Temperature min. 50°F (10°C). Packaged Houseplant Medium or Houseplant Mix #1. Propagation from cuttings. Easy to Cast Iron. 80 species of which 4 grown indoors.

The genus includes one of the most decorative and enduring foliage plants, the Ming or Parsley Aralia, *P. fruticosa.*

P. balfouriana. New Caledonia. Tree to 20' (6 m) but rarely grown indoors taller than 5' (1.5 m). Branches numerous, short, covered with leaves that are very broad heartshaped, finely toothed, 4" (10 cm) wide and long; notched at the base; often blotched with white. Stalks 6" (15 cm) long, upright. The variety with white markings is usually called var. *marginata.* Min. 50°F (10°C).

'Pennockii' is much more beautiful, the leaves being slightly larger and longer than wide, cupped and somewhat quilted by depressed veining.

Variegated with a thick powdering of ivory. Slow growing and woodier than the species. It accepts a limited amount of pruning. Partial sun, min. 60°F (16°C). Humidity min. 50%. A gorgeous plant when well grown.

P. filicifolia. Fern Leaf Aralia. A variable species with a very spreading habit. Branches purplish. Leaves compound to 1' (30 cm) long, the leaflets widely spaced, 4–5 pairs and a tip subleaflet; each long-triangular, simple to edged with sharp triangular sub-segments (the usual form). Culture as for *P. fruticosa.*

'Marginata' and 'Variegata'. Leaflets white edged.

Useful as a screening plant when tall and well grown.

P. fruticosa. Ming or Parsley Aralia. Widespread S. Asia. Leaves are divided and crisped in the manner of coarse parsley. Highly variable. Branches upright, numerous, gnarled with age.

'Elegans' and 'Plumata' are more compact plants and especially good for pseudo-bonsai.

Though a shrub that can attain 10' (3 m) or more, it is so receptive to pruning and underpotting that it can be kept for years no higher than 1' (30 cm) and is a fine subject for pseudo-bonsai. The growth habit is naturally suggestive of oriental design, and this quality can be enhanced by training. Soil and light needs are minimal. Tip cuttings root in plain water within a week or two.

Why, then, is it not more popular? That is difficult to discover. Perhaps the public is unimpressed by its uniform greenness. Nurserymen say that it loses leaves excessively in transit. It is a simple matter to shake the plant and bring the dead leaves down; within a short time they are replaced. We have grown it for many years and never encountered either pests or diseases. What more can one ask of a plant? We recommend it for all types of indoor situations.

P. guilfoylei. Geranium Leaf Aralia. Polynesia. Shrub to 15' (4.5 m). Leaves compound, with 3–4 pairs and a tip leaflet. Leaflets thin, cupped, elliptical, various toothed from shallow to deep, to 4" (10 cm) long. Branches few and the arrangement rather undisciplined.

'Laciniata'. With more leaflets that are more deeply cut.

'Victoriae'. Somewhat more compact. Leaflets grayish green with white edges.

A plant difficult to maintain in good condition as leaves become brown spotted or drop if humidity is below 50% or the plant is exposed to drafts or very high temperatures. Rarely seen in prime condition.

P. guilfoylei quinquefolia 'Elegans'. Still more compact than the above and behaves better indoors. Leaflets green.

'Elegans Variegata'. Young leaflets lemon yellow aging to green. Smaller. Young plants woodier with a corky bark.

P. paniculata. Shrub to 15' (4.5 m). Leaflets shiny dark green, oval.

'Marginata'. Leaflets coarsely toothed.

'Variegata'. Leaflets irregularly marked with areas of buff and cream.

Very diffuse and spreading.

Portulacaria. **Portulacaceae.** Elephant Bush. South America. Succulent shrub. Temperature min. 40°F (4°C). Houseplant Mix #1 with lime. Propagation from cuttings. Easy. 1 species.

Potulacaria afra. A shrub very much like a dwarf branched Crassula. The leaves are max. ½" (12.5 mm) in diameter, smooth, waxy, disklike, borne in clusters on short twigs attached to the thicker branches. Grow in Succulent Mix #1 and water only when completely dry. Fertilize three or four times a year with a balanced fertilizer.

These shrubs are very popular in Mediterranean countries where they are grown in stone troughs. Although a height of 15' (4.5 m) can be attained, they are trimmed and starved to stay at no more than a foot (30 cm) high but spreading.

Leaves of the species are jade green but the preference is for cultivars (variegata) with zones of green and ivory or even gray-green. Still more scarce, but beautiful, is a cultivar, occasionally available, which has a rim of pink on each leaf. Carefully trimmed and trained it is quite possibly the best of the succulents for bonsai. They can look exactly like very fine Chinese mineral jade trees.

Psuederanthemum. **Acanthaceae.** C. and S. America and W. Pacific. Herbs and shrubs. Filtered to partial sun. 300–800 fc. Temperature min. 60°F (16°C). Humidity min. 50%. Houseplant Mix #3. Propagation by cuttings. Fairly easy. 60 species of which 4 grown indoors.

P. alatum. Chocolate Plant. Single-stemmed herbs with opposite-alternate pairs of lanceshaped leaves, 5 × 2½" (12.5 × 6.26 cm), thin, the upcurving veins depressed. Surface cocoa colored, a series of irregular gray triangles down the midrib. Stalks to 1½" (3.75 cm), distinctly winged. A most unusual color. The blades horizontal. Grows about 12" (30 cm) high. Small flowers in a spike, a rich purple. Treat as an annual and renew with rooted cuttings.

P. atropurpureum. Very similar to *Graptophyllum* and used for hedges in the same way. A shrub growing to 4' (1.20 m), the blades to 5" (12.5 cm) long, elliptic. The colors are generally darker than those of *Graptophyllum.*

'Curruthersii'. Blades purple, leathery.

'Rubrum'. To 2" (5 cm) wide, spoonshaped, maroon.

'Tricolor'. Blades lanceshaped; purple zoned in gray green and pink.

'Variegatum'. Blades pink, gray-green and off-white.

These are selected colors but in the tropics various combinations of the basic hues are common, and nurseries here apply various cultivar names.

The plants start out with watery stems which become woody later on. It is rather difficult indoors to grow more stems from the base or to keep them until

Peperomia incana

Peperomia columella

Peperomia sp.

Peperomia caperata tricolor

PLATE 65

Peperomia dolabriformis

Pereskia aculeata **var.** *Godseffiana*

Persea americana. Avocado

Philodendron eichleri

PLATE 66

Philodendron oxycardium aureum

Philodendron verrucosum

Philodendron 'Petit Point'

Philodendron soderoi

PLATE 67

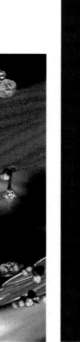

Phyllanthus angustifolius

Phyllanthus sp.

Pilea. Jamaica sp.

Pilea 'Silver Tree'

PLATE 68

Pilea numullariifolia

Pilea microphylla. Artillery Plant

Pilea cadierei. Aluminum Plant

Pilea 'Moon Valley'

PLATE 69

Pimenta dioica. Allspice

Piper ornaturm

Piper 'Quilted Velour'

Pistia stratiotes. Water Lettuce

PLATE 70

Pithecelobium flexicaule. Texas Ebony

Pittosporum tobira

Plectranthus oertendahlii. Swedish Ivy

Plectranthus pentherii

PLATE 71

Plectranthus mentho-eucalyptol (Coleus?)

Plectranthus. Variegated cv.

Podocarpus macrophyllus

Polyscias crispata (?) 'Ruffles'

PLATE 72

Polyscias balfouriana 'Marginata'

Polyscias fruticosa 'Elegans.' Ming Aralia

Portulacaria afra-variegata. Elephant Bush

Pseuderanthemum atropurpureum

PLATE 73

Pseuderanthemum atropurpureum 'Tricolor'

Pseuderanthemum reticulatum

Pseuderanthemum reticulatum 'El Dorado'

Psilotum nudum. Whisk Fern

PLATE 74

Rhaphidophora decursiva

Raphidophora sp.

Reineckia carnea

Rhektophyllum mirabile

PLATE 75

Rhoeo spathacea. Moses in the Bulrushes

Rhoeo bermudensis variegata

Rhoicissus thunbergii

Rosmarinus officinalis. Rosemary

PLATE 76

Ruscus hypoglossus. Butcher's Broom

Sageretia thea

Sanchezia nobilis (speciosa)

Sansevieria 'Bantell's Sensation'

PLATE 77

Sansevieria cylindrica

Sansevieria trifasciata 'Moonshine'

Sansevieria.'Golden Hahnii'

Sansevieria suffruticosa

PLATE 78

Schismatoglottis calyptrata. Drop-Tongue

Scindapsus pictus argyraeus

Senecio macroglossus variegatus

Senecio crest.'Ken'

PLATE 79

Senecio scaposus

Serissa foetida

Setcreasea pallida

Soleirolia soleirolii. Baby's Tears

PLATE 80

they become filled out with branches and woody. Trim and be patient.

P. reticulatum. Shrub to 3′ (90 cm). Leaves lanceshaped to 10 × 1½″ (25 × 3.75 cm), scallop edged; dark green with a network of yellow veining.

P. sinuatum. To 10″ (25 cm) high, with many short branches and leaves. Leaves 3″ (7.5 cm) long, thin, very narrow, distantly lobed, like *Dizygotheca* but rich reddish purple.

The flowers of these species are 5-lobed, white with purple spots.

Psilotum. **Psilotaceae.** Whisk Fern. Southern U.S.A. Semiaquatic herb. Shade to filtered sun. 100 fc. Temperature min. 50°F (4°C). Houseplant Mix #3. Propagation from spores and by division. Easy. 2 species, 1 grown indoors.

P. nudum. Whisk Fern. A very primitive plant. Shallowly rooted with numerous rubbery, shiny stems, branches and twigs, triangular in cross-section. The spiky, tiny leaves are hardly noticeable. Yellow balls of spores are borne at the joints throughout the year. To 2′ (60 cm).

Keep moist at all times and fertilize lightly with a high nitrate formula no more than once every two months. Pest and disease free. Easily divided. Spore seedlings appear in other pots occasionally, but results from sowing are poor. Very long lasting and very tolerant. Curious and charming plants for pot culture.

Rademachera. **Bignoniaceae.** Southern Asia and western Pacific. Small trees. Filtered sun or 500 fc 12 hours daily. Temperature min. 60°F (16°C). Humidity min. 40%. Packaged Houseplant Mix. Propagation by cuttings. Moderately easy. 30 species of which 1 grown indoors.

R. sinica. South China. Small tree to 20′ (6 m) with compound leaves, the leaflets lanceshaped to 2″ (5 cm) long.

Grown in the past mainly for its 3″ (2.5 cm) bright yellow trumpet flowers but has recently attracted attention as a foliage plant capable of being maintained in relatively low light. It is also said to grow rapidly; a boon to nurserymen but of doubtful value for long-term plantscaping. There are other similar Radermacheras, especially from the Philippine Islands, that may be adaptable to indoor conditions.

Raphidophora. **Araceae.** S.E. Asia and Western Pacific. Vines. 60 species of which a half dozen grown indoors. See *Philodendron* for culture.

Raphidophora is a genus that seems invented, like a few others in the family, only to create confusion. As such plants are rarely brought to bloom, herbarium specimens are often inaccessible and botanists frequently disagree as to their identification, it is no wonder if nurserymen use a bit of guesswork in labeling. The difficulties are compounded by plants producing differently shaped leaf blades at the stages from seedling to maturity.

R. cavalieri (?) 'Exotica' (?), 'Silver Streak' (?). Possibly *Epipremnum falcifolia.* Lanceshaped leaves to 8 × 1½″ (20 × 3.75 cm), leathery, green with gray streakings, held out stiffly on channeled stalks to 6″ (15 cm). We have grown this or a very similar plant. It is a low-light climber and quite easy and attractive.

R. celatocaulis. Shingle Plant. A vigorous vine with alternate, leathery leaves. First heartshaped to 8 × 4″ (20 × 10 cm) with a very short, narrow notch, then elongated to 12–15 × 5″ (30–37.5 × 12.5 cm) with undulating edges, finally oblong to 2′ (60 cm) or more long, the upper part of the blade cut into rectangular lobes half way to the midrib, like a *Monstera.* Stalks at first short then as long or longer than the blades.

R. decursiva. Southern Asia. Rampant vine with compound leaves, probably to 2′ (60 cm) long, consisting of 8–12 pairs and a tip leaflet, the leaflets starshaped. Stalk as long as the leaf.

R. peepla. Similar to *R. celatocaulis* but leaves longer, more pendant and veins depressed.

R. pinnata. See *Epipremnum pinnatum.*

R. silvestris. Tall-growing vine. Blades lanceshaped, 5 × 1″ (12.5 × 2.5 cm). Stalks short, channeled.

Reineckia. **Liliaceae.** China and Japan. 1 species. See *Ophiopogon* for culture.

R. carnea. Leaves 12 × ¼″ (30 cm × 6.25 mm), opposite in a row. Colonizing by runners.

'Variegata'. Striped with white.

Plants should be well established in 4″ (10 cm) pots as smaller, younger ones are too weak to adjust quickly to indoor conditions.

Rhektophyllum. **Araceae.** West Africa. Warm house. Filtered sun. 300–500 fc 14 hours daily. Temperature min. 65°F (18.5°C). Humidity min. 60%+. Long-fiber sphagnum moss or Houseplant Mix #3. Propagation by division or from cuttings. Difficult. 2 species; 1 grown indoors.

R. mirabile (Nephthytis picturata). Leaves of young plants are outstandingly elegant. Clambering vine to 30′ (9 m). Grown as a pot plant to max. 4′ (1.20 m) indoors. Blades long triangular with a deep notch at the base and long blunt lobes, to 14 × 4″ (37.5 × 10 cm). Younger leaves broader in respect to length. Edge undulating; texture rather thin. The patterning is extremely complicated. Midrib and the many major and minor side veins are deep green and depressed. The surface between the minor veins is therefore very quilted. The quilting is ivory with a fine dusting of green dots and quite translucent. The lighter colored pattern is like a pointed, compound leaf, and the clubshaped leaflets are oriented in the direction of the base even on the lobes. Each compound leaf pattern, therefore, is broadest near the edge of the blade with the point nearest to the base.

The stalks are cylindrical, dark green and 12–20″ (30–50 cm) long. A very tender plant. High humidity is essential. Subject like most of these plants to spider mite infestation.

Rhodospatha. **Araceae.** Tropical America. Vines. Philodendron culture. 6 species; 3 occasionally grown indoors.

R. hastata (?). Possibly an *Epipremnum.* The leaves are not at all hastate (with spreading basal lobes) at least in the mature stage. They are strapshaped and pointed, 15 × 2″ (37.5 × 5 cm). Stalks short and winged.

'Jet Streak'. Could well belong to another genus. Introduced from Columbia. Slow growing. Blades 18 × 5″ (45 × 12.5 cm), elliptic, slightly notched at the base. Midrib white. Lateral veins depressed. Stalks stiff, as long as blades.

R. latifolia. Brazil. Blades elliptic, 18 × 10″ (45 × 25 cm), edges undulating. Veins horizontal, very numerous. The surface corrugated. Stalks as long as blades; light green.

R. picta. Brazil. Stems to 30″ (75 cm). Leaves spiraled, elliptic, 24 × 8″ (60 × 20 cm), the surface mottled with yellow-green. Stalks short and clasping the stem.

Rhoeo. **Commelinaceae.** W. Indies and C. America. Semisucculent herb. Filtered to full sun. Temperature min. 45°F (7°C). Humidity min. 50%. Sterilized Garden Soil with peat. Propagation by division. Easy. 1 species.

Rhoeos are grown for their curious, boatshaped and colorful leaf arrangement. The cluster of flowers in the center is inconspicuous. They are excellent for low mass plantings wherever sufficient sun is available. Very easy and long lasting.

R. spathacea. Moses in the Cradle. Stems short. Leaves 12 × 3″ (30 × 7.5 cm), stiff, pointed, folded down the center, clasping and overlapping the stems. Dark green above and purple beneath. Colonizing by underground runners.

R. spathaceae concolor vittata. Oyster Plant. Leaves streaked with yellow on upper surface.

R. spathacea nana (*R. bermudensis* ?). Leaves shorter and spiraled; the whole plant lower.

R. spathaceae vittata (?) Leaves arranged in a rosette. Blades striped with yellow on both sides.

Dry between waterings. Fertilize sparingly.

Rhoicissus. **Vitaceae.** S. Africa. Vines. Shade to partial sun. 150–800 fc. Temperature min. 50°F (10°C). Sterilized Garden Soil with peat. Houseplant Mix #2. Propagation from cuttings. Cast Iron. 10 species of which 2 grown indoors.

R. capensis. Cape Grape. Tuberous rooted vines with wiry stems. Leathery blades to 8″ (20 cm) broad and almost as long. The three major lobes are approximately rectangular forming an inverted T (the base being almost straight) with a few broad scallops; green above, reddish-woolly beneath.

R. thunbergii. Compound leaves with three leaflets; oval, leathery; dull reddish brown above, reddish green beneath. Compact.

Both make excellent basket plants. *R. capensis* requires a min. 12″ (30 cm) basket as the leaves are coarse and the branches long. *R. thunbergii,* being

much more compact, needs less space. It is the more ornamental of the two.

Rosmarinus. **Labiatae.** Rosemary. Mediterranean. Woody shrubs. Filtered to full sun. 300–1,000 fc 14 hours daily. Temperature min. 40°F (4°C). Sterilized Garden Soil with lime or Houseplant Mix #1 with lime. Propagation from cuttings. 3 species of which one grown indoors.

Rosemary is an excellent culinary herb with very pungent, needle leaves on a woody, long-lived shrub.

The frequently heard advice to allow the soil to dry out between waterings is misleading. Even one day of complete dryness is lethal, and they are very heavy drinkers in the bargain, so that they must be closely watched. If watering is not neglected the rest of culture is simple as the plants are tolerant of low and high temperatures. They grow best in full sun but manage with less and do well under fluorescent light. Use a high-middle-number fertilizer once a month throughout the year.

Trim for the kitchen and for shape. Rosemary is a splendid subject for indoor bonsai, developing gnarled, barked trunks with age. Maximum height and width indoors is about 2½′ (75 cm).

R. officinalis grows to max. 6′ (1.8 m), is much branched and blanketed with needles to 1″ (2.5 cm) long that vary considerably in small, but significant, details and range from blue to deep green in color. Growth form is also exceedingly variable. Normal *R. officinalis* is erect and hangs over the side of a pot but there are many transitional types. Cultivar labels are of little help. It is best to pick out plants personally at nurseries. Beware of plants that have been forced. These have wide spaces between the joints.

Maintain smaller sizes by frequent trimming and, as the trunk and roots develop, moving them gradually to larger pots. The most frequent cause of loss, besides failure to water, is pot-binding, which causes strangulation. The only means of maintaining in the same pot for very long is to trim roots at the same time as branches.

Ruscus. **Liliaceae.** Mediterranean, Azores and Madeira. Shrubs. Filtered to full sun. Min 400 fc. Temperature min. 45°F (7°C). Sterilized Garden Soil. Houseplant Mix #1. Propagation from cuttings. Easy. 3 species.

These small shrubs grow all over southern Europe and the Middle East in dry, exposed situations. They are quite different from most of the Lily Family except for the related *Semele,* which is a vine. The branches are thin, upright, rigid and dry. The apparent leaves, shiny, thin, brittle, are really modified branchlets (called cladophylls). The tiny flowers grow from the midveins and lie as singles on top of them. They are tolerant of fairly low light, are drought resistant and need hardly any feeding indoors. Give high nitrate formula once a month during the warm season. They are tough and slow growing; excellent, long-lived pot plants, especially kept trimmed to shape and very amusing in appearance.

R. aculeatus. Butcher's Broom. To 3′ (90 cm). Leaves (cladophylls) elliptical, with a spiny tip, to 1½ × ¾″ (3.75 cm × 18.5 mm), dark green. Flowers greenish.

R. hypoglossum. To 18″ (45 cm). Leaves 4 × 1½″ (10 × 3.75 cm). Flowers yellow.

R. hypophyllum. To 12″ (30 cm). Leaves 3″ (7.5 cm) long and half as wide. Flowers white.

Sageretia. **Rhamnaceae.** East Asia and N. America. Shrubs. Filtered to partial sun. 400–800 fc 14 hours daily. Temperature min. 50°F (10°C). Houseplant Mix #2. Propagation by cuttings and seeds. Easy. 30 species of which 1 grown indoors.

S. thea. Much-branched, woody shrub to 4 × 2′ (1.20 m × 60 cm). Branches long, wiry, drooping. Paired leaves an inch (2.5 cm) long, with a small notch at the base; dark, shiny green. Stalks tiny. Berry purple.

Fertilize with high nitrate formula once a month. Keep evenly moist. Looks even more attractive in a basket, if the stem is permitted to grow no more than a foot (30 cm) high, than in a pot.

Sanchezia. **Acanthaceae.** C. & S. America. Herbs and shrubs. Partial sun. Min 500 fc 15 hours daily. Temperature min. 55°F (13°C). Humidity min. 50%. Packaged Houseplant Medium or Sterilized Garden Soil with peat. Propagation from cuttings and division. Easy. 60 species. 1 grown indoors.

S. speciosa (nobilis). Canes to 6′ (1.80 m). Blades elliptical to 1′ (30 cm) on stalks of the same length. Width usually 4″ (10 cm) but variable. Midrib and veins yellow, rimmed with mustard. Potted plants are showy, usually to 2½′ (75 cm) and equally broad. Keep constantly moist and fertilize once a month April to October with balanced formula. They do not tolerate pruning. Separate offsets annually to pot up as replacement.

An unnamed cultivar that is a splendid rosette plant as a juvenile is grown in Caribbean nurseries. No more than 10″ (25 cm) high, it has a spread of over 2′ (60 cm). It could prove most useful for massing in beds.

Sansevieria. **Agavaceae.** Bowstring Hemp. Mostly Africa. Leaf succulent. Filtered to full sun. 300–1,000 fc. Temperature min. 40°F (4°C). Sterilized Garden Soil or Packaged Houseplant Medium or Houseplant Mix #2. Propagation from offsets and leaf cuttings. Cast Iron. More than 60 species of which only one commonly grown indoors.

It could well be that there are more Sansevierias growing in American homes than any other plant. This is possible because their numbers are constantly accumulating, one species, *S. trifasciata,* the Snake Plant, being long-lived and able to survive severe abuse and neglect. In the last few years botanical explorers have sent home, almost all from Africa, a bewildering array of related plants that have attracted widespread interest among amateurs and collectors. Flower spikes are whitish, open only at night and are penetratingly sweet perfumed.

The new acquisitions have revealed that the genus of this common leaf succulent is one of the most extraordinary in the entire plant world. The common Snake Plant has rosettes of thick, sword-shaped leaves. Many species have been found with different surface patterns. But a sensation has been created by the discovery of a very large number with quite different shapes; a complete set of transitional mutations that terminate in leaves that are hard and tubular.

The leaves of *S. trifasciata* have a pointed tip resulting from the in-rolling and fusing of the two edges. Other plants have longer tips and the process continuing downward eventually forms a cylinder for the entire length. That it is truly a leaf becomes apparent when it dries out and then becomes thin and flat. Thin longitudinal channels are simply depressed veins. This unique phenomenon is due to the precise adaptation of the genus to variations in rainfall from near normal to the most severe aridity. It has also affected their sizes which range from a few inches high to leaves that are 5′ (1.5 m) long.

The inundation of new material has led to the utmost confusion in identification. Save for familiar plants and some unmistakeably different ones, all labels supplied by collectors and nurseries are suspect. Our own list is a mix of certainties and guesses. The newer plants should be seen before purchase.

The genus offers a great variety of pot plants of all sizes that require a minimum of attention.

The larger, cylindrical types are very modern-sculptural and can be valuable as accents. Smaller plants can be massed. Upkeep is no problem.

Although accustomed to exposed situations, they are all (even the most succulent species) tolerant of filtered sun, and a few can be grown in shade. The more succulent the plant, the less water it needs. Those with cylindrical leaves can do without for at least a month or two even in hot weather. Only the variegated cultivars need brighter light and may contract fungal diseases if overwatered. All should, nevertheless, be watered during the cold months only after the soil is dry. Fertilizer is almost unnecessary. A balanced formula applied 2 or 3 times a year is more than sufficient. Plants can be shipped out-of-pot without damage if packed dry.

The number and frequency of offsets varies. These are easily cut loose and potted up. Sections of thicker leaves root in moist soil at 80°F (27°C) in partial sun. Cuttings of partly or completely cylindrical leaves produce pups that are rosettes of leaves bearing no resemblance to the mature plants. Mature plants vary, some producing pups with a maturely formed leaf; others start out as simple leaf rosettes. A few smaller, cylindrical leaf plants develop branches between the leaves of the rosette that, in nature, elongate and eventually root when they come into contact with the soil. These can be cut off when relatively short and planted in moist soil like other cuttings.

In general small, shallow pots are sufficient, but

allowance must be made for the taller plants that can become top heavy. Speed of growth varies, but all are relatively slow in comparison with most other plants.

Plants with Normal Leaves.

They are usually thick, waxy surfaced and shiny.

S. aethiopica. Rosettes of up to 30 stiff, blue-green, pointed-strapshaped leaves, 12 × ½″ (30 × 1.25 cm), the tip 1″ (2.5 cm). The reddish edges are somewhat rolled inward. Surface mottled with light and dark green horizontal bands.

S. arborescens (bagamaylensis). Colonies of erect stems to 3′ (90 cm) high. Spiraled leaves, 3 to a turn, stalkless, thick, stiff, lanceshaped, to 8 × ½″ (20 × 1.25 cm) indoors, the edges brown. The stems are easily divided but look their best when growing in a clump. A quick grower, offsetting frequently. Unique in the genus.

S. aubrytyana (?). Leaves swordshaped like *S. trifasciata* but broader. The dark green surface is profusely mottled with lighter, oval spots.

S. dooneri. Rosettes of flat, narrow-swordshaped, arching leaves to 12 × ½″ (30 × 1.25 cm), tan-green. Thin. Good basket plant with several cultivars.

S. ehrenburgii. A magnificent plant that is exasperatingly slow in growth and therefore both rare and costly. Starts as a rosette of thick, swordshaped leaves. Leaves 12 or more on one shoot, arranged opposite each other like a fan, to 4½′ × 3″ (1.35 m × 7.5 cm), stiffly folded in a V along the midrib for the entire length. Keep quite dry except when obviously growing. Partial to full sun.

S. guinensis (?) *variegata.* Grown for its superb variegation. The thick, channeled pseudo-stalk to 1′ (30 cm) widening gradually to the 1′ × 3″ (30 × 7.5 cm) blade; gray-green with broad golden border and fine golden stripes near center. Very slow growing and sensitive to overwatering. Pot snugly.

S. kirkii (metallica). Striking rosettes of up to 7, flat-spreading, undulating, very hard-textured, stiff leaves, 15 × 3″ (37.5 × 7.5 cm), gorgeously mottled gray-green, beige and tan. The flat flower cluster on an erect, long stalk is the finest in the genus. Very slow growing. It somewhat resembles an oversize *Cryptanthus.*

S. parva. Leaves thick, in a rosette of 6–10, max. 15 × ½″ (37.5 × 1.25 cm), sides curved upward to form a channel. The fused tip is 3″ (7.5 cm) long. Runners are thin and long. An excellent basket plant. Offshoots grow out of the sides and bottom.

S. trifasciata. The common Snake Plant. This is by far the most popular species because of its large, decorative leaves and trouble-free culture. Colors, markings and dimensions of the leaves are affected by slight changes in the environment or treatment. Even single individuals produce offsets different from the parent. Thus there are numerous variations.

The "normal" plant has leaves growing in a rosette of 6–8 leaves, swordshaped, the bottom end narrowing and clasping; waxy surfaced, tough, gray to light, medium or dark green with alternating, zigzag, light and dark colored bands. A fairly quick grower with frequent offsets. Use shallow, snug pots at first to force offshoots close to parents. Increase width when pot-bound. Tolerant of shade, low temperatures and general neglect.

'Futura', 'Moonshine', 'Moonglow', etc., are gray with few or no darker bands; max. 2′ × 3–4″ (60 cm × 7.5–10 cm). Very showy at first but turning dull green as the leaves age. The plants were common a few years ago but less so recently.

'Laurentii'. Thicker, broader and more waxy than the species with a broad, yellow border. Popular and easy. The clones with broader yellow bands are very striking.

Dwarf Cvs. They generally go by the name of 'Hahnii' for the originator. They are rosettes max. 6″ (15 cm) high, tightly cusped, with broad leaves no more than 5″ (12.5 cm) long.

'Hahnii' is marked like a typical *S. trifasciata.*

'Golden Hahnii'. One of the showiest of dwarf foliage plants. Yellow, striped in various amounts of gray-green. Grows slowly and must be watered sparingly. Partial sun.

'Silver Hahnii'. Leaves gray with a few dark bands. Occasionally pure gray plants turn up.

S. zeylanica. A doubtful label used frequently for plants similar to *S. trifasciata.*

Leaves Partly or Entirely Cylindrical.

However fully fused into a tube shape, all these leaves must clasp other leaves or stems for support and therefore widen suddenly at the base. They run the gamut of channeling from half way up the leaf to no more than the spread at the bottom. Many plants are transitional forms and have not been definitely identified though they may carry names applied by the nurseryman.

When the cylindrical form is complete the leaf is like a stiff piece of cable, frequently with an exceedingly hard point. At maturity the cross section may be round or oval with the surface smooth or grooved. Some are solid green and others banded light and dark.

S. canaliculata. Two or more dark green, cylindrical leaves per growth; to 30″ (75 cm) long, ¾″ (18.5 mm) thick. Marked with deep vertical channels. Tip very sharp. Spiraled. Flower stalk short.

S. cylindrica. Leaves 6–16, to 3′ (90 cm) long. Smooth, marked with horizontal light and dark bands.

'Patula'. Leaves opposite, layered, to 4′ (1.20 m) or more. A fantastic sculptural plant. We have grown a specimen with 20 opposite leaves, considerably more than it is supposed to have.

S. gracilis. Leaves in rosettes of 8–10, spiraled, 12–15″ (30–37.5 cm) long, ½″ (12.5 mm) or less thick. Channeled below, cylindrical above with a sharp point. A confused species, some plants in trade being different.

S. singularis. Starts out as a short, rosette plant, very thick, rough surfaced and channeled; richly banded and with a dark edge. They are very handsome at this stage. Mature cylindrical leaves are erect, produced singly in a more or less straight line. They attain 6′

(1.80 m) in height.

S. stuckyii. A grab bag for medium length-leaved plants not labeled *S. cylindrica.* Arranged in a spiral or opposite in a fan. Oval in cross-section. Usually there are 6–12 leaves, finely grooved, 2′ (60 cm) long with a hard, short point.

S. suffruticosa. Cylindrical stem to 15″ (37.5 cm), with 15–18 spiraled, 2′ (60 cm) leaves with exceedingly hard, sharp tips.

This is only a sampling of the type.

Dwarfs. There now exists a whole tribe of more or less cylindrical-leaved plants, some of dwarf size, that have not been identified. Many of these bear only the explorers' names, most notably Bally and Lavranos and their collection numbers. Some are very handsome with unusually bright coloring of alternating bands in light and dark green.

Schismatoglottis. **Araceae.** Drop Tongue. Tropical Asia and the Americas. Herbs. Filtered to partial sun. 300–600 fc. Min. 60°F (16°C). Humidity min. 60%. Packaged Houseplant Medium. Propagation from offshoots. 100 species of which about 6 grown indoors.

Plants attributed to the genus are in a sort of limbo between other aroid genera and seemingly closest to Homalomenas. The specific distinction seems to be a very thin-textured spathe that drops immediately leaving the spadix naked. Culture is as for *Anthurium.*

S. calyptrata. Runners creeping. Stalks erect to 20″ (50 cm), the sheaths pinkish. Blades heartshaped, 6–10″ (15–25 cm) long and half as wide.

S. neoguinensis. Blades broader than the above and thinner. Irregularly blotched with light green or yellow.

S. ornata. To 8″ (20 cm). Blades heartshaped, to 6 × ½″ (15 × 3.75 cm), velvety, dark green with a gray-green midvein. Stalks to 6″ (15 cm).

S. picta. Painted Tongue. Similar to *S. calyptrata* but with larger leaves; lanceshaped to 8 × 5″ (20 × 12.5 cm) with center and edge feathered dark green enclosing a longitudinal gray area of varying width.

S. rutteri. Lanceshaped to triangular blades, 12 × 6″ (30 × 15 cm). Bright green. Stalks to 12″ (30 cm).

S. picta. Painted Tongue. Similar to *S. calyptrata* but with broader, larger leaves, that are 10–18″ (25–45 cm) long, lanceshaped or oval-pointed, 8 × 5″ (20 × 12.5 cm) with center and edge feathered dark green enclosing longitudinal gray area of varying widths.

S. rutteri. Lanceshaped to triangular blades to 12 × 6″ (30 × 15 cm). Bright green. Stalks 12″ (30 cm).

Scindapsus (Epipremnum). **Araceae.** Malay Archipelago. Vines. Shade. 150 fc. Temperature min. 65°F (18.5°C). Humidity 50%. Packaged Houseplant Medium. Propagation from stem cuttings. Easy. 20 species of which at least one grown indoors.

S. pictus. A thin-stemmed vine to 30′ (9 m), but usually grown in small pots. Leaves broadly heartshaped to 5″ (12.5 cm) long, velvety green with irregular gray-green markings. Var. *argyraeus;* Leaves

to 2½″ (6.25 cm), the surface velvety and the splotches silvery. The form commonly grown Probably a juvenile form.

A popular, easily grown plant for low-light situations. Fertilize occasionally with 20-20-20 and keep moist. High humidity is not necessary for ordinary maintenance.

It is attractive for trellised wall coverings and the edgings of balconies.

'Aluminum Leaf'. Possibly a species. Described as being a long vine with "waxy, silvery-turquoise leaves."

'Exotica'. Possibly a species. Smooth, lanceshaped, 3″ (7.5 cm) long, leathery blades, bright gray with dark green along the depressed midvein and in irregularly distributed streaks.

'Siamense'. Leaves heartshaped. Veins depressed resulting in tubular quilting. Silver with uneven dark green stripes along the midrib and random spotting elsewhere.

Senecio. **Compositae.** Worldwide. Leafy herbs, vines and succulents. Partial to full sun. 500–1,000 fc. Temperature min. 50°F (10°C). Houseplant Mix #2. Propagation stem or leaf cuttings and seed. Easy to difficult. As many as 3,000 species of which some 50 or more are grown indoors.

Senecio is mainly a flowering genus similar to many other daisylike plants of the family. *Cineraria (Senecio × hybridus)* is a standard florists' gift plant in the spring. As an indoor foliage genus it is of limited importance. There are only two leafy vines worth mentioning. The large number of succulent species are primarily grown by hobbyists. Of the latter we will describe a few.

Leafy Vines.

S. macroglossus. Wax Vine. The thick, waxy leaves are very similar in shape to some Ivies. Leaves triangular, 2½″ (6.25 cm) long, usually with 3 acute-angled lobes. Stalks to 2″ (5 cm). Stems pink. Bears showy, yellow, daisy flowers in bright light.

'Medio-picta'. Center of leaf with an area of bright yellow.

'Variegatus'. Bordered with creamy yellow.

They are not as tolerant of cold as true Ivies, and more sensitive to improper watering. During the warm months keep evenly moist. In winter allow the soil to dry out between waterings. Fertilize sparingly with a high nitrate formula—every 6 weeks in summer and not at all in winter. The plants are subject to spider mite and mealybug infestation. A handsome basket plant but very temperamental. Keep cool in summer.

S. mikanoides. German Ivy. South Africa. Vigorous vine, also resembling *Hedera.* Leaves with 5–7 acute angled lobes and broadly notched at the base; 2½–3″ (6.25–7.5 cm) long. Stalks to 6″ (15 cm). It survives 40°F (4°C). The leaves are very shapely. The stems can be trimmed to make a small shrub for a pot. However its need for cool conditions in summer (not over 80°F (27°C) makes it difficult for most. This probably accounts for its lack of popularity.

221

Cuttings of both species grow roots in water or barely moist sterilized sand.

Thick-leaved Succulents.

The succulent Senecios, now including all the former genus *Kleinia,* are very numerous. Some rely on their stems for water storage while others depend on their leaves. We list only the latter. All are pot plants of low stature. Newly acquired plants should be watched for signs of season reversal, in which case they will be dormant in summer and active in winter. Older strains, not recently imported, have usually adjusted to our season.

All prefer partial to full sun, a sandy medium with some peat and very careful watering. Do not water when leaves are plump. Allow the soil to dry between waterings. Fertilizer is not advisable indoors. Leaves and stem cuttings with leaves attached root in slightly moistened sand but only during the growing season. The erect plants described here rarely achieve the size indoors of those grown in the wild.

S. articulatus. Stems and branches gray-green, fleshy, consisting of cylindrical sections to 6 × ½″ (15 × 1.25 cm), easily broken apart at the narrowed joints. Leaves spiraled at branch tips; blades 2″ (5 cm) long, 3 segmented, the middle 3-lobed and acutely angled, the 2 side ones oval-pointed. Stalks 1½″ (3.75 cm) long. Plants grow to 10–12″ (25–30 cm) indoors.

S. berbertonensis. A small, branching plant, usually no taller than 6″ (15 cm). The dense clusters of nearly white, very narrow, cylindrical leaves at the branch tips, resemble sea anemones. Each leaf to 2″ (5 cm) long and curved upward. This lovely little plant is extremely delicate and demands the most expert attention to watering. Grow cool.

S. fulgens possesses a tuberous root that can be raised above soil level for show. Leaves spiraled, spoonshaped, 3 × 1″ (7.5 × 2.5 cm) or somewhat longer. The green surface is violet tinted.

S. galpinii. Similar to but taller than the above. Leaves grayish-powdery, 4–6″ (10–15 cm) long. Stem finger thick.

S. implexus and *S. jacobsenii.* Both from Kenya. Creepers with longish stems to 20″ (50 cm), with thick, stalkless, spoonshaped leaves, gray-green; 1–2¼″ (2.5–5.6 cm) for *implexus* and twice as big for *jacobsenii.* Very pretty trailing from a small pot.

S. medley-woodii. Small shrub having reddish stems covered with wool. Leaves spiraled, thin, light green with a purplish gray dusting, spoonshaped, the upper end delicately toothed.

S. scaposus. Much like *S. berbertonensis* but with fewer leaves, somewhat flattened at the wider tip. Young leaves are covered with cobwebby hairs. Adult leaves without them and dark green.

S. tropaeolifolius. Roots tuberous. Stems leafy. Blades like those of nasturtiums with the stalk attached near the center; 1″ (2.5 cm) in diameter; shallowly 8 sided with small, reddish teeth at the angles. Stalks to 2″ (5 cm).

With Beadshaped Leaves. All are wiry-stemmed creepers bearing fleshy, beadlike leaves at the closely set joints. In baskets or pots the stems trail over the sides like a beaded fringe. The unique leaves are fleshy, mostly green, with parallel, translucent lines marking the surface. Long-stalked white flowers have a short season.

S. citriformis. Leaves cylindrical in cross-section, elliptical in outline, like a lemon. To ¾″ (18.5 mm) long.

S. herreianus (or herreanus). Stems to 15″ (37.5 cm). Leaves cylindrical, ⅝ × ⅜″ (15.5 × 9.25 mm). Sometimes tinted with red.

S. radicans. Leaves cylindrical in cross-section, broad at the base and narrowing to the point; 1″ (2.5 cm) long, like a high-domed acorn.

S. rowleyanus. String of Pearls. Frequently seen in the shops. Leaves round, green, ⅜″ (9.25 mm) in diameter. Stems hang to 1′ (30 cm).

Serissa. **Rubiaceae.** Southeast Asia. Small shrub. Filtered to partial sun. 400 fc. Temperature min. 55°F (13°C) 12 hrs. daily. Packaged Houseplant Medium. Propagation from cuttings. Fairly easy. 1 species.

Serissa foetida. A favorite bonsai shrub. Much branched to 1′ (30 cm). Leaves elliptical to ¾″ (18.5 mm) long with very short stalks. The side of the blade are raised over the midrib. Flowers small, white.

'Pink'. Pink flowers.

'Snow Rose'. The white flowers are double.

'Variegata'. Edges of blade unevenly white.

Setcreasia. **Commelinaceae.** Mexico. Straggling herb. Partial to full sun. 500–900 fc. 15 hrs. daily. Temperature min. 50°F (10°C). Packaged Houseplant Medium. Propagation from cuttings. Easy. 6 species; 1 grown indoors.

S. pallida. Leaves elliptical to lanceshaped, stalkless, to 6 × 1″ (15 × 2.5 cm), distantly spiraled and clasping the thin, canelike stems. The whole plant green to deep purple and with sparse long hairs. Requires cool winters. Max. 78°F (26°C) by day, lower at night. The small flowers are pink to purple.

'Purple Heart'. Reliable purple variety.

'Purple Scimitars'. Stem erect and leaves shorter. Blue flowers.

'Tampicana'. As large as the species but the purple with a bronze sheen.

The cultivars make good basket plants but require bright light. They bloom mostly in winter.

Siderasis. **Commelinaceae.** Brazil. Low herb. Shade to filtered sun. 100–500 fc. 12 hrs. daily. Temperature min. 65°F (18.5°C). Humidity min. 60%. Packaged Houseplant Medium. Propagation by offsets. Moderately difficult. 1 species.

S. fuscata. Stemless herbs with few-leaved rosettes of closely packed, horizontally carried leaves, elliptic to 8 × 3–4″ (20 × 7.5–10 cm), brown with a rusty red plush surface and a broad silver band down the midrib. An aristocratic plant for terrarium conditions. Fertilize once a month in the warm season with high nitrate formula. Colonizes by means of short runners. Separate new plants and pot up. The small, 3-petalled, purplish flowers grow at the base of the leaves.

Soleirolia. (*Helxine*). **Urticaceae.** Baby's Tears. Mediterranean. Creeping ground cover. Shade. 100 fc. 12 hrs. daily. Temperature min. 50°F (10°C). Humidity min. 50%. Packaged Houseplant Medium or Sterilized Garden Soil. Propagation by division. Fairly easy. 1 species.

S. soleirolii. Charming and relatively easy little, mat-forming plant. Blades alternate, ¼" (6.25 mm), kidneyshaped, lively green on short stalks. It spreads rapidly and is easily divided. A good, decorative covering for soil in larger pots. Must be kept moist and rather cool. Safer in a covered container.

Sonerila. **Melastomataceae.** Tropical Asia. Low creeping terrarium herb. 400 fc. 14 hours daily. Temperature 70–80°F (22–27°C). Humidity min. 65%. Houseplant Mix #2 with lime. Propagation from stem cuttings. Difficult. More than 100 species of which 1 grown indoors.

S. margaritacea. Exquisite, very tender herb. Blades lanceshaped to broadly elliptical, $4 \times 1''$ (10×2.5 cm), facing upward; rich silver between the intricately patterned veins; purple below.

'Argentea'. Leaves wine red, veined with silvery pink between.

'Hendersonii'. Leaves reddish with silver spots.

This is strictly a terrarium plant.

Spathiphyllum. **Araceae.** Mostly tropical America. Leafy herbs. Shade to partial sun. Min. 100 fc. 12 hrs. daily. Temperature min. 60°F (16°C). Houseplant Mix #3. Propagation by division. Cast Iron. 35 species; 8 or 10 in cultivation.

Of all the aroids, Spathiphyllums are the most versatile in meeting the need for large-leaved plants of medium height and spread. They can be used individually or in masses with imposing effect for many different situations. Though Aglaonemas, the only competition, have more colorful leaves, in most other respects Spathiphyllums are superior. Especially in commercial plantings their use has usually been dictated by the appropriateness of their foliage rather than their white spathe flowers. They are amazingly tolerant and tough. We know of plants growing for long periods in restaurants under weak ceiling illumination. They thrive in windows with northern exposures.

Short stems bear long-stalked leaves in tight spirals. The stalks are stiff, the blades long and flexible, curving over gracefully and thereby keeping even the largest plants under 3' in height indoors. Expanding by means of short runners they are easily kept under control by the simple expedient of removing the newer growths, which can be potted up separately.

Given a little attention to their needs they respond with a tremendous display of lush foliage. An organic soil, warmth, regular moisture and some daylight or artificial light is all they need. Low humidity does little harm, though 50% produces richer, larger leaves. Fertilizer is unnecessary, but a monthly feeding with a balanced formula speeds growth and contributes to a healthy appearance.

Hybridization has been rampant and the effects not all beneficial. Recent cultivars are a mixed lot, some of which lack the former ability to withstand abuse. Improper culture results in plants with weak root systems. Both amateurs and professionals should beware of spaced-out joints and lax leaf blades indicating forcing. It is best to stick to the old cultivars until the new ones have been well tested under adverse conditions.

S. blandum. Blades elliptic, $12 \times 4''$ (30×10 cm). Stalks 12" (30 cm).

S. cannifolium. Blades spoonshaped, $15 \times 5''$ (37.5×12.5 cm), rounded toward the top, stalks to 15" (37.5 cm).

S. cochlearisphathum and *friedrichsthalii.* Similar, large plants, rarely grown. The first to 5' (1.5 m), the blades oblong to 30" (75 cm), the depressed veins horizontal. The second smaller, with elliptic leaves 15" (37.5 cm) long, the veins ascending.

S. floribundum. The source of many cultivars. Leaves closely spiraled, the blades of good substance, $1'' \times 4½''$ (30×11.25 cm), elliptical, fluted near the stalk, which is 8" (20 cm) in length. Blades face upward, the surface velvety green.

'Variegatum Mini'. 6–8" (15–20 cm) high with blades to 5", elliptical, a broad, brushed whitish band down the midrib. It has been found difficult to maintain for long.

S. kochii. Like *S. blandum,* but leaves rounded at both ends.

The following cultivars are among those most frequently seen in the shops.

'Clevelandii'. The basic florists' *Spathiphyllum,* notable for its lush foliage and vigorous growth. Long lasting and exceedingly tolerant.

'Duchess'. A large-leaved, sturdy hybrid of 'Mauna Loa' and *S. wallisii* (?).

'Marion Wagner'. A large-leaved hybrid of *S. cochlearisphathum* and 'Clevelandii'.

'Mauna Loa'. Similar to 'Clevelandii' but the leaves $15 \times 4½''$ (37.5×11.25 cm).

There are several new, promising dwarf cultivars.

Stenotaphrum. **Graminiae.** Circumglobal tropics and subtropics. Colonizing grass. Partial to full sun. 600–1,000 fc. 15 hrs. daily. Temperature min. 40°F (4°C). Sterilized Garden Top Soil. Houseplant Mix #1 with sand plus lime. Propagation by division and rooting at the joints. 6 species, 1 grown indoors.

S. secundatum. St. Augustine Grass. Branching grass, the leaves opposite. Blades strapshaped to $4 \times ¼''$ (10 cm $\times$ 6.25 mm). Tips blunt. It grows like Basket Grass (*Oplismenus*). Stalks to 3", clasping stems.

'Variegatum'. Blades striped with white.

Attractive in a basket in bright light. Plant several to a basket. Joints root and tufts can be separated. Dry between waterings. Feed monthly with 15-30-15. It needs good air movement. Individual tufts are not long lasting and must be replaced.

Strelitzia. **Strelitziaceae.** Subtropical S. Africa. Both herbaceous and treelike. Filtered to partial sun. 400–800 fc. Humidity min. 50% Temperature min. 50°F (10°C). Houseplant Mix #3. Propagation by division. Not difficult if sufficient space available. 3 species, all cultivated.

Strelitzias are favorite cut flowers and popular with greenhouse growers. They are rarely grown beyond the juvenile state indoors because of their size and rarely bloomed there, despite advertisements to the contrary—except in the Deep South. Their importance as decorative foliage plants is mainly in set plantings or in tubs in public places where the leaves create an exotic effect. They are valuable as a climax for arrangements of aroids. Being of heavy substance, the leaves last rather better than many other, more shade-tolerant, tropicals.

S. alba and *nicolai* are similar, the latter growing much taller. Both have trunks to 18' (5.40 m) or more with 4' (1.20 m) rounded oblong leaves on long, stiff stalks.

S. reginae is stemless, spreading with clumps of 3' (90 cm) leaves, 6" (25 cm) wide, rounded-oblong, grayish beneath. Leaves spread in a fairly symmetrical pattern which is very ornamental and is proving excellent for focal points of arrangements of aroids and similar foliage material.

Strobilanthes. **Acanthaceae.** Burma, Assam. Small shrubs. Filtered sun. 400 fc. 14 hrs. daily. Temperature min. 65°F (18.5°C). Humidity min. 50%. Packaged Houseplant Medium. Propagation by stem cuttings. Fairly easy. Possibly 300 species of which 2 or 3 grown indoors.

S. dyeranus. Persian shield. Narrowly elliptical leaves to 6" (15 cm) long, finely toothed; ascending and transverse veins, the space between the latter quilted, the surface rich purple, the quiltings iridescent blue. Must be kept warm. A beautiful plant but branches with difficulty.

'Exotica' Still narrower blades, long-pointed at both ends, the markings very prominent.

S. isophyllus. Willowleaf Persian Shield. A still more leggy plant grown for the lavender-blue flowers.

S. lactatus (maculatus). Possibly a *S. dyeranus* variety. The blades blue-green with silver plumes on either side of the midrib. To 8" (20 cm) high, the leaves tightly spiraled. Low light tolerant.

Stromanthe. **Marantaceae.** Tropical South America. 10 species of which 2 or 3 grown indoors.

See *Calathea* for culture. These plants are partially dormant in winter.

S. amabilis (?) (possibly *Ctenanthe amabilis*) Blades oblong with rounded corners to 6" (25 cm) long. Gray, upward-curved bands following the veins against a green background. Grayish beneath. Stalks in an Iris arrangement.

S. porteana. To 6' (1.80 m). Blades oblong to 1' × 5" (30 × 12.5 cm). Green with silvery lateral veins; purple beneath.

S. sanguinea. To 5' (1.5 m). Blades oblong, 20 × 6" (50 × 15 cm), green above, purple beneath.

Synadenium. **Euphorbiaceae.** Southern Africa. Leafy shrub. Partial sun. 500 fc 12 hours daily. Temperature min 50°F (10°C). Humidity 50%. Houseplant Mix #1 with sand. Fairly easy. 13 species, one grown indoors.

S. grantii. African Milkbush. Shrub to 3' (90 cm) indoors. Leaves spoonshaped 4–6" (10–15 cm) long. Stalk very short.

'Rubra'. Leaves dull red. The plant that is usually grown.

Prune early on to cause branching. Heavy drinker. Keep moist, but not wet. High nitrate fertilizer monthly in summer. Partially dormant in winter.

A good-looking, sturdy shrub but not suitable for commercial plantings indoors except in permanent garden installations with natural light.

Syngonium (*Nephthytis*). **Araceae.** Tropical America. Vines. Shade to filtered sun. Min. 100 fc. 12 hrs daily. Temperature min. 60°F (16°C). Humidity 30–60%. Packaged Houseplant Medium or Houseplant Mix #1. Propagation from cuttings. Easy. 20 species of which 7–10 grown indoors.

As is the case with so many other vining aroids, these are grown indoors mostly as young plants. The leaves at this stage are shieldshaped, heartshaped, 3-segmented halberdshaped; in short, with considerable variation. The genus name *Nephthytis* persists in the trade for shieldshape-leaved plants.

At the time when cedar and tree fern slabs and stakes were popular, *Syngonium podophyllum* vied with Philodendrons for public favor. Now the plants are most often seen in small pots, and the larger ones have almost disappeared.

They are rapidly growing vines with tendrils and rather spaced-out joints. They can be pruned to some degree but soon become woody and deteriorate unless allowed to grow on a support. Recently plants with almost entirely white blades have become popular but cannot be maintained for long, the leaves lacking substance and being very subject to disease. Most revert to green later on. The normally green-leaved plants are tolerant of low light and a great deal of neglect.

It was ease of culture that attracted attention to Syngoniums in the first place and that continues to be their greatest advantage. They can be maintained in a north window and under fluorescent light. High humidity produces larger leaves, but dry air causes little damage. To slow growth it is advisable to fertilize sparingly (once a month with a balanced formula) and keep in small containers until potbound. When stems become unmanageable, take cuttings with tendrils at the joints and root in water. Keep the temperature above 60°F (16°C). They will survive lower levels but become vulnerable to fungus.

S. angustatum. Handshaped leaves with 3–5 elliptic segments, the middle one long, to 6" (15 cm) or more on 10" (25 cm) stalks. Veins yellowish. The 3-leaflet stage is often sold as *S. podophyllum.*

'Ruth Fraser'. Rich green leaflets with silvery veins.

S. auritum. Five Fingers. Leaves of 3–5 leaflets, the middle one much larger and the basal ones appearing as wings. They are broader than those of *S. angusttatum* and the midleaflet grows to 10" (25 cm) or more long. Basal leaflets often have little "ears" attached near the stalks.

'Fantasy'. Variegated with pale green to greenish ivory areas.

S. erythrophyllum. Copper Nephthytis. The leaves have 3 leaflets in the adult stage, but the plant is usually seen as a juvenile, with the leaves narrowly arrowshaped, 5" (12.5 cm) long. There are small, roundish basal lobes. Veins radiate from the jointure of stalk and leaf. Coppery surfaced and reddish beneath. Not spiraled but separated along the stem. Must trail or be supported.

S. podophyllum. The familiar Arrowhead Vine of the stores, invariably sold as a juvenile and represented by cultivars that are too numerous to list in their entirety. It is tough, undemanding and slow growing in the house. When it becomes too high for a pot it must be supported or pruned.

Adult plants have handshaped leaves with 5–9 leaflets or segments.

Older varieties of *S. podophyllum* have 3 segmented blades to 7" (17.5 cm) long, segment lanceshaped and at least twice the length and width of the basal ones which are scimitarshaped and often twisted. All 3 segments have a vein that parallels the edges. The surfaces are medium green with depressed veins. The low quilting is lighter green with a dusting of darker dots. Depending on the clone and the culture the variation in the shape and the surface features is considerable.

'Albo-variegatum'. White Arrowhead. Leaves shield or arrowshaped to 6" (15 cm) or more. Pure white with green patches.

'Albo-Virens'. A lovely, much neglected plant. First halberdshaped with a narrow cleft, the color light green, close to chartreuse throughout except for a dark vein along the edge. Later the leaves become 3 segmented.

'Gold Butterfly'. Blades irregularly marked with yellow.

'Gordon's Favorite'. Surface lightish green with a dusting of tiny lighter green to gray dots. Veins darker green. Reverts to green rather quickly.

'Green Gold'. The tip segment narrow with a chartreuse center.

'Imperial White'. Center of blade line white with the edge dark green.

'Mottled Arrowhead'. Deep green blade, the tip segment wider than most, mottled with yellow-ochre.

'White Butterfly'. A nearly white dwarf with green edge. Produced in large quantities for market, this is one of those plants that is grabbed by the impulse buyer. It is a weakling that rarely lasts long indoors and, if it does, tends to go green or splotchy. A fine

example of industry touting of a plant easier to grow in the nursery than in the home.

S. standleyanum. Leaves achieve mature phase very early. Leaves matte green, 3-parted. Middle segment elliptic, 10 × 4" (25 × 20 cm). Basal segments spreading, 9 × 3" (22.5 × 7.5 cm), with bottom edge curved.

S. wendlandii. With three leaflets, the middle one 7 × 3" (12.5 × 7.5 cm), lanceshaped. Lower leaflets horizontal, curved below. Mid and side veins prominently silvery. Surface satiny. A very fine species, little grown.

Syzygium (Eugenia). **Myrtaceae.** Southern Asia and Australia. Trees. Filtered to partial sun. Min. 600 fc. 12 hours daily. Temperature min. 50°F (10°C). Houseplant Mix. Propagation from seed or cuttings. Easy. 500 species of which 10–15 grown for ornament or fruit.

S. paniculatum (Eugenia myrtifolia) var. *globulosa.* (?) This variety with variegated leaves is widely grown. Leaves are elliptic, 2 × 1" (5 × 2.5 mm), somewhat waxy; irregularly bordered with white. Young plants are shrubby. The species, *S. paniculatum,* is more leafy and lightish green with brown branches. Frequently used for bonsai. Treat with high-first-number fertilizer.

Several other Syzygiums are similar and turn up as juvenile pot plants.

Tamarindus. **Leguminosae.** Tamarind. India. Partial sun. 600 fc. 12 hours daily. Temperature min. 60°F (16°C). Sterilized Garden Soil. Cactus & Succulent Mix #2. Propagation from seeds. Easy. One species.

The jellylike filling of the large seed pods is used in chutneys and, with sweetening, as a refreshing drink. The young trees are highly decorative for mass plantings as fine background screening material.

Plant the large seeds in moist milled sphagnum moss as they are very subject to mildew. Once rooted and potted up, the plant grows well and can be pruned. Keep evenly moist and fertilize with high-middle-number formula with every other watering. It is occasionally attacked by spider mites.

T. indica. An 80' (24 m) tree with compound leaves consisting of up to 18 opposite pairs of 1" (2.5 cm) oblong leaflets.

Tetrapanax. **Araliaceae.** Rice Paper Plant. China, Taiwan. Shrub. Filtered to partial sun. 150–600 fc. 12 hours daily. Temperature min. 45°F (7°C). Houseplant Mix #3. Propagation from cuttings. Rather difficult. 1 species.

T. papyriferus. A single-stemmed plant with roundish leaf blades facing upward; about 15" (37.5 cm) in diameter. The pointed, partly jagged, lobes 5–15 and finely toothed. White felted beneath. When young, rusty with age. Stalks stiff, to 2' (60 cm).

This is a cool-growing plant, preferring max. 80°F (27°C). Fertilize with high nitrate formula once a month. Does not take kindly to trimming.

'Variegatus'. Splotched here and there with white.

Tetrastigma. **Vitaceae.** Tropical and subtropical Asia. Vines. Filtered sun. 300 fc. 14 hrs. daily. Humidity min. 40%. Temperature min. 60°F (16°C). Propagation from cuttings. Cast Iron. 90 species of which 3 or 4 grown indoors.

T. harmandii. Philippines. Big climbing tendriled vine. Leaves irregularly handshaped with 3–7 lanceshaped leaflets, 6 × 2″ (15 × 5 cm) strung along at the end of 1′ (30 cm) stalks. Finely and distantly toothed.

T. obovatum. So. China. Brown-felted, handshaped leaves with 5 leaflets to 8″ (20 cm) long, spoonshaped, wavy edged, the veins depressed.

T. voinierianum. Chestnut Vine. Viet Nam. Coarse, big vine with drooping, brown-hairy branches. Leaves handshaped with 5 leaflets, broadly oval, toothed, drooping; to 8 × 3″ (20 × 7.5 cm), pale green, fuzzy beneath. A very impressive basket plant.

Suitable for large baskets and for covering trellised walls in relatively low light. Very vigorous and must be kept trimmed. Provide a high nitrate fertilizer and keep constantly moist.

Tradescantia. **Commelinaceae.** N. & S. America. Herbs. Shade to partial sun. 100–500 fc. 12 hours daily. Temperature min. 55°F (13°C). Humidity min. 40%. Packaged Houseplant Medium. Propagation from cuttings. Easy. At least 20 species of which a half dozen grown indoors.

The tropical Tradescantias are trailers very similar to other small-leaved **Commelinaceae** and are grown mostly in baskets although single plants look well in pots. Even moisture and monthly fertilizing with a balanced formula keep them in good shape. Like all of their kind, they must be trimmed and old plants replaced with new ones as the lower parts of the stems become unsightly. Cuttings root in water and any moist medium. Like the others their leaves are striped and crystalline surfaced, reflecting with a sparkling glow which is very attractive when viewed nearby but is ineffective at a distance. In commercial installations they must be replaced frequently and regroomed.

T. albiflora. Giant Inch Plant. Stems trailing and rooting at the joints. Leaves alternate, hairy, clasping the stems, lanceshaped to 3 × 1″ (7.5 × 2.5 cm), smooth and green above and below. Regarding cultivars we have followed *Hortus Third,* though the trade places them under *T. fluminensis.* It is a moot question as to who is right.

'Albovittata'. Blades finely striped with white.

'Aurea'. Blades light yellow.

'Aureo-striata'. With yellow stripes.

'Laekenensis'. Light green, striped with white and purple.

'Variegata'. Striped with yellow and white.

There are many variations in width of stripings and colors.

T. blossfeldiana. Flowering Inch Plant. Despite the common name and the pretty white and purple flowers, it is grown principally for its foliage. Stems trailing, purplish and white hairy. Leaves stalkless, alternate, elliptical to 4 × 1½″ (10 × 3.75 cm), smooth, green above, purplish and hairy beneath.

T. fluminensis. Inch Plant. Like *T. albiflora,* which see. Leaves half the size. Also very similar to *Zebrina pendula.*

T. navicularis. Chain Plant. Smaller than the others and best for pot culture. Leaf blades, thick, alternate, clasping the stem in a stepladder fashion; partly folded down the midrib; 1″ (2.5 cm) long. Requires less water than the others and partial sun.

T. sillamontana. White Velvet Plant. Mexico. Stems thick, to 10″ (25 cm). Leaves clasping like *T. navicularis,* but broadly lanceshaped, 2½ × 1″ (6.25 × 2.5 cm). The whole plant is gray-green because of the heavy cobwebbing of all parts. A pot plant. Keep cool in winter.

Trevesia. **Araliaceae.** Southern Asia. Large-leaved shrubs or small trees. Filtered to partial sun. 400–800 fc. 14 hours daily. Temperature 60–80°F (16–27°C). Humidity min. 60%. Houseplant Mix #3 or sphagnum moss. Propagation by seeds or cuttings. Difficult. Four species of which 3 grown indoors.

If Trevesias were more adaptable, their magnificently designed leaves would make them instant favorites for large tropical plantings. Unfortunately, they are difficult to grow in commercial quantities, difficult to ship and store and a challenge for amateur growers to maintain for long.

The seed has a very short viability, requiring shipment in moist packing and immediate sowing on arrival. Heel cuttings root readily in terrarium conditions. Subject to spider mites.

Fertilize with 20-20-20 at every watering. Keep constantly moist. Because of the single stem from which the leaf stalks grow directly, pruning is not advisable. Growth is quite rapid.

They might be considered for southern plantscapes, with pools providing high humidity.

T. burckii (T. sanderi). Shrub to 5′ (1.5 m). Very leafy, the blades very similar to *T. palmata,* but parts of the compound leaves are waved and crinkled; 2′ (60 cm) in diameter.

T. palmata. Snowflake Plant. Tree to 20′ (6 m). The compound up-facing leaves are magnificent and most difficult to describe. Each leaflet is broadly lanceshaped and divided into 5–9 jagged lobes. The 2 lower ones are rounded at the base. Below the blades of the segments, the midribs are connected by a broad tissue, like the feet of a duck. Stalks to 2½′ (75 cm). Young leaves are felted and light in color.

Var. *micholitzii* has nearly white young leaves.

Grow in a 12″ (30 cm) or larger, pot or tub.

T. sundaica. Small tree to 25′ (7.5 m). Stalks to 3′ (90 cm) bearing leaves 2½′ (75 cm) in diameter with 9 leaflets, elliptic or sometimes fiddleshaped, with several lobes; drooping at the tips.

Triolena. (Bertolonia). Tropical America. Low, leafy herbs. See *Bertolonia* for culture. 50 species, 1 grown indoors.

T. pustulata (Bertolonia pustulata). Low, colonizing

herb; hairy. Leaves broadly elliptic to 5 × 2½″ (12.5 × 6.25 cm). Midrib with two longitudinal veins on either side and many transverse veins, puffed between. Green with a brownish red central stripe.

Tristania. **Myrtaceae.** S.E. Asia and Australia. Shrubs and Trees. Filtered to partial sun. 400–800 fc. 14 hours daily. Temperature min. 50°F (10°C). Houseplant Mix #2 with sand. Propagation from seeds or cuttings. Easy. 20 species of which one grown indoors.

T. conferta. Brisbane Box. Tree to 150′ (45 m) Indoors to 8′ (2.4 m). Leaves spiraled at ends of branches. Blades 6 × 2″ (15 × 5 cm), elliptic with base and tip attenuated. Stalks 2″ (5 cm).

'Aureo-variegata'. Golden yellow variegation in jagged splotches like *Graptophyllum.*

Keep evenly moist and feed with a balanced fertilizer once a month. Underpot and trim for shrubby growth.

The species *lactiflua,* a smaller tree, and *laurina,* a shrub with green leaves also from Australia, might be considered as houseplant and plantscaping material.

Tupidanthus. **Acanthaceae.** Southern Asia. Shrub. Filtered to partial sun. 300–800 fc. Temperature min. 60°F (24°C). Humidity min. 50%. Houseplant Mix #3. Propagation from cuttings. Easy. 1 species.

T. calyptratus. To 12′ (3.6 m), spreading to 5′ (1.5 m) or more. Leaves compound, handshaped, arranged in a circle. Leaflets drooping, 12 × 2″ (30 × 5 cm) with narrow tips. Stalks to 18″ (45 cm). Similar to *Brassaia actinophylla.* An impressive tub plant for large rooms.

Vriesea. **Bromeliaceae.** Tropical America. Rosette herbs. Partial to full sun. 800–1,000 fc. Min. 65°F (18.5°C) 15 hrs. daily. Humidity min. 60%. Terrestrial Orchid Mix. Propagation by offsets. Moderately difficult. 246 species of which at least 30 in cultivation indoors. See *Aechmea* for additional culture.

Vrieseas are remarkable for their long-lasting, showy flowers. *V. splendens,* Flaming Sword, is a favorite florists' gift plant. They are almost equally cherished for their patterned foliage that is most effective in mass plantings where sufficient light and humidity are available. The tight rosettes create the "vases."

We list a few of the most attractive foliage species. There are numerous named hybrids of varying merit.

V. erythrodactylon. Leaves erect to 12 × 1″ (30 × 2.5 cm), swordshaped. Purple or chartreuse with maroon near the base.

V. fenestralis. Handsome, mounded rosettes, the leaves curving out and downward, swordshaped, 15 × 3″ (37.5 × 7.5 cm); pale green with numerous vertical, thin, dark green veins and irregular horizontal hatchings. Spotted with red near the base.

V. fosterana. Leaves spreading, blunt tipped, to 2′ × 3½″ (60 × 8.75 cm). Bluish green, banded with maroon hatchings.

V. guttata. The vase erect; the leaves 10 × 2½″ (25 × 6.25 cm), light green, randomly spotted top and bottom with brown.

V. hieroglyphica. Leaves blunt tipped and straight sided, 18 × 4″ (45 × 10 cm), light green with very dark green zigzag, horizontal bands.

'Marginata'. A magnificent cultivar. The leaves more numerous and decorated with a broad ivory border.

V. imperialis. A huge plant, the leaves growing to 4½″ (1.35 m). Most frequently grown as a juvenile when the blades become red in bright light.

V. simplex rubra. Leaves long elliptical, 14 × 2½″ (35 × 6.25 cm); very curved. Burgundy in bright light.

V. splendens. Flaming Sword. Vase erect with leaves turned down at the tips. Blades 15 × 2½″ (37.5 × 6.25 cm) with a short point at the tip. Green, with distinct, broad, horizontal brown bands. A number of varieties with very sharp patterning are recognized. 'Chantrieri' is especially popular.

V. triangularis. A dwarf plant with an erect, symmetrical vase; the leaves to 8″ (20 cm), olive green, the base maroon and the tips reddish.

Xantheranthemum. **Acanthaceae.** Peru. Filtered to partial sun. 400–800 fc. 12 hrs. daily. Temperature min. 50°F (10°C). Humidity minimum 60%. Houseplant Mix #1 or 2. Propagation by offsets and cuttings. 1 species.

Chamaeranthemum × Eranthemum igneum. Low, colonizing herb with closely set, upward-facing, velvety leaves, 4 × 1½″ (10 × 3.75 cm), oval to spoonshaped, brownish green with red to burnt orange midrib and veins, the design appearing like fish bones. Edges turned down. Stalks short.

Xanthosoma. **Araceae.** Yautia. Malanga. Tropical America. Tuberous herbs. Filtered to partial sun. 400–800 fc. 14 hrs. daily. Temperature 60–80°F (16–27°C). Humidity 60%. Houseplant Mix #3. Propagation by tubers and offsets. Rather difficult. 40 species of which about 8 occasionally grown indoors.

Xanthosoma is closely related to *Caladium,* and some species also produce edible tubers. Keep plants warm and moist but with good air movement. Partially dormant in winter. Fertilize at every watering with 20-20-20 at ¼ strength. Store tubers until they sprout. Offsets can be separated and potted up.

X. atrovirens. Leaf blades heartshaped with a deep, narrow notch, the basal lobes broad, with tips turned outward; to 3′ (90 cm) long but usually much less indoors. Green above, grayish beneath stalks to 2′ (60 cm).

'Albomarginatum' and 'Albo-marginatum monstrosum'. Curious plants. The blades of the first are contorted and bear blotches of white along the edges. The second has the same markings, but, in addition, the edges of the tip are fused forming a triangular sack with an elongated, narrow point. Blades rarely grow more than 6–8″ (15–20 cm) in length. Both are very temperamental and require high humidity.

X daguense. Narrowly arrowshaped blades with a deep notch, to 12″ (30 cm). Stalks twice as long.

X lindenii. Magnificent leaves to 18 × 5″ (45 × 12.5 cm). Somewhat halberdshaped, swelling in the center and narrowed above the basal lobes, the edges turned down. Basal lobes short, broad, curved outward. The wide midrib and side veins are brilliantly white and depressed. The substance is heavy. Stalks as long as the blades.

'Albescens'. Blades narrower and basal lobes somewhat longer.

'Magnificum'. Blades yellow-green; the white veining broader still and reaching to the edges.

This is a superb plant that can be maintained indoors, but only with difficulty. High humidity and moderate warmth must be maintained. Partly dormant in winter.

X sagittifolium. Like *X atrovirens* but the notch broader. Blades to 3′ (90 cm). It produces edible tubers.

X violaceum. Blue Taro. Similar to *A. sagittifolium* but with edges and some veins tinged with violet. Stalks to 5′ (1.5 m). Edible tubers.

Allow ample pot or tub space for the large roots of these plants.

Xenophya. (Schizocasia). **Araceae.** Moluccas and New Guinea. Leafy herb. Filtered to partial sun. 150–400 foot candles, 14 hrs. daily. Temperature min. 55°F (13°C). Humidity min. 60%. Houseplant Mix #3. Propagation by division. Somewhat difficult. 2 species; one in cultivation.

X. lauterbachiana. Tight spirals of erect leaves to 4′ (1.20 m). Blades to 20 × 4″ (50 × 10 cm), swordshaped; each vein tipped by a lobe with an upward curving hook; satiny blue-green above, silvery purple beneath. Stalk stiff, channeled, to 2′ (60 cm) but usually shorter than the blade.

A superb, rarely grown decorative plant. Pups arise at some distance from the mother plant unless a small diameter container is used. Leaves on the stalk grow one out of the other. It is difficult to maintain more than three at a time. A host to mites.

Yucca. **Agavaceae.** Southern U.S.A. and Mexico. Desert trees. Full sun. Temperature min. 45°F (7°C). Cactus & Succulent Mix #2 with lime. Propagation from stems, runners, offsets and roots. 40 species. Several can be grown indoors.

The warm-growing Yuccas look much alike when young and are attractive in desert-style plantings where sufficient sun is provided. A number have variegated cultivars. The species below came into the market in large numbers a few years ago and disappeared equally quickly. The plants were sold for ordinary home use and, without adequate sunlight, slowly deteriorated from the moment they were purchased and installed. A number of Yucca species are still used where conditions permit and as temporary decoration in commercial situations. They must have illumination of at least 1,000 fc.

Y. elephantipes. A branching tree to 30′ (9 m) high. Leaves to 4′ × 4″ (1.20 m × 10 cm). The plants supplied to the market have had stiff, 3′ (90 cm),

swordshaped leaves in compact rosettes.

The semihardy and hardy Yuccas are probably unsuitable for indoor culture.

Zamia. **Zamiaceae.** Subtropical and tropical America. Low, palmlike plants. Filtered to full sun. Min. 500 fc. 12 hrs. daily. Temperature min. 45°F (7°C). Humidity min. 40%. Houseplant Mix #2 with gritty sand. Propagation from offsets. Moderately easy. 40 species of which 8 or more grown indoors.

The family **Zamiaceae** has been separated by some authorities from the **Cycadaceae.** The foliage difference is that the leaflets have more numerous longitudinal veins but no midrib.

The genus consists of plants with very short trunks or even completely submerged in the soil. They have relatively few compound, palmlike leaves. The appearance is both odd and sculpturally attractive. Leaflets show considerable variation in shape.

Keep evenly moist in bright sun during the warm months. Fertilize once a month with high nitrate formula. In winter dry out for a few days between waterings. The plants produce offsets or suckers. Cut free in wintertime or when the plant is not growing, remove the leaves and plant in gritty sand. Keep at 72–80°F (23–27°C) and mist until they sprout new leaves. They spread 3 to 5′ (90 cm to 1.50 m), but make better pot plants than some of their bigger relatives.

Z. angustifolia. Cuba. Short, almost round stem. Leaves to 36″ (90 cm) long. Leaves opposite in 12 to 30 pairs, 10″ (25 cm) long by ½″ (1.25 cm) wide or less. Stalks, wiry, narrow, to 15″ (37.5 cm).

Z. debilis. Trunk cylindrical, 6″ (15 cm) high. Leaves to 30″ (75 cm). Leaflets in 12 to 25 pairs, very narrowly lanceshaped. W. Indies.

Z. fischeri. Mexico. Trunk 8″ (20 cm) high, cylindrical. Leaves to 20″ (50 cm), the stalks short, leaflets alternate, with up to 20 pairs, lanceshaped, 5 × 1″ (12.5 × 2.5 cm). It produces more leaves than most and is a very graceful, compact plant.

Z. floridana. Coontie. Trunk very short. Leaves to 2′ (60 cm) long, upright, with up to 24 pairs of leaflets, 6 × ¼″ (15 cm × 6.2 mm); very stiff and dry in texture. Stalk to 4″ (10 cm)

Z. furfuracea. See *Z. pumila.*

Z. integrifolia. Florida and W. Indies. Trunk 1½′ (45 cm) high. Stalks angled. Leaflets consisting of 6–18 pairs.

Z. kickxii (?). Cuba. Possibly a variety of *Z. pygmaea.* Very short trunk. Leaves to 15″ (37.5 cm) with 10–15 pairs of short, spoonshaped to nearly wedgeshaped leaflets 2 × 1″ (5 × 2.5 cm).

Z. ottonis. Cuba. Similar to *Z. kickxii.* Brownish-fuzzy beneath leaves.

Z. pumila. Florida, Mexico and W. Indies. Trunk to 6″ (15 cm). Leaves to 4′ (1.20 m). As many as 15 pairs of leaflets, mostly lanceshaped but variable; to 6″ (15 cm) long, toothed toward the tip. Stalks finely toothed.

Z. pygmaea. Cuba. Leaves 4 to 10″ (10–25 cm) long. 8 pairs of leaflets, 2 × ½″ (5 × 2.5 cm) long, lanceshaped. The smallest of the cycads.

Zamioculcas. **Araceae.** Tropical Africa. Shade to partial sun. 100–500 fc. 12 hours daily. Temperature min. 50°F (10°C). Humidity 40%. Packaged Houseplant Medium or Houseplant Mix #2. Propagation by division and from leaf cuttings. Cast Iron. One species.

Z. zamiifolia. Leaves to 3' (90 cm) arise directly from tuberous runners. Stalks stout, cylindrical, much thickened toward the base. Leaflets opposite, very leathery, elliptical, in pairs, to 6" (15 cm) long.

Z. lanceolata (?). Probably just a dwarf of the above. Stalks shorter and leaves smaller.

These unique aroids have a rather undisciplined habit. The tuberous roots can be raised for display. The smaller variety is better for pot culture. Drought resistant, but keep moist for healthy leaves. Fertilize 2 or 3 times a year with high nitrate formula.

Separate the tuberous runners and pot up. Handle the plant with care as leaves break off easily. Planted with the base a half inch deep in moist mix they root rapidly.

A very carefree houseplant.

Zebrina. **Commelinaceae.** Inch Plant. Central America. Trailing herbs. Filtered sun. 300 fc. 12 hours daily. Temperature min. 55°F (13°C). Packaged Houseplant Medium. Propagation from cuttings. Easy. 2 species of which one grown indoors.

Zebrina is a basket plant made attractive by the crystalline shimmer of the leaf surfaces and their colored stripings. Keep soil evenly moist as, otherwise, lower leaves turn brown. Fertilize weekly with ⅛-strength balanced formula. It is relatively free from pests. The stems are very watery and weak. Trim when they elongate excessively. Cuttings root in water. Stems and roots are not very long lasting. Pull out the old plants and fill in with rooted cuttings.

Z. pendula. Trailing to 3' (90 cm) root at the joints. Leaves 1–3" (2.5–7.5 cm) long, narrow to broadly lanceshaped, the base clasping the stem; greenish purple with two vertical silver stripes. Purple below.

'Daniel's Hybrid'. Thickish all purple leaves.

'Discolor'. Tricolor Inch Plant. Crystalline green with narrow silver stripes edged purple and tinted red. Leaf somewhat longer. Purple beneath.

'Discolor Atropurpurea'. Leaves purple with delicate silver stripes.

'Discolor multicolor'. Green, striped with very light pink, irregularly spotted with rusty red. Purple beneath.

'Minima'. Leaves half the length of typical *Z. pendula.*

'Quadricolor'. Leaves striped with purple, green, silver, white and soft pink. To 3¼" (8.1 cm) in length.

'Purpusii'. Leaves purplish brown with silver spots.

Some of the cultivars are unstable. Remove stems on which leaves revert to green or to a less definite striping.

FERNS
Fern Culture

Low Light
100–400 footcandles
Alglaomorpha
Alsophila
Asplenium
Cyrtomium
Humata
Lygodium
Polypodium/Campyloneuron
Polypodium/Phlebodium
Polystichum

Cool. 45°F (7°C).
Alsophila
Asplenium (some)
Cyrtomium
Davallia canariensis
Lygodium
Pellaea
Polypodium/Microsorium scandens
Polypodium/Phlebodium
Polypodium/Polypodium
Polystichum
Polypodium/Microsorium
Pteris
Rumohra
Selaginella

High Light
400–800 footcandles
Adiantum
Davallia
Nephrolepis
Pellaea
Polypodium/Microgramma
Polypodium/Microsorium
Polypodium/Polypodium
Pteris
Rumohra
Selaginella

Warm. 60°F (16°C).
Adiantum
Aglaomorpha
Asplenium (some)
Davallia
Drynaria
Humata
Nephrolepis
Platycerium
Polypodium/Campyloneuron
Polypodium/Microgramma

Low Humidity
30–50%
Asplenium
Polypodium/Phlebodium
Polypodium/Polypodium
Pteris (some)
Rumohra

High Humidity
50%+
Adiantum
Aglaomorpha
Alsophila
Davallia
Drynaria
Nephrolepis
Platycerium
Polypodium/Campyloneuron
Polypodium/Microgramma
Polypodium/Microsorium
Polystichum
Pteris (some)
Selagginella

Adiantum. **Polypodiaceae.** Mostly tropical America but worldwide from the tropics to the warm temperate zones. Temperature; half hardy to tropical, the latter min. 55°F (13°C). Humidity min. 50%. Houseplant Mix #2 or equal parts Sterilized Garden Topsoil and well-rotted Leafmold. Propagation from spores and divisions. Moderately difficult. 200 species of which 4 or 5 widely grown and many others by collectors.

The Maidenhair Ferns are marvels of dynamic delicacy. Growing from creeping runners, wiry, blackish stalks carry lanceshaped to swordshaped compound leaves with numerous branchlets and alternate or opposite thin, wedgeshaped or rhombic, irregularly lobed leaflets that float in the air like a Calder "Mobile." They would, undoubtedly, be among the top favorite pot and basket plants were it not for the special environments they require: bright but indirect sunlight; a very porous, organic medium; and high humidity.

The widespread assumption that they are easy is misleading. The culture is confined to greenhouses and terrarium containers except where, as in the South, the natural environment supplies conditions for maintenance in windows or under fluorescent light. In cities with heavy aerial pollution they are doubly difficult to manage. Terrariums then become the only safe environment.

It is said that they suffer in high humidity, but this, we believe, is true only if the correct minimum or maximum temperature, which varies according to the origin, is exceeded. A primary requirement is very even moisture which is achieved in a terrarium or in the open, through frequent watering of a very porous medium. The mix should not be compacted; just take care that air holes are eliminated. The roots, as with most ferns, are sensitive to the burning action of fertilizers. High percentage formulas must be drastically diluted. With *Adiantum* an application once a month during the warm season is sufficient. Apply a high nitrate formula such as 30-10-10 at the rate of ⅛ tsp. per gallon (3.6 liters) of water. Fish emulsion may be used at the rate of ¼ tsp. per gallon.

At least once a year old tufts of root must be removed and replaced with new material. Pack rooted divisions in the bare spaces.

A large number of species and cultivars are stocked by specialist nurseries. As the geographical range of some species is very large, the tenderness or partial hardiness is not always predictable. We can list only a few; mostly those from warmer environments.

A. capillus-veneris. Venus Maidenhair. Circumglobal temperate to tropical. The species has airy flights of wedgeshaped and notched leaflets. Stalks are up to 2′ (60 cm) long and 10″ (25 cm) across. Branchlets to 6″ (15 cm) with 6–8 pairs of leaflets max. 1″ (2.5 cm) across. There are cool- as well as warmgrowing varieties and clones, with a range of 40–80°F (4–27°C) and 55–85°F (13–30.5°C). Check requirements with the grower.

'Fimbriatum', Leaflets broader and more toothed. Stalks more rigid.

'Imbricatum'. Leaflets are frilled and overlapping, forming tighter clusters of foliage.

'Scintilla'. A smaller plant with erect stalks, the leaflets ruffled and toothed.

A. caudatum. Walking Maidenhair Fern. Old World tropics. Leaves 1½′ (45 cm) long, trailing, little branched, the tips elongated terminating with plantlets. Leaflets oblong, bluntly toothed, pale green. Min. 60°F (16°C). Humidity 50%.

A. hispidulum. Australian Maidenhair Fern. Old World tropics. Stalks to 1½′ (45 cm). Leaves consisting of several leaflets in a circle, each 6–12″ (30 cm) long with up to 20 pairs of square subleaflets, pinkish at first, turning green. 50–80°F (10–27°C).

A. macrophyllum. Tropical America. Stalks stiff, erect, to 1′ (30 cm) with 3 × 1½″ (7.5 × 3.75 cm) triangular, leaflets. Virtually unbranched. Typical of a number of larger leafleted species. They are handsome but rarely grown.

A. raddianum. Brazil. Most of the Adiantums in cultivation belong to this species. The many cultivars vary in ease or difficulty of culture and especially in temperature preference. The distinguishing feature of the species, accounting for its popularity, is the tight clustering of the upright stalks and the massing of leaflets on the branchlets of broadly trangular leaves whose weight bends the stems into a graceful curve. Thus the aspect of the total plant is a mound of foliage consisting of incredibly numerous, overlapping, delicate leaflets.

The bare stalks are 6″ (15 cm) or more long. The leaves range, according to cultivar, from 6–12″ (15–30 cm) long and sometimes as wide at the base. Leaflets wedge shaped to 1″ (2.5 cm) across.

Temperature 60–80°F (16–27°C). Humidity min. 60%.

The following cultivars vary in sensitivity and ease or difficulty of culture. There are fine but noticeable differences in growth habit and size and shape of leaves and leaflets.

A. raddianum cvs: 'Californicum'; 'Cardosa Gardens'; 'Decorum'; 'Deflexum'; 'Excelsum'; 'Fragrantissimum'; 'Fritz Luthii'; 'Gracillimum'; 'Ideal'; 'Kensington Gardens'; 'Lawsonianum'; 'Legrandii'; 'Maximum'; 'Ocean Spray'; 'Pacific Maid';

'Pacotti'; 'Pelican'; 'Thread Leaf'; 'Tinctum'; 'Tuffy Tips'; 'Victoria's Elegance'; 'Weigandii'.

A. tenerum. C. America and northern S. America. The compounding of the leaves is similar to that of *A. raddianum,* but the arrangement of stems is looser and the leaflets more fanshaped than regular lobing and crimping, to ¾″ (18.5 cm) in diameter. In some cultivars young growth is pinkish. Culture as for *A. raddianum,* warm growing and suitable for terrariums.

'Farleyense' is larger than others of the species with leaves to 2′ (60 cm) or more, the leaflets and subleaflets crested and pink when young.

A. trapeziforme. Diamond Maidenhair. 3″ (7.5 cm) brilliant green, irregularly diamondshaped leaflets. Leaves drooping.

Aglaomorpha. **Polypodiaceae.** Tropical Asia. Partial sun. 600–800 fc. Temperature min. 60°F (16°C). Humidity min. 50%. Houseplant Mix #3 with sand. Or 4 parts leafmold, 1 part garden topsoil and 1 part sand. Propagation from spores and division. Easy to difficult. 10–15 species of which a few grown indoors.

Aglaomorphas are coarse, tropical ferns growing as erect rosettes with mostly simple segmented stalkless leaves from masses of reddish, furry runners (rhizomes). They live in the joints and on the boughs of trees where the bases act as catch basins for the fallout of vegetable trash which the runners hold firmly in place, building mounds of fibrous material. The lower sections of the leaves are plain; the upper parts coarsely and usually deeply toothed.

Young plants are manageable and attractive in pots. The more mature ones make superb basket plants with a spread of 4–6′ (1.20–1.80 m). They are of relatively easy culture. Dry out completely after thorough waterings. Do not fertilize unless growth slows. At most, apply high nitrogen formula at ⅛th recommended dosage 3–4 times a year. Do not overpot.

A. coronans. Subtropical Asia. Leaves 2–4′ (60 cm–1.20 m) long, erect, the base thick. The upper part of the leaves are divided into alternate segments to 8 × 1½″ (20 × 3.75 cm) with a tip leaflet.

A. heracleum. W. Pacific Islands. Leaves to 6′ (1.80 m), erect. Segments triangular-attenuated.

A. meyeniana. Bear's Paw Fern. Very similar to *A. cornans* but the mass of furry runners very thick and reddish. It must be well dried out after watering. Tolerant of low humidity.

A. pilosa (?). Leaves narrowed at the base are thin and leathery. Not more than 2′ (60 cm) long.

A. superbum(?) (nitidum?). Also sold as *A. pilosa.* Leaves max. 18″ (45 cm), the bases flaring widely and clasping. The surfaces of segments corrugated.

Alsophila (Cyathia) **Cyathaceae.** Mostly Australia and New Zealand. Tree ferns. Filtered to partial sun. Mostly min. 40°F (4°C). Humidity 60%. Sterilized Garden soil with peat. Or Packaged Houseplant Medium. Propagation by spores and sections of trunk. 230 species of which one occasionally grown indoors.

Note: For *A. australis* and *A. cooperi* see *Sphaeropteris*.

A. tricolor (Cyathia dealbata). Silver Tree Fern. New Zealand. To 30' (9 m). Leaves to 6' (1.80 m) Subleaflets at 3" (7.5 cm) the reverse whitish powdered. Stalks and ribs covered with woolly brown scales.

Handsome ferns for large plantings where natural light is available and night temperatures are cool.

The tree ferns are among the most magnificent of tropical foliage plants; the fronds like those of palms but more delicate. A few species are sold as bare chunks of the trunk which sprout when kept moist or partly buried in moist soil. They are short-lived indoors but spectacular decorations while they last. As rooted plants in large containers they are suitable only for spacious indoor plantscapes with sufficient light and high humidity.

Asplenium. **Polypodiaceae.** Spleenwort. Worldwide. Hardy and tropical ferns. Filtered to partial sun. 300–800 fc. Tropical species 50–80°F (10–27°C). 12 hrs daily. Houseplant Mix #3. Propagation by spores and division. Most rather difficult. 700 species, but few of which grown indoors.

Asplenium is a very large and extraordinarily varied genus with species as different from each other as Bird's-nest Fern (with simple, unsegmented leaves) and the Mother Fern (divided subleaflets). Very demanding of specific environments and care.

With simple leaves.

A. nidus (nidus-avis). Tropical America and western Pacific. Symmetrical rosette of simple leaves growing from a fibrous mass. Leaves spoonshaped to 3' × 6", green, shiny, edges wavy. The center of the circle of leaves is a black, fibrous knob. A popular and easy plant to maintain but subject to browning of leaf edges unless high humidity is maintained. It is a slow drinker and should not be watered until at least ¾ dry. Fertilize once a month with a balanced formula at ¼ recommended dilution. Temperature range 50–80°F (10–27°C). Filtered sun to 400 fc.

A. antiquum, the Japanese Crested Bird's-nest grows half as tall as the leaves are frequently split into tassels at the tips.

Leaves with bulblets or plantlets. Possibly the most feathery of all ferns, the leaves like dropping green plumes. They all have the appearance of being very tropical, but, as their origins indicate, most are cool growing but require high humidity and filtered sun. These should not be exposed to higher than 80°F (27°C) with a 10°F (6°C) drop at night.

A. belangieri. Malaysia. One of the exceptions. Long, narrow, 1½' × 4" (45 × 10 cm). Leaflets ¼" (6.25 mm) long. Bulblets in the joint of the leaflets and the stalk. Terrarium culture, min. 60°F (16°C).

A. bulbiferum. Mother Fern. New Zealand and Australia. Tufted plant with leaves triangular, 4 × 1' (1.20 m × 30 cm). Leaflets lanceshaped; subleaflets to 3" (7.5 cm), toothed and lobed. Bulblets or plantlets

grow in the joints. Var. *laxum* is smaller in all parts.

A. daucifolium. (A. viviparum). Mauritius. Leaves 2' × 8" (60 × 20 cm), very finely divided, rather like the leaves of carrots. Bulblets in the joints. The last 2 species are cool-growing plants and cannot be recommended as houseplants except, perhaps, in the Pacific Northwest. They are especially sensitive to aerial pollution in cities. Young plants can be grown in terrariums.

Blechnum. **Polypodiaceae.** Mostly Southern Hemisphere tropics and subtropics. Terrestrial stemless and stemmed ferns. Partial sun. 500–700 fc. Temperature min. 60°F (16°C). Humidity min. 50%. Houseplants Mix #2 or 3. Propagation by spores and division. Difficult. At least 200 species of which 2 or 3 grown indoors.

We hesitated to include these ferns as they are difficult to maintain. However, their coppery or reddish young leaves are so irresistible that they are worth a try in the hope of solving their problems.

B. brasiliense. Brazil. With a 3' (90 cm) trunk at maturity. But potted plants are stemless juveniles. Tightly, symmetrically spiraled leaves to 3' × 15" (90 × 37.5 cm). The stalks thick. Leaflets simple, narrow, with undulating edges, to 4 × ½" (10 × 1.25 cm), the arrangement very neat and regular. Young leaves red. A vigorous, handsome plant.

B. gibbum. Western Pacific Islands. At maturity the trunk attains 5' (1.50 m). But young plants having no trunks and leaves are, at most, 2½' (75 cm) long. Segments much like the previous species but more irregular in length, 3 × ½" (7.5 × 1.25 cm).

B. occidentale. Hammock Fern. A creeper, colonizing by runners. Leaves 18 × 6" (45 × 15 cm), long triangular. Leaflet-pairs closely set. Red when young. Requires min. 50% humidity and constant moisture.

These ferns should be suited to commercial exploitation. They are superbly symmetrical in growth. We suspect that the only real problem is the selection of clones which demonstrate greater adaptability to indoor conditions.

Cyrtomium. **Polypodiaceae.** Asia, Pacific Islands. Filtered to partial sun. 400 fc. Temperature min 40°F (4°C) indoors. Houseplants Mix #2. Propagation by division. Fairly easy. 10 species of which 1 popular indoors.

C. falcatum. Holly Fern. A semihardy fern that does well in a coolish greenhouse or home. Leaves stiffly spreading, to 2' (60 cm) long, the leaflets coarse, crowded, roughly triangular with a long sharp point, shiny dark green, to 4" (10 cm) long. Indifferent to humidity. Dry out between waterings.

'Butterfieldii'. Leaflets coarsely toothed.

'Compactum'. A dwarf form.

'Mayii'. The leaflets forked at the tip.

'Mandaianum'. Leaflets more evenly triangular.

'Rochefordianum'. The most frequently grown cultivar.

Edges of leaflets fringed.

Sonerila margaritacea

Spathicarpa sagittifolia

Spathiphyllum clevelandii. Photo Gordon Courtright

Spathiphyllum cv.

PLATE 81

Stenotaphrum secundatum. St. Augustine Grass

Stromanthe amabilis

Synadenium cupulare

Synadenium grantii

PLATE 82

Syngonium albo-virens

Syngonium 'Gordon's Favorite'

Syngonium hoffmannii

Syngonium 'Frosty'. Photo Karen McElhinney, Glasshouse Works.

PLATE 83

Syngonium 'French Marble'

Syzygium paniculatum. Bush Cherry

Tamarindus indica. Tamarind

Syzygium paniculatum 'Globulus'

PLATE 84

Tetrapanax papyriferus. Rice Paper Plant. Photo Gordon Courtright

Tradescantia navicularis

Trevesia palmata

Tristania conferta

PLATE 85

Tupidanthus calyptratus. Photo Gordon Courtright

PLATE 86

Vriesea splendens

Xantherantherum igneum

Xanthosoma lindenii

Xanthosoma atrovirens var. *monstrosa*

PLATE 87

Xenophya lauterbachiana

Yucca elephantipes

Zamia floridana

Zamioculcas zamiifolia

PLATE 88

Adiantum raddianum. Photo A. James Downer

Aglaomorpha coronans

Aglaomorpha coronans. Photo Lois Rossten

Alsophila australis. Photo Gordon Courtright

PLATE 89

Asplenium nidus. Birds-nest Fern

Blechnum sp.

Davallia fejeensis

Davallia embolstegia

PLATE 90

Drynaria rigidula var. *whitei*. Photo A. James Downer.

Humata tyermannii. Photo A. James Downer

Nephrolepis exaltata 'Wanamaka'

Nephrolepis exaltata 'Norwoodii'

PLATE 91

Nephrolepis exaltata 'Petticoat'

Nephrolepis exaltata 'Frizzie Lizzie'

Nephrolepis biserrata furcans

Nephrolepis 'Kinky'

PLATE 92

Pellaea viridis.

Platycerium bifurcatum. Photo A. James Downer

Polypodium aureum

Platycerium coronarium (biforme). Photo A. James Downer

PLATE 93

Polypodium formosanum

Polypodium lycopodioides

Pteris cretica 'Wimsettii'

Pteris ensiformis 'Victoriae'

PLATE 94

Rumohra adiantiformis. Leather Fern

Selaginella. Tobago sp.

Selaginella uncinata. Peacock Moss

Selaginella pallescens

PLATE 95

PALMS

Caryota mitis. Fishtail Palm

Areca vestiaria. Photo Lois Rossten

Chamaedorea elegans. Parlor Palm

Chamaedorea erumpens

PLATE 96

Davallia. **Polypodiaceae.** Tropical Africa and Asia. Creeping Basket Ferns. Shade to partial sun. Temperature min. 50°F (10°C). Houseplant Mix #1. Osmunda fiber or 1 part leafmold to 1 part sand. Propagation by cuttings or rooting of the runners (rhizomes). Easy to difficult. 35 species; about 5 grown indoors.

Davallias, and the very similar *Humata tyermannii*, are favorite medium-size basket ferns with triangular, lacy leaves and furry-scaled, branching runners (rhizomes) that blanket the surface of the soil and hang over the edges of containers. People speak of hairs or fur rather than scales because that is what is noticed. But, actually, the hairs are only the tips of the very thin, overlapping, scaly platelets, as you can see for yourself if you pull apart a dry runner.

Davallias are a manageable size for growing in windows, and culture is simple. Some clones can manage with shade or a north exposure, but most do much better with filtered or partial sun.

They are rarely used in commercial plantings because they are sensitive to aerial pollution and the very light soil makes it difficult to water them without spillage. Also, hanging them above eye level is ineffective for decorative reasons. Their leaves are best seen at eye level or below.

Line baskets with sheet moss or long fiber sphagnum. Water when the soil is dry. High humidity is unnecessary, but a daily misting of leaves and runners is beneficial especially in hot weather. Fertilize monthly with a balanced formula.

Grow the plants in azalea pots, tree fern baskets, slatted cedar baskets or on the surface of chunks of tree fern. The last must be watered very often. When runners stray from the surface attach them with hairpins or wire prongs.

To propagate, cut and dig up the roots of sections of runner. Plant in medium with the roots buried. With time the runners become interwoven on the surface. Break off any dead pieces. When the space for growth is nearing exhaustion, decant the whole plant, pull apart or cut away sections and replant with new medium. During the adjustment period maintain a temperature of min. 70°F (22°C).

D. canariensis. Canary Islands and W. Africa. The runners are covered with brown fur tipped with white; ¾" (18.6 mm) thick. Leaves 1½ × 1' (45 × 30 cm). Leaves with divided subleaflets blunt at the tip. Cool growing: 45–80°F (7–27°C). Usually plants so labeled are *D. trichomanoides.*

D. fejeensis. Rabbit's Foot Fern. Fiji Islands. A warm-growing species more suited to greenhouse than indoor culture. Of the several cultivars some are dormant in winter but retain most of their leaves. Leaves triangular, to 2' (60 cm), with divided subleaflets. Deep green, a little rubbery, lax.

'Major'. Somewhat larger. Said to have no dormancy.

'Plumosa'. Leaves to 2' (60 cm) but the subleaflets more numerous than the species. The runners narrow. Very graceful.

'Minor'(?) Runners reddish and leaves somewhat smaller.

D. mariesii (D. bullata?). Squirrel's Foot Fern or Japanese Ball Fern. E. Asia to Japan. Relatively cool growing. Runners are thick and covered with brown furry scales. With age and frequent trimming they can become ½" (1.25 cm) thick or more. They are very fast growing so that the leaves are relatively far apart. Leaves are 4–8" (10–20 cm) long and wide triangular. Winter temperature should be below 75°F (24.5°C). By no means an ideal houseplant.

'Stenolepis'. Fast growing and vigorous.

D. solida. Polynesian Davallia. Runners at least ½" (1.25 cm) thick, covered with brown fur. Leaves thick textured, to 2½ × 1' (75 × 30 cm). A large, spreading, somewhat coarser fern than the others.

'Major' is larger still, with upright leaf stalks. Fast growing and requiring a large basket.

D. trichomanoides. Squirrel Foot Fern. Malay Archipelago. Similar to but larger than *D. mariesii*, the runners ½" (1.25 cm) thick, white to brown.

'Barbata'. Runners reddish.

'Lorrainii'. Runners coarsely gray furry. Semideciduous. Leaves black-green.

'Ruffled Ornata'. Leaflets crimped.

'Philippines Ornata'. Leaves broad on short stalks.

Drynaria. **Polypodiaceae.** Oak Leaf Fern. Old World tropics. Large basket ferns. Partial to full sun. Temperature min. 60°F (16°C). Houseplant Mix #3. Propagation by division. Moderately easy. 20 species, all relatively rare.

Drynarias are still quite rare plants but have the same uses as the Staghorn Ferns and *Polypodium (Phlebodium) aureum.* Like the Staghorns these have two distinct types of leaves. The sterile leaves are short, broad, segmented with some similarity to an oak leaf. The fertile leaves, on long stalks, have pairs of segments and are much longer. They, too, grow in baskets and on chunks of tree fern. Culture is much the same as for *Platycerium,* which see, except that even more care must be given to watering. Allow to dry but water immediately. Daily misting is advisable. The species also require somewhat more light than the Staghorns. Despite these warnings they are attractive, showy and quite manageable in sunny locations.

D. quercifolia. S. E. Asia to Australia. Fertile leaves with long stalks, to 3' (90 cm), the well separated pairs of segments, to 6" (15 cm) long. Sterile leaves stalkless to 1' (30 cm).

D. rigidula. Polynesia. Fertile leaves to 4' (1.20 m) long, the leaflets alternate, narrow, to 5" (12.5 cm), much like a Boston Fern, but more erect. Sterile leaf to 9" (22.5 cm).

D. sparsisora. Sterile leaves to 10" (25 cm), relatively shallowly lobed. Fertile leaves to 3' (90 cm), the paired segments thick, shiny, lanceshaped with a lengthened point, to 6" (15 cm), undulating and drooping at the tip.

Humata. **Polypodiaceae.** Madagascar to western Pacific. Easy. 50 species, 1 grown as a basket plant indoors. See *Davallia* for culture.

H. tyermannii. Bear's Foot Fern. Leaves to 12" (30 cm), triangular, growing from runners covered with furry white scales that turn light brown.

In appearance this plant is very much like *Davallia trichomanoides.* It tolerates a wide range of temperature and light: One of the easiest of the footed ferns to maintain and quite as attractive as any of the others.

Lygodium. **Schizaeaceae.** Worldwide tropics and subtropics. Vines. Filtered to partial sun. 400–800 fc. Temperature min. 40°F (4°C), max. 80°F (27°C). Packaged Houseplant Medium. Propagation mainly from spores. Moderately difficult. 45 species of which on grown indoors.

L. japonicum. Temperate Asia. Japanese Climbing Fern. Leaves triangular to 8 × 4" (20 × 10 cm). Leaflets alternate, triangular. Subleaflets lobed, the fertile more than the sterile ones. Stem to 3' (90 cm) or more, climbing by spiraling; hairy. New foliage grows from buds at the joints to replace the old. Provide good air movement.

An attractive decoration on a small trellis but purely a house pot plant. It can also grow in garden topsoil. There are a number of more tropical vining species that might do well in warm homes.

Nephrolepis. **Polypodiaceae.** Sword Fern. Worldwide tropics and subtropics. Pot and basket ferns. Shade to partial sun. 100–800 fc. Temperature mostly min. 50°F (10°C). Humidity min. 30. Houseplant Mix #2 or 3 or Packaged Houseplant Medium. Propagation by division or offsets. Cast Iron to difficult. 30 species of which about 5 grown indoors.

The genus is of major importance because of one species, *N. exaltata*, the Boston Fern, and its cultivars. It has become by a large margin the most popular of ferns. Commercial production and sales are probably as large as those for any foliage houseplant. It is, in fact, an almost unique species. Propagation is very simple, growth rapid, light requirement low, temperature tolerance considerable, tolerant of low humidity, tolerance of neglect (of some cultivars) ditto, resistance to disease and pests almost complete. Furthermore there are cultivars that supply a very wide range of sizes with textures from moderately coarse to infinitely delicate. It is, therefore, the first choice of both amateurs and of professional indoor plantscapers as a pot or basket plant.

In the 19th century *N. exaltata*, a very large, vigorous, coarse, Florida fern was shipped to florists in considerable numbers as medium-sized plants. They were sold in large pots and displayed on pedestals. Toward the turn of the century a shipment to Boston was found to include some plants that differed from previous deliveries. These were at first judged to belong to a different species. But when further cultivation yielded other plants that bore little resemblance to the species, nurserymen began to realize that they were dealing with a plant that displayed an astonishing propensity to variation, quite unique among the ferns. All the plants acquired the common name of Boston Fern and cultivar names were supplied to the different forms.

We list *N. exaltata* first. A few other species follow.

N. exaltata. Stiff, nearly vertical leaves with thick stalks, to 5' × 6" (1.50 cm × 15 cm). Leaflets wingshaped to 4" (10 cm) long. Finely toothed. We doubt that the species is still cultivated indoors.

Most of the Boston Ferns do well in normal house temperatures and humidity, even during the hottest days of summer weather. In winter the temperature should not go below 50°F (10°C). Central heating if excessive can do some harm but rarely kills the plants unless watering is neglected. Misting is good protection against its effects. Keep evenly moist for best results, but a couple of days of complete dryness are not lethal. Feed with a balanced formula every 2 months for maintenance. An average temperature range of 60–80°F (16–27°C) and 50% or more humidity, does improve the appearance of the foliage and speed growth.

As roots are shallow use azalea-type pots or shallow baskets. However, the plants put out many threadlike runners (stolons) that root at the tips. Allowing room around the plants encourages spreading and colonizing. Individual tufts can be removed and potted up. As the runners are long enough to hang over the edges of pots and baskets they can be propagated in separate containers. Place small pots within their reach and pin the tips in moist medium. Divide plants that have grown too large.

In any colony of Boston Ferns the tufts at the center are the oldest and the first to deteriorate. Dig out the dead roots and stems and fill the space with rooted divisions.

Scale is the principal pest. Wash the plant under a strong stream of water. After the leaves and stems have dried treat with a recommended pesticide. If a single application is not sufficient, repeat the process.

Boston Fern Cultivars

Nursery listings of cultivars run to 60 names or more of which some are old, some new. New cultivars appear yearly and old ones are revived. It is impossible to estimate the total number, which must be very great. When a variation occurs the nursery often has no means of identifying it with certainty and slaps on its own label. Thus plants are constantly appearing and disappearing from the trade. It is not only the look of the plants that changes but also the vigor and degree of sensitivity to the environment. Some are so delicate as to need terrarium culture. But the looks are not a dependable guide to culture. Some of the most exotic feathery cultivars are remarkably adaptable.

The most popular Boston Ferns have been the relatively simple-leaved types. Other cultivars that are more decorative could, in our opinion, be popular if produced in greater quantities so that the public becomes familiar with them.

For convenience in comparing the plants we have arranged the cultivars in five categories.

Primary Cultivars

'Bostoniensis'. Leaves to 2½' (75 cm), crowded, arching. Leaflets wingshaped, toothed. Dark green.

'Bostoniensis Compacta'. Leaves to 1½' (45 cm), crowded, arching. This has been the common Boston Fern of the shops for a long time. Cast Iron and vigorous. They are the least costly ferns of their size on the market and are mostly sold in hanging baskets. They are frequently seen as greenery in restaurants where they survive in near shade and are cheap to replace.

Simple-leaved Cultivars

Some of these are very close to 'Bostoniensis'. Others vary in size, form of leaflets and spread. Leaflets are twisted, curled, ruffled or crowded on the stalk.

'Aurea'. Like 'Bostoniensis Compacta' but leaves uniformly yellowish, tending to chartreuse. Requires filtered to partial sun.

'Dallas'. A new cultivar that has considerable commercial potential. Leaves to 1' (30 cm), very crowded, arching. Leaflets wingshaped to 1 × ½" (2.50 × 1.25 cm), wingshaped, medium dark green, finely toothed. Very vigorous and adaptable and producing many runners. It makes a good pot plant as well as a basket.

'Dreyeri'. Leaves to 2' (60 cm) with a spreading habit. Leaflets very close together, to 2" (5 cm), light green, drooping at the tips.

'Giatrasii'. Diffuse growth. Leaves to 1½' (45 cm). Leaflets broad, undulating.

'Maasii'. Leaves to 2½' (75 cm). Leaflets to 3" (7.5 cm), rather narrow so that they appear more separated. Very vigorous, spreading to 3' (90 cm). Cast Iron.

'M. P. Mills'. Leaves very erect, stiff, narrow, to 2½" (6.25 cm) long. Cast Iron. It tolerates temperatures of 45°F (7°C).

'New York'. Widely spreading growth, shiny green. Leaves shorter than 'Bostoniensis' and longer than 'Bostoniensis compacta'. Light green.

'Porteri'. Dark green leaves to 1½' (45 cm). Leaflets very twisted. Sturdy.

'Randolphii'. Leaves to 2' (60 cm). Leaflets wavy and twisted. Spreading to 3' (90 cm) or more.

'Rooseveltii'. Leaves long-triangular to 2½' (75 cm). Leaflets to 2½' (6.25 cm) and broader at the base than 'Maasii', otherwise nearly identical.

'Scottii'. Diffuse growing, the leaves to 1½' (45 cm), narrow-rectangular in outline. Leaflets short and wide. Yellowish green.

'Teddy Junior'. Smaller and more compact than 'Rooseveltii'. Leaflets broad, wavy and somewhat ruffled. Compact but unsymmetrical growth.

'Viridissima'. Leaves to 1½' (45 cm), narrow rectangular. Leaflets very closely packed, narrow and somewhat ruffled. Tight symmetrical growth. Bright green.

'Wagneri'. Very erect leaves, dark green, to 15" (37.5 cm) long, leathery. Leaflets twisted. Coarse and vigorous.

'Wanamaka'. About the size of 'Bostoniensis'. Leaflets wavy and twisted. A strong grower.

These brief descriptions demonstrate the close relationship of these plants. In some the wingshape is more evident than in others where the leaflets are more rectangular or long-triangular. But even on a single leaf the leaflets may vary to a considerable extent. Only those very familiar with the plants can tell them apart except by size and sometimes by color. There are many other cultivars of the type.

Forked and/or Crested Leaflets

'Childsii'. No more than 6" (15 cm) high and a slow grower. The leaves lightish green. Leaflets tightly packed along the stalks, overlapping, very much crested and distorted. Habit very unsymmetrical with leaves growing in every direction. Tough.

'Compacta Cristata'. Crested form of 'Bostoniensis Compacta'.

'Craigii'. Leaves to 1' (30 cm) with some simple and others with distorted, ruffled or crested leaflets. Compact and easy.

'Falcata'. Similar to 'Scottii' except that some leaflets are forked once or twice at the tips.

'Fluffy Ruffles'. Very tightly packed, upright leaves to 12" (30 cm) long. Dark green. The leaflets are much curled, distorted and forked; leathery in texture. The stalks are very brittle. A basically disorderly and ugly plant that does poorly indoors but has attracted the impulse buyer by its odd appearance and low price. Its popularity has waned.

'Fringed Vase'. Erect, leathery leaves, the leaflets crested and/or tasseled. A recent introduction.

'Gretnae'. Leaves to 3' (90 cm) long or more, arching. Leaflets rectangular or forked; narrower than N. biserrata 'Furcans'.

'Hillii' (or 'Hillsii'). The size of N. 'Bostoniensis'. Leaves erect. Leaflets overlapping, deeply lobed, ruffled and crisped. Very strong grower. A classic plant.

'Hubbardii'. Dwarf plant to 10" (30 cm) with crested leaflets.

'Muscosa'. Leaves to 12" (30 cm). Leaflets frilled and ruffled but also producing simple leaves.

'Rooseveltii Plumosa'. Like 'Rooseveltii', the leaflets crested at the tips.

'Wicheri'. Unruly, spreading plant with leaves to 36" (96 cm); variously forked and frilled leaflets.

Lacy-leaved cultivars

It stretches the limits of our credulity when we are assured that these plants, with multilayered, plumelike fronds are merely variations derived from the preceding cultivars. Even the forked and crested types give no inkling of the extreme degree of change. The finely dissected foliage of ferns in other genera are the characteristic of particular species. Here we are faced with enormous variation that appears to have occurred spontaneously. What is strange, for instance, is the way the normal leaflets of N. exaltata have been metamorphosed from their wing or oblong shapes into ones that are triangular or narrowly oblong and, instead of a toothed edge, have closely set scallops, lobes or segments. The substance is also different, being much thinner.

'Angel Hair'. Extremely delicate dwarf with leaves to max. 6" (15 cm), the stalks like green threads and very numerous, the leaflets thin and tiny. As the leaves are not at all stiff they grow every which way forming inextricable puffs of soft greenery.

This is a plant best grown in a terrarium with min. 60°F (16°C) and min. 50% humidity. Bright shade or 100–300 fc are sufficient. The mix should be very light and well aerated. Avoid temperatures above 80°F (27°C). Do not fertilize.

'Anna Foster'. Leaves to 12" (30 cm), very broadly triangular and spreading. A curious mix of simple 'Bostoniensis' leaflets and lacy subleaflets. A 'Bostoniensis' variation.

'Brooklyn'. Narrowly triangular leaves to 3' (90 cm) long, carried quite erect. Most leaves partly frilled but others with the upper part plain. This and the previous cultivar represent intermediate stages in the transformation from coarse to fine leaflets. Neither is of particular merit except for their culture being Cast Iron.

'Elegantissima'. An old cultivar with leaves to 20" (50 cm) long, the leaflets broad, overlapping; the subleaflets crowded and somewhat fringed.

'Fluffy Duffy'. This is a true lacy fern similar to 'Norwoodii' but much smaller. The broadly triangular leaves are only 4–6" (10–15 cm) in length, the stalks very crowded. In other respects it is so much like 'Norwoodii' that we refer to the description of that plant in respect to culture. Other plants of this size and type turn up at nurseries, and when small differences are noted they are sometimes given cultivar names.

'Norwodii'. The perfect lacy fern. The leaves grow to 18 × 8" (45 × 20 cm), with a graceful, spreading habit. The leaflets are 4" (10 cm) long. These measurements are approximate. Under ideal conditions the length and spread can be greater. The leaflets are so crowded that they are all forced into a position at right angles to the stalk and overlap very closely. The tiny subleaflets are usually either very narrowly lanceshaped or wedgeshaped, and they, in turn, are notched, lobed or segmented. Because of this structure the plume may achieve a thickness of close to an inch (2.5 cm). An approximate measurement of the subleaflets is ⅛–¼" (3–6 mm), but that is a maximum.

Our own current plants of this cultivar are descendants of one we acquired 20 years ago and of which we have given away thousands of propagations.

Despite its delicacy 'Norwoodii' is as tough as any plant we have grown. The light requirement is bright shade or filtered sun. 100–400 fc. Temperature min. 50°F (10°C). Humidity 30%. Houseplant Mix #3. Even moisture, though it will withstand a day or two of complete dryness. Fertilize once a month with high nitrate formula.

'Ostrich Plume'. About the size of 'Norwoodii' but less lacy, the leaflets not so overlapping; more open and spreading. It suffers from the brittleness of 'Fluffy Ruffles' and a tendency to revert to simple leaflets.

'Piersonii'. An early medium-sized cultivar. The

tips of the simple leaflets divide into tufts of compound subleaflets.

'Scholzelii'. Leaves 15 × 4" (37.5 × 10 cm). The laciness is like 'Norwoodii' but more irregular, and the growth habit is more confused. Leaves are erect rather than spreading.

'Smithii'. Even more finely lacy than 'Norwoodii', but the stalks are less sturdy, the leaflets less definite in form, the leaves crowded and drooping on weak stalks. A beautiful plant for the sheer delicacy of the soft green, misty piling up of foliage to 12" (30 cm). Sensitive to low humidity and temperature. Requires very even moisture, any excess leading to root rot.

'Trevillian'. Related to 'Elegantissima' but the leaves more lacy, to 20" (50 cm) long, more erect and the arrangement more symmetrical. Strong growing and tolerant.

'Verona' and 'Manda's Verona'. In type related to 'Whitmanii'. The leaves to 1½' (45 cm); the stalks somewhat stiff; the leaves broadly triangular. The distinctive appearance derives from the greater separation of the leaflets and the subleaflets being less complex than in 'Norwoodii'. Thus it is less lacy and has a crisper, rather neater look. Very tolerant of low light, low humidity and temperature. But we have found it less sturdy and long lasting than 'Norwoodii'.

'Victori'. A strong-growing, medium-sized plant, tha stalks black and the leaflets mostly fringed at the tip.

'Whitmanii'. Lace Fern. A splendid cultivar. The leaves to 18" (45 cm) long, the leaflets and subleaflets partly overlapping and very lacy but less delicate than 'Norwoodii', the color darker green. Halfway between 'Verona' and 'Norwoodii'. It requires, however, min. 65% humidity for good growth.

A curious plant in this group is one that has been questionably labeled 'Courtney Ann'. The leaves are max. 12" (30 cm) long, narrow. The stalks are thin and flexible. It has leaflets only to ¼' (6.25 cm) long, but these are regularly scalloped. Very airy and loose in appearance but as adaptable as many of the coarser ferns. Very much like some finer-leaved garden ferns.

Tasseled Plants

The true tasseled plants have simple leaves from the tips of which grow a number of substalks bearing tiny leaves in such numbers that the stalks are weighted down and a solid curtain of tassels hangs below the basket.

'Ming'. It forms a solid mound of greenery 6–8" (15–20 cm) high. Only 3 inches (7.5 cm) of the leaf is simple; the rest is a tuft of spreading branchlets with tiny subleaflets. Quite extraordinary, but essentially a collector's plant and not easy. It requires high humidity.

'Petticoat'. A plant the size of 'Bostoniensis' suitable only for a large basket. The 4–5" (12–12.5 cm) tassels are produced in great numbers. A most spectacular basket plant requiring partial to full sun and min. 65% humidity. The plants will survive and tassel in normal home conditions, sheer maintenance being easy, but the display will be less impressive. It should

236

be grown in greenhouse and used only for temporary indoor decoration.

Other Nephrolepis Species

N. acuminata. Malay Peninsula. Leaves spreading to 3' × 6" (90 × 15 cm). Leaflets narrowly wingshaped, alternate, with a zigzag pattern. A sturdy fern but requiring min. 60°F (16°C).

N. biserrata (N. ensifolia). Subtropics. Leaves to 4 × 1' (1.20 m × 30 cm). Leaflets to 5" (12.5 cm) long, narrow, opposite, finely toothed, drooping.

'Furcans'. Fishtail Fern. Size same as the species but leaflets alternate, broadly rectangular and with 2 or more triangular forks. A very large, handsome, coarse fern that is virtually Cast Iron, tolerating low light and humidity and some neglect of watering.

N. cordifolia (cordata). Subtropical. The runners bear tubers. Leaves erect, 2' × 2½–4" (60 cm × 6.25–10 cm). Leaflets 1–2" (2.5–7.5 cm) long, mostly opposite, bluntly rectangular. The species and cultivars are relatively cool growing to 45°F (7°C) and require partial sun. Another variable species adapting on average to a 45°F (7°C), a lower temperature than *N. exaltata* cultivars.

'Floral Fantasy'. The size of the species with leathery leaflets crimped and ruffled.

'Foxtail'. Monstrous crimpling and ruffling carried to the point where the leaflets are tufted and almost cylindrical.

'Plumosa'. Tassel Fern. Dark green. The same size as the species. Leaves simple to the tips which extend with smaller crowded leaflets to double the length or more.

'Tesselata'. Petticoat Sword Fern. The ends of the leaves are tasseled as with *N. exaltata* 'Petticoat' but not as full. The leaves are more erect and coarser. Cool growing.

Pellaea. **Polyodiaceae.** Cliff Brake. Subtropical. Filtered sun. 400 fc. Temperature 45–80°F (7–27°C). Houseplant Mix #2 with lime. Propagation from spores and division. Moderately difficult. 80 species of which 3 grown indoors.

Many of the Pellaeas are hardy, and even those that are warmer growing still prefer cool temperatures indoors. The frequent failure of these ferns can usually be attributed either to excessively high temperatures or to an acid soil. Keep evenly moist and fertilize monthly with high phosphate/potash formula.

P. falcata. S. Asia to New Zealand. Leaves on thin, short stalks, pendant, to 2' × 3" (60 cm × 7.5 cm). Leaflets wingshaped nearly even in length; 1½" (3.75 cm).

P. rotundifolia. New Zealand. Frequently displayed in broad azalea pots in the shops. Spreading by prostrate wiry runners. The leaves prostrate or pendant on thin black stalks; to 12" (30 cm) long. Leaflets alternate, round or broadly oval, very dark green, to ⅜" (9.37 mm) in diameter. Very sensitive to overheating.

P. viridis. (Pteris adiantoides). Africa. Leaves to 2' (60 cm) long. Stalks black, upright. Leaves wingshaped triangular or with an additional pair of subleaflets. Forma *macrophylla* has larger leaflets, more widely spaced. Vigorous, rapid grower but must be grown cool.

Platycerium. **Polypodiaceae.** Staghorn Fern. Africa, Southern Asia, Australia and the Western Pacific. Aerial Ferns. Filtered to partial sun. Temperature min. 60°F (16°C). Humidity min. 40%. Houseplant Mix #3. Long-fiber sphagnum moss. Propagation from spores or pups. 18 species of which 2 grown indoors.

The Staghorn Ferns are quite monstrous considering they have no stems or branches but only leaves. They are a feature of most botanical gardens where they hang vertically attached to a basket or chunk of tree fern seemingly altogether too small to accommodate the roots for their 6–8' (1.80–2.40 m) diameter. Even the big bromeliads are dwarfed.

They have no conceivable uses in public planting except for temporary display in a tropical setting. One of the smaller species, *P. bifurcatum,* as a young pot plant, is quite common in the shops and, because of its curious appearance achieves ready sale. Disillusion for most buyers is a foregone conclusion.

The problem is that, like Orchids, they require different treatment from other plants so that unfamiliar skills must be acquired in order to maintain them.

Platyceriums have both sterile and fertile leaves. The sterile leaf, the first to appear, is kidneyshaped and the same texture as the fertile leaves. Later, in the larger species, it becomes footlike, the short lobes having the appearance of toes or pleated-fanshaped, often also forked and very broad but always in a vertical position above the fertile leaves. Its base is plastered to the host tree in nature; beneath is a tangle of fine roots that act as attachments. Sterile leaves die off seasonally and are replaced and covered by new ones, thereby building constantly thicker layers of dead leaves that act as accumulators of moisture and nutrition.

From the notch or the center of the sterile leaves grow more or less pendant, fertile leaves that are usually longer and fanshaped or split into antlerlike prongs. The texture is thick, leathery, stiff, velvety, scurfy or covered with fine stiff hairs. The color is yellowish or greenish gray.

Fine runners produce sterile leaves close to the mother plant. These can be cut loose and potted up.

Fill shallow clay azalea pots part way with shards; pack with houseplant mix and cover with a layer of long-fiber sphagnum moss. Hold everything in with chicken wire and poke the base of the sterile leaf through a hole into the mix. Gently tie against the chicken wire making sure that it is in contact with the moss. Do not use plastic pots.

Young plants can be grown upright in pots but later on they must be suspended vertically.

Treat baskets and half baskets in the same way. Cedar slat baskets are frequently used. On sections of cork, wood or tree fern place a pad of moist sphagnum moss under the sterile leaf and bind on tightly with a soft cord.

Watering is the most critical element in maintenance. The condition of the sterile leaf pad is the test. Before watering it should be quite dry. If the layer is very thin make sure that the sphagnum moss beneath it is dry. Some growers even wait until the fertile leaves begin to droop. Others can tell by the weight of the basket or pot. Pressing the sterile leaves also reveals the degree of remaining moisture. If the pads and leaves are dry, soak thoroughly.

High humidity is not essential. Fertile leaves should not be watered, but a fine misting in warm weather is beneficial. *P. bifurcatum* is somewhat cooler growing than the other species, but all suffer from protracted temperatures above 85°F (29.5°C) and the tropical ones from exposure to temperatures below 60°F (16°C).

Apply very mild solutions of high nitrate or balanced liquid fertilizer at 3-week intervals during the warm months; at 5-week intervals in winter. Be sure that the fertilizer is in complete solution.

P. bifurcatum. (P. alcicorne). Western Pacific. The common Staghorn Fern of the shops. Sterile leaves kidneyshaped, max. 1' (30 cm) in diameter. Fertile leaves to 3' (90 cm), triangular, split in the upper half into long, narrow segments in sets of 3 or 4. Grayish green, scurfy. The splitting of the leaves is exceedingly variable, and clones are frequently give cultivar names. Protect against temperatures over 80°F (27°C) in summer.

'Majus' has shorter segments.

'Netherlands'. With heavier leaves, more irregularly split and somewhat shorter.

'Ziesenhenne'. Leaves to 1½' (45 cm) and slow growing but adaptable.

The last two are the cultivars most frequently seen in the shops.

P. coronarium. S.E. Asia. Sterile leaves to 1½' (45 cm), upright, fanshaped-pleated, with blunt, short segments. Fertile leaves dangling to 3' (90 cm), much branched, with long, narrow segments.

P. hillii. Australia. Sterile leaf kidneyshaped to 1' (30 cm) in diameter. Fertile leaves to 3' (90 cm) broadening from a tubular base into handshaped pads with 6" (15 cm) lanceshaped segments. Leaves very leathery. Cultivars with more divided leaves.

P. superbum. (P. grande). S.E. Asia, Malaysia. A stupendous plant at maturity. The sterile leaves at first kidneyshaped; later in enormous pleated fans with deeply cut segments forming a massive half umbrella to 3' (90 cm) high and 4' (1.20 m) or more across. Sterile leaves dangling, channeled, much branched to 5' (1.50 m) or more. Overall length to 9' (2.7 m).

P. vassei. Similar to *P. bifurcatum* but fertile leaves stiffer and more erect.

P. veitchii. Australia. Fertile leaves thick, to 2' (60 cm) long, narrowly split into 6–8 segments. Whitish scurfy beneath.

P. wilhelmina-reginae. About the same size as *P. superbum.* The sterile leaves huge, broad and tall, to 3' (90 cm) or more with 4 blunt segments each. Fertile leaves to 6' (1.80 m) long, divided into 2 long and 2 much shorter segments.

P. willinckii. Java. Sterile leaves footshaped with short-toothed segments. Fertile leaves to 2½' (75 cm), gray-green, drooping and divided into many long, unequal, strapshaped segments.

'Pygmaeum' is a dwarf form.

Polypodium. **Polypodiaceae.** Worldwide. Ferns with runners; tropical species mostly aerial plants. Shade to partial sun. 100–800 foot candles. Temperature min. 55°F (13°C). Packaged Houseplant Medium or Houseplant Mix #3 with some sand. Propagation from spores, runners, division. Easy to difficult. 75 species of which about 40 in cultivation indoors.

The **Polypodiaceae** are the largest fern family, with some 7,000 species. Most of the genera, though involving instances of overlapping, are generally accepted. But when we come to *Polypodium* which, though of worldwide distribution, has only about 75 species (compared, for instance, with Asplenium's 700 and Pteris' 280) but with huge populations, we become enmeshed in an area of unremitting controversy which has caused *Hortus Third* to omit its usual estimate of the number of species.

To present both sides of the issue and indicate the variety of material available, we have retained *Polypodium* for the general heading and assigned the species to the principal proposed generic names, viz.; *Campyloneurum,* *Microgramma,* *Microsorium,* *Phlebodium* and *Polypodium.* Most of the popular plants will be found under *Phlebodium.*

Campyloneurum. American tropics. These are exclusively Strap Ferns, the leaves relatively narrow, nearly straight sided but coming to a point at either end. They grow in tufts, colonizing by means of runners beneath the soil. Of this leaf type *Asplenium nidus* has been preferred for its more symmetrical growth, but culture is much the same.

C. angustifolium. Narrow-leaved Strap Fern. Leaves strapshaped, erect, 2' × ⅝" (60 cm × 15.5 mm). Texture very thin and papery.

'Corkscrew'. Leaf edges undulating.

'Narrow'. Half as wide; like a light green grass.

C. glaucophyllum (?).

'Villa Tenaril'. Thin bluish green runners on the surface bear rectangular dwarf leaves rounded at the tips.

C. phyllitidis. Strap leaves to 3' × 4" (90 × 10 cm). Runners short and leaves crowded. Easy.

C. punctatum (Microsorium polycarpon). Indian Strapleaf. Leathery, thick leaves, 3' × 3" (90 × 7.5 cm). Very erect.

'Cristatum'. The tips of blades widened into crested forkings.

C. sphenodes. Leaves to 2½' (75 cm), shiny, yellowish green. Leaves crowded.

Microgramma. Tropical America and Africa. Creepers with short, oval or elliptic leaves. Plant in shallow, wide pots. Temperature min. 55°F (13°C). Max 80°F (27°C). Humidity min. 50%. Fine terrarium plants. They can also be grown on tree fern slabs. Interesting small plants that deserve to be better known. Do not fertilize.

M. heterophyllum. Runners creeping and branching. Leaves upright, elliptical or spoonshaped, 1″ (2.5 cm) long. Shade to filtered sun. 150 fc 10 hours daily.

M. lycopodioides. Runners like hairy strings, creeping and dangling. Leaves to 2″ (5 cm), elliptical, lime green with distinctly darker veining.

M palmerii. Runners flat, large, silvery-furry. Leaves spoonshaped to 8 × 3″ (20 × 7.5 cm). Easy. A good small basket plant.

M. piloseloides. Matting plant, the leaves very close, making a complete ground cover. Runners branching. Leaves to 2″ (5 cm) long; elliptical.

M. squamulosum. Leaves 1″ (2.5 cm). Runners thin, white.

M. vaccinifolium. Runners white. Fast growing. Leaves lanceshaped, 2″ (5 cm) long.

Our own experience is that all the above species can be maintained in long-fiber sphagmum moss.

Microsorium. Medium to larger ferns with strap or lanceshaped leaves. Not easy. We do not list those that are hardy or semihardy. Asia and western Pacific.

M. elegans.(?) Like *C. punctatum* 'Cristatum' or *M. polycarpon* 'Grandiceps' (Oh, wonderful confusion!). This one is one third the size, 12–15″ (30–37.5 cm), erect, the tips with multiple forkings.

M. integrifolium (?) (*punctatum* (?)).

'Cristatum'. Strap leaves to 2½′ (75 cm), the forking and cresting overlapping.

'Serrulatum' (?). Cresting the full length of the leaf.

M. musifolium. Banana Leaf Fern. Leaves to 2½′ (75 cm). Runners black. Leaves to 3′ (90 cm) by 4″ (10 cm). Light, creamy green, the spreading veins dark. Min. 65°F (18.5°C). Humidity min. 65%.

M. polycarpon. Climbing Bird's-nest Fern. Leaves 3′ × 3″ (90 × 7.5 cm), leathery, shiny, the tips rounded.

'Grandiceps'. Terrestrial Elkhorn Fern. Leaves erect and heavily crested.

'Grandiceps Compactum'. Leave 12′ (30 cm), also crested. Considered easier to maintain than the species.

P. scandens (pustulatum). Fragrant Fern. Australia and New Zealand. Runners short, branched. Leaves to 9 × ⅝″ (22.5 cm × 15.5 mm). Light green with darker veins very prominent. Cooler growing than the others. Min. 50°F (10°C).

P. scolopendrium. Wart Fern. Leaves leathery to 2′ (60 cm). With 10 or more pairs of deeply cut segments. However there appears to be also a simple-leaved form and one with merely undulating edges. Runners small, green, very much branched, handing from pot or basket as in *Davallia.*

Phlebodium. Tropical America. Only 2 species but one of these has long been popular, understandably so, as it is one of the most spectacular of ferns and among the easiest to grow. Widespread in the tropics; many varieties have been discovered.

P. aureum. Bear's Paw Fern. Florida to Argentina. A large, coarse-leaved but gorgeous fern, with pairs of segments on long stalks. Bare stalks to 18″ (45 cm). Blades lanceshaped to 2′ (60 cm). Segments blunt, paired, undulating wit tip leaf, to 1′ × 1½″ (30 × 3.75 cm); the midrib prominent. Branched runners that cling to the soil or climb over the sides of pots, are up to 1″ (2.5 cm) thick, covered with a fur of reddish brown scales; the growing tips white.

Use 10″ (25 cm) diameter or larger, pots, large baskets or tree fern pots. The species requires partial to full sun, the cultivars filtered to partial sun. Artificial light 400–1,000 fc. Temperature min. 40°F (4°C) for a short period. Keep soil evenly moist but will survive several days of complete dryness.

An excellent way to grow it is in tree fern pots. With time the runners cover the soil and the entire outer surface. In pots the runners of older plants blanket the soil with their wool. Fast growing.

The plant is magnificent displayed in large pots on tall pedestals. The spread is up to 5′ (1.5 m). It can hang in a window. But it is not easy to use it in ground level plantings. We list a few cultivars. Filtered to partial sun.

'Areolatum'. Leaflets narrower. Leaves intense bluish green.

'Areolatum Cristatum'. Mexican Tassel Fern. Leaves are forked and crested. Greenish blue.

'Ekstrandii'. Blue with silver highlights. Crested and undulating.

'Mandaianum'. The most popular cultivar. Segments forked for their entire lengths. Very graceful, robust grower, the leaves spreading and drooping. Virtually Cast-Iron culture.

'Samoa'. Stalks more upright; very crested and fringed.

P. decumanum. Even bigger than *P. aureum*; to 6′, (1.80 m). The edges of segments are parallel. Runners heavy and short. Variable.

Polypodium. Circumglobal. This section includes numerous hardy ferns along with tropical species. The leaves are mostly leathery, lanceshaped, with paired segments and a tip segment. It includes a range of sized from miniature to very large and spreading.

P. formosanum. Leaves erect to 2′ (60 cm). Segments bluish green. Although considered hardy, it does well indoors in a coolish house. Temperature range 50–80°F (10–27°C). Tolerant of low humidity. Keep evenly moist.

'Cristatum'. The runners are matforming. Segments moderately crested.

P. fraxinifolium. Tropical S. America. Ash Leaf Polypody. Leaves to 4′ × 1½′ (1.20 m × 45 cm). Segments long. Runners small, wiry. Leaf grayish.

P. polypodioides. Resurrection Fern. American subtropics. Leathery leaves to 7 × 2″ (17.5 × 5 cm). Evergreen but goes dormant when dry, then revives when watered. Frequently sold as a novelty plant but not especially attractive and difficult to maintain.

P. subauriculatum. Jointed Pine Fern. Leaves to 3′ (90 cm). Runners blackish. Segments long-triangular and very undulating. Stalks spreading. A handsome fern of easy culture as long as temperatures above 85°F (29.5°C) are avoided.

'Knightiae'. The segments very much fringed; the narrow teeth irregular in length.

Polystichum. **Polypodiaceae.** Shield Fern. Worldwide temperate zones. Filtered to partial sun. Temperature hardy. Sterilized Garden Soil with peat. Propagation by division and spores. Difficult. 135 species of which one occasionally grown indoors.

These are attractive garden plants for mild temperate climates but too cool growing for most indoor environments. The reason we include the genus at all is because *P. tsus-simense* have been touted and sold as a houseplant which, like the other species, it is not.

It may be grown in our Northwest and in Canada in cool, well-ventilated homes and in terrariums exposed to cool temperatures throughout the year, max. 80°F (27°C) with no practical lower limit.

P. tsus-simense. Tsusima Holly Fern. Leaves narrowly triangular to 1½' (45 cm), the leaflets wingshaped, the subleaflets lanceshaped and evenly lobed. Neat spreading habit.

Pteris. **Polypodianceae.** Table Fern. Worldwide tropics. Medium-sized pot and basket ferns. Filtered to partial sun. 400–700 fc. Humidity min. 40%. Temperature min. 60°F (16°C). Houseplant Mix #3. Propagation by division. Easy to difficult. 280 species of which 5 or 6 grown indoors.

The colorful, variegated cultivars continue to be popular with impulse buyers despite their record of failing suddenly after a few months in windows or under fluorescent light. They are often used in dish gardens. The showiest of the crested or split-leaved fern cultivars, that used to be very common in the shops, are rarely seen nowadays because, though easy to produce in humid, warm greenhouses, they are difficult to maintain indoors. The plainer cultivars are sometimes much easier and suffer from undeserved neglect.

Most of the Pteris must be kept within the range of 60–80°F (16–29.5°C), being very intolerant of both cold and excessive heat. Maintain even moisture, as a single day of completely dry soil may kill them. They respond best to high humidity, without which the thin leaflets soon turn brown. Fertilizer is unnecessary unless they lose their bright green color. A balanced fertilizer at ⅛th the recommended concentration applied 2–3 times in summer is sufficient to cure this condition. To avoid a harmful build-up of salts in the soil, leach well every 6 months.

P. cretica. Leaves to 1½'(45 cm) long. Stalks stiff, wiry. Leaflets widely spaces apart on the stalks. Leaflets dark green, 2–4 at a joint, to 4" (10 cm) long, narrowly elliptical, the rib prominent, the edges very finely crimped; with a terminal leaflet.

The species has disappeared from horticulture, replaced by dozens of cultivars, some of them so variable that they become look-alikes of each other.

'Albo-lineata'. A beautifully variegated fern. As usually sold the leaves are 1' (30 cm) long, consisting of a stalked terminal leaflet and below it opposite pairs without stalks in a bow tie arrangement. The tip leaflet to 4" (10 cm) long, the upper of the pairs to 3" (7.5 cm) and the lower to 1½" (3.75 cm). A broad white stripe extends the length of the leaflets. Difficult indoors.

'Cristata'. Leaflets long and narrow in pairs; irregularly sized and shaped projections along their edges with some leaflets remaining plain. Some of the tips are crested. Leaflets narrower than 'Wimsettii', but they are virtually undistinguishable.

'Distinction'. Stalks erect and crowded. Leaflets in clustered tufts, crested, frilled, finely divided, formless. An oddity.

'Gautheri'. Not crested but with leaflets lined with deep, irregular toothing.

'Major'. Leaflets to 6" (15 cm) or more, simple, crimped. They are closer together on the stalks so that the plant has a homogeneous appearance lacked by some others. Spiky looking because the tips of the leaflets are long-pointed.

'Ouvrardii'. Similar to the species but leaflets to 6' (15 cm), the surface brighter. Growth is more vigorous but undisciplined like the species.

'Parkeri'. With fewer leaves than the previous cvs. The terminal leaflet consists of three segments; those below are in opposite pairs of which there are not more than 3 or 4. Leaflets to 3½ × ½" (8.75 × 1.25 cm), broadly elliptic with a thin tip.

'Rivertoniana'. Broad leaves to 1½' × 10" (45 × 25 cm). Leaflets to 5" (12.5 cm) with spiky excrescences to 1' (2.50 cm) for their entire length.

'Wilsonii'. Narrow, straightsided leaflets with monstrous cresting at the tips.

'Wimsettii'. Like 'Cristata' but larger leaflets somewhat broader. This, like others of the type, is virtually Cast Iron, though undisciplined and hardly a beauty. Its spores find their way all over an indoor garden and produce sporelings in quantity. A cheerful plant that is quite carefree as it endures very low light and needs to be kept only reasonably moist. It is indifferent to humidity.

P. ensiformis. Sword Brake. S.E. Asia. Warmgrowing ferns requiring high humidity. Difficult.

'Victoriae'. The most popular of the variegated Table Ferns. To 18" (45 cm) but usually half as tall indoors. Lower pairs of leaflets divided into 3–5 subleaflets, the upper simple and with a, usually, triple terminal leaflet. Leaflets to 4" (10 cm). Subleaflets long-narrow to broadly elliptical. Edges wavy. With a broad, feathered white stripe down the middle. The leaves are few in number and erect. Difficult to maintain.

P. multifida. China. Leaves 1½' × 10" (45 × 25 cm). The pairs of leaflets opposite or alternate to 4 or 5" (10–12.5 cm), extremely narrow and straightsided. The pairs are set well apart on the stalks which are crowded. Very cool growing.

There are a number of cvs., but these are rarely grown these days, at least in this country. Cvs:

Chamaerops humilis

Howea fosterana. Photo A. James Downer

Licuala grandis

Licuala spinosa

PLATE 97

Phoenix roebelinii. Photo Lois Rossten

Phoenix reclinata. Photo Lois Rossten

Pritchardia thurstonii

Reinhartia sp.

PLATE 98

Rhapis excelsa dwarf 'Koban'

Rhapis excelsa dwarf 'Zuiko-Lutino'

Rhapis excelsa dwarf 'Zuiko-Nishiki'

Rhapis humilis

PLATE 99

Veitchia merrillii. Photo Lois Rossten

PLATE 100

'Charlesworthii', 'Cristata'. 'Nana', 'Variegata' and 'Voluta'.

P. quadriaurita. Tropics. Leaves to 3′ × 1½′ (90 × 45 cm). Leaflets to 6″ (15 cm) or more, lower pairs facing downward, the others horizontal. Very narrow and straightsided but closely and deeply toothed along the edges.

'Argyraea'. Usually sold as a pot plant, no more than 12″ (30 cm) high.

The arrangement is the same as for *P. cretica*'Albo-lineata'. The leaflets, however, are broad, the sub-leaflets wingshaped and set so close together as to appear segmented, silvery on both sides of the stalk and the lower part of the leaflets. Difficult.

Rumohra. **Polypodiaceae.** Leather Fern. Southern Hemisphere tropics. Pot and basket fern. Filtered sun. 200 fc. Temperature min. 50°F (10°C). Houseplant Mix #3. Propagation by division. Easy. 1 species.

R. adiantiformis. The leaves being long lasting when cut, they are used by florists in arrangements.

Leaves triangular to 3′ (90 cm) but usually much shorter indoors, to 1′ (30 cm). They grow from a brown, crawling runner.

A fine pot fern, very tolerant and adaptable. Propagation by division is easy.

Selaginella. **Selaginellaceae.** Spike Moss. World-wide. Fernlike terrarium plants. Shade. Min. 50 fc. Temperature min. 50°F (10°C). Humidity min. 65%. Houseplant Mix #3. Propagation by division. Easy to difficult. Min. 700 species of which a half dozen grown indoors.

These are exquisite fern relatives, some colonizing to form flat mats, others almost shrubby in appearance, the leaflets tiny on complexly divided, flat branches, the compound leaves branched again. They are mostly green but some take on a reddish hue or variegation.

They are strictly terrarium plants. Because of the restrictions on space that this imposes, many gorgeous species are overlooked. We list only tropical, small-growing species. The many hardy ones are not cultivated.

Care is minimal for the terrarium plants, as long as the soil is organic and porous. Maintain acid conditions of 5.5–6 pH with the medium maintained barely moist. Do not fertilize, but if the pH of the soil is higher it must be adjusted by using aluminum sulphate or some other acidifier with care. Propagate by division.

S. erythropus. Tropical America. Erect plant to 1′ (30 cm) high, bronzy red, the fronds triangular, much divided and fernlike. A vigorous plant, magnificent in a large terrarium. Var. *major (S. umbrosa)* is even larger and the leaves very flattened.

S. cuspidata. See *S. pallescens.*

S. emmeliana. See *S. pallescens.*

S. kraussiana. S. Africa. Spreading Clubmoss. Mat-forming plant like a large moss, creeping, the stems to 12″ (30 cm) long. Bright green. Leaves narrow, the leaflets tiny. Var. *Aurea:* leaves and leaflets golden. Var. *brownii:* much smaller, mounded, not as spreading.

There are a number of other varieties. This is probably the most popular *Selaginella* as it is easy to maintain and sufficiently small for covered pots or small terrariums.

C. martensii. Mexico. Partly erect stems, the lower halves rooting; 12″ (30 cm) long. Rather diffuse, the leaves branched. There are several variations.

S. pallescens. Subtropical N. America to northern S. America. Sweat Plant. Large, beautiful mounds of foliage to 1′ (30 cm), the leaves very crowded, complex and multilayered; green with white tips. Vigorous and spectacular.

S. plana. Plume Clubmoss. Tropical America. To 1′ (30 cm). Stems erect with spaced leaves verging to chartreuse. Some have grown this plant outside a terrarium with 50% humidity.

S. tamaracina. Central and southern Japan. The Japanese have selected a large number of named cultivars of this somewhat cooler-growing species that is unusually variable. Small, low, matforming plants display many shades of green, some with yellow or golden variegation and some with white. Rare in this country.

S. uncinata. Peacock Moss. China. Exquisite trailer, the stems to 2′ (60 cm) long, rooting at the joints, but easily confined in a large bowl or a terrarium. The narrow, long leaves with tiny leaflets are brilliant, metallic blue-green. It must be kept below 85°F (29.5°C) in summer.

S. victoriae. The erect stems topped with broad leaves. Described as "iridescent green and maroon." A strong grower that must be kept underpotted in a terrarium.

PALMS
Palm Culture

Low Light 150–600 footcandles	Cool. 35 F+ (1.5 C+).	High Light 600–1,000 footcandles	Warm. 50 F+ (10 C+).
Chamaedorea	Arecastrum	Areca	Areca
Chrysalidocarpus	Butia	Archontophoenix	Archontophoenix
Howea	Chamaedorea*	Arecastrum	Caryota
Licuala	Chamaerops	Butia	Chamaedorea*
Livistona	Chrysalidocarpus	Caryota	Licuala
Reinhardtia	Howea	Chamaerops	Pritchardia
Rhapis	Livistona	Phoenix	Reinhardtia
Pritchardia	Phoenix		Rhapis*
Veitchia	Rhapis*		Veitchia
Washingtonia	Washingtonia		

*Both Chamaedorea and Rhapis can be grown cool or warm.

Archontophoenix. **Palmae.** King Palms. Northern Australia. Tall single stemmed palms. Partial to full sun. Temperature min. 50°F (10°C). Packaged Houseplant Medium. Propagation from seed. Easy. 2 species, both occasionally grown indoors.

These are very tall palms with rapid seed germination and growth, useful to nurserymen but making for a relatively short useful life indoors except in big plantscapes. Seed not usually available in quantity.

A. alexandrae. To 80' (24 m). Fronds to 10' (3 m) or more with an enlarged base. Leaflets many and narrow, 2" (5 cm) wide. Grayish beneath.

A. cunninghamiana (Seaforthia elegans). Same size as above but leaflets wider, 4" (10 cm).

Areca. **Palmae.** S. Asia and W. Pacific. Single and clustered palms. Partial sun. Min. 60°F (16°C). Houseplant Mix #2 with sand. Propagation by seeds or division. Moderately easy. 50 species of which 2 possibly grown indoors. The common name Areca Palm has been misapplied to *Chrysalidocarpus lutescens.*

The species can be grown as young plants in pots, but the few leaves and broad leaflets are less decorative than those of other indoor palms. The seed is viable only a short time.

A. catechu. Source of the betel nut. A single-stemmed palm to 100' (30 m). Leaves to 6' (1.80 m) long. Leaflets broad, lax. Needs near shade when young. Seed germinates in 80 days.

A. triandra. Malay Pen. A cluster palm to 12' (3.6 m). Leaves to 4' (1.20 m), leaflets broadly elliptical. Tolerant of cool temperatures.

A. vestiaria. Same size and growth as above. Leaf stalks with orange sheaths. Leaflets in 8 to 15 pairs, broadly elliptical. Rarely grown indoors but a good prospect.

Arecastrum. **Palmae.** Brazil and Argentina. Queen Palm. Single-stemmed palm. Partial to full sun. Temperature min. 40°F (4°C). Sterilized Garden topsoil. Propagation from seed. Rather difficult. 1 species.

Arecastrum romanzoffianum. (Cocos plumosa). Much planted in Florida. Trunk to 40' (12 m). Fronds to 15' (4.5 m) and leaflets to 3' (90 cm), very narrow. The leaflets are arranged in several rows rather than on one plane. This results in a somewhat bushy effect. Not ideal for indoors except possibly suitable for very cool situations

Butia. **Palmae.** Pindo Palm. Brazil and Argentina. Single-stemmed palms. Partial to full sun. Temperature min. 45°F (7°C). Houseplant Mix #2 with sand. Propagation from seed. Moderately difficult. 12 species of which one occasionally grown indoors.

B. capitata. To 20' (6 m). Trunk thick. Leaves with leaflets bluish gray angled upward and outward in a V, the tip of the leaf curved downward. Seed takes 3–4 months to germinate.

C. mitis. Clustered Fan Palm. Naturally clustering, producing several stems to 30' (9 m) but grown indoors to max. 8' (2.40 m) high. The fronds 3–4' (90 cm to 1.20 m) long. Leaflets to 12" (30 cm) or more. Subleaflets up to 12 pairs and a tip, to 4" (10 cm) long. Plants can be propagated by division.

C. urens. Single stemmed to 40' (12 m). Leaves to 20' (6 m). Indoors height is limited to 12' (3.6 m) and fronds to 6' (1.80 m) or less. Leaflets and subleaflets like *C. mitis* but less pleated, narrower wedgeshaped and more irregular.

Caryota. **Palmae.** Fishtail Palm. S. Asia and W. Pacific. Cluster and single-stemmed palms. Partial to full sun. Min. 800 fc. Temperature min. 50°F (10°C). Packaged

Houseplant Medium or Houseplant Mix #3 with sand. Moderately difficult. 5–10 species of which 2 grown indoors.

The unique feature of the Fishtail Palms is their fronds, consisting of a number of opposite or alternate leaflets that are short, broad, unevenly wedgeshaped and pleated. If it were not for their large size, they could be taken for those of a fern.

A fast rate of growth recommends them for commercial production. It is a disadvantage indoors where they soon outgrow their tubs. The high light requirement has caused them to deteriorate in most situations where they have been used. For a while they were very common in the shops, and large specimens were impressive in lobby and other public places. Their vogue seems to have passed.

They are more attractive as single-stemmed trees where sufficient light is available. Clusters in tubs serve only as temporary decoration.

Water thoroughly after the soil is completely dry. Fertilize sparingly in order to slow growth.

Chamaedorea. **Palmae.** Mexico and Central America. Small trees. Shade to partial sun. 75–800 fc. Temperature min. 40°F (4°C). Houseplant Mix #2 with sand. Propagation by seed and division. Easy to Cast Iron. 100 species of which about 8 frequently cultivated indoors.

Most Chamaedoreas attain a maximum height of 12' (3.6 m). They have thin stems with ringed joints at intervals of an inch (2.5 cm) or more from which grow short fronds with narrow leaflets. From Victorian days forward they have been the most popular house palms, especially *C. elegans,* the Parlor Palm. Juveniles of tall palms grow rapidly, usually having a short period of use indoors. Chamaedoreas, on the other hand, are natural dwarfs that grow slowly. Accustomed to the shade of forest canopy, they need relatively little light. Warm growing, some species are nevertheless tolerant of low temperatures.

Thus, with good reason, these palms have remained in public favor up to the present day, but a change has taken place recently in the way they are used. For large, public, indoor gardens taller palms are in better proportion. For homes single stems, topped by fronds, have gone out of style. What is wanted is foliage masses. Partly this is a matter of price. To meet this demand nurseries plant more than one plant of single-stemmed species to a pot, so the clustering palms are preferred to the Parlor Palm for the purpose; more plant for the money. They continue to be ideal for low-light situations.

Maintain even moisture to assure a maximum number of fronds, but a short period of completely dry soil usually causes no harm. Fertilize with a balanced formula twice a month at ¼ the concentration indicated on the label. Leach soil thoroughly at least once a year. When potting be careful to pack the soil firmly around the stiff roots. Use a potting stick to fill in empty spaces.

Like most palms, these are often attacked by mites.

A gray look to the leaves and white powder beneath them is the giveaway. Set the tree or cluster on its side and direct a strong stream of water at the undersides of the leaves. Repeat at 2-week intervals until examination with a magnifying glass shows no further evidence of the pests.

Chamaedoreas have also been subject to nematode infestations. The nursery should guarantee against this scourge. If present, the plant and its soil must be discarded and the container thoroughly sterilized before reuse.

Chamaedoreas are easily produced from seed or suckers. They can also be air-layered, a rarity among palms which allows one to start over again with plants that have grown too tall. Remove old stalk sheaths from the ring joints just below the lowest fronds. Procede as recommended in our section on Propagation. When roots have formed, sever the stem just below them and pot up.

C. cataractarum. Forming clumps of narrow stems, growing to 4–5' (2.30–1.50 m). The stalks of the fronds are erect and have 12–16 leaflets 11 × 1½" (27.5 × 3.75 cm), with a vein on either side of the rib. Flowers are on long, pendant ropes carried by stalks longer than the fronds.

C costaricana. Thin stems in clustered to 10' (3 m). The fronds few and separated, to 3' (90 cm) with up to 40 lanceshaped leaflets.

C. elegans (Neanthe bella, Collinia elegans). Parlor Palm. It has enjoyed greater popularity for a longer period than any other indoor palm. Formerly grown singly, it is now frequently planted several to a pot or tub. Not only does it remain small, growing usually no higher than 6' (1.80 m), but, even in very low light, it constantly produces clusters of powdery yellow flowers like a miniature mimosa. Few plants can take more punishment than this one. Fronds are about 2' (60 cm) long with 12–20 pairs of leaflets 8 × ⅜" (20 × 9.37 cm). Pot snugly to induce slow growth. When planted several to a pot do not transplant to a larger container unless pot binding is very severe.

C. ernesti-augusti. A rarely grown species, different from the others and most attractive. The short stem, max. 6' (1.80 m), is topped by a rosette of wedgeshaped leaves 1' (30 cm) long, divided by a cleft for a third of the length and prominently ribbed. Somewhat less tolerant of cool temperatures than most. A fine, small tub plant for a display below eye level.

C. geonoformis from Honduras, *C. metallica* and *C. nana* also have simple cleft leaves. *C. nana* is very dwarf and *C. metallica* leaves are deep green with a bronzy overcast.

C. erumpens. Bamboo Palm. Increasingly popular with nurserymen and decorators because of its natural clustering growth and distinctive leaflets. Maximum height 10' (3 m), the fronds with 5–15 pairs of leaflets to 10" (25 cm) long but usually shorter and broadly elliptic, the terminal pair twice as borad as the others, blunt tipped and jointed to the rib for much of their length. Relatively fast growing. Suckering readily. Germination time up to 9 months.

C. klotzschiana. Single stemmed to 10′ (3 m). Peculiar in having the leaflets in groups of 4, the pairs facing in opposite directions.

C. microspadix. Clustering to 8′ (2.40 m). Leaflets 9–10 pairs, 10 × 1¼″ (25 × 3.12 cm), the 2 at the tip broader and longer. Velvety green above and matte green below. Tolerant to 40°F (4°C). More resistant to nemotodes.

C. seifrizii. Clustering like *C. erumpens* but faster growing and the canes more slender, the fronds further apart, fewer and very narrow. To 6′ (1.80 m). Leaflets virtually strapshaped, pointed. Very graceful. Best used as a screening plant. Cold tolerant.

Chamaerops. **Palmae.** Mediterranean Fan Palm. Mediterranean. Shrubby palm. Partial to full sun. Min. 40°F (4°C). Sterilized Garden Topsoil with peat. Propagation from seeds and suckers. One species.

Chamaerops humilis. A sturdy, quite hardy, shrubby fan palm, usually growing to no more than 5′ (1.50 m) and freely suckering, forming large clumps. Leaves 2–3′ (60 to 90 cm) wide. Leaf segments very narrow, cut almost to base. Easily propagated but slow growing. As stalks are short to 2½′ (75 cm), the clumps are compact and moundshaped. Suitable for cool situations with natural light.

The Japanese, with their usual superior skill, have succeeded in producing superb dwarf display plants by means of severe underpotting, root trimming and limiting action of suckers. The very beautiful small fans, semicircles of narrow leaf segments, are reduced in number and grow symmetrically from a thickened trunk. In this state they are seen to perfection at eye level.

Chrysalidocarpus. **Palmae.** Madagascar. Single-stemmed and clustering palms. Filtered to partial sun. Temperature min. 40°F (4°C). Houseplant Mix #2 with sand. Easy. 20 species of which only 1 frequently grown indoors.

C. lutescens. Butterfly Palm. Areca Palm. A clustering palm very different in appearance and use when juvenile and mature. As a juvenile the foliage is light and airy, the stalks very long and thin, the leaflets very long, thin and attenuated toward the tips, so that it can act as a screening plant and be seen below or at eye level to best effect. As a mature plant 12–30′ (3.6–9 m) high, the leaves arch and the leaflets are closely arranged in a V, overlapping like a fine lattice. It is then seen best from below, that is, with the fronds above eye level.

Keep moderately moist. Though capable of withstanding short spells close to freezing (0°C) it is best maintained at 50°F (10°C) or higher. Fertilize with 20-20-20 formula once a month in summer and supply a dose of chelated iron (Sequestrene) twice a year. Plants are easily divided.

Clusters of juvenile plants should be allowed to become very pot-bound before moving to a larger container or dividing, thereby slowing the rate of growth.

Howea. *(Kentia).* **Palmae.** Lord Howe Island, Australia. Single-stemmed palms. Filtered to partial sun. Min. 40 fc. Temperature min. 45°F (7°C). Houseplant Mix #2 with sand. Propagation from seed. Easy. Two species, both grown indoors.

Slender, elegant, slow growing, thriving in cool temperatures, carefree, the Howeas have long been standard greenhouse and house palms. They were already popular in England before the turn of the century. They are no longer readily available because they are dependent on seeds for propagation and these are off-years when they are not plentiful. Their slow growth has also inhibited commercial production. As pot plants they are more decorative than Chamaedoreas but the latter have other, outweighing, advantages.

H. belmoreana. To 40′ (12 m). The leaves arching to 7′ (2.10 m). Leaflets crowded, arching from the stalk, 1″ (2.50 cm) wide.

H. fosterana. To 70′ (21 m) The leaves to 9′ (2.7 m). Leaflets fewer, broader than the above, very long elliptic, to 2″ (5 cm) wide. Drooping from the stalk.

Both plants are grown as 15–25′ specimens for large plantings. In pots or tubs 2 or 3 are frequently planted together. max. height 4½′ (1.45 m). Spread about the same.

Licuala. **Palmae.** S. Asia and W. Pacific. Small fan palms. Filtered to partial sun. 400–700 fc. Temperature min. 50°F (10°C). Humidity min. 50%+. Houseplant Mix #3. Propagation from offsets or seed. Moderately difficult. Over 100 species of which 3 or 4 grown indoors.

These are handsome small fan palms that are definitely tropical, requiring constant moisture and high humidity. They are very well worthwhile trying as young plants.

L. grandis. New Hebrides Island. Single-stemmed trees to 6′ (1.80 m). Leaves single, nearly round, pleated by the numerous radiating veins, almost 3′ (90 cm) in diameter. The tips of the veins produce a saw-toothing of the edge.

L. pumila. Java. To 5′ (1.50 m). Leaves divided into narrow, 2-ribbed segments, 12″ (30 cm) long. There may be from a few to 24. Usually offsetting.

L. spinosa. S.E. Asia and W. Pacific islands. Clustering stems to 12′ (3.50 m). Leaves nearly round to 3′ (0 cm) in diameter, divided into as many as 15, narrowly wedgeshaped leaflets to 15″ (45 cm) long. Requires a very moist and humid environment.

Livistona. **Palmae.** S.E. Asia, Philippines, Australia. Fan Palms. Filtered to partial sun. Min. 150 fc. Temperature min. 45°F (7°C). Humidity min. 40%. Houseplant Mix with lime. Moderately easy. Propagation from seed. 30 species; 1 grown occasionally indoors.

L. rotundifolia. 80′ (24 m) or more. The tallest of these palms is also the one that makes the best pot and tub plant, developing its fans when only 2′ (60 cm) tall. Leaves are up to 5′ (1.5 cm) across in mature leaves but, at most, 2½′ (75 cm) in tub plants. They are nearly round, concave, with many relatively short 6″ (15 cm), segments curving downward at the tips.

Nurserymen can produce marketable plants rather quickly. On the other hand, users are able to slow growth rates by pot-binding and withholding fertilizer. Low light, of which it is fairly tolerant indoors, also helps to keep the size manageable.

Where a widely spreading and elegant show plants can be accommodated, this one has proved a good choice for decorators. In larger plantscapes older trees are both symmetrical and exotic features.

Phoeniz. Palmae. Date Palm. Tropical and subtropical Africa and Asia. Short to tall trees. Filtered to full sun. Temperature min. 40°F (4°C). Houseplant Mix #2 with sand. Mostly easy. Propagation from seed and divisions. 17 species of which 3 grown indoors.

P. canariensis, the Canary Island Date and *P. dactylifera,* the Date Palm of agriculture, are similar as young plants. Both are single stemmed with stiff, spreading leaves, the leaflets very numerous but extremely narrow and separated, stiff, with hard points. The full-grown trees, their leaves seen at a distance, are magnificent. But juvenile plants are bare looking; hardly suitable for indoor landscaping.

The dried *P. dactylifera* dates from health stores usually contain viable seeds that germinate in a month or two at 75°F (24.5°C). We had no trouble growing an 8′ (2.40 m) tree with 6′ (1.80 m) leaves from seed in about 5 years, despite filtered light well back of a window with southern exposure.

P. roebelinii. Miniature Date Palm. Most cultivars are clustering and can be divided with care after thorough rooting of the pups. It is very slow growing, eventually reaching a height of 6′ (1.80 m). The fronds are 3′ (90 cm) long, carried nearly horizontal. The leaflets are very numerous, closely set on one plane, shiny, very dark green, 10 × ⅜″ (25 cm × 9.37 mm).

It prefers temperatures min. 50°F (10°C) and humidity min. 40%. It thrives best in partial to full sun and is sensitive to overwatering. Surprisingly, it is more difficult to grow than the other 2 species. On the other hand it is very decorative when it can be placed to be seen from above.

Pritchardia. Palmae. Fiji Islands. Small trees. Filtered sunlight. 600 fc. Min. 50°F (10°C). Humidity min. 30%. Packaged Houseplant Medium. Propagation by seeds. Easy. 36 species, 1 occasionally grown indoors.

P. thurstonii. Thin stemmed, to 15′, spreading 6–8′ (1.80–2.40 m). Indoors the height is usually no more than 4–5′ (1.20–1.50 m). The umbrella leaves are 2½′ (75 cm) in diameter with up to 70 segments much shorter than the blade. Magnificent for display at or below eye level. Of most graceful habit. Slow growing. Fans form when stem is only 1½′ (45 cm) high. Keep moist and fertilize sparingly with a balanced formula.

The other Pritchardias are taller trees but may well prove adaptable to indoor use.

Reinhardtia. Palmae. Central America. Dwarf clustering palm. Shade to filtered sun. Min. 100 fc. Temperature min. 60°F (16°C). Humidity min. 50%. Houseplant Mix #3. Moderately difficult. Propagation by division. 5 species of which one grown indoors.

B. gracilis. A fabulously decorative little palm that grows to a maximum of 8′ (2.4 m) but is usually 3–4′ (90 cm–1.20 m). Slow. The stems are stout and the stalks short, bearing the oddest of leaf blades. Each consists of 4 short, broad segments, 7 × 6″ (17.5 × 15 cm), one pair facing upward and the other downward. Each segment has about 10 prominent, parallel veins. At the upper end these produce a coarse, saw toothed edge. Along the stalk the veins are bare, leaving rows of 1″ (2.5 cm) windows on either side. They are curiously like the vanes of a communications satellite.

This is a palm requiring constant warmth, moisture and high humidity but adapted to low lighting such as fluorescent. Where these conditions can be matched it will thrive but it is not recommended to the plantscaper, except in southern locations with near-greenhouse environments. Rooted pups can be separated and potted up.

Rhapis. Palmae. Lady Palm. China. Dwarf trees. Shade to filtered sun. Min. 75 fc. Temperature min. 40°F (4°C). Humidity min. 30%. Houseplant Mix #3 with or without sand. Propagation by division. Cast Iron. 9 species of which 2 or 3 grown indoors.

R. excelsa. A palm that may, in the coming years, take a leading place as a standard foliage houseplant. Its only negative feature, from a production standpoint, is slow growth. For the consumer this is offset by a number of distinct advantages only matched, to some degree, by *Chamaedorea.*

1. It is well filled out with foliage 1½–12′ (45 cm–3.6 m) in height. Plants are available in the full range of sizes. Pots, 5″ (12.5 cm) in diameter and up.

2. Growth is columnar because the leaves are relatively short. Spread 1½–4′ (45 cm–1.20 m). The leaves are long-lasting. The top is flat and spreading.

3. Slow growth is an advantage indoors. The plants are very long lived. Growth rate 6–8″ (15–20 cm) per year; that of the dwarfs 3–4″ (7.5–10 cm).

4. Yearly production of 2–5 pups that can be separated after rooting or left in place to form compact colonies. Not dependent on a seed crop.

5. Lowest light requirement of any palm including the Parlor Palm.

6. Adapts to 30% humidity.

7. Unaffected by low or very high temperatures. Can tolerate short periods below freezing (0°C).

8. Is satisfied with ordinary houseplant media.

9. Normal, even moisture.

10. Not attacked by spider mites as are most palms; occasionally by scale.

11. Relatively disease free.

245

12. The palm that displays in its cultivars the greatest degree of variegation in the form of white, cream or yellowish vertical striping on broad leaves. a handsome, consistently decorative growth habit. *R. excelsa* never becomes spindly like *Chamaedorea*.

Though carefree these are the most aristocratic of palms and bear comparison with any other foliage plants in the repertory. Both architectural and sculptural in form. For temporary displays and permanent plantings. Fine in rows as dividers and singly in mixed plantings; big enough to serve as background massed foliage.

A small clustering palm to 15' (4.5 m). Stems sturdy, heavily clothed with coarse brown fibers. Stalks green, thin, tough, to 10" (25 cm). Leaves handshaped to 15" (37.5 cm) in diameter. Segments to 6–14, cut so close to the attachment of the stalk that they appear to be leaflets; to 8 × 1½" (20 × 3.75 cm), long wedgeshaped. The tips are squared off and toothed, conforming to the max. 5, prominent vertical veins. The edges are turned down, the shape distinctly convex. The texture is stiff and hard; the surface dark, lacquered green. Note that browning of the toothed tips is normal.

Dwarf *Rhapis excelsa* cultivars. This exquisite category deserves special attention. Only recently have Americans become aware of them, though they have been grown in Japan for almost 300 years based on stock originally imported from China and Taiwan. There is flourishing Dwarf Rhapis Society which holds exhibits and competitions. Of the 100 named cultivars that it has certified are some variegated plants that are among the rarest and costliest in the world. A good selection of green and variegated cultivars is now being grown in the U.S., and interest in them has been increasing rapidly.

The little trees grow 1½–6' (45 cm–1.80 m) in height and are propagated from their offshoots. The green cultivars have fewer, shorter and broader segments than the species; usually 2–4, resulting in a mound of foliage which is best observed at or below eye level. The leaves of the variegated plants range from narrow to very broad. Cast-Iron culture is the same as for the species.

It is pointless to attempt detailed descriptions of the leaf and growth patterns of these cultivars. We like 'Koban' and 'Gyokuho' best of the green palms. 'Zuikonishiki' is spectacularly variegated with cream or light yellow. Pot them all in shallow, neutral matte brown or decorative glazed oriental ceramic pots.

R. humilis. Slender Lady Palm. The stems are more slender and covered with less finer fiber than those of *R. excelsa.* The leaves have *pointed* segments, 10–30 in number and 1" (2.5 cm) wide. The texture of the leaves is thin. Light requirement min. 500 fc or partial sun. Min. 40% humidity. The tree reached 12–15' (3.6–4.5 m). Pups are produced but division is difficult. Seed is irregularly available.

This is an airier, less sculptural plant than *R. excelsa.* There are some variegated cultivars, but these are less spectacular as the segments are narrower.

R. subtilis (?) (*R.* 'Thailand'). To 8' (2.40 m). To 6' (1.8 m) indoors. Closer in appearance to *R. excelsa* but segments pointed and irregular in width. It is usually grown from seed. Several young plants are usually potted together in a pot or tub. Min. humidity 60%. A very heavy drinker. Very susceptible to mite infestation. It can be recommended only for temporary displays.

Veitchia (Adonidia). **Palmae.** Western Pacific Island. Partial to full sun. 500–1,000 fc. Temperature min. 45°F (7°C). Sterilized Garden Soil with peat. Propagation from seed and growths on stem. Fairly easy. 18 species of which 1 grown indoors.

Veitchia is popular in Florida and the West Indies. Indoors it grows well and looks well as a juvenile, up to a height of 4–5' (1.20–1.50 m) at which time, unless receiving nearly full sunlight, it begins to decline.

It is a good tree for large installations with bright natural light.

V. merrillii. Palawan Islands. Christmas Palm. A slender tree to 18' (5.4 m), the trunk prominently ringed. Leaves stiff, arching to 5' (1.5 m), the 50 or more pairs of narrow leaflets elevated.

Culture much the same as *Chamaedorea* except that older plants need more sunlight. Seed has a short viability; however, small offshoots with incipient aerial roots develop on the stem near the base when the plants are 4–5 years old. These can be separated from the stem and planted. This is recommended only to the amateur because production of seed is small. It is much quicker than seed.

Washingtonia. **Palmae.** So. California and Mexico. Tall Fan Palm. Partial sun. Min. 600 fc. Temperature min. 40°F (4°C). Houseplant Mix #2 with lime. Easy. Propagation by seeds. 2 species.

W. filifera. Desert Fan Palm. To 80' (24 m). Fast growing as a juvenile. Fans to 3' (90 cm) in diameter with many deeply cut, narrow segments.

W. robusta. To 90' (27 cm) with a narrower trunk. Segments longer and more pendant.

Suitable for large plantscapes with bright light and where there is considerable temperature variation. Tough.

Part III

25

GLOSSARY

Plant Classification

Aerial. (Epiphytic). A plant that grows on trees. We have substituted the common word for the technical term.

Aquatic. A water plant, for example, *Myriophyllum*. Semiaquatic plants are dependent on water-soaked roots, for instance, *Acorus*.

Clone. A plant produced by asexual reproduction (propagation). In horticulture the word is frequently used to designate particular strains of propagated plants possessing unusual or untypical, usually favorable, characteristics. Many cultivars are clones. Even among cultivars, however, growers recognize some plants as "superior" or "inferior" to the average. Clones cannot be produced with uniformity from seed.

Cross. Hybrid

Cultivar. Any plant in cultivation differing from the typical wild species. Cultivars usually possess regressive characteristics, however attractive these may be. Such plants do not usually survive long in the wild. Where atypical plants have been found in the wild and cloned, they are often given the designation of forms or varieties. We have usually preferred to list such plants in cultivation as cultivars.

Family. A division of the plant world whose members cannot be successfully cross-fertilized with members of other families because of the incompatibility of the sex organs. The family includes one or more genera.

Genus. Major division of a family, consisting of one or more species. Originally it was believed that cross-fertilization between species belonging to different genera of the same family was impossible. However, intergeneric hybridization does take place in nature, notably among the orchids. Improvements in artificial cross-fertilization techniques have resulted in intergeneric hybridization being more common.

Species. A division of the genus. Plants within a genus that share principal characteristics but differ in greater or lesser detail. Most hybrids are made between species.

Subtropical. Plants surviving temperatures close to 32°F (0°C).

Succulent. Xerophyte. Desert plant. Leaf succulents store water mainly in their leaves. Stem succulents store water mainly in their stems.

Temperate. Plant that survives temperatures below 32°F (0°C) but not below 0°F (−18°C).

Terrestrial. Plant whose roots grow in the soil in nature.

Tropical. Plant requiring a minimum temperature of about 60°F (16°C).

Plant Description

Cane. Thin, flexible stem, with or without branches. Ex: Bamboo.

Caudex. A thick, woody, under- or aboveground stem or trunk, usually of a succulent but also applied to palms. During dormancy the caudex of succulents is bare. The stem or stems of annual growth emerge from the caudex. We usually employ the term, "thickened stem."

Cluster, clustered, clustering. Applied to stems and leaves that grow crowded together.

Colonizing. Plants that spread by means of offsets or runners.

Creeping. Plants with prostrate stems.

Erect. More or less vertical growth.

Herb. A nonwoody plant. The term also applies to medicinal or culinary or aromatic plants.

Joint. Node or axil. The place on a stem or branch from which leaves or branches grow. The joint is visible as a narrow thickening of a stem or branch. When leaves die, the bare joint is usually still capable of producing either a leaf or a branch.

Matforming. Growing as a low ground cover.

Node. *See* Joint.

Offset. Pup. A growth on or very close to the base of a stem capable of developing its own stem, leaves and roots so that it can be cut free and potted up.

Pendant. Branches, leaves, runners or stolons that hang down.

Prostrate. Stems and branches that grow more or less horizontally close to or on the ground.

Pup. *See* Offset.

Runner. Stolon. Runners are shoots above or below soil level especially equipped to produce new plants at some distance from the mother plant. The runner may have joints from which growths may arise, or it may be a stolon which is specifically adapted to seeking out suitable places to root, producing plantlets only at the tips. Thus, only the tips of stolons can be used for cuttings.

Shrub. Woody plant with short stems or clustered canes. Usually branched.

Stalk. Petiole. We use stalk only for the more or less long connection between a leaf and a stem or branch. Petiole is the botanical term.

Stalkless. Sessile. In botanical language a sessile leaf is one that is directly attached to a stem or branch. We use the word stalkless when the leaf lacks the "more or less long connection" in the last definition.

Stem. Trunk. Primary support of branches and leaves.

Stemless. Acaulescent. The stem absent or very short. Growing directly from the root. Some aroids are called stemless, the apparent short stem being considered a continuation of the root.

Stolon. *See* Runner.

Sucker. *See* Offset.

Thickened stem. *See* Caudex.

Trailing. Prostrate on the ground, or hanging from the sides of pots or baskets. Pendant.

Tree. Woody plant with tall stem or trunk when grown outdoors. Indoors, young trees often look like shrubs.

Trunk. The thick stem of a tree. Applied indoors only to tall specimens.

Tuber. A thickened stem, acting as water storage, usually below ground and bearing "eyes" like a potato. As tuber, bulb and corm are frequently used interchangeably, we define them here. Bulbs are underground, modified leaf buds. The incipient leaves are fleshy and closely packed. Confined mostly to the Amaryllidaceae and Liliaceae. Not occurring in this book. Corms are swollen subterranean or surface parts of a stem, typical of Gladiolus.

Tufted. Applied to colonizing plants producing closely packed clusters of leaves or stems directly from the roots.

Alternate. Single leaves at each joint alternating between one direction and its opposite.

Alternate pairs. Pairs of leaves, on opposite sides of a joint, alternating in direction at each joint.

Horizontal pairs. Leaves in pairs on the same plane lining a branch. Leaflets in pairs along the stalk of a leaf. Subleaflets in pairs along the stalk of a leaflet. And so forth.

Iris arrangement. Leaves opposite, overlapping at the base as with the leaves of Iris. Often extended as with some of the Calatheas, Marantas, etc.

Opposite/alternate. *See* Alternate pairs.

Opposite layered. Usually stemless plants. The arrangement is the same as that of the Iris but leaves are horizontal and layered on top of each other.

Paired alternate. *See* Alternate pairs.

Rosette. Leaves arranged like the petals of a rose, overlapping in a circle, like Bromeliads and Aeonium.

Leaf Arrangement

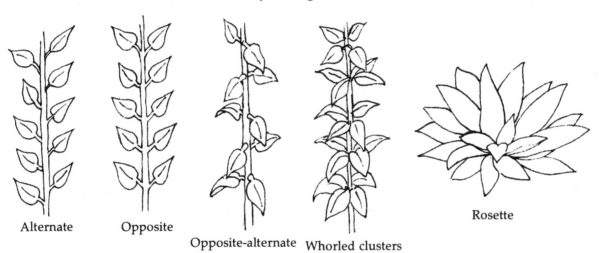

Alternate   Opposite

Opposite-alternate   Whorled clusters

Rosette

The Leaf

Base. The part of the blade of a leaf that is nearest to the stem, branch or stalk. Note that when leaves, especially large ones, curve downward the tip is seen as lower than the base.

Blade. The broad or expanded part of the leaf or leaflet. The part of the leaf above the stalk.

Boatshaped. Carinate. Applied mostly to leaf succulents. The thick blade is triangular in cross-section; broad on top and coming to a point below.

Bottom. Base. Or the the reverse of a leaf blade.

Channelled. Applies to narrow, longish leaves whose edges are evenly higher than the center line in the shape of half of a tube.

Clasping. Many foliage plants, especially those that are stemless, have leaves whose bases overlap tightly. In this way they form a pseudo-stem, usually short, but quite sturdy.

Cleft. The space between basal lobes, especially in heartshaped leaves. Also used to describe the depth of the cut between segments.

Compound. A leaf divided into leaflets, subleaflets, etc. Palms, Ferns, Aroids.

Concave. Describes leaf blades that are low in the center with raised edges.

Convex. Describes blades that are high in the center with edges turned down. The reverse of concave.

Cupped. Deeply and evenly concave.

Cylindrical. Solid, fleshy leaves, round or oval in cross-section. Tubular in shape. Sansevierias.

Edge. The outer limits of a leaf blade.

Frond. Leaf. Applied to the leaves of palms and occasionally to ferns.

Hullshaped. Thick leaves, the bottom (reverse) rounded. Not boatshaped—pointed.

Leaflet. A major division of a compound leaf.

Lobe. A rather loosely used term to describe rounded or pointed projection from a leaf blade. The basal lobes of a heartshaped or halberdshaped leaf. Relatively shallow divisions of the upper edge of a leaf blade. Prominent projections of the edges.

Margin. Edge.

Midrib. The principal vertical vein of a leaf, thicker than the side veins. A continuation of the stalk into the blade.

Notch. Cleft. A shallow cleft, usually basal.

Segment. A deeply cut lobe. The divisions are stalkless, hence not separate leaflets. In hand-shaped leaves the divisions that are stalked are leaflets; those that are connected at the base are segments. The difference between a segment and a leaflet is that the former is connected at the base to other segments while the latter is stalked and therefore separate.

Stalk. Petiole. The support of the blade of a leaf.

Stalkless. Sessile. Leaf base directly attached to stem or branch.

Subleaflet. A stalked blade attached to a leaflet in compound leaves. A further division of the subleaflet is the divided subleaflet (in Ferns).

Substalk. The stalk of a subleaflet or smaller division.

Tip. Apex. The part of the blade of a leaf furthest from the base, stalk, stem or branch.

Top. Tip. Also the upper surface of the blade.

Vein. The circulatory system of the blade, originating from the midrib.

Vein, Connecting or Transverse. The shorter, subsidiary veins, running, usually vertically, between the major veins, frequently forming a network.

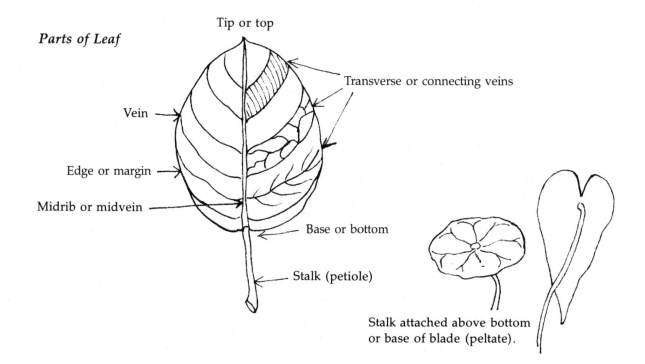

Parts of Leaf

Tip or top

Transverse or connecting veins

Vein

Edge or margin

Midrib or midvein

Base or bottom

Stalk (petiole)

Stalk attached above bottom or base of blade (peltate).

252

Arrowshaped. Broad at the base, without separate lobes, but the edge curved upward between the pointed or rounded tips. The sides rather straight, coming to a sharp or rounded point.

Elliptic. With curved sides meeting at a point both at base and tip. May be broad or long. The most common shape.

Fiddleshaped. Pandurate. With a large, rounded tip; the lower sides with 2 or more rounded lobes.

Halberdshaped. With two broadly or narrowly attached basal lobes. The tip lobe larger.

Handshaped (Digitate). The segments or leaflets like spread fingers. The outline of the leaf is usually like a fan or is circular. Very common among the compound leaves.

Heartshaped. Cordate. With a broad or narrow, deep or shallow basal notch or cleft. The 2 basal lobes, usually rounded but sometimes pointed. The sides curve inward to the tip. *See Anthurium* and other aroids.

Kidneyshaped. The shape of a lima bean, rounded on one side, 2 shallow lobes on the other and a small notch in the middle. Wider than long.

Lanceshaped. Rounded and broader at the base, curving toward the tip. Narrow or broad. Very common.

Needle-leaved or Needleshaped. Having very narrow leaves with parallel edges; less than ⅜ in. (9.35 m) wide. Like a pine needle but sometimes broader. Ex.: *Rosmarinus.*

Oblong. Rectangular with rounded corners.

Oval. Blade longer than broad and more or less evenly rounded at both ends.

Round. Orbicular, Orbiculate. Some simple leaves are actually quite round. We also use the term for the outline of compound leaves when the segments or leaflets describe an approximate circle with their tips.

Scimitarshaped. One side of the leaf blade is curved; the other side is straight or slightly curved in the same direction as the other side.

Spoonshaped. Obovate. Short or long leaves that are narrow at the base and expand toward a rounded or short pointed tip. Very common.

Strapshaped. At least 6 times as long as broad; narrow, with parallel sides and blunt or pointed tip. At least ½ in. (1.25 cm) wide.

Swordshaped. A long, usually stiff, relatively narrow leaf with nearly parallel sides coming to a point at the tip. Frequently clasping at the base. Very common.

Triangular. Like Arrowshaped. But we use the term when the broad base or sides are absolutely straight.

Trident. With 3 spreading leaflets or segments.

Wedgeshaped. The opposite of Arrowshaped and Triangular. A leaf blade with a narrow base and straight sides that widen to the tip which is broad or more or less straight.

Leaf Shapes

1. Arrowshaped

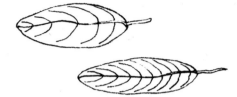

2. Elliptic

3. Fiddleshaped

4. Halberdshaped

5. Handshaped
(left with leaflets; right with segments)

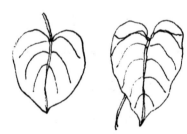

6. Heartshaped

8. Lanceshaped

7. Kidneyshaped

9. Needleshaped

10. Oblong

254

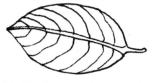

11. Oval or oval pointed
(referring to the tip)

12. Round

13. Spoonshaped

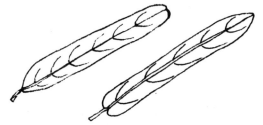

14. Strapshaped

15. Swordshaped

16. Wedgeshaped

Compound Leaves

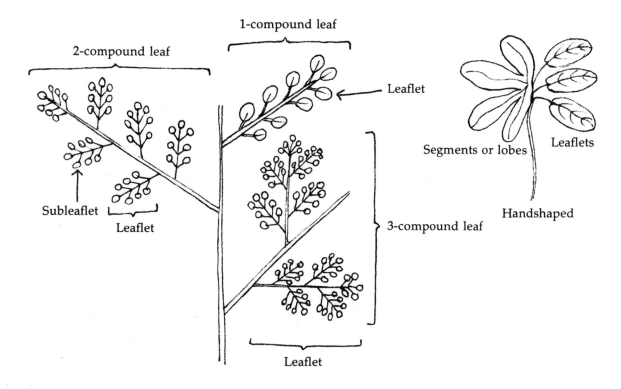

255

Leaf Surfaces

The latinized jargon of surface features of leaves is highly specialized. We use very simple adjectives or similes to indicate them. Such expressions as bright, shiny, lacquered, smooth, matte, rough, etc., are self-explanatory. Fine differences in surface textures are frequently most difficult to suggest with any great degree of accuracy.

Corrugated. When the transverse or connecting veins of a blade are depressed, causing a close pattern of quilting in stripes, the term corrugated seems appropriate and suggestive.

Hairy. Hairiness takes many forms on leaves and plants. We use velvety, felted, woolly, long-hairy, stiffly hairy and even scurfy.

Pleated. The blade is molded in a series of tight folds.

Puckered. Bullate. The surface is raised in many small points, frequently with hairs growing from the tips.

Quilted. The surface is raised and rounded because the veins are depressed.

Wrinkled. Surface irregularly crinkled as in some Peperomias.

Leaf Edges

We have kept our descriptions of edges quite simple. The details between species or cultivars are often so fine that words are of little use. Only exact drawings of the leaves of each species and cultivar would differentiate them. Often these features vary on the leaves of the same plant.

Blunt toothed. Teeth broad.

Crimped. Edge gathered in small rounded pleats.

Rippled. A closely scalloped edge.

Ruffled. Crisped. Like parsley leaves.

Sawtoothed. Teeth acute angled and evenly spaced.

Scalloped. With rounded protuberances or miniature lobes strung along the edges.

Thorn. Thornlike. Hard, thick point. Like *Sansevieria cylindrica* or *suffruticosa*.

Tooth. Toothed. Like two sides of a triangle. Usually small. Or jagged cuts, sometimes large.

Spine. Thin, fine, sharp, needlelike. Usually growing on edges or ribs. Ex: Holly leaves.

Undulating. Edges curved up and down. Not lobed.

Leaf Edges

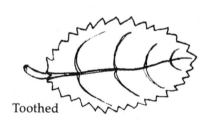
Toothed

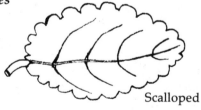
Scalloped

Lobed (3-lobed)

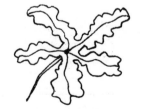
Handshaped, lobed or segmented
(5-lobed or segmented)

Jagged lobed

26

PLANT AND SEED SOURCES

Large commercial consumers of indoor foliage plants have easy access to all sources through their trade organizations. There are numerous nurseries with large productions, especially in Florida and California. Hence, a list for the trade would be superfluous here.

Plant decorators and interiorscapers for domestic customers are as often limited in the quantities they can buy as amateur houseplant growers. They, too, are obliged to confine their purchases to local nurseries or the same mail order ones favored by amateurs. Mail order suppliers are relatively few. However, they have the advantage of very large collections of general or specialized plants. Nurseries with greenhouses are common in many parts of the country. They frequently mass produce a few popular decorative houseplants, but the vast majority also have at least a few exotics. One should investigate these local sources carefully for they often have tucked away, interesting old varieties or novelties which are for sale at modest prices. Try the regional nurseries first and then go over to mail order across the country and abroad according to your needs.

For some it will come as a surprise that there are so few foreign sources. One might expect to find shippers from various parts of Africa, India, Southeast Asia, Indonesia, the Philippines and especially Japan, which has a huge and very sophisticated foliage industry. Up to now, unfortunately, it has been difficult for small professional firms and amateurs to find reliable suppliers in these areas.

Alberts & Merkel Bros., Inc. 2210 S. Federal Highway, Boynton Beach, FL 33435. Wide selection of tropical plants. Tropical plant and bromeliad catalogs $1.00 each.
Anything Grows Greenhouse. 1609 McKean Rd., Ambler, PA 19002. Tropical plants, variegates. Lists free.
B&T Associates. Whitnell House, Fiddington, Bridgewater, Somerset, England TA5 IJE. Tropical seeds. Send $2.00.
The Bamboo Tree. 715 Northampton St., Easton, PA 18042. Tropical seeds and plants. Catalog $.75.
Boojum Unlimited. P.O.B. 1175, Cortaro, AZ 85852. Succulents of Southwest and Baja. Catalog $1.00.
Brudy Exotics, John. 3411 Westfield Dr., Brandon, FL 33511. Tropical seeds. Catalog $1.00.
Brussel's Bonsai Nursery. 8365 Center Hill Rd., Olive Branch, MS 38654. Tropical and sub-tropical bonsai. Catalog $1.00.
Bushland Flora. P.O.B. 189, Hillarys, Australia 6025. Australian seeds. Send $3.00 for lists.
Cape Seed & Bulb Co. P.O.B. 4063, Idas Valley, Stellenbosch, Cape, South Africa 7609. Plants and seeds. Catalog $4.00.
Cornelison Bromeliads. 225 San Bernardino St., North Ft. Myers, FL 33903. Bromeliads. Catalog $1.00.
D. Oriell, Seed Exporters. 45 Frape Avenue, Mt. Yokine, WA, Australia 6060. Lots of native plants from the West. Catalog $3.00.

Dow Seeds Hawaii. Box 30144, Honolulu, HI 96820. N.Z. and Austr. and worldwide tropical and subtropical seeds. Catalog free. Also try Peter B. Dow Co., Gisborne, New Zealand.

Exotica Seeds Co. & Rare Fruit Nursery. P.O.B. 160, Vista, CA 92083. Catalog free. Tropical seeds and plants.

Four Winds Growers. P.O.B. 3538. Fremont, CA 94539. Dwarf citrus trees. Catalog free.

Garden of Delights. 2018 Mayo St., Hollywood, FL 33020. Seeds and plants of tropical fruits and nuts. Catalog $2.00.

Garden World. 2503 Garfield St., Laredo, TX 78043. Tropical plants, especially bananas. Catalog $1.00.

Glasshouse Works. P.O.B. 97., Steward, OH 45778-0097. Tremendous collection of tropical foliage. Catalog $1.50. Many rarities and variegates.

Highland Succulents. Eureka Star Route, Box 133, Galipolis, OH 45631. Superior succulents. Catalog $2.00.

Jerry Horne. 10195 SW 70 St., Miami, FL 33173. Many tropical plants. Send long SASE.

J. L. Hudson Seedsman. P.O.B. 1058, Redwood City, CA 94064. Big list of seed worldwide. Catalog $1.00.

International Seed Supplies. P.O.B. 538, Nowra, NSW, Australia 2541. Native seeds. Catalog $3.00.

Ivies of the World. P.O.B. 408, Highway 42, Weirsdale, FL 32695. Ivies. Catalog $1.50.

K&L Cactus Nursery. 2712 Stockton Blvd., Galt, CA 95652. Cacti & Succulents. Catalog $2.00.

Kartuz Greenhouses. 1408 Sunset Drive, Vista, CA 92083. Begonias, exotic shrubs and vines. Catalog $2.00.

Lake Odessa Greenhouses. 1123 Jordan Lake St., Lake Odessa, MI 48849. Pelargoniums. Catalog Free.

Lauray of Salisbury. Undermountain Rd., Salisbury, CT 06068. Begonias and other exotics. Catalog $2.00.

Logee's Greenhouses. 55 North Street, Danielson, CT 06239. Great collection of exotic plants. Begonias, shrubs, vines, herbs. Fine Catalog $3.00.

Mellinger's Inc. 2310 W. South Range Rd., North Lima, OH 44452. Grab bag collection of supplies and exotic plants. Big free catalog.

Monrovia Nursery Co. 18331 East Foothill Blvd., Azusa, CA 91702. Shrubs and trees of all sizes, many subtropical or tropical. Catalog $10.00.

Nindethana Seed Service. RMB 939, Washpool Rd., Woogenilup, Australia 6324. Native plants. The end of the world. Send $2.50 for catalog.

The Pan Tree. 1150 Beverly Drive, Vista, CA 92084. Succulents. Catalog $.50.

The Plant Kingdom. P.O.B. 7273, Lincoln Acres, CA 92047. Tropical plants including bonsai. Catalog $1.00.

Rainforest Flora Inc. 1927 Rosecrans Ave., Gardena, CA 90249. Tropical Plants. Long SASE for catalog.

Rhapis Gardens. Box 287, Gregory, TX 78359. Superb dwarf *Rhapis excelsa* and *R. humilis,* cycads, *Polyscias* and *Cissus.* Acclimated to indoors. Catalog $1.50.

Rhapis Palm Growers. P.O.B. 84, 31350 Alta Vista Dr., Redlands, CA 92373. Importers of fine Rhapis palms. Catalog $2.00.

SLO Gardens. 4816 Bridgecreek Rd., San Luis Obispo, CA 93401. Hoyas. Catalog $1.00.

Seaborn Del Dios Nursery. Rte 3, Box 455, Willow Lane, Escondido, CA 92025. Bromeliads and other tropicals. Catalog.

Shady Hill Gardens. 821 Walnut Street, Batavia, IL 60510-2999. Pelargonium plants and seeds. Catalog $1.00.

Singer's Growing Things. 17806 Plummer St., Northridge, CA 91325. Caudex plants and other succulents. Catalog $1.00.

South Florida Seed Supply. 16361 Norris Rd., Loxahatchee, FL 33470. Wholesale tropical seeds. Catalog free.

South Seas Nursery. P.O.B. 4974, 1419 Lino Ave., Ventura, CA 93004. Plants of tropical fruits. Catalog for SASE.

Southern Exposure. 35 Minor St., Beaumont, TX 77702. Cryptanthus. Catalog $.75.

Southwest Seeds. 200 Spring Rd, Kampston, Bedford, England MK42 BND. Desert plant seeds worldwide. Catalog $2.00.

Stallings Exotic Nursery. 910 Encinitas Blvd., Encinitas, CA 92024. Tropical and Subtropical plants. Catalog $2.00.

Sunset Nursery Inc. 4007 Elrod Ave., Tampa, FL 33636-1610. Bamboos. Catalog for long SASE.

Sunshine Caladium Farms. P.O.B. 905, Sebring, FL 33870. Caladiums. Free catalog.

Thompson & Morgan. P.O.B. 1308, Jackson, NJ 08527. Huge worldwide seed listing. Free catalog.

Varga's Nursery. 2631 Pickertown Rd., Warrington, PA 18976. Hardy and Tropical ferns. Catalog $1.00.

Westside Exotics Palm Nursery. P.O.B. 156, 6030 River Rd., Westley, CA 95387. Palms. Long SASE for listing.

Wrinkle Exotic Plants, Guy. 11610 Addison St., North Hollywood, CA 91601. Tropicals mostly from Africa. Catalog $1.00.

Young's Mesa Nursery. 2755 Fowler Lane, Arroyo Grande, CA 93420. Pelargoniums. Catalog $2.00.

SOURCES OF INDOOR GARDENING SUPPLIES

Certain indoor gardening supplies may be purchased from local hardware stores, florists and garden centers. Electrical supply shops sell fluorescent tubes and, less commonly, reflector units with ballasts or table top units. These are the places of first resort.

The number of mail order firms offering gardening equipment of all kinds is staggering. And there is hardly a catalog that does not contain something of value for indoor gardening. Decorative and useful accessories turn up also on many household equipment catalogs. Items not specifically manufactured for gardening can, with a little imagination, be adapted to new uses. There is no purpose, then, in listing or rather attempting to list so many sources. Write away for a few of the major catalogs and your mailbox will soon be stuffed with numerous others, as these firms exchange and sell lists.

Our own list is selective, concentrating on basic indoor trays, pots, fertilizers, etc. and on growth lighting equipment which is not always easy to find.

Agrilite. P.O.B. 12, 93853 River Road, Junction City, OR 97448. Growth lighting equipment and indoor gardening supplies.

Bonsai Associates, Inc. 3000 Chestnut Ave., #106, Baltimore, MD 21217. Bonsai supplies and starter plants. Catalog $2.00.

Brighton By-Products Co., Inc. P.O.B. 23, New Brighton, PA 15066. Growing supplies. Catalog $5.00.

Brookstone Co. 127 Vose Farm Rd., Peterborough, NH 03458. These free catalogs offer such variety that you are almost bound to find useful supplies.

Cape Cod Violetry. 28 Minot Street, Falmouth, MA 02540. Catalog for SASE. Pots, trays, fertilizers.

Charley's Greenhouse Supply. 1569 Memorial HWY., Mt. Vernon, WA 98273. Supplies and lights. Catalog $2.00.

Floralite Co. 4124 E. Oakwood Rd., Oakwood, WI 53154. Light Stands. Catalog Free.

Floralight Gardens Canada, Inc. P.O.B. 247, Station A., Willowdale, ON, Canada M2N 5S9. Floralight plant stands and indoor gardening supplies. Catalog free.

Florist Products, Inc. 2242 North Palmer Dr., Schaumburg, IL 60173. Gardening supplies including light units. Catalog free.

Gardener's Eden. Box 73007, San Francisco, CA 94120-7307. Decorative and useful items for the indoor garden. Catalog free.

The Green House. 1432 W. Kerrick St., Lancaster, CA 93534. Tiered lighting unit, the 'Gro-Cart'. Catalog free.

Gro-N-Energy. P.O. Box 1114, Matthews, NC 28106-1114. Growing supplies. Stamped envelope.

H.P. Supplies, Inc. P.O.B. 2053, Livonia, MI 48150. Light gardening carts and supplies. Catalog free.

Indoor Gardening Supplies. P.O.B. 40567, Detroit, MI 48240. We consider this tops for light gardening equipment and supplies. Catalog free.

Janco Greenhouses. 9390 Davis Avenue, Laurel, MD 20707. Superior greenhouses and lean-tos. Catalog $2.00.

Mellinger's Inc. 2310 W. South Range Rd., North Lima, OH 44452. Lots of supplies as well as plants. Catalog free.

OFE International, Inc. Box 161302, Miami, FL 33116. Growing supplies for tropical exotics. Catalog $2.00.

Public Service Lamp Corp. 410 W. 16th Street., New York, NY 10011. The 'Wonderlite' is still, in our estimation, the only effective growth bulb for the home. Catalog free.

Sun Tek Ink. 130 Speedwell Ave., Morristown, NJ 07960. Made-to-order redwood greenhouses, window gardens, etc. Catalog free.

Tropical Plant Products, Inc. P.O.B. 547754, 17-15 Silver Star Rd., Orlando, FL 32804. Orchid and bromeliad growing supplies. Send long SASE.

Tusker Press. Order Department. P.O.B. 1338 Sebastopol, CA 95473. *Gardening By Mail* by Barbara J. Barton. Best Source book to date for gardeners indoors or out.

Verilux, Inc. P.O.B. 1512, Greenwich, CT 06836. Sole source of Verilux 'Tru Bloom' fluorescent tubes. In our opinion, none are better. Catalog free.

The Violet House. P.O.B. 1274, Gainesville, FL 32601. Very good for all houseplant supplies. Catalog free.

Volkmann Bros. Greenhouses. 2714 Minert St., Dallas, TX 75219. Light gardening supplies. Catalog free.

Walter Nicke Company. P.O.B. 433, Topsfield, MA 01983. General supplies galore. Catalog $.50.

✣✣✣ 28 ✣✣✣

A SHORT BIBLIOGRAPHY

There is no lack of reference literature that includes information on foliage plants now being cultivated indoors. However, few of these are of much value to anyone but a botanist or a commercial grower. There are plenty of botanies of different tropical and subtropical countries along with extensive monographs that deal with the revision of the taxonomy of various plant families. The botanies are wide ranging, covering plants found only in the wild or a mix of wild and cultivated plants. They may be restricted to indigenous species or include imports that have adjusted and flourished in the new environment.

These books are helpful in tracking down plants in our collections whose country of origin is known. But they are not as reliable as one might expect. Not all botanists are attached to the same nomenclatural systems or trust in the same authorities. Thus the same plant may receive a different name in different countries or in the books of different authors. Older publications are superseded by recent studies that are frequently hard to track down. Sheer competition among taxonomists puts many names of the larger genera in constant jeopardy. Finally, important families and genera remain without serious study for years as the work is time consuming and costly. Thus errors and contradictions are not corrected. For all but the specialist this is very confusing and frustrating.

The many publications on the commercial uses of ornamental plants generally overlap in respect to plant material and cultural information.

It is unfortunate that economic necessity frustrates the efforts of conscientious authors, severely limiting space and illustration. Thus the majority of cultivars in horticulture are neither described in detail nor illustrated.

The books we list below are among the few that are useful and readily available.

Begonias. Mildred L. and Edward J. Thompson. Times Books, 1981.

Botanical Latin William T. Stearn. Thomas Nelson & Sons, Ltd., 1966. Essential for vocabulary.

1) *Common Trees of Puerto Rico and the Virgin Islands.* Elbert L. Little, Jr. and Frank H. Wadsworth. USDA Handbook No. 249, 1964.

2) *Trees of Puerto Rico and the Virgin Islands.* Elbert H. Little, Jr., Roy O. Woodbury and Frank H. Wadsworth. USDA Agriculture Handbook 449, 1974.
   Invaluable references.

Exotica 4. 11th Ed. Dr. Alfred Byrd Graf. Roehrs Co. East Rutherford, NJ 07073.
   The best-illustrated work on tropicals. We would also recommend the same author's *Tropica* except that the color printing is so poor.

Fern Growers Manual. Barbara Joe Hoshizaki. Alfred A. Knopf, New York, 1976. *Faute de mieux.* Good cultural section but description of plant form left to a numerical system that doesn't work.

Hortus Third. Liberty Hyde Bailey Hortorium. Macmillan, 1976. A lexicon of cultivated plants.
   The best general reference available.

Lexicon of Succulent Plants. Hermann Jacobsen. Blandford Press, London.

The World Weather Guide. E. A. Pearce and C. G. Smith. Hutchinson & Co. (Publishers) Ltd., London, 1984. Very useful to growers of newly acquired species.

Timber Press. 9999 SW Wilshire, Portland, OR 97225. Outstanding source of reference works on botany and horticulture.

SUBJECT INDEX

INDEX OF SYNONYMS

It is unnecessary to list our genus headings in an index because they appear in alphabetical order. Not so, the synonyms. These are generic or species names that exist in a sort of limbo, the older ones replaced but not entirely discarded and the newer ones not quite accepted by the botanical community. The public has a tendency to resist new names for well-known plants. Publication by a reputable botanist is no guarantee of universal recognition. English horticultural catalogers, quite sensibly, delay introducing changes in case they don't hold up. To make clear what we are talking about: you might be looking up *Achyranthes*, the old name of a genus in the family *Amaranthaceae*. You will not find it in our alphabetic list. But, if you turn to this index, you will be referred to the pages 139 and 192 where *Achyranthes* is now divided between the genera *Alternanthera* and *Iresine*. Hallelujah! You will find your plant—if we list the species at all.

INDEX OF COMMON NAMES

The only remotely reliable system for identifying plants by names is Linnaeus' Latin binomial system. The popular way of identifying is with common names. These are of local origin, obeying no rule whatsoever, usually understood in just one language or dialect and not infrequently only in restricted geographic and ethnic areas of any country. Thus the same plant and its flower have different names in every language. It means that a Frenchman, Indian, Englishman, Japanese or Italian will not understand each other when they use the common name of a plant. Latin acts as the bridge. Furthermore, the binomial system is subject to internationally accepted rules.

That is why we list our plants alphabetically by genus, and why we must list the common names separately, as they do not match the same sequence as the Latin names. A large proportion of our plants have no common name in English. That is because they have not yet gained sufficient popularity to be labeled differently from their Latin names. What is a relatively rare or recent plant for us may be common enough in some other country, but we have not had time to either adopt the foreign name or invent one of our own. Then there are also the plants that use a Latin name as the common one, either the same or so similarly as not to need repetition. For instance, *Rosa* is Latin and Rose is English; nobody need refer to an index for that. Some genera have acquired names, and some species that are popular have different ones. Hence the list below.

INDEX OF COLOR PLATES

The dimensions of foliage plants used for indoor decoration are very restricted. Numerous plants we list are far too big when mature to fit into enclosed surroundings. Indoors they are grown in pots or tubs as young plants. Photographs of the full-grown shrubs and trees, therefore, give a false impression of their true appearance and potential for use in the home or, for that matter, atrium. Differentiating small leaves in distant photos becomes quite impossible.

Closeups which show detail are the solution. Unfortunately, the lens and film of cameras deal far more realistically with, say, individual flowers that individual or grouped leaves because of the shallow focal depths at short distances from the subject. Nevertheless, such photographs are much more useful in identification and visualization than illustrations made purely for show.

When it comes to cultivars, we cannot always guarantee the reliability of our identifications because labeling by nurserymen is sometimes either careless or capricious. Illustrations of the more unusual cultivars serve the purpose of suggesting some of the variations important genera can assume and the potential for unusual decorative uses.

Herbs, Shrubs and Trees

Abromeitiella chlorantha Pl. 1
Acalypha wilkesiana. Photo Gordon Courtright Pl. 2
Acanthus mollis Pl. 3
Acorus gramineus variegatus Pl. 4
Adansonia digitata. Baobab. Photo Gregory A. Koob Pl. 5
Adenia 'Snowflake' Pl. 6
Adenia spinosa Pl. 7

Aechmea 'Burt' Pl. 8
Aechmea 'Mend' Pl. 9
Aechmea chantini Pl. 10
Aechmea ornata. Porcupine Plant Pl. 11
Aeonium arboreum 'Schwarzkopf' Pl. 12
Aeonium haworthii Pl. 13
Aeonium tabulaeforme Pl. 14
Aeschynanthus marmoratus Pl.

15
Agave americana marginata Pl. 16
Agave angustifolia marginata Pl. 17
Agave colorata Pl. 18
Agave horrida Pl. 19
Agave parrasana Pl. 20
Aglaonema commutatum Pl. 21
Aglaonema nitidum 'Curtisii' Pl. 22